www.wadsworth.com

www.wadsworth.com is the World Wide Web site for Wadsworth and is your direct source to dozens of online resources.

At www.wadsworth.com you can find out about supplements, demonstration software, and student resources. You can also send email to many of our authors and preview new publications and exciting new technologies.

www.wadsworth.com
Changing the way the world learns®

The Psychology of Women

MARGARET W. MATLIN
SUNY Geneseo

THOMSON

WADSWORTH

Australia • Canada • Mexico • Singapore • Spain • United Kingdom • United States

THOMSON

WADSWORTH

Sponsoring Editor: *Marianne Taflinger*
Assistant Editor: *Dan Moneypenny*
Editorial Assistant: *Nicole Root*
Technology Project Manager: *Darin Derstine*
Marketing Manager: *Lori Grebe*
Marketing Assistant: *Laurel Anderson*
Advertising Project Manager: *Brian Chaffee*
Project Manager, Editorial Production: *Paula Berman*
Print/Media Buyer: *Kris Waller*
Permissions Editor: *Elizabeth Zuber*

Production Service: *Hockett Editorial Service*
Text Designer: *Roy Neuhaus*
Photo Researcher: *Linda Sykes Picture Research*
Copy Editor: *Mimi Braverman*
Illustrator: *Lotus Art*
Cover Designer: *Denise Davidson*
Cover Image: *Kevin Dodge/Masterfile*
Text and Cover Printer: *Webcom*
Compositor: *Lachina Publishing Services*

For more information about our
products, contact us at:
Thomson Learning Academic Resource Center
1-800-423-0563

For permission to use material
from this text, contact us by:
Phone: 1-800-730-2214
Fax: 1-800-730-2215
Web: http://www.thomsonrights.com

Library of Congress Control Number: 2002117118

ISBN 0-534-57964-7

Wadsworth/Thomson Learning
10 Davis Drive
Belmont, CA 94002-3098
USA

Asia
Thomson Learning
5 Shenton Way #01-01
UIC Building
Singapore 068808

Australia/New Zealand
Thomson Learning
102 Dodds Street
Southbank, Victoria 3006
Australia

Canada
Nelson
1120 Birchmount Road
Toronto, Ontario M1K 5G4
Canada

Europe/Middle East/Africa
Thomson Learning
High Holborn House
50/51 Bedford Row
London WC1R 4LR
United Kingdom

Latin America
Thomson Learning
Seneca, 53
Colonia Polanco
11560 Mexico D.F.
Mexico

Spain/Portugal
Paraninfo
Calle/Magallanes, 25
28015 Madrid, Spain

This book is dedicated to
The Students in My Psychology of Women Classes

Brief Contents

Detailed Contents

■ C H A P T E R   5

Gender Comparisons in Cognitive Abilities and Attitudes About Success   142

■ C H A P T E R   8

Love Relationships   244

■ C H A P T E R   9

Sexuality   286

■ CHAPTER 10

Pregnancy, Childbirth, and Motherhood   320

■ C H A P T E R   11

Women and Physical Health   351

■ C H A P T E R   12

Women and Psychological Disorders   385

■ C H A P T E R **13**

Violence Against Women   416

■ C H A P T E R **14**

Women and Older Adulthood   456

■ C H A P T E R   15

Moving Onward . . . 485

Preface

My friend Gail has been a social justice advocate for many decades. Recently, she asked me, "Isn't it discouraging to teach a course like Psychology of Women when the students are now so conservative?" The question surprised me, and it forced me to consider whether my approach to this course had changed. Yes, the current students are living in a more conservative context than feminists had envisioned in the mid-1970s, when I taught my first course in the psychology of women. However, my students—and I assume all students who are reading this preface—still have the same sense of fairness. And they have the same sense of outrage when people are treated unfairly because of their gender, their ethnicity, or some other social category. My students also demonstrate the same empathy and compassion as the students from previous eras. The evening before writing this preface, I taught the final session of the fall semester's course in psychology of women, and students energetically supplied examples of the invisibility of elderly women in our society. Fortunately, this course is just as exciting and just as rewarding as it was almost three decades ago!

Some characteristics of the psychology of women have actually improved over the years. When the first edition of this textbook was published in 1987, the research on many aspects of women's lives was limited. In addition, the research did not always feature women's own perspectives. I couldn't locate much information about women of color, and cross-cultural studies were even less common. In the twenty-first century, it's a unique challenge to keep up with the hundreds of books and thousands of articles published on this subject each year!

This fifth edition of *The Psychology of Women* provides a synthesis that will guide readers through important facets of women's lives. I have made a special effort to include significant topics that are omitted or abbreviated in most other textbooks: the development of gender-typing, women and work, love relationships, pregnancy and motherhood, women with disabilities, and later adulthood. The resources cited here represent only a fraction of the literature I examined in preparing this book. In the first edition of this textbook, I commented that the meager information on the psychology of women made writers reluctant to tackle a textbook in this area. The explosion of research during the past decade has made the task rewarding, but we now face a different challenge. When writing the fifth edition, I often asked myself, "How can I possibly discuss all these dimensions of women's lives without creating a textbook of encyclopedic proportions?"

Text Features and Organization

The fifth edition of *The Psychology of Women* combines both developmental and topical approaches. In an introductory chapter, I present general concepts and several important cautions about research methods and biases. In the second chapter, we will explore some stereotypes that help shape gender-related expectations and behavior. In the next two chapters, we examine female development throughout infancy, childhood, and adolescence.

In the next nine topical chapters (Chapters 5–13), we delve into components of women's lives, such as gender comparisons, work experiences, love relationships, sexuality, childbirth, physical and psychological health, and violence against women. These chapters primarily provide perspectives on adult women and older women. For example, I examine older women's experiences in Chapter 8 (long-term romantic relationships), Chapter 9 (sexuality and aging), and Chapter 11 (women's health). In addition, most of these topical chapters are relevant for women of all ages; these include Chapter 7 on the topic of work, Chapter 8 on love relationships, and Chapter 12 on psychological disorders. Following these nine topical chapters, in Chapter 14 we focus more specifically on women who are middle-aged and elderly. In the concluding chapter of this textbook, we assess the current status of women, women's studies, and gender relations as we move through the early twenty-first century.

Organization is an important component of both my teaching and my textbooks. For example, the combination of life-span and topical approaches seems to provide a cohesive framework that my own students appreciate. However, every chapter is self-contained. Instructors who prefer a different approach can easily rearrange the sequence of topics. The two to five sections within each chapter all have their own summaries, to allow further flexibility.

A second organizational feature is that I develop four general themes about the psychology of women that can be traced through the many components of women's lives. These themes help to provide continuity for an area that might otherwise seem overwhelming to both instructors and students.

I have retained the special features that were praised in the first four editions of *The Psychology of Women:*

- **Topical outlines** provide students with an overall structure before reading each chapter.
- **True-false questions** at the beginning of each chapter encourage student interest and foreshadow many of the key issues to be examined.
- The **writing style** is clear and interesting; I try to engage readers by including many examples and quotations that reflect women's experiences.
- **Boldface type** identifies new terms, which are defined within the same sentence. To accommodate professors who would like to assign chapters in a nonlinear order, a new term that is used in several chapters (e.g., *social constructionism*) is redefined each time it appears. In addition, the correct pronunciation is provided for terms with potentially ambiguous pronunciations.

- Small-scale **demonstrations** are included to encourage active involvement and to clarify the procedures for key research studies.
- **Section summaries** (two to five in each chapter) help students review key concepts in a chapter section before they begin new material.
- A list of **new terms** at the end of each chapter invites students to test themselves on important vocabulary words and phrases.
- The **end-of-chapter review questions** encourage students to clarify and synthesize concepts. These questions also offer instructors a wide range of discussion topics or written assignments for students.
- The lists of **recommended readings** suggest extra resources for students who want to explore in greater detail the topics in each chapter. In addition, I have annotated each reference.

This book is intended for students from a variety of backgrounds. I have included extensive learning aids, to make it readable for students who have taken only an introductory course in psychology. However, *The Psychology of Women* should also be useful for advanced-level students because the coverage of topics is complete and the references are extensive. This textbook is primarily designed for courses in psychology of women, psychology of gender, psychology of gender comparisons, and psychology of gender roles. Instructors who focus on the psychology of gender may wish to supplement the book with one of several textbooks currently available on the psychology of men.

Features of the Fifth Edition

This fifth edition continues the special features and writing style that students and professors admired in the earlier editions. Professors who reviewed the fourth edition were pleased with its overall structure. Accordingly, I retained the same topic sequence for the fifth edition. However, readers should note the following changes:

- Whenever possible, I have expanded coverage on women of color who live in the United States and Canada.
- I now include more information on cross-cultural perspectives, reflecting the exciting recent progress in this area. This information provides a broader view of women's lives in many parts of the globe.
- "Women's voices" are more widely included. Quotations from girls and women enrich and supplement the quantitative research.
- Each chapter is introduced with a vignette or anecdote that represents a perspective on the chapter's content.
- This fifth edition is a thoroughly revised and updated textbook featuring more than 2,556 references. Furthermore, I have emphasized new research; 1,434 of those references were published in 1998 or later. This new revision reflects changes in women's lives, changes in their views of themselves, and changes in society's attitudes toward women's issues.

New Coverage in Specific Chapters

For professors familiar with the fourth edition, here is a brief guide to some of the major changes in this new textbook:

- **Chapter 1** has been rearranged, with new perspectives added on social class and on U.S.-centered nationalism.
- **Chapter 2** is somewhat shortened, with androgyny no longer covered as a separate section; I have expanded the coverage of cross-cultural issues.
- **Chapter 3** is reorganized so that the order of the topics is more consistent with children's developmental patterns; the chapter also includes updated research on parental influences and on children's gender stereotypes.
- **Chapter 4** now includes information about the development of feminist identity, gender comparisons in self-esteem, and lesbian women's coming-out experiences.
- **Chapter 5** provides additional information on gender similarities in cognitive abilities; it also examines the research on stereotype threat.
- **Chapter 6** includes expanded discussion of the social constructionist approach, interruption patterns, and altruism in real-world settings.
- **Chapter 7** is one of the most extensively revised chapters, with about 150 new references; updated topics include women and welfare, sweatshops, and the effects of employment on personal adjustment.
- **Chapter 8** now has more information on ethnicity and cross-cultural research; the section on lesbian relationships emphasizes recent research on the fluidity of female sexual orientation and the "intimate careers approach."
- **Chapter 9** now elaborates on the social construction of women's sexuality, with less emphasis on anatomy and biological processes.
- **Chapter 10** includes more information about cross-cultural perspectives, factors associated with women's responses to pregnancy, and returning to work after childbirth.
- **Chapter 11** has updated coverage on women of color and on women in developing countries, as well as new information about gender biases in health care.
- **Chapter 12** provides new perspectives on gender differences in depression, in addition to new subsections on binge-eating disorder and on psychotherapy with lesbian and bisexual women; the section on anxiety-related disorders has been deleted.
- **Chapter 13** has been extensively updated, especially in the discussions of reactions to rape, child sexual abuse, and society's response to the abuse problem.
- **Chapter 14** provides new information on the double standard of aging, retirement, and economic issues; the discussion of hormone replacement therapy includes the recent research about the potential dangers of this treatment.
- **Chapter 15** includes updated coverage of the number of women in psychology, as well as the men's movement and women's studies on the international level.

Acknowledgments

I especially enjoy writing the acknowledgments section of a book because it gives me the opportunity to thank the people who have provided ideas, references, perspectives, and encouragement. Lucinda DeWitt, a long-time co-author on my textbook ancillaries, read every chapter carefully and noted unclear passages, topics that are challenging to students, and updated references.

I especially appreciated the useful suggestions and insights about organization, content, current research, and presentation that were provided by psychologists who reviewed the manuscript for the fifth edition:

Alice Alexander, *Old Dominion University, Norfolk, Virginia*
Carole Beal, *University of Massachusetts, Amherst*
Cheryl Bereziuk, *Grande Prairie Regional College, Grande Prairie, Alberta, Canada*
Gloria Cowan, *California State University, Santa Barbara*
Amanda Diekman, *Purdue University, West Lafayette, Indiana*
Claire Etaugh, *Bradley University, Peoria, Illinois*
Gilla Family, *Bishop's University, Lennoxville, Quebec, Canada*
Margaret Gittis, *Youngstown State University, Youngstown, Ohio*
Michele Hoffnung, *Quinnipiac College, Hamden, Connecticut*
Laura Madson, *New Mexico State University, Las Cruces*
Nina Nabors, *Eastern Michigan University, Ypsilanti*
Agnes O'Connell, *Montclair State University, Upper Montclair, New Jersey*
Carla Reyes, *University of Utah, Salt Lake City*
Janis Sanchez-Hucles, *Old Dominion University, Norfolk, Virginia*
Hannah Steinward, *Cégep Vanier College, St. Laurent, Quebec, Canada*
Noreen Stuckless, *York University, Toronto, Ontario, Canada*
Lori Van Wallendael, *University of North Carolina, Charlotte*

My continuing thanks go to the reviewers of the first four editions: Harriet Amster, Linda Anderson, Julianne Arbuckle, Illeana Arias, Nancy Betts, Beverly Birns, Krisanne Bursik, Joan Chrisler, Gloria Cowan, Mary Crawford, Kay Deaux, Lucinda DeWitt, Sheri Chapman De Bro, Nancy DeCourville, Joan Fimbel DiGiovanni, Elaine Donelson, Susan K. Fuhr, Grace Galliano, Margaret Gittis, Sharon Golub, Beverly Goodwin, Chris Jazwinski, Linda Lavine, Liz Leonard, Wendy Martyna, Maureen O'Neill, Michele A. Paludi, Letitia Anne Peplau, Jean Poppei, Rebecca Reviere, Barbara Sholley, Linda Skinner, Myra Okazaki Smith, Susan Snelling, Beverly Tatum, Barbara S. Wallston, Dolores Weiss, Yvonne V. Wells, Barbara J. Yanico, and Cecilia K. Yoder. I also acknowledge the numerous contributions of Mary Roth Walsh, who died in February 1998. Over a period of nearly 20 years, Mary generously shared with me her perspectives, resources, and insights on the psychology of women. I continue to miss our conversations.

I'm delighted that Lucinda DeWitt could continue to co-author the Instructor's Manual/Test Bank for this fifth edition! Lucinda has written the test item file or instructor's manual for three previous textbooks. I am consistently impressed with her organizational skills and her expertise in the psychology of women, as well as her ability to track down information for the ancillary section called "Women's Issues Web Sites."

I would also like to thank friends, relatives, and colleagues for suggesting many important references: Susan Arellano, Christine Beard, Lawrence Casler, Jacques Chevalier, Johanna Connelly, Joanna Cotton, Lisa Elliot, Hugh Foley, Joanne Goodrich (from the About Canada Project), Jennifer Gullo, Diane Halpern, Marion Hoctor, Andrea James, Jamie Kerr, Arnold Matlin, Kathy McGowan, Stuart J. McKelvie, Murray Moman, Patricia Murphy, Josephine Naidoo, Thaddeus Naprawa, Lisa Naylor, George Rebok, Philip Smith, Helen S. White, and Diony Young.

Many students gave valuable suggestions and feedback: Kate Bailey, Marcia Barclay, Laurie Ciccarelli, Kelly Crane, Patty Curry, Kathryn Delaney, Michael Derrick, Jennifer Donlon, Amy Jo Eldred, Susan Flood, Lori Gardinier, Charlie Gilreath, Myung Han, Erik Jacobsen, Lisa Kaplan, Karen Kreuter, Kari Kufel, Heidi Lang, Christine Lauer, Laura Leon, Yau Ping Leung, Amy Liner, Zorayda Lopez, Tracy Marchese, Kathleen Matkoski, Erin Mulcock, Torye Mullins, Cory Mulvaney, Cathleen Quinn, Ralph Risolo, Marriane Rizzo, Bridget Roberts, Stephanie Roberts, Kristen Setter, Jennifer Swan, Emily Taylor, Marcie Trout, and Cindy Zanni. The students enrolled in my psychology of women courses have also given me numerous ideas and suggestions.

Constance Ellis, Carolyn Emmert, and Diane Sinnott provided numerous services that permitted me to devote more energy to writing. Four students—Allison Katter, Stacy Fravel, Emily Kreuger, and Elizabeth Zhe—were especially helpful in locating references and performing clerical tasks. The members of the Milne Library staff at SUNY Geneseo demonstrated their professional expertise in tracking down elusive references, documents, and information. My thanks go especially to Paula Henry, Harriet Sleggs, Diane Johnson, and Judith Bushnell.

I also want to thank several editors who have guided *The Psychology of Women* through its development and production. Tracy Napper, formerly of Harcourt College Publishers, is a superb developmental editor who helped to shape the fourth edition as well as several chapters of the fifth edition. I greatly admire Tracy's organizational skills and her helpfulness in pursuing elusive information.

In 2001, Wadsworth acquired *The Psychology of Women*. I soon had the opportunity to work with many Wadsworth staff members who were both skilled and experienced. Marianne Taflinger, my sponsoring editor, provided numerous creative perspectives and suggestions for new textbook features. With the move to Wadsworth, I was also delighted to work once again with three wonderful editors with whom I had worked on previous textbooks. Special thanks to Susan Badger (President/CEO), Sean Wakely (Senior Vice President, Editorial), and Eve Howard (Vice President/Editor-in-Chief, Editorial)!

Nicole Root, the Wadsworth editorial assistant for the fifth edition, deserves enthusiastic praise for her skills and efficiency, as well as her abilities as a photo researcher. Assistant editor Dan Moneypenny was especially helpful in working with Lucinda DeWitt and me on the *Instructor's Manual*.

Other Wadsworth folks who deserve my gratitude include text designer Roy Neuhaus and cover designer Denise Davidson. I also appreciate the talents of two especially skilled marketing staff members, Lori Grebe and Chris Caldeira.

In the world of entertainment, the top stars win public praise and standing ovations. If this were a world where justice prevailed, the production team for my *Psychology of Women* textbook would receive a similarly enthusiastic public acknowledgment! I would like to offer my extremely enthusiastic—though less public—gratitude to several individuals. Paula Berman, the project manager, arranged the production schedule and skillfully answered all my questions. Rachel Youngman of Hockett Editorial Service provided superb advice and coordinated the flow of edited manuscript and page proofs. Copyeditor Mimi Braverman, a gifted expert in the fine points of the English language, also provided many details that enhance the quality of this textbook. Authors seldom praise the typesetters who have worked on their books. However, Sona Lachina and Ronn Jost of Lachina Publishing Services produced superbly balanced page proofs that were remarkably error free. Extended applause for my Production Dream Team!

Linda Webster prepared the indexes for this book. Linda and I have now worked together on 10 textbooks, and I continue to admire her ability to produce such detailed and thoughtful resources.

Finally, I thank the most important people in my life for their help, suggestions, love, and enthusiasm. My parents—whose photo you will see on page 244—provided an ideal home for raising three strong daughters. My mother, Helen Severance White, taught me to value learning and to love language. She also continues to send me interesting articles about feminist topics. My father, Donald E. White, provided a model of a scientist who cared deeply about his profession in geology research. Dad also taught me the phrase *terminal velocity*. In fact, I was completing the final draft on this manuscript when he died on November 20, 2002.

I was fortunate to marry a feminist before "feminism" was a word in my daily vocabulary. Arnie Matlin and I have now been married for 36 years, and his encouragement and optimism continue to inspire and support me when I encounter roadblocks. Our daughters and their spouses now live on opposite coasts of the United States. Beth and Neil Matlin-Heiger are in Boston, Massachusetts; Sally Matlin and Octavio Gonzalez live in Oakland, California. Their appreciation and pride in my work continue to make writing textbooks a joyous occupation!

Margaret W. Matlin
Geneseo, New York

Introduction

Nicole Katano/PictureQuest

T R U E   O R   F A L S E ?

_____ 1. If a corporation refuses to consider hiring a male for a receptionist position, that corporation is showing sexism.

_____ 2. Feminism is based on the principle that women should be highly regarded as human beings.

_____ 3. Feminists disagree among themselves about whether men and women are very different from each other or whether the two genders are fairly similar.

_____ 4. Ironically, most female psychologists in the early 1900s conducted research designed to demonstrate that men are more intellectually competent than women.

_____ 5. Research on the psychology of women grew especially rapidly in the 1950s in both the United States and Canada because so many women were earning Ph.D.'s in psychology.

_____ 6. If a box of crayons has one crayon labeled "flesh-colored"—and that color is light pink—this is an example of the White-as-normative concept.

_____ 7. Native Americans in the United States have more than 200 different tribal languages.

_____ 8. Many large-scale medical studies on important health topics have been conducted using only male participants.

_____ 9. A problem in research on gender is that researchers' expectations can influence the results of the study.

_____ 10. Gender differences are larger when researchers observe people in real-life situations rather than in a laboratory setting.

Consider the following items, reported in recent months:

• On December 4, 2001, Tom Brokaw announced on the *NBC Nightly News* that one of the segments would honor the heroines of the September 11 disaster. Firefighter Lieutenant Brenda Bergman described how she raced into the flames, risking her own life to save other people. Why was this report unusual? It was the first major broadcast to feature women rescue workers, and almost three months had passed since the disaster. As Bergman said, "The fact that the faces of women haven't been in the news or . . . in the media is not reflective of reality" (Pozner, 2001b, p. 23).

• A Web site specializes in selling T-shirts with the insignia "Wife-Beater." Men can receive a special discount if they send proof of their conviction for domestic violence. Shirts are also available in children's sizes, including one for infants labeled "L'il Wife-Beater" (McNamara, 2001).

• Amina Lawal is an unmarried woman in Nigeria who recently gave birth to a daughter. According to the laws of the region, she committed adultery and therefore must be condemned to death by stoning. Meanwhile, her partner has been released; for him to be convicted, four other men would need to testify that they had actually witnessed the adultery (Amnesty International, 2002).

These examples illustrate a pattern that we will encounter throughout this book. Even in the twenty-first century, women are frequently treated in a biased fashion. This biased treatment is often relatively subtle, but it can also be life-threatening.

Furthermore, women and issues important to them are frequently neglected by the popular media and the academic community. For example, I searched for topics related to women in the index of a popular introductory psychology text-book. Pregnancy isn't mentioned, but the index has an entry for a relatively rare insect: "praying mantis, and hearing." The topic of rape is similarly missing from the index, but the listings under the letter *R* include multiple references to reflexes, racetrack handicappers, and the resting potential of neurons.

The reason we study the psychology of women is to explore a variety of psychological issues that specifically concern women. Some life events are directly experienced only by women; these include menstruation, pregnancy, childbirth, and menopause. Other experiences are inflicted almost exclusively on women, such as rape, domestic violence, and sexual harassment. When we study the psychology of women, we can also focus on women's experiences in areas that are usually approached from the male point of view, such as achievement, work, sexuality, and retirement. Still other topics compare females and males. For example, what factors in childhood encourage little girls and boys to behave differently? Do women and men differ substantially in their intellectual abilities or their social interactions? Are women and men *treated* differently? These important topics, which are neglected in most psychology courses, will be our central focus throughout this book.

Our exploration of the psychology of women begins with some important concepts in the discipline; next, we'll briefly consider the history of the psychology of women. In the third section of the chapter we'll provide a background on women of color, to give you a context for the discussion of ethnicity in later chapters. Next, we'll explore some of the problems and biases that researchers face when they study the psychology of women. In the final section, we'll describe the themes of this book as well as several features that can help you learn more effectively.

CENTRAL CONCEPTS IN THE PSYCHOLOGY OF WOMEN

Let's first consider two interrelated terms, *sex* and *gender,* that are crucial to the psychology of women. Other central concepts we'll examine are several forms of bias, various approaches to feminism, and two psychological viewpoints on gender similarities and differences.

Sex and Gender

The terms *sex* and *gender* have provoked considerable controversy (e.g., Pryzgoda & Chrisler, 2000). **Sex** is a relatively narrow term that refers only to those inborn biological characteristics relating to reproduction, such as *sex chromosomes* or *sex organs* (Howard & Hollander, 1997).

In contrast, *gender* is a broader term. **Gender** refers to psychological characteristics and social categories that are created by human culture. For example, a friend showed me a photo of her 7-month-old son, whom the photographer had posed with a football. This photographer is providing gender messages for the infant, his mother, and everyone who sees the photo. As you might guess, the North American understanding of gender is likely to differ strongly from the gender concept in Kenya, China, or Brazil (Howard & Hollander, 1997). Because in this textbook we focus on psychology, rather than on biology, you'll see the word *gender* more often than the word *sex*. For example, you'll read about gender comparisons, gender roles, and gender stereotypes.

Unfortunately, the distinction between sex and gender is not maintained consistently in psychology articles and books (Howard & Hollander, 1997). For instance, a highly regarded scholarly journal is called *Sex Roles,* although a more appropriate title would be *Gender Roles.*

A useful related phrase is *doing gender* (C. West & Zimmerman, 1998a). According to the concept of **doing gender,** we express our gender when we interact with other people; we also perceive gender in these other people. We give gender messages to others through factors such as our appearance, tone of voice, and conversation. At the same time, we perceive the gender of a conversational partner, and we typically respond differently to a male than to a female. The phrase *doing gender* emphasizes that gender is a dynamic process rather than something that is stable and rigid.

Social Biases

An important term throughout this book is *sexism* (which probably should be renamed *genderism*). **Sexism** is bias against people on the basis of their gender. A person who believes that women cannot be competent lawyers is sexist. A person who believes that men cannot be competent nursery school teachers is also sexist. Sexism can reveal itself in social behavior, in media representations of women and men, and in job discrimination. Sexism can be blatant. For example, Yale Law School students distributed a flyer that rated the physical appearance of five women students and described them in sexual terms (Benokraitis, 1997a). Sexism can also be more subtle, as in using the word *girl* to refer to an adult woman.

Numerous other biases permeate our social relationships. For example, **racism** is bias against differing racial or ethnic groups. For instance, many White college students report that their parents had not allowed Black friends to visit their homes when they were younger (Tatum, 1992). Like sexism, racism provides special privileges to some humans, based on their social category (Burnham, 1994). As we'll see throughout this book, sexism and racism combine in complex ways. For example, the experiences of women of color may be quite different from the experiences of European American men.

We'll also examine several other forms of bias in which a person's category membership can influence his or her social position. For example, **classism** is bias on the basis of social class, defined in terms of factors such as income, occupation, and education (Howard & Hollander, 1997). Unfortunately, psychologists have paid little attention to social class, even though this factor has a major impact on people's lives (Ocampo et al., 2003; Saris & Johnston-Robledo, 2000; A. J. Stewart, 1998). During your high school years, for example, you probably noticed that students from relatively wealthy families had different experiences and expectations than students from low-income families did. In Chapter 11, we'll see that social class has a profound effect on people's health and expected life span.

Another important problem is **heterosexism,** or bias against lesbians, gay males, and bisexuals, three groups that are not exclusively heterosexual. Heterosexism is revealed in the behaviors of individuals, and it is also found in the policies of institutions, such as the legal system (Herek, 1994). Because of heterosexism, male-female romantic relationships are considered normal, and therefore people in same-gender relationships do not have the same rights and privileges. In Chapters 2 and 8 we will explore heterosexism in detail, and in Chapters 4, 9, 10, and 12 we will also discuss psychological aspects of lesbians' lives.

An additional bias is **ableism,** or bias based on an individual's disability. In Chapter 11, we'll see how ableism can create inequalities for people with disabilities, both in the workplace and in personal relationships.

We emphasize **ageism,** or bias based on chronological age, in Chapter 14. Ageism is typically directed toward elderly people (Whitbourne, 2001). Individuals can reveal ageism in terms of biased beliefs, attitudes, and behaviors. For example, a teenager may avoid sitting next to an elderly person. Institutions can also exhibit ageism, for instance, in their hiring policies.

Feminist Approaches

A central term throughout this book is *feminism,* the principle that women should be highly regarded as human beings. **Feminism** is a belief system in which women's experiences and ideas are valued; feminists argue that women and men should be socially, economically, and legally equal (Hunter College Women's Studies Collective, 1995; L. A. Jackson et al., 1996).

We must emphasize several additional points about feminists. First, reread the definition of feminism and notice that it does not exclude men. Indeed, men as well as women can be feminists. Many current books and articles discuss feminist males (e.g., Enns & Sinacore, 2001; M. S. Kimmel, 2000; Levant & Pollack, 1995; O'Neil & Nadeau, 1998). Think about some men you know who advocate feminist principles more than some of the women you know. (We'll discuss male feminists and the growing discipline of men's studies in the final chapter of this book.)

Second, many of your friends would probably qualify as feminists, even though they may be reluctant to call themselves feminists (Liss et al., 2000). You have probably heard someone say, "I'm not a feminist, but I think men and women should be treated the same." This person may mistakenly assume that a feminist must be a person who hates men or a person who believes that all males in positions of power should be replaced by females. However, remember that the defining feature of feminism is a high regard for women, not antagonism toward men.

Third, feminism encompasses a variety of ideas and perspectives, not a single feminist viewpoint. Let's consider three different theoretical approaches to feminism: liberal feminism, cultural feminism, and radical feminism.

1. **Liberal feminism** focuses on the goal of gender equality, giving women and men the same rights and opportunities. Liberal feminists argue that this goal can be achieved by reducing our culture's rigid gender roles and by passing laws that guarantee equal rights for women and men (Enns & Sinacore, 2001; Humm, 1995). Liberal feminists emphasize that gender differences are relatively small; these differences would be even smaller if women had the same opportunities as men.

2. **Cultural feminism** emphasizes the positive qualities that are presumed to be stronger in women than in men—qualities such as nurturing and caretaking. Cultural feminism therefore focuses on gender differences that value women rather than on the gender similarities of liberal feminism (Bohan, 1997; Henley et al., 1998). Cultural feminists often argue that society should be restructured to emphasize cooperation rather than aggression (Enns & Sinacore, 2001; Kimball, 1995).

3. **Radical feminism** argues that the basic cause of women's oppression lies deep in the entire sex and gender system rather than in some superficial laws and policies (D. Bell & Klein, 1996; Tong, 1998). Radical feminists argue that sexism permeates our society, from the personal level in male-female relationships to the national and international level (Hunter College Women's Studies Collective, 1995). Radical feminists often argue that our society needs to dramatically change its policies on sexuality and on violence against women. They maintain that the oppression of women is so pervasive that massive social changes will be required to correct the problem (Enns & Sinacore, 2001; Percy, 1998; Tong, 1998).

In Chapter 15, we'll further explore perspectives on feminism and women's studies. A central point, however, is that feminism isn't simply one unified point of view. Instead, feminists have created a variety of perspectives on gender relationships and on the ideal pathways for achieving better lives for women. To clarify the three feminist approaches we discussed in this section, try Demonstration 1.1 on page 7.

Psychological Approaches to Gender Similarity and Difference

Psychologists interested in women's studies and gender usually adopt either a similarities perspective or a differences perspective. Let's explore these two approaches.

DEMONSTRATION 1.1 ■ ■ ■ ■ ■ ■ ■ ■ ■ ■ ■ ■ ■ ■ ■ ■ ■ ■ ■

Differentiating Among the Three Approaches to Feminism

Imagine that, in a discussion group, each of these six individuals makes a statement about feminism. Read each statement and write down whether the approach represents liberal feminism, cultural feminism, or radical feminism. The answers are on page 33.

1. Cora: "The way marriage is currently designed, women are basically servants who spend most of their energy improving the lives of other people." _____

2. Nereyda: "Laws must be made to guarantee women the right to be educated the same as men; women need to reach their full potential, just like men do." _____

3. Sylvia: "My goal as a feminist is to value the kind of strengths that have traditionally been assigned to women, so that women can help society learn to be more cooperative." _____

4. María: "Society needs to change in a major way so that we can get rid of the oppression of women." _____

5. Stuart: "I think women should be given exactly the same opportunities as men with respect to promotion in the workplace." _____

6. Terry: "Because women are naturally more peaceful than men, I think women need to organize and work together to build a peaceful society." _____

Source: Based on Enns (1997).

The Similarities Perspective. Those who emphasize the **similarities perspective** believe that men and women are generally similar in their intellectual and social skills. These psychologists argue that social forces may create some temporary differences. For example, women may be more submissive than men in the workplace because women typically hold less power in that setting (Kimball, 1995; Lott, 1996). Supporters of the similarities perspective also tend to favor liberal feminism; by reducing gender roles and increasing equal rights laws, they say, the gender similarities will increase still further.

If the similarities perspective is correct, then why do women and men often *seem* so different? Let's consider an explanation called the social constructionist perspective. First, however, read the following passage:

Chris was really angry today! Enough was enough. Chris put on the gray suit, marched into work, and went into the main boss's office and yelled: "I've brought in more money for this company than anybody else and everybody gets promoted but me!" . . . The boss saw Chris's fist slam down on the desk. There was an angry look on Chris's face. They tried to talk but it was useless. Chris just stormed out of the office in anger. (Beall, 1993, p. 127)

Most people envision that Chris is a man, although Chris's gender is not stated. Instead, readers *construct* a gender, based on their cultural information about gender.

According to **social constructionism,** individuals and cultures construct or invent their own versions of reality based on prior experiences, social interactions, and beliefs (Howard & Hollander, 1997; Hyde, 1996b; Marecek, 2001a; Pleck et al., 1998). A young woman develops a female identity, for example, by learning about gender through her social interactions and other experiences in her culture.

Social constructionists argue that we can never objectively discover reality because our observations will always be influenced by our beliefs. (In Chapter 2, we'll show how our thought processes are colored by our culture's myths and practices.) As a result, we tend to perceive, remember, and think about gender in a way that exaggerates the differences between women and men. The views in this textbook (and most other current psychology of women textbooks) support both the similarities perspective and the social constructionist view.

The Differences Perspective.   In contrast, other psychologists interested in women's studies emphasize the **differences perspective,** which argues that men and women are generally different in their intellectual and social skills. Feminist psychologists who support the differences perspective usually emphasize the positive characteristics that have been undervalued because they are associated with women. These psychologists might emphasize that women are more likely than men to be concerned about human relationships and caregiving (Kimball, 1995; Tavris, 1992). As you might imagine, those who favor the differences perspective also tend to be cultural feminists. Critics of this perspective point out that an emphasis on gender differences will simply strengthen people's stereotypes about gender (Clinchy & Norem, 1998).

People who endorse the differences perspective believe that gender differences can be explained by essentialism. **Essentialism** argues that gender is a basic, stable characteristic that resides *within* an individual. According to the essentialist perspective, all women share the same psychological characteristics, which are very different from the psychological characteristics that all men share. Essentialism also emphasizes that women's psychological characteristics are universal and can be found in every culture—a proposal that is not consistent with cross-cultural research (Wade & Tavris, 1999). The essentialists point out that women are more concerned than men about caregiving because of their internal nature, not because society currently assigns women the task of taking care of children (Bohan, 1993; Hare-Mustin & Marecek, 1994; Kimball, 1995). We'll explore essentialist views on caregiving in more detail in Chapter 6.

SECTION SUMMARY ■

Central Concepts in the Psychology of Women

1. *Sex* refers only to physiological characteristics related to reproduction (e.g., sex chromosomes); *gender* refers to psychological characteristics (e.g., gender roles). The term *doing gender* means that we display gender in our social interactions and that we perceive gender in other people during those interactions.

2. Some of the social biases to be discussed in this book include sexism, racism, classism, heterosexism, ableism, and ageism.

3. Feminism emphasizes that women and men should be socially, economically, and legally equal. Women and men who hold these beliefs are feminists; however, many people endorse feminist principles, even if they do not identify themselves as feminists.

4. Three feminist perspectives discussed in this section are liberal feminism, cultural feminism, and radical feminism.

5. Psychologists typically support either a gender similarities perspective (combined with social constructionism) or a gender differences perspective (combined with essentialism).

A BRIEF HISTORY OF THE PSYCHOLOGY OF WOMEN

Psychology's early views about women were generally negative (Bohan, 1992). Consider the perspective of G. Stanley Hall, who founded the American Psychological Association and pioneered the field of adolescent psychology. He also led the movement in the United States against coeducation (Minton, 2000). Specifically, Hall opposed college education for young women because he believed that academic work would "be developed at the expense of reproductive power" (G. S. Hall, 1906, p. 592). As you might imagine, views like Hall's helped promote biased research about gender. Let's briefly examine some of this early work, then trace the emergence of the psychology of women, and finally outline the discipline's current status.

Early Studies of Gender Comparisons

Most of the early researchers in psychology were men, although a few women made valiant attempts to contribute to the discipline of psychology (Pyke, 1998; Scarborough & Furumoto, 1987). The early research on gender specifically focused on gender comparisons, and it was often influenced by sexist biases. Helen Thompson Woolley (1910), an early woman psychologist, claimed that this early research was permeated with "flagrant personal bias, . . . unfounded assertions, and even sentimental rot and drivel" (p. 340).

For example, one early hot topic focused on the relative size of structures within male and female brains. Early scientists believed that the highest mental capacities were located in the frontal lobes of the brain. Not surprisingly, early researchers reported that men had larger frontal lobes than women (Shields, 1975). However, researchers often revised their earlier statements to match whatever brain theory was currently fashionable.

During this early period in psychology's history, dozens of researchers assessed gender differences in areas as diverse as fear responses, reading speed, intelligence, and color preferences (Milar, 2000; Morawski, 1994). In that same era, two female psychologists conducted important gender-fair research. Helen Thompson Woolley discovered that men and women had similar intellectual abilities and that women actually received superior scores on some memory and thinking tasks (E. M. James, 1994; H. B. Thompson, 1903). Leta Stetter Hollingworth (1914) demonstrated that the menstrual cycle had little effect on intellectual abilities (Benjamin & Shields, 1990), a finding that we'll discuss in Chapter 4. This first generation of female psychologists used their research findings to argue that women and men should have equal access to a college education (Milar, 2000).

The Emergence of the Psychology of Women as a Discipline

Most psychologists paid little attention to research on gender in the early years of psychology. During the 1930s, women constituted roughly one-third of the members of the American Psychological Association (M. R. Walsh, 1987). However, most of these women were employed in applied areas and social services. Women were seldom hired for faculty positions at research universities—the primary location for conducting psychological research and constructing theories (Furumoto, 1996; Scarborough, 1992). As a result, the psychology of women did not move forward substantially during the first half of the twentieth century (Morawski & Agronick, 1991).

By the 1970s, a greater number of women had entered psychology. Feminism and the women's movement had gained recognition on college campuses, and colleges added numerous courses in women's studies (Brownmiller, 1999; Howe, 2001a; Rosen, 2000). This rapidly growing interest in women had an impact on the field of psychology. For example, the Association for Women in Psychology was founded in 1969. In 1973, a group of American psychologists established an organization that is now called the Society for the Psychology of Women; it is currently one of the largest divisions within the American Psychological Association.

In 1972, a group of Canadian psychologists submitted a proposal for a symposium—called "On Women, By Women"—to the Canadian Psychological Association. When they learned that the organization had rejected their proposal, they cleverly decided to hold this symposium at a nearby hotel (Pyke, 2001). Shortly afterward, the Canadian Psychological Association Task Force on the Status of Women in Canadian Psychology was formed (Pyke, 1994, 2001).

In both the United States and Canada, the psychology of women was increasingly likely to be a standard course on college campuses. Many psychologists found themselves asking questions about gender that had never occurred to them before. For example, I recall suddenly realizing in 1970 that I had completed my undergraduate degree in psychology at Stanford University and my Ph.D. in psychology at the University of Michigan with only one female professor during my entire academic training! I wondered why these universities hadn't hired more women professors and why so little of my training had focused on either women or gender.

During the mid-1970s, the field of the psychology of women expanded dramatically. Researchers eagerly explored topics such as women's achievement motivation, domestic violence, and other topics that had previously been ignored (A. J. Stewart, 1994, 1998).

Looking back on the 1970s from the perspective of the twenty-first century, many people have remarked on that decade's sense of excitement and discovery. However, the work done in the 1970s typically had two problems. First, we did not realize that the issue of gender was extremely complicated. Most of us optimistically thought that just a handful of factors could explain, for example, why so few women held top management positions. Now we realize that the explanation encompasses numerous factors, as you'll see in Chapter 7.

A second problem with the 1970s framework is that women were sometimes blamed for their own fate. In trying to determine why women were scarce in management positions, researchers typically constructed two answers. Women were (1) not assertive enough and (2) afraid of success. The alternative idea—that the *situation* might be faulty—received little attention (Henley, 1985; Unger, 1983). Researchers and the popular media often emphasized that the fault rested in women's personalities rather than in social structure, stereotypes, and institutions. Gradually, however, many researchers shifted their focus from gender differences to gender discrimination and sexism (Unger, 1997).

The Current Status of the Psychology of Women

In the current era, we have learned that questions about the psychology of women are likely to generate complex answers. Research in this area continues to increase rapidly. For example, a search of a library resource called PsycINFO for 1990 to 2001 revealed that 69,641 scholarly articles, books, and chapters mention the topics of women, gender, or feminism. Three journals that are especially likely to publish relevant articles are *Psychology of Women Quarterly, Sex Roles,* and *Feminism & Psychology.*

A related development is that psychologists are increasingly aware of how factors such as ethnicity, social class, and sexual orientation interact in complex ways with gender. As you'll see throughout this book, we typically cannot make statements that apply to *all* women. Contrary to the essentialist approach, women are far from a homogeneous group. As we'll note in Chapter 12, for example, the incidence of eating disorders seems to depend on factors such as ethnic group and sexual orientation.

The current field of the psychology of women is also interdisciplinary. In preparing all five editions of this book, I consulted resources in areas as varied as biology, medicine, sociology, anthropology, history, philosophy, media studies, economics, political science, business, education, religion, and linguistics. In preparing this current edition, I accumulated a stack of reprints that was literally more than 7 feet tall, in addition to more than 600 relevant books, all published in the past 4 years!

Still, research on the psychology of women is relatively young, and several important issues are not yet clear. At many points throughout this textbook, you will read a sentence such as "We don't have enough information to draw conclusions." My students tell me that these disclaimers irritate them: "Why can't you just tell us what the answer is?" In reality, however, the conflicting research findings often cannot be summarized in a clear-cut statement (Unger, 1997).

Another issue is that our knowledge base continues to change rapidly. Because new research often requires revision of a previous generalization, this current edition of your textbook is substantially different from the four earlier editions. For example, the coverage of gender comparisons in cognitive abilities bears little resemblance to the material on that topic in the first edition. Other areas that have changed dramatically include adolescence, women and work, and substance abuse.

The field of psychology of women is especially challenging because both women and men continue to change as we move into the new century. We'll see, for example, that the number of women working outside the home has changed dramatically. On many different dimensions, women in 2003 are psychologically different from women in 1953. It is fascinating to contemplate the future of the psychology of women toward the end of the twenty-first century!

SECTION SUMMARY ■

A Brief History of the Psychology of Women

1. Most early research on gender examined gender differences and emphasized female inferiority, although Helen Thompson Woolley and Leta Stetter Hollingsworth conducted gender-fair research.

2. Gender research was largely ignored until the 1970s, when the psychology of women became an emerging field in both the United States and Canada. However, researchers in that era did not anticipate the complexity of the issues; blame for the low status of women was often placed on the women themselves.

3. In the current era, research on gender is widespread and interdisciplinary; the knowledge base continues to change as a result of this research.

WOMEN AND ETHNICITY

Earlier in this chapter, we introduced the term *racism,* or bias against certain ethnic groups. In this section, we'll specifically focus on ethnicity, in order to provide a framework for future discussions. In exploring the psychology of women, we need to explore ethnic diversity so that we can establish an accurate picture of women's lives, rather than simply White women's lives. We also need to appreciate how women construct or make sense of their own ethnic identity (Madden & Hyde, 1998). Let's begin by exploring a concept called "White as normative" and then consider some information about ethnic groups. Our final topic is U.S.-centered nationalism, a kind of bias in which people believe that the United States holds a special status that is superior to other countries.

The White-as-Normative Concept

According to Peggy McIntosh (1998), our culture in the United States and Canada is based on the hidden assumption that being White is normative or "normal." According to the **White-as-normative concept,** White people have certain privileges that they often take for granted (M. Fine, 1997b). For example, if a White woman acts in an impolite manner, people will not assume that her impolite behavior is characteristic of all White people. She can use a credit card or write a check and not arouse suspicions about its legitimacy.

Our school systems also assume that Whites or European Americans are normative. (At present, our terminology for ethnicity is in flux; I will use the terms *Whites* and *European Americans* to refer to White individuals who are not Latinas/Latinos.)

Consider this example of the White-as-normative concept: McIntosh reports that, as a White woman, she can be certain that her children will be taught material that focuses on their ethnic group. In contrast, a child from any other ethnic background has no such guarantee. For instance, Aurora Orozco (1999) was born in Mexico and came to California as a child. She recalls a song the students sang in her new U.S. school:

> The Pilgrims came from overseas
> To make a home for you and me
> Thanksgiving Day, Thanksgiving Day
> We clap our hands, we are so glad. (p. 110)

Orozco felt as though her own ethnic heritage was invisible in a classroom where children were supposed to clap their hands in celebration of their Pilgrim ancestors.

Another component of the White-as-normative concept is that White individuals often think that Blacks, Latinas/os, Asian Americans, and Native Americans belong to ethnic groups—but that European Americans do not (Peplau, Veniegas et al., 1999; Weedon, 1999). In fact, each of us has an ethnic heritage. Can you think of other hidden assumptions that are customary in our White-as-normative culture?

Women of Color

Figure 1.1 shows the estimated number of U.S. residents in the major ethnic groups, as reported in the 2000 census. Figure 1.2 indicates the ethnic origins of people who live in Canada.

As Figure 1.1 reveals, Latinas/Latinos are currently the second-largest ethnic group in the United States. At present, most individuals in this ethnic group pre-

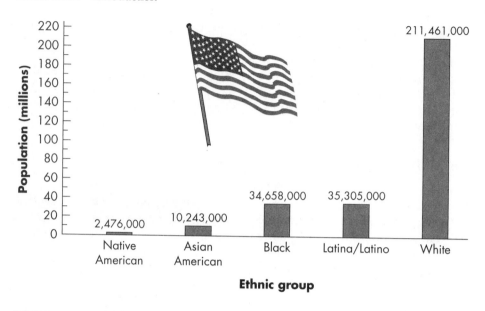

FIGURE 1.1 ■ U.S. population, by ethnic group and Hispanic origins, based on the 2000 census.

Source: U.S. Census Bureau (2001a).

fer this term rather than *Hispanic,* the term often used by governmental agencies (Espín, 1997; E. Martínez, 1997). The problem is that *Hispanic* focuses on Spanish origins rather than on Latin American identity. Unfortunately, though, the term *Latinos* has an *-os* ending that renders women invisible when speaking about both males and females. I will follow the current policy of using *Latinas* to refer to women of Latin American origin and *Latinas/os* to refer to both genders. (Some Latin American feminists use a creative nonsexist alternative that incorporates both the *-as* and the *-os endings;* it is written *Latin@s.*) Incidentally, Mexican Americans often refer to themselves as *Chicanas* or *Chicanos,* especially if they feel a strong political commitment to their Mexican heritage (D. Castañeda, 2000b).

Any exploration of ethnicity must emphasize the wide diversity of characteristics and experiences within every ethnic group (Peplau, Veniegas et al., 1999). For example, Latinas/os share a language and many similar values and customs. However, a Chicana growing up in a farming community in central California has different experiences from a Puerto Rican girl living in Manhattan. Furthermore, a Latina whose family has lived in Iowa for three generations has different experiences from a Latina who recently left her Central American birthplace because her family had been receiving death threats.

Donna Castañeda (2000b) described how she and other Latinas must navigate two cultures, frequently crossing borders between their Latina heritage and the European American culture in which they now live. As she writes,

> The notion of border crossing has a deep resonance for me each time I go home to visit my family. In a family of seven children, I have been the only person to go to

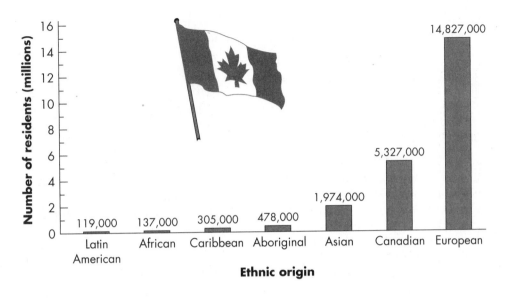

FIGURE 1.2 ■ Self-reported ethnic origins of Canadians, based on the 1996 census.

Source: Statistics Canada (2001c).

college, and on top of that I went on to get a Ph.D. As the eldest daughter in a family that places great value on children . . . not only do I not have any children, but I am also unmarried! Each homecoming is like moving from one world into another, from one self to another. The transitions are now much smoother for me than in earlier years, but only after a process of coming to understand that at any point in time I am more than one person, one dimension. (p. 205)

If you reexamine the U.S. data in Figure 1.1, you'll see that Blacks constitute the third-largest ethnic group in the United States. Blacks may include people who live in cities, suburbs, and rural areas. Some may have arrived recently from Africa or the Caribbean, whereas the families of others may have lived in North America since the 1700s.

Every non-White ethnic group has encountered racism, and this book will provide many examples of racial bias. In the United States, however, Black people's experiences with racism have been especially well documented. For example, Patricia Hill Collins recalls how her personal identity as a Black female changed during childhood as she grew to understand racism:

When I was five years old, I was chosen to play Spring in my preschool pageant. Sitting on my throne, I proudly presided over a court of children portraying birds, flowers, and other, "lesser" seasons. Being surrounded by children like myself—the daughters and sons of laborers, domestic workers, secretaries, and factory workers—affirmed who I was. When my turn came to speak, I delivered my few lines masterfully, with great enthusiasm and energy. I loved my part because I was Spring, the season of new life and hope. All of the grown-ups told me how vital my part was and congratulated me on how well I had done. Their words and hugs made me feel that I was important and that what I thought, and felt, and accomplished mattered.

As my world expanded, I learned that not everyone agreed with them. . . . I saw nothing wrong with being who I was, but apparently many others did. My world grew larger, but I felt I was growing smaller. I tried to disappear into myself in order to deflect the painful, daily assaults designed to teach me that being an African-American, working-class woman made me lesser than those who were not. And as I felt smaller, I became quieter and eventually was virtually silenced. (P. H. Collins, 2000, p. vi)

Incidentally, Collins's book uses two terms—*Black* and *African American*—to refer to her own ethnicity. In general, I'll use the term *Black* because it is more inclusive (Boot, 1999). *African American* seems to exclude many North Americans who feel a strong connection to their Caribbean roots (e.g., in Jamaica, Trinidad, or Haiti) as well as Blacks who live in Canada. As the Black Poet Laureate Gwendolyn Brooks said in an interview, she likes to think of Blacks as family who happen to live in countries throughout the world. *Black* is a welcoming term, like an open umbrella (B. D. Hawkins, 1994).

Like Hispanics, Asian Americans come from many different countries. Asian Americans include Chinese, Filipinos, Japanese, Vietnamese, Koreans, South Asians (i.e., people from countries such as India, Pakistan, and Bangladesh), and about 20 other ethnic-cultural groups. Consider a Laotian woman who is one of the 10,000 refugees belonging to the Hmong tribe and now living in Minnesota. She may have little in common with a Taiwanese woman living in Toronto's Chinatown or a South Asian woman who is a physician in New Jersey. Although many Asian American women have professional careers, women who are Filipino, Korean, and Chinese garment workers experience some of the most stressful labor conditions in North America (Kato, 1999).

Asian Americans are often stereotyped as the ideal minority group, and they are often academically successful. For example, Asian American women are twice as likely as European American women to earn a college degree (Root, 1995). However, we'll see throughout this book that women from an Asian background face many roadblocks. For instance, Dr. Madhulika Khandelwal describes her experiences as a professor at the University of Massachusetts, Boston: "Stereotypically [Asians] are presumed to have had limited access to English before arriving in America. They are considered followers rather than leaders. And the women are seen as either downtrodden or sexual 'exotics.'" She recalls being praised once after a lecture because she "spoke so well." In fact, India was colonized by the British, so Dr. Khandelwal had grown up speaking English as her first language (Collison, 2000, p. 21).

Native Americans and First Nations people[1] may share a common geographic origin and a common history of being invaded, dispossessed, and regulated by White North Americans. However, their languages, values, and current

---

[1] In referring to people who lived in Canada before the arrival of European Americans, Canadians use two terms, *First Nations* and *Aboriginal;* the two terms are used somewhat interchangeably, although Canadian colleagues have told me that *First Nations* is used somewhat more in Eastern Canada and that *Aboriginal* is used somewhat more in Western Canada.

lifestyles may have little in common (Daly, 2001; LaFromboise et al., 1990). In fact, they may represent the most diverse of all ethnic groups. In the United States, for example, Native Americans have more than 200 different tribal languages and more than 500 separate native backgrounds (Daly, 2001).

Many Native American women struggle as they try to integrate their own aspirations with the values of their culture. For example, a Native American teenager explained this conflict: "As a young woman, I should have been starting a family. When Grandma told them I was going to college, they'd look away. But in my eyes, going to college wasn't going to make me less Indian or forget where I came from" (Garrod et al., 1992, p. 86).

We have seen that each ethnic group consists of many different subgroups. Even if we focus on one specific subgroup—perhaps Chinese Americans—the variability within that one subgroup is always greater than the variability between groups (Bronstein & Quina, 1988; Kowalski, 2000). In examining how the various ethnic groups differ from one another, keep in mind the difficulty of drawing any generalizations that also reflect this within-group diversity. As we noted at the beginning of this section, we must reexamine the perspective that routinely considers European Americans to be normative. As Elsa Brown (1990) wrote, most European American students have learned a perspective in which the "normal human" is White, middle class, and North American.

Most current research about the psychology of women still describes the experience of White middle-class people, but the focus of the discipline is broadening. For example, groups such as the Society for the Psychology of Women sponsor numerous conferences and presentations on women of color. Whenever possible, in the chapters in this book, we will examine the diversity of experiences for all women.

U.S.-Centered Nationalism

Earlier in this section, we emphasized the White-as-normative concept. Now let's focus on a related bias, in which the United States is considered normative. Michiko Hase (2001) teaches a course in global gender issues at the University of Colorado. She has found that students are fascinated by topics such as female genital mutilation in Africa. In contrast, she explains:

> [My students] show little interest in the ways in which the United States—its government, its corporations, and U.S.-dominated international institutions—shapes (and even dictates) the process of globalization. I have encountered much student resistance when attempting to engage my students in the latter perspective and issues. A disturbing pattern emerged: the American students I have taught showed lack of interest in the negative impact of policies and actions of the U.S. government, U.S. corporations, and U.S.-dominated international agencies (like the IMF and the World Bank) on the rest of the world. (p. 94)

According to the principle of **U.S.-centered nationalism,** the United States dominates over all other countries in the world, who are believed to have lower status. U.S.-centered nationalism reveals itself in many ways that may be invisible to U.S. residents. For example, my colleagues in Canada have e-mail addresses that end in "ca." The e-mail address for Japanese residents ends in "jp," and those in Greece end in "gr." In contrast, residents of the United States do not need to add any additional letters to their e-mail addresses because our country occupies a position of privilege. We are "normal," whereas the other countries have less prominence. On a more harmful level, the United States believes that it can force its political policies on other sovereign countries. For example, when I was writing this section of your textbook in 2001, the U.S. ambassador to Nicaragua had just announced that the United States would be unhappy if Nicaraguans chose a member of the Sandinista party during their presidential elections in October rather than a member of the U.S.-favored right-wing parties. If this policy seems acceptable to you, consider how you would react if an ambassador from another country (perhaps England or Japan) announced that you must vote for a particular presidential candidate.

U.S.-centered nationalism is a challenging topic to discuss in the United States. As Hase (2001) noted, it is difficult for her students to hear their country criticized. In part, this attitude may be strengthened by students' educational experiences. If you grew up in the United States, for example, students at your high school were probably encouraged to respect and value people from ethnic groups other than their own. However, were you taught to value other countries equally—or did everyone simply assume that the United States had a special, privileged status compared with the rest of the world? Throughout this book, we will explore biases such as sexism, racism, and ageism—situations in which one group has a more powerful position than other groups. We need to keep in mind that U.S.-centered nationalism creates similar problems of inequality—on an international level rather than on the interpersonal or intergroup level.

SECTION SUMMARY ■

Women and Ethnicity

1. In North American culture, being White is normative; as a result, White individuals may mistakenly believe that they do not have an ethnic heritage.

2. Latinas/os share a language as well as many values and customs, but other characteristics vary tremendously; Latinas often comment that they must frequently cross boundaries between Latina culture and European American culture.

3. Blacks constitute the third-largest ethnic group in the United States; Blacks differ from one another with respect to their residential community and their family background.

4. Asian Americans also come from diverse backgrounds. Although they are considered the ideal minority, they often experience discrimination and stressful work conditions.

5. Even though Native Americans and Canadian Aboriginals share a common geographic origin and history, they are perhaps the most diverse of all ethnic groups.

6. The variability within any ethnic group—or subgroup—is always greater than the between-group variability.

7. Another form of bias that is related to ethnic bias is U.S.-centered nationalism, in which the United States has higher status than other countries; for example, the United States government believes that it can make decisions about the politics of other countries.

PROBLEMS AND BIASES IN RESEARCH

Earlier in this chapter, we mentioned the biased research that characterized the early history of the psychology of women. Let's now focus on the important topic of contemporary research in this discipline. Specifically, we'll explore the kinds of problems that sometimes arise when people conduct research on gender or the psychology of women.

Anyone conducting research in psychology faces the problem of potential biases. However, biases are a particular problem in research on the psychology of women because researchers are likely to have strong preexisting emotions, values, and opinions about the topics being investigated. In contrast, consider people who conduct research in the area of visual shape perception. As they were growing up, they probably did not acquire strong emotional reactions to topics such as the retina and the visual cortex! Preexisting reactions to gender issues may be especially strong in connection with research on women who do not conform to the traditional feminine stereotypes (e.g., unmarried women or lesbian mothers).

Figure 1.3 shows how biases and inappropriate procedures can influence each step of the research process. Psychologists are trained to carefully consider each phase of research in order to eliminate these problems. Although most current studies avoid obvious flaws, students must learn how to evaluate psychological research. Let's look at each phase of this research in more detail, and then we'll consider the more general issue of critical thinking in psychology.

Formulating the Hypothesis

Researchers are often strongly committed to a certain psychological theory. If this theory is biased against women, then the researchers may be predisposed to biased findings before they even begin to conduct their study (Caplan & Caplan, 1999; McHugh & Cosgrove, 1998). For example, one of Sigmund Freud's theories argued that women actually enjoy suffering. Psychologists who endorse this concept will be biased when they conduct research about women who have experienced domestic violence.

A second problem is that psychologists may formulate a hypothesis based on previous research that is unrelated to the topic they want to study. Several decades ago, for example, researchers wanted to determine whether children were psychologically harmed when their mothers worked outside the home. Psychologists' own biases against employed mothers led them to locate studies showing that children raised in low-quality orphanages often developed psychological problems. The situation of a child whose mother works outside the home

I. Formulating the hypothesis

    A. Using a biased theory
    B. Formulating a hypothesis on the basis of unrelated research
    C. Asking questions only from certain content areas

II. Designing the study

    A. Selecting the operational definitions
    B. Choosing the participants
    C. Choosing the experimenter
    D. Including confounding variables

III. Performing the study

    A. Influencing the outcome through experimenter expectancy
    B. Influencing the outcome through participants' expectancies

IV. Interpreting the data

    A. Emphasizing statistical significance rather than practical significance
    B. Ignoring alternate explanations
    C. Making inappropriate generalizations
    D. Supplying explanations that were not investigated in the study

V. Communicating the findings

    A. Leaving out analyses that show gender similarities
    B. Choosing a title that focuses on gender differences
    C. Journal editors rejecting studies that show gender similarities
    D. Secondary sources emphasizing gender differences instead of
       gender similarities

FIGURE 1.3 ■ How bias can influence research during five different stages.

is quite different from the situation of a child raised in an institution without a mother or father. Still, these early researchers argued that the children of employed mothers would develop similar psychological disorders.

    The final way that biases can influence hypothesis formulation concerns the nature of researchers' questions. For example, researchers who are studying Native American women typically examine issues such as alcoholism or suicide. Because of a biased attitude that these women are somehow deficient, researchers fail to ask questions that can reveal the strengths of these women. For example, do women with extensive tribal experience have more positive attitudes about growing old?

So far, we have reviewed several ways in which biases can operate in the early stages of hypothesis formulation. Specifically, biases can influence the theoretical orientation, the previous research that psychologists consider relevant, and the content areas that are investigated.

Designing the Study

An important early step in designing a research study is selecting the operational definitions. An **operational definition** tells exactly how a **variable** (or characteristic) in a study will be measured. Consider a study investigating gender differences in **empathy,** which means that you experience the same emotion that someone else is feeling. For our operational definition, we might decide to use people's answers to questions such as "When your best friend is feeling sad, do you also feel sad?" In other words, we will measure empathy in terms of self-report.

This operational definition of empathy may look perfectly innocent until we realize that it contains a potential bias. Women and men may really be equal in their empathy, but men may be more hesitant to *report* that they feel empathic. Gender stereotypes emphasize that men should not be overly sensitive. Perhaps if we had used another measure (maybe watching people's faces as they watch a sad movie), we might have reached a different conclusion about gender differences in empathy. In fact, a hypothesis should ideally be tested with several different operational definitions to provide a richer perspective of the research question.

The second source of bias in research design is the choice of participants. Some researchers have studied men more than women (McHugh & Cosgrove, 1998). Several decades ago, for instance, medical researchers included only male participants in many large-scale studies on important health questions. In more recent years, psychologists have examined roughly equal numbers of men and women (Ader & Johnson, 1994). However, psychologists typically conduct research with participants who are European American middle-class individuals—most often, college students (S. Graham, 1997). As a result, we know relatively little about people of color and people who are economically poor (Reid & Kelly, 1994; Yoder & Kahn, 1993). The choice of research topics also influences the choice of participants. Studies on welfare mothers or on female criminal behavior have typically focused on African American women and Latinas, but studies on body image or equity have usually been limited to European Americans.

A third source of bias in designing a study is the choice of the experimenter who will conduct the study. The gender of the experimenter may make a difference (e.g., F. Levine & Le De Simone, 1991). Let's imagine that a researcher wants to compare women's and men's interest in babies. If the experimenter is a man, males may be embarrassed to demonstrate a strong interest in babies; gender differences may be large. The same study conducted by a female experimenter could produce minimal gender differences.

A final source of bias is the inclusion of confounding variables. A **confounding variable** is any characteristic, other than the central variable being studied, that is not equivalent under all conditions; this confounding variable has the potential to influence the study's results. In studies that compare women and men, a confounding variable is some variable other than gender that is different for the two groups of participants. For example, if we want to compare the mathematics performance of college men and women, a potential confounding variable is the number of courses in mathematics and science they have taken. Because college men are likely to have taken more of these courses, any gender difference in math performance might be traceable to the discrepancy in the number of previous math courses rather than to a true difference in the actual mathematics ability of college women and men.

The reason we want to be wary of confounding variables is that we need to compare two groups that are as similar as possible in all characteristics except the central variable we are studying. Careless researchers may fail to take appropriate precautions. For example, suppose that researchers want to study whether sexual orientation influences psychological adjustment, and they decide to compare married heterosexual women with women who are lesbians. The two groups are not appropriate for comparison (Herek et al., 1991). For example, some of the lesbians may not currently be in a committed relationship. Depending on the goals of the researchers, a more appropriate study might compare single heterosexual women in a committed relationship and single lesbians in a committed relationship.

Each of these problems in designing a study may lead us to draw inadequate or inappropriate conclusions. The underrepresentation of females in some research means that we do not know much about their behavior in certain areas. Furthermore, decisions about operational definitions, the gender of the experimenter, and the inclusion of confounding variables may influence the nature of the conclusions.

Performing the Study

Further complications arise when the study is actually performed. One source of bias at this point is called experimenter expectancy (R. Rosenthal, 1976, 1993). According to the concept of **experimenter expectancy,** or **researcher expectancy,** the biases that researchers bring to the study can influence the outcome. If researchers expect males to perform better than females on a test of mathematics ability, they may somehow treat the two groups differently. Males and females may therefore respond differently (Halpern, 2000). Any researcher—male or female—who has different expectations for males and females can produce these expectancy effects.

Other areas of psychology also encounter the problem of experimenter expectancy. However, researchers in those areas can often reduce the effect by designing the study so that the experimenter is not aware of which participant is in which condition. If the experimenters in a study on memory don't know which people received a special memory-improvement session and which did not, they won't have different expectations for the two groups. However, in gender research, the investigators can't help noticing which participants are female and which are male! Suppose that researchers are rating female and male adolescents on their degree of independence in working on a difficult task. These ratings may reflect the researchers' expectations and stereotypes about female and male behavior rather than reality. These researchers may rate male adolescents higher than female adolescents on a scale of independence, even though an objective frequency tally of their actual behavior would reveal no gender differences.

Participants, as well as researchers, are likely to have absorbed expectations and stereotypes about their own behavior (Jaffee et al., 1999). For example, many women have learned that they are supposed to be moody and irritable just before their menstrual periods. If a woman is told that she is participating in a study on how the menstrual cycle affects mood, she may supply more negative ratings during the premenstrual phase of the cycle. If she had been unaware of the purpose of the study, her responses might have been different. When you read about a study that uses self-report, keep this potential problem in mind.

In summary, the expectations of both the researchers and the participants may bias the results so that they do not accurately reflect reality.

Interpreting the Data

The data from studies on gender and the psychology of women can be misinterpreted in many ways. For example, some researchers confuse statistical significance and practical significance. As we'll discuss in Chapter 5, a difference between male and female performance on a math test may be *statistically* significant. **Statistical significance** means that the results are not likely to occur by chance alone. The mathematical formulas used in calculating statistical significance are influenced by sample size. For example, almost any gender difference is likely to be statistically significant if a study has tested 10,000 males and 10,000 females.

Suppose that a standardized geometry test was given to 10,000 males and 10,000 females. Closer inspection reveals that the males received an average score of 40.5, in contrast to the females' average score of 40.0. The difference would almost certainly be statistically significant. However, this difference has minimal *practical* significance. **Practical significance,** as the name implies, means that the results have some meaningful and useful implications for the real world (Halpern, 2000). A half-point difference in these hypothetical geometry scores would have no imaginable implications for how males and females should be treated with respect to mathematics. Unfortunately, researchers often discuss only statistical significance, when they should also discuss whether a gender difference has practical significance.

When researchers interpret the data they have gathered, another potential problem is that they may ignore alternative explanations. For example, suppose researchers claim that males' superior performance on a math test is due to their superior math ability. The researcher may be ignoring an alternative explanation that we mentioned earlier: Males often take more math courses than females do. Consider another example. Suppose that females score higher on a test measuring anxiety. This difference might really be caused by males' reluctance to *report* anxiety that they feel, rather than by any gender differences in true anxiety. Unbiased research considers alternative interpretations.

An additional problem occurs when researchers make inappropriate generalizations. For example, researchers may sample unusual populations and draw conclusions from them about the psychological characteristics of normal populations. For instance, after investigating infants who had been exposed to abnormally high levels of male hormones before they were born, researchers might overgeneralize and draw conclusions about the way that male hormones influence normal infants (Halpern, 2000). Other researchers might examine a sample of European American female and male college students and then assume that their findings apply to all people, including people of color and people who have not attended college (Reid & Kelly, 1994).

In summary, the interpretation phase of research contains several additional possibilities for distorting reality. Researchers have been known to ignore practical significance, bypass alternative explanations, overgeneralize their findings, and supply explanations that were never properly tested.

Communicating the Findings

After researchers conduct the planned studies and perform the related analyses, they usually want to report their findings in writing. Other sources of bias may now enter. One important point to keep in mind is that a gender similarity is seldom considered startling psychological news (Caplan & Caplan, 1999). Therefore, when researchers summarize the results of a study, they may leave out a particular analysis showing that females and males had similar scores. However, they are likely to report any gender *difference* that was discovered. As you can imagine, this kind of selective reporting underrepresents the gender similarities that are found in research and overrepresents the gender differences.

Biases are even likely to influence the choice of a title for a research report. Until recently, titles of studies focusing on the psychological characteristics of men and women were likely to include the phrase *gender differences*. Thus, a study examining aggression might be titled "Gender Differences in Aggression," even if it reported one statistically significant gender difference and five comparisons that showed gender similarities. The term *gender differences* focuses on dissimilarities, and it suggests that we should search for differences. Accordingly, I prefer to use the more neutral term *gender comparisons.*

After researchers have written a report of their findings, they send their report to journal editors, who must decide whether it deserves publication. Journal editors, like the researchers themselves, may be more excited about gender differences than about gender similarities (Clinchy & Norem, 1998; Halpern, 2000). Selective publication therefore overrepresents gender differences still further, so that gender similarities receive relatively little attention.

Even further distortion occurs when the published journal articles are discussed by secondary sources, such as textbooks, newspapers, and magazines. For example, an introductory psychology textbook might discuss one study in which men are found to be more aggressive than women and ignore several other studies that report gender similarities in aggression.

The distortion of results is typically even more blatant when research on gender is reported in the popular press. For example, an article on women and men who own businesses showed a small number of gender differences in decision-making style and a large number of gender similarities (National Foundation for Women Business Owners, 1994). However, the article summarizing this report in *The Washington Post* carried the headline "Different Strokes for Different Genders" (Mathews, 1994). Similarly, a newsletter intended for college educators featured the headline "Gender Affects Educational Learning Styles, Researchers Confirm" (1995), even though the original research did *not* find a statistically significant gender difference (Philbin et al., 1995).

In an attempt to entice their audience, the media may even misrepresent the species population. A study on response to pain in male and female mice was later summarized for the *Los Angeles Daily News* with the following leap to the human species: "Women have a gender-specific, natural pain-relief system that depends on estrogen, say researchers at UCLA" ("Gender-Specific Pain Relief," 1993, p. C1; Mogil et al., 1993). Try Demonstration 1.2 to see whether you find similar media biases.

Critical Thinking and the Psychology of Women

As we have discussed, people must be cautious when they encounter information about gender; they need to inspect published material for a variety of potential biases. This vigilance is part of a more general approach called critical thinking. **Critical thinking** requires you to:

1. Ask good questions about what you see or hear;
2. Determine whether conclusions are supported by the evidence that has been presented; and
3. Suggest alternative interpretations of the evidence.

One of the most important skills you can acquire in a course on the psychology of women and gender is the ability to think critically about the issues. Unfortunately, the popular culture does not encourage this skill. We are often asked to believe what we see or hear without asking good questions, determining whether the evidence supports the conclusions, or suggesting other interpretations.

Consider, for example, a scenario described by psychologist Sandra Scarr (1997). She had been invited to discuss the topic of mothers' employment on

---

DEMONSTRATION 1.2 ■

Analyzing Media Reports About Gender Comparisons

Locate a magazine or a newspaper that you normally read. Look for any reports on gender comparisons or the psychology of women. Check Figure 1.3 as you read each article. Can you discover any potential biases? Can you find any areas in which the summary does not include enough information to make a judgment (e.g., the operational definition for the relevant variables)?

National Public Radio, and she described eight recent research studies, all showing that maternal employment had no impact on infants' emotional security. The other female guest on the show was a psychotherapist, the author of a new book arguing that mothers should stay home. The source of her evidence was her own clients, who reported that they had been emotionally harmed by having a caretaker other than their mother. The psychotherapist argued that she must speak for young infants, because she knows their pain and they are too young to express their distress.

Scarr reported that both the talk-show host and those who called the show seemed to consider her research evidence and the other guest's intuitive evidence to be equally persuasive. Critical thinkers, however, would ask good questions, examine the evidence, and think of other interpretations. For example, they might ask whether we should generalize from the retrospective reports of a small number of therapy clients in order to draw conclusions about infants in the current era. They might also ask whether the psychotherapist ever directly measured distress in the young infants she claimed to represent. Naturally, critical thinkers would also examine Scarr's more research-based findings for evidence of potential bias.

Because accuracy is an important aim of research, we must identify and eliminate the sources of bias that can distort accuracy and misrepresent women. We must also use critical thinking skills to examine the research evidence. Only then can we have a clear understanding about women and gender.

SECTION SUMMARY ■

Problems and Biases in Research

1. When researchers formulate their hypotheses, biases can influence their theoretical orientation, the research they consider relevant, and the content areas they choose to investigate.

2. When researchers design their studies, biases can influence the choice of an operational definition, the choice of participants, the choice of the experimenter, and the inclusion of confounding variables.

3. When researchers perform their studies, biases may include experimenter expectancy as well as the participants' expectations.

4. When researchers interpret their results, biases may include ignoring practical significance, ignoring alternative explanations, overgeneralizing the findings, and supplying explanations that had not been tested.

5. When researchers communicate their findings, gender differences may be overreported; the title of the paper may emphasize gender differences; articles that demonstrate gender difference may receive preference; and the popular media may distort the research.

6. Being alert for potential biases is part of critical thinking, which requires asking good questions, determining whether the evidence supports the conclusions, and proposing alternative interpretations for the evidence.

ABOUT THIS TEXTBOOK

I designed this book to help you understand and remember concepts and information about the psychology of women. Let's first consider the four themes of the book, and then we'll examine some features that will help you learn more effectively.

Themes of the Book

The subject of the psychology of women is impressively complex, and the discipline is so young that we cannot point out a large number of general principles that summarize this diverse field. Nevertheless, you'll find that several important themes are woven throughout this textbook. Let's discuss them now, to provide a framework for a variety of topics you will encounter.

Theme 1: Psychological Gender Differences Are Typically Small and Inconsistent. The earlier section on research biases noted that published results may represent gender differences as being larger than they really are. However, even the published literature on men's and women's abilities and personalities shows that gender similarities are usually more impressive than gender differences. In terms of permanent, internal psychological characteristics, women and men simply are not that different (Aries, 1996; Basow, 2001; Hyde & Plant, 1995). In gender research, one study may demonstrate a gender difference, but a second study—apparently similar to the first—may demonstrate a gender similarity. As Rhoda Unger (1981, 1998) has remarked, gender differences often have a "now you see them, now you don't" quality.

You'll recognize that Theme 1 is consistent with the similarities perspective discussed on page 7. Theme 1 also specifically rejects the notion of essentialism. As we noted earlier, essentialism argues that gender is a basic, stable characteristic that resides within an individual.

Let's clarify two points, however. First, I am arguing that men and women are *psychologically* similar; obviously, their sex organs make them anatomically different. Second, men and women acquire some different skills and characteristics in our current culture because they occupy different social roles (Aries, 1996; Eagly, 2001). Men are more likely than women to be chief executives, and women are more likely than men to be secretaries. However, if men and women could have similar social roles in a culture, those gender differences would be almost nonexistent.

Throughout this book, we will see that gender differences may appear in some situations but not in others. Gender differences are most likely to occur in these three contexts (Basow, 2001; Unger, 1998):

1. When people evaluate themselves rather than when a researcher records behavior objectively;
2. When people are observed in real-life situations (where men typically have more power) rather than in a laboratory setting (where men and women are fairly similar in power);
3. When people are aware that they are being evaluated by others.

In these three kinds of situations, people drift toward stereotypical behavior. Women tend to respond the way they think women are supposed to respond; men tend to respond the way they think men are supposed to respond.

Theme 1 focuses on **gender as a subject variable,** or a characteristic within a person that influences the way she or he acts. We will see that the gender of the participant or subject (i.e., the person who is being studied) typically has little impact on behavior.

Theme 2: People React Differently to Men and Women. We just pointed out that gender as a subject variable is usually not important. In contrast, gender as a *stimulus variable* is important. When we refer to **gender as a stimulus variable,** we mean a characteristic of a person to which other people react. When psychologists study gender as a stimulus variable, they might ask, "Do people react differently to individuals who are female than to people who are male?"

Gender is an extremely important social category—perhaps the most important social category—in North American culture (Bem, 1993). To illustrate this point, try ignoring the gender of the next person you see!

Throughout the book, we will see that gender is an important stimulus variable. In general, we will see that males are more valued than females. For example, many parents prefer a boy rather than a girl for their firstborn child. In addition, men are typically more valued in the workplace. In Chapter 2, we will also discuss how males are represented more positively in religion and mythology as well as in current language and the media.

If people react differently to men and women, they are illustrating that they believe in gender differences. We could call this phenomenon "the illusion of gender differences." As you will see, both men and women tend to exaggerate these gender differences.

Theme 3: Women Are Less Visible Than Men in Many Important Areas. Men are typically featured more prominently than women in areas that our culture considers important. A quick skim through your daily newspaper will convince you that males and "masculine" topics receive more emphasis. In Chapter 2, we will discuss the research on all forms of media, confirming that men are seen and heard more than women are. Another example is the relative invisibility of girls and women in the classroom, which arises because teachers tend to ignore females (Sadker & Sadker, 1994). Females may also be relatively invisible in the English language. In many respects, our language has traditionally been **androcentric:** The male experience is treated as the norm (Basow, 2001; Bem, 1993, 1996). Instead of *humans* and *humankind,* many people still use words such as *man* and *mankind* to refer to both women and men.

Psychologists have helped to keep some important topics invisible. For example, several major biological events in women's lives have received too little attention from psychology researchers. These events include menstruation, pregnancy, childbirth, and breast-feeding. Women *are* visible in areas such as women's magazines, advertisements for laundry soap, the costume committee for the school play, and low-paying jobs. However, these are all areas that our culture does not consider important or prestigious.

As we noted in a previous section, women of color are even less visible than White women. In Chapter 2, we will emphasize how women of color are absent in the media. Psychologists have only recently paid attention to this invisible group (Guthrie, 1998). When was the last time you saw a newspaper article or television show about women who are Asian American, Latina, or Native American?

Theme 4: Women Vary Widely from One Another.   In this textbook, we explore how women differ from one another in their psychological characteristics, their life choices, and their responses to biological events. In fact, individual women show so much variability that we often cannot draw any conclusions about women in general. Notice that Theme 4 contradicts the essentialism perspective, which argues that all women share the same psychological characteristics that differentiate them from men.

Think about the variability among women you know. They probably differ dramatically in their aggressiveness or in their sensitivity to the emotions of others. Women also vary widely in their life choices in terms of careers, marital status, sexual orientation, desire to have children, and so forth. Furthermore, women differ in their responses to biological events. Some women have problems with menstruation, pregnancy, childbirth, and menopause; others find these experiences neutral or even positive.

In the previous section, we discussed ethnicity and we noted that the diversity within each ethnic group is remarkable. Throughout this book, when we examine the lives of women in countries outside North America, we will gather even further evidence that women vary widely from one another.

We have emphasized that women show wide variation. As you might imagine, men show a similarly wide variation among themselves. These within-gender variabilities bring us full circle to Theme 1 of this book. Whenever variability *within* each of two groups is large, the difference *between* those two groups is not likely to be statistically significant. In Chapter 5, we will discuss this statistical issue in more detail. The important point to remember now is that women (and men) show wide variability.

How to Use This Book Effectively

This textbook has been designed to provide many features that will help you learn the material more effectively. Read this section carefully to make the best use of these features.

Each chapter begins with a set of 10 true-false questions. You can find the answers at the end of each chapter together with the page number where each item is discussed. These questions will encourage you to think about some of the controversial and surprising findings you'll encounter in the chapter.

The second feature in each chapter is an outline. When you start a new chapter, be sure to read through the outline to acquaint yourself with the scope of the chapter.

The chapters themselves contain a number of demonstrations, such as Demonstrations 1.1 (page 7) and 1.2 (page 25). Try them yourself, or invite your friends to try them. Each demonstration is simple and requires little or no equipment. The purpose of the demonstrations is to make the material more concrete and personal. Research on memory has demonstrated that material is easier to remember if it is concrete and is related to personal experience (Matlin, 2002; T. B. Rogers et al., 1977).

In the text, new terms appear in boldface type (e.g., **gender**) and are defined in the same sentence. I have also included some phonetic pronunciations, with the accented syllable appearing in italics. (My students tell me that they feel more confident about using a word in discussion if they know their pronunciation is correct.) Concentrate on these definitions. An important part of any discipline is its terminology.

Many textbooks include summaries at the end of each chapter, but I prefer section summaries at the end of each major section. For example, this chapter has five section summaries. This feature helps you review the material more frequently, so that you can feel confident about small, manageable portions of the textbook before you move on to new material. At the end of each section, you may wish to test yourself to see whether you can recall the important points. Then check the section summary to see whether you were accurate. Incidentally, some students have mentioned that they learn the material more effectively if they read one section at a time, then take a break, and review that section summary before reading the next portion.

A set of chapter review questions appears at the end of each chapter. Some questions test your specific recall, some ask you to interrelate information from several parts of the chapter, and some ask you to apply your knowledge to everyday situations.

At the end of each chapter is a list of the new (boldface) terms, in the order in which they appear in the chapter. You can test yourself to see whether you can define each term; this list of terms also includes page numbers, so that you can check on the terms you find difficult. Each of these terms also appears in the subject index at the end of the book.

A final feature, also at the end of each chapter, is a list of several recommended readings. These are important articles, books, or special issues of journals that are particularly relevant to that chapter. These readings should be useful if you are writing a paper on one of the relevant topics or if an area is personally interesting to you. I hope you'll want to go beyond the information in the textbook and learn on your own about the psychology of women!

SECTION SUMMARY ■

About This Textbook

1. Theme 1 states that psychological gender differences are typically small and inconsistent; gender differences are more likely (a) when people evaluate themselves, (b) in real-life situations, and (c) when people are aware that they are being evaluated by other people.

2. Theme 2 states that people react differently to men and women (e.g., males are typically more valued).

3. Theme 3 states that women are less visible than men in many important areas; for instance, our language is androcentric.

4. Theme 4 states that women vary widely from one another, for example, in psychological characteristics, life choices, and responses to biological processes.

5. Features of this book that will help you learn more effectively include true-false questions, chapter outlines, demonstrations, boldfaced new terms, section summaries, chapter review questions, new-terms lists, and recommended readings.

■ ■ ■ ■ ■ ■ CHAPTER REVIEW QUESTIONS ■ ■ ■ ■ ■ ■

1. The terms *sex* and *gender* have somewhat different meanings, although they are sometimes used interchangeably. Define each term, and then decide which of the two terms should be used in connection with each of the following topics: (a) how boys learn "masculine" body postures and girls learn "feminine" body postures; (b) how hormones influence female and male fetuses; (c) a comparison of self-confidence in adolescent males and females; (d) how body characteristics develop during puberty, such as pubic hair and breasts in females; (e) people's beliefs about the personality characteristics of women and men.

2. Apply the two terms *feminism* and *sexism* to your own experience. Do you consider yourself a feminist? Can you identify examples of sexism you have observed during the past week? How do the terms *feminism* and *sexism*, as used in this chapter, differ from the popular use in the media? Also, define and give an example for each of the following terms: racism, classism, heterosexism, ableism, ageism, U.S.-centered nationalism, and the White-as-normative concept.

3. Describe the three kinds of feminism discussed in this chapter. How are the similarities perspective and the differences perspective (with respect to gender comparisons) related to those three kinds of feminism? How are social constructionism and essentialism related to these two perspectives?

4. Describe the early research related to gender and the psychology of women. In the section on problems in research, we discuss biases that arise in formulating hypotheses. How might these problems be relevant in explaining some of this early research?

5. Briefly trace the development of the psychology of women from its early beginnings to the current state of the discipline.

6. Imagine that you would like to examine gender comparisons in leadership ability. Describe how a number of biases might influence your research.

7. Suppose that you read an article in a news magazine that concludes, "Women are more emotional than men." From a critical thinking perspective, what questions would you ask to uncover potential biases and problems with the study? (Check Figure 1.3 to see whether your answers to Questions 6 and 7 are complete.)

8. Turn back to Figures 1.1 and 1.2. Does the information about the diversity of racial and ethnic groups match the diversity at your own college or university? If not, what are the differences? How does the information on ethnicity relate to two of the themes of this book?

9. Describe each of the four themes of this book, providing an example for each theme. Do any of the themes contradict your previous ideas about women and gender? If so, how?

10. What is the difference between gender as a subject variable and gender as a stimulus variable? Suppose that you read a study comparing the aggressiveness of men and women. Is gender a subject variable or a stimulus variable? Suppose that another study examines how people judge aggressive men versus aggressive women. Is gender a subject variable or a stimulus variable?

NEW TERMS

*sex (4)
*gender (4)
 doing gender (4)
*sexism (4)
*racism (4)
 classism (5)
*heterosexism (5)
*ableism (5)
*ageism (5)
*feminism (5)
*liberal feminism (6)
 cultural feminism (6)
*radical feminism (6)
*similarities perspective (7)
*social constructionism (7)
*differences perspective (7)

*essentialism (7)
 White-as-normative concept (13)
 U.S.-centered nationalism (17)
*operational definition (21)
*variable (21)
*empathy (21)
*confounding variable (21)
 experimenter expectancy (22)
 researcher expectancy (22)
 statistical significance (23)
 practical significance (23)
*critical thinking (25)
 gender as a subject variable (28)
 gender as a stimulus variable (28)
*androcentric (28)

The terms asterisked in the New Terms section serve as good search terms for InfoTrac® College Edition. Go to http://infotrac.thomsonlearning.com and try these added search terms.

RECOMMENDED READINGS

Caplan, P. J., & Caplan, J. B. (1999). *Thinking critically about research on sex and gender* (2nd ed.). New York: Longman. Paula Caplan is a well-known psychologist whose work on the psychology of women is discussed throughout this textbook. She and her son Jeremy wrote this excellent book on applying critical thinking principles to the research on gender.

Clinchy, B. M., & Norem, J. K. (Eds.). (1998). *The gender and psychology reader.* New York: New York University Press. This book has 41 chapters written by the prominent researchers and theorists in the area of gender; I recommend it for anyone who would like an in-depth exploration of important topics related to gender.

Scarborough, E., & Furumoto, L. (1987). *Untold lives: The first generation of American women psycholo-*

gists. New York: Columbia University Press. If you are searching for interesting women in the early history of psychology, this book is ideal. It focuses not only on these important women but also on the forces that shaped their lives.

Unger, R. (Ed.). (2001). *Handbook of the psychology of women and gender.* New York: Wiley. I strongly recommend this handbook, which contains 27 chapters on topics such as gender comparisons, gender and language, and older women.

Worell, J. (Ed.). (2001). *Encyclopedia of women and gender.* San Diego: Academic Press. This two-volume encyclopedia is an excellent resource for current information about gender, with more than 100 entries written by prominent psychologists.

ANSWERS TO THE DEMONSTRATIONS

Demonstration 1.1: 1. radical feminism; 2. liberal feminism; 3. cultural feminism; 4. radical feminism; 5. liberal feminism; 6. cultural feminism.

ANSWERS TO THE TRUE-FALSE QUESTIONS

1. True (p. 4); 2. True (p. 5); 3. True (pp. 7–8); 4. False (pp. 9–10); 5. False (p. 10); 6. True (p. 13); 7. True (p. 17); 8. True (p. 21); 9. True (p. 22); 10. True (p. 27).

Gender Stereotypes and Other Gender Biases

AFP/Corbis

Biased Representations of Women and Men

Gender Biases Throughout History

Gender Biases in Language

Gender Biases in the Media

People's Beliefs About Women and Men

The Content of Stereotypes

The Complexity of Contemporary Sexism

Heterosexism

The Social Cognitive Approach to Gender Stereotypes

Gender Stereotypes and Behavior

Internalizing Gender Stereotypes

TRUE OR FALSE?

_____ 1. Historians and archeologists have typically paid more attention to men's lives, ignoring contributions made by women.

_____ 2. Before about 1900, all the prominent philosophers maintained that women were clearly inferior to men.

_____ 3. When people hear a sentence such as "Each student took his pencil," they understand that the word "his" refers to both males and females.

_____ 4. In the current era, women in television programs are frequently shown in employment settings.

_____ 5. Black women and men are fairly well represented on television, but Latinas and Latinos account for less than 5% of all characters on prime-time television.

_____ 6. In general, men tend to have more traditional gender stereotypes than women do.

_____ 7. People are especially likely to be biased against women's competence when women are acting in a stereotypically masculine fashion.

_____ 8. Current surveys indicate that at least 50% of lesbians and gay males have been verbally harassed about their sexual orientation.

_____ 9. Most contemporary psychologists explain gender stereotypes as an unconscious desire to discriminate against women.

_____ 10. Current research suggests that men rate themselves very differently from women on gender-related characteristics such as self-reliance and independence.

D r. Taraneh Shafii, the chief resident at a children's hospital in Louisville, Kentucky, frequently notices the impact of stereotypes. One day, in the emergency department, she introduced herself to the father of a sick child: "Hi, I'm Dr. Shafii." Then she proceeded to ask detailed questions about the child's illness. When it came time for the physical exam, the father said, "Come on, get up for the nice nurse." Later that day, another parent watched Dr. Shafii examine her children and then asked, "Can you tell me when the doctor will be in?" A third time that day, Dr. Shafii again introduced herself and examined a patient, a teenage boy. As she was preparing to put a splint on his broken hand, the boy asked, "So, how long did you have to go to school to be a nurse?" As Dr. Shafii explains, she admires nurses, and she also has many friends and relatives who are nurses. However, her patients often fail to understand that a woman can be a doctor rather than a nurse. Apparently, their gender stereotype—that a woman cannot be a doctor—is so powerful that it overrides the "Dr." in her name, the "M.D." on her name tag, and all her medical expertise (Shafii, 1997).

Gender stereotypes are organized, widely shared sets of beliefs about the characteristics of females and males (Golombok & Fivush, 1994). Notice that a stereotype is a *belief*. In other words, stereotypes refer to thoughts about a social group, which may not correspond to reality. Even when a gender stereotype is partly accurate (e.g., in describing women), it still won't apply equally to every individual woman (Eagly et al., 2000; Kunda, 1999). As Theme 4 points out, individual differences in psychological characteristics are large; no stereotype can accurately describe everyone in a particular social category.

Several additional terms are related to stereotypes. **Prejudice** is a biased attitude or emotional reaction toward a group of people—such as women—especially when these people try to move into new roles (Eagly, in press). **Discrimination** refers to action against a person or a group of people. A person can discriminate against an individual woman by making degrading remarks. Social institutions can also discriminate against groups of women, for example, when an organization has an unwritten policy that women cannot be promoted to the executive level (Lott & Maluso, 1995). Table 2.1 contrasts these three terms. The most general term, **gender bias,** includes all three issues: gender stereotypes, gender prejudice, and gender discrimination.

Let's begin our examination of gender stereotypes by noting how women have been represented in history, philosophy, and religion and how they are currently represented in language and the media. In the second section of this chapter, we focus on the content of contemporary stereotypes: What are the current stereotypes? How are these stereotypes related to thought processes? How can stereotypes influence behavior? How do people sometimes apply these gender stereotypes to themselves, so that they adopt a gender-stereotyped identity? How can people create a self-identity that is not constrained by these rigid categories?

BIASED REPRESENTATIONS OF WOMEN AND MEN

A systematic pattern emerges when we look at the way women are portrayed. As we'll see in this section, women are the "second sex" (de Beauvoir, 1961). Consistent with Theme 2, women are often represented as being inferior to men. In addition, consistent with Theme 3, women are frequently invisible. As you read about gender biases in history, language, and the media, be sure to think about how they may have shaped your own beliefs about women and men.

Gender Biases Throughout History

A few pages of background discussion cannot do justice to a topic as broad as our legacy of gender bias. However, we need to summarize several topics in order to appreciate the origin of current views about women.

The Invisibility of Women in Historical Accounts.   In recent decades, scholars have begun to realize that we know little about how half of humanity has fared

TABLE 2.1 ■ Comparing Three Kinds of Gender Bias

Term	Brief Definition	Example
Stereotype	Belief about women	Chris believes that women aren't very smart.
Prejudice	Attitude or emotions about women	Chris doesn't like female lawyers.
Discrimination	Behavior toward women	Chris won't hire a woman for a particular job.

throughout history (Stephenson, 2000). What *have* women been doing for all these centuries? Archeologists interested in prehistoric humans typically focused their research attention on tools associated with hunting, which was most often men's activity. They ignored the fact that women provided most of the diet by gathering vegetables and grains. Women also built and repaired the huts (Hunter College Women's Studies Collective, 1995; Stephenson, 2000).

Similarly, what were the women doing while the men of Europe were enjoying the Renaissance period? Did they also have a Renaissance? One important goal of women's studies is to look for missing information about women. Women have been invisible in our history books. We need to know about women food providers, artists, and philosophers.

Women have been left out of many history books because their work was confined to home and family. Women artists often expressed themselves in music, dance, embroidered tapestries, and quilting. These relatively fragile and anonymous art forms were less likely to be preserved than men's artistic efforts in painting, sculpture, and architecture. In addition, few women had the opportunity or encouragement to become artists.

In addition, many of women's accomplishments have been forgotten. Did you know that women often presided over monasteries before the ninth century (Hafter, 1979)? Did your history book tell you that the Continental Congress chose Mary Katherine Goddard to print the official copy of the Declaration of Independence in 1776? Traditional historians, whether consciously or unconsciously, have ensured women's invisibility in most history books. Scholars interested in women's history, however, are uncovering information about women's numerous accomplishments. Many college history courses now focus on women's experiences, making women central rather than peripheral.

Philosophers' Representation of Women.   Philosophers throughout the centuries have commented on women but have typically depicted them as inferior to men. For example, the Greek philosopher Aristotle (384–322 B.C.) believed that women's inferiority was biologically based (Book IX, Chapter 1, cited in C. Miles, 1935, p. 700). He believed that women could not develop fully as rational beings. Aristotle also believed that women are more likely than men to be envious and to tell lies (Dean-Jones, 1994; Stephenson, 2000).

Philosophers since the classical Greek period have adopted the same framework. For instance, Jean-Jacques Rousseau (1712–1778) argued that the function of women was to please men and to be useful to them (Hunter College Women's Studies Collective, 1995). In other words, this prominent Enlightenment philosopher was not enlightened about the roles of women! Rousseau's views were echoed by political figures. The French emperor Napoléon Bonaparte (1769–1821) wrote: "Nature intended women to be our slaves. . . . They are our property. . . . Women are nothing but machines for producing children" (cited in Mackie, 1991, p. 26).

Before the twentieth century, perhaps the only well-known philosopher whose views would be acceptable to current feminists was John Stuart Mill (1806–1873), a British philosopher whose viewpoint was strongly influenced by his wife, Harriet Taylor Mill (1807–1858). John Stuart Mill argued that women should have equal rights and equal opportunities. They should be able to own property, to vote, to be educated, and to choose a profession. John Stuart Mill is prominently featured in philosophy textbooks, but his views on women were omitted until recently (Hunter College Women's Studies Collective, 1995).

Images of Women in Religion and Mythology.   We've seen that history and philosophy have not been kind to women. In general, women are also treated differently from men in religion and mythology.

For example, Jews and Christians share the story of Adam and Eve. In this account, God created man "in His own image." Later, God made Eve, constructing her from Adam's rib. In other words, women are made from men, and women are therefore secondary in the great scheme of things. In addition, Eve gives in to temptation and leads Adam into sin. Women's moral weakness therefore contaminates men. When Adam and Eve are expelled from Paradise, the curses they receive show an interesting asymmetry. Adam's curse is that he must work for food and survival. Eve's curse is that she must endure the pain of bearing children, and she must also obey her husband.

In Judaism, further evidence of the position of women can be found in the traditional prayer for men, "Blessed art Thou, O Lord our God, King of the Universe, that I was not born a woman." Furthermore, the Torah specifies 613 religious rules, but only 3 of them apply to women. In these important Jewish traditions, women are relatively invisible (Ruth, 2001; R. J. Siegel et al., 1995). In addition, women must sit apart from men during Orthodox religious services.

For Christians, many parts of the New Testament treat men and women differently. For example, a letter of St. Paul notes that "the women should keep silence in the churches. For they are not permitted to speak, but should be subordinate, as even the law says" (1 Corinthians 14:34).

As the twenty-first century begins, Jewish women have become rabbis and scholars (R. J. Siegel et al., 1995). Women have also assumed leadership responsibilities in Protestant religions. However, women typically constitute less than 10% of the clergy in both the United States and Canada (Ruether, 1994).

Other religions promote negative views of women. Consider the yin and yang in traditional Chinese beliefs. The feminine yin represents darkness, ignorance, and evil. The yang, the masculine side, represents light, intellect, and goodness (Levering, 1994; Pauwels, 1998).

In Hinduism, a woman is defined in terms of her husband. As a consequence, an unmarried woman or a widow has no personal identity (R. J. Siegel et al., 1995). The Hindu goddess Kali is a dark monster with fangs, crossed eyes, and bloodstained tongue, face, and breasts. Hindus believe her wild dancing brings death on the world.

When we combine views of women from various religions and from traditional Greco–Roman mythology, we can derive several views of women:

1. *Women are evil.* Women can bring harm to men, as Eve did to Adam. Women may even be bloodthirsty, like the goddess Kali.
2. *Women are terrifying sorceresses.* Women can cast spells, like the wicked witches and evil stepmothers in fairy tales. Scylla, in Greek mythology, was a six-headed sea monster who squeezed men's bones together and ate them.
3. *Women are virtuous.* Women can also be virtuous and saintly, especially when they nurture men and small children. For example, the Virgin Mary represents the essence of caring and self-sacrifice, showing that women must never demand anything for themselves. Mythology may also represent women as "earth mothers" who are fertile and close to nature (Mackie, 1991; Sered, 1998).

Notice that these images are sometimes negative and sometimes positive. However, each image emphasizes how women are *different* from men. These traditions can be called **androcentric** or **normative male**: Men are normal; women are "the second sex."

Gender Biases in Language

Language, like religion, encourages a second-class status for women. Specifically, people often use subordinate or negative terms to refer to women. In addition, women are often invisible in language, for example, when the term *he* is used in reference to both men and women. Incidentally, we'll consider a related topic in Chapter 6 when we compare how men and women use language.

Terms Used for Women.   In many situations, people use different terms to refer to men and women, and the two terms are not parallel (Gibbon, 1999). For example, John Jones, M.D., will be called a *doctor,* whereas Jane Jones, M.D., may be called a *lady doctor.* This usage implies that being a male doctor is normal and that a female doctor is an exception.

Sometimes, the female member of a pair of words has a much more negative or trivial connotation than the male member does. Think about the positive connotations of the word *bachelor:* a happy-go-lucky person, perhaps with many romantic partners. How about *spinster?* Here the connotation is much more negative; no man wanted to marry her. Similarly, compare *master* with *mistress, major* with *majorette, sculptor* with *sculptress,* and *wizard* with *witch* (Gibbon, 1999; Penelope, 1990). Language may also infantilize women. For example, women are often referred to as *girl* or *gal* in situations where men would not be called *boy.* When these biased terms are used to refer to a woman, she is judged to be less competent than when she is referred to in gender-neutral terms (Dayhoff, 1983).

The Masculine Generic.   A cognitive psychology textbook with a 1998 copyright begins with this introduction: "Who and what are we? What is the mind and how does it function? . . . Such questions certainly have been with us as long as man has existed." As I read these sentences, I wondered: Were women really included in the author's term *man?* Women have surely pondered these same questions!

The example of *man* illustrates a problem called the masculine generic. The **masculine generic** (sometimes called the **androcentric generic**) is the use of masculine nouns and pronouns to refer to all human beings—both males and females—instead of males alone. Table 2.2 shows some of these masculine generic terms. A teacher may have told you that *his* really includes *her* in the sentence "Each student took his pencil." Essentially, you were supposed to consider *his* in this sentence as gender neutral, even though any female content is invisible (Pauwels, 1998; Romaine, 1999).

Researchers have now provided clear evidence that these masculine generic terms are not really gender neutral. More than 40 studies have demonstrated that terms such as *man* and *he* produce thoughts about males rather than thoughts about both genders (e.g., Crawford, 2001; Ivy et al., 1995; Romaine, 1999; Switzer, 1990). The issue is no longer simply a grammatical one; it has become both political and practical.

Demonstration 2.1 illustrates part of a representative study, conducted by John Gastil (1990). Gastil presented a number of sentences that used a masculine generic pronoun (e.g., "The average American believes he watches too much TV"). Other sentences used a gender-neutral pronoun (e.g., "Pedestrians must be careful when they cross the street"). Gastil asked the participants to describe the mental image evoked by each sentence.

As Figure 2.1 shows, female participants reported four times as many male images as female images when they responded to sentences containing *he.* In contrast, females reported an equal number of male and female images (i.e., a 1:1 ratio) when they responded to sentences containing *they.* Figure 2.1 also shows that males, in responding to the *he* sentences, reported an astonishing 13 times as many male images as female images, but only a 4:1 ratio in response to the *they*

TABLE 2.2 ■ Examples of Masculine Generic Terms

businessman	manpower
chairman	master of ceremonies
forefather	Neanderthal man
fraternal twins	patronize
he/his/him (to refer to both genders)	salesman
mankind	workmanship
man-made	

Sources: American Psychological Association (2001) and Doyle (1995).

DEMONSTRATION 2.1 ■ ■ ■ ■ ■ ■ ■ ■ ■ ■ ■ ■ ■ ■ ■ ■ ■

Imagery for Masculine Generic and Gender-Neutral Pronouns

Ask a friend to listen as you read sentence 1 aloud. Then ask the friend to describe out loud any image that comes to mind. Repeat the process with the remaining sentences. For each of the target (T) sentences, note whether your friend's image represents a male, a female, or some other answer.

	1.	Fire hydrants should be opened on hot days.
(T)	2.	The average American believes he watches too much TV.
	3.	The tropical rain forests of Brazil are a natural wonder.
(T)	4.	Pedestrians must be careful when they cross the street.
	5.	The apartment building was always a mess.
(T)	6.	After a patient eats, he needs to rest.
	7.	In the corner sat a box of worn-out shoes.
(T)	8.	Teenagers often daydream while they do chores.

Did your friend supply more male images for sentences 2 and 6 than for sentences 4 and 8? To obtain a broader sample of replies, try this demonstration with several friends, or combine data with a number of other classmates.

Source: Based on Gastil (1990).

---

sentences. In short, masculine generic terms do indeed produce more thoughts about males than do gender-neutral terms.

Other research has shown that the masculine generic issue has important implications for people's lives. For example, Briere and Lanktree (1983) presented students with different versions of a paragraph describing careers in psychology. Students who had seen the gender-neutral version rated psychology as a more appealing career for women than did those who had seen the masculine generic version. M. E. Johnson and Dowling-Guyer (1996) reported a related finding: College students rate psychology counselors more positively if the counselors use gender-neutral language rather than masculine generic language.

The use of gender-biased language has clearly decreased in recent years. For example, most writers now use the term *people* rather than the masculine generic term *man*. In fact, some observers have stated that the shift to avoid the masculine generic may be one of the most important changes in the English language in the past four centuries (C. Miller et al., 1997).

In general, college students tend to prefer nonsexist language (Parks & Roberton, 1998a, 1998b, 2000). Also, researchers have found that high school students

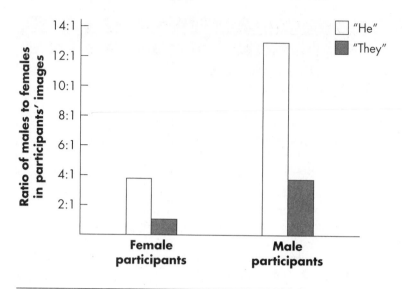

FIGURE 2.1 ■ Ratio of male images to female images, as a function of the pronoun condition and the gender of the participant.
Source: Based on Gastil (1990).

can easily increase their use of nonsexist language after they have seen appropriate examples (Cronin & Jreisat, 1995). Parks and Roberton (1998a) reported that some male students have made positive comments about gender-neutral terms. For example, a male college student reported:

> Being a male myself, it's easy to think that people are making mountains out of molehills. . . . But I think that if the roles were reversed, I would want change. . . . It wouldn't be fair if I was part of womankind, so it shouldn't be fair for women to be part of mankind. We should all be part of humankind. (p. 451)

Organizations such as the American Psychological Association strongly caution against gender-biased language. In addition, many books and articles have been written about substitutions for gender-biased language (e.g., American Psychological Association, 2001; Foertsch & Gernsbacher, 1997; Gibbon, 1999; Pauwels, 1998; Russo, 1999). Table 2.3 provides some suggestions.

Language change does require some effort, and we may find ourselves slipping back into the masculine generic. For example, a truck driver once passed my car when the visibility was poor, and I shouted, "What in the world does he think he is doing?" My daughter, then 9 years old, gently reminded me, "Or *she*, Mom."

Gender Biases in the Media

An advertisement for perfume in an upscale magazine shows a woman reclining with her eyes closed, adorned by flowers, as if it is her funeral. Another ad shows a women who appears to be about 20, and she is applying antiwrinkle cream;

TABLE 2.3 ■ **Suggestions for Nonsexist Language**

1. Use the plural form. "Students can monitor their progress" can replace "A student can monitor his progress."

2. Use "you." The sentence "Suppose that you have difficulty recalling your Social Security number" is less sexist—and also more engaging—than "Suppose that a person has difficulty recalling his Social Security number."

3. Use "his or her" or "her or his," as in the sentence "A student can monitor her or his progress." The order of these pronouns may sound awkward, but females do not always need to appear second.

4. Eliminate the pronoun. "The student is typically the best judge of the program" can replace "The student is usually the best judge of his program."

Source: Based on American Psychological Association (2001).

the text says to use this cream *before* your first wrinkle! Can you imagine switching the genders—using a corpselike male model to advertise men's cologne or running an ad to encourage 20-year-old men to purchase an antiwrinkle cream? If you want to test whether an advertisement is sexist, switch the genders and note whether the revision seems bizarre.

In Chapter 3, we'll consider media directed at children. In the present chapter, let's first examine gender stereotypes found in media directed at adults, and then we'll discuss the effects of these stereotyped representations.

Stereotyped Representations.   Hundreds of studies have examined how women are represented in the media. You may find an occasional example of nurturant dads and intellectual moms. However, the research generally demonstrates the following eight conclusions, which support both Theme 2 (differential treatment of women) and Theme 3 (invisibility of women).

1. *Women are relatively invisible.* Recent studies show that women are underrepresented in the media. For example, women are relatively invisible in the news. Studies of the front pages of newspapers in the United States and Canada show that the articles refer to women only 15–25% of the time (Bridge, 1994; United Nations, 1995; Wheeler, 1994). On television, women report only about 20% of the news stories about economic, political, or international issues (Grieco, 1999; Hoynes, 1999).

Men also dominate entertainment. Consider, for example, the main character in films that have won an Oscar for best motion picture. Between 1965 and 2001, only three focused on a woman—and all these women were European American (A. G. Johnson, 2001). An analysis of characters on TV shows found 2.4 times as many males as females (Gerbner, 1997). In addition, we rarely see women athletes on TV. In fact, television coverage of women's sports is only 10% of the total sports coverage (R. L. Hall, 2000; Koivula, 1999).

One place where women *are* seen is in television advertisements, where the numbers of females and males are roughly equal (Furnham & Skae, 1997; Signorielli & Bacue, 1999). As we'll see, however, the ads portray women in sexist contexts.

2. *Women are relatively inaudible.* Women are not seen much, and they are *heard* even less. For example, only 5% of radio talk-show hosts are women (Flanders, 1997). Women are also inaudible in advertisements. Try to recall a typical television ad. Whose voice of authority is praising the product's virtues? As it turns out, it is almost always a man's voice. The percentage of males in these voice-overs has remained reasonably constant in recent years. Studies in the United States report that 70–90% of voice-overs are male; similar data are reported in Great Britain, Portugal, France, Denmark, and Australia (Bartsch et al., 2000; Furnham & Mak, 1999; Furnham & Skae, 1997; Hurtz & Durkin, 1997; Neto & Pinto, 1998).

3. *Although most women are employed, they are seldom shown working outside the home.* For example, television advertisements and popular magazines are much more likely to show men rather than women in an employment setting (Coltrane & Adams, 1997b; Hurtz & Durkin, 1997; Vigorito & Curry, 1998). In television programs, ironically, women and men are both likely to be described as having professional careers—lawyers, doctors, and architects—an employment pattern that doesn't reflect the real-life distribution of jobs (Kolbe & Albanese, 1997; Signorielli & Bacue, 1999). In addition, women on television shows are seldom shown actually *working* on the job.

In Chapter 4, we'll see that adolescent girls may have ambitious career plans. However, they frequently abandon these plans as they work on cultivating romantic relationships. Several analyses of magazines such as *Seventeen* have shown a similar emphasis (Peirce, 1990; Schlenker et al., 1998; Willemsen, 1998). The articles on physical appearance and finding a boyfriend consistently outweigh the articles about career planning and independence. In magazines intended for adult women, the articles on love relationships, food, cosmetics, and home products far outnumber the articles on careers and other serious topics (S. H. Alexander, 1999; French, 1992).

4. *Women are shown doing housework.* Here, unfortunately, the percentages probably capture reality quite accurately. For example, the women in the Sunday comics are much more likely than the men to be cleaning the house (Brabant & Mooney, 1997). Television and radio commercials seldom show men taking care of children or performing household chores, whether the sample is gathered in North America, Europe, Asia, or Africa (Bartsch et al., 2000; Furnham & Mak, 1999; Furnham & Thomson, 1999; Furnham et al., 2000; G. Kaufman, 1999; Mwangi, 1996; Vigorito & Curry, 1998). For instance, a cartoon portrayed a male advertising executive explaining why he won't use a female copywriter's proposed layout for an ad: "Destereotyping the housewife can't be done overnight, Angela. Be a good kid and let her sing to her mop in this one, and I promise next time she can do something else with it" (Rhode, 1997, p. 71).

5. *Women and men are represented differently.* The media are likely to treat men more seriously than women. Consider Hillary Clinton's 2000 senatorial campaign in New York. It was difficult to find a newspaper article that did not mention her hairstyle, her "figure flaws," or her clothing choices (Pozner, 2001a). The media also portray women and men as having different personalities. The women are relatively powerless and passive, and the men are often aggressive and macho, both on television and in the movies (Haskell, 1997; Scharrer, 1998).

In addition, male characters on TV tend to move away from women twice as often as they move away from men (Lott, 1989; Lott & Maluso, 1995). In other words, men keep their attention focused on other men, but they soon turn away from women.

6. *Women's bodies are used differently from men's bodies.* Magazines and television rarely show images of overweight women (G. Fouts & Burggraf, 1999; Lin, 1998). In action comic books, the women have exaggerated bodies, with enormous breasts and tiny waists. They also wear short skirts or clinging bodysuits (Fraser, 1997; Massoth, 1997). Furthermore, if you glance through magazine advertisements, you'll notice that the women are more likely than the men to serve a decorative function. Women recline in seductive clothes, caressing a liquor bottle, or they drape themselves coyly on the nearest male. In contrast, the men are strong and muscular, and they typically adopt a rigid, dignified body posture (Kolbe & Albanese, 1996; Millard & Grant, 2001). The research confirms that women are frequently shown lying down or bent at an angle, whereas men are posed to look more dignified (Belknap & Leonard, 1991; Jones, 1991). Also, women's whole bodies are typically shown, whereas a photo of a man is likely to show only his face (C. C. I. Hall & Crum, 1994; M. J. Levesque & Lowe, 1999).

7. *Women of color are underrepresented, and they are often shown in a particularly biased way.* On television, people of color appear primarily in situation comedies (C. C. Wilson & Gutiérrez, 1995). Blacks are now represented in a reasonable number of TV programs and advertisements. However, other ethnic groups are virtually invisible (Boston et al., 2001; Coltrane & Messineo, 2000). For example, Latinas/os are the fastest-growing ethnic group in the United States, and they now represent about 12% of the U.S. population. However, they account for only about 2% of all characters on prime-time television shows and people in magazine advertisements (Espinosa, 1997; Kilbourne, 1999). Most often, these Latinas/os are featured only in minor supporting roles (Cortés, 1997; C. E. Rodríguez, 1997). Native American women are especially rare in the media (S. E. Bird, 1999).

In the earlier discussion of women and religion, we noted that religions represent women as either saints or sinners. The same polarized representation is often true for women of color in the media. Most women of color are either "good girls" or "bad girls"—either asexual or sexpots. The characters are seldom well enough developed to reveal the interesting combination of traits depicted in the media for European American individuals (Coltrane & Messineo, 2000; Espinosa, 1997; C. E. Rodríguez, 1997; Vargas, 1999).

In summary, women of color are both underrepresented and misrepresented by the media.

8. *Lower-social-class women are underrepresented, and they are often shown in a particularly biased way.* Surprisingly, media researchers have paid remarkably little attention to the issue of social class. In fact, five recent books about television and magazines do not even list the term *social class* in the index (Brunsdon et al., 1997; Cortese, 1999; Dow, 1996; Kilbourne, 1999; Shanahan & Morgan, 1999). However, the research shows that prime-time television features middle-class or wealthy individuals. If you are looking for low-income women on television,

you'll need to watch the afternoon talk shows, such as *The Jerry Springer Show*. After all, it's considered acceptable to include low-income women if they are promiscuous or if they come from dysfunctional families. In newspapers or magazines, you'll rarely find any article about low-income women unless it describes a mother receiving public assistance. These articles seldom capture the difficulty of raising a family under these conditions (Bullock et al., 2001).

Now that you are familiar with some of the ways in which women are represented in the media, try Demonstration 2.2. Also, start analyzing magazine advertisements to assess stereotyped representations. Pay particular attention to any nontraditional advertisements. Is the female lawyer who is arguing the case looking both confident and competent? How about the father who is changing the baby's diaper?

You may want to share your views with the advertisers. (You can obtain the addresses from the World Wide Web.) Sponsors are often attuned to public opinion. For example, I once wrote to the chief executive of a hotel after seeing its extremely sexist ad in *Toronto Life*. He replied that the advertisement had already been discontinued as a result of complaints from the public. You should also be ready to compliment companies about nonstereotyped ads.

The Effects of Stereotyped Representations.   Does the biased representation of women in the media simply *reflect* reality, or does it actually *influence* reality? We have evidence for both effects. The media reflect the reality that women are often unseen and unheard and that they are more likely than men to do housework. The media also reflect the reality that women are too frequently believed to be decorative and subservient. However, the ads certainly do *not* reflect reality in other respects. For example, do you have any female friend who obsesses about ring-around-the-collar or who invites neighbors in to smell her toilet bowl?

Research evidence also suggests that the media may be important in influencing reality. Stereotypes in magazines and on television actually do change some people's behaviors and beliefs. In one classic study, researchers found that college women who had seen a nontraditional version of a TV advertisement were much more self-confident than college women who had seen a traditional version (Jennings et al., 1980). Other research investigated women's self-images. When women looked at advertisements showing beautiful female models, they tended to be less satisfied with their own attractiveness (Richins, 1991; Wolf, 1991).

Advertisements can also influence gender-role attitudes. For example, men who are initially nontraditional are likely to become even more nontraditional after looking at nonstereotyped ads. In contrast, men who look at stereotyped ads become more traditional (Garst & Bodenhausen, 1997). Other research shows that both men and women hold less feminist attitudes after viewing stereotyped ads (MacKay & Covell, 1997).

Furthermore, people who have been exposed to sexually aggressive media are more likely to believe that violence against women is acceptable (J. D. Johnson et al., 1995; Lanis & Covell, 1995; MacKay & Covell, 1997; Wester et al., 1997). In other words, people who have watched violent music videos or videos that show women in subordinate roles may be more likely to believe that women are largely responsible for being raped.

DEMONSTRATION 2.2 ■ ■ ■ ■ ■ ■ ■ ■ ■ ■ ■ ■ ■ ■ ■ ■ ■

The Representation of Women and Men on Television

Keep a pad of paper next to you during the next five television programs you watch so that you can monitor how women and men are represented. Use one column for women and one for men, and record the activity of each individual who appears on screen for more than a few seconds. Use simple codes to indicate what each person is doing, such as working at a job (W), doing housework (H), or performing some activity for other family members (F). In addition, record the number of female and male voice-overs in the advertisements. Can you detect any other patterns in the representations of women and men, aside from those mentioned in the text?

How are social class and ethnicity represented on these shows? Can you identify any nonstereotypical examples?

The media can also influence how we judge other people. For example, J. L. Knight and Giuliano (2001) asked students to read an article about a female athlete and rate her on a number of dimensions. They rated her higher in talent, aggressiveness, and heroism if the article had emphasized her athletic skills rather than her attractiveness. Even subtle differences in the representation of women and men can have an important effect on people's stereotypes (M. J. Levesque & Lowe, 1999). More optimistically, the media also have the power to create new possibilities for nontraditional gender roles.

SECTION SUMMARY ■

Biased Representations of Women and Men

1. A gender stereotype is an organized, widely shared set of beliefs about the characteristics of females and males. Prejudice refers to negative attitudes, and discrimination refers to biased behavior.

2. We have little information about women's activities throughout history. In general, philosophers emphasized women's inferiority.

3. Judaism and Christianity both perpetuate women's inferiority; traditional Chinese beliefs and Hinduism also portray negative images of women. Various religions and ancient myths have represented women as evil people, sorceresses, and virtuous mothers.

4. The terms used for women often emphasize their secondary status, or these terms may be negative or infantilizing.

5. Numerous studies have demonstrated that the masculine generic encourages people to think about males more often than females; gender-neutral terms can be easily substituted.

6. The media represent women in a stereotyped fashion. Women are seen and heard less than men are. They are seldom shown working outside the home, although they are shown doing housework. The media treat men more professionally, and male TV characters distance themselves from women; women's bodies are also represented differently.

7. Women of color are particularly likely to be underrepresented or to be represented in a stereotypical fashion. Low-income women are also underrepresented; when they are shown, they are portrayed in a negative fashion.

8. The media's stereotyped representations of women promote stereotyped behaviors, self-images, and attitudes. Sexually aggressive media tend to promote the view that violence against women is acceptable. Finally, we judge women to be less talented and competent if they have been portrayed in a gender-stereotyped fashion.

PEOPLE'S BELIEFS ABOUT WOMEN AND MEN

In the first section of this chapter, we looked at the ways in which women and men are represented in history, philosophy, religion, mythology, language, and the media. These representations certainly help to shape people's beliefs about gender. Let's now turn to the man and woman on the street—or, more likely, on the college campus. What is the nature of their gender stereotypes? Why is sexism such a complex topic? What kinds of thought processes produce these stereotypes and keep them powerful? How can gender stereotypes influence people's behavior? Finally, do people adopt these stereotypes, so that women tend to describe themselves with "feminine" terms, whereas men prefer "masculine" terms?

The Content of Stereotypes

Before you read any further, look at Demonstration 2.3 on page 49. Notice that this demonstration does not ask you to assess your own stereotypes or beliefs about men and women. Instead, you must try to guess what *most people* think. You will probably find that your answers are accurate.

If you check the list of characteristics associated with women and with men, you'll see that those two lists are somewhat different. Theorists use the term **agency** to describe a concern with one's own self-interests. Terms associated with agency (such as *self-confident* and *competitive*) are usually stereotypically masculine. In contrast, the term **communion** emphasizes a concern for one's relationship with other people. Terms associated with communion (such as *gentle* and *warm*) are usually stereotypically feminine (Eagly, 2001; Kite, 1996).

DEMONSTRATION 2.3 ■ ■ ■ ■ ■ ■ ■ ■ ■ ■ ■ ■ ■ ■ ■ ■ ■ ■

Stereotypes About Women and Men

For this demonstration, you are asked to guess what *most people* think about women and men. Put a W in front of those characteristics that you believe most people associate with women more than with men. Put an M in front of those characteristics associated with men more than with women.

M	self-confident	m	fickle
W	gentle	m	greedy
W	kind	W	warm
m	competitive	W	nervous
m	active	W	capable
W	emotional	W	talkative
W	loud	m	show-off
W	compassionate	W	patient
W	modest	m	courageous
m	inventive	m	powerful

The answers appear at the end of the chapter and are based on responses that researchers have obtained (Cota et al., 1991; Street, Kimmel et al., 1995; J. E. Williams & Best, 1990; J. E. Williams et al., 1999).

Interestingly, these stereotypes have remained fairly consistent across time, especially the stereotypes about men (Diekman & Eagly, 2000; Glick & Fiske, 1999; Holt & Ellis, 1998; Hosoda & Stone, 2000). Furthermore, in studies that examined general stereotypes about men and women, college students and college faculty members shared almost identical stereotypes about men and women (Street, Kimmel et al., 1995; Street, Kromrey et al., 1995). Let's now look at the stereotypes about men and women from various ethnic groups. Then we'll consider how certain variables influence our stereotypes.

Stereotypes About Women and Men from Different Ethnic Groups. We humans move beyond simple stereotypes about women and men, and we create stereotypes about women and men from different ethnic groups (Deaux, 1995). For example, Yolanda Niemann and her colleagues (1994) asked college students from four ethnic groups to list the first 10 adjectives that came to mind when they thought of particular categories of people. These target categories included males and females from four different ethnic groups, so that each rater provided adjectives for a total of eight groups. Table 2.4 combines the data from all participants and shows the three most commonly listed terms for each group. As you

TABLE 2.4 ■ The Three Most Frequently Supplied Adjectives for Females and Males from Four Different Ethnic Groups

European American Females	European American Males
Attractive	Intelligent
Intelligent	Egotistical
Egotistical	Upper-class

African American Females	**African American Males**
Speak loudly	Athletic
Dark skin	Antagonistic
Antagonistic	Dark skin

Asian American Females	**Asian American Males**
Intelligent	Intelligent
Speak softly	Short
Pleasant/friendly	Achievement-oriented

Mexican American Females	**Mexican American Males**
Black/brown/dark hair	Lower-class
Attractive	Hard workers
Pleasant/friendly	Antagonistic

Source: Based on Niemann et al. (1994).

can see, people do not have one unified gender stereotype that holds true for all four ethnic groups. Instead, gender and ethnicity combine to produce a variety of gender stereotypes.

In reality, however, we probably create subtypes within each of these gender-ethnicity categories. For example, the stereotypes often distinguish between the "good women" and the "bad women" in each ethnic group. Ethnic studies scholars note that Black women are stereotyped as either warm but sexless "mammies"—a stereotype preserved since the slavery era—or sexually promiscuous females (Comas-Díaz & Greene, 1994; C. M. West, 2000). Latinas are portrayed, with similar polarization, as either chaste virgins or promiscuous women (Comas-Díaz & Greene, 1994; Peña, 1998). Asian American women are seen as either shy and submissive young women or as threatening and manipulative "dragon ladies" (Okazaki, 1998).

Interestingly, we don't know much about people's stereotypes about Native American women. Niemann and her colleagues (1994) did not study Native Americans, so they are not listed in Table 2.4. When most people hear the term *Native American* or *Indian*, they think of a male, or they may possibly think of Pocahontas. In any event, residents in most regions of North America do not have clear stereotypes about this least visible group of women of color (Comas-Díaz & Greene, 1994).

The research on ethnic subtypes within gender stereotypes illustrates the complexity of these stereotypes. There is no simple, unified stereotype that represents all women. Instead, we've created subtypes to reflect social class, ethnicity, and other characteristics of the group we are judging (Lott & Saxon, 2002).

Factors Influencing Stereotypes.   We've just seen that various characteristics of the target—the person we are judging—can influence our stereotypes. For example, ethnicity as a *stimulus* variable can affect these stereotypes. Now let's switch gears and examine characteristics of the *subject*—the person who holds these stereotypes. Subject variables are often important in research about gender. (You may want to review the distinction between stimulus variables and subject variables on page 28.)

Are stereotypes influenced by subject variables such as gender, ethnicity, and the culture in which we are raised? Alternatively, do we all share the same gender stereotypes, no matter what our own background may be? The answer seems to be somewhere between these two possibilities.

Consider the influence of the respondents' gender. Typically, men and women hold similar gender stereotypes, but men's stereotypes are somewhat more traditional (e.g., Levant & Majors, 1997; Spence & Hahn, 1997; Twenge, 1997). Within each gender, however, there are substantial individual differences in the strength of these stereotypes (Theme 4). For example, some women hold strong gender stereotypes; other women believe that men and women are quite similar.

In contrast, the respondents' ethnicity does not have a consistent influence on gender stereotypes (Dugger, 1996; R. J. Harris & Firestone, 1998; Levant & Majors, 1997; Levant et al., 1998). For example, Levant and his colleagues (1998) discovered that Southern Black men had stronger gender stereotypes than Southern White men; in the Northeast, however, Black men and White men had similar stereotypes. The researchers speculated that Black men in metropolitan regions of the Northeast would have more exposure to contemporary ideas about gender roles. In any event, gender stereotypes are much more complicated than we originally thought (Deaux, 1999; LaFromboise et al., 1990)!

Do people in other countries differ in their stereotypes? Cross-cultural research presents a unique set of challenges. As Gibbons, Hamby, and Dennis (1997) have pointed out, some tests that are commonly used to measure gender stereotypes cannot be easily used in some cultures. Consider the item, "It is all right for a girl to want to play rough sports like football." In many parts of the world, football means soccer; in other parts of the world, the game that Americans call football is unknown. A test containing this item would not be valid in many cultures outside North America.

The most extensive cross-cultural research on gender stereotypes has been conducted by Deborah Best and John Williams (Best & Williams, 1993; J. E. Williams & Best, 1990; J. E. Williams et al., 1999). They assessed gender stereotypes for 100 university students (50 females and 50 males) in each of 25 countries. In general, people in these diverse cultures shared similar gender stereotypes. For instance, men were typically believed to be more conscientious, outgoing, and emotionally stable, whereas women were believed to be more agreeable (J. E. Williams et al., 1999).

In summary, factors such as gender, ethnicity, and culture have complex influences on people's gender stereotypes. Overall, however, the consistency of the gender stereotypes is more prominent than any differences among the groups.

The Complexity of Contemporary Sexism

At the beginning of this chapter, we introduced three intertwined concepts: stereotypes, prejudice, and discrimination. In the previous discussion, we focused on stereotypes. Now we'll consider both prejudice and discrimination, and we'll also explore the complexity of gender biases in the current era.

In 1989, a Texas state senator remarked, "Do you know why God created women? Because sheep can't type" (Armbrister, cited in Starr, 1991, p. 41). This quotation is clearly sexist—no doubt about it! Present-day sexism is typically less obvious and more subtle, elusive, and complex (Brant et al., 1999). Let's consider three components of prejudice: (1) attitudes toward women's competence, (2) attitudes toward women's "pleasantness," and (3) a related topic, a recent scale designed to test the complicated ambivalent sexism that is now fairly common. Finally, we'll consider several studies that focus on discrimination against women in interpersonal interactions.

Attitudes Toward Women's Competence.   Dozens of studies conducted in the past 35 years have focused on people's attitudes toward women's achievements (e.g., Goldberg, 1968; Swim et al., 1989). For example, S. Beyer (1999b) asked college students to estimate the grade point averages (GPAs) of male and female students at their university. They greatly overestimated the GPAs for men, but they only slightly overestimated the GPAs for women.

In other research, students are asked to make judgments about either a male or a female under well-controlled circumstances. For example, Haley (2001) asked White undergraduate students to examine a fictitious application for a college scholarship. This application included a completed application form and a two-page essay. As part of this study, some students received an application in which the form specified that the student was a White male; other students received an identical application, only the form specified that the student was a White female. The students were instructed to indicate how much money should be awarded to the person described in the application. Haley's results showed that the White males specified much larger scholarships (about $1,900 more) when they read the application of a White male rather than that of a White female. In contrast, the White females specified only slightly larger scholarships (about $300 more) for the White female applicant than for the White male applicant.

Janet Swim and her colleagues (1989) reviewed 123 studies that focused on gender prejudice in the evaluation of competence. Overall, they found no convincing evidence for prejudice against women. Even when the stimulus material was concerned with a stereotypically masculine area, the gender of the presumed author produced only a modest bias. The analysis did suggest, however, that people rate women less favorably than men when they have little additional information about the person's qualifications.

Researchers have tried to identify the circumstances in which women's competence is likely to be devalued. For example, Haslett and her colleagues (1992) pointed out that evaluators who have expertise in an occupation are especially likely to devalue women. According to this perspective, students would not be very biased—and research using students is especially common for studies similar to Haley's (2001) research. In contrast, in real-life occupational settings, women are more likely to be evaluated by "experts," who may be quite biased. In addition, women's competence is likely to be devalued when the evaluators are men rather than women (Eagly et al., 1992; Eagly & Mladinic, 1994; Haley, 2001).

So far, we have seen that bias against women is most likely in the following conditions: (1) when little information is available about a person's qualifications, (2) when experts are doing the evaluating, and (3) when males are doing the evaluating. Another factor—perhaps one of the most important—is that (4) bias may be strongest when a woman is acting in a stereotypically masculine fashion (Eagly et al., 1992; Eagly & Mladinic, 1994; Fiske et al., 1993).

Consider the case of gender discrimination that accountant Ann Hopkins brought to court (Fiske et al., 1991; Fiske & Stevens, 1993). Hopkins was working at a prestigious accounting firm. She was being considered for promotion to partner, the only woman among 88 candidates that year. She had brought in business worth $25 million, the top amount of the 88 candidates. However, the company did not promote her. The firm claimed that Hopkins lacked interpersonal skills, and they branded her "macho" because of her hard-driving managerial style. A sympathetic coworker suggested that she would improve her chances if she would "walk more femininely, talk more femininely, dress more femininely, wear makeup, have her hair styled, and wear jewelry" (Fiske et al., 1991, p. 1050).

Notice that this bias against strong women presents a double bind. On the one hand, if these women act stereotypically feminine and gentle, then they are unlikely to be persuasive. Would Ann Hopkins have brought in $25 million in business if she had worn frilly blouses and acted submissive? On the other hand, if these women act masculine and assertive, then their superiors give them negative evaluations. Also, notice that the accounting firm was operating against its own best interests in order to provide a message about how females must behave. The company didn't promote someone who brought in millions of dollars to the company, and they also had to pay additional millions of dollars when they lost the legal case in the Supreme Court (Clinchy & Norem, 1998).

Attitudes Toward Women's Pleasantness. People don't think that women are especially competent, but they *do* think that women are generally pleasant and nice. A series of studies was conducted by Alice Eagly, whose work on gender comparisons forms the core of Chapter 6. In this research, college students were asked to rate the category "men" and the category "women" on scales with labels such as "pleasant–unpleasant," "good–bad," and "nice–awful" (Carter et al., 1991; Eagly, 2001; Eagly & Mladinic, 1994; Eagly et al., 1991). Compared to men, women typically receive more positive ratings on these scales. For example, the subtype "macho men" receives the lowest rating; these men are rated as much less pleasant than the comparable female subtype "sexy women."

We also know that people are not equally positive about all kinds of women. G. Haddock and Zanna (1994) asked Canadian college students to rate their attitude toward two groups of women, "housewives" and "feminists." Figure 2.2 shows their responses on a scale from 0 to 100, where 100 was labeled "extremely favorable" and 50 was labeled "neither favorable nor unfavorable." As you can

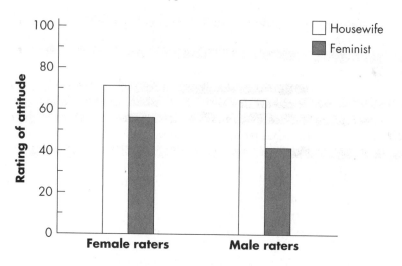

FIGURE 2.2 ■ Attitudes toward housewives and feminists, as a function of respondents' gender. (Note: 100 = extremely favorable; 50 = neither favorable nor unfavorable.)

Source: Based on G. Haddock and Zanna (1994).

see, females gave higher ratings to both groups of women than did males. Also, both females and males gave higher ratings to housewives than to feminists, a finding that has been replicated with U.S. college students (Kite & Branscombe, 1998).

Before you read any further, look at Demonstration 2.4 on page 55.

Ambivalent Sexism. We have seen that contemporary sexism is complicated. Women may not be judged to be very competent, but they *are* judged to be fairly nice—unless they happen to be feminists.

Peter Glick and Susan Fiske (1996, 1997, 2001a, 2001b) have tried to capture the complexity of sexism with a scale they call the Ambivalent Sexism Inventory. They argue that sexism is a prejudice based on a deep ambivalence toward women rather than on a uniform dislike of women. This scale contains items that tap two kinds of sexism: hostile sexism and benevolent sexism. **Hostile sexism,** the more blatant kind of sexism, is based on the idea that women should be subservient to men and should "know their place." **Benevolent sexism** is a more subtle kind of sexism that argues for women's special niceness and purity; however, it still emphasizes that women are *different* from men and that they are also weaker.

Notice that these two different kinds of sexism are consistent with the two different representations of women in religion and mythology (pp. 38–39) as well as with the mixture of negative and positive attitudes we have just discussed (pp. 52–54). All of these general tendencies reflect an ambivalence toward women.

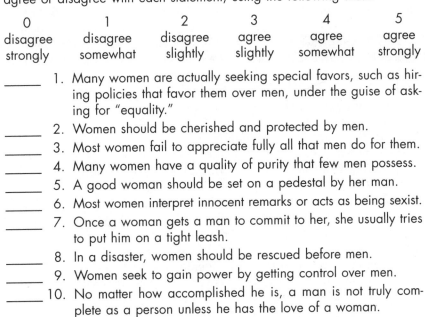

DEMONSTRATION 2.4

The Ambivalent Sexism Inventory

The following items are selected from Glick and Fiske's (1996) Ambivalent Sexism Inventory. For each item, indicate the degree to which you agree or disagree with each statement, using the following scale:

0	1	2	3	4	5
disagree strongly	disagree somewhat	disagree slightly	agree slightly	agree somewhat	agree strongly

_____ 1. Many women are actually seeking special favors, such as hiring policies that favor them over men, under the guise of asking for "equality."

_____ 2. Women should be cherished and protected by men.

_____ 3. Most women fail to appreciate fully all that men do for them.

_____ 4. Many women have a quality of purity that few men possess.

_____ 5. A good woman should be set on a pedestal by her man.

_____ 6. Most women interpret innocent remarks or acts as being sexist.

_____ 7. Once a woman gets a man to commit to her, she usually tries to put him on a tight leash.

_____ 8. In a disaster, women should be rescued before men.

_____ 9. Women seek to gain power by getting control over men.

_____ 10. No matter how accomplished he is, a man is not truly complete as a person unless he has the love of a woman.

When you have finished this test, check the scoring instructions at the end of the chapter on page 71. You may also want to ask friends to take the test, to see whether you obtain the same gender differences that Glick and Fiske did.

Note: The complete test includes 22 items, some of which are worded so that a highly sexist person would disagree with them. Readers should be aware that this shortened version of the Ambivalent Sexism Inventory has not been validated. Anyone who is interested in using the scale for research or assessment purposes should refer to Glick and Fiske (1996).

Source: From Glick and Fiske, _Ambivalent Sexism Inventory._ Copyright © 1995 by Peter Glick and Susan T. Fiske.

You tried a short version of Glick and Fiske's (1996) Ambivalent Sexism Inventory in Demonstration 2.4. In the United States, many studies with this inventory have shown that men typically score higher than women on the benevolent sexism subscale, but the gender differences are even larger on the hostile sexism subscale (Glick & Fiske, 1996, 2001b).

The Ambivalent Sexism Inventory has also been tested with 15,000 men and women in 19 different countries throughout the world (Glick et al., 2000). Both hostile sexism and benevolent sexism have been found in all these countries. The studies also confirmed that gender differences are larger on the hostile sexism subscale than on the benevolent sexism subscale. Glick and his colleagues also obtained data from the United Nations about gender equality in each of these 19 countries (based on measures such as women's share of the earned income and the percentage of high governmental positions held by women). In countries with low gender equality, the respondents tended to be high in both hostile sexism and benevolent sexism. This finding is easy to understand for hostile sexism: When people believe that women should be subservient to men, women will probably receive low salaries and hold few government positions. The relationship between gender equality and benevolent sexism is more subtle. However, benevolent sexism also helps justify gender inequality. After all, women are pleasant, helpless people whom men must protect from having too much responsibility in the workplace (Glick & Fiske, 2001a, 2001b).

In short, the research on the Ambivalent Sexism Inventory highlights both the subtlety and the complexity of contemporary sexism. It also illustrates that the two different kinds of sexism are widespread throughout the world.

Discrimination in Interpersonal Interactions.   So far in this section, we've looked at the nature of stereotypes and prejudice. We'll now explore gender discrimination. As you'll see, people in North America behave differently toward men and women, both in laboratory research and in real life; in addition, we'll see that gender discrimination even has life-threatening consequences in some countries.

The classic laboratory research was conducted by Bernice Lott, who examined discrimination in a basic kind of interpersonal situation (Lott, 1987; Lott & Maluso, 1995). Pairs of unacquainted students were observed from behind a one-way mirror while they worked together to build a structure. This research showed that women seldom responded negatively to their partners (either male or female). However, the men made many more negative comments to their female partners than to their male partners. In another similar study, men reported that they would prefer to work with other men rather than with women on a variety of tasks (Lott et al., 1990).

The conclusions from these laboratory studies are echoed in research on real-life gender discrimination (e.g., Landrine & Klonoff, 1997; Swim et al., 2001). For example, Janet Swim and her colleagues (2001) conducted a series of studies in which undergraduate women were asked to keep track of the number of nontrivial sexist remarks and behaviors they encountered during a 2-week period. They reported that these events occurred an average of once or twice a week. The specific kinds of sexist encounters fell into three basic categories: (1) Some women reported traditional gender-stereotyped remarks (e.g., "You're a woman, so fold my laundry"). (2) Others noted demeaning comments and behaviors (e.g., a woman who was talking with friends was told by a man, "Yo bitch, get me some beer!"). (3) Still others reported sexual comments and behaviors (e.g., one woman reported on a conversation with two male friends in which they agreed that females were okay only if they were "easy").

In Chapter 7, we will explore other forms of interpersonal discrimination when we look at sexism in the workplace. In Chapter 12, we'll see that interpersonal discrimination may contribute to the relatively high rate of depression in women (Landrine & Klonoff, 1997; Swim et al., 2001). In other words, the interpersonal discrimination that women experience does not evaporate quickly. Instead, these gender-biased experiences often reduce the overall quality of women's lives. In short, this section provides abundant evidence for Theme 2: Women are often treated differently from the way men are treated.

Most of the research discussed in this textbook focuses on the United States, Canada, and other English-speaking cultures. In many countries, however, the kind of discrimination we've discussed—such as negative remarks to a female coworker—would be considered relatively minor.

Several years ago, the country that practiced the greatest discrimination against women was Afghanistan. In the course of a turbulent history, an extremist Muslim group called the Taliban took control of this country in 1994. The Taliban's rules prohibited women from working outside the home. As a result, unmarried women who had previously worked as teachers, doctors, and nurses were often forced to beg in the streets in order to feed themselves, or they became prostitutes (W. Anderson, 2001; Physicians for Human Rights, 1998; Vollmann, 2000). Girls and women were also forbidden to attend school. In addition, females usually could not seek health care. For example, only 10% of pregnant Afghan women received any prenatal care or care during childbirth (Physicians for Human Rights, 1998). As a result, many women died at home during labor.

When out in public, Afghan women were required to wear a burqa, a garment that covers the entire body, with only a small mesh portion in front of the eyes that allows the wearer to see (see Photo 2.1). Women were often beaten if part of their body was exposed. For example, one woman described how her great aunt was flogged by a Taliban militia member when her ankle was accidentally exposed. He beat her with a metal cable, breaking her leg in the process. As you can imagine, the restrictions in work, school, health care, and clothing had serious consequences for the mental health of Afghan women. According to a study conducted by Physicians for Human Rights (1998), 97% of their sample met the criteria for major depression, and 86% met the criteria for an anxiety disorder.

As you probably know, the United States destroyed most of the Taliban leadership during the war that followed the tragedies of September 11, 2001. You may not know that the United States had been sending billions of dollars to the Taliban during the 1990s, to help them fight troops from Russia. Unfortunately, the U.S. government was willing to ignore the Taliban's mistreatment of women.

On the other end of the spectrum, women in Scandinavian countries experience less discrimination than women in the United States. For example, the percentage of women in Parliament (the highest government assembly in these countries) ranges from 24% in Iceland to 39% in Finland and Norway (Solheim, 2000). The current percentage of women in the Canadian Senate is 35%, in contrast to only 13% in the U.S. Senate. The U.S.-normative perspective encourages U.S. citizens to assume that women are especially well treated in our society.

PHOTO 2.1 ■ These Afghan women were begging for money for food, because the Taliban prohibited women from paid employment outside the home. (Note that the women are wearing burqas, which allow only a limited view of the world.)

In many cases, this perspective is true. Sadly, however, this textbook will identify many exceptions to this assumption.

Heterosexism

In the previous discussion of contemporary sexism, we saw that people make a major distinction between men and women. People may be hostile toward women or they may be benevolent toward women, but an important conclusion is that they think women are psychologically different from men. As we also emphasized in our discussion of Theme 2, people react differently to men and women. We'll see throughout this chapter that people divide the world into two categories, male and female.

This gender categorization has an important implication for love relationships. Specifically, gender categorization encourages people to believe that a person from the category "male" must fall in love with a person from the category "female." Most people are troubled by same-gender love relationships (Bem, 1995).

A **lesbian** is a woman who is psychologically, emotionally, and sexually attracted to other women. A **gay male** is a man who is psychologically, emotionally, and sexually attracted to other men. A **bisexual** is someone who is psychologically, emotionally, and sexually attracted to both women and men. In Chapter 8, we will discuss potential explanations for sexual orientation as well as the love relationships of women who are lesbians and bisexuals.

In this section, however, let's focus on heterosexism. As we noted in Chapter 1, **heterosexism** is bias against lesbians, gay males, and bisexuals—or any group that is not exclusively heterosexual. A related term is **sexual prejudice,** a negative attitude toward someone because of her or his sexual orientation (Herek, 2000). An older term, *homophobia,* is less useful because it suggests that the problem is found in individual people, rather than in the general culture, and that it is an irrational fear of gay people, rather than a negative attitude (Fernald, 1995; Herek, 2000). As a result, we'll typically use the terms *heterosexism* and *sexual prejudice* throughout this book. Let's consider some examples of heterosexism and then see what factors are correlated with it.

Examples of Heterosexism.   Some types of heterosexism are relatively subtle, but they still reveal that our culture values people who love someone from the other gender category rather than someone from the same gender category. Consider Jane and her longtime partner Marilyn, who were guests at the wedding of Jane's cousin. After the ceremony, Jane's aunt was gathering family members together for a photo. The aunt called out to Jane to join them, but she didn't call Marilyn (Berzon, 1996). From the aunt's perspective, a longtime lesbian relationship didn't have the same status as a heterosexual relationship.

In many instances, heterosexism is more intentionally hurtful. For example, surveys suggest that between 50% and 90% of lesbians and gay males have been verbally harassed about their sexual orientation (Pilkington & D'Augelli, 1995). For example, Carla was the president of her senior class when she told her classmates she was gay. The next day, someone had spray-painted "Carla will die" in big red letters across one of the walls of the school building (Owens, 1998).

Surveys also indicate that between 10% and 40% of lesbians and gay males have been chased or followed and that between 10% and 50% have been assaulted (Herek et al., 1997; Pilkington & D'Augelli, 1995). For instance, a lesbian college student named Jaime described how she was walking with her girlfriend when some men from a college fraternity approached them with a baseball bat. The men first struck Jaime, breaking two of her ribs. Then they hit her girlfriend with the butt of the bat, breaking her nose (Owens, 1998).

We've seen that gays and lesbians frequently experience interpersonal discrimination—heterosexist biases, verbal harassment, and physical assault—because of their sexual orientation. They also face institutional discrimination; that is, the government, corporations, and other institutions discriminate against gays, lesbians, and bisexuals. For example, the U.S. military does not currently permit its members to discuss their sexual orientation. Most insurance companies deny benefits to same-gender partners. I recall a friend discussing with irony that her insurance benefits could not cover her lesbian partner, with whom she had lived for 20 years. In contrast, a male colleague's wife could receive benefits even though the couple had been married less than three years and were now separated.

Factors Correlated with Heterosexism.   Attitudes toward lesbians, gays, and bisexuals are complex. In the current era, U.S. and Canadian residents generally believe that homosexuals should be allowed equal rights in terms of job opportunities. However, most argue that homosexuality is morally wrong (Fernald, 1995).

In general, men are more negative than women in their attitudes toward gays and lesbians (Herek & Capitanio, 1999; Kite & Whitley, 1996). In addition, people with traditional gender roles are more likely than nontraditional people to express sexual prejudice (Basow & Johnson, 2000; Whitley & Ægisdóttir, 2000). As you know, men are more likely than women to endorse traditional gender roles, a factor that may explain the gender difference in sexual prejudice (Kite & Whitley, 1996, 1998; LaMar & Kite, 1996). Furthermore, people generally have more negative attitudes toward gay men than toward lesbian women (Herek, 2000; Schellenberg et al., 1999).

In general, people with heterosexist attitudes tend to be politically and religiously conservative. They also tend to be racist (Fernald, 1995; Kite & Whitley, 1998). However, students often become more tolerant and less heterosexist as they go through college (Lottes & Kuriloff, 1994; Schellenberg et al., 1999). It's worth mentioning, though, that college courses in gay and lesbian studies are relatively rare (Austria, 2000). According to one estimate, only 59 colleges offer a social science course on this topic (Marketing Services Group Inc., 2000). To assess your own attitudes toward lesbians and gay men, try Demonstration 2.5.

The Social Cognitive Approach to Gender Stereotypes

The social cognitive approach provides a useful theoretical explanation for gender stereotypes, heterosexist stereotypes, and stereotypes based on categories such as ethnicity, social class, and age. According to the **social cognitive approach, stereotypes are belief systems that guide the way we process information, including information about gender** (D. L. Hamilton & Sherman, 1994; Kunda, 1999).

One cognitive process that seems nearly inevitable is our tendency to divide the people we meet into social groups (Banaji & Hardin, 1996; Fiske et al., 1999; Macrae & Bodenhausen, 2000). We categorize people as females or males, White people or people of color, people with high occupational status or people with low occupational status, and so forth.

The social cognitive approach argues that stereotypes help us simplify and organize the world by creating categories (Kunda, 1999; Macrae et al., 1994; Snyder & Miene, 1994). The major way we categorize people is on the basis of their gender (Glick & Fiske, 1998). This process of categorizing others on the basis of gender is habitual and automatic. If you doubt that statement, after you finish reading today, try *not* to pay attention to the gender of the first person you meet!

The problem, however, is that this process of categorizing and stereotyping often encourages us to make errors. These errors, in turn, produce further errors. That is, because we have a stereotype, we tend to perceive women and men differently, and this perception adds further "evidence" to our stereotype. A strengthened stereotype leads to an even greater tendency to perceive the two genders differently. As a result, stereotypes are especially resistant to change (Barone et al., 1997; Macrae & Bodenhausen, 2000).

DEMONSTRATION 2.5 ■ ■ ■ ■ ■ ■ ■ ■ ■ ■ ■ ■ ■ ■ ■ ■ ■ ■

Attitudes Toward Lesbians and Gay Men

Answer each of the following items either yes or no. (Please note that the original questionnaire was designed for heterosexuals, so some items may seem inappropriate for lesbian, bisexual, and gay male respondents.)

1. I would not mind having gay friends.
2. I would look for a new place to live if I found out that my room-mate was gay.
3. I would vote for a gay person in an election for a public office.
4. Two people of the same gender holding hands in public is disgusting.
5. Homosexuality, as far as I'm concerned, is not sinful.
6. I would mind being employed by a gay person.
7. I would decline membership in an organization if it had gay members.
8. I would not be afraid for my child to have a gay teacher.
9. Gay people are more likely than heterosexuals to commit deviant sexual acts, such as child molestation.
10. I see the gay movement as a positive thing.

To obtain a rough idea about your attitudes, add together the number of yes answers you provided for items 1, 3, 5, 8, and 10. Next, add together the number of no answers you provided for items 2, 4, 6, 7, and 9. Then, add these two subtotals together; scores close to 10 indicate positive attitudes toward gay people.

Source: Based on Kite & Deaux (1986).

Let's look at several topics in the area of the social cognitive approach and gender stereotyping:

1. People tend to exaggerate the contrast between women and men.
2. People tend to see the male as normative and the female as nonstandard.
3. People often make biased judgments on the basis of stereotypes.
4. People often selectively remember information that is consistent with gender stereotypes.

Exaggerating the Contrast Between Women and Men. We tend to exaggerate the similarities *within* a group and exaggerate the contrast *between* groups. When we divide the world into two groups—male and female—we tend to see all males as being similar, all females as being similar, and the two gender categories as being different; this tendency is called **gender polarization** (Bem, 1993). Gender polarization forces us to condemn individuals who deviate from this rigid role definition. As we saw in the discussion of gender discrimination, accountant Ann Hopkins experienced job discrimination because she did not have typically feminine mannerisms.

As we will emphasize throughout this textbook, the characteristics of women and men tend to overlap. Unfortunately, however, gender polarization often creates an artificial gap between women and men. People tend to believe that gender differences in psychological characteristics are larger than they really are (B. P. Allen, 1995; J. A. Hall & Carter, 1999; C. L. Martin, 1987). Human cognitive processes seem to favor clear-cut distinctions, not the blurry differences that are more common in everyday life. Our contemporary culture especially encourages distinctions based on gender.

The Normative Male.   As we discussed earlier in this chapter, the normative male concept (or androcentrism) means that the male experience is considered the norm, that is, the neutral standard for the species as a whole. In contrast, the female experience is a deviation from that supposedly universal standard (Basow, 2001; Bem, 1993, 1996). One example of the normative male principle is that when we hear the word *person*, we tend to believe that this individual is a male rather than a female (M. C. Hamilton, 1991a; Merritt & Kok, 1995). Similarly, D. T. Miller and his colleagues (1991) asked people to visualize a "typical American voter"; 72% of their participants described a male.

The normative male principle also reveals itself when people discuss gender differences (Tavris, 1992). As you'll learn in Chapter 5, men and women sometimes differ in their self-confidence. However, the research typically assumes that males have the "normal" amount of self-confidence and that females are somehow defective. In other words, men are serving as the standard of comparison (McGill, 1993). However, the truth may be that females actually have the appropriate amount of self-confidence; they may judge the quality of their performance fairly accurately. From that perspective, males would be *over*confident and overly self-serving.

We have already seen evidence of androcentrism in Chapter 1; the early history of the psychology of gender assumed that the male is normative. Our discussion of masculine generic language and the representation of gender in the media also reflects androcentrism. In addition, androcentrism is apparent in the workplace, family life, and medical care (Basow, 2001), as we will see in later chapters of this book.

Making Biased Judgments About Females and Males.   Our stereotypes may also lead us to interpret certain behaviors in a biased manner. After all, social behavior is often ambiguous and can be interpreted in several different ways (Fiske et al., 1999; D. L. Hamilton et al., 1990). For example, people display stereotyped interpretations when they make judgments about emotional reactions. M. D. Robinson and Johnson (1997) asked college students to read a variety of short scenarios. A representative scenario described a typical woman (or man) who was becoming concerned about the future of an important relationship that the person did not want to end. When the participants were making judgments about a woman, they tended to say that she would feel "emotional." In contrast, when making judgments about a man, the participants tended to say that he would feel "stressed." These gender stereotypes were much more influential when participants evaluated other people than when they evaluated themselves (M. D. Robinson et al., 1998). Once again, the stereotypes about gender differences are larger than the actual gender differences.

Naturally, our tendency to make stereotyped judgments is influenced by several variables. Specific information about individuals can sometimes be so persuasive that it overrides a stereotype (Kunda & Sherman-Williams, 1993). A woman may be so well qualified for a job that her strengths outweigh the "problem" that she is female. However, we are especially likely to apply a stereotype if we are busy working on another task at the same time (Macrae & Bodenhausen, 2000; Valian, 1998).

Many studies have been conducted on a particular kind of judgment called attributions. **Attributions** are explanations about the causes of a person's behavior. Chapter 5 discusses how people make attributions about their own behavior. In this current chapter, we'll discuss how people make stereotypical attributions about the behavior of other individuals.

The research on attributions is both extensive and complex. It shows that people often think that a woman's success on a particular task can be explained by the fact that she tried hard (Swim & Sanna, 1996). For example, researchers have examined parents' attributions for their children's success in mathematics. When a daughter does well in math, parents attribute her success to hard work. In contrast, they attribute their son's success to his high ability (Eccles, 1987; Eccles [Parsons] et al., 1982). Notice the implications of this research: People think that females need to try harder to achieve the same level of success as males.

The same "effort and hard work" explanation may be used when people are trying to explain the success of other groups that are commonly believed to be inferior. For example, people were asked to judge why a White male in a scenario had become a successful banker; they attributed his success to his high ability (Yarkin et al., 1982). However, they showed a different attributional pattern when judging a White female, a Black male, or a Black female. For those three individuals, hard work and luck were judged to be the most important reasons for success. I'm reminded of a highly successful Black couple I know. She's a professor, and he's a surgeon. They were visiting their son's math teacher to discuss the young man's less than ideal performance. The teacher said to them, "Well, I wouldn't worry too much. You're both overachievers." In the teacher's eyes, the only way these two Black individuals could have achieved their professional prominence was by hard work, not by natural intelligence and ability.

Let's review what we know so far about the social cognitive approach to gender stereotypes. We know that stereotypes simplify and bias the way we think about people who belong to the social categories "female" and "male." Because of gender stereotypes, we exaggerate the contrast between women and men. We also consider the male experience to be normal, whereas the female experience is the exception that requires an explanation. We also make biased judgments about females and males, for instance, when we judge whether they are feeling emotional or stressed. Research in the area of social cognition also emphasizes one final component of stereotypes: people's memory for stereotyped characteristics.

Memory for Personal Characteristics.   People sometimes, but not always, recall gender-consistent information more accurately than gender-inconsistent information (e.g., Cann, 1993; Furnham & Singh, 1986; Halpern, 1985; T. L. Stewart & Vassar, 2000). For instance, Dunning and Sherman (1997) asked participants to read a sentence such as "The women at the office liked to talk around the water cooler." During a later memory test, the researchers presented a series of sentences and asked the participants to decide whether each sentence was old (that is, seen in exactly the same form on the initial presentation) or new. The most interesting results concerned their judgments about new sentences that were *consistent* with the gender stereotype implied by a sentence presented earlier (e.g., "The women at the office liked to gossip around the water cooler"); they erroneously judged that 29% of these sentences were old. In contrast, when they saw new sentences that were *inconsistent* with a gender stereotype (e.g., "The women at the office liked to talk sports around the water cooler"), they erroneously judged that only 18% of these sentences were old. Apparently, when people saw the original sentence about women talking around the water cooler, they often made gender-consistent inferences (e.g., that the women must be gossiping). As a result, when they later saw a sentence that explicitly mentioned gossiping, that sentence looked familiar!

The research in social cognition shows that we are especially likely to recall stereotype-consistent material when we have other tasks to do at the same time, such as remembering other information, and when we have a strong, well-developed stereotype (Burn, 1996; D. L. Hamilton & Sherman, 1994; Hilton & von Hippel, 1996). When we have nothing else to do and when stereotypes are weak, we may sometimes remember material inconsistent with our stereotypes.

Gender Stereotypes and Behavior

We began this section by discussing the content of gender stereotypes and the complex nature of contemporary sexism. The social cognitive approach helps us to understand how errors in our thinking can arise and how these errors, in turn, generate further errors. However, if we focus entirely on our thought processes, we may forget an extremely important point: Stereotypes can influence people's behavior. That is, stereotypes can influence actions and choices, in other people and in ourselves.

Stereotypes can influence behavior through a **self-fulfilling prophecy:** Your expectations about someone may lead him or her to act in ways that confirm your original expectation (R. Rosenthal, 1993). For example, if parents expect that their daughter will not do well in mathematics, she may become pessimistic about her ability in that area. As a result, her math performance may drop (Eccles et al., 1990; Jussim et al., 2000).

Self-fulfilling prophecies are difficult to study, but let's consider a representative study. Skrypnek and Snyder (1982) arranged to have pairs of students participate in an experiment without ever seeing or talking to each other. One member of each pair was male and the other member was female, but this fact was not revealed to the participants. These researchers found that females chose more masculine tasks to perform when their male partners had been led to believe they were working with other males. In contrast, the females tended to select feminine tasks when the male partners believed they were working with females. Presumably, the men's stereotypes influenced the way they treated their partners; they used different strategies toward people whom they believed to be male rather than female. The women then behaved in a fashion that was consistent with the men's expectations.

Think of occasions when self-fulfilling prophecies may operate in your own life. As Burn (1996) pointed out, a man might believe that women are not good drivers. If he states this belief to a woman while she is driving, she may become so nervous that she indeed does not drive well. His stereotype will be confirmed, even though his opinion indirectly influenced her behavior.

A related problem is called **stereotype threat:** If you belong to a group that is hampered by a negative stereotype—and someone reminds you about your group membership—you may become anxious and your performance may suffer (Jussim et al., 2000; C. M. Steele, 1997). Consider some research by Shih and her colleagues (1999), in which all the participants were Asian American women. In North America, one stereotype is that Asian Americans are "good at math" (compared to other ethnic groups). In contrast, another stereotype is that women are "bad at math" (compared to men). Some of the participants in this study were asked to indicate their ethnicity and then answer several questions about their ethnic identity; they then took a challenging math test. These women answered 54% of the questions correctly. Other participants did not answer any questions beforehand; they simply took the same math test. The women in this control group answered 49% of the questions correctly. Still others began by indicating their gender and then answering several questions about their gender identity; then they took the same math test. These women answered only 43% of the questions correctly. Apparently, when Asian American women are reminded of their ethnicity, they perform relatively well. However, when Asian American women are reminded of their gender, they experience stereotype threat and they perform relatively poorly.

However, people are not always at the mercy of gender stereotypes (Fiske, 1993; Jussim et al., 2000). We are not marionettes, with other people pulling our strings. Our own self-concepts and abilities are usually stronger determinants of behavior than are the expectancies of other people. Furthermore, the three groups of students in the math study did not have wildly different math scores (Shih et al., 1999). Still, we should be concerned about the potentially powerful effects of gender stereotypes. As Jussim and his colleagues (2000) stated, these stereotypes "may contribute to the continuing inequalities in power, status, and resource distribution between men and women" (p. 384). In other words, stereotypes have the power to keep both women and men from living up to their potential.

Internalizing Gender Stereotypes

In this chapter we have explored the representation of gender stereotypes in religion, language, and the media as well as the nature of people's current gender stereotypes. However, stereotypes not only describe our perceptions about the characteristics of women and men. They also describe how women and men *ought* to behave (Clinchy & Norem, 1998; Eagly, 2001). According to the traditional view, women *should* try to be "feminine" and men *should* try to be "masculine." Do people actually adopt these stereotypes, so that women and men have very different standards about the ideal person they should be?

Assessing Self-Concepts About Gender.   Several different scales have been developed to assess people's ideas about their own gender-related characteristics. For example, Sandra Bem (1974, 1977) designed the Bem Sex-Role Inventory (BSRI), a test in which people rate themselves on a variety of psychological characteristics. The BSRI provides one score on a femininity scale and one score on a masculinity scale. A person who scores high on both scales would be classified as androgynous (pronounced an-*drah*-jih-nuss). In the 1970s, psychologists often urged both women and men to develop more androgynous characteristics.

Hundreds of studies have been conducted to try to discover whether androgynous individuals might possess any unusual advantages; several resources provide reviews of the research (e.g., Auster & Ohm, 2000; Holt & Ellis, 1998; Matlin, 2000; C. J. Smith et al., 1999; Stake, 1997, 2000; C. A. Ward, 2000). You will still hear about the concept of androgyny, especially in the popular press.

In contrast to the media, however, contemporary psychologists have become disenchanted with androgyny. They argue that the concept of androgyny has several problems. For example, the research shows that androgynous people are not more psychologically healthy than other people. Critics have also argued persuasively that the theory behind androgyny is flawed. For instance, androgyny tempts us to believe that the solution to gender bias lies in changing the individual, whereas the reality is that we should try instead to reduce institutional sexism and discrimination against women. In 1983, Sandra Bem herself argued against the concept of androgyny, and she urged psychologists to turn their attention to a different question explored throughout this textbook: Why does our culture place such a strong emphasis on gender?

Do People Internalize Gender Stereotypes?   Although the specific concept of androgyny is no longer popular with psychologists, many researchers continue to explore whether people incorporate gender stereotypes into their own concepts about themselves. In the workplace, for example, many people reject the traditional gender stereotypes. For example, Stake (1997) asked people to describe real-life situations they had encountered at work. One woman described her job as a bookkeeper; she was expected to work on her own accounting tasks in a competent and efficient manner while also answering, in a sensitive and helpful manner, questions from the professional staff about their own projects. In addition, J. A. Harvey and Hansen (1999) conducted a survey of male clinical psychologists and found that these therapists emphasized both nurturance and competence when working with their clients.

You won't be surprised, however, to learn that many people do internalize gender stereotypes into their own self-concepts. For instance, C. J. Smith and her colleagues (1999) administered the BSRI to college students in the United States. In the first task of this study, the students filled out the questionnaire according to how well each characteristic described them in general. Under these neutral instructions, 30% of the female students could be classified as stereotypically feminine and 63% of the male students could be classified as stereotypically masculine. Notice, therefore, that females were substantially less likely than males to adopt the stereotypical gender role.

After students in this study had completed the BSRI with the general instructions, Smith and her colleagues (1999) asked the students to imagine that they were in a specific setting. The students then rated how well each characteristic would describe them in each of these settings. This research demonstrated that the social context clearly influences whether people act in a manner consistent with traditional gender stereotypes. For example, women were especially likely to report that they would act stereotypically feminine if they were in a social situation where most people were strangers. In contrast, men were especially likely to report that they would act in a stereotypically masculine fashion when they were with other men.

Cross-cultural research suggests that people in some ethnic groups may not adopt the gender stereotypes held by European Americans. For example, Sugihara and Warner (1999) administered the BSRI to Mexican American college students and found that only 22% of the female students could be classified as stereotypically feminine and that only 22% of the male students could be classified as stereotypically masculine. Furthermore, Sugihara and Katsurada (1999, 2000) studied gender self-concepts among college students in Japan. The male students scored significantly higher than the female students on the masculine scale of the BSRI, but males and females had similar scores on the feminine scale of the BSRI. In addition, both males and females scored significantly higher on the femininity scale than on the masculinity scale.

Are Gender Stereotypes Personally Important?   So far, we've seen that people show some tendency to incorporate gender stereotypes into their own self-concepts. But do they believe that these gender stereotypes are crucial aspects of their own personality? Auster and Ohm (2000) asked U.S. undergraduates to complete the BSRI with the instructions to "rate each characteristic according to how important you feel it is/would be for you to have this characteristic" (p. 504). Table 2.5 lists the 10 characteristics that each gender judged to be most important. As you can see, the lists are remarkably similar. In fact, seven items appear on both the women's and the men's lists.

Conclusions About Internalizing Gender Stereotypes.   In this discussion, we've seen that people often adopt flexible self-concepts about gender. However, studies suggest that European Americans often do adopt gender-stereotypical characteristics, especially among males and especially in some social settings. Extensive cross-cultural research has not yet been conducted, but the current evidence suggests that females and males in some other cultures may be similar in many gender-related characteristics. Furthermore, U.S. female and male

TABLE 2.5 ■ Top 10 Traits That Female and Male U.S. Students Consider Most Important for Themselves

Female Students	Male Students
1. Loyal	1. Loyal
2. Independent	2. Defends own beliefs
3. Individualistic	3. Willing to take a stand
4. Defends own beliefs	4. Understanding
5. Self-sufficient	5. Independent
6. Understanding	6. Ambitious
7. Ambitious	7. Willing to take risks
8. Self-reliant	8. Self-reliant
9. Sensitive to the needs of others	9. Self-sufficient
10. Compassionate	10. Has leadership abilities

Source: Auster, C. J., and Ohm, S. C. (2000). Masculinity and femininity in contemporary American society: A reevaluation using the Bem Sex Role Inventory. *Sex Roles, 43,* 499–528.

students are remarkably similar in the characteristics that they consider personally important.

We saw in the first section of this chapter that men and women are represented differently throughout history, in language, and in the media—a finding that parallels Theme 2 of this textbook. Although we should not oversimplify the conclusions in our current discussion about internalized gender stereotypes, it seems clear that women and men often have similar views about their gender-related characteristics. Consistent with Theme 1, gender differences in psychological characteristics are usually small. As we'll emphasize throughout this textbook, women and men do not live on different psychological planets with respect to their beliefs, abilities, and personal characteristics.

SECTION SUMMARY   ■

People's Beliefs About Women and Men

1. People believe that men and women differ substantially on a number of characteristics. Men are considered to be higher in agency, and women are considered to be higher in communion. These stereotypes have remained fairly consistent throughout recent decades.

2. People have different stereotypes about women from different ethnic groups; in most cases, however, the stereotypes include both "good women" and "bad women" within each ethnic group.

3. The strength of a person's gender stereotypes may be influenced by such factors as his or her gender, ethnicity, and culture. However, the overall consistency of stereotypes is impressive.

4. Women's competence is likely to be downgraded when little other information is available, when the evaluators are experts, and when the evaluators are

males. Women are also evaluated negatively when they act in a stereotypically masculine fashion.

5. People typically rate women higher than men on scales assessing pleasantness, but they tend not to rate feminists favorably.

6. Men score higher than women on both the benevolent sexism and the hostile sexism subscales of the Ambivalent Sexism Inventory.

7. Research shows evidence of gender discrimination in interpersonal interactions (e.g., negative statements about women or reports of sexist comments). Sexism in cultures such as Afghanistan has more serious consequences than it does in North America.

8. Heterosexism is encouraged by strict gender categorization, and it includes both interpersonal and institutional discrimination. Men often show more sexual prejudice than women, and people with traditional gender roles are also likely to show more sexual prejudice.

9. According to the social cognitive approach to stereotypes, people tend to (a) exaggerate the contrast between women and men, (b) consider the male experience to be normative, (c) make biased judgments about females and males, and (d) remember gender-consistent information more accurately than gender-inconsistent information.

10. Stereotypes can influence behavior through self-fulfilling prophecies, according to research on topics such as parents' expectations for their children's mathematical skills and people's choice of work tasks. Also, the research on stereotype threat shows that people's own gender stereotypes can undermine performance in situations in which gender is emphasized.

11. People often adopt flexible self-concepts about gender rather than completely internalizing gender stereotypes; cross-cultural differences have been reported with respect to the personal emphasis on gender stereotypes; women and men tend to rate themselves similarly to traits related to gender.

▪ ▪ ▪ ▪ ▪ ▪ CHAPTER REVIEW QUESTIONS ▪ ▪ ▪ ▪ ▪ ▪

1. How would you define the term *gender stereotype*? Based on the information in this chapter, would you suppose that the stereotype of a female can accurately represent a specific woman you know? Why or why not?

2. In this chapter, we examined how women have been left out of history. Discuss the kinds of topics related to women that scholars have previously ignored. Mention several reasons why women have not received much attention in history books.

3. We discussed in this chapter how women often seem invisible; for example, men are normative, whereas women are secondary. Summarize the information about women's invisibility, mentioning history, religion, mythology, language, the media, and relevant parts of the social cognitive approach to stereotypes.

4. In this chapter, we pointed out that people often hold more positive views about men than about women. Discuss this statement, citing support from philosophers, religion, mythology,

language, and the media. Then point out why the issue is more complicated when we consider current research on people's stereotypes and attitudes regarding women (e.g., ambivalent sexism).

5. What does the research show about people's stereotypes regarding women from various ethnic groups (i.e., ethnicity as a stimulus variable)? Similarly, what does the research show about how a person's ethnicity influences his or her gender stereotypes (i.e., ethnicity as subject variable)?

6. What is heterosexism, and how are gender stereotypes related to heterosexism? The social cognitive approach proposes that our normal cognitive processes would encourage people to develop stereotypes about lesbians and gay males. Describe how some of the cognitive biases would encourage these exaggerated stereotypes.

7. The social cognitive approach proposes that stereotypes arise from normal cognitive processes, beginning with the two categories

"men" and "women." Describe some of the cognitive biases that would encourage people to believe that women are more talkative than men (a stereotype that actually is not correct).

8. What is a self-fulfilling prophecy? Why is it relevant when we examine how stereotypes can influence behavior? Identify one of your own behaviors that is more gender stereotyped than you might wish, and point out how a self-fulfilling prophecy might be relevant.

9. Women and men are represented differently in the media and in people's gender stereotypes, yet people may not incorporate these stereotypes into their own self-concepts. Discuss this statement, using material from throughout the entire chapter.

10. Throughout this chapter, we discussed cross-cultural research. How do gender stereotypes and other gender biases operate in cultures outside North America? When are gender differences substantial in other cultures, and when are they relatively small?

NEW TERMS

*gender stereotypes (36)
*prejudice (36)
*discrimination (36)
*gender bias (36)
*androcentric (39)
 normative male (39)
 masculine generic (40)
 androcentric generic (40)
 agency (48)
*communion (48)
 hostile sexism (54)

 benevolent sexism (54)
*lesbian (58)
*gay male (58)
*bisexual (58)
*heterosexism (59)
*sexual prejudice (59)
*social cognitive approach (60)
*gender polarization (62)
*attributions (63)
*self-fulfilling prophecy (64)
*stereotype threat (65)

The terms asterisked in the New Terms section serve as good search terms for InfoTrac College Edition. Go to http://infotrac.thomsonlearning.com and try these added search terms.

RECOMMENDED READINGS

Brehm, S., Kassin, S., & Fein, S. (2002). *Social psychology* (5th ed.). Boston: Houghton Mifflin. I recommend this book to anyone who wants a clear, comprehensive introduction to the topic of stereotyping in social psychology.

Frieze, I. H., & McHugh, M. C. (Eds.). (1997). Measuring beliefs about appropriate roles for women and men [Special issue]. *Psychology of Women Quarterly, 21*(1). This special issue is devoted entirely to measuring stereotypes and attitudes toward women; it's an excellent resource for current research.

Meyers, M. (Ed.). (1999). *Mediated woman: Representations in popular culture.* Cresskill, NJ: Hampton Press. Here's an excellent book about the representation of women in films, television, magazines, and newspapers; several chapters focus on the representation of women of color.

Swann, W. B., Jr., Langlois, J. H., & Gilbert, L. A. (Eds.). (1999). *Sexism and stereotypes in modern society: The gender science of Janet Taylor Spence.* Washington, DC: American Psychological Association. Janet Taylor Spence has had a long-standing influence on the research about gender stereotypes. This volume was written in honor of Spence's contributions; especially relevant to the present chapter are the chapters written by Deaux and by Glick and Fiske.

ANSWERS TO THE DEMONSTRATIONS

Demonstration 2.3: Most people believe that the following items are characteristics of women (W): gentle, kind, emotional, compassionate, modest, fickle, warm, nervous, talkative, patient. They also believe that the following items are characteristic of men (M): self-confident, competitive, active, loud, inventive, greedy, capable, show-off, courageous, powerful.

Demonstration 2.4: Add together the total number of points from the following items: 1, 3, 6, 7, 9. These items represent the hostile sexism subscale. Then add together the total number of points from the following items: 2, 4, 5, 8, 10. These items represent the benevolent sexism subscale. Adding these two subscale scores together provides an index of overall sexism.

ANSWERS TO THE TRUE-FALSE QUESTIONS

1. True (p. 37); 2. False (p. 38); 3. False (pp. 40–41); 4. False (p. 44); 5. True (p. 45); 6. True (p. 51); 7. True (p. 53); 8. True (p. 59); 9. False (p. 60); 10. False (p. 68).

Infancy and Childhood

Arnold H. Matlin, M.D.

T R U E   O R   F A L S E ?

_____ 1. During the first few weeks of prenatal development, females and males have similar sex glands and external genitals.

_____ 2. People living in the United States and Canada have strong preferences about the gender of their firstborn child; more than two-thirds would prefer a son rather than a daughter.

_____ 3. When adults think they are interacting with a baby boy, they typically hand this baby a football; if the same baby is introduced as a baby girl, people typically hand this baby a doll.

_____ 4. Children's gender development can be almost entirely explained by the fact that parents reward gender-consistent behavior and punish gender-inconsistent behavior.

_____ 5. Parents consistently criticize aggressive girls more than they criticize aggressive boys.

_____ 6. In research on three major ethnic groups, Latina mothers almost always send the strongest gender messages to their children, European American mothers send moderately strong messages, and Black mothers treat their daughters and sons in a relatively gender-fair fashion.

_____ 7. Teachers typically give more educational feedback to boys than to girls.

_____ 8. Research conducted during the past 10 years shows that boys and girls are now almost equally represented in children's television programs and that children rarely act in gender-stereotyped ways in these programs.

_____ 9. By the age of 6 months, infants can perceive that a female face belongs in a different category from a series of male faces.

_____ 10. In general, girls are more likely than boys to prefer an occupation that is considered nontraditional for their gender.

One hot summer day, a little girl was attending the birthday party of another preschooler. The children managed to stay cool by taking off their clothes and wading in the backyard pool. The little girl's mother picked her up from the party, and the two began discussing the afternoon's events. The mother asked how many boys and how many girls had attended the party. "I don't know," the child replied. "They weren't wearing any clothes" (C. L. Brewer, personal communication, 1998). As we'll see in this chapter, children's conceptions of gender are often surprisingly different from adult perspectives. However, we'll also see that children can be quite knowledgeable. For example, even preschoolers are well informed about our culture's gender stereotypes.

In this chapter, we will discuss a process called gender typing. **Gender typing** includes how children acquire their knowledge about gender and how they develop their personality characteristics, preferences, skills, behaviors, and self-concepts (Bem, 1983; Eckes & Trautner, 2000b). We'll start by considering the early phases of development, during the prenatal period and infancy, and then we'll consider some theoretical explanations of gender typing. Next, we'll examine a variety of factors that contribute to children's gender typing. These factors, such as the school system and the media, virtually guarantee that children growing up in North America will be well trained about the importance of gender in our culture. In the final part of this chapter, we'll focus on children's knowledge and stereotypes about gender; as we'll see, even infants can create some basic categories based on gender.

BACKGROUND ON GENDER DEVELOPMENT

Some important components of gender—specifically, the sex organs—develop during the **prenatal period,** the time before birth. Many gender messages are conveyed during **infancy,** the period between birth and 18 months of life. An adequate theory about gender development must be sufficiently complex to explain the societal forces that encourage children's gender typing. The theory must also emphasize that children also contribute to their own gender typing, by actively working to master the lessons of gender.

Prenatal Sex Development

At conception, an egg with 23 chromosomes unites with a sperm, which has 23 chromosomes. Together, they form a single cell that contains 23 chromosome pairs. One of those pairs is called the **sex chromosomes,** that is, the chromosomes that determine whether the embryo will be genetically female or male. The other 22 chromosome pairs determine numerous additional physiological and psychological characteristics.

The egg from the mother always supplies an X sex chromosome. The father's sperm, which fertilizes the egg, contains either an X chromosome or a Y chromosome. If the egg is fertilized by an X chromosome, then the chromosome pair is symbolized XX, and the child will be a genetic female. If the egg is fertilized by a Y chromosome, then the chromosome pair is symbolized XY, and the child will be a genetic male. The situation is ironic: A characteristic that our culture considers so important—whether someone is an XX person or an XY person—is determined simply by whether an X-chromosome-bearing sperm or a Y-chromosome-bearing sperm is the first to penetrate the egg cell!

Typical Prenatal Development.   Until about 6 weeks after conception, female and male embryos are virtually identical. (Only their chromosomes differ.) For instance, each human fetus has two sets of primitive internal reproductive systems. The internal female system, called Müllerian ducts, will eventually develop into a uterus, egg ducts, and part of the vagina in females. The internal male system, called Wolffian ducts, will eventually develop into the male internal reproductive system, which includes structures such as the prostate gland and the vesicles for semen.

The sex glands (or **gonads**) of males and females also look identical during the first weeks after conception. If the embryo has an XY chromosome pair, a tiny segment of the Y chromosome guides the gonads to develop into male testes, beginning about 6 weeks after conception. In contrast, if the embryo has an XX chromosome pair, the gonads begin to develop into female ovaries, beginning about 10 weeks after conception (Fausto-Sterling, 2000; J. Marx, 1995; Ruble & Martin, 1998).

In about the third month after conception, the fetus's hormones encourage further sex differentiation, including the development of the external genitals. In males, the testes secrete two substances. One of these, the Müllerian regression hormone, shrinks the (female) Müllerian ducts. The testes also secrete **androgen,** one of the male sex hormones. Androgen encourages the growth and development of the Wolffian ducts (Breedlove, 1994; Collaer & Hines, 1995). Androgen also encourages the growth of the external genitals (Figure 3.1). The genital tubercle becomes the penis in males.

At about the same time, the ovaries in females begin to synthesize large quantities of **estrogen, one of the female sex hormones.** Consistent with the invisible female theme, we know much less about prenatal development in females than in males (Fitch et al., 1998). However, some researchers argue that estrogen encourages the growth and development of the Müllerian ducts while shrinking the Wolffian ducts. Estrogen also seems to encourage the development of the external genitals in females. Note in Figure 3.1 that the genital tubercle develops into the clitoris in females.

In summary, typical sexual development follows a complex sequence before birth. The first event is conception, when genetic sex is determined. Female and male embryos are anatomically identical for the first weeks after conception. As we have seen, four further processes then begin the differentiation of females and males: (1) the development of the internal reproductive system, (2) the development of the gonads, (3) the production of hormones, and (4) the development of the external genitals.

Atypical Prenatal Development.   The scenario we've just examined is the typical one. However, this elaborate developmental sequence sometimes takes a different pathway. The result is an intersexed infant whose biological sex is not clearly female or male. An **intersexed individual** is someone who does not have a matching chromosomal pattern, internal reproductive system, gonads, hormones, and external genitals. In other words, the world does not have just two sex categories, female and male (Golden, 2000; S. J. Kessler, 1998). In fact, Fausto-Sterling (1993, 2000) estimated that intersexed individuals represent 2–4% of the general population.

One atypical pattern is called **androgen-insensitivity syndrome,** a condition in which genetic males (XY) produce normal amounts of androgen, but a genetic defect makes their bodies not respond to androgen (Breedlove, 1994; Fausto-Sterling, 2000). As a result, the genital tubercle does not grow into a penis; the external genitals look female. These children are usually labeled girls because they lack a penis. However, they have a shallow cavity instead of a complete vagina, and they have no uterus. They also do not menstruate. Individuals with

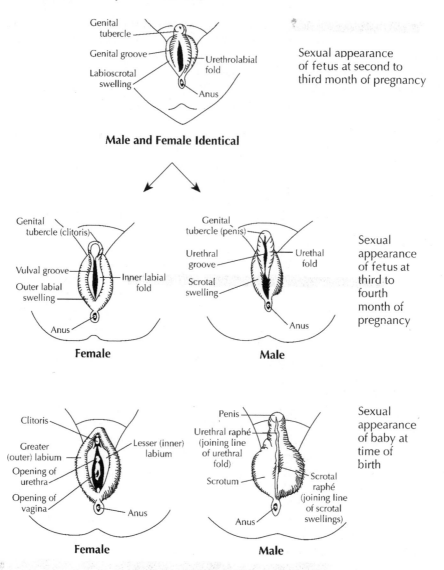

FIGURE 3.1 ■ Prenatal development of the external genitals.

Source: Based on Money & Ehrhardt (1972).

androgen-insensitivity syndrome who are raised as girls generally play with stereotypically feminine toys and appear satisfied with the female gender role (Ruble & Martin, 1998).

A second atypical pattern is called **congenital adrenal hyperplasia,** a condition in which genetic females (XX) receive too much androgen during prenatal development. The excess androgen causes their genitals to look somewhat masculine at birth. The traditional medical treatment is surgery, so that the genitals look more feminine (Fausto-Sterling, 2000).

To me, the most interesting aspect of atypical prenatal development focuses on some important questions: Why does our culture force all infants into either the female category or the male category (Dreger, 1998; Golden, 2000; S. J. Kessler, 1998)? Why can't we accept that some people are intersexed, neither female nor male? Why do physicians typically recommend surgery for intersexed individuals, so that the external genitals can appear to be either clearly feminine or clearly masculine?

Many adult intersexed individuals now argue that such children should *not* be forced to adopt one gender just because it is socially acceptable (Colapinto, 2000; M. Diamond & Sigmundson, 1999; Fausto-Sterling, 2000; Golden, 2000). As one intersexed person writes:

> I was born whole and beautiful, but different. The error was not in my body, nor in my sex organs, but in the determination of the culture. . . . Our path to healing lies in embracing our intersexual selves, not in labeling our bodies as having committed some "error." (M. Diamond, 1996, p. 144)

We pointed out in the previous two chapters that gender polarization forces us to see the two genders as being very different from one another. Can we overcome this polarization and accept the fact that we humans are not limited to just two options?

How People Respond to Infant Girls and Boys

We consider a person's gender—the label "female" or "male"—to be very important, as noted in previous chapters and in the discussion of intersexed individuals. You won't be surprised to learn about people's first reactions when they hear that a baby has been born. In a study by Intons-Peterson & Reddel (1984), researchers stood by as the parents of newborns telephoned friends and relatives to announce that their baby had been born. In 80% of the calls, the first response to the announcement was some variation on the classic question, "Is it a boy or a girl?" To some parents, sex and gender are so important that their own child may be a tragic disappointment. In fact, a friend of mine once shared a room on a maternity ward with a woman who was planning to give up her infant girl for adoption. She and her husband had wanted a boy.

Parental Preferences About Sex of Children. Several decades ago, researchers in the United States and Canada found that most men and women preferred a boy for their firstborn child. More recent research shows no clear-cut pattern of infant-sex preferences (M. C. Hamilton, 1991b; Marleau & Saucier, 2002; McDougall et al., 1999). Try Demonstration 3.1, which focuses on gender preferences.

In some other cultures, however, parents do have strong preferences for boys. Favoritism toward boys is so strong in India that traveling "sonogram doctors" move from village to village, conducting prenatal sex determinations. The mother typically requests an abortion if the fetus is female (Bellamy, 2000; Kishwar, 1995).

Selective abortion and female infanticide are also common in China, where the discrepancy in the female population has important social consequences.

DEMONSTRATION 3.1 ■ ■ ■ ■ ■ ■ ■ ■ ■ ■ ■ ■ ■ ■ ■ ■ ■ ■ ■

Preferences for Males Versus Females as the Firstborn Child

You've just read that most North Americans no longer have clear-cut preferences for the sex of their offspring. However, some individuals you know may have strong opinions on the topic. To perform this demonstration, locate 10 women and 10 men who do not have children, and ask them whether they would like a boy or a girl as their firstborn child. Be sure to select people with whom you are comfortable asking this question, and interview them one at a time. After noting each person's response, ask for a brief rationale for the answer. Do your male and female respondents differ in their preferences? Do you think their responses would have been different if they had filled out an anonymous survey?

In some regions of China, for instance, the preference is so strong that only 70 infant girls are born for every 100 boys. This pattern of selective abortion means that many Chinese men of marrying age will not be able to find a spouse. As a consequence, thousands of women from other regions of China—as well as Vietnam and Korea—have been kidnapped to serve as wives (Beach, 2001; Pomfret, 2001). Researchers have estimated that India and China together have about 80 million fewer females than would be expected if these countries did not demonstrate such clear gender preferences. This preference for male babies is an important example of Theme 2 of this book: People often respond differently to males and females.

The preference for male babies is also revealed in other cultures, even those that do not practice selective abortion. For example, C. Delaney (2000) reported that residents of Turkish villages consider girls to be temporary guests in the family home, because they leave when they marry. In contrast, boys remain in the house after marriage, and they eventually inherit the property. A common saying in this region is "A boy is the flame of the hearth, a girl its ashes" (p. 124).

A preference for male babies may also have important health consequences. For example, I know a female student, now in her mid-20s, who had been born in Korea, in a premature delivery. Her father recently told her that the family had decided not to put her in an incubator because she was a girl but that they would have chosen the incubator option if she had been a boy. Fortunately, she survived anyway.

People's Stereotypes About Infant Girls and Boys.   Do people think baby girls and baby boys have different characteristics, and do they treat them differently? Consider a representative study by Katherine Karraker and her colleagues (1995).

These researchers investigated 40 mother-father pairs two days after their infant son or daughter had been born. All the parents were asked to rate their newborn infant on a number of scales. Each scale was anchored with a masculine adjective (e.g., *strong*) on the left and a feminine adjective (e.g., *weak*) on the right.

Even though the boys and girls were objectively similar in terms of size and health, the parents rated them differently (Figure 3.2). Parents of girls rated their daughters as being relatively weak, whereas parents of boys rated their sons as being relatively strong. Parents also distinguished between daughters and sons on three other dimensions: (1) large featured versus fine featured; (2) hardy versus delicate; and (3) masculine versus feminine. Mothers and fathers responded similarly in this study; in other research, we'll see that fathers often have stronger gender stereotypes.

Parents also arrange different environments for their infant sons and daughters. They typically decorate boys' rooms with animal themes and bold colors. In contrast, girls' rooms are likely to have pastels, lace, and ruffles (A. Pomerleau et al., 1990). Youngsters' toys also differ. In one study, for example, boys had an average of 12 toy vehicles, in contrast to 5 for girls. Girls owned an average of 4 dolls, in contrast to 1 for boys (A. Pomerleau et al., 1990).

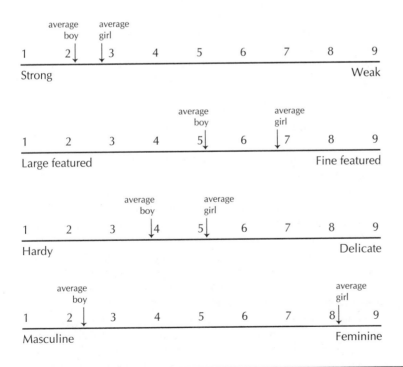

FIGURE 3.2 ■ Average ratings for newborn girls and boys on four dimensions.
Source: Based on Karraker et al. (1995).

We've noted that parents sometimes react differently to their infant girls than to their infant boys. Strangers show this same tendency to make distinctions based on gender. For instance, have you ever assumed an infant was a boy, and then learned it was a girl? Most of us find this experience puzzling. We try to maintain a nonsexist perspective, yet we find ourselves immediately justifying this gender transformation: "Oh, of course, I didn't notice that she has long eyelashes," or "Yes, her hands are so delicate." In general, the research evidence confirms that people judge infants differently when they are perceived to be female rather than male (e.g., Condry & Condry, 1976; Delk et al., 1986; Demarest & Glinos, 1992; C. Lewis et al., 1992).

We should emphasize, however, that adults do not universally view infants through gender-stereotyped lenses. For example, Plant and her colleagues (2000) studied women and men enrolled in a childbirth-education course—a group of people who would certainly consider babies relevant to their lives! The participants watched a short video, which showed a 9-month-old infant who looked gender neutral. The infant was playing with a card. Next, an off-screen adult took the card away, and then the baby cried for the remainder of the video. Before watching the video, half of the participants were told that they would see a girl named Karen, and half were told that they would see a boy named Brian. (Otherwise, both the "Karen" group and the "Brian" group were identical.) After seeing the video, everyone rated the baby's emotions.

A previous study had shown that people who thought they were watching a boy rated the baby as being quite angry compared to the group who thought they were watching a girl (Condry & Condry, 1976). In other words, they attributed this characteristically masculine emotion to infant boys rather than to infant girls. In their more recent study, Plant and her colleagues found that male participants who had strong gender stereotypes about emotions were indeed likely to provide higher anger ratings for the "boy" than for the "girl." However, the remaining participants provided similar ratings in the two gender conditions. We must note that people who are enrolled in a childbirth-education course in a liberal community (Madison, Wisconsin) probably do not represent the general North American population. Still, it's encouraging that relatively few adults in this study revealed gender stereotypes.

So far, we've just looked at adults' *judgments* about infants. Do they actually *interact* differently with girls and boys? Some research has demonstrated that people hand different toys to infants based on their perception of the infants' gender. In one study, college students who thought they were playing with a baby girl handed "her" a doll 80% of the time and a football 14% of the time. Students who thought they were playing with a baby boy handed "him" a doll 20% of the time and a football 64% of the time (Sidorowicz & Lunney, 1980). Unfortunately, repeated play with stereotyped toys may keep children from developing broader competencies.

Marilyn Stern and Katherine Karraker (1989) reviewed the research in which infants are given male or female labels. More than two-thirds of the studies showed at least one gender-label effect. In general, gender labels make the greatest difference when people judge infants' activities and physical characteristics or when people actually interact with the infants. In contrast, gender labels are less likely to influence judgments of developmental achievements and personality characteristics (Golombok & Fivush, 1994).

In addition, relatives and friends may convey gender stereotypes through their choice of greeting cards. Figure 3.3 illustrates a typical contrast between cards intended for parents of newborn girls and those intended for parents of newborn boys. In general, cards for boys show physical activity and action toys, whereas the cards for girls emphasize the baby's sweetness. In addition, cards for boys were more likely to mention how happy the parents must be (Bridges, 1993). Parents therefore receive a strong gender message as soon as they open the envelopes!

Notice that these studies on adults' treatment of infants tend to support a social constructionist approach. As we discussed in Chapter 1, **social constructionism** argues that we tend to construct or invent our own versions of reality based on our prior experiences and beliefs. For example, when we are told that an infant is female, we tend to see delicate, feminine behavior. When we are told that the same infant is male, we tend to see sturdy, masculine behavior. That is, we create our own versions of reality based on our prior beliefs about gender.

FIGURE 3.3 ■ Representative cards to be sent to the parents of a baby boy or a baby girl. (Note: The original card for the boy is blue, and the card for the girl is pink.)

This discussion suggests that gender typing can be explained at least partly by the way people respond to infant girls and boys: Both parents and strangers make some gender distinctions. However, differential treatment by adults is not a complete answer. As we'll see in the remainder of this chapter, part of the explanation comes from girls' and boys' own ideas about the importance of gender. They acquire these ideas initially from adults, other children, the school system, and the media, and they exaggerate these ideas still further through their own patterns of thought.

Theories of Gender Development

How can we account for the development of gender? What theories explain how children acquire their knowledge about gender as well as how they acquire their gender-related personality characteristics, preferences, skills, behaviors, and self-concepts? One early explanation of gender development was Sigmund Freud's elaborate psychoanalytic theory. However, that theory has not been supported by the research, and it is seldom discussed in contemporary explanations for the development of gender (Bussey & Bandura, 1999; Jacklin & Reynolds, 1993; Robins et al., 1999). If you are interested in the topic, you can consult other resources (e.g., Callan, 2001; Whyte, 1998).

In this discussion of gender development, we will focus instead on two contemporary perspectives. These perspectives emphasize two different processes that operate during child development: the social learning approach and the cognitive developmental approach. Two decades ago, these two approaches were considered rival theories. We now acknowledge that gender development is such a complex process that neither explanation is sufficient by itself. In fact, children acquire their information about gender by both of these important methods (Bem, 1981, 1985, 1993; Powlishta et al., 2001; Ruble & Martin, 1998):

1. In the social learning approach, children learn gender-related *behaviors* from other people.
2. In the cognitive developmental approach, children actively synthesize and create their own *thoughts* about gender.

The Social Learning Approach.   The social learning approach argues that traditional learning principles explain an important part of gender development (Lott & Maluso, 2001; Mischel, 1966, 1970). More specifically, the **social learning approach** proposes two major mechanisms for explaining how girls learn to act "feminine" and how boys learn to act "masculine":

1. Children are rewarded for "gender-appropriate" behavior, and they are punished for "gender-inappropriate" behavior; and
2. Children watch and imitate the behavior of other people of their own gender.

Let's first see how rewards and punishments might operate through direct learning experiences. Jimmy, age 2, grabs a toy truck. He races it back and forth, producing an impressive rumbling motor sound. The doting parents smile, thereby rewarding Jimmy's "masculine" behavior. His parents would not respond so positively if he donned his sister's pink tutu and waltzed around the dining room. Instead, his parents would probably make active efforts to discourage him. Now imagine how Sarah, also age 2, might win smiles for the pink tutu act but possible frowns for the roaring truck performance. According to this first social learning component, children directly learn many gender-related behaviors by trial and error; they notice and modify their behavior based on responses from other people. As we'll soon see, adults and other children may respond differently to girls' behavior than to boys' behavior (Fabes & Martin, 2000).

According to the second of the two social learning components, children also learn by watching others and imitating them, a process called **modeling**. Children are especially likely to imitate a person of their own gender or a person who has been praised for a behavior (Carli & Bukatko, 2000; Leaper, 2000; Lott & Maluso, 2001). For example, a little girl would be particularly likely to imitate her mother, especially if someone praised her mother for her actions. Children frequently imitate characters from books, films, and television as well as real people. As we'll discuss later, gender-stereotyped models in the media help to explain why children reared in strongly feminist homes may still develop stereotyped views. For instance, a woman who is a physician overheard her young son telling the child next door, "No, ladies can't be doctors; they gotta be nurses."

Direct learning, by means of rewards and punishments, is the major way that very young children learn "gender-appropriate" behavior. As children grow older, the second component (modeling) becomes active. Children can now observe the behavior of others, internalize that information, and imitate that behavior at a later time (Bussey & Bandura, 1999; Lott & Maluso, 2001; Trautner & Eckes, 2000). In addition, as we'll see in the next part of this chapter, our gender schemas and other cognitive processes contribute to a lifetime of learning about gender.

The Cognitive Developmental Approach.   Whereas the social learning approach focuses on behaviors, the cognitive developmental approach focuses on thoughts. More specifically, the **cognitive developmental approach** argues that children are active thinkers who seek information from their environment; children also try to make sense of this information and organize it in a coherent fashion (Coltrane & Adams, 1997a). A **schema** (pronounced *skee*-mah) is a general concept that we use to organize our thoughts about a topic. Cognitive psychologists point out that we acquire schemas from our past experience. For example, you have a schema for a professor's office; your general knowledge suggests that the office should have a desk, a chair, and books but not a pet rabbit or a waffle iron. Schemas help both children and adults to process information rapidly (Zemore et al., 2000). Notice that the cognitive developmental approach to children's gender typing is consistent with the social cognitive approach we considered in connection with adults' gender stereotypes (see Chapter 2, pp. 60–64).

Sandra Bem (1981, 1985, 1993) argued that children develop powerful **gender schemas;** children organize information about themselves and about the rest of the world according to the definitions of maleness and femaleness found in their culture. These gender schemas include everything children know about gender, and they encourage children to think and act in gender-stereotyped ways that are consistent with the gender schemas (G. D. Levy & Fivush, 1993). With repeated use, these gender schemas become automatic (Zemore et al., 2000). As children grow older, their gender schemas become more complex and also more flexible (C. L. Martin & Dinella, 2001).

Sandra Bem (1981, 1985, 1993) also proposed that children evaluate their own adequacy in terms of the gender schema. For example, Mary realizes that she should be gentle and attentive to her baby brother in order to rate high on the nurturance dimension, which adults will use to evaluate her. Bem observed that a culture determines what kind of schema is most important. In the United States and Canada, gender is emphasized more than other social categories. For example, teachers often instruct their students to form boys' lines and girls' lines when they leave for lunch. Teachers do not line up the children according to race. We try to deemphasize racial distinctions, but we continue to emphasize gender distinctions. In some other cultures, where boys and girls are treated similarly, children's gender schemas may be less powerful (Lott & Maluso, 2001).

The cognitive developmental approach to gender development was originally developed by Lawrence Kohlberg (Kohlberg, 1966; Kohlberg & Ullian, 1974). Kohlberg proposed that children actively work to make sense of their own gender. One of the first major steps in gender development is **gender identity:** a girl's realization that she is a girl and a boy's realization that he is a boy. Most children are accurate in labeling themselves by the time they are 2 or 3 years old.

Soon after children label themselves accurately, they learn how to classify other males and females. At this point, they begin to prefer people, things, and activities that are consistent with their own gender identity (Kohlberg, 1966; Powlishta et al., 2001). A child who realizes that she is a girl, for example, likes feminine objects and activities. A woman in one of my classes provided a vivid example of these preference patterns. Her 4-year-old daughter asked about the sex of every dog she met. If it was a "girl dog," she would run up and pat it lovingly. If it was a "boy dog," she would cast a scornful glance and walk in the opposite direction. Girls prefer stereotypically feminine activities because these activities are consistent with their female gender identity, according to Kohlberg.

General Comments About Theories of Gender Development.   We have explored two major theoretical approaches to development; both of these theories are necessary to account for children's gender typing. Together, they suggest the following:

1. Children's behavior is important, as proposed by social learning theory.
   a. Children are rewarded and punished for gender-related behavior.
   b. Children model their behavior after same-gender individuals.
2. Children's thoughts are important, as suggested by cognitive developmental theory.
   a. Children develop powerful gender schemas.
   b. Children use gender schemas to evaluate themselves and the people around them.

Psychologists generally favor a combination of both the learning and the cognitive approaches (e.g., Bussey & Bandura, 1999; Reid et al., 1995; Ruble & Martin, 1998). However, it's unclear exactly how these two approaches blend together. Most theorists propose that children *behave* before they *think*. In other words, the two components of social learning theory may begin to operate before children have clear gender schemas or other thoughts about gender (Warin, 2000). However, in turn, children's cognitive development probably enhances their ability to learn gender-typed behavior, through direct learning and modeling.

For the remainder of the chapter, we turn our attention to the research about children's gender development. We'll first consider the external forces that encourage gender typing, including the parents and teachers who reward and punish children's gender-related behavior and the media that provide models of gender-stereotyped behavior. Then we'll consider how children's thoughts about gender develop from infancy to late childhood.

SECTION SUMMARY

Background on Gender Development

1. During typical prenatal development, male and female embryos initially look identical; male testes begin to develop at 6 weeks, and female ovaries begin to develop at 10 weeks.

2. An embryo's initially neutral external genitals grow into either female or male genitals during prenatal development.

3. In atypical prenatal development, an intersexed infant is born; this child is neither clearly male nor clearly female. For example, genetic males with androgen-insensitivity syndrome may have external genitals that look female. Also, genetic females with congenital adrenal hyperplasia (too much androgen) have external genitals that look masculine.

4. The research demonstrates that our culture is uncomfortable with intersexed infants, because they do not fit into one of the two "acceptable" gender categories.

5. Most parents no longer have a strong preference for male offspring in the United States and Canada; gender preferences are so strong in some other countries (e.g., India and China) that female fetuses may be aborted.

6. Parents tend to have different initial reactions to sons and daughters and to buy different room furnishings and toys for their sons and daughters.

7. Strangers often judge babies differently, depending on whether they believe a baby is a boy or a girl; they also interact differently with infants, depending on the infant's perceived gender.

8. Gender typing can best be explained by combining two approaches: (a) the social learning approach (in which children are rewarded for "gender-appropriate"

behavior and punished for "gender-inappropriate" behavior and in which children imitate the behavior of same-gender individuals) and (b) the cognitive developmental approach (in which children's active thought processes encourage gender typing, and children use gender schemes for evaluation).

FACTORS THAT SHAPE GENDER TYPING

In the previous section, we discussed two explanations for gender typing. The social learning approach emphasizes that parents often reward gender-typed behavior more than "gender-inappropriate" behavior; also, parents and the media typically provide models of gender-typed behavior. The cognitive developmental approach emphasizes that children actively construct their gender schemas based on messages they learn from parents and other sources of information. Let's look in closer detail at these factors that shape gender typing, beginning with parents and then moving on to peers, schools, and the media.

Parents

In an earlier section, we saw that parents react somewhat differently to male and female infants. Those reactions tend to be stereotyped because parents do not yet know their infants' unique characteristics (Jacklin & Maccoby, 1983). By the time children become toddlers, however, the parents know much more about each child's individual personality (Lott & Maluso, 1993). Therefore, parents often react to toddlers on the basis of personality characteristics rather than on the basis of gender.

In this section, we'll see that parents sometimes encourage gender-typed activities and conversational patterns. They also treat sons and daughters somewhat differently with respect to two social characteristics: aggression and independence. However, parents often do not make as strong a distinction between boys and girls as you might expect (Fagot, 1995; Lytton & Romney, 1991; Ruble & Martin, 1998). In this section, we'll also consider the factors related to parents' gender-typing tendencies.

Gender-Typed Activities.   According to the research, parents often encourage their children to develop gender-typed interests by providing different kinds of toys for daughters than for sons (Caldera & Sciaraffa, 1998; Coltrane & Adams, 1997a; Fisher-Thompson, 1990, 1993). However, one study provided an interesting perspective. When parents rated toys without the child present, they had gender-typed opinions about the toys. In contrast, when a child was present and actively engaged in playing with the toys, parents showed less stereotypical behavior (Idle et al., 1993). In other words, if parents notice that 3-year-old Tanya likes playing with the Fisher-Price gas station, they won't interfere by handing her a doll. Parents and adults may have gender stereotypes, but they also are sensitive to each child's individual preferences (Fisher-Thompson et al., 1995).

Parents also encourage gender-typed activities when they assign chores to their children. As you might expect, girls are more likely to be assigned domestic chores, such as washing the dishes or dusting the furniture, whereas boys are typically assigned outdoor work, such as mowing the lawn or taking out the garbage (Antill et al., 1996; Coltrane & Adams, 1997a).

Perhaps an even stronger force than encouragement of gender-typed activity is parents' *discouragement* of activities they think are inappropriate. They are particularly likely to discourage sons, rather than daughters, from playing with "gender-inappropriate" toys. That is, parents are much more worried about boys being sissies than about girls being tomboys (Campenni, 1999; Sandnabba & Ahlberg, 1999).

Why are parents more worried about a boy who puts on lipstick and wears high heels than about a girl who outlines a mustache above her lip and wears cowboy boots? To some extent, "gender-inappropriate" behavior in boys may be more anxiety arousing because we tolerate a wider range of dress in adult women than in adult men. Adult women can wear cowboy boots as well as underwear for women that mimics men's jockey shorts. However, the men's stores do not offer pink lace bikinis for males! A possible explanation is that adults tend to interpret feminine behavior in a boy as a sign of gay tendencies, but they are less likely to view masculine behavior in a girl as a sign of lesbian tendencies (Sandnabba & Ahlberg, 1999).

Theme 2 of this book, that males are more valued than females, is another reason why people are more concerned about "gender-inappropriate" behavior in boys. A boy who doesn't act masculine is failing to show the traits and behaviors that our culture values most highly (M. Crawford, personal communication, 1984).

Just as male children are the most likely recipients of messages about "gender-appropriate" behavior, male adults are more likely than females to offer these messages (Bussey & Bandura, 1998; Coltrane & Adams, 1997a; Leve & Fagot, 1997). For example, fathers are more likely than mothers to encourage their daughters to play with stereotypically feminine items such as tea sets and baby dolls and to encourage their sons to play with stereotypically masculine items such as footballs and boxing gloves.

In summary, parents do seem to promote some gender-typed activities in their children. As we'll soon see, however, many parents conscientiously try to treat their sons and daughters similarly.

Conversations About Emotions.   Another kind of gender-typed activity focuses on conversations. Parents are more likely to talk with their daughters than with their sons about other people and about emotions (S. Adams et al., 1995; Fivush et al., 2000; Flannagan & Perese, 1998).

Perhaps the most interesting aspect of parent-child conversations is that parents typically discuss different emotions with daughters than with sons (Chance & Fiese, 1999; Fivush & Buckner, 2000). In the section on infancy, we mentioned that some adults tend to judge that a crying baby boy is angry, whereas a crying baby girl is afraid. Related research examined mothers' conversations with children between the ages of $2\frac{1}{2}$ and 3 years. During a session that lasted about half an hour, 21% of mothers discussed anger with their sons, whereas 0% of mothers discussed anger with their daughters. Instead, they talked with their daughters about fear and sadness (Fivush, 1989). In other studies, mothers are especially likely to discuss sadness in detail with their daughters, in order to discover exactly why their daughters had been sad on a particular occasion (Fivush & Buckner, 2000).

Additional studies confirm that fathers, as well as mothers, are much more likely to discuss sadness with their daughters than with their sons (S. Adams et al., 1995; Fivush & Buckner, 2000; Fivush et al., 2000). Not surprisingly, then, studies of 3- and 4-year-olds show that girls are more likely than boys to spontaneously talk about sad experiences (Denham, 1998; Fivush & Buckner, 2000). In Chapter 12, we'll see that when women are sad, they may spend time trying to figure out the precise nature of their sadness, an activity that may lead to higher rates of depression in women than in men (Nolen-Hoeksema, 1990). Early family interactions may encourage these gender differences during adulthood.

Attitudes About Aggression.   In popularized accounts of gender-role development, you may read that parents discourage aggression in their daughters but tolerate or even encourage aggression in their sons. This description may be intuitively appealing. However, the research findings are inconsistent. Some studies show that parents are more likely to discourage aggression in their daughters than in their sons, but other studies show no differences (Lytton & Romney, 1991; Powlishta et al., 2001; Ruble & Martin, 1998). Try Demonstration 3.2 when you have a chance. Do your own observations show that parents respond differently or similarly to aggressive daughters and to aggressive sons?

In Chapter 6, we'll discuss how adult males are more aggressive than adult females in some kinds of interpersonal interactions. Apparently, most of this difference cannot be explained by parents' rewarding and punishing boys differently from girls.

DEMONSTRATION 3.2 ■ ■ ■ ■ ■ ■ ■ ■ ■ ■ ■ ■ ■ ■ ■ ■ ■ ■ ■

Tolerance for Aggression in Sons and Daughters

For this demonstration, you will need to find a location where parents are likely to bring their children. Some possibilities include grocery stores, toy stores, and fast-food restaurants. Observe several families with more than one child. Be alert for examples of verbal or physical aggression from the children directed toward either a parent or a sibling. What is the parent's response to this aggression? Does the parent respond differently to aggression as a function of a child's gender?

We need to emphasize, however, that parents can provide information about aggression and power in other ways. As the second component of social learning theory emphasizes, boys can learn to be aggressive by imitating their aggressive fathers. Furthermore, the structure of the family provides information for children's thoughts about proper "masculine" and "feminine" behavior, as emphasized by cognitive developmental theory. Children notice in their own families that fathers make decisions and announce which television show will be watched. Fathers may also use physical intimidation to assert power. By watching their parents, children often learn that aggression and power are "boy things," not "girl things."

Attitudes About Independence.   According to popularized accounts of gender-role development, parents encourage their sons to explore and do things on their own, but they overprotect and overhelp their daughters. Once again, the evidence is not as clear-cut as the media suggest.

In some situations, parents do encourage more independence in boys than in girls. In research on toddlers, boys are more often left alone in a room, whereas girls are more likely to be supervised and chaperoned (Fagot, 1978; Grusec & Lytton, 1988). Also, a study of mothers showed that they allowed their sons more independence than their daughters in a variety of everyday activities (Pomerantz & Ruble, 1998). However, parents give the same kind of verbal directions and suggestions to their sons and their daughters (Bellinger & Gleason, 1982; Leaper et al., 1998). It's frustratingly difficult to draw conclusions about the topic of independence, especially because we have little recent research on the topic. Parents apparently allow their sons more independence than their daughters on some tasks and in some contexts, but in other situations, they treat their sons and daughters somewhat similarly (Lytton & Romney, 1991; Powlishta et al., 2001; Zemore et al., 2000).

Individual Differences in Parents' Gender Typing.   We have seen that parents may encourage gender-typed activities. They often spend more time talking about sadness with their daughters than with their sons. However, they do not consistently encourage aggression or independence in their sons more than in their daughters (Lytton & Romney, 1991; Powlishta et al., 2001; Ruble & Martin, 1998).

Consistent with Theme 4 (individual differences), parents vary widely in the kinds of gender messages they provide to their children. Some parents treat their sons and daughters very differently, whereas others actively try to avoid gender bias. For example, Tenenbaum and Leaper (1997) studied Mexican American fathers interacting with their preschool children in a feminine setting: playing with toy foods. Fathers who had traditional attitudes toward gender did not talk much with their children in this setting. In contrast, nontraditional fathers asked their children questions such as "What is on this sandwich?" and "Should we cook this egg?" By asking these questions, the fathers are sending a message to their children that men can feel comfortable with traditionally feminine tasks.

Several studies have focused specifically on ethnic differences in parents' treatment of sons and daughters. As might be expected when the variability is so great within each ethnic group, the results are often contradictory (L. W. Hoffman & Kloska, 1995; P. A. Katz, 1987; Price-Bonham & Skeen, 1982).

Dorothy Flannagan and San Perese (1998) conducted a study that highlights the complexity of the research on ethnicity and parents' gender messages. Specifically, their research showed that we need to know a family's social class before we can draw conclusions about the relationship between ethnicity and gender messages. These researchers asked mothers from three ethnic groups in the region of San Antonio, Texas, to make a tape recording of a conversation they had with their preschool or kindergarten child. The researchers then analyzed the conversations for the number of times that the conversation referred to emotions.

If we consider just the lower-social-class participants in Flannagan and Perese's (1998) study, we would draw one kind of conclusion: European American mothers discuss emotions equally with their sons and their daughters, whereas Black and Latina mothers discuss emotions much more often with their daughters than with their sons. However, if we consider just the higher-social-class participants, Black mothers discuss emotions equally with their sons and daughters, whereas European American and Latina mothers discuss emotions much more often with their daughters than with their sons. These complex results are puzzling. For instance, why should higher-social-class Black mothers talk so frequently with their sons about emotions, and why don't the higher-social-class European American and Latina mothers encourage these emotional conversations with their sons? In any event, Flannagan and Perese's research provides convincing evidence that we cannot find clear-cut, overall ethnic differences with respect to mothers' gender-related behavior.

You won't be surprised to learn that parents' personal ideas about gender can have a significant effect on the kind of messages they give their sons and daughters. For example, Fiese and Skillman (2000) studied a group of parents, most of whom were European American. Each parent was instructed to tell a story to her or his 4-year-old child, focusing on the parent's own childhood experience. Mothers who had stereotypically feminine personal characteristics and fathers who had stereotypically masculine personal characteristics tended to interact with their children in a gender-stereotypical fashion. That is, they told about three times as many stories about achievement to their sons as they did to their daughters. However, parents who had a mixture of stereotypically feminine and masculine personal characteristics tended to interact in a nonstereotypical fashion. Specifically, they told about the same number of achievement-related stories to their daughters and to their sons.

Some parents make impressive efforts to treat their children in a gender-fair manner. We have discussed the theories developed by Sandra Bem in connection with the topic of androgyny in Chapter 2 and have explored the idea of gender schemas in the current chapter. Bem (1998) wrote a book called *An Unconventional Family*, which provides details about the nonstereotyped way that she and Daryl Bem had raised their daughter and son.

> For example, we took turns cooking the meals, driving the car, bathing the baby, and
> so on, so that our own parental example would not teach a correlation between sex
> and behavior. This was easy for us because we already had such well-developed

habits of egalitarian turn-taking. In addition, we tried to arrange for both our children to have traditionally male and traditionally female experiences—including, for example, playing with both dolls and trucks, wearing both pink and blue clothing, and having both male and female playmates. This turned out to be easy, too, perhaps because of our kids' temperaments. Insofar as possible, we also arranged for them to see nontraditional gender models outside the home. (p. 104)

Sandra Bem (1998) interviewed her daughter Emily, age 22, about whether she has managed to transcend gender. Emily responded, "I think I transcend gender in my head all the time. I don't look at other people as boys or girls. I put myself in their shoes and consider what they're feeling or how they're thinking or why they're acting the way they are" (p. 195). Clearly, it would be interesting to conduct a large-scale study of children who had been reared by egalitarian parents. Would they be more likely than other children to become nontraditional adults?

In summary, this discussion about individual differences in parents' gender typing demonstrates that ethnicity has a complex influence on parents' treatment of daughters and sons. Parents who endorse nontraditional gender beliefs in their own lives may indeed treat their sons and daughters in a gender-fair fashion. When discussing factors that influence parents' gender typing, however, we need to reemphasize the general conclusions about parents. Specifically, parents often encourage gender typing by their reactions to their children's "masculine" and "feminine" activities. They also discuss emotions, especially sadness, more with their daughters than with their sons. In contrast, they often treat their daughters and sons similarly with respect to aggression and independence. Taking everything into account, parents are not as consistent about encouraging gender typing as articles in the popular media would suggest. We need to consider additional forces that are responsible for gender typing. Let's therefore examine three factors that reveal greater gender bias: peers, schools, and the media.

Peers

Once children in the United States and Canada begin school, a major source of information about gender is their **peer group,** that is, other children of approximately their own age. A child may have been raised by relatively nonsexist parents. However, on the first day of class, if Jennifer wears her hiking boots and Johnny brings in a new baby doll, their peers may respond negatively.

Peers encourage gender typing in four major ways: (1) They reject children who act in a nonstereotypical fashion; (2) they encourage gender segregation; (3) they are prejudiced against children of the other gender; and (4) they treat boys and girls differently. As you read this discussion, notice how social learning theory would explain each topic's contribution to children's gender typing.

Rejection of Nontraditional Behavior.   In general, children tend to reject peers who act in a fashion that is more characteristic of the other gender (C. P. Edwards et al., 2001). For example, children tend to think that girls should not play aggressive, "fighting" electronic games (Funk & Buchman, 1996). Also, girls who dominate discussions are downgraded as being too bossy (Zucker et al., 1995). Women who had been tomboys as children often report that their peers were influential in convincing them to act more feminine (B. L. Morgan, 1998).

Nontraditional boys experience even stronger rejection (Fagot et al., 2000). For example, elementary school children are much more positive toward a boy who watches Superman cartoons and plays with racing cars than toward a boy who watches Powerpuff Girls cartoons and plays with Barbie dolls (Zucker et al., 1995). Pollack (1998) suggested that peers contribute to an unwritten boys' code, a set of rigid rules about how boys should speak and behave. He proposed that the code explicitly forbids boys from talking about anxieties, fear, and other "sensitive" emotions.

Gender Segregation.   The tendency to associate with other children of the same gender is called **gender segregation.** Children in the United States and Canada begin to prefer playing with same-gender children by age 3 or 4 years, and this tendency increases until early adolescence (C. P. Edwards et al., 2001; H. W. Gardiner et al., 1998; Maccoby, 1998). In one study, for instance, 86% of 5-year-old children chose a same-gender playmate (P. A. Katz & Kofkin, 1997). On the school playground or in the cafeteria, the peer pressure can be so strong that a girl who plays with a particular boy in her neighborhood may refuse to say hello to him once they reach school (Thorne, 1993).

One problem with gender segregation is that these single-gender groups encourage children to learn gender-stereotyped behavior (Maccoby, 1998). Boys learn that they are supposed to be physically aggressive and not admit that they are sometimes afraid. Girls learn to focus their attention on clothing and glamour rather than on competence. Both groups learn that the boys' group has greater power. This inequality encourages a sense of **entitlement** among the boys; the boys will feel that they *deserve* greater power simply because they are male rather than female (Golden, 1998; L. M. Ward, 1999). Another major problem with gender segregation is that children who grow up playing with only same-gender peers will not learn the broad range of skills they need to work well with both females and males (Fagot et al., 2000).

This preference for friends of the same gender continues to increase until about the age of 11 (Maccoby, 1998). As romantic relationships develop in early adolescence, boys and girls then increase their time together.

Gender Prejudice.   A third way in which peers encourage gender typing is with prejudice against members of the other gender (Boyatzis et al., 1999). As we discussed in connection with gender schema theory, children develop a preference for their own gender. For example, Powlishta (1995) showed 9- and 10-year-old children a series of brief videotaped interactions between children and adults. After viewing each video, the children rated the child in the video, using a 10-point scale of liking that ranged from "not at all" to "very, very much."

As you can see in Figure 3.4, girls liked the girl targets in the videos better than the boy targets, and boys preferred the boy targets to the girl targets. This

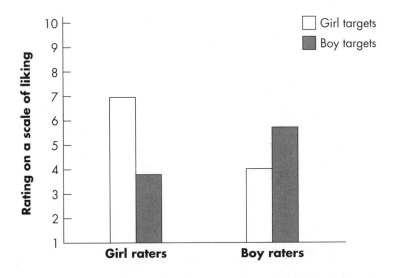

FIGURE 3.4 ■ Ratings supplied by female and male children for the girls and boys in videos. The data show prejudice against the other gender.

Note: 1 = most negative; 10 = most positive.

Source: From Powlishta, K. (1995). Intergroup processes in childhood. *Developmental Psychology, 31,* 781–788. © 1995 by the American Psychological Association. Reprinted with permission.

kind of prejudice arises from children's clear-cut gender schemas, and it reinforces children's beliefs that females and males are very different kinds of people.

Differential Treatment.   A fourth way in which peers promote gender typing is that they use different standards in their interactions with boys than with girls. One of the most interesting examples of differential treatment is that children respond to girls on the basis of their physical attractiveness, but attractiveness is largely irrelevant for boys. Gregory Smith (1985) observed middle-class European American preschoolers for 5-minute sessions in a classroom setting on 5 separate days. He recorded how other children treated each child. Were the other children prosocial—helping, patting, and praising the child? Or were the other children physically aggressive—hitting, pushing, or kicking the target child? He then calculated how each child's attractiveness was related to both prosocial and aggressive behavior.

The results showed that attractiveness (as previously rated by college students) was correlated with the way the girls were treated. Specifically, attractive girls were much more likely to receive prosocial treatment. Figure 3.5 shows a strong positive correlation. In other words, the "cutest" girls were most likely to be helped, patted, and praised. In contrast, the less attractive girls received few of these positive responses. However, Smith found no correlation between attractiveness and prosocial treatment of boys; attractive and less attractive boys received a similar number of prosocial actions.

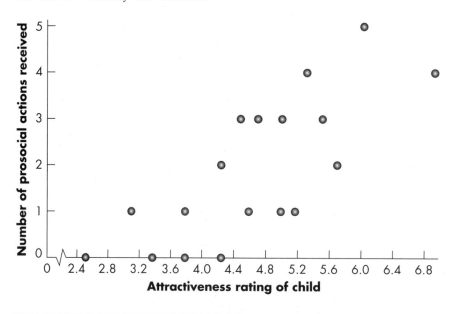

FIGURE 3.5 ■ Positive correlation between attractiveness and prosocial treatment of girls (r = +0.73).

Source: G. J. Smith (1985).

Gregory J. Smith (1985) also found a comparable pattern for physical aggression scores. That is, the less attractive girls were more likely to be hit, pushed, and kicked, whereas the cutest girls rarely received this treatment. However, attractiveness was not related to the aggression directed toward boys. Young girls learn a lesson from their peers that will be repeated throughout their lives: Physical attractiveness is important for females, and pretty girls and women will receive better treatment. Boys learn that physical attractiveness is not really relevant to their lives.

The influence of peers on gender typing has not been examined as thoroughly as the influence of parents (Jacklin & Baker, 1993). However, we have seen that, in several ways, children can influence others who are their own age. Specifically, they can reject nontraditional behavior in their peers. They can encourage gender segregation, so that boys and girls have minimal contact with one another. They can also express prejudice against children of the other gender. Finally, they can respond differently to girls and boys, for example, by emphasizing attractiveness for girls but not for boys.

School

The typical elementary school child in North America spends more waking hours in school with teachers than at home with family members. As a result, teachers and schools have numerous opportunities to influence gender typing.

Even the structure of a school provides evidence that males are treated differently and valued more than females (Theme 2). Specifically, the principal and other high-prestige officials are typically male, whereas those who teach "the little kids" are usually female (Fischman, 2000). Let's investigate how teachers' behavior may reinforce this same message. Then we'll consider how gender-fair programs can encourage children to become less gender stereotyped. Finally, we'll consider the serious problem that occurs in some developing countries, where girls are much less likely than boys to receive a good education.

Teachers' Behavior.   Beginning in the early 1990s, the media finally began to publicize some information that many of us had been reporting for years: Girls do not receive equal treatment in the classroom (AAUW Educational Foundation, 1992; Sadker & Sadker, 1994). The publicized reports highlighted the invisibility of girls in the educational system, a point that is clearly consistent with Theme 3 of this textbook. According to the reports, classroom activities are often selected to appeal to boys, teachers typically pay more attention to boys in the classroom, and females are absent or misrepresented in the textbooks and other teaching materials.

More specifically, the research suggests that boys generally receive more positive feedback in the classroom. They are also more likely to be recognized for their creativity, called on in class, and included in class discussions (American Institutes for Research, 1998; Basow, 2000; DeZolt & Hull, 2001; Lott & Maluso, 2001). Sadker and Sadker (1994) discussed a typical example: The teacher asks, "What is an adjective? Maria?" Maria answers appropriately, "A word that describes something." Simultaneously, Tim calls out, "Adjectives describe nouns." The teacher responds, "Good, Tim" (p. 74). Notice how the teacher reinforces Tim, ignoring Maria's correct answer. A moment later, the teacher asks the children to identify the adjective in a sentence. Donna appropriately answers "Beautiful," but the teacher doesn't even comment that she is correct. Teachers also tend to offer more specific suggestions to boys than to girls (American Institutes for Research, 1998).

Teachers may also encourage girls to become dependent and polite. This emphasis on girls' "niceness" was illustrated in the class awards one teacher distributed at kindergarten graduation. The "Boys' Awards" were listed as "Very Best Thinker, Most Eager Learner, Most Imaginative, Mr. Personality, and Hardest Worker." The "Girls' Awards" were "All-Around Sweetheart, Sweetest Personality, Cutest Personality, Best Manners, and Best Helper" (Rhode, 1997, p. 55).

Female students of color are especially likely to be ignored in the classroom. If Black girls speak up in the classroom, their assertiveness may be discouraged. In fact, they may become more passive and quiet (Basow, 2000). Furthermore, Black girls often assume adultlike social roles in elementary classrooms, distributing material to other students and keeping them in line when the teacher must leave the classroom. However, teachers don't seem to encourage Black girls to take on *academic* responsibilities, such as tutoring or showing a new student how to prepare an assignment (L. Grant, 1994).

In short, several factors in the school system operate so that girls are often shortchanged. They may be ignored, they may not be given appropriate feedback, and they may be encouraged to be dependent or socially skilled rather than academically competent. Hilary Lips (2001) pointed out how girls' relative powerlessness in the elementary classroom encourages them to expect a life in which women have less power than men.

Encouraging Change. So far, our exploration of gender and education has emphasized that school structure and teachers' behavior are likely to favor boys over girls. Fortunately, however, the North American educational scene may be gradually changing. Many colleges and universities that train teachers now require courses that focus on gender and ethnic diversity. Media coverage of the "silenced female" problem has also alerted teachers about the need for more equal attention to girls and boys (Streitmatter, 1994).

Some programs have been designed to change children's stereotypes (Bigler, 1999a; Gash & Morgan, 1993; Tozzo & Golub, 1990). For instance, teachers can help children become less stereotyped by deemphasizing gender schemas. For example, Bigler (1995) assigned 6- to 9-year-old children either to control classrooms or to gender-emphasized classrooms during a four-week summer school program. Teachers in the control classrooms were instructed not to emphasize gender in their remarks or in their treatment of the children. Meanwhile, teachers in the gender-emphasized classrooms used gender-segregated seating, with girls' and boys' desks on opposite sides of the classroom. The teachers also displayed girls' and boys' artwork on different bulletin boards, and they frequently instructed boys and girls to perform different activities.

The most interesting results concerned those children who did not have strong gender schemas before the program began. Those enrolled in classrooms that did not emphasize gender were 50% less likely than those in the gender-emphasized classrooms to make stereotyped judgments about which jobs males and females could hold. In contrast, children were not influenced by the nature of the program if they already had strong gender schemas before the program began.

Unfortunately, we cannot expect that a life history of learning gender stereotypes can be erased with one simple, brief intervention. Many programs have been unsuccessful (Bigler, 1999a). From similar research on racial stereotypes, we know that school programs work more effectively if they emphasize peer collaboration. Children change their stereotypes more dramatically when they work together on an issue rather than when an adult tries to persuade them to change perspectives (Aboud & Fenwick, 1999; Bigler, 1999b). The approach to gender and education must be more sophisticated, keeping in mind that children actively construct their gender schemas; they do not simply acquire information by means of the more passive social learning approach (Bigler, 1999a).

Educators must also emphasize a more comprehensive approach toward gender, so that teachers from kindergarten onward are encouraged to pay equal attention to girls and to reduce inappropriate stereotypes about gender. One 4-year-old girl revealed her awareness about gender equity when she explained why her class had changed the words to a song about "Mr. Sun." As she pointed out, "You've just gotta sing about Mrs. Sun to make it fair" (K. R. Bailey, 1993, p. 100).

Gender and Education on the International Level. At the international level, we often encounter a more extreme problem about education for young girls. In many countries, girls are much less likely than boys to be enrolled in school. For example, in many parts of India, boys are encouraged to go to school, but girls are kept at home to care for younger siblings. As a result, the literacy rate in India is 64% for males and 35% for females (Bellamy, 2000).

United Nations data show that developing countries have 538 million illiterate women, in contrast to 302 million illiterate men (Sweetman, 1998a). Where food and other essentials are limited, the education of females is considered a luxury. An additional problem in some developing countries is that the educational system may encourage exaggerated gender stereotypes (Bellamy, 2000; R. Gordon, 1998).

Literacy rates for women in developing countries vary greatly. For example, 96% of women in Cuba can read, in contrast to 41% in nearby Haiti (Bellamy, 2000). Some countries (or regions within countries) have recently begun literacy campaigns (Gold, 2001; Nussbaum, 2000; Seymour, 1999; Sweetman, 1998b). In the rural regions of Iran, for instance, girls' enrollment in primary schools rose from 60% to 80% in just 5 years (Bellamy, 2000).

Unfortunately, women who have not been educated will experience a lifelong handicap. They will not be able to read newspapers, write checks, sign contracts, or perform numerous other activities that can help make them independent and economically self-sufficient (Nussbaum, 2000). In addition, uneducated women have far higher birth rates than educated women, and their children are less likely to be healthy. The gap between developing countries and wealthy countries continues to widen (Bellamy, 2000). In addition, the governments of wealthy countries rarely subsidize literacy programs or other socially responsible projects that could make a real difference in the lives of women in developing countries.

One woman living in the Canary Islands, off the coast of North Africa, described why she regrets that she never learned to read:

> The greatest treasure that exists in life is to read and understand what one is reading. This is the most beautiful gift there is. All my life I have wished to learn to read and write, because, to me, knowing how to do so meant freedom. (Sweetman, 1998a, p. 2)

The Media

So far, we have considered how parents, peers, and schools treat girls and boys differently. Children also receive gender messages from many additional sources. For example, children learn about gender through video games, but females are entirely absent from 41% of the games with human characters (Cassell & Jenkins, 1998; Dietz, 1998). "Barbie Fashion Designer" is currently one of the most successful interactive games designed for girls (Subrahmanyam et al., 2001), and this game sends a clear gender message. Occasionally, we'll see a creative alternative, such as the software program *The Adventures of Josie True*, featuring an 11-year-old Chinese American girl detective (Donovan, 2000; the Web site is http://www.josietrue.com). In general, though, the large number of masculine video games encourages boys to develop more extensive computer skills than girls.

Even Halloween costumes convey messages about gender: Girls can be beauty queens, princesses, or cuddly animals, whereas boys can be warriors, superheroes, or monsters (A. Nelson, 2000). Most of the research on gender and the media examines how males and females are represented in books and television, so we'll explore these two areas in more detail.

Books.   You won't be surprised to learn that most of the main characters in children's picture books are males, usually by a ratio of about 2 to 1 (R. Clark et al., 1993; Kortenhaus & Demarest, 1993; Tepper & Cassidy, 1999). Males also appear much more often in the books' illustrations (R. Clark et al., 1993; Tepper & Cassidy, 1999).

What are the males and females *doing* in these books designed for young children? Males are portrayed in a wider variety of occupations compared to females (Crabb & Bielawski, 1994; McDonald, 1989). Also, boys help others, solve problems independently, and play actively. In contrast, girls need help in solving their problems, and they play quietly indoors (Kortenhaus & Demarest, 1993; Spitz, 1999). In one quantitative study, for example, males were almost three times as likely as females to be accomplishing goals, and females were almost five times as likely as males to be shown in passive or dependent activities (Kortenhaus & Demarest, 1993). Surprisingly—in light of our earlier discussion about gender and emotions—a sample of books aimed at preschoolers showed males and females as being similar in their fear and also similar in their anger (Tepper & Cassidy, 1999). Books designed for older children, however, reinforce the gender stereotypes: Males are typically aggressive, argumentative, and competitive, whereas females are typically affectionate and emotionally expressive (L. Evans & Davies, 2000).

As you've been learning about the general lack of female role models in children's literature, perhaps you felt uneasy. Should we really worry about what children read? As it turns out, these biases do have important consequences for children. For example, Ochman (1996) designed a study in which children watched videotapes of an actor reading a series of stories. Each story required the main character to solve a problem, which then enhanced this character's self-esteem. The same stories were presented to classrooms of 7- to 10-year-olds; however, the main character was a boy for half of the classes and a girl for the remaining classes.

A standard measure of self-esteem was administered at the beginning of the study. Then the children saw the videotaped stories over a period of about six weeks, and the self-esteem measure was administered a second time. The researchers then calculated the change in the children's self-esteem. As Figure 3.6 shows, girls had a greater increase in self-esteem if they heard the stories about an achieving girl rather than an achieving boy. The boys showed a comparable pattern; their self-esteem increased after they heard stories about an achieving boy rather than an achieving girl.

Think about the implications of Ochman's research. If children hear stories about strong, competent boys, but not girls, the boys are likely to experience a boost in self-esteem. Meanwhile, the girls' self-esteem will not be improved.

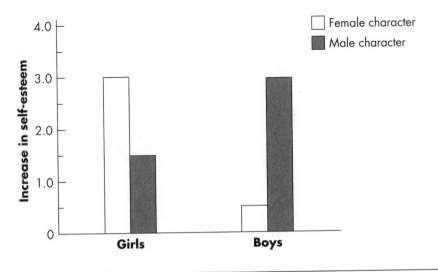

FIGURE 3.6 ■ Improvement in girls' and boys' self-esteem (compared to baseline) after hearing stories about a female character or a male character.

Source: Based on Ochman (1996).

Conscientious parents and teachers can review the books that children will see and can make sure that competent females are well represented (Bem, 1998). They can also be alert for new resources. For example, a feminist magazine called *New Moon* is edited by girls and young women (see Figure 3.7).

Television. Preschoolers average more than 20 hours of television per week (Paik, 2001). By the time teenagers graduate from high school, they have spent about 18,000 hours in front of the TV set, in contrast to about 12,000 hours in classroom instruction (Singer & Singer, 2001). In Chapter 2, we examined stereotyping in programs intended for adult audiences. Now let's consider the television programs and advertisements aimed at children. As we'll see, 18,000 hours of television can provide a strong education in gender stereotypes.

Males are shown much more frequently than females in children's television programs (R. F. Fox, 2000; Furnham et al., 1997; Huntemann & Morgan, 2001). For example, a sample of network and cable cartoon programs contained 106 major female characters and 326 major male characters (T. L. Thompson & Zerbinos, 1995). Many cartoon programs have no female characters (Golombok & Fivush, 1994). I recall seeing an adventure cartoon in which the only female was the young male hero's mother. She fainted within the first five minutes and never appeared again. *Sesame Street* has more than twice as many male characters as female characters (Hallingby, 1993).

Males and females also perform different activities on television. For example, males are more likely to be shown in the workplace, whereas females are

FIGURE 3.7 ■ *New Moon*, a magazine for girls and young women, discusses issues such as gender, racism, and ecology.

Reprinted, with permission, from New Moon®: The Magazine for Girls and Their Dreams; Copyright New Moon Publishing, P.O. Box 3620, Duluth, MN 55803-3587. Subscriptions $29.00/ 6 issues. Call 1-800-381-4743 or visit http://www.newmoon.org.

shown as caregivers (T. L. Thompson & Zerbinos, 1995). Just as we saw in the analysis of children's books, males are more likely to show leadership, ingenuity, and aggression. In contrast, females are more likely to be affectionate and helpless (T. L. Thompson & Zerbinos, 1995).

Another problem is that boys and girls are shown playing with different toys in the advertisements. In a sample of 135 toy ads from Saturday morning children's programs, the 15 depicting action figures showed only boys. Of the ads for dolls, 52 showed only girls, 10 showed both boys and girls, and 1 showed only a boy (Rajecki et al., 1993). Perhaps we should be happy that 11 ads showed a boy interacting with a doll. However, even children reared by nonsexist parents will quickly understand the television message that girls and boys are supposed to enjoy playing with different kinds of toys.

We have seen that females are underrepresented. We've also seen that females and males are shown in different roles. Again, skeptics might ask whether children even notice the gender patterns on television. T. L. Thompson and Zerbinos (1997) asked 4- to 9-year-olds about the number of boy and girl characters who appeared on the television shows they watched. The researchers found that 78% of the children reported more boy characters, 12% reported more girl characters, and 10% reported the same number of boy and girl characters. In general, then, children do notice that males are more common in the cartoons.

But can children learn gender-role stereotypes by watching television? Let's consider a careful study conducted by Signorielli and Lears (1992). These researchers studied 530 fourth- and fifth-graders, using a sample of ethnic groups that resembled the distribution in the United States. Each child completed a test of gender stereotyping. A typical question on this test asked whether a chore, such as washing dishes, should be done by girls only, boys only, or either girls or boys. Signorielli and Lears found that the children who watched many hours of television were significantly more likely than other children to be highly gender stereotyped.

If you are considering some of the potential research problems we raised in Chapter 1, you might wonder whether those results might be explained by confounding variables. For example, maybe well-educated parents limit their children's television viewing and also discourage gender stereotypes. However, Signorielli and Lears (1992) conducted a second analysis in which they statistically controlled for potential confounding variables such as gender, ethnic group, reading level, and parents' education. The correlation between TV viewing and gender stereotyping still remained statistically significant, although it was not very strong. In general, the research tends to show a modest relationship between television viewing and gender stereotypes (e.g., C. P. Edwards et al., 2001; Gunter & McAleer, 1997; Huntemann & Morgan, 2001).

Cautious parents who want to raise nonstereotyped children should limit television viewing. Parents should also encourage their children to watch programs in which women are shown as competent people and men are shown in nurturant roles. Parents can also select educational and entertaining videos that avoid stereotypes and feature competent females. Furthermore, parents can occasionally stop these videos at appropriate intervals to discuss gender-related issues with their children (Gunter & McAleer, 1997). Television and videos have the potential to present admirable models of female and male behavior, and they *could* even make children less stereotyped. So far, unfortunately, the media have not lived up to that potential.

SECTION SUMMARY   ■

Factors That Shape Gender Typing

1. Parents tend to encourage gender-typed activities (e.g., toy choice and chore assignment), and they discuss different emotions with daughters than with sons; they also treat sons and daughters somewhat differently with respect to children's aggression and independence, but the differential treatment is not consistent.

2. Parents differ widely in their differential treatment of girls and boys; the relationship between ethnicity and differential treatment is complicated because of important factors such as social class. However, parents can devise creative ways to treat their children in a gender-fair fashion.

3. Peers react negatively to another child's nonstereotypical behavior; peers also encourage gender segregation; they are prejudiced against children of the other gender; and they use different standards when interacting with girls rather than boys.

4. North American schools encourage gender typing through the distribution of men's and women's occupations. Boys also receive more attention and useful feedback in the classroom compared to girls. Some programs have been developed to help children reduce stereotypes, but these programs must be both comprehensive and sophisticated in order to have an important impact. In many developing countries, boys are more likely than girls to attend school and to learn to read.

5. Children's books and television continue to underrepresent females and to show males and females in stereotyped activities. According to research, children's ideas about gender can be influenced by reading books and watching television.

CHILDREN'S KNOWLEDGE ABOUT GENDER

We've just outlined several important ways in which children receive gender messages from the surrounding culture. Now let's see how well children learn their gender lessons: What do they know about gender, and what kind of stereotypes do they hold? In Chapter 2, we explored adults' stereotypes; we'll see that these ideas about gender are well established before children begin kindergarten. Keep in mind a point we emphasized in connection with the cognitive developmental explanation of gender typing: Children actively work to create gender schemas, and these schemas encourage them to act in a manner that is consistent with their gender.

Interestingly, even infants as young as 6 months of age know something about gender; they can place males and females in different categories (Fagot et al., 2000; P. A. Katz & Kofkin, 1997; C. L. Martin & Dinella, 2001). In a typical study, researchers showed each infant a series of slides of the heads and shoulders of different women. (The slides showed a variety of clothing, hairstyles, facial expressions, and so forth.) After a number of slides, the infant lost interest in these female stimuli. Then the researchers presented a test slide, showing either a male or a female. P. A. Katz and Kofkin (1997) found, for example, that 6-month-olds looked significantly longer at a slide of a male than at a slide of a female. This looking pattern tells us that young infants recognize that the new slide belongs to a different category than the slides previously shown. (Infants also looked longer at a slide of a female after seeing a series of slides showing males.) This series of studies shows us that—long before they are able to say their first word or take their first step—infants divide people into two categories on the basis of gender.

As you can imagine, gender knowledge is much easier to test in children who are old enough to talk. For instance, 68% of 2-year-olds and 93% of 3-year-olds can correctly identify whether they are a girl or a boy (P. A. Katz, 1996).

However, as illustrated in the birthday party anecdote at the beginning of this chapter, children's ideas about gender often differ from adults' perspectives. Young children often agree with that little girl, arguing that clothing is the most accurate way to determine a person's gender (Ruble & Martin, 1998).

Let's begin by examining children's knowledge about gender-stereotyped activities and occupations. Then we'll discuss their knowledge about gender-stereotyped personality characteristics, a more abstract kind of distinction. We'll also examine some factors that influence the strength of children's stereotypes.

Children's Stereotypes About Activities and Occupations

At an early age, children have clear ideas about the activities that are gender consistent. As the cognitive developmental approach argues, children actively construct gender schemas. For instance, when 4- and 5-year-olds are given a choice of a picture to color, 75% of boys select a picture of a car, a baseball player, or some other masculine scene, whereas 67% of girls select a picture of a cat, a ballet dancer, or some other feminine scene (Boyatzis & Eades, 1999). Also, 4-year-olds know that boys are "supposed to" like toy tools, whereas girls are "supposed to" like toy dishes (Raag, 1999). Many boys also report that their fathers would think that it would be wrong if they played with toy dishes (Raag & Rackliff, 1998). Furthermore, adults have difficulty persuading children to play with toys considered appropriate for the other gender (Fisher-Thompson & Burke, 1998).

In addition, children remember activities better when they are consistent with their own gender. Girls remember stereotypically feminine activities better than boys do, and boys remember stereotypically masculine activities better than girls do (Conkright et al., 2000; Signorella et al., 1997). As Sandra Bem (1985, 1993) theorized, children categorize objects and activities according to their gender schemas. And as Kohlberg (1966) proposed, children show favoritism for items that match their own gender.

These gender schemas extend to occupations. Gary Levy and his colleagues (2000) interviewed younger children (ages 3 to 4) and older children (ages 5 to 7), using questions such as the ones shown in Demonstration 3.3 on page 104. As in this demonstration, the study required a forced choice; children were instructed to respond either "a woman" or "a man."

As you can see from Table 3.1 on page 105, even the younger children had well-developed gender stereotypes about occupations. However, notice an interesting pattern in the judgments of the older children. Their judgments about stereotypically feminine occupations are about the same as the judgments of younger children, but their judgments about stereotypically masculine occupations shift dramatically, compared to the younger children's judgments: Men are much better suited for these occupations than women!

Sadly, children also show strong stereotypes when thinking about their own future occupations. For example, in another part of the study by G. D. Levy and his colleagues (2000), children were asked to choose which emotion they would feel if they grew up to have each of the four occupations described in Demonstration 3.3. Girls were likely to say that they would be happy with a stereotypically feminine occupation and angry or disgusted with a stereotypically masculine occupation. Boys showed the opposite response pattern, except that they were even happier with a gender-stereotyped occupation, and they were even more angry and disgusted with a stereotypically feminine profession. We have seen throughout this chapter that gender roles constrict boys more than they

DEMONSTRATION 3.3 ■ ■ ■ ■ ■ ■ ■ ■ ■ ■ ■ ■ ■ ■ ■ ■ ■

Children's Beliefs About Men's and Women's Occupations

With a parent's permission, enlist the help of a child who is between the ages of 4 and 7 years. Then ask the child each of the following questions. After listening to each answer, ask the child, "Why do you suppose that a (man/woman) would be best for that job?"

1. An airplane pilot is a person who flies an airplane for other people. Who do you think would do the best job as an airplane pilot, a woman or a man?
2. A clothes designer is a person who draws up and makes clothes for other people. Who do you think would do the best job as a clothes designer, a woman or a man?
3. A car mechanic is a person who fixes cars for other people. Who do you think would do the best job as a car mechanic, a woman or a man?
4. A secretary is a person who types up letters and mails things for other people. Who do you think would do the best job as a secretary, a woman or a man?

After asking all four questions, ask the child which job she or he would like best and which one would be worst. (For younger children, you may need to remind them what each employee does.)

Source: Based on G. D. Levy et al. (2000).

constrict girls, and other research confirms this tendency with respect to future occupations (Etaugh & Liss, 1992; Helwig, 1998). For instance, Etaugh and Liss (1992) found that not one single boy in their study of kindergartners through eighth-graders named a "feminine" career choice.

Children's Stereotypes About Personality

Children's stereotypes about personality are somewhat slower to develop than their stereotypes about activities, perhaps because personality characteristics are more abstract than activities and occupations (Powlishta et al., 2001). Even so, children between the ages of 2½ and 4 show some tendency to believe that strength and aggression are associated with males and that softness and gentleness are associated with females (G. Cowan & Hoffman, 1986; J. E. Williams & Best, 1990; J. E. Williams et al., 1975).

TABLE 3.1 ■ **Children's Judgments About the Relative Competence of Women and Men in Four Gender-Stereotyped Occupations**

	Child's Age Group	
	Younger (3- to 4-year-olds)	Older (5- to 7-year-olds)
"Feminine" occupations		
Percentage who judged women more competent	75%	78%
Percentage who judged men more competent	25%	22%
"Masculine" occupations		
Percentage who judged women more competent	32%	7%
Percentage who judged men more competent	68%	93%

Source: G. D. Levy et al. (2000).

In a representative study focusing on children's stereotypes, 8- to 10-year-old children looked at a series of photographs of women, men, girls, and boys (Powlishta, 2000). The children rated each photo on several gender-related personality characteristics, such as "gentle" and "strong." Consistent with previous research, the children rated female photos significantly higher than male photos on the stereotypically feminine characteristics, and they rated male photos significantly higher than the female photos on the stereotypically masculine characteristics.

Factors Related to Children's Gender Stereotypes

Several factors influence the strength of children's stereotypes. We mentioned earlier that boys have stronger stereotypes about career choices than girls do. Ethnicity and social class probably have a complex relationship with children's gender stereotypes. You may recall from page 90 that ethnicity and social class are not related in a clear-cut fashion to the way that mothers discuss emotions with their sons and daughters (Flannagan & Perese, 1998). Unfortunately, I've been unable to locate similarly recent, large-scale studies that examine the stereotypes of children from different ethnic groups and different social classes. However, cross-cultural research shows that children in different countries are generally similar to North American children in their views of the personality characteristics associated with males and females (Best & Williams, 1993; Gibbons, 2000; J. E. Williams & Best, 1990). Another cross-cultural finding is that children have consistently stronger stereotypes about males than about females. Once again, masculine stereotypes are relatively rigid.

Are children's gender ideas influenced by their family's views? In general, parents who have strong gender stereotypes about child rearing are likely to have children with stronger gender stereotypes (Ex & Janssens, 1998; Fagot & Leinbach, 1995; O'Brien et al., 2000; Powlishta et al., 2001).

As you might expect, children's age has an important effect on the nature of their stereotypes (Durkin & Nugent, 1998; Lobel et al., 2000; Powlishta et al., 2001). Some studies assess children's *knowledge* about culturally accepted gender stereotypes. The older children clearly know more than the younger children. After all, the older children have had more opportunities to learn their culture's traditional notions about gender. However, other studies have assessed the *flexibility* of children's stereotypes. A typical question might be: "Who can bake a cake? Can a woman do it, can a man do it, or can they both do it?" Older children were generally more flexible than younger children; that is, they were more likely to reply, "Both can do it." We can conclude that older children know more about gender stereotypes, but they are also aware that people do not need to be bound by them (Fagot & Rodgers, 1998).

SECTION SUMMARY ■

Children's Knowledge About Gender

1. Even 6-month-olds show some ability to distinguish between males and females.

2. Children have well-developed stereotypes about women's and men's activities and occupations, as well as their personality characteristics.

3. The strength of children's gender stereotypes is influenced by such factors as their gender and their age; these stereotypes are fairly consistent across cultures; parents who have traditional ideas about gender generally have children with stronger gender stereotypes.

■ ■ ■ ■ ■ ■ **CHAPTER REVIEW QUESTIONS** ■ ■ ■ ■ ■ ■

1. Early in prenatal development, infant boys and girls are similar. By the time they are born, they differ in their gonads, internal reproductive systems, and external genitals. Discuss how these three kinds of differences emerge during normal prenatal development.

2. According to a well-known proverb, beauty is in the eye of the beholder. Apparently, the masculinity or femininity of an infant is also in the eye of the beholder. Discuss how both parents and strangers provide evidence for this statement.

3. Five-year-old Darlene is playing with a doll. Discuss how current psychological theory would explain her behavior. Be sure to mention the two mechanisms proposed by social learning theory as well as the central ideas of the cognitive developmental approach.

4. Imagine that a family has twins, a girl named Susan and a boy named Jim. Based on the information on families and gender typing, how would you predict that their parents would treat Susan and Jim? Discuss four topics: (a) gender-typed activity, (b) discussion of emotion, (c) aggression, and (d) independence.

5. Discuss four ways in which peers encourage gender typing. How might a skillful teacher minimize gender typing? What other precautions should this teacher take to make certain that females and males are treated fairly in the classroom?

6. Describe as completely as possible how books and television convey gender stereotypes. Also describe how these media can influence children's toy preferences and other activities.

7. A friend who has a 2-year-old child asks you: "What can I do to encourage my child *not* to be restricted by gender stereotypes?" How would you reply?

8. Suppose that you are working at a day care center and that you interact with children between the ages of 6 months and 5 years. How do researchers know that the 6-month-olds already have some information about gender? Also describe what the older children of different ages will know about gender and gender stereotypes.

9. As children grow older, they know more about gender stereotypes, but these stereotypes are also more flexible. Describe the research that supports this statement. What implications does this statement have for the influence of peers on gender typing?

10. At several points throughout the chapter, we mentioned that gender stereotypes are more restrictive for boys than for girls and that fathers are more likely than mothers to encourage these stereotypes. Discuss this issue, being sure to mention parents' reactions to their children's gender-related activities, children's ideas about occupations, and any other topics you consider relevant.

NEW TERMS

* gender typing (73)
* prenatal period (74)
* infancy (74)
* sex chromosomes (74)
* gonads (75)
* androgen (75)
* estrogen (75)
* intersexed individual (75)
* androgen-insensitivity syndrome (75)
* congenital adrenal hyperplasia (76)

* social constructionism (81)
* social learning approach (82)
* modeling (83)
* cognitive developmental approach (83)
* schema (83)
* gender schemas (83)
* gender identity (84)
* peer group (91)
* gender segregation (92)
* entitlement (92)

The terms asterisked in the New Terms section serve as good search terms for InfoTrac College Edition. Go to http://infotrac.thomsonlearning.com and try these added search terms.

RECOMMENDED READINGS

Eckes, T., & Trautner, H. M. (Eds.). (2000a). *The developmental social psychology of gender.* Mahwah, NJ: Erlbaum. I strongly recommend this handbook, which features 14 chapters on topics such as gender socialization, theories of gender development, children's gender stereotypes, and cross-cultural research.

Maccoby, E. E. (1998). *The two sexes: Growing up apart, coming together.* Cambridge, MA: Harvard University Press. Eleanor Maccoby's book is especially strong in exploring gender segregation, children's play patterns, and the implications of these behaviors.

Powlishta, K. K., et al. (2001). From infancy through middle childhood: The role of cognitive and social factors in becoming gendered. In R. K. Unger (Ed.), *Handbook of the psychology of women and gender* (pp. 116–132). New York: Wiley. Here's a concise yet comprehensive chapter about children's knowledge about gender stereotypes, their gender-typed behavior, and factors that contribute to gender typing.

Ruble, D. R., & Martin, C. L. (1998). Gender development. In N. Eisenberg (Ed.), *Handbook of child psychology,* v. 4, *Social, emotional, and personality development* (pp. 933–1016). New York: Wiley. Diane Ruble and Carol Martin are two prominent researchers in the field of gender; this chapter traces the development of gender-related concepts and behaviors and includes a detailed exploration of gender-development theories.

Sweetman, C. (Ed.). (1998b). *Gender, education, and training*. Oxford, England: Oxfam. Fortunately, a number of resources are now available about the education of girls and women in developing countries. This book is my current favorite because it emphasizes political aspects of gender equity, focuses on a variety of countries, and includes informative data about this pervasive problem.

ANSWERS TO THE TRUE-FALSE QUESTIONS

1. True (p. 75); 2. False (p. 77); 3. True (p. 80); 4. False (p. 83); 5. False (p. 88); 6. False (pp. 89–90); 7. True (p. 95); 8. False (pp. 99–100); 9. True (p. 102); 10. True (pp. 103–104).

Adolescence

PictureQuest

T R U E   O R   F A L S E ?

_____ 1. Researchers believe that there is no physical explanation for menstrual pain.

_____ 2. A clear-cut cluster of symptoms, often called premenstrual syndrome (PMS), typically affects between 35% and 50% of North American adolescent females.

_____ 3. According to surveys, European American adolescents are more concerned about their ethnic identity than adolescents of color are.

_____ 4. Recent research confirms that females are much lower than males in their self-esteem, beginning in childhood and continuing through middle age.

_____ 5. During the current era, schools, teachers, and peers offer strong support for young women who want to pursue careers in math and science.

_____ 6. For all major ethnic groups in the United States, women are more likely than men to attend college.

_____ 7. Adolescent males and females are interested in pursuing careers that are similar in level of prestige.

_____ 8. According to research, most adolescents get along fairly well with their parents.

_____ 9. The friendships of adolescent men have been consistently shown to be just as intimate as the friendships of adolescent women.

_____ 10. Young lesbians are more likely to "come out" to their mothers than to their fathers.

Thirteen-year-old Aisha is a Black girl who lives in Seattle, Washington. She describes why she likes talking and arguing with other people. As she comments:

> It's not about convincing people to see things my way; it's about learning another perspective, which ultimately makes both of us smarter. I talk with my friends about the work we do at school and what we think is useful, as well as the things we think are not useful. . . . I'm not interested in being intimidated; I'm interested in being myself. So I look for people who are smart and who don't try to make me feel bad about being smart too. (Carroll, 1997, p. 85)

Aisha's narrative shows us how girls and young women in the present era can construct a thoughtful life for themselves—a life that is not constrained by stereotypical views of gender. In this chapter, we'll explore physical and psychological changes during adolescence, focusing on the changes where gender plays a particularly important role. In human development, **adolescence** is defined as a transition phase between childhood and adulthood. Adolescence begins at **puberty,** the age at which a young person is physically capable of sexual reproduction (McClintock & Herdt, 1996). For females, a major biological milestone of puberty is **menarche** (pronounced meh-*nar*-key), or the beginning of menstruation. No specific event marks the end of adolescence and the beginning of adulthood. We usually associate the beginning of adulthood with milestones such as living separately from our parents, completing college, holding a job, and finding a romantic partner. However, none of these characteristics is essential for adulthood.

Adolescents often find themselves caught between childhood and adulthood. Adults may sometimes treat adolescents as children—a mixed blessing that eases their responsibility but limits their independence and their sense of competence (Zebrowitz & Montepare, 2000). Adults also give adolescents mixed messages about issues of sexuality and the transition into adulthood. Parents tell them not to grow up too quickly. On the other hand, their role models tend to be adolescents who *have* grown up too quickly: sexy teenage television and movie stars, teenagers in advertisements, and maybe even the girl next door.

In this chapter, we will examine four important topics for adolescent females: (1) puberty and menstruation, (2) self-concepts, (3) education and career planning, and (4) interpersonal relationships. We'll mention other relevant topics (such as cognitive abilities, sexuality, and eating disorders), but those will be discussed more completely in later chapters.

PUBERTY AND MENSTRUATION

Let's begin by discussing the physical changes that girls experience as they enter adolescence. We'll briefly consider puberty before we look at menstruation in greater detail.

Puberty

Most girls enter puberty between the ages of 10 and 15; the average age at menarche is 12 (Adair & Gordon-Larsen, 2001; Obeidallah et al., 2000; O'Sullivan et al., 2001). Black and Latina girls in the United States reach menarche somewhat earlier than European American girls, and Asian American girls reach menarche somewhat later than other ethnic groups (Adair & Gordon-Larsen, 2001; Obeidallah et al., 2000; O'Sullivan et al., 2001). Unfortunately, data are not currently available for Native American girls. Researchers have not yet uncovered a satisfactory explanation for ethnic differences, but body weight is an important factor (Adair & Gordon-Larsen, 2001; Obeidallah et al., 2000).

Emotional reactions to menarche vary widely (Graber & Brooks-Gunn, 1998). In part, these reactions depend on girls' understanding of menstruation and the reaction of family and friends. Some young women report that their peers envied them when they began to menstruate (J. Lee & Sasser-Coen, 1996). In contrast, young women who are not informed about menstruation may react with panic. When a young Egyptian woman awoke to find blood on her thighs, she assumed that a man had crept into her bedroom and had somehow harmed her (Saadawi,

1998). In short, the varied emotional reactions to menarche provide evidence for the individual differences theme of this textbook.

During puberty, young women experience the most dramatic physical changes they have undergone since infancy. Specifically, they experience a transformation in their **secondary sex characteristics,** or the parts of the body related to reproduction but not directly involved in it. For instance, breast development precedes menarche by about two years. Looking back on adolescence, many women report that they had felt self-conscious about breasts that they considered either too large or too small (K. A. Martin, 1996; P. Robinson, 1997). During puberty, young women also accumulate body fat through the hips and thighs—often a source of resentment in a culture that emphasizes slender bodies (Fredrickson & Roberts, 1997; Steinberg & Morris, 2001).

Biological Aspects of the Menstrual Cycle

Let's briefly examine the biological components of menstruation and the sequence of events in the menstrual cycle. The average woman menstruates about 450 times during her life. Naturally, then, this information on the menstrual cycle is relevant for most women for about 40 years after menarche—decades beyond adolescence. For the sake of continuity, however, let's discuss a variety of topics related to menstruation.

Structures and Substances Responsible for Menstruation.   The hypothalamus, a structure in the brain, is crucial in menstruation because it monitors the body's level of estrogen during the monthly cycle. When estrogen levels are low, the hypothalamus signals a second brain structure, the pituitary gland. The pituitary gland produces two important hormones: follicle-stimulating hormone and luteinizing hormone.

In all, four hormones contribute to the menstrual cycle:

1. Follicle-stimulating hormone acts on the follicles (or egg holders) within the ovaries, making them produce estrogen and progesterone.
2. Luteinizing hormone is needed for the development of the follicles.
3. Estrogen, primarily produced by the ovaries, stimulates the development of the uterine lining.
4. Progesterone, also primarily produced by the ovaries, regulates the system by inhibiting overproduction of the luteinizing hormone.

Several major structures in menstruation are illustrated in Figure 4.1 together with other important organs in the female reproductive system. The two **ovaries,** which are about the size of walnuts, contain the follicles that hold the **ova,** or eggs, and produce estrogen and progesterone. Midway through the menstrual cycle, one of the eggs breaks out of its follicle. It moves from an ovary into a fallopian tube and then into the uterus. The **uterus** is the organ in which a fetus develops. The lining of the uterus, called the endometrium, can serve as a nourishing location for a fertilized egg to mature during pregnancy. If a fertilized egg is not implanted, the endometrium is shed as menstrual flow, and the egg disintegrates on its way out of the uterus.

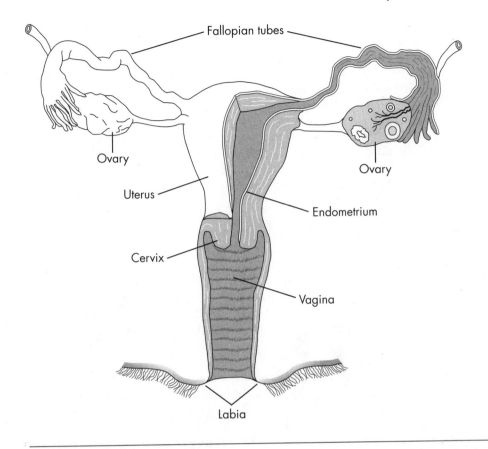

FIGURE 4.1 ■ Female internal reproductive organs. (Note: On the right-hand side of the diagram, you can see the interior of the ovaries, the fallopian tube, and the uterus.)

The Events in the Menstrual Cycle.   Now that you know some of the important components of the menstrual cycle, let's see how they interact. The important thing to remember is that brain structures, hormones, and internal reproductive organs are carefully coordinated to regulate the menstrual cycle. They operate according to a **feedback loop:** When the level of a particular hormone is too low, a structure in the brain is signaled, and the chain of events that follows produces more of that hormone. Later on, when the level of a hormone is too high, a signal to a structure in the brain begins a chain of events that decreases that hormone. Here are the major events in this monthly cycle:

1. In response to a low estrogen level, the hypothalamus signals the pituitary gland.
2. The pituitary gland responds by releasing follicle-stimulating hormone, which stimulates the follicles to become more mature; this hormone also signals the ovaries to increase their production of estrogen.

3. The increased level of estrogen stimulates the development of the endometrium (essentially preparing for possible pregnancy every month). It also signals the pituitary gland to stop producing follicle-stimulating hormone.
4. The pituitary gland stops producing follicle-stimulating hormone and starts producing luteinizing hormone.
5. Luteinizing hormone usually suppresses growth in all follicles except one; therefore, only one egg typically reaches maturity.
6. The follicle then releases the ovum, or egg, on approximately the 14th day of the menstrual cycle, a process called **ovulation** (pronounced ov-you-*lay*-shun).
7. The empty follicle matures into a round structure called the corpus luteum, which secretes progesterone and estrogen. The levels of both of these hormones rise after ovulation.
8. The high level of progesterone inhibits the production of additional luteinizing hormone, resulting in the decomposition of the corpus luteum.
9. When the corpus luteum decomposes, the production of both progesterone and estrogen falls rapidly. With such low levels of hormones, the endometrium can no longer be maintained in the style to which it has grown accustomed. The endometrium is sloughed off, and it passes out of the vagina as menstrual flow.
10. The low level of estrogen signals the hypothalamus, causing a new cycle to begin.

Notice the checks and balances that are required to orchestrate the menstrual cycle (L. L. Alexander et al., 2001). This complex set of interactions encourages the production of an egg, leads to menstrual flow if no fertilized egg is implanted, and then begins another cycle.

Most people are amazed to learn that a woman typically loses only about 3 to 6 tablespoons of blood during each menstrual period (Emans, 1997). However, this relatively trivial blood loss is often accompanied by menstrual pain and is sometimes associated with a variety of premenstrual reactions. Let's examine these two phenomena.

Menstrual Pain

Menstrual pain, or **dysmenorrhea** (pronounced diss-men-or-*ree*-ah), typically refers to painful cramps in the abdominal region. It may also include headache, nausea, dizziness, fatigue, and pain in the lower back (Crooks & Baur, 2002; A. E. Walker, 1998). (Dysmenorrhea is *not* the same as premenstrual syndrome, or PMS, which will be discussed in the next section.)

How common is menstrual pain? Estimates range from 50% to 75% for high school– and college-age women (Golub, 1992; A. E. Walker, 1998). Dysmenorrhea is also the leading cause of young women's absence from school or work (Golub, 1992). Consistent with Theme 4 of this book, women's reactions to life events, such as menstruation, vary widely. Pain during menstruation is certainly common, but it is *not* inevitable.

In our culture, women expect that menstruation will be painful, but menstrual pain is clearly *not* "all in the head." The contractions of the uterus that cause menstrual pain are encouraged by prostaglandins (pronounced pross-tuh-*glan*-dins). **Prostaglandins** are substances produced by the body in high concentrations just before menstruation, and they cause severe cramps. However, the relationship between prostaglandins and menstrual pain is complex. The two factors are strongly correlated, but some women with severe dysmenorrhea do not have elevated prostaglandin levels (Golub, 1992; A. E. Walker, 1998).

Researchers have also discovered that highly anxious women report having more menstrual pain than less anxious women. Perhaps anxious women focus more attention on their cramps, which could increase their intensity (Sigmon, Rohan et al., 2000). However, we must think critically about correlational results such as these. Another possibility may be that women who experience relatively strong menstrual pain (and perhaps other forms of pain) become more anxious as a consequence of these unpleasant experiences. Looking at all the evidence, menstrual pain is probably caused by a combination of physiological and psychological factors.

Many different treatments have been used to reduce menstrual pain. Some drugs are helpful, including those that inhibit the synthesis of prostaglandins (e.g., ibuprofen). Oral contraceptives can be useful in severe cases, but they may bring unwanted side effects. Exercise, a heating pad, muscle relaxation, adequate sleep, and dietary changes often produce additional relief (Golub, 1992; Hyde & DeLamater, 2003).

The Controversial Premenstrual Syndrome

Menstrual pain is well accepted as being part of the menstrual cycle. In contrast, premenstrual syndrome is controversial among both professionals and laypeople (Chrisler, 2000; Figert, 1996). **Premenstrual syndrome (PMS)** is the name given to a variety of symptoms that may occur a few days before menstruating. These symptoms often include headaches, breast soreness, swelling in some body regions, increased sensitivity to pain, acne, and various psychological reactions. These psychological reactions typically include depression, irritability, anxiety, and lethargy (Chrisler, 1996; Gottheil et al., 1999).

One reason that PMS is controversial is that researchers do not agree on its definition (Chrisler, 2000; Figert, 1996). Read the previous list of symptoms once more, and add other symptoms that you've heard about in popular accounts of PMS. Some critics have discovered as many as 200 different symptoms presumably connected with PMS (Gottheil et al., 1999). Think of the problem created by this confusion. One researcher may be studying women whose primary symptom is anxiety; another may be studying women with depression. How can researchers study PMS systematically when we don't even have a clear-cut operational definition for the problem? As you can imagine, no blood test or other biological test can be used to assess whether a woman is experiencing PMS (Gottheil et al., 1999).

Another reason PMS is so controversial is that some experts claim that virtually all menstruating women experience it (see Chrisler, 2000). This claim is unfair because it suggests that all women are at the mercy of their "raging hormones" (Chrisler, 2002). An alternative view argues that PMS is entirely a myth created by our culture. This view, if taken too far, would be equally unfair because some women do experience genuine symptoms more often premenstrually than at other times in their cycle.

Our discussion of PMS takes an intermediate position between the two extremes of the biologically driven explanation and the psychological-cultural explanation. Apparently, a small percentage of women (maybe 5%) have significant symptoms that are related to their menstrual cycle (Hardie, 1997; Jensvold & Dan, 2001; S. R. Johnson, 1995). Other women do not. This is an example of the general theme of large individual differences among women. We cannot make a statement that holds true for all women.

Let's examine the aspect of PMS that has received the most attention: the presumably dramatic mood swings during the menstrual cycle. We'll also consider methods of coping with PMS and a different perspective, called menstrual joy.

Mood Swings.   Much of the research that supposedly supports the concept of PMS is plagued by biases. For example, many researchers ask women to recall what their moods had been during various times throughout previous weeks of the menstrual cycle. Problems with this kind of retrospective study are easy to anticipate. For example, women may recall their moods as being more negative premenstrually than they actually were.

During the current era, most of the research has produced results that should make us skeptical about the mood-swings component of PMS (e.g., Chrisler, 2002; Nash & Chrisler, 1997; Oinonen & Mazmanian, 2001). For example, Klebanov and Jemmott (1992) examined the effects of expectations on PMS symptoms. They gave women a fictitious medical test that misinformed the women that they were either midcycle or premenstrual. Then the women took a standard scale called the Menstrual Distress Questionnaire. Those who believed that they were premenstrual, even if they were not, reported more symptoms than did those who thought they were midcycle.

Let's consider another study that is critical of the PMS concept. Hardie (1997) asked 83 menstruating women who were employed by a university to keep records in a booklet titled *Daily Stress & Health Diary.* Each day, for 10 weeks, they recorded their emotional state, stress level, general health, exercise, laughter, crying, menstrual bleeding, and so forth. At the end of the 10 weeks, the women completed a questionnaire about women's health issues. Included in this questionnaire was a crucial item: "I think I have PMS."

To assess PMS, Hardie used a definition that several others have used. The definition specifies that a woman's mood during the premenstrual phase needs to be more depressed and emotional than during other parts of her menstrual cycle. Not one of the 83 women met this criterion for two menstrual cycles during the 70-day study. In addition, the women who believed they had PMS did *not* have more negative emotions premenstrually than did the women who reported no PMS. In other words, both groups actually reported similar cyclic changes.

Researchers who endorse the psychological-cultural explanation for PMS argue that our current culture clearly accepts PMS as an established fact (Figert,

---

DEMONSTRATION 4.1 ■ ■ ■ ■ ■ ■ ■ ■ ■ ■ ■ ■ ■ ■ ■ ■ ■ ■

Positive Symptoms of Menstruation

If you are a female who has menstrual cycles, complete the following questionnaire, which is based on the Menstrual Joy Questionnaire (Chrisler et al., 1994; J. Delaney et al., 1988). If you do not have menstrual cycles, ask a friend if she would be willing to fill out the questionnaire.

Instructions: Rate each of the following items on a 6-point scale. Rate an item 1 if you do not experience the feeling at all when you are menstruating; rate it 6 if you experience the feeling intensely.

_____ high spirits   _____ affection

_____ sexual desire   _____ self-confidence

_____ vibrant activity   _____ creativity

_____ revolutionary zeal   _____ power

_____ intense concentration

Did you or your friend provide a positive rating for one or more of these characteristics?

1996; A. E. Walker, 1998). You've probably heard dozens of jokes and references to PMS, such as, "What is the difference between a pit bull and a woman with PMS?" The answer? "A pit bull doesn't wear lipstick" (Figert, 1996, pp. 12–13). With this kind of cultural endorsement, women believe that PMS is normal. If a woman is feeling tense and she is premenstrual, she blames her emotions on PMS (Cosgrove & Riddle, 2001a; Hardie, 1997). For example, one woman explained how she often interprets her emotions: "I feel irritable for some reason and then I'll think about why I am irritable and then I'll think, oh, well, it's the week before my period and sometimes I'll say, well, maybe that's what it is" (Cosgrove & Riddle, 2001a, p. 19). (Incidentally, try Demonstration 4.1 before you read further.)

Hormonal factors may indeed cause premenstrual problems in a small percentage of women (Hardie, 1997; Schmidt et al., 1998). However, two other factors are probably more important:

1. Psychological factors, such as anxiety and strong endorsement of traditionally feminine gender roles (Sigmon, Dorhofer et al., 2000; Sigmon, Rohan et al., 2000); and
2. Cultural factors, such as our culture's belief that PMS is a well-established fact and its emphasis on biological explanations (Chrisler, 2000; Cosgrove & Riddle, 2001b).

Coping with Premenstrual Syndrome.   It's difficult to talk about coping with or treating PMS when we have no clear-cut definition of the problem and no comprehensive theory about its origins (Golub, 1992; A. E. Walker, 1998). The research suggests that women should monitor their emotional reactions throughout the menstrual cycle to determine whether anxiety and tension are equally likely to occur during phases that are not premenstrual. The best strategy may be to figure out how to reduce the problems that create those emotions at *all* phases of the menstrual cycle. When the problems are severe, psychotherapy may be helpful for developing these strategies.

Physicians—and other health professionals who believe that PMS is a genuine, biologically driven problem—often recommend exercise as therapy. They also suggest avoiding fat, salt, sugar, alcohol, and caffeine (Futterman & Jones, 1998; A. E. Walker, 1998). None of these remedies can hurt, although their value has not been established. Some physicians are currently recommending low doses of antidepressants such as Prozac (Futterman & Jones, 1998; A. E. Walker, 1998). These drugs can cause side effects, and they are not necessary for most women (A. E. Walker, 1998). Most psychologists who currently conduct research on PMS would not recommend antidepressants unless a woman and her health care provider are convinced that she has serious premenstrual problems.

Menstrual Joy

Go ahead; read the title of this section again. Yes, menstrual *joy.* Joan Chrisler and her colleagues noticed that the typical questionnaires focused only on negative aspects of menstruation. Furthermore, the popular press had generated hundreds of articles on the negative—and often exaggerated—aspects of changes associated with the menstrual cycle (Chrisler, 2002; Chrisler & Levy, 1990; Chrisler et al., 1994). Surely some women must have *some* positive reactions to menstruation! Therefore, Chrisler and colleagues (1994) administered the Menstrual Joy Questionnaire (Delaney et al., 1988), which is similar to Demonstration 4.1. Interestingly, women who first completed the Menstrual Joy Questionnaire were likely to rate their level of arousal more positively when they later completed a questionnaire about menstrual symptoms. Compared to women who hadn't been encouraged to think about the positive side of menstruation, these women were more likely to report feelings of well-being and excitement and bursts of energy (Chrisler et al., 1994). Chrisler and her colleagues do not anticipate that they can convince the world that menstruation is truly joyous rather than unpleasant. However, isn't it interesting that so little research has been conducted on the potentially positive side of menstruation?

Women's personal accounts about menstruation sometimes provide more positive images. Anne Frank wrote a passage in her diary that captures the bittersweet emotions she felt about her menstrual periods:

> Each time I have a period . . . I have the feeling that in spite of all the pain, unpleasantness, nastiness, I have a sweet secret and that is why, although it is nothing but a nuisance to me in a way, I always long for the time that I shall feel that secret within me again. (A. Frank, 1972, p. 117)

A friend of mine mentioned another positive image: Menstruation represents sisterhood to her. When she is menstruating, she is reminded that women all over the world, of different races, ethnicities, shapes, and ages, are menstruating as well. Less poetically but nonetheless significantly, many women greet a menstrual period with joy because it means they are not pregnant. Menstrual cramps and other problems will not disappear if you simply adopt a more positive attitude. However, the issues are easier to deal with if you know their cause and remind yourself that other women share similar experiences.

Cultural Attitudes Toward Menstruation

Throughout this book, you'll often see a contrast between people's beliefs about women and women's actual experiences. For example, people's stereotypes about women (Chapter 2) often differ from women's actual cognitive skills (Chapter 5) and women's social characteristics (Chapter 6). Similarly, we will see in this discussion that cultural attitudes about menstruation often differ from women's actual experiences.

Some cultures have a taboo against contact with menstruating women. For example, contemporary Creek Indians in Oklahoma do not allow menstruating women to use the same plates or utensils as other tribe members (A. R. Bell, 1990). Many similar menstrual practices reflect a belief in female pollution and the devaluation of women (A. E. Walker, 1998). In other cultures, such as the Mayans who live in Guatemala, young girls are not informed about menstruation before they reach menarche. Their first experience with menstrual blood must be both frightening and puzzling (Gardiner et al., 1998). These attitudes toward menstruation are consistent with Theme 2 of this book: Something associated with women—in this instance, their menstrual periods—will often be negatively evaluated by the cultural community (Chrisler, 2000).

The topic of menstruation is also relatively invisible in our popular culture, consistent with Theme 3 of this book. We usually do not speak openly about menstruation. Instead, we enlist euphemisms, or more pleasant ways of saying the same thing. For example, you'll rarely hear the word *menstruation* on television. An ad referring to "that time of the month" probably does not mean the date the car payment is due! Some common euphemisms include "on the rag" and "I've got my friend" (M. Gordon, 1993; A. E. Walker, 1998). Even the customary term *period* is actually a euphemism that manages to avoid the word *menstruation.*

Young girls' attitudes may be shaped by advertisements in the teen media. Debra Merskin (1999) examined the advertisements in the popular magazines *Seventeen* and *Teen.* Most readers of these magazines are probably in early puberty, so the advertisements may have a strong influence on young women's attitudes at the time of menarche. Merskin found that an especially important message in these ads is secrecy: The advertised product can conceal the fact that a young woman would have the poor taste to be menstruating. In preparing this chapter, I examined an issue of the teen magazine *Jump.* In addition to the usual ads for menstrual products, *Jump* featured an article titled "Seeing Red, Feeling Blue?

Cramps! Bloating! Breakouts!" (Marston, 1998). I read two paragraphs before seeing the word *menstruation,* although "the Curse" was prominent and the article firmly endorsed PMS and hormone-dependent emotions. As you might imagine, no hint of menstrual joy appears in those teen magazines!

SECTION SUMMARY ■

Puberty and Menstruation

1. Adolescence begins at puberty; for females, menarche is the crucial milestone of puberty, and young women vary greatly in their reactions to menarche.

2. The menstrual cycle requires a complex coordination of brain structures, hormones, and internal reproductive organs.

3. Dysmenorrhea, or menstrual pain, is common in young women. Dysmenorrhea is partly caused by prostaglandins, but psychological factors also play an important role.

4. Premenstrual syndrome (PMS) is a controversial set of symptoms that presumably includes headaches, breast soreness, depression, and irritability. PMS is challenging to study because it cannot be clearly defined. PMS-related mood swings are difficult to document.

5. The psychological-cultural explanation of PMS suggests that psychological factors play a role and that cultural expectations encourage women to use PMS as an explanation for negative moods that occur on the days before their menstrual period.

6. Because of the controversy about the origins and nature of PMS, it's difficult to make recommendations about treating it; some physicians have proposed medications with significant side effects.

7. Some women actually report positive reactions to menstruation.

8. Menstrual myths are found in many cultures; these myths demonstrate the negative evaluation of women's bodily processes. Euphemisms have been created to refer to menstruation, and media directed at adolescent females suggest that menstruation should be kept secret.

SELF-CONCEPT AND IDENTITY DURING ADOLESCENCE

We have seen that adolescent females are aware of the changes in their bodies during puberty and that they experience a major transition when they reach menarche. Adolescents have the cognitive capacity to think abstractly, so they can begin to ask complex questions such as "Who am I?" (Steinberg & Morris, 2001). **Identity** refers to an individual's self-rating of personal characteristics along with biological, psychological, or social dimensions (Whitbourne, 1998). We'll consider four components of identity in this section: body image, feminist identity, ethnic identity, and self-esteem.

Body Image and Physical Attractiveness

In Chapter 3, we saw that attractiveness is more important for preschool girls than for preschool boys. Compared to less attractive little girls, cute little girls are more likely to be patted and praised—and less likely to be hit and pushed. However, attractiveness is generally irrelevant for little boys (G. J. Smith, 1985).

This same emphasis on female attractiveness is exaggerated during adolescence. Young women constantly receive the message that good looks and physical beauty are the most important dimension for females (Brumberg, 1997; Steinberg & Morris, 2001). Their skin must be clear, their teeth straight and gleaming, and their hair lustrous. They must also be slender. Attractiveness may be an especially important attribute in the United States and in other relatively wealthy countries (Gibbons, Brusi-Figueroa et al., 1997).

Some North American adolescents are so concerned about being slender that they develop life-threatening eating disorders. (We will discuss these disorders and our culture's emphasis on thinness in more detail in Chapter 12.) This intense focus on body weight extends beyond those with eating disorders; it also has a substantial impact on the general population of adolescent females. For example, Polce-Lynch and her colleagues (1998) asked adolescents in the southeastern United States to name some things that made them feel bad about themselves. In this sample, 38% of the eighth-grade girls reported dissatisfaction with their bodies, in contrast to only 15% of the eighth-grade boys.

The media encourage this emphasis on beauty and slenderness, and young women are well aware of this message (Higginbotham, 1996; Milkie, 1999). Try Demonstration 4.2 on page 122 to appreciate the narrow view that teen magazines provide to female adolescents.

Your investigation of magazines in Demonstration 4.2 probably will not reveal many young women of color, even though teen magazines sell well when their covers feature Black women (Higginbotham, 1996). Women of color realize that they are relatively invisible in the pages of these magazines. Melissa Milkie (1999) asked adolescent females to describe the kind of image that people would form about young women if they had access only to teen magazines. As one teenager said, "I think this is mainly toward . . . white females. . . . You really wouldn't see too many black people in here—so if this is all you saw, you'd be kinda scared when you saw one like me or something" (p. 197). Ironically, these idealized images of White women may actually allow women of color to escape the constraints of imitating the women in the advertisements, because women of color do not identify with those idealized women. Of course, some women of color develop a concept of beauty consistent with their own racial or ethnic features. One Black woman wrote:

> Through solidarity with other women and my reading, I learned to develop a positive self-image. I went through a period of being born again black, of experiencing a

DEMONSTRATION 4.2 ■■■■■■■■■■■■■■■■■

Representation of Females in Teen Magazines

Locate several magazines intended for adolescent women. (In the current era, *Seventeen, YM, Jump, Twist Magazine*, and *Teen* are popular.) Glance through the magazine for photos of women in either advertisements or feature articles. What percentage of these women would be considered overweight? How many look nearly anorexic? Then inspect the magazines for ethnic representation. If you find any women of color, are they pale-skinned, with features typical of White women, or do they seem typical of their own ethnic group?

Notice the body posture of the women pictured. Would a young man look ridiculous in these positions? What percentage of the photos seems aimed at encouraging sexual relationships? How many of the women look competent? What other messages do these images provide for high school females?

transformation. My relaxed hair was changed to an Afro look. . . . This was the beginning of a period in my life of feeling the rage, coming to terms with the guilt, healing the shame, and breaking the silence. (Valcarcel, 1994, p. 290)

Unfortunately, young women's general self-concepts are often shaped by whether they believe they are attractive. In one study, physical appearance was the strongest predictor of self-worth in females (Kwa, 1994). For males, athletic competence was the strongest predictor of self-worth. Notice, then, that females feel valued for how their bodies look. In contrast, males feel valued for how their bodies *perform* in athletics and other activities that enhance their self-image.

In recent years, researchers have begun to discover that girls who participate in athletics can often escape from the dominant images presented to adolescent females. Not surprisingly, women athletes often have higher self-esteem than their nonathlete peers (Richman & Shaffer, 2000; J. Young & Bursik, 2000). They may even enjoy long-term health benefits (Rongé, 1996).

Young women's participation in sports has increased dramatically during recent decades. For example, Erkut and her colleagues (1996) collected information on 362 females from the five major ethnic groups. In response to the question "What activities make you feel good about yourself?" almost half mentioned an athletic activity. The media are now more likely to feature female athletes, and these images of strong women might make a difference. Adolescent women watching the victorious women athletes in sports such as basketball and soccer may realize that women's bodies can be competent and athletic rather than anorexic (Dowling, 2000; Strouse, 1999). Now try Demonstration 4.3 before you read further.

DEMONSTRATION 4.3 ■ ■ ■ ■ ■ ■ ■ ■ ■ ■ ■ ■ ■ ■ ■ ■ ■

Assessing Feminist Identity

If you are a woman, rate each of the following items using a 5-point scale. (Rate an item 1 if you strongly disagree; rate the item 5 if you strongly agree.) If you are a man, think of a woman you know well who shares your ideas about women's issues, and try to answer the questionnaire from her perspective.

_____ 1. I want to work to make the world a more fair place for all people.

_____ 2. I have become increasingly aware that society is sexist.

_____ 3. I am very interested in women writers and other aspects of women's studies.

_____ 4. I think that most women feel happiest being a wife and mother.

_____ 5. I do not want to have the same status that a man has.

_____ 6. I am proud to be a strong and competent woman.

_____ 7. I am angry about the way that men and boys often treat me.

_____ 8. I am glad that women do not have to do construction work or other dangerous jobs.

_____ 9. I owe it to both women and men to work for greater gender equality.

_____ 10. I am happy being a traditional female.

Note: These items are similar to the 39-item Feminist Identity Development Scale (FIDS), developed by Bargad & Hyde (1991). The reliability and validity of the items in this shortened version have not been established.

Feminist Identity

In Chapter 1, we emphasized that **feminism** is a belief system in which women's experiences and ideas are valued. Feminists argue that women and men should be socially, economically, and legally equal (Hunter College Women's Studies Collective, 1995; L. A. Jackson et al., 1996). In that chapter, we also identified several different approaches to feminism. In Chapter 2, we briefly noted that people have less favorable attitudes about feminists than about housewives. In the present chapter, we noted that adolescents have the capacity to think abstractly and to contemplate their personal identity. As a consequence, they can think about abstract questions such as "What do I believe about women's roles?" and "Am I a feminist?" Most of the research about feminist values and identity has been done with college students in late adolescence. We would welcome research on the development of a feminist identity from early adolescence through late adulthood, using a more diverse sample of young women.

In general, people are likely to say that they support feminist ideas, but they are reluctant to claim a **feminist social identity,** to say, "Yes, I am a feminist" (Twenge & Zucker, 1999). For example, Anastasopoulos and Desmarais (2000) studied women at a university in Ontario and found that 30% called themselves feminists. An additional 48% of the women said that they believed in equality, but they did not label themselves as feminists. Burn and her colleagues (2000) surveyed female and male students at a college in California and found that only 17% of the women (and 4% of the men) called themselves feminists. An additional 44% of the women (and 37% of the men) said that they agreed with most or all of the objectives of the feminist movement, but they did not call themselves feminists.

Researchers have identified several factors that are associated with feminist beliefs. For example, people who support feminist beliefs are more advanced in their ego development than those who don't support them (Bursik, 2000). **Ego development** is a kind of psychological growth in which people develop a more complex view of themselves and of their relationships with other people.

We know somewhat more about people who have a feminist social identity and are willing to use the term *feminist* to describe themselves. Not surprisingly, those with a feminist social identity are more likely to have had extensive exposure to feminism, through friends, through college classes, or through feminist magazines and books. They are also more likely to have a positive evaluation of feminists (Henley et al., 1998; Liss et al., 2001; Myaskovsky & Wittig, 1997; R. Williams & Wittig, 1997). In addition, they are more likely to be female than male (Burn et al., 2000; R. Williams & Wittig, 1997).

Now assess your answers to Demonstration 4.3 by looking at the end of the chapter (page 141). Also, answer one additional question: Do you consider yourself a feminist?

Ethnic Identity

Ethnic identity can be defined as people's sense that they belong to an ethnic group as well as their attitudes and behaviors toward that group (Yeh, 1998). People learn about their ethnic identity at an early age (Deaux, 2001b). You probably thought about your ethnic background long before you considered the question "Am I a feminist?"

Researchers have examined whether female and male adolescents differ in the strength of their ethnic identity. However, no consistent gender differences have been found (Ethier & Deaux, 1990; Phinney & Alipuria, 1990; Rotheram-Borus et al., 1996; Waters, 1996).

Other researchers have focused on the growth of adolescents' ethnic identity rather than on gender comparisons. In general, European American adolescents are not concerned about their ethnic identity (Peplau, Veniegas et al., 1999; Waters, 1996). When being White is considered standard or normative, White individuals don't notice their privileged status.

Some young women of color may initially try to reject their ethnicity. Consider, for example, an African American woman's description of herself:

> For a long time it seemed as if I didn't remember my background, and I guess in some ways I didn't. I was never taught to be proud of my African heritage. Like we talked about in class, I went through a very long stage of identifying with my oppressors. Wanting to be like, live like, and be accepted by them. Even to the point of hating my own race and myself for being a part of it. Now I am ashamed that I ever was ashamed. I lost so much of myself in my denial of and refusal to accept my people. (Tatum, 1992, p. 10)

When some young women of color explore their family's history, they discover that their roots are deep, as a Mexican American woman explained:

> I also think of people as flowers. . . . The reason why I say this is because there are things in our lives constantly. But it goes farther back than my life here. It goes deeper into our past interior, and I think of that as my past history. And all those things impact me. I don't know all those things. But some I've been told about, and I can see the way my great-grandmother interacts with me, I hear the stories of my great-great-aunt, and it's all impacted me. (Ford, 1999, p. 85)

However, some adolescents find that their ethnic identity may clash with their nontraditional ideas about gender (Dasgupta, 1998). For instance, a young South Asian woman commented:

> My parents are sort of old-fashioned, so they tell me that I have to do things. . . . Like I am a girl so I am always sent to the kitchen to cook. . . . I am more Americanized and I don't believe in that girl thing. We end up in an argument and it does not get solved. (Phinney & Rosenthal, 1992, p. 153)

Researchers are just beginning to explore these complex issues about identity that arise at the intersection of ethnicity and gender (Peplau, Veniegas et al., 1999).

Self-Esteem

Self-esteem refers to your evaluation of yourself on a scale that ranges from negative to positive (Kling & Hyde, 2001). Do adolescent males and females differ in their self-esteem? As with ethnic identity, we cannot reach a clear-cut conclusion because the answer seems to depend on several important factors.

During the 1990s, several popular books concluded that self-esteem drops sharply for females, relative to males, during high school (Pipher, 1994; Sadker & Sadker, 1994). Indeed, many researchers have reported a modest gender difference in adolescents' self-esteem (e.g., K. Kelly & Jordan, 1990; Quatman & Watson, 2001; Widaman et al., 1992). However, other researchers have reported that adolescent females and males have similar self-esteem, at least under some conditions (e.g., Kling & Hyde, 2001; Knox et al., 2000; Polce-Lynch et al., 2001; A. J. Rose & Montemayor, 1994).

With mixed results like these, how can we draw any conclusions? Fortunately, researchers who study gender comparisons can use a technique called meta-analysis. **Meta-analysis** provides a statistical method for integrating numerous studies on a single topic. Researchers first locate all appropriate studies on the topic. Then they perform a statistical analysis that combines the results from all these studies. The meta-analysis yields a single number that tells us whether a particular variable has an overall effect. For example, for self-esteem, a meta-analysis can statistically combine numerous previous studies into one enormous superstudy that can provide a general picture of whether gender has an overall effect on self-esteem.

Two prominent meta-analytic studies have now been conducted on gender comparisons of self-esteem, each study based on more than 200 different gender comparisons (Kling et al., 1999; Major et al., 1999). Both studies concluded that the average male scores slightly—but significantly—higher in self-esteem than the average female. However, when these two groups of researchers took a closer look, they found that the gender differences are minimal in childhood, early adolescence, and later adulthood; during late adolescence, gender differences are somewhat larger. Also, the gender differences were relatively large for European Americans, whereas Black females and Black males were generally more similar in their self-esteem. These findings are consistent with other reports that Black females are higher in self-esteem than females from other ethnic groups (Eccles et al., 1999; Erkut et al., 1999). Finally, Major and her colleagues (1999) found that gender differences are relatively large among lower-class and middle-class participants but that upper-class females and males from well-educated families are usually somewhat similar in their self-esteem.

In other words, gender differences in self-esteem are inconsistent, and they depend on several personal characteristics. We know that age is an important characteristic; a young woman in her late teens may feel especially constrained by our culture's gender roles (Major et al., 1999). Ethnicity is also important; Black women may use different cultural standards than other women when assessing their self-worth (Major et al., 1999). Social class is similarly important; well-educated families may conclude that gender bias is unfair, so female adolescents raised in these families may be encouraged to break through these gender roles (Major et al., 1999).

SECTION SUMMARY ■

Self-Concept and Identity During Adolescence

1. Physical attractiveness is emphasized for adolescent women, and the current emphasis on thinness can lead to eating disorders. The focus on European American models in the media may help some young women of color to ignore those media images.

2. People who say they are feminists are likely to be familiar with feminism and to evaluate feminists positively; females are more likely than males to say they are feminists.

3. Young women of color may initially ignore their ethnic identity but strengthen it during adolescence; some adolescents may experience conflict between ethnic identity and nontraditional gender roles.

4. The average male scores slightly higher in self-esteem than the average female; this gender difference is relatively large in late adolescence, in European Americans, and in people with relatively little education.

EDUCATION AND CAREER PLANNING

In Chapter 3, we saw that young girls are often relatively invisible in the elementary school classroom, whereas boys receive more attention. Now we'll examine young women's educational experiences and career planning. Then, after investigating cognitive skills and achievement motivation in Chapter 5 and social and personality characteristics in Chapter 6, we will be in a good position to discuss women and employment in Chapter 7. In the current section, we'll be tracing young women's experiences in middle school and high school, early encounters with math and science, experiences in higher education, career choices, and the discrepancy between aspirations and reality.

Young Women's Experiences in Middle School and High School

A female seventh-grader described the complex challenge of blending school and social roles:

> For school we got an open mind, good grades, participation, we've got the attitude, a certain perspective. You have to suck up sometimes, you have to be quiet, you have to know certain people, you have to be yourself, you have to be attentive, on task, you have to study a lot. And for the crowd you have to wear the right clothes, you have to have the attitude, you have to be willing to bully people, you also have to suck up to, like, your friends or whatever, you have to be outgoing, daring, you have to know certain people . . . and sometimes you have to be mean. (Cohen et al., 1996, p. 60)

Some of the adolescent characteristics we've discussed in this chapter make it especially challenging for young women to achieve academic success. Their bodies are changing, they may be preoccupied with their physical appearance, and they may be tempted to starve themselves. They may also have low self-esteem. Many females in middle school (junior high) and high school feel invisible in the classroom (Levstik, 2001). As one educator wrote, "Some girls lose opportunities for learning if they do not learn to express themselves in academic situations, ask questions when concerns arise, and clarify issues they may not understand" (S. M. Reis, 1998, p. 114). When the academic environment emphasizes traditional femininity, many young women will not select a challenging career, choose rigorous courses, or study diligently (Arnold et al., 1996; L. M. Brown, 1998; Kerr, 1994).

Young women are most likely to maintain their academic aspirations if their middle school or high schools make gender equality a priority, institute a mentoring system, have high expectations for young women, and encourage them to become leaders (Cohen et al., 1996; Erkut et al., 2001).

Early Experiences in Math and Science

Zelda Ziegler remembers sitting in a high school classroom, preparing to take an engineering exam. She was the only female among those taking the test. The proctor stood in front of the room and announced that the exam would be reasonable. "Nobody would have trouble with it except for one person—and she knows who she is" (J. Kaplan & Aronson, 1994, p. 27). Fortunately, Ziegler was not discouraged by these words. She went on to earn a Ph.D. in chemistry and now acts as a mentor for young women interested in science.

Most young women do not face such overt sexism, but they typically experience subtle biases that discourage all but the most persistent students. For example, math and science teachers may interact more frequently with male students than with female students (Duffy et al., 2002). They may also give males more helpful feedback. Some teachers select mostly males to perform classroom demonstrations (J. Kaplan & Aronson, 1994; S. M. Reis, 1998). Teachers may also emphasize examples that are more familiar to males than to females. In addition, teachers may fail to encourage talented females to pursue careers in math and science. Middle school is often the crucial time at which young women start to form negative attitudes toward these traditionally male courses (Eccles, 1997; Hanson & Johnson, 2000). As a consequence, students may then take only the required math and science courses in high school.

Several additional factors contribute to the gender differences in pursuing math and science: (1) Male peers may tease and harass females interested in these areas (J. Kaplan & Aronson, 1994); (2) females are less likely to join extracurricular groups that focus on math and science (S. M. Reis, 1998); and (3) females often feel less competent and effective in these courses, even though they may actually perform very well (Betz, 1997; Erchick, 2001).

Some school systems have developed innovative programs to bring females into the sciences—and to keep them there. For example, some school districts encourage high school females to enroll in special science schools. Other schools encourage young women to participate in science clubs. A few schools have developed summer programs in which talented young women can conduct science research with a mentor (Betz, 1997; S. M. Reis, 1998). In these settings, they can learn to take risks, make mistakes, and enjoy being successful in a nontraditional area.

In addition, parents can support their daughter's interest in nontraditional fields by seeking nonsexist career guidance. They can also encourage her college plans and value her academic interests (Kerr, 1994; Song, 2001). Furthermore, teachers can identify young females who are gifted in science and math, and the teachers can then encourage parents to support their daughter's interest in these areas (Eccles et al., 2000; S. M. Reis, 1998).

Higher Education

In North America, women are currently more likely than men to pursue higher education. For example, women now constitute 56% of university graduates in Canada (Girvan, 2000). Women also constitute 56% of students enrolled in U.S. colleges and universities ("The Nation: Students," 2001). As Table 4.1 shows, this gender difference holds for all five major ethnic groups, although the gap is largest for Black women and men.

In contrast to the gender ratio for students, relatively few college professors are women. At present, only 35% of all full-time faculty members at U.S. colleges and universities are female ("The Nation: Faculty and Staff," 2001). Consequently, female students may receive a message that they have entered a male-dominated environment. Is the college environment somewhat hostile to women? And what is college like for women of color?

The Academic Environment.   In the early 1980s, some observers suggested that female students in higher education were experiencing a chilly classroom climate (e.g., R. M. Hall & Sandler, 1982). Where the concept of the **chilly classroom climate** persists, faculty members treat men and women differently in the classroom and women may feel ignored and devalued. As a result, some women may participate less in discussions and may be less likely to feel academically competent (Pascarella et al., 1997).

Several resources provide reports of the chilly classroom climate in higher education (S. L. Murray et al., 1999; "Notebook," 1999; Pascarella et al., 1997; S. M. Reis, 1998). For example, when a female nursing student asked a question about the topic a male professor had just discussed, the professor leaned over to one of the male students and said, "Whoa, that went right over her head, didn't it?" (Shellenbarger & Lucas, 1997, p. 156). According to one survey of undergraduate students, 55% of women and 44% of men reported that they had heard a faculty member using sexist language, humor, or comments (Shepela & Levesque, 1998).

Research has not found consistent evidence for a chilly classroom climate (Brady & Eisler, 1995; Crawford & MacLeod, 1990). For example, in a recent

TABLE 4.1 ■ Male and Female Enrollment in U.S. Colleges and Universities in 1999, as a Function of Ethnic Group

	Number of Students	
Ethnic Group	**Women**	**Men**
European American	5,722,600	4,539,900
Black	1,037,700	603,000
Latina/o	754,400	562,300
Asian	474,400	435,300
Native American	86,800	58,500

Source: Based on "The Nation: Students" (2002).

study, Kristine Brady and Richard Eisler (1999) invited faculty members at a large university to participate in a study of classroom interaction patterns. The researchers observed 24 college classrooms, ranging from stereotypically masculine courses, such as engineering, to stereotypically feminine courses, such as child development. The results showed that professors called on female and male students equally. Also, females and males participated equally in the class discussions. Finally, females and males had similar perceptions about how they were treated in the classroom.

As Brady and Eisler (1999) pointed out, a qualitative study might discover that professors use different voice tones or different feedback when interacting with males as opposed to females. Furthermore, professors who volunteer for any observational study are likely to be good teachers who are also relatively unbiased. In any event—fortunately!—we do not currently have compelling evidence for a widespread chilly climate in college classrooms.

Women of Color and Higher Education.   We mentioned earlier that Black women are much more likely than Black men to attend college. The reasons for this discrepancy are not clear, but theorists suggest that part of the problem is a cultural climate that values athletic ability and high salaries more than academic achievement in young males (B. D. Hawkins, 1996; Roach, 2001).

Students of color often receive the message that they do not fit well in a college setting (Gruber, 1999; Reid & Zalk, 2001). As one young Puerto Rican woman said, "People sort of see me differently because I'm Hispanic and I'm smart. I feel sometimes that they want to put me down. I have had several incidents where people will look at my skin color and think I'm dumb, and they immediately think 'She's not bright, she's not smart'" (S. M. Reis, 1998, pp. 157–158).

Students of color face multiple additional barriers. For instance, Asian families may be reluctant to let their daughter attend a college far from home (Zia, 2000). Financing a college education is often an issue for women of color, especially in immigrant families (De las Fuentes & Vasquez, 1999; hooks, 2000c).

A small number of universities offer special programs for people of color. For example, Pennsylvania State University's American Indian Leadership Program was designed to train leaders in the field of education. Napier (1996) describes the experience of nine Native American women who received doctoral degrees through this program. The women encountered resistance from family members. One elderly father said, "You've got enough education. Why do you want to go there? It's so far away" (p. 139). However, support from helpful faculty members—and from each other—provided a warm academic climate rather than a chilly one.

Our discussion so far has focused on the difficulty of blending school with peer relationships, early experiences in math and science, and the challenges of higher education. Now let's turn to women's career plans.

Career Aspirations

A variety of studies have asked adolescents about their career aspirations. In general, adolescent females and males have similar career goals. Here are some of the findings:

1. Adolescent males and females have equivalent aspirations with respect to advanced degrees, and they also aspire to similarly prestigious careers (e.g., Abele, 2000; Astin & Lindholm, 2001; S. M. Reis et al., 1996).
2. Adolescent females are more likely than adolescent males to choose careers that are nontraditional for their gender (Bobo et al., 1998). For example, S. M. Reis and her colleagues (1996) surveyed gifted adolescents. Of the females, 37% aspired to be doctors, whereas fewer than 1% of the males aspired to be nurses.
3. Adolescent females are more likely than adolescent males to emphasize the importance of marriage and children (Debold et al., 1999; Eccles, 1994; S. M. Reis et al., 1996).
4. Parents are more likely to let daughters make their own decisions about careers. In one study of middle school students, 88% of girls, compared with only 38% of boys, said that their parents had been allowing them to make their own occupational choices (S. M. Reis, 1998).

What personal characteristics are typical for women who aspire to high-prestige, nontraditional careers? Not surprisingly, they receive high grades in school (Betz & Fitzgerald, 1987; Holms & Esses, 1988). They also tend to be independent, self-confident, assertive, emotionally stable, and satisfied with their lives (Astin & Lindholm, 2001; Betz, 1994; Eccles, 1994). Notice that these nontraditional women typically have characteristics that should serve them well in a traditionally masculine occupation. In addition, their emotional stability and life satisfaction indicate that they are well adjusted. They also tend to express feminist attitudes and to transcend traditional gender roles (Flores & O'Brien, 2002; Song, 2001; Vincent et al., 1998).

Women who plan on prestigious nontraditional careers are likely to have parents who are well educated and from middle- or upper-class backgrounds (Kastberg & Miller, 1996). Their mothers are also likely to be employed outside the home and to have feminist beliefs (Belansky et al., 1992; J. Steele & Barling, 1996). Other influential background characteristics include a supportive and encouraging family, female role models, and work experience as an adolescent (Betz, 1994; Flores & O'Brien, 2002).

In this section, we have explored women's aspirations about future careers and the factors associated with nontraditional career choices. But how well do women's aspirations match their actual career pathways?

Career Aspirations Versus Reality

Young women may enter middle school or high school with admirable life goals. However, they may absorb the cultural messages about finding a boyfriend, so that they lose sight of these goals (S. M. Reis, 1998). For example, a seventh-grader commented about this topic:

> I don't know what has happened to some of my friends. Consider Lisa. She acts so different around boys. She gets all giggly and silly and seems to act like such a jerk. She's cooing and trying to be all sweet and everything. She's started to act like she isn't smart at all. Her grades are horrible and she just isn't herself any more. (S. M. Reis, 1998, p. 130)

As you may recall from previous chapters, boys and men hold more traditional views about gender than do girls and women. As a result, a young woman in a romantic relationship may find that her boyfriend does not support her career ambitions, and she becomes a less dedicated student (Basow & Rubin, 1999).

Women may also be more likely than men to downscale their dreams as they move through college (Betz, 1994). For example, one study followed the lives of a group of Black women and a group of White women while they progressed through two universities in the South (Holland & Eisenhart, 1990). In two-thirds of both groups, the women's aspirations about careers diminished during their college years. Instead, they spent a great deal of time and energy on romantic relationships. In a cyclical fashion, increased attention to romance produced more boredom with schoolwork and further erosion of their career identities. Ultimately, their romantic relationships became far more important than their career-related education.

Most of the research in this area examines the career paths of relatively affluent women who can afford to go to college. Columnist Molly Ivins (1997) reminds us that the aspirations of these individuals are not relevant for many young women. Ivins described the situation of Shanika, who is 24 and unmarried and has three children. She has no high school degree, no job, and little prospect of obtaining either. When asked what she had dreamed before her children were born, she replied, "You know, I really didn't have a dream."

SECTION SUMMARY ■

Education and Career Planning

1. Adolescent females must negotiate the conflicting demands of schoolwork and social interactions.

2. Teachers and school systems may treat young women in a biased fashion, which can discourage them from careers in science and math; however, some schools offer innovative programs to promote these nontraditional careers for women.

3. Women in higher education may sometimes encounter a chilly classroom climate, but current research has not documented widespread discrimination against college women.

4. Women of color sometimes report that they do not feel comfortable in academic environments, but some universities offer programs designed to be supportive.

5. Adolescent females are similar to adolescent males with respect to their aspirations for advanced degrees and prestigious careers, but females are more likely to choose nontraditional careers, to emphasize marriage and children, and to experience less parental pressure to choose a particular career.

6. Factors associated with women's choice of a prestigious nontraditional career include high grades, self-confidence, emotional stability, and feminist beliefs.

Other factors include parental education, mothers' employment and feminist beliefs, and supportive adults.

7. As women advance through middle school, high school, and college, they are likely to adopt less ambitious plans; romantic relationships may interfere with academic achievement.

INTERPERSONAL RELATIONSHIPS DURING ADOLESCENCE

So far in this chapter, we have explored three clusters of issues that are important to young women: (1) puberty and menstruation; (2) self-concept and identity; and (3) education and career planning. However, as we suggested in the third section, adolescent females are perhaps most concerned about their social interactions.

Consider Ruby, a 14-year-old African American, who has six younger siblings. Her narrative illustrates the centrality of interpersonal relationships for adolescent females. For example, she describes the circle of support offered by the women in her family when she wants to discuss her future plans: "[My mother] says if I want something, I can always accomplish it. I believe that, too. And my aunt and my grandmother. There's lots of people" (Taylor et al., 1995, p. 42). However, Ruby also emphasizes the support offered by her classmates, for example, when they elected her to a special team in her history class: "The kids are all—I guess they accepted me for that, so maybe they like me. . . . You know you're wanted" (p. 42).

In this final section of the chapter on adolescence, we will begin by exploring relationships with family members. Then we'll examine connections with peers, specifically in friendships and in love relationships.

Family Relationships During Adolescence

If you believe the popular media, you might conclude that adolescents and their parents inhabit different cultures, interacting only long enough to snarl at each other. The data suggest otherwise (Zebrowitz & Montepare, 2000). Most adolescents, both females and males, actually get along quite well with their parents. Although they may disagree on relatively minor issues such as music or messy rooms, they typically agree on more substantive matters such as religion, politics, education, and social values (Graber & Brooks-Gunn, 1999; J. Kaufman, 1999; Smetana, 1996).

The family is likely to be a strong basis of identification for adolescent females of color, especially if the family can serve as a source of resiliency when these young women experience ethnic or gender discrimination (Vasquez & De las Fuentes, 1999). The research also suggests that both in North America and in other cultures, adolescent females typically feel closer to their mothers than to their fathers (Gibbons et al., 1991; A. G. Kaplan et al., 1991; Vitulli & Holland, 1993).

In most areas, female and male adolescents report similar family experiences. However, you may remember that parents tend to discuss fear and sadness with their daughters but that they talk about anger with their sons (Chapter 3). Interestingly, adolescent females are much more likely than adolescent males to endorse statements such as "In our family, it's okay to be sad, happy, angry, loving, excited, scared, or whatever we feel" (Bronstein et al., 1996). Family discussions about emotions may encourage young women to think about them and to experience them. We'll explore some of the consequences of this emphasis on emotions in Chapter 12, when we discuss depression.

As young women mature, they may begin to notice gender issues in their families. For example, J. M. Taylor and her colleagues (1995) reported that the young Latina and Portuguese American women in their study complained that their parents gave their brothers many more privileges and much more freedom. Their parents also emphasized that young women must be modest about their bodies and not sexually interested. The parents' concerns have important implications for young women's romantic relationships, a topic we'll discuss at the end of this chapter.

Friendships During Adolescence

In Chapter 6, we'll examine gender comparisons in friendship patterns during adulthood. We have somewhat less information about adolescent friendships. In general, females' friendships seem to be somewhat closer and more intimate than males' friendships. However, the gender differences are not enormous (e.g., L. M. Brown et al., 1999; Zarbatany et al., 2000).

A more interesting question focuses on the importance of close friendships in the lives of adolescent females. Loyalty and trust are considered essential in these friendships (B. B. Brown et al., 1997; L. M. Brown et al., 1999). For example, Lyn Mikel Brown (1998) studied a group of lower-class European American teenagers. These young women reported that their relationships with girlfriends provided a support system in an environment that often seemed hostile.

Another important part of young women's friendships is intimate conversations. A Latina teenager discusses her best friend: "I go to her because I wouldn't feel comfortable telling other people, you know, like, real deep personal things" (Way, 1998, p. 133). Similarly, Gilligan (1990) asked young European American females to identify the worst thing that could happen in a relationship. Most mentioned some aspect of failing to talk openly. One student responded that the worst thing would be

> that you grow up, or sideways, and not be able to talk to each other, especially if you depend on being able to talk to someone and not being able to. That hurts a lot, because you have been dependent on that. It is like walking fifty miles for a glass of water in a hot desert and you have been depending on it for days and getting there and finding it is not there anymore; you made the wrong turn ten miles back. (Gilligan, 1990, p. 24)

DEMONSTRATION 4.4 ■ ■ ■ ■ ■ ■ ■ ■ ■ ■ ■ ■ ■ ■ ■ ■ ■ ■

Gender and Love Relationships

For each of the following quotations, try to guess whether the person describing the love relationship is a male or a female. Then check the answers, which are listed at the end of the chapter.

_____ Person 1: "Um, we're both very easygoing. Um, we like a lot of affection. Um, not like public affection, but um, just knowing that we, we care for each other. Um, uh, it doesn't even have to be physical affection, just any type. We like cuddling with each other. Um, we enjoy going out and doing things with each other and each other's friends. . . . We enjoy high action things together. Um, pretty much, we have a very open relationship, and we can talk about anything."

_____ Person 2: "I think after a while, like, (person) following me around, and wanting to be with me all the time, and maybe the fact that I had a lot to say and had the power . . . I'd just, like, I don't know, I still think like that. I don't know why but (person) . . . was getting too serious by following me around all the time and, you know, wanting to spend every minute of the day. . . . You know I'm, like, 'I do have friends I need to talk to.' . . . I was just, like 'Aaah! Go away!'"

_____ Person 3: "It's like . . . you know . . . we love each other so much . . . it's great. We have so much fun. We get mad at each other sometimes, and, you know, we make up, and, you know, we hug. It's great. I mean (person) is wonderful! . . . We, like, we just have a lot of fun, and we have a lot of heartache, but it's perfect because of that, you know. If it was all fun all the time, what's wrong? And if it's bad all the time, something's wrong. It's right in the middle. It's right where it should be."

_____ Person 4: "I'm not really a relationship person. If I meet someone, I want to be able to, you know, to uh, you know . . . not have any restraints or anything. Basically, I run into someone who I think is cool and all that about twice a month. . . . The friends before are friends after. Most of them are probably physical. Um, I don't have any regrets."

Source: Based on Feiring (1998).

Adolescent females face a major challenge as they try to develop a clear sense of themselves in relationships with others. Some emphasize interdependence with others; these young women may spend so much attention on their friends that they fail to take care of their own needs. Other young women are more autonomous in relation to others; they are concerned about other people, but they do not compromise their own integrity for the sake of friends (Lyons, 1990).

The research on friendships illustrates a central choice that weaves through women's lives. At many turning points, from youth through old age, women will be faced with conflicts between doing something that is best for themselves or doing something for another person—a parent, a female friend, a male friend, or a spouse (Eccles, 2001).

In two later chapters of this book, we attend to topics related to women's focusing on themselves: cognitive ability and achievement (Chapter 5) and work (Chapter 7). Several other chapters emphasize women in relationships: social characteristics (Chapter 6), love relationships (Chapter 8), sexuality (Chapter 9), and pregnancy, childbirth, and motherhood (Chapter 10). We'll see that women frequently have to balance their own needs and priorities against the wishes of other people who are important in their lives.

Romantic Relationships During Adolescence

For most individuals, adolescence marks the beginning of romantic relationships. We'll explore these experiences in more detail in Chapter 8, but let's consider some of the issues that young women face in heterosexual and lesbian relationships during adolescence. Before you read further, try Demonstration 4.4 on page 135, which focuses on early heterosexual romances.

Heterosexual Relationships. As you recall from Chapter 3, young girls and boys practice gender segregation; they inhabit different worlds for many years. As a result, they reach early adolescence with only limited experience regarding the other gender (Feiring, 1998).

How do young women figure out how they should interact with these unfamiliar young men in a romantic relationship? An important source of information is the media: movies, television, music, books, and computer games (B. B. Brown et al., 1997; Feiring, 1998). Not surprisingly, the media typically portray gender-stereotyped romances. The media also suggest that a boyfriend is an absolutely necessity for a high school female. Consider the title of a recent article in a magazine aimed at adolescent women: "Why Don't I Have a Boyfriend? (And How Do I Get One?)" (2001). This article suggests, for example, that if a young woman is too busy studying to meet a boyfriend, she should look around the library to find a likely candidate. Furthermore, about half of teen magazine articles are devoted to the topics of beauty, fashion, and romance (Currie, 1999; Mazzarella, 1999; Rennells, 2001). The magazines proclaim that, with hard work and self-sacrifice, a young woman can transform herself into someone who is extremely thin and flawlessly beautiful (Kilbourne, 1999). Also, as we'll see shortly, these magazines focus exclusively on heterosexual relationships—lesbian relationships do not exist in those glossy pages!

Adolescent romantic relationships have only recently attracted the attention of serious researchers (Steinberg & Morris, 2001). The researchers report tremendous individual differences in the gender typing of adolescents' romantic relationships, consistent with Theme 4 of this book (Feiring, 1998; Hartup, 1999). For example, if you check the answers to Demonstration 4.4, you're likely to find that some adolescents behave in a gender-stereotypical fashion but that some clearly transcend these stereotypes.

Research on early heterosexual romances suggests that these relationships typically last an average of about 4 months (Feiring, 1996). Both females and males are likely to describe their romantic partners in terms of positive personality traits, such as nice or funny. However, males are more likely to mention physical attractiveness, whereas females are more likely to emphasize personal characteristics, such as support and intimacy (Feiring, 1996, 1999b). In Chapter 8, we'll see that males' emphasis on attractiveness in a dating partner continues through adulthood.

In Chapter 9, we'll examine in some detail an important component of heterosexual romantic relationships during adolescence: decision making about sexual behavior. As we'll see, these decisions can have a major impact on a young woman's life, especially because they may lead to pregnancy and life-threatening sexually transmitted diseases.

Romantic relationships can also have an important influence on academic performance and career planning. Young women often spend many hours each week dreaming about romance, discussing romantic relationships with friends, and pursuing these relationships (Rostosky et al., 1999). Once a woman finds a boyfriend, she may arrange her life to be available to her boyfriend, to help her boyfriend, and to participate in social activities chosen by her boyfriend (Holland & Eisenhart, 1990).

However, when a young woman has a boyfriend who respects her and who values her ideas, these romantic relationships can encourage her to explore important questions about her identity and self-worth (Larson et al., 1999). She can notice how her own personality is affected by her interactions with this boyfriend (Feiring, 1999a). She can also contemplate what she truly wants in an ideal long-term relationship (W. A. Collins & Sroufe, 1999). Clearly, this self-exploration will have an important impact on personal values—as well as on romantic relationships—during adulthood.

Lesbian Relationships.   In Chapter 8, we will examine many aspects of lesbian relationships during adulthood. Adolescent women who are just beginning to discover their lesbian identity rarely have the opportunity to see positive lesbian images in the movies or on television (O'Sullivan et al., 2001). Psychology researchers also pay more attention to adolescent gay males than to adolescent lesbians. As Theme 3 points out, females are less visible than males. In addition, psychologists typically focus on observable problems, and young lesbians are not at high risk for health problems such as pregnancy or AIDS (Welsh et al., 2000).

However, young lesbians are likely to hear negative messages about lesbians and gay males from their peers. By fourth or fifth grade, the words *queer, dyke,* and *fag* are serious insults. Adolescent lesbians are likely to be threatened or attacked (Owens, 1998; Prezbindowski & Prezbindowski, 2001). They may also receive negative messages from their parents, who sometimes believe that being gay or lesbian is a sin. However, some fortunate adolescents may find a school or community support group for lesbian, gay, and bisexual young people (L. M. Diamond et al., 1999).

After a period of questioning their sexual orientation, young lesbians are most likely to "come out" to a friend. If they choose to come out to their parents, they are more likely to disclose to their mother rather than to their father. Surveys suggest that two-thirds of lesbian and gay youth are out to their mother, whereas one-half are out to their father (Savin-Williams, 1998, 2001).

Consistent with Theme 4, young women have widely varying experiences when they come out to their parents. At first, parents may react with shock or denial, as in the case of one young woman who told her mother she was a lesbian: "Mother went white and stark cold. When I told her she just looked away; she couldn't look me in the face. It scared her out of her freaking mind. She screamed lots of questions; said it was unnatural" (Savin-Williams, 2001, p. 89). In contrast, another young woman reported about her mother, "We've always been very close, very close, and talk about everything. No secrets from her! . . . This gave me hope in coming out to her. Shortly thereafter I told her I was dating Naomi. . . . But you know, she seemed to know it before I did!" (Savin-Williams, 2001, p. 67). Fortunately, most parents eventually become tolerant or even supportive of their daughter's lesbian relationships (Savin-Williams & Dubé, 1998).

As we'll see in Chapter 8, lesbians typically overcome most negative messages from their community and family, and they construct positive self-images. Consider the words of 'Lizabeth, who came out as a lesbian when she was 18 years old:

> I have a sense of peace about me that I've never had. I don't have to play any games. I don't have to pretend that I'm straight when I'm not. It's like a weight had been lifted off my shoulders. . . . My mother keeps telling me that the heterosexual norm would be so much easier. . . . But I had to live that way for eighteen years and it wasn't easier. It was screwing me up in my head. (Owens, 1998, p. 224)

In Chapter 3 and in this chapter, we have considered how children and adolescents develop gender typing. We pointed out in Chapter 3 that children develop elaborate ideas about gender throughout their childhood, especially because their family, their peers, their schools, and the media often provide clear gender messages. In this chapter, we have examined how puberty and menstruation help define young women's views of themselves. We have also noted that gender may influence an adolescent's body image, feminist identity, ethnic identity, and self-esteem. Gender also has important implications for an adolescent's career planning and interpersonal relationships.

In the following chapters, we will change our focus in order to examine adult women. We'll first explore gender comparisons in cognitive and achievement areas (Chapter 5) and in personality and social areas (Chapter 6). Then we'll consider women in work settings (Chapter 7) as well as in social relationships (Chapters 8, 9, and 10). In Chapters 11, 12, and 13, we will focus on issues women face with respect to health, psychological disorders, and violence. We will return to a developmental framework in Chapter 14, when we consider women's journeys during middle age and old age. In our final chapter, we'll examine some trends in gender issues that we are facing in the twenty-first century.

SECTION SUMMARY ■

Interpersonal Relationships During Adolescence

1. Adolescent women generally get along well with their families; they typically feel closer to their mothers than to their fathers.

2. Compared to adolescent men, adolescent women may have somewhat more intimate friendships.

3. Adolescents' heterosexual relationships show wide individual differences in the extent to which they are gender stereotyped. Young women spend a great deal of time in their romantic relationships; these relationships can encourage them to explore important questions about identity.

4. Adolescent lesbians often hear negative messages from classmates, community members, and parents; experiences differ widely when lesbians come out to their parents. Negative messages must be overcome in order to develop a positive self-image.

■ ■ ■ ■ ■ ■ CHAPTER REVIEW QUESTIONS ■ ■ ■ ■ ■ ■

1. In the section on menstruation, we examined two topics that are occasionally mentioned in the popular media: menstrual pain and premenstrual syndrome (PMS). What did you learn in this section that was different from the impressions the media convey?

2. At several points in this chapter, we discussed our culture's emphasis on young women's attractiveness. Summarize this topic, and relate your material to several adolescent women you know.

3. Throughout this book, we have discussed the social constructionist perspective, in which people construct or invent their own versions of reality based on prior experiences and beliefs. How does this perspective help explain the following issues: (a) premenstrual syndrome, (b) young women's emphasis on slenderness, and (c) how romantic relationships "should" be?

4. We emphasize in this textbook that research findings about gender comparisons often vary, depending on operational definitions. How is this statement relevant when we consider the research on feminist identity and ethnic identity and on the chilly classroom climate?

5. In this chapter we have argued that some people—but not everyone—may treat young women in a biased fashion during the process of guiding and educating them. Summarize the information on these issues. If you were conducting a large-scale study on gender biases during high school and college, what other issues, not mentioned here, would you consider examining?

6. In portions of this chapter, we examined ethnic comparisons. Describe information about relevant comparisons, including age of menarche, reactions to media images, self-esteem, and experiences with higher education.

7. Compare adolescent males' and females' career aspirations. What factors modify these aspirations for young women? Although we do not have similar research on young men, speculate about whether these same factors influence the aspirations of adolescent males.

8. Relate the material in the section on self-concept to the material on career aspirations and to the material on social interactions. Focus on the struggle between commitment to one's own pursuits and commitment to social relationships.

9. We mentioned parents in connection with nontraditional careers, family relationships, and romantic relationships. Discuss this information and speculate how parents can also be important in a young woman's attitudes toward menstruation, feminist identity, and ethnic identity.

10. Imagine that you are teaching high school and that a group of teachers has obtained a large grant for a program on improving the lives of female adolescents. Review the topics in this chapter, and suggest 8 to 10 important topics that should be addressed in this program.

NEW TERMS

*adolescence (110)
*puberty (110)
*menarche (111)
*secondary sex characteristics (112)
*ovaries (112)
*ova (112)
*uterus (112)
*feedback loop (113)
*ovulation (114)
*dysmenorrhea (114)

*prostaglandins (115)
*premenstrual syndrome (PMS) (115)
*identity (120)
*feminism (123)
*feminist social identity (124)
*ego development (124)
*ethnic identity (124)
*self-esteem (125)
*meta-analysis (125)
*chilly classroom climate (129)

The terms asterisked in the New Terms section serve as good search terms for InfoTrac College Edition. Go to http://infotrac.thomsonlearning.com and try these added search terms.

RECOMMENDED READINGS

Currie, D. H. (1999). *Girl talk: Adolescent magazines and their readers.* Toronto: University of Toronto Press. Here's an excellent overview of issues concerned with magazines intended for adolescent females; topics include idealized images of women, the emphasis on materialism, advice columns, and interviews with readers.

Furman, W., Brown, B. B., & Feiring, C. (Eds.). (1999). *The development of romantic relationships in adolescence.* New York: Cambridge University Press. This intriguing book examines numerous topics related to adolescent romance, including emotional responses, peers' reactions, and cognitive components of relationships.

O'Reilly, P., Penn, E. M., & deMarrais, K. (Eds.). (2001). *Educating young adolescent girls.* Mahwah, NJ: Erlbaum. The scope of this book is broader than the standard meaning of education, because it also includes chapters on young women with disabilities, adolescent lesbians, and romantic relationships.

Reis, S. M. (1998). *Work left undone: Choices and compromises of talented females.* Mansfield Center, CT: Creative Learning Press. I recommend this book for anyone interested in the educational experiences of girls and women, especially because the volume discusses both the relevant research and suggestions for improving education.

Walker, A. E. (1998). *The menstrual cycle.* New York: Routledge. Here's an excellent account of the biology of menstruation, premenstrual syndrome, and the effects of the menstrual cycle on cognitive performance.

ANSWERS TO THE DEMONSTRATIONS

Demonstration 4.3: You can informally assess your feminist identity by adding together the ratings that you supplied for Items 1, 2, 3, 6, 7, and 9 and by subtracting the ratings that you supplied for Items 4, 5, 8, and 10. Higher scores indicate a stronger feminist identity.

Demonstration 4.4: Person 1 is a male; Person 2 is a female; Person 3 is a female; Person 4 is a male.

ANSWERS TO THE TRUE-FALSE QUESTIONS

1. False (pp. 114–115); 2. False (pp. 115–116); 3. False (p. 123); 4. False (pp. 125–126); 5. False (pp. 127–128); 6. True (p. 129); 7. True (p. 131); 8. True (p. 133); 9. False (p. 134); 10. True (p. 138).

Gender Comparisons in Cognitive Abilities and Attitudes About Success

Pictor International/PictureQuest

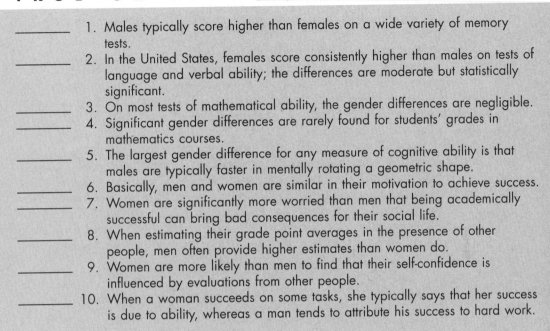

T R U E   O R   F A L S E ?

_____ 1. Males typically score higher than females on a wide variety of memory tests.

_____ 2. In the United States, females score consistently higher than males on tests of language and verbal ability; the differences are moderate but statistically significant.

_____ 3. On most tests of mathematical ability, the gender differences are negligible.

_____ 4. Significant gender differences are rarely found for students' grades in mathematics courses.

_____ 5. The largest gender difference for any measure of cognitive ability is that males are typically faster in mentally rotating a geometric shape.

_____ 6. Basically, men and women are similar in their motivation to achieve success.

_____ 7. Women are significantly more worried than men that being academically successful can bring bad consequences for their social life.

_____ 8. When estimating their grade point averages in the presence of other people, men often provide higher estimates than women do.

_____ 9. Women are more likely than men to find that their self-confidence is influenced by evaluations from other people.

_____ 10. When a woman succeeds on some tasks, she typically says that her success is due to ability, whereas a man tends to attribute his success to hard work.

An article in *USA Weekend* is titled "Sex and Brain Differences: Why the Female Brain Is Like a Swiss Army Knife" (1999). The accompanying sketch shows a man whose thoughts are represented by a large chopping knife; this knife can presumably perform only one function. A woman sitting next to him on a bench is simultaneously reading and tending her baby. Her thoughts are represented by a multifunction Swiss Army knife, which includes a can opener, a screwdriver, a knife blade, scissors, and six other tools. The article begins by describing "half a dozen proven differences between male and female brains" (p. 8), and it then discusses the presumably well-established gender differences in brain structure and cognitive performance. So I was not surprised when a professor in the English Department told me, several months later, "But I've read that the research proves that women can do many things at the same time, but men have to concentrate on just one thing."

When the popular media discuss gender comparisons in thinking, they almost always emphasize gender differences, ignoring the evidence for gender similarities. People who study the psychology of women need to know the research in this area, because it demonstrates that men and women are remarkably similar in most of these cognitive skills (Theme 1). Consistent with our culture's current emphasis on biology, the popular media also highlight biological explanations for the small number of gender differences. You need to know, however, that social and cultural explanations seem to play a more important role.

In the present chapter, we will explore two broad questions regarding gender comparisons:

1. Do women and men differ in their cognitive abilities?
2. Do women and men differ in their patterns of achievement motivation?

By addressing these two questions, we will gain the background information needed to answer another important question. In Chapter 7, we'll see that men and women tend to pursue different careers; for example, men are much more likely than women to become engineers. Can we trace this gender difference in career choice to major cognitive differences (such as ability in math) or to major motivational differences (such as an interest in achieving)?

We will focus in this chapter on the school-related comparisons that assess intellectual abilities and achievement motivation. In contrast, in Chapter 6, we will emphasize more interpersonal gender comparisons, specifically, social and personality characteristics. Can we trace gender differences in career preferences to gender differences in some important personality qualities, such as communication patterns, helpfulness, and aggressiveness?

BACKGROUND ON GENDER COMPARISONS

Before we address any of these specific gender comparisons, we need to consider some research issues that are relevant here and in Chapter 6. We'll first examine some cautions about the way research in psychology is conducted and interpreted. Then we'll briefly describe two approaches for summarizing a large number of studies that focus on the same topic.

Cautions About Research on Gender Comparisons

As pointed out in Chapter 1, a variety of biases can have a powerful effect when psychologists conduct research about women or research about gender comparisons. In addition, we need to be cautious about interpreting the results. Let's consider four specific cautions that are relevant to the current chapter:

1. Expectations can influence results.
2. Biased samples can influence results.
3. The scores of males and females typically produce overlapping distributions.
4. Gender differences are not likely to be found in all situations.

Let's look at each caution in more detail.

1. *Expectations can influence results.* As we noted in Chapter 1, biases can interfere at every stage of the research process. For example, researchers who expect to find gender differences will often tend to find them. Participants also have expectations, including expectations about cognitive gender differences (Caplan & Caplan, 1999).

2. *Biased samples can influence results.* Almost all the research on cognitive abilities focuses on college students (Halpern, 2000). We know almost nothing about adults who don't attend college. In addition, most of the research on gender comparisons examines U.S. and Canadian samples (Archer, 1996; McGuinness, 1998). Our conclusions about gender comparisons might be different if the research participants were more diverse.

3. *The scores of males and females typically produce overlapping distributions.* To discuss the concept of overlap, we need to consider frequency distributions. A **frequency distribution** tells us how many people in a sample receive each score. Imagine that we give a vocabulary test to a group of women and men and that we use their scores to construct the frequency distribution for each gender, as shown in Figure 5.1. Notice the tiny section in which the frequency distribution for the males overlaps with the frequency distribution for the females. In Figure 5.1, males and females received the same scores only in one small region, roughly between 54 and 66. When the two distributions show such a small overlap, we know that the two distributions are very different. As you can see in this figure, the average woman received a score of 80, whereas the average man received a score of 40.

In real life, however, distributions of female and male characteristics rarely show the separation illustrated in Figure 5.1. They are much more likely to show a large overlap (Geary, 1998; Hyde & Mezulis, 2001), as illustrated in Figure 5.2. Notice that males and females receive the same scores in the large region that extends roughly between 35 and 85. As we have often emphasized in our discussion of Theme 1, men and women are reasonably similar, which means that their scores will overlap considerably. Notice in Figure 5.2 that the average woman received a score of 63 and that the average man received a score of 57. This

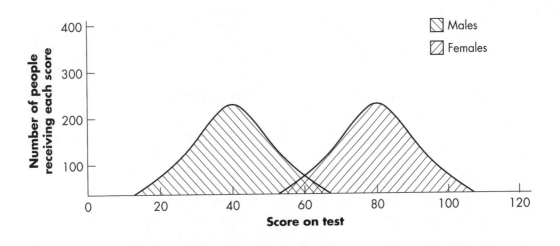

FIGURE 5.1 ■ Scores achieved by males and females on a hypothetical test. The small overlap indicates a large gender difference.

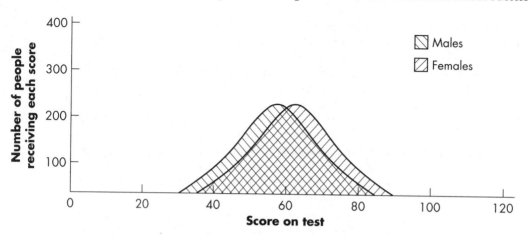

FIGURE 5.2 ■ Scores achieved by males and females on a hypothetical test. The large overlap indicates a small gender difference.

6-point difference between the average scores looks trivial when we compare it to the difference *within* each distribution, a range of about 50 points. As Theme 4 emphasizes, women differ widely from one another; men also show wide variation.

4. *Gender differences are not likely to be found in all situations.* You are certainly familiar with this issue from our earlier discussion of Theme 1. Throughout this chapter as well, you will notice that we cannot make general statements about gender differences. Instead, the gender differences often disappear when we test certain kinds of people or when we look at particular situations (Hyde & Mezulis, 2001; Lott, 1996). This observation suggests that gender differences can be modified; they are not inevitable. In short, many men and women have remarkably similar psychological characteristics in many situations.

Two Approaches to Summarizing Multiple Studies

When psychologists want to obtain an overview of a specific topic, they typically review the research by examining all the studies on that topic. For many years, psychologists who wanted to draw general conclusions about gender comparisons used the box-score approach to reviewing research. When using the **box-score approach** (also called the **counting approach**), researchers read through all the appropriate studies on a given topic and draw conclusions based on a tally of their outcomes. Specifically, how many studies show no gender differences, how many show higher scores for men, and how many show higher scores for women? Unfortunately, however, the box-score approach often produces ambiguous tallies. Suppose that researchers locate 16 relevant studies; 8 of these studies find no gender differences, 6 show higher scores for men, and 2 show higher scores for women. One researcher might conclude that no gender differences exist, whereas another might conclude that men score somewhat higher. The box-score approach does not provide a systematic method for combining individual studies.

A newer alternative, called the **meta-analysis** technique, provides a statistical method for integrating numerous studies on a single topic. Researchers first try to locate all appropriate studies on the topic. Then they perform a statistical analysis that combines the results from all these studies. The meta-analysis yields a single number that tells us whether a particular variable has an overall effect (Hyde & Mezulis, 2001). For example, for verbal ability, a meta-analysis can combine numerous previous studies into one enormous superstudy that can provide a general picture of whether gender has an overall effect on verbal ability.

A meta-analysis yields a number known as effect size, or d. Psychologists tend to use the following guidelines: A d value less than 0.35 indicates that the variable being studied (e.g., gender) has only a small influence. A d value close to 0.50 is generally considered a moderate difference. A d value greater than 0.65 is considered a large difference (Cohen, 1969; Hyde & Plant, 1995).

To provide a yardstick for effect size, consider that the d for the gender difference in height is 2.0. This is a huge difference; in fact, the overlap between the male and the female distributions is only 11% (Kimball, 1995). Compared to a d of 2.0, the d values for psychological gender comparisons are relatively small. In fact, Hyde and Plant (1995) examined 171 different meta-analyses that focused on psychological gender comparisons. Their study showed that 60% had small effect sizes (d less than 0.35), 27% had medium effect sizes ($d = 0.36$ to 0.65), and only 22% had large effect sizes (d greater than 0.65). Only 3% had d values greater than 1.0. With all these important methodological issues in mind, let's now consider the actual research.

SECTION SUMMARY ▪

Background on Gender Comparisons

1. In considering research on gender comparisons, we need to emphasize that (a) expectations and biased samples can influence results; (b) frequency distributions for the scores of males and females typically overlap, so that most females and males receive similar scores; and (c) gender differences are often present in some situations and absent in others.

2. In contrast to the earlier box-score approach, the meta-analysis technique provides a systematic statistical method for integrating studies on a single topic and for drawing conclusions about that topic.

COGNITIVE ABILITIES

We'll begin our examination of the research by focusing on cognitive abilities. Topics related to achievement motivation will be discussed later in the chapter. In this current section, we'll first examine some areas that show gender similarities, and then we'll focus on three kinds of cognitive abilities for which we have some evidence of gender differences: (1) verbal ability, (2) mathematics ability, and (3) spatial ability.

Throughout this chapter, however, we must emphasize a practical point: Each gender difference that has been identified is relatively small, and so it should *not* be considered when people are making career choices. For example, women's scores may be slightly lower than men's scores on tasks that require spatial skills. Specifically, 7% of males and 3% of females place in the top 5% of the population (Hyde, 1981). In other words, 38% of the people with superior spatial abilities are female.

Some people argue that women seldom pursue careers in engineering because they lack spatial skills. At present, only 10% of U.S. engineers are women, that is, about 1 female to 10 males (U.S. Census Bureau, 2001b). This 10% is much lower than the 38% we would expect if high spatial ability were the only requirement for becoming an engineer. We need to search for additional explanations if we want to account for the small number of women in such fields as engineering.

Cognitive Abilities That Show No Consistent Gender Differences

Before we examine the three areas that show occasional gender *differences*, let's first consider some general categories where gender *similarities* are typically observed.

General Intelligence.   One major area in which females and males are similar is general intelligence, as measured by total scores on an IQ test (e.g., Geary, 1998; Halpern, 2001; Stumpf, 1995). Many intelligence tests have been constructed by eliminating items on which gender differences are found. As a result, the final versions of the intelligence tests usually show gender similarities. Other research also shows gender similarities in general knowledge about history, geography, and other basic information (Meinz & Salthouse, 1998).

Memory.   In general, men and women are similar in memory ability, although occasional studies report that women are somewhat more accurate (Herlitz et al., 1997, 1999; Meinz & Salthouse, 1998). We'll have to wait for an appropriate meta-analysis to figure out whether gender differences are likely to emerge in certain tasks. For example, the nature of the items may make a difference. Herrmann and his colleagues (1992) gave men and women a list of items to remember. The list was labeled either "Grocery store" or "Hardware store." The items on the list were equally likely for both settings (e.g., brush, nuts, salt, chips). Women remembered more items than men did when the list was labeled "Grocery store," but men remembered more items than women did when it was labeled "Hardware store."

Complex Cognitive Tasks.   A variety of other challenging intellectual tasks show no overall gender differences. For example, males and females are equally competent when they form concepts and when they solve a variety of complex problems (Kimura, 1992; Meinz & Salthouse, 1998). Males and females are also similar in their performance on a variety of creativity tasks (J. Baer, 1999; Ruscio et al., 1998; Singleton, 1987). Furthermore, in the United States, men and women earn similar grades in college courses (Shoichet, 2002).

We have seen that women and men are typically similar in their general intelligence, memory, and complex cognitive abilities. Keep these important similarities in mind as we explore the three areas in which modest gender differences have sometimes been identified.

Verbal Ability

Females score somewhat higher than males on a small number of verbal tasks, although the overall gender similarities are more striking. Let's look at three areas of research: the general studies, standardized language tests, and the research on language disabilities.

General Research. Some research suggests that girls have larger vocabularies than boys have before the age of 2, but these gender differences disappear by 3 years of age (N. Eisenberg et al., 1996; Huttenlocher et al., 1991; Jacklin & Maccoby, 1983). The similarities are more striking than the differences when we consider young school-age children (Cahan & Ganor, 1995; Maccoby & Jacklin, 1974). Therefore, if you plan to teach elementary school, the girls and boys in your class should be comparable in their language skills.

When we consider adolescents and adults, the research shows gender similarities in such areas as spelling, vocabulary, and reading comprehension (Collaer & Hines, 1995; Feingold, 1993; Halpern, 1997; Hedges & Nowell, 1995). In some specific areas, the gender differences demonstrate statistical significance but not practical significance (see page 23). For example, females seem to be somewhat better at **verbal fluency,** or naming objects that meet certain criteria, such as beginning with the letter *S* (Halpern, 2000, 2001; Halpern & Tan, 2001). Females also score somewhat higher on tests of writing ability (Geary, 1998; Halpern, 2000; Pajares et al., 1999).

We emphasized earlier that meta-analysis is the ideal statistical tool for combining the results of a number of studies on a specific topic. Janet Hyde and Marcia Linn (1988) conducted a meta-analysis on overall gender comparisons in verbal ability. The average effect size (d) was only 0.11, just slightly favoring females. This value is so close to 0 that Hyde and Linn concluded that overall gender differences do not exist. Other researchers have reached the same conclusions, based on standardized test scores for U.S. students (Feingold, 1988; Hedges & Nowell, 1995; Willingham & Cole, 1997). Ironically, the one general area in which females occasionally have the advantage—verbal abilities—has been studied less extensively than spatial or mathematical skills (Halpern, 2000). An up-to-date meta-analysis would help us understand whether any gender differences in verbal ability are noteworthy.

Standardized Language Tests.   You may have taken the Scholastic Achievement Test (SAT) when you applied for college admission. The verbal portion of this test covers skills such as reading comprehension, verbal analogies, and sentence completion. Gender differences on the SAT are minimal. For example, in 2002, the average SAT verbal score was 502 for women and 507 for men (J. R. Young, 2002). Gender differences are also minimal for the Advanced Placement tests in English language, English literature, and all foreign languages (Stumpf & Stanley, 1998).

We've looked at general verbal ability and at performance on standardized tests of verbal skills. Let's explore the related topic of language disabilities.

Reading Disabilities.   Some research suggests that males are more likely than females to be labeled as having language problems. For instance, school systems report reading disabilities about five times as often for boys as for girls (Halpern, 2000).

An important study by S. E. Shaywitz and her colleagues (1990) used more objective methods to categorize students. These researchers pointed out that the term **reading disability** refers to poor reading skills that are not accounted for by the level of general intelligence. Accordingly, they defined reading disability in objective, statistical terms.[1] The target population for this study included children in 12 cities throughout the state of Connecticut.

As Figure 5.3 shows, when the school systems evaluated the two gender groups, they classified roughly four times as many boys as having reading disabilities. This ratio was consistent with earlier reports (Halpern, 2000). In contrast, when the *objective* test scores were measured, roughly the same number of boys and girls met the criterion of having reading disabilities.

Why do the schools identify reading problems in so many more boys than girls? S. E. Shaywitz and her colleagues (1990) proposed that teachers target more active, less attentive boys as having reading disabilities. These boys may be referred to a reading clinic on the basis of their behavior, not their reading skills. Equally disturbing is that many girls probably have genuine reading disabilities, but they sit quietly in their seats and hide their disabilities (J. T. E. Richardson, 1997a). These well-behaved, neglected girls will miss out on the additional tutoring in reading that could help them thrive in school. As Chapter 3 emphasized, girls are often invisible in our schools, and they lose out on educational opportunities.

Throughout this section on verbal skills, we have seen a general pattern of minimal gender differences, based on a variety of measures. In addition, gender differences in reading disabilities can be traced, at least partly, to a bias in teachers' referrals to reading clinics.

---

[1] Specifically, a child's IQ was used to predict what his or her score should be on a standardized test of reading achievement. Any child whose actual score on the reading test was more than 1.5 standard deviations below the predicted score was categorized as having a reading disability. A score that was 1.5 standard deviations below the prediction meant that the child had a reading score in the bottom 7% of all those children at his or her IQ level.

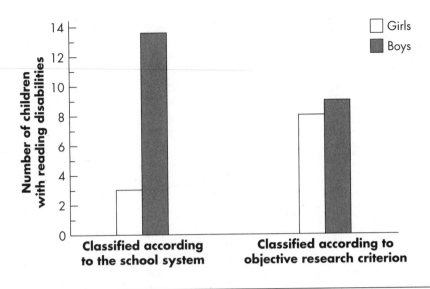

FIGURE 5.3 ■ Number of boys and girls with reading disabilities, according to the schools' criterion and the objective research criterion.

Source: Based on S. E. Shaywitz et al. (1990).

Mathematics Ability

Of all the topics associated with cognitive gender differences, mathematics receives the most attention from researchers and from the popular press. Media reports would lead you to expect large gender differences favoring males. Instead, as you'll see, most of the research shows gender similarities in math ability, and females actually receive higher grades in math courses. Males perform substantially better than females only on the mathematics section of the SAT.

General Research. Most comparisons of males' and females' ability on mathematics achievement tests show gender similarities (Feingold, 1988; Hedges & Nowell, 1995). Consider, for example, a meta-analysis of 100 studies, based on standardized-test scores of more than 3 million people. (This analysis did not include math SAT scores, which we'll consider shortly.) By averaging across all samples and all tests, Hyde and her colleagues (1990) found a *d* of only 0.15, which is illustrated in Figure 5.4. As you can see, the two distributions are almost identical. Studies conducted in the United States, Canada, the United Kingdom, Ireland, Spain, and Korea also report minimal gender differences (Beller & Gafni, 2000; Duffy et al., 1997; Randhawa & Hunter, 2001).

Researchers have found some interesting patterns in the data on math ability (Geary, 1998; Hyde et al., 1990). For example, females perform somewhat better than males in elementary school and middle school on complex arithmetic problems. Males perform somewhat better than females during late adolescence and

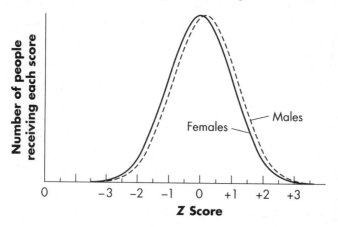

FIGURE 5.4 ■ Performance of females and males on all mathematics tests except the SAT, showing an effect size (*d*) of 0.15.

Source: From Hyde, S. J., et al. (1990). Gender differences in mathematics performance: A metaanalysis. *Psychological Bulletin, 107,* 139–155. © 1990 by the American Psychological Association. Reprinted with permission.

adulthood, especially on tests that measure mathematical problem solving and geometry.

Grades in Mathematics Courses. I often ask students in my classes to raise their hands if they have heard that males receive higher average scores on the math section of the SAT. The hands fly up. Then I ask how many have heard that females receive higher average grades in mathematics *courses.* The hands all drop. In fact, representative studies show that females earn higher grades in fifth-, sixth-, and tenth-grade mathematics as well as in college math courses (S. Beyer, 1999a; Frome & Eccles, 1998; S. E. Smith & Walker, 1988). Females also earn higher grades in related areas, such as high school science courses and college-level statistics (C. I. Brooks, 1987; Brownlow et al., 2000; M. Stewart, 1998).

Meredith Kimball (1989, 1995) reviewed the research on grades in mathematics courses. She found fairly consistent evidence that females receive higher grades in their math classes; Willingham and Cole (1997), in another comprehensive review, reached the same conclusion. Kimball proposed that females perform better when dealing with familiar situations, such as exams on material covered in a mathematics course. In contrast, males seem to perform better when dealing with unfamiliar situations, especially the kinds of math problems included on the SAT. In any event, Kimball points out that females' high grades in math courses deserve wider publicity. This publicity would encourage females, their parents, and their teachers to have greater confidence in girls' and women's competence in mathematics.

The SAT. Of all the research in cognitive gender differences, the topic that has received the most media attention is performance on the math portion of the

SAT. For instance, Camilla Benbow and her colleagues administered the math SAT test to groups of seventh- and eighth-grade students who had outstanding ability in mathematics (e.g., Benbow, 1988; Benbow & Stanley, 1980; Benbow et al., 2000). In a typical report, for example, females received an average math SAT score of 505, whereas males received an average score of 537 (Benbow et al., 2000). The media widely publicized these gender differences, often including the untested claim that the gender differences were biologically based.

The gender difference in the scores remains about the same when the math portion of the SAT is given to the general high school populations for which it was intended. According to the data for 2002, women received an average score of 500, in contrast to 534 for men (J. R. Young, 2002).

Let's shift now to the more general question of the validity of the math section of the SAT. A test has high **validity** if it measures what it is supposed to measure. For example, the SAT is supposed to predict students' grades in college courses. In general, the SAT is valid, because it does predict college grades (D. K. Leonard & Jiang, 1999; Willingham & Cole, 1997). However, the math SAT has a specific validity problem because it *underpredicts* the grades that women will receive in their college math courses.

Consider, for example, Wainer and Steinberg's (1992) study of roughly 47,000 students at 51 different colleges and universities. These researchers looked at math SAT scores earned by males and females who were matched in terms of the grades they earned in college mathematics courses. Wainer and Steinberg found that the women had received math SAT scores that were an average of 33 points lower than those of the men with whom they were matched. For example, suppose that Susan Jones and Robert Smith both received a B in calculus at College X. Looking back at their math SAT scores, we might find that Susan had a score of 600, compared to 633 for Robert. Susan's math SAT score, relative to Robert's score, had substantially underestimated her grade in calculus (Linn & Kessel, 1995).

A similar analysis showed that more than 200 women were denied admission to the University of California at Berkeley each year because the SAT had underpredicted their college grades (D. K. Leonard & Jiang, 1999). Based on validity studies such as these, some colleges and universities have stopped using the SAT or have modified the math SAT requirements (Linn & Kessel, 1995).

Spatial Ability

Most people are familiar with the first two cognitive abilities discussed in this chapter: verbal ability and mathematics ability. Spatial abilities are less well known. **Spatial abilities** include understanding, perceiving, and manipulating shapes and figures. Spatial ability is important in many everyday activities, such as playing electronic games, reading road maps, and arranging furniture in a dormitory room.

Most researchers agree that spatial ability is not unitary. Instead, it has several quite different components (Caplan & Caplan, 1999; Voyer et al., 1995). Most researchers also agree that the gender difference in the mental rotation component of spatial ability—with males performing better than females—is larger than in any other cognitive area (Crawford et al., 1995; Geary, 1995; Halpern, 2001). Let's consider each of these components separately.

Spatial Visualization.   Tasks that use **spatial visualization** require complex processing of spatially presented information. For example, an embedded-figure test requires locating a particular pattern or object that is hidden in a larger design. Demonstration 5.1a illustrates three examples of an embedded-figure test. As a child, you may have tried similar games, perhaps searching for faces in a picture of a woodland scene.

Many individual studies and meta-analyses have concluded that males and females perform fairly similarly on tasks requiring spatial visualization (e.g., Hedges & Nowell, 1995; Scali & Brownlow, 2001; Scali et al., 2000). For example, one meta-analysis of 116 studies produced a *d* of 0.19, a small gender difference suggesting that males are slightly better on this task (Voyer et al., 1995). Glance again at Figure 5.4 for a graph of a similar effect size (*d* = 0.15). As you can see, the overlap for the two distributions is substantial.

Let's consider one specific aspect of spatial visualization, the ability to learn map information. One study found that males performed better, but a similar study reported no gender differences (Beatty & Bruellman, 1987; Galea & Kimura, 1993). Related research indicated that males were better than females in finding their way back to the starting point from a distant location. However, other measures revealed no gender differences (C. A. Lawton, 1996; C. A. Lawton & Morrin, 1999; C. A. Lawton et al., 1996; Saucier et al., 2002; Schmitz, 1999). Another study suggested that males score higher on tests of geography map skills (Henrie et al., 1997). As you can see, the picture is mixed; gender differences are not consistent.

Spatial Perception.   In **spatial perception** tests, the participants are asked to identify a horizontal or vertical location without being distracted by irrelevant information. One example of this skill, a water-level test, is shown in Demonstration 5.1b. Spatial perception is also assessed by the rod-and-frame test, in which participants sit in a darkened room and look at a single rod, which is surrounded by a rectangular frame. The participants are instructed to adjust the rod so that it is in a true vertical position, without being distracted by the cues from the obviously tilted frame. Meta-analyses of gender comparisons for spatial perception show that males receive somewhat higher scores; effect sizes are in the range of 0.40 (Linn & Petersen, 1986; Nordvik & Amponsah, 1998; Voyer et al., 1995, 2000). However, one study found no gender differences on the water-level test (Herlitz et al., 1999), and another study found that gender differences were erased following a brief training session (Vasta et al., 1996).

Mental Rotation.   A test of **mental rotation** measures the ability to rotate a two- or three-dimensional figure rapidly and accurately. This skill is illustrated in the two problems of Demonstration 5.1c. The mental rotation task produces the largest gender differences of all spatial skills, when measured in terms of performance speed. The effect sizes are generally in the range of 0.50 to 0.90

DEMONSTRATION 5.1 ■ ■ ■ ■ ■ ■ ■ ■ ■ ■ ■ ■ ■ ■ ■ ■ ■ ■

Examples of Tests of Spatial Ability

Try these three kinds of tests of spatial ability.

a. **Embedded-Figure Test.** In each of the three units, study the figure on the left. Then cover it up and try to find where it is hidden in the figure on the right. The left-hand figure may need to be shifted in order to locate it in the right-hand figure.

b. **Water-Level Test.** Imagine that this woman is drinking from a glass that is half-filled with water. Draw a line across the glass to indicate where the water line belongs.

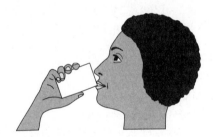

c. **Mental Rotation Test.** If you mentally rotate the figure on the left-hand side, which of the five figures on the right-hand side would you obtain?

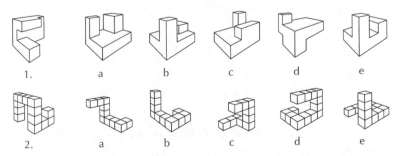

The answers to these three tests appear at the end of the chapter.

(Linn & Petersen, 1985; M. S. Masters & Sanders, 1993; Nordvik & Amponsah, 1998; Voyer et al., 1995). Even though the gender differences for mental rotation tasks are relatively large, we still need to keep the data in perspective. An effect size as large as 0.90 is certainly larger than the other cognitive effect sizes. However, it is trivial compared to the effect size of 2.00 for height, which we discussed earlier (Kimball, 1995). Also, an occasional study reports no gender differences (Halpern & Tan, 2001). In addition, we need to emphasize that females are sometimes just as *accurate* as males on this task, although they may take longer to produce the answer (Loring-Meier & Halpern, 1999).

Furthermore, Favreau (1993) pointed out that statistically significant gender differences often arise from studies in which most males and females actually receive similar scores. Look at Figure 5.5, which Favreau derived from earlier research by Kail and his colleagues (1979). As you can see, most males and females received scores between 2 and 8. The statistically significant gender difference can be traced almost entirely to 20% of the females who had very slow mental rotation speeds (Favreau & Everett, 1996).

Other research shows that gender differences on mental rotation tasks depend on how the task is described to participants. For example, Sharps and his colleagues (1994) found that men performed much better than women when the instructions emphasized the usefulness of these spatial abilities in stereotypically masculine professions, such as piloting military aircraft. When the instructions emphasized how these abilities could help in stereotypically feminine occupations, such as interior decoration, the gender differences disappeared.

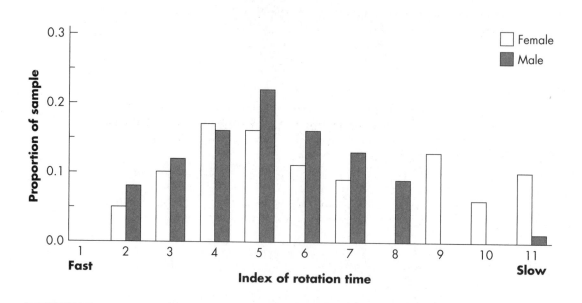

FIGURE 5.5 ■ Amount of time required to mentally rotate a geometric figure, showing a large overlap between males' scores and females' scores. (Note: Faster scores represent better performance.)

Sources: Based on Favreau (1993) and Kail et al. (1979).

What can we conclude about spatial abilities? Even the most well-established gender difference—mental rotation—turns out to be elusive. In fact, any potential deficit is limited to only a small proportion of females, and the gender differences seem to decrease when the instructions emphasize that a spatial skill is related to a traditionally feminine area of interest. In short, this erratic gender difference should not have major implications for women's lives—and it certainly cannot explain why only 10% of U.S. engineers are female!

Explaining the Gender Comparisons

We began this chapter by considering a large number of cognitive skills on which males and females are similar. Then we saw that the gender differences in most verbal skills and most mathematical skills are minimal. The gender differences in mathematical problem solving, spatial perception, and mental rotation are somewhat larger, so we need to consider some potential reasons for the difference. Let's first consider the biological explanations and then turn to the social explanations.

Biological Explanations. It's ironic that the media and some researchers are extremely eager to embrace a biological explanation, even though gender differences are not even well established.[2] In a clear presentation of biological perspectives, Diane Halpern (2000) divided the biological explanations into three major categories: (1) genetics, (2) sex hormones, and (3) brain organization. Let's consider each of these.

1. A genetic explanation suggests that spatial ability might be a recessive trait carried on the X chromosome. However, research has not supported this idea that genetic factors directly produce cognitive gender differences (Halpern, 2000; J. T. E. Richardson, 1997b).

2. Hormones are critically important before birth and during puberty. Could the level of hormones in males and females also account for gender differences in cognitive skills? Here, the results are often complex or contradictory (J. T. E. Richardson, 1997b). For example, men seem to perform better on spatial tasks if they have low levels of male hormones, whereas women seem to perform better if they have high levels of these hormones (Kimura, 1987).

3. The last category of biological explanations focuses on brain organization. Many researchers who favor biological explanations tend to emphasize gender differences in brain lateralization. **Lateralization** means that the two halves (or hemispheres) of the brain function somewhat differently. In humans, the left hemisphere typically specializes in language or verbal tasks, whereas the right hemisphere typically specializes in spatial tasks. (For easy recall, remember that *left* and *language* both begin with the letter *l*.) For most people, either hemisphere

---

[2] Biological factors such as genetics and brain structure are clearly important in accounting for individual differences in various cognitive abilities. For example, these biological factors help explain why some people (both male and female) earn high scores on a math test, whereas other people (again both male and female) earn low scores. As emphasized in this discussion, however, biological factors cannot adequately account for *gender differences*.

can process both language and spatial material. However, the left hemisphere tends to be faster and more accurate on language tasks, and the right hemisphere tends to be faster and more accurate on spatial tasks.

A typical lateralization theory might argue that males use only the right hemisphere to perform spatial tasks, whereas females may use both hemispheres to perform all cognitive tasks (Gur et al., 1999; Halpern, 2000; Kimura, 1999). According to this argument, when females work on a spatial task, a smaller portion of the right hemisphere is available to process spatial information. As a result, they perform the spatial problem more slowly. However, the research does not provide convincing evidence that males actually have more complete lateralization. For example, one study was widely cited as proof that men's brains show more lateralization (B. A. Shaywitz et al., 1995). The popular media failed to emphasize that only 11 of the 19 female participants showed the balanced-hemisphere pattern proposed by lateralization theory (Favreau, 1997).

Still other studies acknowledge gender similarities, but you'll never read about them in your local newspaper. For instance, Gur and his colleagues (1995) concluded that "the two cerebral hemispheres and the brains of men and women are fundamentally more similar than different" (p. 530). In addition, even if we could demonstrate major gender differences in brain lateralization, no one has yet shown that these brain differences actually *cause* the gender differences on cognitive tests (Halpern, 2000; Hyde, 1996b; Hyde & Mezulis, 2001).

Conceivably, at some time in the future, researchers might identify a biological component that helps explain gender differences. However, we need to remember that the differences requiring explanation are neither widespread nor extraordinarily large (Caplan & Caplan, 1999). Indeed, biological explanations may be more powerful than they need to be to explain such small and inconsistent gender differences. Relying on biological explanations is like trying to kill a fly with a baseball bat when a subtler instrument, such as a fly swatter, would be more appropriate.

Social Explanations.   Many theorists have provided social explanations for cognitive gender differences. These explanations can be divided into two categories: (1) different experiences for males and females and (2) different attitudes among males and females.

Experience with a subject clearly influences a person's competence. If you've had frequent experience with maps and other spatial tasks, you'll perform a mental rotation task quickly (Crawford & Chaffin, 1997). Let's examine these gender differences in experience.

1. When elementary textbooks show how people use mathematics, they often include more pictures of boys than girls. The girls may also be shown in helping roles (Kimball, 1995). As Chapters 2 and 3 emphasized, images of competent females can boost the performance of girls and women. If they have more positive images, role models, and experiences, young girls may realize that females can excel in mathematics (D. M. Marx & Roman, 2002; R. L. Pierce & Kite, 1999).

2. Parents and teachers may provide different experiences for males and females. For example, parents spend more time explaining science concepts to their sons than to their daughters (Crowley et al., 2001).

3. Males and females differ in the amount of experience they have with mathematics and spatial activities outside school. Young boys are more likely to play with math and spatial games (Halpern, 2000; J. T. E. Richardson, 1997a; Voyer et al., 2000). Boys are also more likely to belong to a chess club, be members of a math team, learn about numbers in sports, and attend computer summer camp (Hyde, 1996a; L. A. Jackson et al., 1995; Subrahmanyam & Greenfield, 1994).

4. College-bound males are about 10% more likely than their female classmates to take four or more years of high school mathematics. They are also much more likely than females to take science courses, such as physics, which provide extra practice in solving math problems (Catsambis, 1999; Chipman, 1996).

We have reviewed four ways in which males and females may differ in mathematics *experience*. Let's now turn to another social explanation, which focuses on gender differences in *attitudes* about mathematics.

1. Parents' attitudes may influence their children's self-confidence in an indirect fashion. Specifically, if parents hold strong stereotypes about females' poor performance in math, they may convey these stereotypes to their daughters (Frome & Eccles, 1998).

2. By early adolescence, boys perceive themselves as more competent in math than girls do, even though boys may actually receive lower grades (Eccles, Barber, & Jozefowicz et al., 1999; C. M. Steele, 1997). Boys also have more positive attitudes toward mathematics (Eccles, 1994).

3. By high school, many students believe that math, computers, and science are primarily associated with males (Gerrard, 1999; T. J. Smith et al., 2001). As we noted in Chapter 3, people prefer activities that are consistent with their gender role. Accordingly, many females may avoid math because it seems "too masculine." A young woman may say to herself, "Why should I struggle with math when it's a guy thing, and it won't be relevant in my life?"

4. Stereotype threat may decrease females' performance on mathematics and spatial tests. In Chapter 2, we introduced the concept of **stereotype threat;** if you belong to a group that is hampered by a negative stereotype—and you are reminded about your group membership—your performance may suffer (Jussim et al., 2000; C. M. Steele, 1997). Suppose that a young woman is about to take the mathematics test of the SAT. As she sits down, she thinks to herself, "This is a test where women just can't do well." Indeed, her performance may suffer. Be sure to review the important study by Shih and her colleagues (1999) about stereotype threat, discussed on page 65. A later study conducted in Turkey did not find evidence of stereotype threat on a spatial task (Halpern & Tan, 2001). In another study, however, college women in Canada scored lower than men on an SAT-type test when they had been told that the test had previously shown gender differences (M. Walsh et al., 1999). In contrast, no gender differences were found when the students had been

told that the test simply compared Canadian and American students. We cannot yet predict when these gender-related attitudes will influence cognitive performance.

We have examined a large number of biological and social factors that can contribute to the gender differences in spatial and mathematics tasks. We do not currently have a cohesive explanation for the way in which the pieces of the puzzle fit together in accounting for the gender differences. However, as Janet Hyde and Amy Mezulis (2001) concluded, "If the extensive examination of gender differences over the past several decades has taught us anything, it may be that gender differences are (1) often small in magnitude and (2) low in frequency compared with the vast similarities between the sexes" (p. 555). Furthermore, not one of these cognitive gender differences is so substantial that it has major implications for the career performance of women and men, a topic we will explore in Chapter 7.

SECTION SUMMARY ■

Cognitive Abilities

1. No consistent gender differences are found in general intelligence, memory, concept formation, problem solving, or creativity.

2. At present, gender differences in verbal skills and reading disabilities are minimal.

3. Gender differences in mathematics ability are negligible on most tests, although males tend to excel in problem-solving ability after middle school. Females generally receive higher grades than males in their math courses. Males receive higher scores on the SAT mathematics test, a test that underpredicts women's college math grades.

4. Gender differences are minimal on spatial visualization tasks, moderate on spatial perception tasks, and more substantial on mental rotation tasks. Still, most males and females receive similar scores on mental rotation tests. Also, gender differences on spatial tasks disappear when people receive training and when task instructions are altered.

5. Biological explanations for gender differences in cognitive skills include genetics, hormones, and brain organization (e.g., brain lateralization); none of these explanations is strongly supported by the research.

6. Social explanations for gender differences in cognitive skills include several that emphasize gender differences in experience (textbook illustrations, treatment by adults, extracurricular activities, and course work). Several other social explanations focus on math attitudes (parents' attitudes, perceptions of math competence, attitudes toward math, beliefs about math being masculine, and stereotype threat).

ACHIEVEMENT MOTIVATION AND ATTITUDES ABOUT SUCCESS

In the preceding section on gender comparisons in cognitive abilities, we concluded that men and women are generally similar in their thinking skills. The cognitive differences are never large enough to explain the tremendous imbalances in the gender ratios found in many professions. Some observers argue that these imbalances can be traced, instead, to women's lack of motivation; perhaps women simply don't want to achieve. In this part of the chapter, we'll explore **achievement motivation,** which is the desire to accomplish something on your own and to do it well (Hyde & Kling, 2001).

As Kahn and Yoder (1989) noted, many theorists have tried to explain women's absence from certain prestigious fields in terms of personal "deficiencies" that inhibit their achievement. However, you've seen that females actually earn higher grades in math classes than males do and that females are also more likely than males to enroll in college. As we'll see in this section, the research reveals gender similarities in almost every area related to achievement. Personal deficiencies cannot explain the gender differences in career patterns; in Chapter 7, we will explore several other more valid explanations.

Biases in the Research on Achievement Motivation

Before we examine the research on achievement motivation, we should note two interesting biases in this field. First, the tasks on which success is measured are usually stereotypically masculine (Todoroff, 1994). Success may be represented by achievement in a prestigious occupation, academic excellence, or other accomplishments associated with traditionally masculine values. Achievements that are associated with traditionally feminine values receive little or no attention. An adolescent woman may manage to entertain a group of six toddlers so that they are all playing cooperatively. However, psychologists don't typically include this kind of accomplishment among the topics of achievement motivation. Psychologists also don't broaden their views of achievement to include comforting a distressed friend or making a stranger feel welcome. As Theme 3 emphasizes, topics that are traditionally associated with women are underrepresented in the psychological literature.

A second bias applies to most of psychology. Nearly all research on achievement motivation is conducted with college students. These are people who are highly motivated to achieve academic success. Researchers rarely examine achievement motivation in older populations or in nonacademic settings. Furthermore, researchers rarely investigate achievement in people of color or in populations outside North America (Dabul & Russo, 1998; Mednick & Thomas, 1993). Think how achievement motivation might be defined in a different culture (perhaps in Asia or Latin America) that places more emphasis on the well-being of the community. Perhaps achievement motivation might be measured in terms of a person's ability to work well with others or a person's knowledge about the community's history. As you read through this section, keep these limitations in mind.

DEMONSTRATION 5.2   ■

Completing a Story

Write a paragraph in response to one of the following beginning sentences.

If you are a female, complete this sentence with a paragraph: "After first-term finals, Anne finds herself at the top of her medical school class. . . ."

If you are a male, complete this sentence with a paragraph: "After first-term finals, John finds himself at the top of his medical school class. . . ."

Let's begin our exploration of motivation by discussing gender similarities in people's desire for achievement and in their concerns about the negative consequences of success. We'll see that gender differences are sometimes found in self-confidence, although gender similarities are often reported. We'll also see that women and men usually provide similar explanations for their achievements.

Achievement Motivation

Achievement motivation is often measured by asking the study participants to look at drawings of people in various situations and then to create stories based on these drawings. A person receives a high achievement motivation score if these stories emphasize working hard and excelling. The research, conducted with both Black and White participants, shows that males and females are similar in achievement motivation (Hyde & Kling, 2001; Krishman & Sweeney, 1998; Mednick & Thomas, 1993).

Travis and her colleagues (1991) assessed achievement motivation by using another approach. They asked students to recall and describe an event that had occurred in their lives within the past year. Later, the researchers rated the event on a number of scales, such as the extent to which the event described mastering certain skills (e.g., receiving grades or getting a job). Gender differences were not significant; both men and women emphasized mastery in their descriptions.

Try Demonstration 5.2 before reading further.

Fear of Success

So far, our discussion of achievement motivation has emphasized how people are motivated to achieve success. Another strand in the research about achievement motivation focuses on how some people are afraid of this kind of successful achievement. At the end of the 1960s, Matina Horner proposed that women are more likely than men to be afraid of success (e.g., Horner, 1968, 1978). More specifically, Horner proposed that a woman who is high in **fear of success** is afraid that success in competitive achievement situations will produce unpleasant consequences, including unpopularity and a loss of femininity. Men are not afraid of success, Horner said, because achievement is part of the masculine gender role.

When Horner used a technique such as the one illustrated in Demonstration 5.2, she found that women tended to write stories in which a successful woman was socially rejected. Men tended to write stories in which a successful man's hard work brought rich rewards. The popular press was delighted: At last, here was a reason to justify why women were less successful than men!

In the years following Horner's original study, however, the research has shown fairly consistent gender similarities in the fear of success (e.g., Hyde & Kling, 2001; Krishman & Sweeney, 1998; Mednick & Thomas, 1993; Naidoo, 1999). The only fairly recent exception I found was a study of businesswomen and businessmen that used a questionnaire format; many of the questions emphasized negative consequences that people might experience because of gender bias. Not surprisingly, women scored higher on this measure than men did (Fried-Buchalter, 1997). Interestingly, however, a current study shows some good news: Adolescent males and females judge successful women positively (Quatman et al., 2000). In any event, if theorists are searching for a powerful explanation for women's absence from prestigious occupations, they will need to look beyond fear of success (Hyde & Kling, 2001).

Confidence in Your Own Achievement and Ability

Self-confidence is another concept that is intertwined with achievement motivation. As we'll see, gender differences do sometimes emerge in two areas: (1) Men often report more self-confidence than women do, and (2) men's self-confidence may be less influenced by the evaluations provided by other people.

Level of Self-Confidence.   Several studies suggest that men are sometimes more self-confident about their ability than women are[3] (Eccles et al., 1998; Furnham, 2000; Furnham et al., 1999). For example, Furnham and Rawles (1995) found that males estimated their own IQs at an average of 118, in contrast to an estimated average of 112 for females. Other research reveals that males are more likely than females to overestimate their grades on a test of general knowledge (Pulford & Colman, 1997). However, the research on self-confidence typically shows that the specific conditions of a task influence the results. Let's consider several relevant factors:

1. Men are more self-confident than women when making public estimates; gender similarities are found for private estimates (J. Clark & Zehr, 1993; Daubman et al., 1992; Lundeberg et al., 2000). Some interesting research demon-

---

[3] People sometimes assume that women are *under*confident. An alternative viewpoint is that men are *over*confident and that women have the appropriate level of self-confidence (Hyde & Mezulis, 2001; Tavris, 1992).

strates that women are especially likely to give low estimates for their grade point average when another student has already announced that he or she has low grades (Heatherington et al., 1993, 1998). One possible explanation is that women are more likely than men to be modest when they are with other people (Daubman et al., 1992; Wosinska et al., 1996).

2. Men are more self-confident than women on a task that is considered traditionally masculine; gender similarities are found for neutral or traditionally feminine tasks (S. Beyer, 1998; S. Beyer & Bowden, 1997; R. A. Clark, 1993). Brownlow and her colleagues (1998) compared the strategies of contestants on the TV game show *Jeopardy*. On stereotypically masculine topics, men bet a higher percentage of their earnings than the women did. On neutral and stereotypically feminine topics, men and women used similar betting strategies.

3. Men are more self-confident than women when no feedback is provided; gender similarities are found when people are given clear feedback about how they had performed (Sleeper & Nigro, 1987). For example, in one study, students estimated their grades for introductory psychology (S. Beyer, 1999b). For the first test, at the beginning of the semester, male students overestimated their grades more than female students did. When students learned about their grades on this first test, these grades provided feedback about their performance. On subsequent tests, the gender difference decreased.

Try Demonstration 5.3 before reading further.

Self-Confidence and Evaluation Provided by Others. We've seen that gender differences in self-confidence sometimes emerge, especially for public estimates of ability, for traditionally masculine tasks, and for situations when no feedback is provided. Now let's consider a second issue, focusing on the *stability* of a per-

---

DEMONSTRATION 5.3 ■ ■ ■ ■ ■ ■ ■ ■ ■ ■ ■ ■ ■ ■ ■ ■ ■

Reactions to Comments from Other People

Imagine that you have given a presentation on a project to an important group of people. Afterward, someone approaches you and says that you did a very good job: You were clear and articulate, and your ideas were interesting. Someone else rejects everything you had to say and disagrees with all your proposals. Then a third person comments, not on the content of your presentation but on your excellent speaking style.

How much would the feedback from these other people influence your self-confidence? Would your confidence rise or fall, depending on the nature of the comments, or would your self-evaluations tend to remain fairly constant?

Source: Based on T. Roberts (1991, p. 297).

son's self-confidence. Specifically, Tomi-Ann Roberts and Susan Nolen-Hoeksema (1989, 1994) demonstrated that women's self-confidence is influenced by comments from other people. In contrast, men's self-confidence is more stable. Compared to these findings, how did you respond to Demonstration 5.3?

In an important study on responses to others' comments, Roberts and Nolen-Hoeksema (1989) asked students to work on a series of challenging cognitive tasks. After several minutes, the participants rated their self-confidence in terms of the likelihood that they could do well on the task. A few minutes later, half of the participants—chosen at random—received positive comments from the researcher (e.g., "You are doing very well" or "You are above average at this point in the task"). The other half of the participants received negative comments ("You are not doing very well" or "You are below average at this point in the task"). Several minutes later, they all rated their self-confidence a second time.

Figure 5.6 shows the change in self-confidence between the first rating period and the second rating period. Notice that the men's self-confidence ratings were not significantly changed by the nature of the comments other people provided. When the men received positive comments, their self-confidence barely rose;

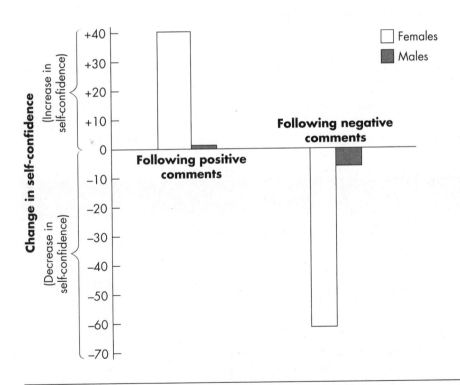

FIGURE 5.6 ■ Change in self-confidence, following either positive or negative comments. (Note: Negative numbers indicate a decrease in self-confidence; positive numbers indicate an increase.)

Source: Based on T. Roberts and Nolen-Hoeksema (1989).

their self-confidence dipped only slightly following negative comments. In contrast, the women's self-confidence rose dramatically after receiving positive comments, and it fell even more dramatically after receiving negative comments. More recent research confirms that women are more likely than men to use other people's evaluations to assess their own achievements (Van Blyderveen & Wood, 2001).

But *why* should men and women react so differently to people's comments? In further research, Roberts and Nolen-Hoeksema (1994) replicated their earlier findings. They also discovered that women were more likely than men to believe that other people's evaluations were accurate assessments of their performance. Women are therefore more likely to use the information from these evaluations in assessing their own performance, even when the evaluations are not accurate.

When I first read about these gender differences in response to others' comments, I confess that I was dismayed. Men apparently trust their own judgments, whereas women seem to adjust their self-confidence in response to whatever comments they happen to hear. But then I recalled the male-as-normative issue, discussed on page 62 in Chapter 2 (Tavris, 1992). Maybe we shouldn't conclude that men are stable and that women are fickle. Instead, men may be overly rigid, trusting their initial judgment, even when it may be inappropriate. In contrast, women may be appropriately flexible, willing to listen and to respond to new information! Ideally, people *should* respond to evaluations from well-informed experts (presumably including the researcher conducting a psychology experiment).

Attributions for Your Own Success

Be sure to try Demonstration 5.4 before reading further. This demonstration asks you to make attributions about your own performance on an achievement task. **Attributions** are explanations about the causes of your behavior. When you

---

DEMONSTRATION 5.4 ■ ■ ■ ■ ■ ■ ■ ■ ■ ■ ■ ■ ■ ■ ■ ■ ■

Explaining Successful Performance

Think about the last time you received a good grade on a test. A number of different factors could have been responsible for your success. Four possible factors are listed below. You have 100 points to divide among these four factors. Assign points to reflect the extent to which each factor contributed to your success; the points must add up to 100.

_____ I have high ability for the subject that was covered on that test.

_____ I put a lot of effort into studying for that test.

_____ The test was easy.

_____ It was just luck.

have been successful on an achievement task, you generally attribute that success to some combination of four factors: (1) ability, (2) effort, (3) task easiness, and (4) luck. Keep your own answers to Demonstration 5.4 in mind as we examine the research on gender comparisons in attribution patterns.

Incidentally, this topic of attributions may seem somewhat familiar, because we examined a similar topic in connection with gender stereotypes in Chapter 2. In that chapter, we saw that the gender of the *stimulus* often influences attributions; specifically, when people make judgments about men, they tend to attribute the success of men to their high ability. In contrast, when people make judgments about women, they tend to attribute the success of women to other factors, such as an easy task or luck. In this chapter, however, we are examining the gender of the *subject*. In particular, we will see whether women and men use different attributions when making judgments about *their own* success.

During the 1970s, several studies suggested that, when males are successful, they give credit to their ability. In contrast, when females are successful, they choose explanations other than ability (e.g., Deaux, 1979). These early studies suggested that a woman who has received a high exam score might say, "Well, this test was relatively easy, and I really studied hard for it, so that's why I received an A."

However, two meta-analyses concluded that gender differences in attributional patterns are minimal (Sohn, 1982; Whitley et al., 1986). Other research and reviews of the literature also conclude that women and men are similar in the reasons they provide for their success or failure (Gaeddert, 1987; Mednick & Thomas, 1993; Travis et al., 1991).

Consider a representative study. Russo and her colleagues (1991) asked public administrators to evaluate the importance of a variety of factors in explaining their own professional success. Both men and women explained their success in terms of ability and hard work, and the two genders supplied similar ratings for these two factors.

In short, attributions for success tend to show the same pattern of gender similarities that we observed in our earlier discussion of cognitive abilities, achievement motivation, and fear of success. (Remember, however, that gender differences are somewhat common in areas related to self-confidence.)

Although gender similarities in attributions are most common, gender differences are found in some social settings and on some kinds of tasks:

1. Women are likely to avoid saying "I did well because I have high ability" when making public statements, whereas men are somewhat more comfortable about mentioning high ability in public. When men and women provide attributions in private, their responses may be similar (J. H. Berg et al., 1981).

2. Men are more likely than women to cite ability as an explanation for their success on stereotypically masculine tasks, such as grades in natural science, mathematics, and business courses (C. R. Campbell & Henry, 1999; Li & Adamson, 1995). However, women are more likely than men to use ability explanations on stereotypically feminine tasks, such as comforting a friend or earning high grades in an English course (S. Beyer, 1998/1999; R. A. Clark, 1993).

3. Women who are low in ability and general achievement motivation—and who support traditional gender roles—are more likely than men to attribute

their success to luck. In contrast, women who are high in ability and general achievement motivation—and who are nontraditional—are fairly similar to men; they typically attribute their success to ability (Crombie, 1983; Eccles et al., 1984).

At the beginning of this section on achievement motivation, we saw that theorists have often favored a "women are deficient" rationale to explain why women are less likely than men to hold prestigious positions in society. However, the discussion of attributions reveals the same pattern we have found throughout most parts of this chapter. Consistent with Theme 1, women and men are typically similar. When gender differences do emerge, they can usually be traced to characteristics of the social setting or the task. With attribution patterns, the gender differences are so small and readily modifiable that a blame-the-person explanation does not seem useful.

We have emphasized in this chapter that women resemble men in both cognitive ability and motivational factors. In Chapter 6, we will continue our search for explanations about the lack of women in prestigious occupations. Specifically, we will consider gender comparisons in social and personality characteristics. Then, in Chapter 7, we will turn our attention to women's work experiences to try to identify external factors that account for gender differences in employment patterns.

SECTION SUMMARY ■

Achievement Motivation and Attitudes About Success

1. The research on topics related to achievement motivation typically focuses on stereotypically masculine tasks and European American college students.

2. Women and men are similar in their achievement motivation.

3. Men and women do not differ in their fear of success.

4. Men are sometimes more self-confident than women on achievement tasks, especially those involving public estimates of self-confidence, traditionally masculine tasks, or no feedback on performance.

5. Women's self-confidence is more likely than men's to be influenced by comments from other people.

6. Women and men tend to use similar attributions when explaining their successes. However, gender differences may emerge when making statements in public and when performing gender-stereotyped tasks; also, traditionally feminine women who have low ability and motivation are likely to attribute their success to luck.

▪▪▪▪▪ CHAPTER REVIEW QUESTIONS ▪▪▪▪▪

1. Suppose that your local newspaper carries the headline: "Test Shows Males More Creative." The article reports that the average male scored 78 on a creativity test compared to 75 for females. Based on the cautions discussed at the beginning of this chapter, why would you be hesitant to conclude that the gender differences in creativity are substantial?

2. We emphasized in this chapter that we should not discourage people from pursuing careers on the basis of their gender. Considering the information about cognitive abilities and topics related to achievement motivation, what evidence do we have for this point?

3. Recall the cognitive abilities for which no consistent gender differences have been reported. Think of several men and several women whom you know well. Do the conclusions about those abilities match your observations about these individuals?

4. Imagine that a third-grade teacher comments to you that the girls in her class have much better verbal abilities than the boys. What would you answer, based on the information in this chapter?

5. The sections on mathematics and spatial abilities showed inconsistent gender differences. Which areas showed the smallest gender differences, and which showed the largest? Which potential biological and social explanations might account for these differences?

6. Suppose that a woman you know has read an article about fear of success in a popular magazine marketed to young businesswomen. She asks you whether the article is correct: Do women have a significantly higher fear of success than men do? Answer her with the information from this chapter.

7. The research on topics related to achievement motivation illustrates how gender differences rarely apply to all people in all situations. Describe some variables that determine whether gender differences will be found in self-confidence and in attributions for one's own success. Although the research on fear of success shows gender similarities, which of these variables could also apply to fear of success?

8. We discussed three factors that influence whether gender differences will be found with respect to self-confidence in achievement settings. Keeping these factors in mind, think of a concrete situation in which gender differences are relatively large. Then think of an example of a situation in which gender differences should be minimal.

9. In Chapter 6, we'll see that, in comparison to men, women are somewhat more attuned to the emotions of other people. How is this sensitivity to emotions related to an observation in the current chapter, that women are somewhat more attuned to social factors and other people's emotions when they make judgments about self-confidence and attributions for success? Also, how is sensitivity to others related to the discussion of self-confidence on pages 163 to 166?

10. To solidify your knowledge in preparation for the chapter on women and work (Chapter 7), think of a profession in which relatively few women are employed. Review each of the cognitive abilities and motivational factors discussed in this chapter. Note whether any of these factors provide a sufficient explanation for the relative absence of women in that profession.

NEW TERMS

*frequency distribution (145)
*box-score approach (146)
 counting approach (146)

*meta-analysis (147)
*verbal fluency (149)
*reading disability (150)

*validity (153)
*spatial abilities (153)
*spatial visualization (154)
*spatial perception (154)
*mental rotation (154)

*lateralization (157)
*stereotype threat (159)
*achievement motivation (161)
*fear of success (163)
*attributions (166)

 The terms asterisked in the New Terms section serve as good search terms for InfoTrac College Edition. Go to http://infotrac.thomsonlearning.com and try these added search terms.

RECOMMENDED READINGS

Caplan, P. J., Crawford, M., Hyde, J. S., & Richardson, J. T. E. (Eds.). (1997). *Gender differences in human cognition.* New York: Oxford University Press. I recommend this book, which contains five chapters on topics such as meta-analyses, social influences on cognitive abilities, and the interesting issue of our culture's enchantment with gender differences.

Clinchy, B. M., & Norem, J. K. (Eds.). (1998). *The gender and psychology reader.* New York: New York University Press. Several chapters in this book are relevant to gender comparisons in cognitive abilities and motivation. I especially recommend the chapters on achievement at the end of the book.

Halpern, D. F. (2000). *Sex differences in cognitive abilities* (3rd ed.). Mahwah, NJ: Erlbaum. Diane Halpern writes about gender comparisons in a clear and interesting fashion; she emphasizes that gender differences arise from a combination of biological and social factors.

Worell, J. (Ed.). (2001). *The encyclopedia of women and gender.* San Diego: Academic Press. I strongly recommend this two-volume encyclopedia for college libraries, especially because the entries are written by prominent researchers and theorists in the field of psychology of women. Especially relevant for the current chapter are the chapters on achievement and gender difference research.

ANSWERS TO THE DEMONSTRATIONS

Demonstration 5.1: a.1: Rotate the pattern so that it looks like two mountain peaks, and place the leftmost segment along the top-left portion of the little white triangle. a.2: This pattern fits along the right side of the two black triangles on the left. a.3: Rotate this figure about 100 degrees to the right, so that it forms a slightly slanted Z, with the top line coinciding with the top line of the top white triangle. b. The line should be horizontal, not tilted. c. 1c, 2d.

ANSWERS TO THE TRUE-FALSE QUESTIONS

1. False (p. 148); 2. False (pp. 149–150); 3. True (p. 151); 4. False (p. 152); 5. True (p. 154); 6. True (p. 161); 7. False (pp. 162–163); 8. True (pp. 163–164); 9. True (pp. 164–165); 10. False (p. 167).

Gender Comparisons in Social and Personality Characteristics

Jon Feingersh/Corbis

Communication Patterns
Verbal Communication
Nonverbal Communication
Potential Explanations
for Gender Differences
in Communication

**Characteristics Related
to Helping and Caring**
Altruism
Nurturance

Empathy
Moral Judgments Concerning
Other People
Friendship

**Characteristics Related to
Aggression and Power**
Gender and Aggression:
The Social Constructionists'
Concerns

Overt Aggression Versus
Relational Aggression
Gender and Aggression:
Other Important Factors
Leadership
Persuasion

TRUE OR FALSE?

_____ 1. Gender differences in social behavior tend to be especially large when people's behavior is measured in terms of self-report.

_____ 2. In most situations, adult women talk significantly more than adult men do.

_____ 3. Women tend to look at their conversational partners more than men do, especially when talking with someone of the same gender.

_____ 4. In general, women are more helpful to other people than men are.

_____ 5. Women are consistently more interested in infants than men are, according to several different measures of interest.

_____ 6. The research shows that women make moral decisions on the basis of caring relationships with others, whereas men make moral decisions on the basis of laws and regulations.

_____ 7. According to self-reports, men are just as satisfied with their friendships as women are.

_____ 8. One consistent gender difference is that men are more aggressive than women.

_____ 9. The current research shows that men and women have very different kinds of leadership styles.

_____ 10. Men are more likely to be persuaded by a woman who uses tentative language than by a woman who uses assertive language.

Shortly after I began revising this chapter, my attention was captured by the cover of *People* magazine. "Heroes Among Us," proclaimed one of the titles. I expected yet another article about heroic men who rescued timid women. However, the stories were refreshingly gender balanced. Yes, Brian Schimpf, an air-traffic controller, continued to guide planes toward a safe landing, even in the midst of an earthquake. Yes, 11-year-old Chris Haney had scrambled up a pine tree to rescue his 9-year-old friend Samantha, who had climbed the tree on a dare—and had received a 7,200-volt shock from a power line. However, the lead story featured 14-year-old Amanda Valance, who had rescued her friend Edna from the jaws of an alligator—while their male classmates ran away. And Norma Bentzel, an elementary school principal, heroically protected her kindergarten students from an angry man who was beginning to attack the children with a machete (N. Charles et al., 2001).

In Chapter 5, we saw that gender similarities are common when we consider cognitive abilities and achievement. In this chapter about social and personality characteristics, we'll once again observe occasional small to moderate gender differences but many gender similarities (Eagly, 2001; M. C. Hamilton, 2001). For example, we'll see that males are somewhat more likely than females to be heroic rescuers, although the overall differences in helping behavior are not large. Also, in this chapter we will explore gender comparisons in communication patterns, characteristics associated with helping and caring, and characteristics associated with aggression and power.

We'll see that the social constructionist perspective is especially useful in examining social behavior, as we have emphasized several times throughout this textbook. According to the **social constructionist approach,** we construct or invent our own versions of reality, based on prior experiences in our culture. The social constructionist approach often focuses on language as a mechanism for categorizing our experiences, for example, our experiences about gender (Cosgrove, 2000).

A colleague provided an excellent example of the way we construct personality characteristics (K. Bursik, personal communication, 1997). Quickly answer the following question: Who are more emotional, men or women? Most people immediately respond, "Women, of course" (J. R. Kelly & Hutson-Comeaux, 2000). But what kinds of emotions did you consider? Only sadness and crying? Why don't we include anger, one of the primary human emotions? When a man pounds his fist into a wall in anger, we don't comment, "Oh, he's so emotional." The fact is that our culture constructs the word *emotional* to refer primarily to the emotions typically associated with women. As we'll see in the final section of this chapter, social constructionism also shapes the way we view aggression; we define the word *aggression* primarily in terms of the kinds of aggression associated with men.

Every day, we construct what it means to be male and female in our society. When social constructionists examine gender, they focus on a central question: How does our culture create gender and maintain it in our interpersonal relationships and communication patterns (Gergen, 2001)?

You and I do not construct gender independently. Instead, our culture provides us with schemas and other information; all this information operates like a set of lenses through which we can interpret the events in our lives (Bem, 1993; Shields, 2002). In Chapters 2 and 3, we examined how the media provide cultural lenses for both adults and children. Females are represented as gentle, nurturant, and submissive, whereas men are represented as independent, self-confident, and aggressive. Our culture has established different social roles for women and men, so we should find that people typically want to uphold these ideals (Eagly, 2001).

As you read this chapter, keep in mind some of the gender comparison issues we raised in Chapter 5. For example, we saw that people's self-confidence and their attribution patterns are influenced by the social setting. Social factors have only a modest impact on cognitive and achievement tasks, because these tasks are typically performed in relative isolation. The social situation is more important when we consider social and personality characteristics. Humans talk, smile, help, and act aggressively in the presence of other people. The social situation provides a rich source of information that people examine in order to make sense out of the world. If the social situation has such an important influence on whether people act in a gender-stereotyped fashion, then a characteristic such as "nurturant" is not an inevitable, essential component of all females. Furthermore, a characteristic such as "aggressive" is not an inevitable, essential component of all males.

Several factors related to the social setting have an important influence on the size of the gender differences in social and personality characteristics (Aries, 1996; Eagly & Karau, 1991; N. Eisenberg & Lennon, 1983; M. C. Hamilton, 2001; J. B. James, 1997). Here are some examples:

1. *Gender differences are largest when behavior is measured in terms of self-report.* Women are more likely than men to *report* that they are extremely nurturant. In contrast, differences are smaller when behavior is measured by some method less influenced by people's ideas about how they should behave. For example, we'll see that women and men are fairly similar when we observe and record their *behavior* objectively.

2. *Gender differences are largest when other people are present.* For instance, women are especially likely to react positively to infants when other people are nearby.

3. *Gender differences are largest when gender is prominent and other shared roles are minimized.* For example, at a singles bar, gender is emphasized strongly, and gender differences are likely to be large. In contrast, at a professional conference of accountants—where men and women occupy the same work role—the work role will be emphasized, and gender differences will be small.

4. *Gender differences are largest when the behavior requires specific gender-related skills.* For example, men might be especially likely to volunteer to change a tire or perform a similar skill traditionally associated with men in our culture.

Notice, then, that gender differences are especially prominent when a social situation encourages us to think about gender and to wear an especially strong set of gender lenses. In other social situations, however, women and men behave with remarkable similarity. Our exploration of social characteristics in this chapter will focus on three clusters: (1) communication patterns, (2) characteristics related to helping and caring, and (3) characteristics related to aggression and power.

COMMUNICATION PATTERNS

The word *communication* typically suggests verbal communication, or communication with words. Many people have strong gender stereotypes about this topic; for example, they often think that women are more chatty. The research results may surprise you.

Communication can also be nonverbal. **Nonverbal communication** refers to all human communication that does not use words, such as eye movements, tone of voice, facial expression, and even how far you stand from another person. Nonverbal communication can effectively convey messages of power and emotion, but we typically pay less attention to nonverbal communication than to verbal communication. Still, research has uncovered some substantial gender differences in nonverbal communication that are worth exploring.

Both verbal and nonverbal communication are essential in our daily interactions. Unless you are reading this sentence before breakfast, you have already seen and spoken to many people, smiled at others, and perhaps avoided eye contact with still others. Let's examine verbal and nonverbal communication for gender comparisons.

Verbal Communication

John Gray's best-selling book, *Men Are From Mars, Women Are From Venus*, claims that men and women "almost seem to be from different planets, speaking different languages" (Gray, 1992, p. 5). Gray's book is based on speculation and informal observations rather than actual research. In reality, within each gender, we find great variation in verbal communication patterns, and social factors influence whether we observe gender differences (Aries, 1998; Bing & Bergvall, 1998; Freed, 1996). Let's consider the research.

Talkativeness.   According to the long-standing stereotype, women chatter for hours (Holmes, 1998). In reality, however, males are typically more talkative, based on data gathered in elementary classrooms, college classrooms, and college students' conversations (Aries, 1998; Crawford, 1995; Romaine, 1999). In one study, Spender (1989) recorded pairs of faculty members in conversation; each pair consisted of one man and one woman. In each pair, the man spoke for more minutes than the woman. Afterward, Spender asked each person whether he or she had contributed a fair share of the conversation. Most of the men believed they had *not* had a fair share, even when they had spoken for 58% to 75% of the time.

Interruptions.   Do men also interrupt more frequently than women? As we've seen throughout this book, the only honest answer is often, "It depends." For example, in this particular case, the answer depends on the operational definition of the word *interruption*. As we noted in Chapter 1, an **operational definition** tells exactly how a variable in a study will be measured. Suppose that you are telling a story about meeting a famous person and a listener interrupts after your first two sentences to say, "Oh, that sounds like the time I . . ." This kind of interruption, called a successful interruption, occurs when the interrupter takes over the conversation. When researchers look only at these intrusive, successful interruptions, they find that men tend to interrupt more than women (K. J. Anderson & Leaper, 1998). Suppose, however, that you are telling a story. The listener appears interested and, from time to time, says "uh-huh." However, the listener makes no attempt to take over the conversation. Some researchers use an operational definition of *interruption* that includes these friendly comments as well as successful interruptions. (Yes, I agree: It doesn't really seem fair!) With this more inclusive definition, the gender differences are negligible (K. J. Anderson & Leaper, 1998).

Also, the research sometimes compares high-status men in conversation with low-status women. This research typically finds that men interrupt more than women do. However, power, not gender, could explain the interruptions (Romaine, 1999). Other studies suggest that men interrupt significantly more often than women do in conversations with relative strangers and in competitive task settings. However, gender differences may be minimal in other situations (Aries, 1996, 1998; C. Johnson, 1994; C. West & Zimmerman, 1998b).

Language Style.   Some theorists suggest that women's language style is very different from men's (e.g., Lakoff, 1990). In reality, the gender differences are subtle (Mulac, 1998). Men *are* likely to curse more often and to use a larger vocabulary of obscene words (Jay, 2000; Winters & Duck, 2001). However, other research shows only minimal gender differences in politeness during conversations or in writing style (Cameron et al., 1993; D. L. Rubin & Greene, 1992, 1994). Carli (1990) studied disclaimers such as "I'm not sure" and "I suppose." When women were talking to other women, they used these disclaimers rarely, as did men in their conversations with other men. However, when women and men are talking with each other, women are much more likely than men to use these disclaimers. Once again, we need to know the social setting before we can draw conclusions about language and other social behavior.

The Content of Language.   We have discussed *how* women and men talk, but what do they talk about? R. A. Clark (1998) asked female and male students at the University of Illinois to report on all topics mentioned in their most recent conversation with a student of the same gender. As you can see from Figure 6.1,

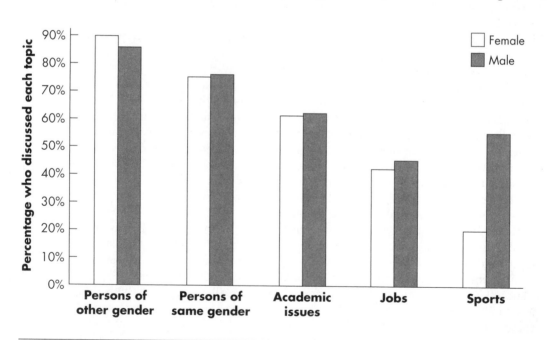

FIGURE 6.1 ■ Percentage of women and men who discussed each of five topics in a recent conversation with a friend of the same gender.
Source: Based on R. A. Clark (1998).

the gender similarities are striking. In fact, the only statistically significant gender difference is in talking about sports.

Let's consider one other important point about conversations. In our list of four generalizations about gender comparisons, we noted that gender differences are small when other roles are emphasized. S. A. Wheelan and Verdi (1992) illustrated this point clearly. They observed professionals in business, government, and service-oriented occupations who were attending a four-day group relations conference. In other words, this was a setting in which work-related roles would be prominent. Men and women were found to be similar in the nature of their verbal contributions to the discussion groups. For example, men and women were similar in the number of statements that challenged the leadership and also in the number of statements that supported other people's remarks.

The groups in Wheelan and Verdi's study met for extended periods, between 4½ and 6 hours; most other studies have recorded relatively brief conversations. In Chapter 2, we saw that stereotypes are especially likely to operate when people have little additional information about a person's qualifications. When people initially meet each other, these stereotypes may suppress a competent woman's comments. As time passes, however, other group members begin to appreciate the woman's remarks, and their expectations become less gender based. As a consequence, gender differences may grow smaller as conversations become longer. By looking at a wide range of conversations, Aries (1998) confirmed that gender is a relatively unimportant factor in conversational content when groups have met for a long time.

Nonverbal Communication

Try turning off the sound on a television game show and observing the nonverbal behavior. You could write down a transcript of the conversation between Mr. Game Show Host and Ms. Contestant, and yet that transcript would fail to capture much of the subtle communication between these two people. The nonverbal aspects of conversation are extremely important in conveying social messages. As we'll note later in this chapter, gender differences are often substantial in certain kinds of nonverbal behavior, such as personal space, body position, and smiling.

Let's examine several components of nonverbal communication, beginning with the nonverbal messages that people send by means of their personal space, body posture, gaze, and facial expression. A fifth topic, decoding ability, examines gender comparisons in interpreting these nonverbal messages. As we'll see throughout this section, gender differences in nonverbal communication are typically larger than other kinds of gender differences (J. A. Hall, 1998). We'll also consider individual differences in nonverbal communication as well as explanations and implications of these gender comparisons.

Now turn the page and try Demonstration 6.1 before you read any further.

DEMONSTRATION 6.1   ■ ■ ■ ■ ■ ■ ■ ■ ■ ■ ■ ■ ■ ■ ■ ■ ■ ■

Gender Differences in Body Posture

Which of these figures is a girl, and which is a boy? What cues did you use to reach your decision?

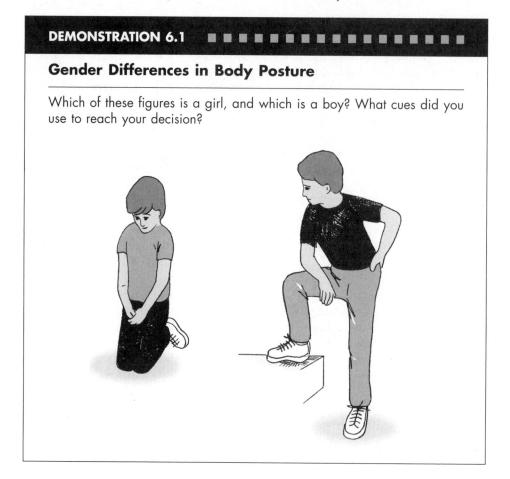

Personal Space. The term **personal space** refers to the invisible boundary around each person that other people should not invade during ordinary social interactions. You are probably most aware of personal space when a stranger comes too close and makes you feel uncomfortable. In general, women have smaller personal-space zones than men (Briton & Hall, 1995; M. LaFrance & Henley, 1997; Payne, 2001). Therefore, when two women are talking to each other, they sit closer together than two men do. In the world of work, high-status individuals occupy larger physical work spaces than low-status individuals (Bate & Bowker, 1997). In general, the executives (mostly men) occupy spacious offices, whereas the low-ranking employees (mostly women) work in relatively crowded conditions.

Body Posture. Gender differences in body posture develop early in life. The drawings in Demonstration 6.1 were traced from yearbook pictures of two fifth-graders, and then other cues about gender were equated. The figure on the left can be easily identified as a girl, whereas the one on the right is clearly a boy. A glance through magazines will convince you of further gender differences in body posture. Notice that females keep their legs together, with their arms and hands close to their bodies. In contrast, males sit and stand with their legs apart, and their hands and arms move away from their bodies. Men look relaxed; even when resting, women keep their postures more tensely contained (Bate & Bowker, 1997; J. A. Hall, 1984).

Notice how this observation meshes with the gender differences we have discussed. Men often use more conversational space in their verbal interactions. Similarly, men use more personal space (distance from other people), and their own body postures require greater physical space. As Demonstration 6.1 illustrates, even young children have mastered "gender-appropriate" body language.

Gaze.   A classic film on gender includes a fairly lengthy interview with a married couple named Richard and Carol, who are doing their best to avoid a gender-stereotyped relationship. However, their gaze patterns reveal that they are still somewhat traditional. When Richard speaks, Carol gazes at him admiringly. When Carol speaks, Richard looks around the room.

Gender as a subject variable is important. Research has shown that females gaze more at their conversational partners than males do (Briton & Hall, 1995; M. LaFrance & Henley, 1997). This gender difference emerges during childhood; even young girls spend more time looking at their conversational partners.

Gender as a stimulus variable seems to be even more powerful than gender as a subject variable. Specifically, people gaze *at* females more than they gaze *at* males (J. A. Hall, 1984, 1987). The result with gazing is that two women speaking to each other are likely to have frequent eye contact. In contrast, two men in conversation are likely to avoid looking at each other for long periods of time. Prolonged eye contact is relatively uncommon between two men.

Facial Expression.   Gender differences in facial expression are substantial. The most noticeable difference is that women smile more than men do (J. A. Hall et al., 2000; Hecht & LaFrance, 1998; Stoppard & Gruchy, 1993). In one meta-analysis of 147 gender comparisons of smiling frequency, the d was 0.40. Consistent with the discussion at the beginning of the chapter, men and women have similar facial expressions when alone in a room. When other people are present, however, substantial gender differences emerge (M. LaFrance & Hecht, 2000).

The magazines you examine in Demonstration 6.2 are likely to reveal smiling women and somber men. An inspection of yearbooks will probably confirm this gender difference (J. Mills, 1984; Ragan, 1982). Ragan examined nearly 1,300 portrait photographs and found that women were nearly twice as likely as men to smile broadly. In contrast, men were about eight times as likely as women to show *no* smile.

The gender difference in smiling has important social implications. For example, we know that positive responses, such as smiling, can have an effect on the person who receives these pleasant messages. Specifically, the recipients begin to act in a more competent fashion (P. A. Katz et al., 1993; Word et al.,

---

DEMONSTRATION 6.2 ■ ■ ■ ■ ■ ■ ■ ■ ■ ■ ■ ■ ■ ■ ■ ■ ■ ■

Gender Differences in Smiling

For this demonstration, you will first need to assemble some magazines that contain photos of people. Inspect the photos to identify smiling faces. (Let's define a smile as an expression in which the corners of the mouth are at least slightly upturned.) Record the number of women who smile, and divide it by the total number of women to calculate the percentage of women who smile. Repeat the process to calculate the percentage of men who smile. How do those two percentages compare? Does the gender comparison seem to depend on the kind of magazine you are examining (e.g., fashion magazine versus news magazine)?

Next, locate a high school or college yearbook. Examine the portraits, and calculate the percentages of women and of men who are smiling. How do these two percentages compare?

1974). When a typical man and woman interact, the woman's smiles may produce feelings of competence and self-confidence in the man. However, the typical man does not smile much to encourage a woman.

The gender difference in smiling also has a dark interpretation. You may have noticed that some women smile bravely when someone makes fun of them, tells an embarrassing joke in their presence, or sexually harasses them. As J. A. Hall and Halberstadt (1986) reported, social tension is the strongest predictor of smiling in women. In other words, women often smile because they feel uncomfortable in the current social setting, not because they are enjoying the social interaction.

So far, our exploration of facial expressions has mentioned only smiling. Another gender difference focuses on the ability to send various nonverbal messages through facial expression. In these studies, the research participants watch a variety of film clips designed to elicit a range of emotions, such as happiness, sadness, disgust, and fear. Compared to men, women typically show greater changes in facial expression (Kring & Gordon, 1998). Also, women are typically better at conveying these emotions to other people (Briton & Hall, 1995; Shields, 1995).

You may recall our earlier discussion of research on adults' biased interpretation of infants' facial expressions. Specifically, when a baby has an unhappy facial expression, adults who believe that the baby is a girl tend to label that expression "fear." In contrast, adults who believe that the baby is a boy tend to label that expression "anger" (Condry & Condry, 1976; Plant et al., 2000). We find a similar effect when people judge adults' facial expressions. Algoe and her colleagues (2000) asked college students to make judgments about the facial expressions of adult males and females in photographs. These photos are part of a standardized set and were carefully chosen so that the males and the females showed similarly intense emotions.

Let's consider a representative portion of the data from the study by Algoe and her colleagues (2000). Specifically, we'll focus on people's interpretations about a photo of an angry person who was described as an employee involved in a workplace incident. Figure 6.2 shows the ratings of this photo, where a rating of 0 represents the lowest amount of an emotion and a rating of 7 represents the highest amount of an emotion. As you can see, the male was judged to be showing somewhat more anger than the female. Even more interesting, however, is that the angry female was judged to be showing a moderate amount of *fear*, much more than the angry male. Apparently, when people look at an angry woman, they perceive that she is actually somewhat afraid.

Decoding Ability.   So far, we have seen evidence of gender differences in several kinds of nonverbal behavior: personal space, body posture, gaze, and facial expression. Decoding ability is somewhat different because it requires receiving messages rather than sending them. **Decoding ability** refers to competence in figuring out, from another person's nonverbal behavior, what emotion that person is feeling. A person who is a skilled decoder can notice a friend's facial expression, body posture, and tone of voice and deduce whether that person is in a good mood or a bad mood.

According to reviews of the research, females are more likely than males to decode nonverbal expressions accurately (J. A. Hall, 1998; M. LaFrance &

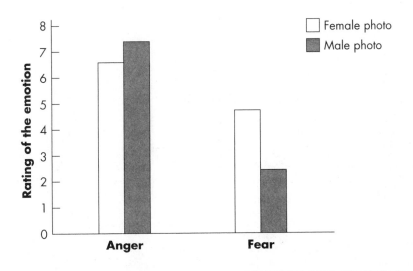

FIGURE 6.2 ■ Ratings of anger and fear when judging the photo of an angry female or male "employee." (Note: Minimum rating = 0; maximum rating = 8.)
Source: Based on Algoe et al. (2000).

Henley, 1997; McClure, 2000). For example, one meta-analysis of the research yielded a moderate effect size ($d = 0.41$); women were better decoders in 106 of 133 gender comparisons (J. A. Hall, 1984; J. A. Hall et al., 2000).

During infancy, baby girls are more skilled than baby boys in visually discriminating between adults' facial expressions, although the explanation for this gender difference is not clear (McClure, 2000). During childhood and adolescence, females are better decoders than males (McClure, 2000). The gender difference also holds true cross-culturally, as evidenced by studies conducted in countries as varied as Greece, New Guinea, Japan, and Poland (Biehl et al., 1997; J. A. Hall, 1984). Incidentally, the research in Canada and the United States typically examines European Americans. It would be interesting to see whether the gender differences are consistent in all ethnic groups.

So far, we have focused on gender differences in decoding emotion from facial expressions. Bonebright and her colleagues (1996) examined people's ability to decode emotion from *vocal* cues. They instructed trained actors to record paragraph-long stories, each time using their voice to portray a specified emotion: fear, anger, happiness, sadness, or neutral emotion. Then, undergraduate students were asked to listen to each recorded paragraph and determine which emotion the speaker was trying to portray. As you can see from Figure 6.3, women were more accurate than men in decoding voices that expressed fear, happiness, and sadness; these gender differences were small but consistent. No gender differences were found for anger—the one emotion where we might have expected men to be more accurate—or for neutral emotions.

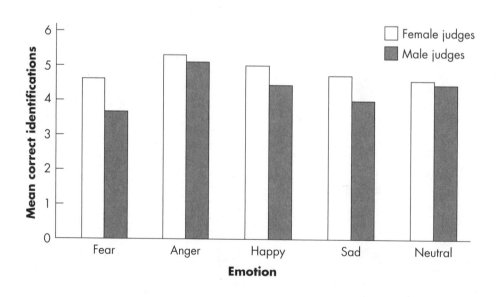

FIGURE 6.3 ■ Male and female accuracy in decoding emotions from vocal cues. (Note: Maximum score = 6.)

Source: From Bonebright, T. L., Thompson, J. L., & Leger, D. W. (1996). Gender stereotypes in the expression and perception of vocal effect. *Sex Roles, 34,* 429–445 (Figure 1). Reprinted with permission.

Individual Differences in Communication Styles.   The gender differences in non-verbal behavior are often larger than other gender differences. However, we must emphasize that many people do not display the nonverbal behavior that is characteristic of their gender. As always, individual differences within each gender are large, and the behaviors of men and women show some overlap. For example, Gallaher (1992) examined a dimension of nonverbal style called expansiveness. She concluded that people who had been rated as being more masculine, "regardless of their sex, were also rated as more expansive: They tend to sit with legs wide apart, walk with a heavy step, and speak in a loud voice" (p. 138). In other words, "masculine" people, whether they are male or female, typically take up more space, both physically and psychologically. In contrast, Gallaher found that "feminine" people are relatively self-contained and quiet, whether they are female or male.

We need to keep in mind the large individual differences within each gender, consistent with Theme 4 of this book. For example, women differ from one another in the size of their personal-space zones, their body posture, gazing, facial expression, and decoding ability. These within-gender variations are so large that you can probably think of several women whose nonverbal behavior is more "masculine" than the average male. For instance, you probably know some women who rarely smile and other women who have no idea what emotions you are feeling unless you make a public announcement.

Potential Explanations for Gender Differences in Communication

Even though individual differences are substantial, we need to explain the gender differences in some kinds of verbal and nonverbal communication. Specifically, men often talk more, have larger personal-space zones, use more relaxed body postures, gaze less, and smile less; they also tend to be less skilled at decoding other people's facial expressions. Given these reasonably large gender differences, we might expect that theorists would have developed a coherent theory for them. Unfortunately, they have not. Let's consider two general approaches, which primarily address the gender differences in decoding ability and in smiling.

Power and Social Status Explanations.   Marianne LaFrance and Nancy Henley (1997) argued that the single most effective explanation for gender differences in communication is that men have more power and social status in our culture. Powerful people are allowed to talk at length; less powerful people must listen. Powerless people should use phrases such as "I'm not sure" and "I suppose" when talking with powerful people. Powerful people also have large personal-space zones that less powerful people should not penetrate. Powerful people can sprawl in a chair in a relaxed body position. Powerful people don't need to smile, whereas low-power people must often smile, even if they do not feel happy (Hecht & LaFrance, 1998).

M. LaFrance and Henley (1997) were especially interested in explaining the gender differences in decoding ability. They argued that low-power individuals must be especially attentive to powerful individuals so that they can respond appropriately (M. Conway et al., 1996). Imagine a male boss and his low-ranking male assistant. The assistant must be vigilant for signs of unhappiness on his boss's face, because those signs suggest that the boss shouldn't be interrupted or brought any bad news. In contrast, the boss doesn't need to be equally sensitive. According to the power-based explanation, the boss has little to gain from decoding his assistant's facial expression.

M. LaFrance and Henley (1997) argued that our current culture usually assigns dominant status to men and subordinate status to women. As a consequence, even when a man and a woman are equivalent in other characteristics, such as age and occupation, the man will generally have more power. With that status, the man will use the verbal and nonverbal communication patterns that are characteristic of bosses, leaving the woman in the position of a relatively submissive assistant.

Social Learning Explanations.   Judith Hall and her colleagues believe that social status and power cannot account for the gender differences in nonverbal decoding ability (J. A. Hall & Halberstadt, 1997; J. A. Hall et al., 2000). For example, Hall and Halberstadt (1994) found that women in low-ranking jobs at a university were *not* more skilled than high-ranking women in decoding men's facial expressions. In another study, Hall and her colleagues (1997) gathered measures of subordination among undergraduates; these measures included social class background, a personality test of subordination, and self-rated social status in high school. In general, the more powerful students were *more* skilled at decoding facial expression than were the more subordinate students—the opposite of the relationship predicted by the power-based explanation.

Instead, Hall and her colleagues argue that our culture provides roles, expectations, and socialization experiences that teach males and females how to communicate (Brody & Hall, 1993; J. A. Hall & Halberstadt, 1997; J. A. Hall et al., 2000). In other words, they emphasize a social learning approach, which we discussed in Chapter 3. As children grow up, for instance, they are reinforced for using nonverbal behavior consistent with their gender. They are also punished for using nonverbal behavior that is more typical of the other gender. Thus, a young girl may be scolded and told, "Let's see a *smile* on that face!" when she has been frowning. If she values others' approval, she will probably smile more often. The girl also notices that females often smile and gaze intently at their conversational partners. In contrast, a boy will be criticized if he uses "feminine" hand gestures, and he can certainly notice stereotypically masculine body movements by watching the men in his family, his community, and the media. Young girls also learn that they are supposed to pay attention to people's emotions, so they are likely to develop sensitivity to facial expressions. In addition, young girls learn that they are supposed to look out for people's emotional well-being, and a smile makes people feel welcome and accepted.

Conclusions.   Like so many debates in psychology, both perspectives are probably at least partially correct. My own sense is that both the power hypothesis and the social learning approach combine fairly well to explain the gender differences in the communications that people *send* to others. However, the social learning approach seems more relevant than the power hypothesis in explaining people's ability to *receive* and decode emotions in other people. Consistent with J. A. Hall and Halberstadt's (1997) argument, I've known some executives and other high-power individuals who are skilled at reading other people's emotions from relatively subtle cues. Social sensitivity makes some people popular, and so they rise to positions of power.

Even if we aren't certain about the explanations, the gender differences remain. What should we do about them? Women do not have to smile when they are unhappy, and they do not need to occupy the smallest possible space on a couch. With respect to verbal communication, they should feel comfortable claiming their fair share of the conversation. Men can stop interrupting, and they can stop invading women's personal space. They can also smile more, and they can sit so that they occupy less space.

In discussing how nonverbal behavior can be changed, we must remember that women should not necessarily strive to be more masculine in their behavior. This reaction would assume that male behavior must be normative. I recall an article in a magazine intended for women executives that illustrated how a woman can master "powerful, masculine nonverbal behavior." However, as Judith A. Hall (1984) pointed out, we should not assume that women's behavior is deviant and in need of change. Instead, we should note that men may be the victims of years of learning. They have much to gain from adopting some of the nonverbal behaviors and decoding skills of women.

SECTION SUMMARY

Communication Patterns

1. The social constructionist perspective helps us understand how language shapes our ideas about gender; it also emphasizes why our culture has different standards for the ideal social behavior of women and men.

2. Gender differences are largest when self-report is used, when other people are present, when gender roles are emphasized, and when gender-related skills are required.

3. Men often talk more than women; in some circumstances, they also interrupt more.

4. With respect to language style, women may be less likely than men to use profanity; also, they use disclaimers (e.g., "I suppose") more in speech with men than in speech with other women.

5. Gender differences in conversational topics are usually minimal.

6. Women generally have smaller personal-space zones than men do, and they are less relaxed in body posture.

7. Compared to males, females often gaze more at their conversational partners, especially when speaking with someone of the same gender.

8. Women usually smile more than men do, but their smiles may indicate social tension rather than pleasure; women are typically better than men at conveying emotions. However, people may misread women's angry facial expressions as being partly fearful.

9. Women are generally better than men at decoding most nonverbal messages sent by other people.

10. Individual differences in nonverbal behavior are large; in general, people of both genders who are "masculine" take up more space than those who are "feminine."

11. Some gender differences in communication can be traced to gender differences in power; social learning explanations (e.g., roles, expectations, socialization) are probably even more important.

12. Suggestions for changing nonverbal behavior emphasize not only the ways in which women should become more "masculine" but also the ways in which men should become more "feminine."

CHARACTERISTICS RELATED TO HELPING AND CARING

Take a moment to form a mental image of a person helping someone else. Try to picture the scene as vividly as possible. Now inspect your mental image. Is this helpful person a male or a female?

In North America, we have two different stereotypes about gender differences in helpfulness. Males are considered more helpful in activities requiring heroism; they are supposed to take risks, even to help strangers. In contrast, females are considered more helpful and generous in offering assistance and emotional support to family members and close friends (Barbee et al., 1993).

For many years, psychologists ignored helpfulness in long-term close relationships, where so many of our everyday interactions occur (Eagly & Wood, 1991). In fact, this helpfulness to friends and family members is likely to be called social support rather than helpfulness. We'll explore how women provide social support in the discussion of child care (Chapter 7), love relationships (Chapter 8), and care of elderly relatives (Chapter 14). Social support is a less noticed kind of helpfulness; it contributes to the relatively low visibility of women (Houston, 1989).

Furthermore, women's paid employment often emphasizes this low-visibility kind of helpfulness. Women are more likely than men to enter occupations in the "helping professions," such as nursing and social work (Schroeder et al., 1995). In summary, helpfulness actually includes both the high-visibility activities that are stereotypically masculine and also the less visible activities that are stereotypically feminine. Let's consider several topics related to helping and caring: altruism, nurturance, empathy, moral judgments involving other people, and friendship.

Altruism

Altruism means providing unselfish help to others who are in need, without anticipating any reward for that assistance (Schroeder et al., 1995). Research has not uncovered consistent, overall gender differences in altruism with either children or adults (N. Eisenberg et al., 1996). One meta-analysis of 182 gender comparisons yielded an overall effect size of only 0.13; men were only slightly more helpful (Eagly & Crowley, 1986). A more refined examination of these data showed that, compared to women, men were substantially more likely to help if the task was perceived to be dangerous to women. For example, men were much more likely to give a ride to a hitchhiker, but men and women were equally likely to place a stamped letter (presumably lost) in a mailbox. Men were also substantially more likely than women to help on tasks for which they had greater experience, such as changing a tire. In other words, men and women probably do not differ in terms of their general helpfulness. However, gender differences emerge on tasks that are dangerous or require expertise (Fiala et al., 1999; M. C. Hamilton, 2001).

Let's consider a representative study in which researchers distributed questionnaires to adult visitors at a Canadian science museum (R. S. L. Mills et al., 1989). Each person read three stories, such as the one in Demonstration 6.3, and was instructed to choose between two specified options. The results of this study showed that both women and men selected the altruistic choice 75% of the time. In other words, the researchers found no gender differences in responses to this hypothetical nondangerous scenario.

DEMONSTRATION 6.3 ■ ■ ■ ■ ■ ■ ■ ■ ■ ■ ■ ■ ■ ■ ■ ■ ■ ■ ■

A Personal Dilemma

Suppose you have been looking forward to watching a special television program that you have wanted to see for quite some time—an old movie you have always wanted to see, a sports championship game, or a special program such as "Masterpiece Theater." Just as you are all settled in and the show is about to begin, your best friend calls and asks you to help with something you had promised several days ago you would do—for example, painting a room or hanging wallpaper. You had assumed that your friend would need you sometime during the week, but had not expected it to be right now. You want nothing else but to stay in your comfortable chair and watch this show, but you know your friend will be disappointed if you do not come over to help. (R. S. Mills et al., 1989, p. 608)

For purposes of this demonstration, assume that you cannot record the program for future viewing. What would you choose to do in this dilemma?

Several studies focus on how people help their friends in real-life settings. These studies often find that women are more helpful (Belansky & Boggiano, 1994; George et al., 1998). For example, George and his colleagues (1998) asked 1,004 community residents to describe a recent situation in which they helped a friend of the same gender. Compared to men, women reported spending more time helping their friend. Also, Belansky and Boggiano (1994) reported gender differences in the *kind* of help people would offer. For example, a scenario in their study described a friend from high school who was considering dropping out of school. Women were likely to say that they would encourage the friend to talk about the situation. Men were likely to use two strategies: the "let's talk about it" strategy and a problem-solving strategy such as encouraging the friend to make a list of pros and cons about dropping out.

Notice the complex relationship between gender and altruism. Gender differences depend on the nature of the task and the nature of the interpersonal relationship as well as on factors such as danger and expertise.

Alice Eagly believes that the pattern of gender differences in helpfulness can be explained by social roles (Eagly, 2001; Eagly & Wood, 1999; Eagly et al., 2000). A **social role** refers to a culture's shared expectations about the behavior of a group that occupies a particular social category, for example, the social category "women." In North America, our culture currently expects that women will be more likely than men to take care of the home and children. Our culture also expects that men will be more likely than women to be the primary family provider.

Furthermore, Eagly emphasizes that physical characteristics help to shape social roles. For example, because women give birth to children, they are more likely to assume caretaking responsibility for children. As a result of this role, women have become associated with unselfishness and concern about other people. In contrast, men typically have greater size and strength than women, which means that they are more likely to perform activities requiring these physical characteristics. As a result of this role, men have become associated with strength and power—both physical power and social power. Eagly argues that gender differences in personality can be traced to the different social roles occupied by women and men. For example, women should be more helpful when the altruistic task requires interpersonal sensitivity. In contrast, men should be more helpful when the altruistic task requires physical strength.

Will the gap close in the future? Only if our culture establishes greater gender equality, so that women and men occupy more similar roles. This gender equality would require men to participate more in caretaking roles at work and at home, and it would require women to continue to enter the paid workforce (Eagly, 2001; Eagly & Diekman, 2002).

Nurturance

Nurturance is a kind of helping in which someone gives care to another person, usually someone who is younger or less competent. The stereotype suggests that women are more nurturant than men. In fact, women actually do rate themselves higher than men do (Feingold, 1994; P. J. Watson et al., 1994). However, researchers often find gender similarities.

According to Deaux and Major (1987), gender similarities are found when the situation requires an obvious helpful response. For example, both men and women will quickly respond to the screams of a child who is clearly in pain. However, gender differences may emerge when the situation is more ambiguous, for example, when a child begins to whimper softly.

Here's a related question: Do females find babies more interesting and engaging than males do? As we've seen before, the answer to this question depends on the operational definitions used by the researchers. For example, women and men are equally responsive to babies when the operational definition requires a physiological measure (e.g., heart rate) or a behavioral measure (e.g., playing with the baby). However, when the operational definition is based on self-report, women rate themselves as being more attracted to babies (Berman, 1980; M. C. Hamilton, 2001).

Judith Blakemore (1998) examined whether preschool girls and boys differ in their interest in babies. She asked parents to observe their children interacting with an unfamiliar baby on three separate occasions, such as in a doctor's office or when a family with a baby came to visit in the home. Each parent was also instructed to find another person who could simultaneously observe the preschoolers' behavior; Blakemore found that the parents' ratings were highly correlated with the other observers' ratings. The analysis of the ratings showed that preschool girls scored higher than boys in their amount of nurturance toward the baby, degree of interest in the baby, and kissing and holding the baby. Interestingly, however, some parents had rated themselves as being tolerant of "girl-like behavior" in their sons. These parents tended to have sons who were highly interested in babies and very nurturant toward these babies. Notice, then, that preschool children often show a gender difference on a behavioral measure of both nurturance and interactions with a baby, although some preschool boys can defy the stereotypes.

Empathy

You show **empathy** when you understand the emotion that another person is feeling and when you experience that same emotion (P. W. Garner & Estep, 2001). An empathic person who watches someone lose a contest can experience the same feelings of anger, frustration, embarrassment, and disappointment that the loser feels. According to the stereotype, women are more empathic than men. However, researchers typically find substantial gender differences only when the results are based on self-reports (N. Eisenberg et al., 1989, 1996; N. Eisenberg & Lennon, 1983; P. W. Garner & Estep, 2001). The findings will remind you of our discussion about responsiveness to babies:

1. *Females and males are equally empathic when the operational definition requires physiological measures.* Specifically, measures such as heart rate, pulse, skin conductance, and blood pressure typically show no gender differences in empathy.

2. *Females and males are equally empathic when the operational definition requires non-verbal measures.* For example, some studies have measured empathy in terms of the observer's facial, vocal, and gestural measures. A typical study examines whether children's facial expressions change in response to hearing an infant cry. Using this nonverbal measure, boys and girls usually do not differ in their empathy.

3. *Females are more empathic than males when the operational definition is based on self-report.* To assess empathy, a typical questionnaire includes items such as "I tend to get emotionally involved with a friend's problems." Studies with children usually find gender similarities. However, studies with adolescents and adults usually find that females report more empathy than do males. Furthermore, males who rate themselves relatively high in "feminine characteristics" also report that they are high in empathy (Karniol et al., 1998). In summary, gender differences in self-reported empathy are far from universal.

As we have seen, we cannot answer the question of whether males or females are more empathic unless we know how empathy is measured and whom we are studying. Once again, we see an illustration of Theme 1: Gender differences certainly are not found in every condition.

Moral Judgments Concerning Other People

Do males and females tend to make different kinds of decisions when they make moral judgments that have implications for other people's lives? This is a controversial topic. We'll explore it in some detail because of its important consequences for helping and caring. First, let's consider some theoretical background, emphasizing the important contributions of Carol Gilligan. Then we'll review other research, which generally supports the similarities perspective. Finally, we'll summarize the issues.

Theoretical Background.   Several prominent feminist theorists have argued that characteristics traditionally associated with women have been undervalued. For example, Judith V. Jordan (1997) summarized the perspective of a group of theorists working at the Stone Center at Wellesley College. According to their **relational model** (sometimes called the **self-in-relation theory**), girls and women grow through their relationships with other people by means of mutual empathy and responsiveness to others; in addition, women are more likely to feel that connections with others are central to their psychological well-being. Other researchers have presented a similar argument: that women consider themselves interdependent, whereas men consider themselves independent (e.g., Cross & Madson, 1997a, 1997b).

The relational model is consistent with the differences perspective emphasized in Chapter 1. Those who favor the **differences perspective** tend to exaggerate gender differences; they view males and females as being different and as having mutually exclusive characteristics. The relational model is also consistent with cultural feminism. As we discussed in Chapter 1, **cultural feminism** emphasizes the positive qualities that are presumably stronger in women than in men—qualities such as nurturing and caring for others.

The **similarities perspective,** in contrast, tends to minimize gender differences, arguing that males and females are generally similar. As you know from Theme 1, this book typically favors a similarities perspective. The similarities perspective is most consistent with the framework of **liberal feminism;** by deemphasizing gender roles and increasing equal rights laws, the gender similarities will increase still further. Those who favor the similarities perspective admire some aspects of the relational model and Gilligan's model, which we'll discuss next. However, supporters of the similarities perspective argue that women and men are fairly similar in their concerns about helping and caring; the two genders do not live on separate planets.

Working in parallel with those who support the relational model, Carol Gilligan eloquently expressed the differences perspective in her 1982 book, *In a Different Voice.* Gilligan's book was partly a feminist response to the research by Lawrence Kohlberg (1981, 1984), who had argued that men are more likely than women to achieve sophisticated levels of moral development. Gilligan (1982) criticized the masculine bias in the moral dilemmas that Kohlberg had tested. For our purposes, however, the most interesting aspect of her book is that she provided a feminist approach to moral development (Clinchy & Norem, 1998). According to Gilligan, women are not morally inferior to men, but they do "speak in a different voice," a voice that has been ignored by mainstream psychology.

Gilligan (1982) contrasted two approaches to moral decision making. The **justice approach** emphasizes that an individual is part of a hierarchy in which some people have more power and influence than others. Gilligan proposed that men tend to emphasize justice and the legal system when making moral decisions. In contrast, the **care approach** emphasizes that individuals are interrelated with one another in a web of interconnections. Gilligan proposed that women tend to favor the care perspective, in which life is based on connections with others.

Numerous feminists, including many from disciplines outside psychology, embraced Gilligan's emphasis on gender differences (described by Kimball, 1995). Others argued that men and women are more likely to show similar styles of moral reasoning. The dissenters also pointed out that if we were to glorify women's special nurturance and caring, men would be less likely to recognize and develop their own competence in that area (H. Lerner, 1989; Tavris, 1992).

Subsequent Research.   A variety of studies have been conducted to examine gender comparisons in moral reasoning. An occasional study reports that women are somewhat more likely than men to adopt a care perspective (e.g., Crandall et al., 1999; Finlay & Love, 1998). However, most of the results support the similarities perspective: Men and women typically respond similarly (e.g., Kunkel & Burleson, 1998; C. L. Martin & Ruble, 1997). For instance, Jaffee and Hyde (2000) found gender similarities in 73% of the 160 studies they examined. The d was 0.28, indicating a small gender difference. In general, the more recent studies have examined participants' responses to standardized hypothetical dilemmas, whereas Gilligan's technique asked individuals to describe moral dilemmas from their own life experiences.

Let's consider a study by Clopton and Sorell (1993), who examined moral reasoning using both standardized dilemmas and participants' own examples. These researchers limited the dilemmas to child-rearing situations, so that all dilemmas focused on comparable circumstances. They tested two standardized moral dilemmas about parent-child relationships. Parents were also asked to describe a dilemma they had faced in parenting their own child. Trained raters assessed the mothers' and the fathers' responses for evidence of both the justice perspective and the care perspective. The results showed no gender differences for either the standardized dilemmas or the participants' real-life dilemmas. These conclusions are consistent with a point we made at the beginning of the chapter: Gender differences are small (or, in this case, nonexistent) when the situation emphasizes roles other than gender. Specifically, when men and women focus on the parenting role, they provide similar moral judgments about child-rearing dilemmas.

Some critics of Gilligan's theory argue that her approach is based on European American values (e.g., Brabeck & Satiani, 2001; Lykes & Qin, 2001; Stack, 1994). For example, Brabeck (1996) interviewed teenage boys in Guatemala. When asked about the characteristics they most valued, they emphasized helping other people and improving the community.

Summary of Moral Judgments.   Carol Gilligan contributed an important framework by emphasizing our responsibility to other people and our interconnections with them. She emphasized that the standard theory had downplayed the ethic of care, a value traditionally associated with women. However, the current research does not support the idea of major gender differences in moral judgment. I'm more persuaded by the research that demonstrates how men and women respond similarly to a wide variety of moral dilemmas. Especially, when people provide judgments about similar moral dilemmas and when we consider the values of people who are not European American, men and women seem to live in the same moral world. We share the same basic values that include both justice and care (Kunkel & Burleson, 1998).

Friendship

For many decades, psychologists ignored the topic of friendship; aggression was a much more popular topic! However, in recent years, many books and articles have been published that are relevant to gender differences in friendship (e.g., H. T. Reis, 1998; Winstead & Griffin, 2001; P. H. Wright, 1998).

Try to create a mental image of two women who are good friends with each other, and think about the nature of their friendship. Now do the same for two men who are good friends. Are female-female friendships basically different from male-male friendships? You can probably anticipate the conclusion we will reach in this section: Although gender differences are observed in some components of friendship, gender similarities are more striking.

DEMONSTRATION 6.4 ■ ■ ■ ■ ■ ■ ■ ■ ■ ■ ■ ■ ■ ■ ■ ■ ■

Characteristics of Friendships

Think about some of the friendships you have with other people of the same gender. What do you mean by the term *intimacy* when it is used in reference to your same-gender friends? In your reply, please indicate how you and your same-gender friends express intimacy in your relationships. This issue will be discussed shortly in the text.

Source: Based on Monsour (1992, p. 282).

We find gender similarities when we assess what friends do when they get together. Specifically, both female friends and male friends are most likely to just talk. They are somewhat less likely to work on a specific task or project together. And they rarely meet for the purpose of working on some problem that has arisen in their friendship (Duck & Wright, 1993; P. H. Wright, 1998). Another gender similarity is that females and males report the same degree of satisfaction with their same-gender friendships (Crick & Rose, 2000).

What does intimacy in a friendship mean to men and women? (To assess your own thoughts, try Demonstration 6.4 before reading further.) Monsour (1992) posed this same open-ended question to undergraduates and then compared the responses supplied by males and females. Both women and men typically said that the most important component of intimacy is **self-disclosure,** or revealing information about oneself to someone else. Both women and men also emphasize emotional expressiveness, communication skills, unconditional support, and trust (Monsour, 1992; P. H. Wright, 1998). However, females also emphasized physical contact with the friend, whereas—no surprise—males mentioned this less often.

Other research suggests that women typically value self-disclosure somewhat more than men. Dindia and Allen (1992) conducted a meta-analysis of 205 studies, which reported on 23,702 people. The d was 0.18, a small effect size, with women disclosing somewhat more than men. Recent studies generally report that women are more self-disclosing (Foubert & Sholley, 1996; H. T. Reis, 1998; Veniegas & Peplau, 1997).

Why should women tend to be more self-disclosing? One reason is that women value talking about feelings more than men do; as we've already discussed, females receive greater training in emotions. In addition, North Americans have gender-related norms about self-disclosure; men are not *supposed* to discuss private feelings with other men, especially if they are guided by our culture's antigay messages (Canary & Emmers-Sommer, 1997; H. T. Reis, 1998; Winstead & Griffin, 2001; P. H. Wright, 1998).

SECTION SUMMARY ▪

Characteristics Related to Helping and Caring

1. Overall gender differences in helpfulness are not strong; men are more likely to help on dangerous tasks and on tasks requiring expertise in masculine areas. When helping friends, gender differences may be minimal or women may help more.

2. According to Eagly's social role theory, the gender differences in helping patterns can be traced to women's and men's current work roles and family responsibilities.

3. In general, women and men do not differ in nurturance or in responsiveness to babies; preschool girls may show more interest in infants than do preschool boys who have been reared in traditional households.

4. In general, women and men do not differ in empathy; gender similarities are found for physiological and nonverbal measures, but women are typically more empathic on self-report measures.

5. The relational model emphasizes growth through relationships with other people, with women being more concerned than men about interpersonal connections. Carol Gilligan (1982), a proponent of the differences perspective, has suggested that men favor a justice approach, whereas women emphasize a care approach.

6. Most research supports a similarities perspective, especially when people make moral judgments about the same kind of situation and when considering the values of cultures other than European American groups.

7. Men and women have similar friendship patterns in terms of the activities that friends engage in when they get together and in terms of satisfaction with their friendships; women are typically somewhat more self-disclosing than men are.

CHARACTERISTICS RELATED TO AGGRESSION AND POWER

We have seen that the research on helping and caring does not allow a simple, straightforward conclusion about gender differences. The situation is similar for attributes associated with aggression and power.

In the previous section, we focused on characteristics that are stereotypically associated with females; in this section, we will focus on characteristics stereotypically associated with males. An important central topic in this cluster is **aggression,** which we'll define as any behavior directed toward another person with the intention of doing harm (J. W. White, 2001).

Let's begin by considering some issues raised by social constructionists about the nature of aggression, and next we'll examine the research on aggression.

Then we'll shift our focus from aggression to power, as we consider the topics of leadership and persuasion.

Gender and Aggression: The Social Constructionists' Concerns

As we saw in the introduction to this chapter, social constructionists argue that we humans actively construct our views of the world. This point holds true for people trying to make sense out of their daily experiences and for theorists and researchers trying to make sense out of human behavior. As a result, researchers who are studying aggression are guided by the way scholars have constructed the categories. The customary language has limited the way researchers tend to view aggression (Jack, 1999a; Marecek, 2001a; J. W. White, 2001). Consequently, the cultural lenses that they wear restrict their vision.

In particular, researchers have constructed aggression so that it is considered a *male* characteristic. To appreciate this point, reread the definition of aggression in the second paragraph of this section. What kinds of aggression do you visualize—hitting, shooting, and other kinds of physical violence? But aggression can be verbal as well as physical. If you are a typical college student, you are much more likely to experience verbal aggression, instead of physical aggression, in your everyday life (Howard & Hollander, 1997). This verbal aggression may not require a trip to the hospital, but a hostile remark can have a profound effect on your self-esteem and on social interactions. However, our cultural lenses do not encourage us to see the kinds of aggression that might be more common in females.

Social constructionists point out that each culture devises its own set of lenses. Peplau and her colleagues (Peplau, Veniegas et al., 1999) argued that each culture shapes a different construction of social behaviors, such as aggression. Consider the egalitarian culture on the island of Vanatinai, a remote island near New Guinea in the South Pacific (Lepowsky, 1998). In this remarkable culture, both girls and boys are socialized to be self-confident but not aggressive. During Lepowski's 10 years of research, she heard about only five acts of physical violence—and women were the aggressors in four of these incidents. In a culture that discourages aggression, gender differences may disappear.

Closer to home, M. G. Harris (1994) reported on female members of Mexican American gangs in the Los Angeles area. The young women she interviewed stated that they had joined the gang for group support but also because of a need for revenge. Commenting on the physical violence, a gang member named Maryann reported, "It's not that you like to fight. You have to fight. But I like fighting" (p. 296). Reselda emphasized, "Most of us in our gangs always carry weapons. Guns, knives, bats, crowbars, any kind. . . . Whatever we can get hold of that we know can hurt, then we'll have it" (p. 297). In a subculture that admires physical aggression, gender differences may disappear as both females and males adopt violent tactics (Jack, 1999a).

Throughout this exploration of aggression, keep in mind the cultural lenses that we wear. Also, remember that the way we ask questions has an important influence on the answers we obtain.

Overt Aggression Versus Relational Aggression

As we have discussed, our cultural lenses typically encourage us to see aggression from a male perspective, which emphasizes physical aggression. **Overt aggression** is aggression that physically harms or could threaten to harm another person. Nicki Crick and her colleagues have explored a different kind of aggression, one that threatens interpersonal relationships (e.g., Crick & Bigbee, 1998; Crick & Rose, 2000; Crick et al., 1997). **Relational aggression** is aggression that harms or threatens to harm another person through intentionally manipulating peer friendships (Crick & Bigbee, 1998). For example, someone may spread a lie about a person or intentionally exclude a person from a group. Relational aggression is often more common in females than in males.

In a representative study, Crick and her colleagues (1997) studied children who attended a preschool program. The preschool teachers were instructed to rate each student on items related to both overt and relational aggression. As you can see from Figure 6.4, the teachers rated the boys higher than the girls on overt aggression, whereas they rated the girls higher than the boys on relational aggression. These results help us to reinterpret the myth of the nonaggressive female.

The research on relational aggression is relatively new, and we do not yet know how often this form of aggression occurs across the life span. However, as children grow older, they develop the cognitive skills that allow them to better understand social relationships. People who are high in relational aggression

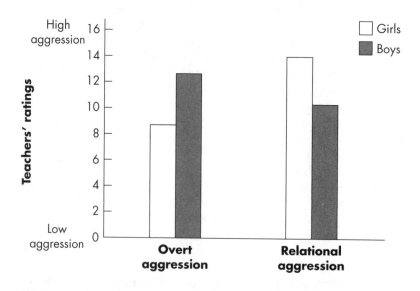

FIGURE 6.4 ■ Teachers' ratings of preschoolers' overt aggression and relational aggression. (Note: Higher numbers indicate more aggression.)
Source: Based on Crick et al. (1997).

probably become more skilled at figuring out clever ways to demonstrate this aggression (Crick & Rose, 2000).

We do have some limited cross-cultural research on relational aggression. Consider verbal attacks, for example. Cross-cultural research in Scandinavia, Tonga (a Polynesian society), and Argentina suggests that females are as likely as males to use verbal indirect aggression, such as excluding people from their group or gossiping. In some cases—consistent with Crick's work—women may even be *more* aggressive on these measures (Björkqvist, 1994; Hines & Fry, 1994; Olson, 1994). Incidentally, in emphasizing gender comparisons in relational violence, we must not lose sight of the harmful consequences of men's physical violence. No one would argue that a woman's gossiping is equivalent to a man's breaking someone's arm.

Let's examine the research on gender comparisons in crime rates, an important index of physical aggression. The data on crime show that men are consistently more likely than women to be the offenders in every category of criminal behavior (G. P. Knight et al., 1996; U.S. Census Bureau, 2001b). For example, men account for 84% of violent crime, including murder, rape, robbery, and assault (J. W. White, 2001). We'll return to this topic in Chapter 13 when we consider domestic violence.

In both Canada and the United States, the media are eager to point out how the number of women in prison has been rapidly rising (Pate, 1999). These media reports may not mention that drug-related offenses are the major reason for the increase in women in prison (P. A. Murphy & Cleeton, 2000). Still, the media are correct in saying that women are increasingly likely to be arrested for violent crimes (P. A. Murphy & Cleeton, 2000; U.S. Bureau of the Census, 1997). Keep in mind, though, that crime rates are still much lower for women than for men.

What can we conclude from these data on criminal behavior? Women are clearly capable of committing atrociously violent murders (Pearson, 1998). They are also somewhat more likely to commit violent crimes now than in earlier eras. Still, the bottom line is that gender differences in physical aggression remain relatively large.

Gender and Aggression: Other Important Factors

Aggression is one of the most popular topics for research on gender comparisons (Brody, 1999), so our discussion of other aspects of this topic will consider only a fraction of the studies. So far, we have seen that females may be relatively high in relational aggression but that males are relatively high in overt physical aggression. For many years, psychologists seemed convinced that males are more aggressive than females. However, a breakthrough in our understanding of gender and aggression came from a classic review of previous studies, conducted by Ann Frodi and her colleagues (1977). According to the studies, males were often found to be more aggressive. However, only 39% of these studies showed males being more aggressive than females for all the research conditions. The analysis by Frodi and her colleagues has now been joined by additional research and meta-analyses (e.g., Bettencourt & Miller, 1996; Brody, 1999;

G. P. Knight et al., 1996). These reports inform us that gender differences depend on factors such as operational definitions and the social context.

1. *Gender differences are relatively large when aggression is measured in terms of self-report.* As we have seen throughout this chapter, people move in the direction of gender stereotypes when they report about themselves. For example, men are more likely than women to report having physically aggressive dreams (Bursik, 1998). Other studies have asked people to rate themselves on a variety of scales that assess aggression (A. H. Buss & Perry, 1992; M. B. Harris & Knight-Bohnhoff, 1996). Men had much higher scores than women did on questions that assessed physical aggression. Men also reported slightly more verbal aggression and hostility.

2. *Gender differences are relatively large when measuring spontaneous aggression.* Men are more likely than women to show spontaneous, unprovoked aggression—the kind of aggression that cannot be traced to a specific cause. In contrast, when people have been insulted—a specific excuse for an aggressive response—both men and women are likely to respond aggressively. With provoked aggression, no gender differences are observed (Bettencourt & Miller, 1996; Brody, 1999).

3. *Gender differences are relatively large when the individuals know each other.* For example, in a study by Lightdale and Prentice (1994), a pair of participants played a video game in which each person dropped bombs on the competitor's target. When the two participants did not know each other beforehand, no gender differences were observed. However, when the participants had briefly met before the game began, men played the game significantly more aggressively than women did. Here's one possible explanation for the gender difference in this condition: Compared to the men, women may have felt more empathy for someone they had met, so the women might have been more reluctant to treat their opponents in an aggressive fashion (Carlo et al., 1999).

When you think about gender and aggression, keep in mind the general principle that the psychological characteristics of males and females always show a substantial overlap. For example, some studies have examined the scores that young boys and girls receive on measures of observed physical aggression (e.g., Favreau, 1993; Frey & Hoppe-Graff, 1994). Gender differences should be relatively large in these studies, because they measure physical violence. Still, most of the boys and girls were similarly nonaggressive, and the gender differences could be traced to a small number of aggressive boys.

Also keep in mind that researchers and theorists emphasize the kinds of aggression that are stereotypically masculine. They seldom explore those domains in which women may be more aggressive. As a result, people tend to believe that females are rarely aggressive. The myth of the nonaggressive female has several disadvantages for North American society:

1. If women see themselves as weak and nonaggressive, they may believe that they cannot defend themselves against men's aggression (J. W. White & Kowalski, 1994).

2. Because competitiveness is associated with aggression, women may be denied access to professions that value competition.

3. Aggressiveness may be seen as normal for males, so men may choose not to inhibit their aggressive tendencies.

In short, both women and men suffer when we hold stereotyped views of the gender differences in aggression.

Leadership

If you attend a college that has both female and male students, notice the gender of the student council leaders. If your college is typical, the leaders are predominantly men, even if most students are women. In general, research shows that male leaders emerge from mixed-gender groups, even when the members of the groups are presumably equal in ability (Eagly & Karau, 1991; V. E. O'Leary & Flanagan, 2001; Sapp et al., 1996). Let's consider two questions about gender and leadership: Do women and men differ in their style of leadership, and do they differ in their leadership effectiveness? But first, try Demonstration 6.5.

DEMONSTRATION 6.5 ■

Persuasion Techniques

Imagine that you have just come down with a nasty cold, and you cannot find any tissue. You go to the convenience store, and just as you turn down the aisle you want, you find that there are no boxes of tissue left on the shelf. Two aisles over, you spot someone who seems to be the only person working in the store; he is frantically stocking items before closing time. After you ask him if he could check the back for a box of tissue, he says, "Look, I've been here all day. I have to get this done, and helping you is not really on the top of my list right now."

Based on your past behavior, rate the likelihood that you would make each of the following four responses. Use a 7-point rating scale (1 = very unlikely; 7 = very likely).

_____ 1. Threaten to complain to his manager.

_____ 2. Explain to him that you really feel lousy and that it would mean a lot to you if he could get the tissue for you.

_____ 3. Offer to put in a good word to his manager if he gets the tissue for you.

_____ 4. Remind him that it is his job to help customers, so he must get the tissue for you.

Source: Based on Carothers and Allen (1999, p. 378).

Leadership Style.   You probably will not be surprised to learn that gender comparisons about leadership performance show a complex pattern. For example, when Eagly and Johnson (1990) analyzed laboratory research, they found that men are somewhat more concerned about getting the job done, whereas women are somewhat more concerned about the feelings of other group members. However, when they analyzed research on men and women who are actually employed as leaders in organizations, they found gender similarities. As noted at the beginning of this chapter, gender similarities are found when a role other than gender is prominent. In this situation, the role of *executive* is prominent, so gender similarities are typical. Furthermore, gender similarities in leadership style are even stronger when we compare men and women who occupy similar roles in an organization (Eagly & Johannesen-Schmidt, 2001).

Another dimension of leadership style is whether the leader behaves democratically or autocratically. **Democratic leadership** allows subordinates to participate in making decisions. In contrast, **autocratic leadership** discourages subordinates from participating in decision making. For both laboratory and organizational studies, Eagly and Johnson (1990) found that the gender differences were small ($d = 0.22$). However, women were somewhat more likely to use democratic leadership, whereas men were somewhat more likely to use autocratic leadership.

Leadership Effectiveness.   Which gender is actually more effective in the leadership role? Eagly, Karau, and Makhijani (1995) performed a meta-analysis on the ratings of leaders in laboratory research and in organizations. Overall, males and females were equally effective leaders ($d = 0.02$). However, males received more positive ratings than females when the people evaluated were employed in a stereotypically masculine profession (e.g., military leadership). Females received more positive ratings than males when they were employed in a stereotypically feminine profession (e.g., educational leadership). Furthermore, female raters were equally positive about male and female leaders. However, male raters were more positive about male leaders than about female leaders. In other words, a female who is a military leader, supervising more men than women, will typically receive a low rating for her performance.

Other research shows that female leaders are rated especially negatively when their leadership style is autocratic or when they claim to be an expert about a stereotypically masculine topic (Eagly et al., 1992; Lips, 2001; J. Yoder et al., 1998).

All this research on leadership ability has important implications for women and work, the topic of our next chapter. Specifically, the research tells us that women and men are typically similar in both their leadership style and their leadership effectiveness—consistent with Theme 1 of this book. In other words, our culture may believe that men and women differ greatly in their leadership characteristics, but this apparent gender difference is really a product of social construction (V. E. O'Leary & Flanagan, 2001). The research also tells us—consistent with Theme 2—that people react differently to male and female leaders.

Unfortunately, however, few of the studies on leadership examine ethnic issues. We don't know, for example, whether Black men and women differ in their leadership style. We also don't know whether ethnicity has an influence on people's ratings of male and female leaders. For instance, would people be especially likely to downgrade an Asian American or Latina woman if she held a leadership position in a traditionally masculine field?

Persuasion

Which strategy did you use most often in Demonstration 6.5? Bobbi Carothers and James Allen (1999) asked students to read a vignette—either the convenience store vignette in Demonstration 6.5 or one describing a conflict on a group project. The participants then rated the likelihood of each of four responses, as you did in the demonstration. The results showed that male and female students who were high in masculinity were more likely than other students to favor the threatening response (Option 1). In a second study, Carothers and Allen (1999) found that women with traditionally masculine occupations were less likely to favor the request response (Option 2) to resolve the conflict when they had been insulted by the clerk rather than treated neutrally. In contrast, women with traditionally feminine occupations were equally likely to favor the request response, whether they had been insulted or treated neutrally. In summary, both personality characteristics and occupational experience can have an effect on the persuasion techniques we select.

How do people respond to the persuasive efforts of men and women? In general, the research shows that men are more persuasive than women (Burgoon & Klingle, 1998; Carli, 2001). This gender difference can be partly traced to stereotypes about women. As we saw in Chapter 2 (p. 53), people think women are friendly and nice, but not especially competent. When women try to influence other people—and they therefore violate this stereotype—they may encounter problems (Carli & Bukatko, 2000).

Our discussion of leadership pointed out that women are downgraded if they appear too masculine. Similarly, women may be less persuasive if they appear too masculine. For example, men are not persuaded by women who use assertive language. Instead, they are persuaded when women use the kind of tentative language we discussed earlier, such as "I'm not sure" (Buttner & McEnally, 1996; Carli, 1990, 2001). Interestingly, though, *women* are often more persuaded by a woman who uses assertive language than by a woman who uses tentative language (Carli, 1990). A female politician who plans to give a persuasive speech to voters therefore faces a double bind: If she is too assertive, she'll lose the males, but if she is too tentative, she'll lose the females!

Other research shows this same pattern of gender differences in response to a competent, assertive woman. For example, Dodd and her colleagues (2001) asked students to read a vignette focusing on a conversation among three friends, one woman and two men. In the story, one of the men makes a sexist comment, and the woman either ignores it or confronts it. The results of the study showed that the male students liked the woman more if she ignored the comment rather than confronted it. In contrast, the female students liked the woman more if she confronted the comment rather than ignored it.

Women also face a problem if they use nonverbal behavior that appears too masculine. An interesting analysis by Linda Carli and her colleagues (1995) compared women who used a competent nonverbal style and men who used the same style. A competent nonverbal style includes a relatively rapid rate of speech, upright posture, calm hand gestures, and moderately high eye contact when speaking. A male audience was significantly more influenced by a man who used this competent style than by a woman who used this same style. Again, behavior associated with high status is not acceptable when used by a person with low status (Carli, 1999; Carli & Bukatko, 2000; Rudman, 1998).

In summary, subtle sexism persists in social interactions. A competent woman finds herself in a double bind. If she speaks confidently and uses competent nonverbal behavior, she may not persuade the men with whom she interacts. But if she speaks tentatively and uses less competent nonverbal behavior, she will not live up to her own personal standards—and she might not persuade other women. Keep this issue in mind when you read about women's work experiences in Chapter 7.

Throughout this chapter, we have compared women and men on a variety of social and personality characteristics. For example, we noted occasional gender differences in communication patterns, helpfulness, and aggression. However, gender similarities are typically more common, and every characteristic we discussed demonstrates a substantial overlap in the distribution of female and male scores. In summary, we can reject the claim that men and women are from different planets and have little in common. The title of John Gray's book, *Men Are From Mars, Women Are From Venus,* was certainly enticing enough to produce a best-seller. However, its message does not properly represent the gender similarities found in the research. Furthermore, in Chapter 7, we'll continue to search for factors that could explain why women are seldom employed in certain high-prestige occupations and why women are treated differently from men in the workplace. In the chapter you've just read, we have seen that the answers cannot be provided by major gender differences in social and personality characteristics.

SECTION SUMMARY ■

Characteristics Related to Aggression and Power

1. According to the social constructionist perspective, North American scholars have emphasized the stereotypically masculine components of aggression. They have typically ignored the kinds of aggression that might be more common in females; they have also paid little attention to gender similarities in other cultures and subcultures.

2. Some researchers are beginning to differentiate two kinds of aggression. Males are often higher in overt physical aggression, whereas females are often higher in relational aggression.

3. Gender differences in aggression are inconsistent. These gender differences are relatively large (a) when measured by self-report, (b) when spontaneous aggression is measured, and (c) when individuals know each other.

4. In general, males are more likely than females to emerge as group leaders; women are somewhat more likely to use a democratic leadership style, whereas men are somewhat more likely to use an autocratic style.

5. Males and females receive similar ratings in terms of leadership effectiveness, although each receives higher ratings when judged in a gender-consistent leadership position. Women are also likely to be downgraded by males (rather than by females), especially if they use an autocratic leadership style.

6. Men and women generally use similar persuasion strategies, but women face a double bind when they want to be persuasive. If they appear stereotypically masculine, they won't persuade men; if they appear less assertive and more stereotypically feminine, they won't persuade women.

▪ ▪ ▪ ▪ ▪ CHAPTER REVIEW QUESTIONS ▪ ▪ ▪ ▪ ▪

1. In the discussion of communication styles, we pointed out that men seem to take up more space than women, whether we use the word *space* to refer to physical space or, more figuratively, conversational space. Discuss this point, making as many gender comparisons as possible.

2. Turn back to Chapter 3, and review the social learning and cognitive developmental approaches to gender development (pages 82 to 84). Point out how this theory could explain each of the gender differences in verbal and nonverbal communication. Then explain how the power explanation and the social status explanation in this chapter (pages 183 to 185) could account for most gender differences.

3. In the section on facial expression, we pointed out that women's smiles often do not match their true emotions. However, women are more accurate than men in decoding the emotions that underlie other people's facial expressions. Speculate how these two points might be related, and then list some practical implications of these two points.

4. The social constructionist perspective emphasizes that our cultural lenses shape the way we ask questions. In particular, these lenses influence our choice of issues to emphasize within each topic. Summarize the topics of helpfulness, aggression, leadership, and persuasion, pointing out how the nature of the results could be influenced by the kinds of issues studied in each area (e.g., aggression in stereotypically masculine areas versus stereotypically feminine areas).

5. According to stereotypes, women care about interpersonal relationships, whereas men care about dominating other people. Like many stereotypes, this contrast contains a grain of truth. Discuss the grain of truth with respect to helping, friendship, aggression, leadership, and persuasion. Then point out the number of similarities shared by males and females.

6. What kinds of factors influence gender differences in aggression? Combining as many factors as possible, describe a situation in which gender differences are likely to be exaggerated and a situation in which they are likely to be minimal.

7. Some researchers argue that gender differences are likely to emerge in areas in which men and women have had different amounts of practice or training. Using the chapter outline on page 171, point out how differential practice can account for many of the gender differences.

8. Page 174 lists four circumstances under which we tend to find large gender differences in social and personality characteristics. Describe what these factors would predict about gender comparisons in the following situations: (a) A male professor and a female professor who have similar status are discussing a professional article they have both read; what are their likely patterns of gaze? (b) A group of male and female students are asked to talk about the nurturing support that they have given to a younger sibling. (c) A lecture hall is filled with people, and the VCR is not working; the speaker asks for volunteers to figure out the problem.

9. In most of this chapter, we focused on the topic of gender of the subject. However, gender of the stimulus was also discussed. How do people react to men and women leaders and to females who are trying to influence other people? Why is the phrase *double bind* relevant to this question?

10. To solidify your knowledge in preparation for the chapter on women and work (Chapter 7), think of a profession in which relatively few women are employed. Review each of the social and personality characteristics discussed in the current chapter. Note whether any of these factors provides a sufficient explanation for the relative absence of women in that profession.

NEW TERMS

social constructionist approach (173)
nonverbal communication (174)
*operational definition (175)
*personal space (178)
*decoding ability (181)
*altruism (187)
social role (188)
*nurturance (188)
*empathy (189)
*relational model (190)
self-in-relation theory (190)
*differences perspective (190)

cultural feminism (190)
*similarities perspective (191)
liberal feminism (191)
*justice approach (191)
care approach (191)
*self-disclosure (193)
*aggression (194)
*overt aggression (196)
*relational aggression (196)
democratic leadership (200)
autocratic leadership (200)

The terms asterisked in the New Terms section serve as good search terms for InfoTrac College Edition. Go to http://infotrac.thomsonlearning.com and try these added search terms.

RECOMMENDED READINGS

Canary, D. J., & Dindia, K. (Eds.). (1998). *Sex differences and similarities in communication.* Mahwah, NJ: Erlbaum. This excellent book explores not only gender comparisons in communication but also relevant topics such as friendship, social support, and influence.

Kowalski, R. M. (Ed.). (2001). *Behaving badly: Aversive behaviors in interpersonal relationships.* Washington, DC: American Psychological Association. Here is an interesting book that focuses on topics associated with aggression—aspects beyond the scope of this chapter—such as thoughtless behavior, hurt feelings, and rumors.

Romaine, S. (1999). *Communicating gender.* Mahwah, NJ: Erlbaum. I recommend this book for anyone who would like to know more about language and gender because it provides a welcome blend of research-based information and interesting real-life examples.

Shields, S. A. (2002). *Speaking from the heart: Gender and the social meaning of emotion.* New York: Cambridge University Press. Stephanie Shields argues that emotion is at the core of our ideas about gender; her book is a concise, interesting exploration of this topic.

ANSWERS TO THE TRUE-FALSE QUESTIONS

1. True (p. 174); 2. False (p. 175); 3. True (p. 179); 4. False (pp. 187–188); 5. False (p. 189); 6. False (pp. 191–192); 7. True (p. 193); 8. False (p. 198); 9. False (p. 200); 10. True (p. 201).

Women and Work

Louise Wadsworth

T R U E   O R   F A L S E ?

_____ 1. Social scientists believe that the 1996 welfare reform policy has been highly successful in helping women get off welfare and find jobs that pay reasonably well.

_____ 2. Researchers have found that the U.S. affirmative action policy has led to numerous cases of reverse discrimination against males.

_____ 3. Although women earn lower incomes than men, the discrepancy can be explained by gender differences in occupation, amount of work experience, and number of years of full-time employment.

_____ 4. Less than 1% of the top 500 U.S. corporations were headed by women in 2001.

_____ 5. A woman making clothes in a U.S. sweatshop (a factory that violates labor laws) typically earns about $13,000 annually if she works full time, with 8-hour days.

_____ 6. Women and men in the same profession, such as medicine, are typically fairly similar in their cognitive and personality characteristics.

_____ 7. Women in blue-collar jobs are usually dissatisfied with their work, especially because their salaries are so low.

_____ 8. Research in both the United States and Canada shows that women perform about two-thirds of household chores.

_____ 9. Children in day-care centers have normal cognitive development compared to children cared for at home by their mothers; however, they have substantially more social and emotional problems.

_____ 10. Because of their heavy responsibilities, employed women are more likely than nonemployed women to experience problems with their physical and psychological health.

Eileen graduated with honors from the University of Pennsylvania, and then she entered a training program for stockbrokers at a large firm in New York City. This firm had only three female stockbrokers, although many women worked in clerical positions. Eileen was the only woman in her training program, and many of the brokers assumed that she was a secretary. They often asked her questions such as "Why are you in this meeting?" or "Will you fax this?" Eileen's supervisor even instructed her to get lunch and babysit for his 8-year-old son, although none of the male trainees received this assignment. Shortly afterward, a senior broker in the firm announced a competition among his trainees to see who could be the first to have sex with Eileen. After Eileen spoke with the company's Human Resources Office, the situation became even grimmer. Supervisors threatened to decrease their trainees' pay if they spoke to Eileen. Not surprisingly, Eileen quit after six months (Center for Gender Equality, 2000).

In this chapter, we'll continue to explore a question we presented in Chapters 5 and 6: Why do women and men frequently have different work experiences? In Chapter 5, we demonstrated that women and men have fairly similar cognitive abilities and motivation to succeed. Eileen's academic success at a prestigious university demonstrates that she is superior in both of these areas. Then, in Chapter 6, we showed that women and men are similar in most social and personality characteristics. However, in that chapter we also discovered a hint about why extremely competent women like Eileen may face discrimination in a work setting. Women may be negatively evaluated if they are competent in a traditionally masculine area, such as being a stockbroker. Consistent with Theme 1, gender differences are often small; consistent with Theme 2, women and men are often treated differently.

We will see throughout this chapter that women often face barriers with respect to hiring, salary, treatment, and advancement in the workplace. However, we will also see that work is becoming an increasingly important part of women's lives. In the United States and Canada, about 60% of women over the age of 15 are currently employed (Bureau of Labor Statistics, 2001c; Statistics Canada, 2001b). Employment rates are lower for women in most other parts of the world: for example, 29% in northern Africa, 39% in Central America, and 49% in eastern Europe (United Nations, 2000).

To remove any confusion, we need to discuss some terms related to work. The general term **working women** refers to two categories:

1. **Employed women,** or women who work for pay. Employed women may receive a salary or be self-employed.
2. **Nonemployed women,** or women who are unpaid for their work. They may work for their families, in their homes, or for volunteer organizations, but they receive no money for these services.

We'll begin this chapter by exploring some background information about women and work, and next we'll consider several kinds of discrimination in the workplace. We'll then explore a variety of traditional and nontraditional occupations. In the final section of the chapter, we'll discuss how women coordinate their employment with family responsibilities.

BACKGROUND FACTORS RELATED TO WOMEN'S EMPLOYMENT

In Chapter 4, we emphasized that a variety of social forces can reduce many young women's life goals. As a result, they may settle for an occupation that does not utilize their full potential.

However, there's also a bright side. In some fields that were once reserved for men, the number of women has increased dramatically. Well into the twentieth century, women were barred from many medical schools. For years, Yale University Medical School clung to men-only admissions by arguing that the facilities did not include women's bathrooms (M. R. Walsh, 1990). As recently as

1979, only 23% of U.S. medical school graduates were women. Currently, 41% of medical school graduates are women (Nonnemaker, 2000). The numbers of women in law schools and veterinary schools have also increased dramatically. We'll be well into the twenty-first century before an equal number of *practicing* doctors, lawyers, and veterinarians are female. However, the large percentage of women currently in the professional pipeline is encouraging.

In this chapter, we will examine areas in which women have made progress in recent decades, as well as areas in which women still face disadvantages. Let's begin this first section by examining women's personal characteristics that are associated with employment. Then we'll briefly explore two issues that are critical for women: welfare and discrimination in hiring.

What Factors Are Related to Women's Employment?

What situations or characteristics predict whether a woman works outside the home? One of the best predictors of women's employment is education. As you can see from Figure 7.1, U.S. women with at least four years of college are more than twice as likely as women with less than four years of high school to be employed outside the home (Bureau of Labor Statistics, 2001c).

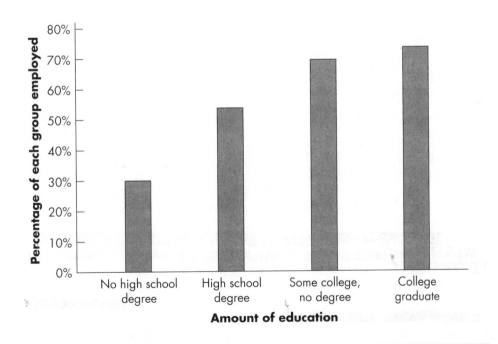

FIGURE 7.1 ■ Percentage of women in the labor force, as a function of education.
Source: Based on Bureau of Labor Statistics (2001c).

Several decades ago, one of the best predictors of a woman's employment was whether she had children. However, the current U.S. data show that married women with children under the age of 6 do not differ from other married women in their rate of employment (U.S. Census Bureau, 2001b).

Ethnicity is not strongly related to participation in the labor force. For example, U.S. data show current employment for 59% of European American women, 56% of Latina women, 63% of Black women, 59% of Asian women, and 55% of Native American women (Costello & Stone, 2001; Hesse-Biber & Carter, 2000).

One group of women who face different barriers to employment are immigrant women. Many of these women are not fluent in the language of their new country. Their educational degrees, professional licenses, and work experience in another country may not be given full credit when they apply for a North American job (Chow, 1994; Naidoo, 2000).

Within any ethnic immigrant group, we can see large variations in personal characteristics. For instance, in the last two decades, 12% of the Asian women who immigrated to the United States had less than a ninth-grade education; the comparable figure for U.S.-born European American women is 5%. These women are likely to find low-paying work on the assembly line or in domestic settings (Hesse-Biber & Carter, 2000; Naidoo, 2000; Phizacklea, 2001). In contrast, immigrants from some Asian countries are unusually well educated. Of the South Asians currently living in Ontario, Canada, 40% have had at least some university education, in contrast to only 20% in the general population (Rajagopal, 1990). Still, these immigrants' salaries are significantly lower than nonimmigrants with comparable training (Hesse-Biber & Carter, 2000).

In summary, education and immigrant status are related to women's employment situation. However, two factors that are unrelated to employment are parental status and ethnicity.

Women and Welfare

In the United States, an important current debate focuses on women who are not employed. If they do not find employment after an "appropriate" period of time, should their welfare payments be suspended? We need to address the myths about welfare, especially because policies have important effects on women's long-term prospects for employment. Before you read further, try Demonstration 7.1.

The Aid to Families with Dependent Children (AFDC) program was created to provide welfare payments for children whose parents could not provide economic support. Although that program was far from perfect, it did benefit numerous low-income families. In August 1996, President Clinton signed legislation that abolished AFDC and created a new program, called Temporary Assistance for Needy Families (TANF). This legislation includes many changes that jeopardize economically poor women. For example, individuals can now remain on welfare for a lifetime maximum of 5 years. In addition, each of the 50 states is now allowed to decide which individuals are desperate enough to need financial assistance (Albelda & Tilly, 1997; Zuckerman & Kalil, 2000).

DEMONSTRATION 7.1   ■ ■ ■ ■ ■ ■ ■ ■ ■ ■ ■ ■ ■ ■ ■ ■ ■ ■

A Quiz About Welfare, Welfare Reform, and Poverty

This quiz tests your knowledge about Aid to Families with Dependent Children (AFDC)—a policy in the United States that was abolished in 1996—as well as the current status of financial aid to impoverished families. Answer the questions, and then check your accuracy by looking at the answers at the end of the chapter.

1. What percentage of the federal budget was allocated to the AFDC program in 1995, just before this program was abolished?

2. The average U.S. mother who received no benefits from AFDC had approximately two children. The average woman receiving AFDC had approximately how many children?

3. What income is specified as the federal poverty line for a family of three (one adult plus two children)?

4. What annual income would a woman earn if she worked full time at the federal minimum wage?

5. What percentage of women workers currently earn wages below the federal poverty line?

6. Of the women who have left welfare and are currently working, what percentage report that their family needed to skip meals because there wasn't enough food?

7. Some politicians claim that the government made the right decision to abolish AFDC, because women's employment rate rose after the change in policy. Explain why we cannot conclude that the change in government policy was responsible for the change in employment.

Sources: Based on Belle (1997), Burnham and Gustafson (2000), Flanders (1997), "Women and Poverty" (2000), and Zuckerman (2000).

The elimination of AFDC has had tragic consequences for many women, especially because most former recipients still live below the U.S. federal poverty line (L. Dodson, 1998; Glenn, 2002; Scarbrough, 2001). For example, suppose that a college student who is a mother wants to escape from an abusive marriage. If she leaves the marriage and applies for welfare to support her children, she will be forced to leave college and earn a minimum wage in a low-level job (Evelyn, 2000; Madsen, 1998).

In another example, a Wisconsin woman was enrolled in a community college program so that she could become a police officer. Previous welfare policies allowed women to enroll in college programs that would make them more employable. However, Wisconsin's revised welfare policy forced her to drop out of college and take a $6.25-an-hour job as a clerk. As she said:

> In class I was so confident and proud because I was going to do this. It's strange. I've gone from this positive, happy person to, I don't know, I'm just so sad. (D. Z. Jackson, 1998, p. 1)

You already know from Figure 7.1 that a woman's education is one of the best predictors of her employment. Compared to college graduates, women without college degrees are 10 times as likely to live in poverty (D. Z. Jackson, 1998). The new TANF policy also has important consequences for the children of these women. Researchers have established that children whose mothers are well educated have fewer cognitive and behavioral problems (Duncan & Brooks-Gunn, 1997; A. P. Jackson et al., 2000). The current welfare reform is obviously shortsighted.

Discrimination in Hiring Patterns

In the 1960s, employers could legally refuse to hire a woman for a specific job simply because she was a woman (Clayton & Crosby, 1992). This overt discrimination is no longer legal, but discrimination often persists. For example, Rhea Steinpreis and her colleagues (1999) wrote to psychology professors, asking them to evaluate the qualifications of a potential job candidate. All the professors received the same, identical resume; however, half the resumes used the name "Karen Miller" and half used the name "Brian Miller." Of those who thought that the candidate was female, 45% said that they would hire her. Of those who thought that the candidate was male, 75% said that they would hire him. Incidentally, female professors were just as likely as male professors to demonstrate this biased hiring pattern.

The term **access discrimination** refers to discrimination used in hiring, for example, rejecting well-qualified women applicants or offering them less attractive positions. Once they have been hired, women may face another kind of discrimination, called treatment discrimination, which we'll discuss later in this chapter.

When Does Access Discrimination Operate?   Several factors determine whether women face access discrimination when they apply for work.

1. *People who have strong gender-role stereotypes are more likely to demonstrate access discrimination.* For example, personnel administrators who were highly gender stereotyped were likely to be biased against women applying for a position as a sports reporter. In contrast, people who were less stereotyped were more likely to judge women fairly (D. Katz, 1987). In addition, people who consider themselves strongly religious are likely to have negative attitudes toward employed women (Harville & Rienzi, 2000).

2. *Access discrimination is particularly likely to operate when women apply for a prestigious position.* For example, Kolpin and Singell (1996) studied the hiring patterns of economics departments in 181 U.S. universities. The departments

that were ranked most prestigious were the least likely to hire female faculty members, even though the female applicants were better qualified than the male candidates. Other research analyzed more than 30,000 employees of financial service organizations (Lyness & Judiesch, 1999). According to the results, men were likely to be hired at senior-level positions. In contrast, women were more likely to be hired at lower positions and, much later, promoted to the higher positions.

3. *Access discrimination often operates for both women and men when they apply for "gender-inappropriate" jobs.* In general, employers select men for jobs when most of the current employees are male, and they select women when most of the employees are female (Clayton & Crosby, 1992; Konrad & Pfeffer, 1991; Lorber, 1994).

For example, Peter Glick (1991) mailed employment questionnaires to personnel officers and career placement consultants. He asked them to read the job applications and make judgments about the applicants' suitability for 35 specific jobs. Glick then calculated the respondents' preferences for female versus male applicants. The respondents showed a clear preference for male applicants when 80% to 100% of the employees in an occupation were male. They showed weaker preferences for a male applicant when about half the employees were male. When the clear majority (80–100%) of employees were female, the respondents actually preferred female applicants. These data suggest that employers would tend to select a male for an executive position in a corporation, but they would prefer a female as a worker in a day-care center. These two examples of discrimination are not really equivalent, however, because the position where the men experience bias pays less and is less prestigious.

4. *Access discrimination is particularly likely to operate when the applicant's qualifications are ambiguous.* For instance, employers will hire a man rather than a woman when both candidates are not especially qualified for a job. In contrast, employers are less likely to discriminate against a woman if they have abundant information that she is well qualified and if her experience is directly relevant to the proposed job (Martell, 1996a).

In summary, a woman is less likely to be considered for a job when the evaluators hold strong stereotypes, when the position is prestigious, and when the job is considered appropriate for males. She is also less likely to be considered when information about her qualifications is insufficient or unclear.

How Does Access Discrimination Operate?   We examined gender stereotypes in some detail in Chapter 2. Unfortunately, people's stereotypes about women may operate in several ways to produce access discrimination (Glick & Fiske, 1998; Heilman, 2001; Martell, 1996a).

1. Employers may have negative stereotypes about women's abilities. An employer who believes that women are typically unmotivated and incompetent will probably react negatively to a specific woman candidate.
2. Employers may assume that the candidate must have certain stereotypically masculine characteristics to succeed on the job. Female candidates may be

perceived as having stereotypically feminine characteristics, even if they are actually assertive and independent. An employer may misperceive a woman as being deficient in these ideal characteristics.

3. Employers may pay attention to inappropriate characteristics when female candidates are being interviewed. The interviewer may judge a woman in terms of her physical appearance, secretarial skills, and personality, and they might ignore characteristics relevant to the executive position she is seeking. In this situation, called **gender-role spillover,** beliefs about gender roles and characteristics spread to the work setting (Cleveland et al., 2000). Employers are likely to emphasize the kinds of stereotypically female traits we discussed in Chapter 2.

Notice that, in each case, stereotypes encourage employers to conclude that a particular position ought to be awarded to a man. In fact, they may decide that a woman would be entirely unsuitable.

What Is Affirmative Action?   Affirmative action is designed to reduce access discrimination and other workplace biases. According to the current federal law in the United States, every company that has more than $50,000 in government contracts—and more than 50 employees—must establish an affirmative action plan. **Affirmative action** means that a company must make special efforts to consider qualified members of underrepresented groups during hiring and promotion decisions (Cleveland et al., 2000; Crosby & Cordova, 2000). Most often, the underrepresented groups are women and people of color.

The term *affirmative action* is often misunderstood (Konrad & Linnehan, 1999; Sincharoen & Crosby, 2001). You are likely to hear talk-show hosts or politicians claiming that the government is forcing companies to hire unqualified women instead of qualified men. They may also claim that the government sets quotas, for instance, about the specific number of Black individuals that a company must hire. Neither of these claims is correct. Instead, affirmative action specifies that companies must encourage applications from the underrepresented groups and that these companies must make a good-faith effort to meet the affirmative action goals they have set. The goal is to make sure that fully qualified women and people of color are given a fair consideration in the workplace, to compensate for past or present discrimination (Cleveland et al., 2000; Vasquez, 1999). For example, a company's administrators may discover that the company employs a smaller number of women than the data indicate to be available for a specific job title. The administrators must then analyze their procedures to see whether or not the hiring procedures are somehow biased (Sincharoen & Crosby, 2001).

Research demonstrates that those U.S. companies with affirmative action programs—and Canadian companies with a similar program called Employment Equity—do indeed have greater workplace equality for women and people of color (Konrad & Linnehan, 1999). Also, women perceive that they are more fairly treated when they work for a corporation that has hired a relatively large number of women (Beaton & Tougas, 1997).

Some people think that affirmative action will produce **reverse discrimination,** in which a woman would be hired instead of a more highly qualified man. However, according to a study of 3,000 U.S. affirmative action court cases, only 3 cases represented reverse discrimination. Unfortunately, though, conservative politicians and commentators distort the truth by claiming that affirmative action is clearly unfair to men (Crosby & Cordova, 2000; Hesse-Biber & Carter, 2000).

SECTION SUMMARY ■

Background Factors Related to Women's Employment

1. Although many factors discourage women from entering prestigious careers, the percentage of women in some professions, such as medicine, has increased dramatically.

2. Women's employment status is influenced by factors such as education and immigrant status; parental status and ethnicity are not strongly related to being employed.

3. Cutbacks in welfare have important consequences for women's lives; for example, women may be forced to leave a career-oriented college program in order to earn money in a low-level job.

4. Access discrimination is most likely to occur when (a) the employer has strong stereotypes, (b) the position is prestigious, (c) a woman is applying for a stereotypically masculine position, and (d) her qualifications are ambiguous.

5. Stereotypes encourage access discrimination because (a) employers have negative stereotypes about women, (b) employers believe that women lack stereotypically masculine characteristics, and (c) employers may pay attention to characteristics that are irrelevant for the positions that women are seeking.

6. Affirmative action policy specifies that companies must make appropriate efforts to consider qualified members of underrepresented groups in work-related decisions.

DISCRIMINATION IN THE WORKPLACE

So far, we've discussed one kind of discrimination against women: the access discrimination women face when they are applying for a job. A second problem, **treatment discrimination,** refers to the discrimination women face after they have obtained a job. We'll examine salary discrimination, promotion discrimination, other workplace biases, and the discrimination experienced by lesbians in the workplace. We'll also consider what people can do to combat workplace discrimination.

Salary Discrimination

The most obvious kind of treatment discrimination is that women earn less money than men do. As of 2000, for example, U.S. women who worked full time earned only 76% of the median[1] annual salary of men (Bureau of Labor Statistics, 2001b). As Figure 7.2 shows, the gender gap in salaries holds true for European Americans, Blacks, and Latinas/os (Bureau of Labor Statistics, 2001d; Hesse-Biber & Carter, 2000). Unfortunately, the Bureau of Labor Statistics does not include Asian American and Native American workers in its salary calculations.

Canadian workers also experience a gender gap. In 1999, Canadian women who worked full time earned only 70% of the average[2] annual salary of men (Statistics Canada, 2001a). Unfortunately, one of the fastest growing employment fields in Canada is in part-time and temporary work, where women's salaries are unpredictable and job security is minimal (De Wolff, 2000). However, in 1999, employed women in Canada won a landmark pay equity lawsuit. The Federal Court ruled that more than 200,000 female clerical workers had been systematically underpaid (Elton, 2000). As a result, the average clerical worker was awarded about $44,000 (Canadian dollars).

Salary discrimination cannot be explained by gender differences in education (Drolet, 2001). Women earn substantially lower salaries at *every* educational level, from no high school education to completion of some graduate work. One analysis showed that female high school graduates made an average of only about $600 more per year than males who had not completed high school (Bureau of Labor Statistics, 2001b).

One important reason for the discrepancy in salaries is that men enter jobs that pay more money. Engineers, who are usually male, earn about twice as much as elementary school teachers, who are usually female (Andriote, 1998).

However, the choice of different kinds of jobs explains only part of the discrepancy. A number of carefully conducted studies demonstrate that women are simply paid less than men, even when other factors are taken into account (Cohn, 2000; D. Robinson, 2001; Roos & Gatta, 1999; Tsui, 1998; Valian, 1998). For example, Baker (1996) studied the salaries of male and female physicians in the United States. He statistically corrected for a variety of factors that could account for gender differences in salary, such as the physicians' specialty, ethnic group, type of medical school, and the income level of the community in which the physician practiced. The analysis showed that, for physicians with at least 10 years of experience, men still earned 17% more than women.

So, which factors are most important in explaining salary discrimination? Looking at a wide variety of jobs, Dunn (1996) estimated that about 35% of the wage gap could be explained by the fact that men are more likely than women to enter occupations that pay well. An additional 15% of the wage gap could be

---

[1] The *median* is the exact midpoint of a distribution; in this case, it is a dollar amount above which half the men were receiving higher salaries and below which half were receiving lower salaries.

[2] In contrast to the median, the *average* is calculated by adding together every person's salary and dividing by the number of people. Because the U.S. data and the Canadian data used different measures to represent the typical salary, they cannot be directly compared.

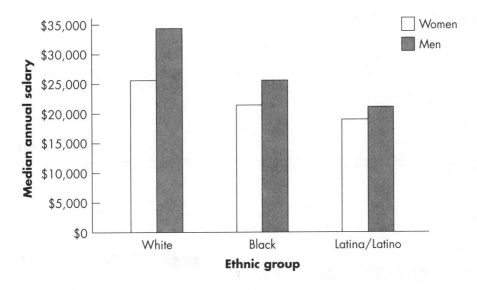

FIGURE 7.2 ▨ U.S. median annual salaries for full-time employment, as a function of gender and ethnic group.

Source: Based on Bureau of Labor Statistics (2001d).

explained by other factors, such as women taking time out to raise children. The rest of the wage gap, about 50%, could be attributed to discrimination (Dunn, 1996).

Similar wage gaps are found in countries other than the United States and Canada (Benokraitis, 1997b; Roos & Gatta, 1999). In Great Britain, Switzerland, and Germany, women earn between 66% and 76% of men's pay. In several countries, such as France, Iceland, and Australia, women earn close to 90% of men's pay (Reskin & Padavic, 1994). The salary gap is smaller in countries in which the government has instituted a policy of pay equity.

Let's look at two more specific aspects of the salary gap: (1) the concept of comparable worth and (2) women's reactions to receiving lower pay.

Comparable Worth.   Most people are willing to agree that a man and a woman with equivalent performance at the same job should receive the same salaries. That is, women and men should receive equal pay for equal work.

Comparable worth is more complicated. The concept of **comparable worth** argues that women and men should receive equal pay for *different* jobs when those different jobs are comparable (England, 1992; D. Robinson, 2001).

People who favor comparable worth legislation point out that much of the gender gap in wages can be attributed to **occupational segregation;** as we noted, men and women tend to choose different occupations. Specifically, "women's jobs" (such as nurses and secretaries) pay less than "men's jobs" (such as auto mechanics and electricians) (Roos & Gatta, 1999). Consistent with Theme 3 of this book, the work women do is devalued in terms of the actual dollar value placed on their accomplishments in the workplace.

In general, the strategy of comparable worth is to pay the same salaries for "men's jobs" and "women's jobs" that have been matched on characteristics such as education, previous experience, skills, dangerousness, and supervisory responsibilities (M. A. Barker, 1996; Roos & Gatta, 1999). By this reasoning, a woman with a bachelor's degree who works with children in a day-care center should earn more than a mechanic with a high school degree who works with air conditioners. If comparable worth legislation were instituted in the United States, the average employed woman would earn $4,205 more each year (Lubin, 1999). So far, however, comparable worth legislation has had only limited success.

Reactions to Lower Salaries.   How do women feel about their lower salaries? One answer to this question comes from research in which women and men decide how much they *ought* to receive for doing a particular job. According to research in both the United States and Canada, women choose lower salaries, suggesting that they are satisfied with less (Bylsma & Major, 1992; Desmarais & Curtis, 1997a, 1997b; Sumner & Brown, 1996). Now try Demonstration 7.2, which illustrates a classic study by Bylsma and Major (1992). These researchers found that male and female undergraduates who received no additional information gave very different salary requests. Specifically, men asked for an average of $6.30, whereas women asked for an average of $5.30. With respect to salary, men

---

DEMONSTRATION 7.2 ■ ■ ■ ■ ■ ■ ■ ■ ■ ■ ■ ■ ■ ■ ■ ■ ■ ■ ■

Gender Comparisons in Salary Requests

Ask a number of friends to participate in a brief study. Ideally, you should recruit at least five males and five females. (Make sure that the two groups are roughly similar in average age and work experience.) Ask them the following question:

> I want you to imagine that you are an undergraduate who has been employed as a research assistant to Dr. Johnson, who is a professor of psychology. You will be working with him all summer, entering data that are being collected for a summer research project. What *hourly* salary do you believe would be appropriate for this summer job?

When you have gathered all the data, calculate the average wage suggested by the males and the average wage suggested by the females. The text lists the salary requests that students provided in a study several years ago. Do you find a similar wage gap in the requests you gathered?

Source: Based on Bylsma & Major (1992).

seem to have a greater sense of **entitlement;** based on their membership in the male social group, they believe that they have a right to high rewards (Steil et al., 2001).

How do women react to the gender gap in wages? Women are typically more concerned about women's lower wages than men are (Browne, 1997; Desmarais & Curtis, 2001)—a finding that should not be surprising. For instance, Reiser (2001) asked 1,000 men and women a variety of questions that focused on anger. She found that 62% of the women and only 38% of the men agreed with the statement "It makes me angry when men have greater job opportunities and rewards than women" (p. 35). Still, isn't it surprising that 38% of the women were not concerned about this inequity?

We have other evidence that women are not especially outraged about their own personal salaries (Clayton & Crosby, 1992; Crosby, 1982; J. A. Roberts & Chonko, 1994; Sincharoen & Crosby, 2001). Faye Crosby and her colleagues report that women typically acknowledge that *women in general* are underpaid. However, women tend to show **denial of personal disadvantage;** they believe that they *personally* are not affected by injustices that harm the disadvantaged groups to which they belong.

Why should women be relatively happy about their low salaries? An important reason is that they want to believe that the world is a just and fair place in which people receive what they deserve (Sincharoen & Crosby, 2001). In contrast, if a woman acknowledges that she is underpaid, then she must explain this inequity. She may be reluctant to conclude that her boss and the organization that employs her are villains. Unfortunately, if she continues to deny her personal disadvantage, she is not likely to work for pay equity and other social justice issues.

Discrimination in Promotions

Alice Huang came to the United States when she was 10 years old, a refugee from China with no money. However, she earned a bachelor's degree from Wellesley College, a doctorate from Johns Hopkins University, and full professor status from Harvard University. She was also elected president of the American Society of Microbiologists. When she was being interviewed for a top-level job at a prestigious college, she realized that the interviewers did not seem enthusiastic about her qualifications. Huang recalled, "I told them that I doubted whether they were going to offer this job, at this time in the history of the institution, to an Asian-American woman" (S. K. Miller, 1992, p. 1224). Two of the interviewers actually nodded their heads, confirming her strong suspicions.

Alice Huang had bumped into the **glass ceiling,** a presumably invisible barrier that seems to prevent women and people of color from reaching the top levels in many professional organizations (Gutek, 2001; Quina et al., 1998). The data persuasively confirm that women encounter glass ceilings in a variety of professions. Compared to men, women are less likely to be promoted to management positions in fields such as college teaching, law, and business (Chiu, 1998; Lawler, 1999; Powell, 1999). The top 500 U.S. corporations are headed by 497 men and 3 women (Pozner, 2001c). Basically, when male managers think about the term *manager,* they typically picture another male. Female managers are usually much less biased (Schein, 2001).

Labor theorists have constructed another metaphor to describe a related situation. The metaphor of the **sticky floor** describes the phenomenon of women who are employed in low-level, dead-end jobs with no chance of promotion (Gutek, 2001). One-third of all employed women perform some kind of office work. Women also work in service professions, as cashiers and waitresses. They are likely to remain in these jobs throughout their work life, never being considered for positions with greater responsibility (Headlee & Elfin, 1996).

A third metaphor describes another component of gender bias. According to the **glass escalator** phenomenon, when men enter fields often associated with women—becoming nurses, teachers, librarians, and social workers—they are often quickly promoted to management positions (Coleman, 1996; C. L. Williams, 1998). The glass escalator whisks them up to a more prestigious position. For example, a male teacher in elementary special education was asked about his career choice. He replied, "I am extremely marketable in special education. That's not why I got into the field. But I am extremely marketable because I am a man" (C. L. Williams, 1998, p. 288).

In short, women generally face discrimination with respect to promotion. The three stereotypes that we mentioned on pages 213–214 in connection with hiring patterns also operate when women want to advance in their occupations (Burn, 1996; Martell et al., 1998). After reviewing a wide range of studies on treatment discrimination, Jerry A. Jacobs (1995) concluded that females have a long way to go before they have the same status as men in the workplace. Specifically, "Women managers continue to trail their male counterparts in both earnings and authority" (p. 172).

Other Kinds of Treatment Discrimination

In addition to discrimination in salary and promotions, women experience treatment discrimination in other areas (Benokraitis, 1998; Cleveland et al., 2000; Lyness & Thompson, 1997). For example, several studies show that women in the workplace are more likely than men to receive a negative evaluation (e.g., Gerber, 2001; Heilman, 2001). You'll recall from Chapter 2 that women sometimes (although not always) are downgraded for their performance. The research on evaluation in the workplace confirms a point we made throughout Chapter 6: Women are especially likely to be downgraded if they are seen as assertive, independent, and unfeminine (Fiske et al., 1993). Other analyses show that women are especially likely to receive negative workplace ratings (relative to men) when the rater is somewhat preoccupied with other tasks or when the rater makes a rating sometime after observing the individual (Martell, 1991, 1996b). In the real world, executives frequently rate their employees under distracted or delayed conditions—with unfortunate consequences for women!

For women teaching at colleges and universities, students provide other forms of treatment discrimination. For instance, male students are generally more likely than female students to give their female college professors poor ratings on their teaching performance, especially in courses considered stereotypically masculine (Basow, 1998). In addition, students often assume that their male professors have had more education than their female professors (J. Miller & Chamberlin, 2000). When students address their female professors who have Ph.D.'s, they are likely to call them "Miss———" or "Ms.———," instead of "Dr.———" (Benokraitis, 1998).

Another form of treatment discrimination is **sexual harassment,** or "deliberate or repeated comments, gestures, or physical contacts of a sexual nature that are unwanted by the recipient" (American Psychological Association, 1990, p. 393). (We'll discuss sexual harassment in detail in Chapter 13.) Women frequently experience this kind of treatment discrimination on the job. Some harassers specifically tell women that sexual favors are a prerequisite for job advancement. Other harassers' messages are more subtle, although no less humiliating. One legal secretary recalled, for example, that her boss instructed one of his clients to ask her to get up and get him a cup of coffee so he could see what great legs she has (J. L. Pierce, 1995).

Another potential kind of treatment discrimination is less dramatic, although it has important implications. Specifically, coworkers may make negative gender-related comments that convey the message that women are second-class citizens (St. Jean & Feagin, 1997). A Black female firefighter recalled her first encounter with her White male supervisor:

> The first day I came on, the first day I was in the field, the guy told me he didn't like me. And then he said: "I'm gonna tell you why I don't like you. Number one, I don't like you cuz you're Black. And number two, cuz you're a woman." And that was all he said. He walked away. (J. D. Yoder & Aniakudo, 1997, p. 329)

You won't be surprised to learn, then, that women are often more likely than men to report negative interactions in the workplace (Blau & Tatum, 2000; Kite & Balogh, 1997). Women often lack a mentor who can offer both advice and support, and they may also be excluded from informal social interactions both at work and after hours. Business may be conducted at these events, and important information may be exchanged (Bronstein & Farnsworth, 1998; Lyness & Thompson, 2000). Furthermore, the friendships that are strengthened outside work may provide access to prestigious assignments, useful hints, and other factors that could lead to career advancement. In addition to facing other forms of discrimination, women certainly do not have equal opportunities in informal social interactions.

Discrimination Against Lesbians in the Workplace

In Chapter 2, we noted that **heterosexism** is a bias against lesbians, gay males, and bisexuals—any group that is not heterosexual. Lesbians frequently face heterosexism in the workplace. A lesbian mortgage broker remarked about the effects of heterosexism on her career:

> I was on the fast track in my company—I was on special committees, getting bonuses, the whole works. Somehow my employer found out that I had a female domestic partner and—*pow!*—it took no time before I was fired. Despite my not being out and being considered an attractive woman, the mere fact of my being a lesbian was enough to get me fired. There was no law to protect me from this. (Blank & Slipp, 1994, p. 141)

Most students are surprised to learn that, in many cases, employers can fire employees for any reason they choose, including being a lesbian (Purcell & Hicks, 1996). As you can guess, many employers refuse to hire individuals who are known to be gay. For example, public schools often discriminate against hiring lesbians, gays, and bisexuals as teachers. The unjustified argument is that these individuals may try to persuade young people to adopt a nonheterosexual orientation (Purcell & Hicks, 1996).

The research suggests that people who are open and accepting of their gay identity are higher in self-esteem (Walters & Simoni, 1993). Sadly, many jobs seem to require that gay individuals remain in the closet. Many lesbians and gay men say they spend so much energy trying to hide their sexual orientation that their work is less productive (Blank & Slipp, 1994). Furthermore, many lesbian professors discover that their colleagues are surprisingly negative about lesbians, even at presumably liberal universities. However, some lesbian professors who teach at presumably conservative institutions report that their colleagues are surprisingly positive (B. Mintz & Rothblum, 1997).

Should lesbians, gay men, and bisexuals disclose their sexual orientation to potential employers? Openness makes sense for people who plan to be "out" in their work setting, especially for people who would not choose to work in a heterosexist environment (Gonsiorek, 1996; Wenniger & Conroy, 2001). However, some lesbians prefer to receive the job offer first and then come out gradually to colleagues. As you know from this chapter, bias is less likely when people are already familiar with an employee's work.

What to Do About Treatment Discrimination

The title of this section is daunting: How can we possibly try to correct all the forces that encourage gender discrimination in the workplace? A few guidelines may be helpful with respect to the actions of both individuals and institutions.

Individuals can have an impact on their own work experiences as well as on the experiences of other women:

1. Women should be aware of the conditions in which stereotypes are least likely to operate, for example, when the job applicant's qualifications are clear-cut rather than ambiguous. Find work you enjoy, and develop skills and experiences that are especially relevant to your occupation (Committee on Women in Psychology, 1998; O'Connell, 2001). You should also know your legal rights.
2. Join relevant organizations, use the Internet, and make connections with other supportive people (Carli, 1998; Wenniger & Conroy, 2001; Zahm, 1998). Feminist organizations may be especially helpful. In a study by Klonis and her colleagues (1997), female psychology professors reported that they experienced feminism as "a life raft in the choppy, frigid waters of gender discrimination" (p. 343).
3. Locate a woman who has achieved success in your profession; ask whether she can serve as a mentor (Bronstein & Farnsworth, 1998; O'Connell, 2001; Quick, 2000). You can also try to enlist the help of male employees who seem to be supportive of women (Benokraitis & Feagin, 1994).

In reality, however, individuals cannot overcome the entire problem of gender discrimination. Institutions must change. It is often in their best interests to become more diversified—more like the real world outside the institution (Cleveland et al., 2000). Many of you probably share my skepticism that government organizations and corporations would genuinely want to eliminate discrimination. However, one important component is already in place: Gender discrimination is legally prohibited. Organizations that are truly committed to change can take the following precautions:

1. Understand affirmative action policies and take them seriously; make sure that women are included in the pool of candidates for hiring and promotion. Develop guidelines within the organization (Bronstein & Farnsworth, 1998; Eberhardt & Fiske, 1998; Reskin, 1998).
2. Appoint a task force to examine gender issues within the organization, and make it clear that the group's recommendations will be valued and carried out (Cleveland et al., 2000; Kite & Balogh, 1997). Incentives should be offered to managers who are successful in meeting diversity goals. Diversity training workshops are also useful (Rynes & Rosen, 1995).
3. Train managers so that they can evaluate candidates fairly, reducing gender stereotypes (Facteau & Dobbins, 1996; Gerber, 2001). Managers who rate employees should be encouraged to ask themselves questions such as "How would I evaluate this performance if the person were a man rather than a woman?" (Valian, 1998, p. 309).

Realistically, creating a gender-fair work experience requires a massive transformation of our culture, beginning with nonsexist child rearing, awareness and acceptance of feminist concerns, and an appreciation for women's contributions. Comparable worth must also become the standard policy (J. D. Yoder, 2000). A truly gender-fair work world would also provide a national child-care plan, and it would ensure that men would perform an equal share of child-care and housework responsibilities—a topic we'll examine at the end of this chapter (Cleveland et al., 2000).

SECTION SUMMARY ▪

Discrimination in the Workplace

1. Women earn lower salaries than men; research demonstrates that the wage gap remains, even when such factors as occupation, education, and experience are taken into account.

2. Comparable worth means that women and men should receive the same pay for occupations that require comparable complexity, education, skill, and responsibility.

3. Men typically feel entitled to a higher salary than women do; also, women may fail to acknowledge that they are underpaid.

4. Women experience discrimination in terms of promotion; three interrelated kinds of discrimination are called the glass ceiling, the sticky floor, and the glass escalator (in which men are more quickly promoted).

5. Women experience other kinds of treatment discrimination, such as lower evaluations from supervisors and (in the case of professors) from students; women may also face sexual harassment and exclusion from social interactions.

6. Lesbians are especially likely to experience workplace discrimination; they may be fired because of their sexual orientation, and they may feel it necessary to hide their sexual orientation.

7. Treatment discrimination can be addressed through the actions of individuals and institutions, but a genuine solution must depend on more widespread societal change.

WOMEN'S EXPERIENCES IN SELECTED OCCUPATIONS

We have seen that women face access discrimination when they apply for work and that they encounter a variety of treatment discriminations once they are employed. In this section, we will examine women's work experiences in several specific occupations.

On the news, we hear about women who are physicians, heads of corporations, and steelworkers. Women who are nurses, cashiers, and cafeteria workers do not make headlines. Even though the majority of employed women may engage in traditional clerical and service occupations, their work is relatively invisible.

Let's begin by discussing some traditionally female occupations. Then we'll examine two areas in which women are employed less often, the traditionally male professions and traditionally male blue-collar work. After discussing why women are so scarce in nontraditional occupations, we'll consider homemakers, who are among the least visible female workers.

Employment in Traditionally Female Occupations

Table 7.1 lists some representative traditional occupations and shows the percentage of workers who are women. Close to half of all female professional or technical workers are in traditional areas such as nursing and precollege teaching. This observation does not imply that something is wrong with traditionally female occupations. In fact, our society's children would probably be better off if occupations such as child care and elementary school teaching were more highly valued. However, women in traditionally female jobs frequently confront real-world problems, such as low income, underutilization of abilities, and lack of independence in decision making.

Similar employment patterns operate in Canada. The 10 most frequent jobs for men include truck driver, janitor, and retail trade manager (Statistics Canada, 1996a). The 10 most frequent jobs for women include secretary, cashier, and nurse (Statistics Canada, 1996b). The only job that appears on both the men's list and the women's list is retail salesperson.

TABLE 7.1 ■ Percentage of Workers in Selected Traditionally Female Occupations Who Are Female

Occupation	Percentage of Workers Who Are Women
Secretary	99%
Speech therapist	94
Registered nurse	93
Elementary school teacher	83
Social worker	72

Source: Bureau of Labor Statistics (2001a).

Keep in mind, though, that the work considered traditional for women may be quite different in developing countries. Most women in Western Europe work in service occupations, but throughout most of Africa, 75% of the women in the labor force work in agriculture (United Nations, 1995). We even see different work patterns within the same continent. For example, consider two African countries. In Sierra Leone, the men are responsible for the rice fields; in Senegal, the rice fields are managed by women (Burn, 1996).

Perhaps the only characteristic that all these traditionally female occupations have in common is that the pay is relatively low. As we discussed in connection with welfare, women who work at many of these jobs earn wages that are below the poverty level. Writer Barbara Ehrenreich (2001) tried to see how she could survive working as a waitress and a hotel maid, for $6 to $7 an hour. She found that the only way to make ends meet was to work seven days a week—and hope that she didn't have to buy a new pair of shoes or repair her car.

Let's consider two traditionally female jobs: domestic work and work in the garment industry. Consistent with Theme 3, this kind of women's work is generally invisible; women do the work, but few people notice (Zandy, 2001). Furthermore, women are especially likely to be exploited in these jobs.

Domestic Work.   Immigrant women from the Caribbean and Latin America often come to the United States to live and work in private homes, doing domestic work until they can earn a green card, which will allow them to find better jobs. Their employers may offer room and board and may pay as little as $120 for a 60-hour work week (Hondagneu-Sotelo, 1997). Colen (1997) described the lives of Caribbean domestic workers in New York City. These women are expected to work long hours for minimal pay. Many of the women described the insults they receive from their employers, who treat them much like modern-day slaves. For example, one woman reported:

> I work hard. I don't mind working hard. But I want to be treated with some human affection, like a human being. . . . I don't get any respect. . . . Since I came here this woman has never shown me one iota of . . . human affection as a human being. (p. 205)

Liba Taylor/Panos Pictures

PHOTO 7.1 ■ Women working in a sweatshop in Bangladesh.

Garment Work.   Most of us wake up in the morning, button up a shirt, and do not consider the life of the person who made that shirt—most often, a woman. About half of all the clothes purchased in the United States have been made in another country, often under inhuman conditions (Zia, 1996). Many of our clothes are made in **sweatshops,** which are defined as factories that violate labor laws regarding wages and working conditions. For instance, workers in Bangladesh in Southeast Asia are paid about 15 cents an hour. In an hour, a woman can usually sew about 10 of the kinds of caps that your university probably sells. In other words, she probably earns 1.5 cents for each cap (National Labor Committee, 2001).

In Latin America, these sweatshops are called *maquiladoras* (pronounced mah-kee-lah-*door*-ahs) or *maquilas,* and they are typically run by U.S. corporations. In addition to the long hours, low pay, and unsafe working conditions, the women who work in these sweatshops often experience sexual harassment and physical abuse. If they try to organize a union, they may be fired; many have even received death threats (C. Barton & Nazombei, 2000; Hesse-Biber & Carter, 2000; "Maquila Workers Attacked for Organizing a Union," 2001).

Illegal sweatshops are operating in some North American cities. These sweatshops are hidden away so that inspectors cannot find them. They employ mostly Latina and Asian immigrants, many of whom are undocumented, so the workers know they cannot protest about the working conditions (Soldatenko, 1999; Zia, 1996). A woman in a sweatshop in New York's Chinatown may earn about $8,000 a year, working 16-hour days (National Mobilization Against

Sweatshops, 2000). Clothing manufacturers also hire women to work at home, where they are even less visible to inspectors looking for labor violations. These women are paid for each completed item, and they may not be aware that a legal factory would pay twice as much. In Toronto, an estimated 4,000 to 8,000 women do garment work in their homes (Bains, 1998).

The sweatshop issue cannot be addressed without looking at our economic system to discover who is making the greatest profits from our clothing industry. If this problem concerns you, call the National Labor Committee at (212) 242-3002 (or visit www.nicnet.org) to find out which companies pay women fairly and which ones have been charged for running sweatshops. Now try Demonstration 7.3.

Employment in Traditionally Male Professions

Ironically, we have more information about the relatively small number of women employed in "the male professions" than we have about the large number of women employed in traditionally female jobs. For example, in preparing this section, I found entire books on women in business and management (D. P. Moore & Buttner, 1997), in college teaching (Aguirre, 2000; L. H. Collins et al., 1998), in college administration (Wenniger & Conroy, 2001), in science (Etzkowitz et al., 2000; Pattatucci, 1998; Schiebinger, 1999), in computer science (Woodfield, 2000), in medicine (Wear, 1997), and in law (Guinier et al., 1997).

Unfortunately, this emphasis on nontraditional professions creates an impression that employed women are more likely to be executives than clerical workers. A more accurate picture of reality is shown in Table 7.2, which lists the percentage of workers who are women in several prestigious occupations. You can glance back at Table 7.1 to compare the two groups.

Incidentally, you'll note that I used the phrase *prestigious occupations* to refer to the male-dominated professions. Glick and his colleagues (1995) asked college students to rate the prestigiousness of a variety of occupations. Those rated most prestigious were all professions in which more men are employed than women.

DEMONSTRATION 7.3 ■ ■ ■ ■ ■ ■ ■ ■ ■ ■ ■ ■ ■ ■ ■ ■ ■ ■

Where Were Your Clothes Made?

Go to your closet or your dresser, and search each item of clothing for a label indicating where it was made. Record each location. What percentage was made in the United States or Canada, and what percentage was made in other countries? Later, when you have the opportunity, look in your college bookstore or other location that sells caps and sweatshirts featuring your college's logo. Where were these items made?

TABLE 7.2 ■ Percentage of Workers in Selected Traditionally Male Professions Who Are Female

Occupation	Percentage of Workers Who Are Women
Engineer	10%
Dentist	19
Architect	24
Physician	28
Lawyer	30

Source: Bureau of Labor Statistics (2001a).

This pattern suggests an interesting prediction. Some professions, such as veterinary medicine and psychology, once had far more males than females. In recent decades, however, the majority of students in veterinary schools and psychology graduate schools have been females (Gose, 1998; Norcross et al., 1996). Will these two career choices become less prestigious as the number of women in these fields increases?

Let's consider some of the characteristics of these women in traditionally male professions. Then we'll examine the climate in which these women work.

Characteristics of Women in Traditionally Male Professions. In general, the women who work in stereotypically masculine occupations are similar to the men in that area. To some extent, this similarity may occur because only those women with personal characteristics appropriate for that occupation would choose it for a career and persist in it (Cross & Vick, 2001).

As we would expect, women and men in the same profession tend to be similar in cognitive skills. For example, Cross (2001) found that men and women in science and engineering had earned similar scores on standardized tests as well as similar grades in graduate school. Other research shows that men and women have similar professional expectations and work involvement (Aven et al., 1993; Burke, 1999; Chiu, 1998). However, one area in which gender differences are often found is self-confidence (Cross, 2001). This finding is not surprising. As we observed in Chapter 5, men may be more self-confident than women in some achievement settings. We also saw in Chapter 6 that women are downgraded if they are too self-confident and assertive; this principle also applies in the world of work (Rudman & Glick, 1999).

The Workplace Climate for Women in Traditionally Male Professions. In Chapter 4, we saw that young female students may face a chilly climate in their academic classrooms. The chilly climate continues for many women in their graduate training and in their professions (Janz & Pyke, 2000). Earlier in this chapter, we noted several forms of treatment discrimination. Unfortunately, treatment discrimination has a clear effect on the professional environment.

For instance, Dr. Frances Conley (1998), a prominent neurosurgeon, described how the male neurosurgeons would attempt to kiss her neck while she was scrubbing up, call her "honey" in front of patients, and brag about their sexual conquests. One neurosurgeon would sometimes invite her to go to bed with him, thrust his pelvis forward, look down at his genitals, and directly ask his genitals whether they would like that experience.

Another problem for women in these traditionally male professions is that men may treat them in a patronizing fashion. For instance, one engineer described how the male engineers would frequently pat her on the head, as if she were a young daughter (McIlwee & Robinson, 1992). Other women in these professions point out that male colleagues are sometimes astonishingly sexist. For example, a male chemistry professor announced out loud to another man, "Why do you bother with women? They're almost as bad as foreigners" (Gleiser, 1998, p. 210). Obviously, this professor showed not only sexism but also U.S.-centered nationalism. In short, women in traditionally male professions receive many messages that they are not really equal to their male colleagues.

Employment in Traditionally Male Blue-Collar Jobs

Several years ago, Barbara Quintela's job as a secretary had paid $10 an hour. When her husband left her—and their five children—she became a displaced homemaker. (A **displaced homemaker** is a woman who has lost her primary source of income because of divorce, widowhood, extended unemployment of her spouse, and similar reasons.) She managed to persuade a school administrator to let her enroll in a high school training program for electricians. After a grueling interview with eight hostile administrators, she was accepted into an apprenticeship program that will eventually pay $22 an hour. As she says, "I like getting dirty, running wires, digging ditches, getting into crawl spaces. I would never want to go back to being a secretary. I can't *afford* to be a secretary" (J. C. Lambert, 2000, p. 6). Most women in blue-collar jobs report that the pay is attractive, especially compared to the salaries for traditionally feminine jobs (Coffin, 1997).

Most of the information on working women describes women in such traditionally male professions as medicine and law. In contrast, the information on women in blue-collar jobs is scanty. Women are slowly entering blue-collar fields, and the percentages are still small. Table 7.3 lists some representative employment rates for women in these jobs.

Women in blue-collar jobs report that they are often held to stricter standards than their male coworkers. For example, a Black woman firefighter was forced by her White male supervisor to recertify after her vehicle skidded into a pole during an ice storm. In contrast, a male colleague received no penalty when his vehicle accidentally killed an elderly pedestrian who was crossing a street (J. D. Yoder & Aniakudo, 1997). Women firefighters frequently comment that they would probably have to keep proving—for the rest of their lives—that they are competent workers (J. D. Yoder & Berendsen, 2001). Men often claim that women are physically unable to handle the work (P. Y. Martin & Collinson, 1998). Another study of women firefighters discovered that only 3 out of 44 women said that

TABLE 7.3 ■ Percentage of Workers in Selected Traditionally Male Blue-Collar Occupations Who Are Female

Occupation	Percentage of Workers Who Are Women
Automobile mechanic	1%
Carpenter	2
Firefighter	3
Truck driver	5
Farm worker	19

Source: Bureau of Labor Statistics (2001a).

they had never experienced sexist reactions on the job (J. D. Yoder & McDonald, 1998).

Sexual harassment is often common (S. Eisenberg, 1998). One woman cab-driver in Canada asked the dispatcher to call her for an early morning shift. Unfortunately, a male driver also heard her request. He called her at 3:40 a.m. and made sexually suggestive remarks (Boyd, 1997).

Fortunately, some women report that they develop good working relationships with their male colleagues. For instance, a White female firefighter described the bond she shared with her Black male coworkers:

> It's neat. Because I think a lot of them . . . we kind of have a bond, too. And they understand more what I go through than a White guy would. So, yeah. They're pretty together guys. They've come through the fire too, I think, in a lot of ways. (J. D. Yoder & Berendsen, 2001, p. 33)

Other women mention additional advantages to blue-collar work, such as a sense of pride in their own strength and satisfaction in doing a job well (Cull, 1997; S. Eisenberg, 1998). Others enjoy serving as a role model and encouraging young women to pursue work in nontraditional areas (Coffin, 1997).

Why Are Women Scarce in Certain Occupations?

Why do relatively few women work in the traditionally male professions or in the traditionally male blue-collar jobs? Researchers have identified two major classes of explanations. According to **person-centered explanations** (also called the **individual approach**), female socialization encourages women to develop personality traits that are inappropriate for these occupations (Hesse-Biber & Carter, 2000; Riger & Galligan, 1980). One example of a person-centered explanation is fear of success—the notion that women have negative reactions to successful achievement. However, according to Chapter 5, women and men are currently similar in their fear of success. Recall, also, that women and men are similar in other areas related to achievement, such as attributions for one's own success or failure. We also saw in Chapter 5 that women and men are similar in their cognitive abilities. Furthermore, in Chapter 6, we saw that women and men are similar in their leadership characteristics.

Most research in the psychology of women supports a second explanation for the scarcity of women. According to **situation-centered explanations** (or the **structural approach**), the characteristics of the organizational situation explain why women are rarely found in these traditionally masculine occupations; personal skills or traits cannot be blamed (Hesse-Biber & Carter, 2000; Riger & Galligan, 1980). For example, access discrimination may block women's opportunities. If women do manage to be hired, they face several kinds of treatment discrimination, such as the glass ceiling that blocks promotion (Cohn, 2000). Also, people in prestigious positions are not likely to help young women.

Notice that the person-centered explanations and the situation-centered explanations suggest different strategies for improving women's employment conditions. For example, if a woman aspires to a management position in a corporation, the person-centered explanations propose that women should take courses in handling finances, conducting meetings, and assertiveness training.

In contrast, the situation-centered explanations propose strategies designed to change the *situation,* not the person. For instance, programs should be instituted to train managers to use objective rating scales (Gerber, 2001). Affirmative action policies should be enforced; and women should be promoted into high-ranking positions (Etzkowitz et al., 2000).

Although these suggestions sound excellent, they are not likely to occur spontaneously. To some extent, organizations may realize that hiring competent women is in their own best interest (Etzkowitz et al., 2000). Also, as more women enter into nontraditional jobs, their coworkers may acknowledge their competence. Furthermore, with larger numbers of women engaged in an occupation, they will be more likely to push for fair treatment of women in the workplace. Now try Demonstration 7.4, if you haven't already.

DEMONSTRATION 7.4 ■ ■ ■ ■ ■ ■ ■ ■ ■ ■ ■ ■ ■ ■ ■ ■ ■ ■

Evaluating a Job Description

Based on the provided description, decide whether you would be tempted to apply for this job:

Help Wanted

Requirements: Intelligence, energy, patience, social skills, good health. *Tasks:* At least 12 different occupations. *Hours:* About 100 hours per week. *Salary:* None. *Holidays:* None (must remain on standby 24 hours a day, 7 days a week). *Opportunities for Advancement:* None (future employees will not be impressed with your work on this job). *Job Security:* None (layoffs are likely as you approach middle age). *Fringe Benefits:* Food, clothing, and shelter generally provided, but any additional bonuses will depend on the financial standing and good nature of the employer. No pension plan.

Source: Based on Chesler (1976, p. 97).

Homemakers

You probably recognized that the unappealing job description in Demonstration 7.4 lists the duties of a wife and mother. A **homemaker** is defined as someone who works full time as an unpaid laborer in the home (Lindsey, 1996). About 20% of adult women in the United States are currently full-time homemakers (Hesse-Biber & Carter, 2000). In the next section of this chapter, we'll see that even women with full-time paying jobs continue to do far more than their share of housework and child care. Here, we will focus on the diversity of responsibilities performed by homemakers.

Little research has been conducted on homemakers. As Theme 3 argues, topics associated almost exclusively with women tend to be invisible. Also, by definition, homemaking is unpaid, and our culture values work that earns money (Hesse-Biber & Carter, 2000; Lindsey, 1996).

We do know that the variety of tasks included in homemaking is so extensive that any list will necessarily be incomplete. Here is just a fraction of the responsibilities: shopping for food; preparing meals; washing dishes; making household purchases; cleaning the house; washing, ironing, and mending clothes; tending to the garden; taking care of the car; preparing children for school; transporting children; preparing children for bed; disciplining children; hiring child-care help; planning for holidays; managing household finances; and volunteering in the community (Lindsey, 1996; Pearce, 1993).

We do not need to dwell on the obviously unpleasant nature of many tasks performed by homemakers. Any job is frustrating if it must be repeated just as soon as it is finished or if it typically has no clear-cut standards of completion. (Is the kitchen floor ever really clean enough?)

In short, our discussion of working women in this chapter must acknowledge the tremendous amount of time and effort women devote to housework. This is work that someone must do. However, the tasks are extensive, repetitious, often frustrating, and low in prestige.

SECTION SUMMARY ■

Women's Experiences in Selected Occupations

1. Most employed women occupy traditional clerical and service jobs.

2. Women are especially likely to be exploited in two traditionally female jobs: domestic work and work in the garment industry.

3. Women who are employed in traditionally male professions are generally similar to the men in these professions in terms of personal characteristics and cognitive skills; however, the women are often lower in self-confidence.

4. Many women in traditionally male professions face sexual harassment, sexist attitudes, and patronizing treatment.

5. Women in blue-collar jobs may face biased treatment from the men on the job, but they value the salary and the sense of pride they gain from their work.

6. Person-centered explanations argue that women are absent from traditionally male occupations because they lack the personality characteristics and the appropriate skills. Situation-centered explanations provide a more accurate account of the findings; they emphasize that the structure of organizations prevents women's success.

7. The work of homemakers is relatively invisible, frustrating, and time consuming.

COORDINATING EMPLOYMENT WITH PERSONAL LIFE

Most college women plan to combine a career with family life (Fitzgerald & Rounds, 1994; Hoffnung, 1993; Novack & Novack, 1996). Yet the popular media claim that the employed woman is a total wreck. Barnett and Rivers (1996) described the media's viewpoint:

> [The employed woman is] so stressed out that she's going to drop dead of a heart attack right at her desk; she's probably chewing hundreds of Tums or thinking of sticking her head in the microwave because she's so prone to anxiety and depression. (p. 24)

Throughout this textbook, we've seen that reality is often different from the myth presented by the media. In this section, we'll see that employed women may find it challenging to combine their many roles, but they are *not* dropping out of their careers by the thousands, as some magazine articles imply. Let's see how employment influences three components of a woman's personal life: (1) her marriage, (2) her children, and (3) her own well-being.

Marriage

In 53% of all married couples in the United States, both the wife and the husband are employed (Bureau of Labor Statistics, 2001b). Try Demonstration 7.5 on page 234 before you read further, and then we'll consider two questions:

1. How do families divide their household responsibilities?
2. Does employment influence marital satisfaction?

Performing Household Tasks.   Throughout this chapter, we've often noted that women are treated unfairly in the world of work. When we consider how married couples divide household tasks, we find additional evidence of unfairness.

Several studies in the United States suggest that women perform between 60% and 70% of the household tasks in two-job families (Bianchi et al., 2000; Coltrane & Adams, 2001a; Perkins & DeMeis, 1996; L. B. Silverstein, 1996). Research in Canada also shows that women do about two-thirds of the housework (Brayfield, 1992; Devereaux, 1993; Statistics Canada, 1995). The same pattern has also been observed in Great Britain, China, and Japan (Brush, 1998).

DEMONSTRATION 7.5   ■ ■ ■ ■ ■ ■ ■ ■ ■ ■ ■ ■ ■ ■ ■ ■ ■ ■

Division of Responsibility for Household Tasks

Think about a married heterosexual couple with whom you are familiar; it might be your parents, the parents of a close friend, or your own current relationship with someone of the other gender. For each task in the following list, place a check mark to indicate which member of the pair is *primarily* responsible. Is this pattern similar to the division of housework we are discussing in this chapter?

Task	Wife	Husband
Shopping for food	_____	_____
Cooking	_____	_____
Washing the dishes	_____	_____
Laundry	_____	_____
Vacuuming	_____	_____
Washing the car	_____	_____
Gardening	_____	_____
Taking out the trash	_____	_____
Paying the bills	_____	_____
Household repairs	_____	_____

Women are much more likely than men to do the cooking, cleaning, laundry, dish washing, and shopping. The only indoor chore that men are more likely to do is household repair (Galinsky & Bond, 1996; Landry, 2000). Another issue is that men seldom take responsibility for noticing when a household task needs to be done; instead, the typical husband waits for his wife to remind him (Coltrane & Adams, 2001a). Also, the men don't seem to acknowledge how little housework they do; only 52% of men in one study agreed with the statement "Men typically don't do their share of work around the house" (Reiser, 2001, p. 35). Earlier in the chapter, we noted a wage gap between the salaries of employed men and women. Here, we notice a leisure gap for employed men and women (Coltrane & Adams, 2001a).

Are household tasks shared more equally when the wife works outside the home rather than when she is a full-time homemaker? Some research suggests that men perform more housework when they are married to employed women, but they still do much less than 50% (Risman, 1998; Spain & Bianchi, 1996). I found only one study focusing on the reverse question: What happens when the woman works outside the home and the husband is not employed? S. K. Davis and Chavez (1995) studied Latina/o families in which the wife was employed outside the home and was considered the primary wage earner in the household. Because the husbands were either unemployed or worked part time, we might expect husbands to take on many household chores. However, wives were still more likely to be responsible for the laundry, dishes, cooking, and cleaning. The leisure gap was therefore particularly striking in this sample. Would it be equally large for other ethnic groups?

How do cultural background and ethnicity influence the division of household tasks? One study reported that housework is more evenly divided among French Canadian couples than among English Canadian couples (Brayfield, 1992). In the United States, two nationwide studies concluded that Black and White families were similar in the way they divided housework (D. John & Shelton, 1997; Landry, 2000). Other research focused on four ethnic groups in Southern California (Stohs, 2000). Black husbands spent more time on household tasks than did Asian or Middle Eastern husbands; Latino husbands spent less time on these tasks.

As Spain and Bianchi (1996) observed, academic researchers seem to be more troubled by the unequal division of housework than are the women they interview. What's going on here? Nevill (1995) reported that college men and women have similar scores on a measure of commitment to home and family. Apparently, however, the men are not committed to housework. How do the men explain their lack of responsibility for household tasks? Although many men may be more sensitive, one man explained, "People shouldn't do what they don't want to do. . . . And I don't want to do it" (Rhode, 1997, p. 150). Earlier in this chapter, we noted that men often feel entitled to higher salaries than women receive. Apparently, many men also feel entitled to leave the housework to their wives (Steil, 2000).

Surprisingly, many women do not express anger toward their greater work in the home (Ferree, 1994). Instead, they tend to show the same "denial of personal disadvantage" that they show for the wage gap. If wives complain to an interviewer that they are doing more housework than their husbands, they frequently add that the discrepancy really isn't very important (Dryden, 1999). Some employed women come home from work and feel guilty that they are not being "wifely" enough (Biernat & Wortman, 1991). Amy, who is employed full time and has two daughters, feels guilty when she falls behind in doing the laundry:

> I'm so ashamed. If I'm behind, or there is something that [my husband] would really like and hasn't had for a week or so, like a flannel shirt, and hasn't seen it around, then he'll probably put a load of laundry in so he can get it. I'm pretty good—sometimes I just get bogged down, and he'll help out. (Hoffnung, 1992, p. 148)

Notice that the laundry is considered to be Amy's problem and that her husband simply helps out. If the women cannot negotiate a more equal division of housework, perhaps they should set lower standards for themselves.

Satisfaction with Marriage.   In general, a woman's employment status does not influence her marital satisfaction or the stability of her marriage (L. W. Hoffman & Youngblade, 1999; Stoltz-Loike, 1992; L. White & Rogers, 2000). For example,

Stacy J. Rogers (1996) analyzed data from a national sample of 1,323 women, all married continuously to the same men and all with at least one child living at home. She found no statistically significant difference in the women's reports of marital quality as a function of being employed or nonemployed.

However, marital satisfaction *is* related to other work-related factors. For example—no surprise!—employed women are usually happier with their marriage if their husbands perform a relatively large percentage of the housework (Coltrane & Adams, 2001b; Hesse-Biber & Carter, 2000; Steil, 2000). In contrast, women whose husbands are doing relatively little housework are at risk for depression (C. E. Bird, 1999), as we'll see in Chapter 12.

In summary, women who work outside the home may be busier than non-employed women. However, they are not necessarily less satisfied with their marriages.

Children

In the United States and Canada, most surveys of young women show that they expect to combine a career with motherhood (Davey, 1998; Hoffnung, 1999, 2000). However, in an occasional study, young women report that they plan to give up their career once they have children (Riggs, 2001). Try Demonstration 7.6, to explore this question with your own friends.

The reality is that most North American mothers do work outside the home. In the United States, 72% of mothers with children under the age of 18 are currently employed (Bureau of Labor Statistics, 2001b). The data are comparable for Canada, where 70% of mothers with children under the age of 16 are currently employed (Statistics Canada, 2001d). These observations suggest two important questions concerning the children of employed women:

1. How are the child-care tasks divided in two-parent families?
2. Does a mother's employment influence children's psychological adjustment?

Taking Care of Children.   In the previous section, we saw that women perform more housework than men do. Who's taking care of the children? The research suggests that fathers have substantially increased their child-care responsibilities since similar studies were conducted 30 years ago. Still, researchers estimate that mothers perform between 60% and 90% of child-care tasks (L. W. Hoffman, 2000; Pleck, 1997; L. B. Silverstein, 1996). If we combine the hours spent on housework and the hours spent on child care, we see that mothers devote many more hours working in the home, in comparison to fathers (Dryden, 1999; M. Fine & Carney, 2001). No consistent ethnic differences have been reported in the proportion of child-care tasks that fathers perform (Pleck, 1997).

When fathers perform a high proportion of the child care, children show greater cognitive and social skills (Coltrane & Adams, 2001; L. W. Hoffman & Youngblade, 1999; Pleck, 1997). Apparently, children benefit from having two caring adults actively involved in their lives. Fathers who spend more time in child care are also healthier and more caring of other people than are uninvolved fathers. In addition, these fathers have better relationships with their chil-

DEMONSTRATION 7.6 ■ ■ ■ ■ ■ ■ ■ ■ ■ ■ ■ ■ ■ ■ ■ ■ ■

College Students' Plans About Careers and Parenthood

Conduct an informal survey of your friends, ideally at least five females and five females. (Note that you must select people who would feel comfortable discussing this topic with you.) Ask them each individually the following questions:

1. After you have finished your education, would you plan to seek employment? How many hours would you expect to work each week?
2. After you have finished your education, do you see yourself becoming a parent? (If the answer is no, you do not need to ask additional questions.)
3. Suppose that you and your partner have had a baby, and the baby is now 1 year old. How many hours a week would you expect to work outside the home? How many hours a week would you expect your partner to work outside the home?
4. How many hours a week would you expect to spend taking care of the baby? How many hours a week would you expect your partner to spend in child care?

Note the percentage of respondents who plan to be employed when they are the parents of a 1-year-old child. If you surveyed both women and men, did you notice any differences in their patterns of responses?

---

dren (Barnett & Rivers, 1996; hooks, 2000a; Pleck, 1997). In other words, both fathers and children seem to benefit from the time they spend together.

Francine Deutsch and her colleagues have studied married couples who share their child-care activities reasonably equally (Deutsch, 1999, 2001; Deutsch & Saxon, 1998a, 1998b). These parents describe the difficulty of breaking out of the traditional patterns of child care. However, many fathers report the unexpected benefits of sharing child care. For example, a fire inspector who is married to a secretary commented:

> [I've gained] time with my wife. I mean it's not much time, but whatever time there is in the evening. If one of us had to do everything, then we wouldn't have the time together. I enjoy spending time with my wife too (as well as the kids). It's crazy sometimes, crazy most days, but I love my life. I love the way it is and I can't see living any other way. (Deutsch, 1999, p. 134)

Many women have no husband who can—even theoretically—share in the care of the children. Mothers who are single, separated, divorced, or widowed typically work outside the home for economic reasons. For these women, the logistic problems of arranging for child care and transporting children become even more complicated. In addition, unmarried mothers usually have sole responsibility for nurturing their children, helping them with homework, and disciplining them.

Maternal Employment and Children.   College students tend to believe that a mother's employment has a negative impact on her children (Bridges & Etaugh, 1994, 1995, 1996). The research contradicts this belief. We need to emphasize that the topic of maternal employment and children's adjustment is complex. The nature of our conclusions depends on a wide variety of variables, such as the quality of the child-care program, the economic background of the family, and the mother's sensitivity to her child's needs (Brooks-Gunn et al., 2002; NICHD Early Child Care Research Network, 1999, 2001, 2002).

In general, the cognitive development of children who have been in a day-care setting is similar to that of children cared for by their mother at home. For low-income families, day care may even provide cognitive advantages, especially when the day care is high quality (L. W. Hoffman, 2000; NICHD Early Child Care Research Network, 2001; Scarr, 1998).

In addition, most infants who spend time in a day-care center have the same kind of emotional closeness to their mothers as do children whose mothers do not work outside the home. The only exception is children who have poor-quality day care and whose mothers are not sensitive to their needs (L. W. Hoffman, 2000; NICHD Early Child Care Research Network, 1999, 2001; Weinraub et al., 2001).

The picture is mixed for some aspects of social behavior (E. Harvey, 1999). For example, children in poor-quality day-care settings may show more aggression than children cared for by their mothers. However, children in high-quality day care are more cooperative, and they have fewer behavior problems (NICHD Early Child Care Research Network, 2001, 2002; Weinraub et al., 2001).

Children whose mothers work outside the home do have one important advantage: Their mothers provide models of competent women who can achieve in the workplace (Coontz, 1997; L. W. Hoffman & Youngblade, 1999). In general, the research shows that children of employed mothers are not as gender stereotyped as children who are cared for in the home by their mothers (Etaugh, 1993; L. W. Hoffman, 2000). Also, college students whose mothers were employed when these students were young are more supportive of maternal employment. These individuals may realize that their mothers' employment had a positive effect on their families when they were growing up (Willetts-Bloom & Nock, 1994).

In short, the overall picture suggests that children's development is not substantially affected by nonmaternal care (Erel et al., 2000; L. W. Hoffman, 2000). However, U.S. families face a problem. Children clearly benefit from good day care, and high-quality child care at a reasonable price is not widely available (Brooks-Gunn et al., 2002; Coontz, 1997; Neft & Levine, 1997). We claim that children are a top priority, yet the government does not subsidize child care. In France, Denmark, and Sweden, parents can enroll their children in a variety of programs at no cost or at a minimal charge (Neft & Levine, 1997). In fact, the United States is one of a few industrialized countries that does not have comprehensive child-care policies (Hesse-Biber & Carter, 2000; L. B. Silverstein & Auerbach, 1999).

Personal Adjustment

We have examined both the marriages and the children of employed women. But how are the women themselves doing? Do they experience role strain? How is their physical and mental health?

Role Strain.   A female physician who directs an inner-city medical clinic for adolescents commented about her life:

> I don't know any professional woman in her 40s who feels her life is balanced. At that age, we are all overcommitted. Perhaps we figure it out in our 50s. (Asch-Goodkin, 1994, p. 63)

This woman is describing **role strain,** which occurs when people have difficulty fulfilling all their different role obligations. A study of Canadian nurses, for example, reported high levels of role strain and burnout (Thorpe et al., 1998).

Employed women often experience role strain in the form of conflict between a job and family responsibilities (Cleveland et al., 2000; Davidson & Fielden, 1999; Hochschild, 1997). However, employed women often say they would miss their work identity if they stopped working outside the home. One mother, who is a well-paid professional, remarked:

> If I just stay at home, I'll kind of lose—I don't want to say my *sense* of identity—but I guess I'll lose my career identity. . . . My friend who stays at home, she had a career before she had her children, but I forget what it was. So that whole part of her, I can't even identify it now. (Hays, 1996, p. 142)

Physical Health.   We might imagine that role strain could lead to poor physical health for employed women. However, the data suggest that employed women are, if anything, healthier than nonemployed women (Barnett & Rivers, 1996; Cleveland et al., 2000). Only one group of employed women has substantial health problems: women who have low-paying or unrewarding jobs, several children, and an unsupportive husband (Barnett & Rivers, 1996; Cleveland et al., 2000; Noor, 1999).

Mental Health.   After reading the earlier section about role strain, you may have a mental image of a bleary-eyed woman who arrives home from a grueling day at work just in time to feed the dog, change the baby's diapers, and set the dinner table. This woman, it would seem, has every right to be depressed and unhappy. However, as we'll see in this section, employed women are typically as happy as nonemployed women. In fact, they are often happier and better adjusted (Barnett & Rivers, 1996; Betz, 1993; L. W. Hoffman, 2000). Many women are excited by the challenge of a difficult task and the enormous pleasure of successfully achieving a long-term occupational goal.

For many women, having multiple roles provides a buffer effect (Barnett, 1997; Barnett & Hyde, 2001; Cleveland et al., 2000). Specifically, employment acts as a buffer against the stress of family problems, and family life acts as a buffer against problems at work. When these roles are generally positive, the benefits of multiple roles seem to outweigh the disadvantages (J. D. Yoder, 2000).

Several studies have demonstrated that women's lives are enhanced by employment. In general, employed women report a greater sense of competence and accomplishment, compared to nonemployed women (Cleveland et al., 2000; P. H. Hoffman & Hale-Benson, 1987).

Little cross-cultural information is available on employed women's multiple roles. One exception is a study conducted in South Korea by Park and Liao (2000). This research compared married female professors with female home-makers who were married to professors. Park and Liao's results showed that the female professors experienced both greater role strain and greater feelings of gratification—similar to the general trend of North American research.

In one large-scale study, Barnett (1997) studied 300 married couples, all of whom worked outside the home. She found that women who had challenging and rewarding jobs coped well with problems at home, such as frustrating child-care issues. However, women who have low-status, unrewarding jobs report lower general life satisfaction and greater levels of distress (Noor, 1996). Another study demonstrated that French Canadian women were significantly higher in self-esteem if their occupations gave them the opportunity to work independently and to feel accomplished. These characteristics of their jobs were more important than salary in determining self-esteem (Streit & Tanguay, 1994).

We cannot ignore the fact that employed women experience a leisure gap; their housework and child-care responsibilities are much greater than those of employed men (Hochschild, 1997). This problem cannot be solved by women learning how to manage their time more effectively (Nevill & Calvert, 1996). Wise couples will negotiate more equitable sharing of the workload at home.

Most important, our society needs to acknowledge the reality of employed women and dual-earner families (Barnett, 2001). As Barnett and Rivers (1996) emphasized:

> The facts are clear: Women are working and will do so in even greater numbers in the near future. They are not going home. Paid employment has a positive impact on the physical and emotional health of women, and trying to get them to work part-time or relinquish their commitment to work will harm—not improve—their health. (p. 38)

SECTION SUMMARY

Coordinating Employment with Personal Life

1. Among North American families, women do about 60% to 70% of the house-hold tasks, although women typically do not express anger about their greater workload.

2. In general, a woman's satisfaction with her marriage is not influenced by whether she works outside the home.

3. North American women perform the clear majority of child-care tasks; fathers' time spent in child care is not consistently related to ethnicity. Both fathers and children benefit from fathers' involvement with child care.

4. In general, children in day care do not experience major disadvantages with respect to cognitive abilities, attachment, or social development, and they may develop more flexible beliefs about gender. The quality of day care has an important influence on children's psychological development.

5. Employed women often experience role strain from conflicting responsibilities.

6. Employed women are as healthy and as well adjusted psychologically as non-employed women; women with satisfying jobs seem to be even healthier and better adjusted.

▪ ▪ ▪ ▪ ▪ ▪ CHAPTER REVIEW QUESTIONS ▪ ▪ ▪ ▪ ▪ ▪

1. Consider several women you know who are between the ages of 25 and 35. Think about the personal characteristics related to women's employment. Do these factors help explain which women are employed and which are nonemployed?

2. Where did you learn your previous information about women and welfare: from other classes, from the media, or from people you know? Which aspects of this chapter's discussion match your previous information, and which aspects are new?

3. Based on this chapter's examination of access discrimination, describe a situation in which a woman would be especially likely to face access discrimination when she applies for a job. What factors would make a woman *least* likely to face access discrimination? How would affirmative action operate in hiring situations?

4. What kinds of treatment discrimination might women face in the workplace? Discuss the research on this topic, and supplement it with some of the factors mentioned in the section on women's experiences in selected occupations.

5. Suppose that a friend claims that the wage gap can be entirely explained by the fact that

women are more likely than men to stop working once they have children and that they have less education. How would you answer this claim, and how would you explain the concept of comparable worth?

6. Compare the experiences of employed women and employed men with respect to the glass ceiling, the sticky floor, the glass escalator, and personality characteristics (of men and women in the same occupation). Also compare women's and men's performance of household and child-care tasks.

7. Outline the two general kinds of explanations that have been offered for women's underrepresentation in certain jobs (pp. 230–231). Review the section summaries in Chapters 5 and 6, and note which explanation is most supported by the evidence from cognitive and social gender comparisons.

8. How does the denial of personal disadvantage apply to a woman's reaction to the wage gap? What similar process operates when a woman considers the gap in the amount of housework and child care that she and her husband perform?

9. Imagine that you are a 25-year-old woman and that you have decided to return to your former job after the birth of your first baby.

A neighbor tells you that your child will probably develop psychological problems if you work outside the home. Cite evidence to defend your decision.

10. Imagine that you are part of a new task force in your state or province. This task force has been instructed to make recommendations to improve the situation of women in the workplace. Based on the information in this chapter, make a list of 8 to 10 recommendations.

NEW TERMS

*working women (208)
*employed women (208)
*nonemployed women (208)
*access discrimination (212)
 gender-role spillover (214)
*affirmative action (214)
*reverse discrimination (215)
 treatment discrimination (215)
*comparable worth (217)
*occupational segregation (217)
*entitlement (219)
*denial of personal disadvantage (219)
*glass ceiling (219)

*sticky floor (220)
*glass escalator (220)
*sexual harassment (221)
*heterosexism (221)
*sweatshops (226)
*maquiladoras (226)
*displaced homemaker (229)
 person-centered explanations (230)
*individual approach (230)
 situation-centered explanations (231)
*structural approach (231)
*homemaker (232)
*role strain (239)

The terms asterisked in the New Terms section serve as good search terms for InfoTrac College Edition. Go to http://infotrac.thomsonlearning.com and try these added search terms.

RECOMMENDED READINGS

Cleveland, J. N., Stockdale, M., & Murphy, K. R. (2000). *Women and men in organizations.* Mahwah, NJ: Erlbaum. This comprehensive textbook provides a clear overview of the topic. Some especially relevant chapters focus on topics related to the workplace such as gender stereotypes, discrimination, power, and stress.

Deutsch, F. M. (1999). *Halving it all: How equally shared parenting works.* Cambridge, MA: Harvard University Press. Here's a fascinating study of professional and blue-collar parents, emphasizing how they negotiate child care as well as other people's reactions to their nontraditional arrangements.

Ehrenreich, B. (2001). *Nickel and dimed: On (not) getting by in America.* New York: Metropolitan Books. This book is ideal for anyone who thinks that a person can survive on the minimum wages paid for service jobs. Ehrenreich is a superb writer, and she compassionately describes both her own work experiences and those of her coworkers.

Eisenberg, S. (1998). *We'll call you if we need you: Experiences of women working construction.* Ithaca, NY: Cornell University Press. Susan Eisenberg's book provides insights into women working in blue-collar jobs. She includes a wonderful blend of the women's own words and a good synthesis of the pluses and minuses of this kind of work setting.

O'Connell, A. N. (Ed.). (2001). *Models of achievement: Reflections of eminent women in psychology.* Mahwah, NJ: Erlbaum. Agnes O'Connell's book includes autobiographies written by 19 contemporary female psychologists. O'Connell's introductory chapters and her final chapter provide background and synthesis about factors influencing the lives of professional women.

ANSWERS TO THE DEMONSTRATIONS

Demonstration 7.1: 1. 1%; 2. two children; 3. $13,423; 4. $10,712; 5. 30% to 35%; 6. 30% to 35%; 7. AFDC was abolished in 1996. However, the economic situation was favorable during the years immediately afterward. As a result, the overall employment rate in the United States was high. Therefore, women's employment probably would have increased substantially, even *without* the abolition of AFDC.

ANSWERS TO THE TRUE-FALSE QUESTIONS

1. False (pp. 211–212); 2. False (p. 215); 3. False (pp. 216–217); 4. True (p. 219); 5. False (p. 226); 6. True (p. 228); 7. False (pp. 229–230); 8. True (p. 233); 9. False (p. 238); 10. False (pp. 239–240).

Love Relationships

Margaret W. Matlin, Ph.D.

T R U E   O R   F A L S E ?

_____ 1. Men are more likely than women to specify that a sexual partner must be attractive.

_____ 2. Some psychologists have argued that evolutionary forces can explain gender differences in characteristics of an ideal romantic partner; however, the evidence for this explanation is not strong.

_____ 3. In about half of current first marriages, the couples had lived together before they were married.

_____ 4. People's satisfaction with their marriage often drops during the first 20 years of marriage, but it typically increases later in life.

_____ 5. Current research shows that most Latina/o couples admire an ideal in which the man is clearly dominant and the woman is passive and long-suffering.

_____ 6. Although divorce may be painful initially, it encourages many women to discover their strengths.

_____ 7. According to recent research, women's sexual orientation is relatively flexible during the late teens and early twenties.

_____ 8. In general, bisexual women feel equal attraction to both women and men in any given time period.

_____ 9. Researchers have discovered compelling evidence that a lesbian sexual orientation is biologically based.

_____ 10. Compared to married women, single women typically have more serious psychological problems.

J ust before I began to write this chapter on love relationships, my husband and I traveled to New York City to see the Metropolitan Opera's production of *Il Pirata*. The plot? A young woman has been forced to marry a man whom she does not love, although many years earlier she had given her heart to a young man who is—you guessed it!—a pirate. On our walk back to our hotel from the opera, we passed by a movie theater that was playing *My Big Fat Greek Wedding*, a popular romantic comedy about a woman from a Greek American family who falls in love with a man from a wealthy, decidedly non-Greek family. Soap operas, like grand operas, specialize in romantic relationships. On *As the World Turns*, will Craig marry Rosanna? This week's *People* features the blissful marriage of Catherine Zeta-Jones and her husband, Michael Douglas.

No matter how many times we hear about "boy meets girl," we go back for more. You can probably think of a few grand operas, soap operas, or movies that feature plots about power or danger or money. However, these are clearly outnumbered by themes about love (Coltrane, 1998). In the previous chapter, we focused on women and work—certainly a central issue in the lives of contemporary women. In Chapters 8, 9, and 10, we'll turn our attention to women's close personal relationships as we consider love, sexuality, and motherhood. Our four major topics in the current chapter about love relationships are (1) dating and living together, (2) marriage and divorce, (3) lesbians and bisexual women, and (4) single women.

DATING AND LIVING TOGETHER

We'll begin by talking about those heterosexual people whose thoughts and feelings are most visible—and audible—in the media. We should note, though, that many heterosexuals report that they never thought much about their sexual orientation. After all, being "straight" is considered normative in our culture. When heterosexual students are asked to describe their thoughts on the issue, they often write comments such as "I never gave consideration to my sexual identity; it just came naturally" (Eliason, 1995, p. 826).

Incidentally, the title of this section uses the word *dating*. However, many adolescents currently report that they are more likely to hang out together or go out with a group of males and females rather than have a formally planned date (Mulhauser, 2001; O'Sullivan et al., 2001). Still, we'll refer to "dating" because popular culture has not yet invented a substitute term.

Let's consider how heterosexual individuals view the ideal romantic partner and discuss two explanations for gender differences in this area. We'll then compare women and men with respect to several characteristics of the love relationship. Our final two topics will be couples who live together and couples who break up.

The Ideal Romantic Partner

Before you read this section on ideal partners, try Demonstration 8.1. You may be convinced that you can tell whether a man or a woman wrote these personal ads, but be sure to check the answers. Let's first consider the North American studies on this topic and then explore several studies from other cultures.

North American Research.   What do women and men want in their romantic partner? The answer depends on whether they are discussing a sexual partner or a marriage partner. Regan and Berscheid (1997) asked undergraduates at a Midwestern university to rank a variety of personal characteristics in terms of their desirability for a partner for sexual activity and a partner for a long-term relationship such as marriage. Table 8.1 shows the five most important characteristics for each type of relationship for females judging males and for males judging females.

As you can see, both women and men emphasized physical attractiveness when judging an ideal sexual partner. In addition, a statistical analysis showed that a greater number of men than women ranked physical attractiveness as the most important characteristic.

DEMONSTRATION 8.1 ■ ■ ■ ■ ■ ■ ■ ■ ■ ■ ■ ■ ■ ■ ■ ■ ■ ■

The Ideal Partner

This demonstration contains excerpts from advertisements in the personals column of *City Newspaper* (Rochester, New York). Each excerpt describes the kind of person the writer of the ad is looking for. I have left out any mention of the gender of the ideal partner; otherwise, this portion of the ad is complete. In front of each description, put an F if you think the writer of the ad is female or an M if you think the writer is male.

_____ 1. I am seeking a friend first and then maybe more. Warmth, intelligence, and sense of humor all pluses.

_____ 2. I'm looking for someone who is successful, but not a workaholic, with great sense of humor, healthy, honest, faithful, able to make commitment.

_____ 3. I am seeking a new best friend to laugh with. Interests include: movies, cards, antiques, the outdoors.

_____ 4. I'm looking for a 30-something nonsmoker. Trail-climbs and off-road bike by day, and share romantic cultured evenings. Friends first.

_____ 5. Looking for fun-loving single White Jewish [person] who enjoys dancing and dining.

_____ 6. I'm seeking a single White Protestant [person], 45–55 years old, who wants to share music, cooking, football Sundays, weekend trips, and holiday fun. Love of walking and biking a plus. Smoking will get you nowhere.

_____ 7. I'm seeking a single White [person] under 34 to share a life of kindness, togetherness, friendship, and love.

_____ 8. [Ad writer] seeks single [person], 26–35, race unimportant. Must like dancing, dining, movies, and cuddling, for exciting Fall romance. Will not be disappointed.

_____ 9. Looking for career-oriented self-confident individual who desires to share a variety of outdoor activities, including bicycling, skiing, backpacking, gardening.

_____ 10. Seeking Black [person] 20's–40's who's honest, intelligent, positive, loving, caring, and tender for a relationship.

Check the accuracy of your answers at the end of this chapter (page 284).

TABLE 8.1 ■ Characteristics That Males and Females Consider Most Important for a Sexual Partner and a Marriage Partner, Listed in Order of Importance

	Females Judging Males	Males Judging Females
Sexual partner	Physically attractive	Physically attractive
	Healthy	Healthy
	Attentive to my needs	Overall personality
	Sense of humor	Attentive to my needs
	Overall personality	Self-confident
Marriage partner	Honest or trustworthy	Overall personality
	Sensitive	Honest or trustworthy
	Overall personality	Physically attractive
	Intelligent	Intelligent
	Attentive to my needs	Healthy

Source: Regan, P. C., & Berscheid, E. (1997). Gender differences in characteristics desired in a potential sexual and marriage partner. *Journal of Psychology & Human Sexuality, 9,* 32 (Table 1). Haworth Press, Inc., 10 Alice Street, Binghamton, NY 13904.

Notice, however, that the preferred characteristics shift when people judge an ideal marriage partner. Here, the gender differences are small, because both women and men value honesty, good personality, and intelligence. Still, you can see that men do mention physical attractiveness as the third most important characteristic for a marriage partner.

Other research confirms that physical appearance is extremely important when people first meet a potential romantic partner. Also, attractiveness and slimness are especially important when men are judging women (Hatfield & Rapson, 1993; Regan & Sprecher, 1995; Travis & Meginnis-Payne, 2001).

How accurate were you in guessing the gender of the people who wrote the personal ads in Demonstration 8.1? You probably hesitated because several of these ads could have been written by either a male or a female. In general, systematic studies of personal ads in both the United States and Canada confirm that men are more likely than women to emphasize physical attractiveness in a partner. Men are more likely than women to describe their own financial status in an ad, but women are more likely to specify financial status in describing their ideal partner. However, both men and women tend to specify that an ideal partner should be warm, romantic, kind, and sensitive and also have a good sense of humor (Green & Kenrick, 1994; Hatfield & Rapson, 1993; Lance, 1998; E. J. Miller et al., 2000).

You may wonder whether women are looking for strong, dominant men or for nice guys. Jensen-Campbell and her colleagues (1995) arranged for female college students to listen to a man whose conversation revealed either high or low levels of altruism. They rated the highly altruistic man as being more physically attractive, socially desirable, and preferable as a date, compared to a less altruistic man. Desrochers (1995) found similar results. Any readers of this text who happen to be kind, considerate males who are in search of a female partner will be pleased to know that nice guys finish first, not last!

Cross-Cultural Research.   Most of the participants in research on ideal partners have been White men and women living in the United States and Canada. A representative study conducted in Holland echoes the North American research; both males and females emphasized interpersonal skills in an ideal partner, but men emphasized physical attractiveness more than women did (Doosje et al., 1999, p. 50).

When we move beyond groups with European origins, we often find different patterns for romantic relationships. For example, young people who live in immigrant communities are typically caught between the cultural traditions of their home country and those of their adopted country (Dasgupta, 1998). Consider the predicament of women who have emigrated from India, where marriages are usually arranged by the couple's parents. These women now live in North America, where romantic love is supposed to be the basis for marriage (K. K. Dion & Dion, 1998; Gourevitch, 1999). For many years, the immigrant Indian community has offered an interesting alternative: The would-be husband—or the family of the would-be wife—places a matrimonial advertisement in newspapers. For instance, one woman's family placed the following ad in *India Abroad:*

> Brahmin professional Punjabi parents seek MD, nonsmoker match; for beautiful, fair daughter, Indian values, 30/5'2", Canadian citizen, MD, Internal Medicine. ("IA Matrimonial Classifieds," 2001, p. 44)

Different cultures value somewhat different characteristics in a marriage partner (Gibbons et al., 1996). In general, however, women are more likely than men to say that a partner should have good financial prospects. In contrast, men are more likely than women to say that a partner should be physically attractive (D. M. Buss & Schmitt, 1993; Sprecher et al., 1994; Winstead et al., 1997).

In a cross-cultural study, Hatfield and Sprecher (1995) asked college students in the United States, Russia, and Japan to rate a number of characteristics that might be important in selecting a marriage partner. Gender similarities were found for many characteristics. However, Figure 8.1 shows that women in all three cultures are more likely than men to emphasize financial prospects in a spouse. Also, Figure 8.2 shows that men in all three cultures are more likely than women to emphasize physical attractiveness.

Explanations for Gender Differences in Preference Patterns

One of the most controversial topics in the research on love relationships is whether evolutionary explanations can account for gender differences in romantic preferences. An approach called **evolutionary psychology** proposes that various species gradually change over the course of many generations so that they can adapt better to their environment. A basic principle of this approach is that both men and women have an evolutionary advantage if they succeed in passing

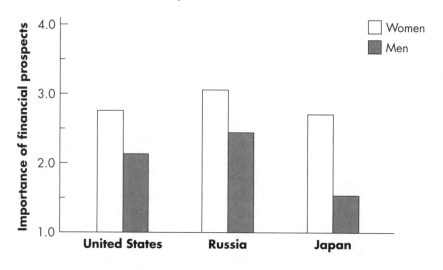

FIGURE 8.1 ■ Importance of financial prospects in a spouse, for women and men in three cultures.

Source: Hatfield and Sprecher (1995).

on their genes to the next generation. Evolutionary psychologists argue that the principles of the evolutionary approach can explain why men and women have somewhat different views about ideal mates (D. M. Buss, 1994, 1995; Geary, 1998). Specifically, men should be driven to prefer young, attractive, healthy-looking women because those women are most likely to be fertile—they will pass on the men's genes to the next generation. Contrary to the evolutionary perspective, however, researchers have found that women's attractiveness is not correlated with being healthy or being fertile (Kalick et al., 1998; Tassinary & Hansen, 1998).

Evolutionary psychologists also propose that women try to select a partner who will be committed to a long-term relationship. After all, not only do women give birth to children, but they also must make sure that the children are provided with financial resources. According to this argument, women look for men who have good incomes and are reliable (D. M. Buss, 1994). Evolutionary psychologists emphasize that culture has little influence on gender differences in mate selection (D. M. Buss, 1998).

Many feminist psychologists object to the evolutionary approach. They argue, for example, that the theory is highly speculative about evolutionary forces that operated many thousands of years ago (Eagly & Wood, 1999). Also, researchers point out that both men and women are highly interested in long-term relationships (L. C. Miller et al., 2002; Popenoe & Whitehead, 2002). In addition, the evolutionary approach argues that gender differences are both large and inevitable (G. R. Brooks, 1997b; Hatfield & Rapson, 1996). As a result, some people may use this argument to justify why women *should* have less power than men (Funder, 2001).

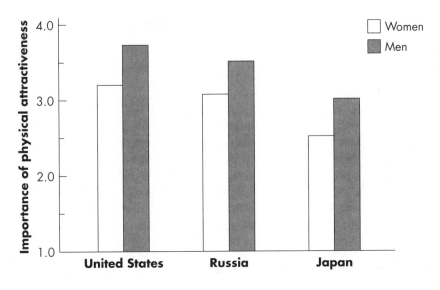

FIGURE 8.2 ■ Importance of physical attractiveness in a spouse, for women and men in three cultures.

Source: Hatfield and Sprecher (1995).

An explanation that sounds much more credible to me—and to most other feminists—emphasizes that social factors can effectively explain gender differences in preference patterns. According to the **social roles explanation,** men and women often occupy different social roles, they are socialized differently, and they experience different social opportunities and social disadvantages (Eagly & Wood, 1999; Hatfield & Sprecher, 1995; Johannesen-Schmidt & Eagly, 2002). For example, women have more limited financial resources in our culture, as we saw in Chapter 7. As a result, women are forced to focus on a partner's ability to earn money.

In support of the social roles approach, research demonstrates that women are especially likely to prefer high-income men if they live in countries where women have limited educational and financial opportunities (Eagly & Wood, 1999; Kasser & Sharma, 1999). In contrast, women from more egalitarian countries can earn their own incomes, so they don't need to seek wealthy husbands. Contrary to the predictions of evolutionary psychology, culture *does* have an effect on mate preferences (Travis & Meginnis-Payne, 2001).

An important argument comes from social roles theorists: Gender differences in mate preferences are *not* inevitable. For example, if women's social status in our own culture improves, women may place less emphasis on financial resources and more emphasis on factors such as physical attractiveness (Hatfield & Sprecher, 1995). A final point favoring the social learning approach is that the differences in mate preferences between cultures are much larger than the differences in mate preferences between genders (K. K. Dion & Dion, 2001b).

Characteristics of Heterosexual Love Relationships

We have looked at women's and men's ideal romantic partners. But how do women and men compare in an established love relationship? What factors predict satisfaction with a love relationship?

Gender Comparisons.   To some extent, women and men emphasize different aspects of love in their current romantic relationships. Sprecher and Sedikides (1993) examined some romantic couples at a university and some in the neighboring community. They found that women are significantly more likely than men to say that they have a relationship based on friendship (K. L. Dion & Dion, 1993; Sprecher & Sedikides, 1993). This same gender difference has been found among deaf European Americans and people of African descent living in Jamaica (Nicotera, 1997). Compared to men, women also report more liking, commitment, and satisfaction—all positive emotions. However, women also report more sadness, depression, hurt, and loneliness. In other words, compared to men, women seem to experience a wider range of both positive and negative emotions (Sprecher & Sedikides, 1993).

In many other respects, however, the gender similarities are more striking. For example, men and women are both likely to say that the essential features of their love relationships are trust, caring, honesty, and respect (Rousar & Aron, 1990). As C. Hendrick and S. Hendrick (1996) concluded, women may emphasize friendship more than men do, but "the structure of women's and men's belief systems about love and relationships appears to be roughly similar" (p. 143).

Factors Related to Satisfaction with the Relationship.   Before you read further, try Demonstration 8.2, which is based on a study by Grote and Frieze (1994). This questionnaire assesses the friendship dimension of a love relationship. We just examined gender differences in emphasizing friendship. Other research suggests that both men and women are more satisfied with their love relationships if they are based on friendship (Grote & Frieze, 1994). People who had friendship-based relationships also reported a greater degree of reciprocal understanding. In addition, relationships based on friendship lasted longer.

In Chapter 6, we saw that women are sometimes more likely than men to disclose personal information about themselves. In their romantic relationships, however, women and men have similar self-disclosure patterns (Hatfield & Rapson, 1993). In addition, both men and women are more satisfied with their love relationship if both partners are skilled at expressing their emotions (Lamke et al., 1994; R. J. Sternberg, 1998). The strong, silent male or the mysteriously uncommunicative female may look appealing in the movies. However, in real life, people prefer a person with sensitivity and other interpersonal skills.

Living Together

The term **cohabitation** refers to unmarried people who live together and who have a continuing emotional and sexual relationship (Rice, 2001b). Some other legal terms include *unmarried-couple household, consensual union,* and *common-law*

DEMONSTRATION 8.2 ■

Friendship-Based Love

If you are currently in a love relationship, rate the following statements based on that relationship. Alternatively, rate a previous love relationship that you experienced or a love relationship of a couple whom you know fairly well. In each case, use a scale in which 1 = strongly disagree and 5 = strongly agree. Then add up the total number of points. In general, high scores reflect a love relationship that is strongly based on friendship.

_____ 1. My love for my partner is based on a deep, long-lasting friendship.

_____ 2. I express my love for my partner through the activities and interests we enjoy together.

_____ 3. My love for my partner involves solid, deep affection.

_____ 4. An important factor in my love for my partner is that we often laugh together.

_____ 5. My partner is one of the most likable people I know.

_____ 6. The companionship I share with my partner is an important part of our love.

_____ 7. I feel I can really trust my partner.

_____ 8. I can count on my partner in times of need.

_____ 9. I feel relaxed and comfortable with my partner.

Source: Based on Grote and Frieze (1994).

relationship. All these terms sound more like a business arrangement than a romantic relationship! According to recent data, about 4 million heterosexual couples in the United States report that they are living together; this number is probably an underestimate (J. Fields & Casper, 2001). Furthermore, Canadian research reports that 13% of women between the ages of 25 and 44 are currently living with a man to whom they are not married (Statistics Canada, 2000). In both countries, the number of couples who are living together has increased dramatically since 1980 (Smock, 2000). However, U.S. data collected on Whites, Blacks, and Latinas/os indicate no ethnic differences in the percentage of couples who live together (H. Rodriguez, 1998).

Just as there is no typical dating or marriage relationship, there is no typical pattern for living together. Some couples live together simply because it is convenient. About 70% engage in sexual activity only with their partner (L. A. Morris,

1997). Some couples choose to live together so that they can determine whether they should consider marriage (Z. Wu, 1999).

In about half of current first marriages in North America, couples had lived together before marriage (H. Rodriguez, 1998; Smock, 2000). Looking at a different dimension, 50% to 60% of all couples who live together will eventually decide to marry (H. Rodriguez, 1998; Smock, 2000).

According to research in the United States and Canada, couples who live together before marriage are more likely to get divorced than those who have not lived together (D. R. Hall & Zhao, 1995; L. A. Morris, 1997; H. Rodriguez, 1998; Smock, 2000). Does this mean that living together is a bad idea because it is likely to cause divorce? A likely alternative explanation is that people who live together before marriage are relatively nontraditional. Nontraditional people may also feel fewer constraints about seeking a divorce (Clarkberg et al., 1995; H. Rodriguez, 1998; Smock, 2000).

For some women, living together may provide an opportunity to have a close, continuous relationship with a man while still preserving the woman's sense of individuality. However, some couples who live together find that they adopt more traditional roles once they become married. As one woman reported:

> It seems that once the marriage contract was official, we began to expect each other to perform the roles of husband and wife rather than two people just wanting to love and live with each other. We didn't think that would happen to us. (L. A. Morris, 1997, p. 47)

Breaking Up

A man and a woman have been dating for about a year. Then they break up. Who suffers more? Try Demonstration 8.3 before you read further.

Choo and her colleagues (1996) have reminded us that any gender differences must be interpreted in the context of widespread gender similarities: "Men and women are more similar than different. In most things, it is not gender, but our shared humanity that seems to be important" (p. 144).

Choo and her coauthors (1996) studied a sample of students at the University of Hawaii. Unlike a typical sample from the continental United States, most of the participants were Asian Americans. The students were asked to think back on a romantic relationship that had broken up and to assess their emotional reactions immediately after the breakup. You may be surprised to learn that women felt more joy and relief following the breakup. However, men and women reported similar negative emotions (anxiety, sadness, and anger) as well as similar guilt.

How can we explain the results? Choo and her colleagues (1996) pointed out that women are usually more sensitive to potential problems in a relationship. In other words, women may have anticipated the breakup and worried about some danger signs. For instance, as you recall from Chapter 6, women are relatively skilled in decoding facial expressions. In contrast, a man may miss signs of sadness or anger in a woman's facial expression. As a result, a woman may be less shocked and more relieved when the breakup does occur.

DEMONSTRATION 8.3 ■ ■ ■ ■ ■ ■ ■ ■ ■ ■ ■ ■ ■ ■ ■ ■ ■ ■

Coping with a Breakup of a Love Relationship

Think about a person you once dated and felt passionate about, but then the two of you broke up. Read each of the items below, and place an X in front of each strategy you *frequently* used to cope with the breakup. (If you have not personally experienced a breakup, think of a close friend who has recently broken up with a romantic partner, and answer the questionnaire from that person's perspective.)

_____ 1. I tried to figure out what I might have done wrong.

_____ 2. I took alcohol or drugs.

_____ 3. I talked to my friends, trying to figure out if there was anything we could do to save the relationship.

_____ 4. I thought about how badly my partner had treated me.

_____ 5. I kept busy with my schoolwork or my job.

_____ 6. I told myself: "I'm lucky to have gotten out of that relationship."

_____ 7. I engaged in sports and other physical activities more than usual.

Source: Based on Choo et al. (1996).

Both women and men are likely to experience ambivalence after the end of a romantic relationship. For instance, a young woman described her emotions when she saw her former high school boyfriend, a year after breaking up:

> I saw Jim for two days before I left for my sophomore year of college. There was something bittersweet about the whole thing. I hadn't seen him in so long and it felt so comfortable to be back with him even if it was for a short time. . . . I was proud that I didn't need him any more. I felt more grown up. Even though I didn't need him, I still wanted him back with me too. I was flooded with memories of the past, some good, some not so good. (N. M. Brown & Amatea, 2000, p. 86)

How do women and men cope with a breakup? Choo and her colleagues (1996) asked their respondents to recall how they had responded to the end of their love relationship. Demonstration 8.3 shows some of the items. The researchers found that women and men were equally likely to blame themselves for the breakup (Questions 1 and 3 of Demonstration 8.3). They were also equally likely to take alcohol and drugs following the breakup (Question 2). However, women were somewhat more likely to blame their partner for the breakup (Questions 4 and 6), whereas men were more likely to try to distract themselves from thinking about the breakup (Questions 5 and 7).

Why were women more likely than men to blame their partner for the breakup? Choo and her colleagues suggested one possibility: Women typically work harder than men do to maintain a relationship. When a breakup occurs, women may realistically blame their partner for not investing more effort in the relationship.

SECTION SUMMARY ■

Dating and Living Together

1. Both women and men value physical attractiveness as an important characteristic for an ideal sexual partner, but men emphasize it more; both women and men value characteristics such as honesty and intelligence in an ideal marriage partner, but men still emphasize attractiveness more than women do.

2. To explain why men emphasize physical attractiveness in a romantic partner—and why women emphasize good financial prospects—evolutionary psychologists theorize that each gender emphasizes characteristics that are likely to ensure passing their genes on to their offspring. The social roles explanation emphasizes that men and women typically occupy different social roles, that they are socialized differently, and that they have different opportunities and costs; furthermore, the differences are not inevitable.

3. Women are somewhat more likely than men to emphasize friendship in a love relationship; gender differences are minimal in other features considered essential in a love relationship.

4. Relationships are more satisfying if they are based on friendship and if both partners can express their emotions.

5. The number of cohabiting couples has increased dramatically in recent years, and about half of these couples will eventually marry.

6. When couples break up, women are more likely than men to experience joy and relief, more likely to blame their partner for the breakup, and less likely to distract themselves from thinking about the breakup.

MARRIAGE AND DIVORCE

Our theme of individual differences in women's lives is especially important when we discuss women's experiences with marriage. Consider how the following two women describe their marriages.

A woman named Linda describes the reality of her marriage compared to her previous dreams about marriage:

> Marriage is struggle, the two words are synonymous. But! We're not told that. I grew up with the lies that marriage is a sweet wonderful thing. . . . I was really brought up by TV and the movies, by advertisements, and the whole culture saying that you melted into each other's arms and had this love relationship that was ever blossom-

ing and growing but somehow never changed. . . . It's not that way at all. (Mayerson, 1996, pp. 29–30)

Contrast Linda's description with the observations of feminist author Letty Cottin Pogrebin (1997) about her own marriage. Recalling her parents' troubled marriage, she had originally vowed to remain single. However, she now describes being happily married for 34 years. As Pogrebin emphasizes, feminists need to acknowledge that marriage can be a source of strength and joy:

> All I know is what I've had—34 years with a devoted partner who is my lover and closest friend. I know how it feels to live with someone whose touch excites, whose counsel calms, whose well-being matters as much as my own. I know that simple contentment is a kind of euphoria, that the familiar can be as intoxicating as the exotic, and that comfort and equality are, over the long haul, greater aphrodisiacs than romanticized power plays. I know how soul-satisfying it is to love someone well and deeply and to be loved for all the right reasons. I know how much more layered life is when everything is shared—sorrow and success, new enthusiasms, old stories, children, grandchildren, friends, memory. . . . We're what's called a good fit. (p. 37)

In the United States, the average ages for a first marriage are 25 years for women and 27 years for men (J. Fields & Casper, 2001). Canadians marry somewhat later, with an average age of 28 years for women and 30 years for men (Statistics Canada, 2000). Figures are also similar for most European countries. However, we find somewhat different patterns throughout the rest of the world; for example, women first marry at the age of 16 in Niger, Mali, and several other African countries (Neft & Levine, 1997).

Approximately half of adult North Americans are currently married. Figure 8.3 shows the percentages of married women in four major ethnic groups of U.S. residents (U.S. Census Bureau, 2000). Unfortunately, these data do not include information about Native Americans.

Let's begin our examination of marriage and divorce by first discussing marital satisfaction. Then we'll look at the distribution of power in marriage and marriage patterns among women of color. Our final topic in this section is the realities of divorce.

Marital Satisfaction

How happy are women with their marriages? Let's see how marital satisfaction changes over time, how men and women compare in terms of marital satisfaction, and how certain characteristics are associated with happy marriages.

Satisfaction During Various Periods of Marriage.   Think of the words *newlywed* and *bride*. These words may suggest associations such as bliss, radiance, obliviousness to the rest of the world, and complete happiness. According to surveys, young married couples are perhaps the happiest people in any age group (McNulty & Karney, 2001; Orbuch et al., 1996).

Most research on marriage focuses on European American couples. However, Jean Oggins and her colleagues (1993) studied 199 Black and 174 White newlywed couples, all of whom were married for the first time. In general, the

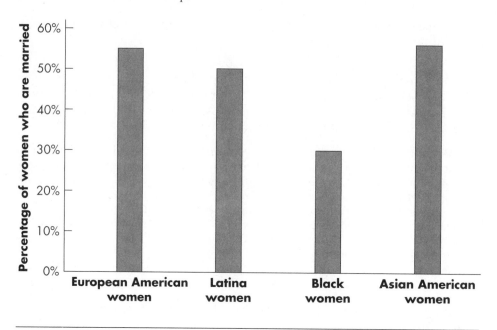

FIGURE 8.3 ■ Percentages of women (age 15 or older) who are married, in four major ethnic groups of U.S. residents.

Source: Based on data from U.S. Census Bureau (2000).

respondents were happiest if they felt that their partners valued them and showed this high regard through both words and behaviors.

After several years, married people sometimes report being unhappy and dissatisfied (Hatfield & Rapson, 1993). Women are likely to resent that they perform more housework than their husbands, an inequity we emphasized in Chapter 7. As we also saw in that chapter, women do even more of the work after children are born; during this period, women may become less satisfied with the marriage (K. K. Dion & Dion, 2001b).

Orbuch and her colleagues (1996) analyzed data from U.S. national surveys. They found that people who had been married 20 to 24 years were the least satisfied with their marriage. However, marital satisfaction generally improves during the next decade, once the children have left home (Koski & Shaver, 1997; Levenson et al., 1994; Orbuch et al., 1996). Couples who have been married at least 35 years also report relatively little conflict in their relationship (Levenson et al., 1994). The reasons for this increased satisfaction are not clear, but they may include factors such as reduced conflict over parenting issues after the children leave home and an increase in economic resources.

Gender Comparisons in Marital Satisfaction.   A survey of college students asked them to estimate what percentage of their future identity would be devoted to being a marriage partner. Both women and men supplied an average figure of 30% (Kerpelman & Schvaneveldt, 1999).

Once people are married, however, how do women and men compare? This topic is more complex than you might expect. The problem is that women report more extreme levels of emotion than men do. Specifically, women report more positive emotions (W. Wood et al., 1989). However, women are also more likely than men to report major depression, as we'll see in Chapter 12.

Regarding satisfaction with marriage, women are more likely than men to report that their marriage did not live up to their visions of an ideal relationship (Vangelisti & Daily, 1999). Also, women are more sensitive than men to problems in their marital relationships (K. K. Dion & Dion, 2001b; R. J. Sternberg, 1998; W. Wood et al., 1989). This sensitivity is consistent with our earlier observation that women are better than men at anticipating potential problems in a dating relationship.

A related issue is whether marriage has a similar effect on men's and women's happiness. Wendy Wood and her colleagues (1989) conducted a meta-analysis on the effects of gender and marital status on well-being. These researchers found that both men and women were happier if they were married than if they were not. For men, the effect size, d, was 0.49; for women, d was 0.54. In this analysis—as well as in others—men and women profit about equally from being married (Mookherjee, 1997; Myers, 1999). Incidentally, both men and women are also likely to live longer if they are married rather than divorced (Fincham & Beach, 1999; Friedman et al., 1995).

Characteristics of Happy Marriages. In a happy marriage, both the wife and the husband feel that their emotional needs are fulfilled, and each partner enriches the life of the other. Both people understand and respect each other, as noted in Pogrebin's (1997) comment at the beginning of this section. Each partner is concerned about the other's happiness and welfare.

Researchers have found that a variety of psychological characteristics are correlated with happy, stable marriages (N. M. Brown & Amatea, 2000; Cobb et al., 2001; Fincham & Beach, 1999; Myers, 1999; Steil, 2001; R. J. Sternberg, 1998):

1. Communication skills and understanding,
2. More positive comments, rather than negative comments,
3. Conflict-resolution skills,
4. Trust in the other person,
5. Mutual support,
6. Flexibility,
7. Equal sharing of household tasks,
8. Equal sharing in decision making.

Happily married couples even interpret their spouse's actions differently than unhappy couples do. For example, suppose that Jack gives a gift to his wife, Mary. If Mary is happily married, she is likely to think to herself, "How wonderful! Jack wanted to do something nice for me!" However, if Mary is unhappily married, she might think, "He's probably giving me these flowers just so he can spend money on himself." Unpleasant interactions can also be explained in either a positive or a negative light. These explanatory patterns could make a happy marriage even happier, but they could encourage more conflict in an unhappy marriage (N. M. Brown & Amatea, 2000; Fincham & Bradbury, 1990, 1992; McNulty & Karney, 2001).

Responsibility and Power in Marriage

In Chapter 7, we discussed how women are increasingly likely to work outside the home. Still, the responsibility of providing everyday services within the family home rests primarily with women. However, husbands typically have more power in a marriage than wives do. Let's explore how men's and women's salaries can influence the balance of power in a marriage. Then, we'll discuss three patterns of power distribution that are found in North American marriages.

Salary and Power.   My students are often skeptical about the influence of crass factors such as salary on intimate, romantic relationships. However, the research suggests that, at least to some extent, money *is* power (N. M. Brown & Amatea, 2000; Steil, 1997).

According to recent reviews of the literature, the more husbands earn (relative to their wives' salaries), the more power they have in decision making and the less domestic work they do. Wives who are employed have more power in decision making than nonemployed wives have. However, women who earn more than their husbands still do not have an equal voice in financial matters. In other words, these women bring the family more income than their husbands do, but their husbands still make most of the financial decisions (Steil, 1997, 2001).

Three Patterns of Power Distribution.   We have emphasized individual differences throughout this book. The variation in marital roles is substantial. In a classic article, Peplau (1983) classified North American married couples in terms of three patterns of marital roles: (1) a traditional marriage, (2) a modern marriage, and (3) an egalitarian marriage. Not every couple fits neatly into a single pattern. However, this classification system helps us appreciate the variety of relationships found in North American marriages (N. M. Brown & Amatea, 2000).

According to Peplau (1983), in a **traditional marriage** the husband is more dominant than the wife, and both partners maintain traditional gender roles. The wife is not employed, and the husband controls the money. The wife makes decisions about housework and child care, but the husband has the ultimate authority in family decisions. In 1998, the delegates to the Southern Baptist Convention passed a resolution stating that a wife should "submit graciously to her husband's leadership" (Wingert & Snow, 1998), providing a guideline for a traditional marriage.

In a **modern marriage,** the husband is less dominant and the wife serves as a "junior partner" (N. M. Brown & Amatea, 2000). Modern couples say that husbands and wives should share equally in making decisions, yet husbands still tend to be more powerful. Traditional gender roles are modified somewhat. The husband may encourage his wife's employment, but her work is secondary to his. (For example, she will miss work if their child is ill.) The term *modern marriage* is appropriate. As we saw in Chapter 7, most married women do work outside the home, yet husbands and wives do not have similar power. Furthermore, most husbands in a modern marriage are reluctant to try to solve the gender inequities in their marriages (Dryden, 1999; Steil, 2000).

In an **egalitarian marriage,** the partners share power equally, without traditional gender roles. The wife and the husband have equal responsibility for housework, child care, finances, and decision making. Egalitarian marriages also emphasize companionship and sharing. These marriages are based on a true friendship in which both partners really understand and respect one another. They share many of the same interests, and they know how to resolve conflicts fairly; yet the two partners retain their unique styles and strengths (P. Schwartz, 1994). A husband who had been married 16 years remarked:

> I started out pretty traditional. But over the years it made sense to change. We both work, and so we had to help each other with the kids. . . . And we worked together at church, and we both went whole hog into the peace program. So that got shared. I don't know; you can't design these things. You play fair, and you do what needs doing, and pretty soon you find the old ways don't work and the new ways do. (P. Schwartz, 1994, p. 31)

Marriage and Women of Color

We do not have a large number of systematic studies about marriage patterns for people from ethnic groups that are not European American. However, some resources provide partial information.

Latinas.   One of the key concepts often discussed in connection with Latinas/os is *machismo.* Social scientists have traditionally defined **machismo** (pronounced mah-*cheez*-mo) as the belief that men must show their manhood by being strong, sexual, and even violent—clearly dominant over women in relationships (Ybarra, 1995).

The parallel concept for women is *marianismo.* Social scientists have traditionally defined **marianismo** (pronounced mah-ree-ah-*neez*-mo) as the belief that women must be passive and long-suffering, giving up their own needs to help their husbands and children (Chin, 1994; Ehlers, 1993). (*Marianismo* is based on the Catholic representation of the Virgin Mary.) M. Fine and her colleagues (2000) described how *machismo* and *marianismo* complement each other in a traditional Latina/o marriage:

> Love and honor your man—cook his meals, clean his house, be available and ready when he wants to have sex, have and care for his children, and look the other way at marital infidelities. . . . In return, he will agree to protect you and your children, work, pay the bills. (p. 96)

How well do *machismo* and *marianismo* capture the relationship between Latinos and Latinas in the current era? Latinas/os do report less egalitarian attitudes than Whites or Blacks, especially among recent immigrants (Steil, 2001;

P. L. Taylor et al., 1999). However, the stereotype of the dominant husband and the submissive wife does not hold up (Baca Zinn & Wells, 2000; D. Castañeda, 1996; Leaper & Valin, 1996; Roschelle, 1998). Fewer than half of Latinos and Latinas believe that marriages should adopt this pattern of inequity. Furthermore, both Latina women and Latino men believe that they can effectively influence their partners by being honest and by talking with their partners (Beckman et al., 1999).

The *marianismo* model also fails to describe women's roles for the millions of economically poor Latinas who must take a job to survive (Ehlers, 1993). When women work in factories or pick crops, they cannot remain passive and totally focused on their husbands and children. In short, many Latinas and Latinos have created marital patterns that are different from the models suggested by *marianismo* and *machismo* values.

Black Women.   In the 1960s, U.S. government officials coined the term **Black matriarchy** to refer to women's domination in Black families. Women in Black families were supposed to be so dominant that they presumably emasculated Black men and encouraged other family problems (Gadsden, 1999; Staples, 1995; R. L. Taylor, 2000).

Much of the early research focused on the most economically poor Black families, typically those without a husband/father living in the home (Gadsden, 1999; L. B. Johnson, 1997). The researchers then generalized from that selected sample to all Black families. Basically, Black women were being unfairly criticized for having the stamina to work outside the home and still be strong figures in their own homes (P. H. Collins, 1990; L. B. Johnson, 1997).

The current research does not support the idea of a Black matriarchy (J. E. Dodson, 1997; L. B. Johnson, 1997). For example, Oggins and her colleagues (1993), in a study of newlyweds, showed that both Black families and White families saw husbands as having slightly more power than wives. McAdoo (1993) specifically focused on decision-making power in a group of middle-income African American families living in the Baltimore area. The picture that emerged from this sample showed families that were close to the egalitarian model. The husband and the wife contributed equally to decisions about what car to buy, what house to buy, children's curfews, and other similar issues. However, husbands had somewhat more power regarding the final decisions about what jobs they would take. In summary, the Black matriarchy is *not* a useful concept in explaining Black families in the current era.

Asian American Women.   Ethnicity typically has an important impact on a person's choice of a marriage partner. Research on Korean Americans documents this emphasis among Asian Americans. A study on marriages within the Korean community in Los Angeles found that only 8% involved someone who was not Korean by birth or descent (Min, 1993). About 60% married a Korean partner who had been living in the United States. However, about 30% brought their marriage partners from Korea. Marriages between Korean Americans and people who have just emigrated from Korea are likely to have many adjustment problems. For example, many Korean American men who have only a high school education bring in brides who have been college educated in Korea. The result is typically a significant gap in their relationship. Furthermore, Korean American women who bring in husbands from Korea are likely to find that their spouses have extremely traditional ideas about gender roles.

Conflict between traditional customs in the home country and contemporary gender roles in North America undermines many marriages of recent immigrants (K. K. Dion & Dion, 2001a; Naidoo, 1999; Tang & Dion, 1999). Consider a Korean couple who immigrated to the United States and now work together in a family business. The husband comments:

> After she started working her voice got louder than in the past. Now, she says whatever she wants to say to me. She shows a lot of self-assertion. She didn't do that in Korea. Right after I came to the U.S., I heard that Korean wives change a lot in America. Now, I clearly understand what it means. (Lim, 1997, p. 38)

In contrast, consider his wife's comments:

> In Korea, wives tend to obey their husbands because husbands have financial power and provide for their families. However, in the U.S., wives also work to make money as their husbands do, so women are apt to speak out at least one time on what they previously restrained from saying. (Lim, 1997, p. 38)

We've noted the relative power of the wife and the husband in Latina/o, Black, and Korean couples. When couples immigrate to the United States from India, the traditional wife is supposed to quietly obey her husband and in-laws. She should also be self-sacrificing and uncomplaining (Gupta, 1999; C. G. Tran & Des Jardins, 2000). These couples divide decision-making power along gender-stereotypical lines. Specifically, wives are primarily responsible for decisions concerning food and home decoration. In contrast, husbands are primarily responsible for decisions requiring large sums of money, such as buying a car and deciding where to live (Dhruvarajan, 1992).

In summary, Latina/o, Black, and Asian American families are guided by cultural traditions that vary widely, consistent with Theme 4 of this book. However, in this discussion, we have seen how women from all three cultures are creating their own marriage styles that differ greatly from these traditions.

Divorce

So far, most of our discussion has focused on relatively upbeat topics such as dating, living together, and marriage. As you know, however, divorce has become more common in recent years. Between 40% and 50% of first marriages recently taking place in the United States and Canada will end in divorce (Kitzmann & Gaylord, 2001; Neft & Levine, 1997; Popenoe & Whitehead, 2002). In the United States, the different ethnic groups have somewhat different divorce rates, with the highest rate for Blacks, then Latinas/os, then European Americans, and then Asian Americans (Kitzmann & Gaylord, 2001).

Even though attitudes toward divorce are not as negative as they were several decades ago, the divorce experience is still traumatic for most people. Let's consider three aspects of divorce: (1) the decision to divorce, (2) psychological effects, and (3) financial effects.

The Decision to Divorce.   Who is more likely to seek divorce, men or women? Folk wisdom might suggest that the men are most eager to leave a marriage. However, you'll recall that women are more likely to foresee problems in a dating relationship. Similarly, women typically complain more about the marriage than their husbands do (Amato & Rogers, 1997; Kitson, 1992). The data also show that wives initiate divorce more often than husbands do (Rice, 2001a). In some cases, women initiate divorce because they have experienced physical violence or psychological abuse; we'll discuss violence against women in depth in Chapter 13.

Psychological Effects of Divorce.   Divorce is especially painful because it creates so many different kinds of transitions and separations in addition to the separation from a former spouse (Ganong & Coleman, 1999). When a woman is divorced, she may be separated from friends and relatives previously shared by the couple. She may also be separated from the home she has known and from her children. In addition, people are likely to judge a divorced woman negatively (Etaugh & Hoehn, 1995).

Divorce is one of the most stressful changes a person can experience (Kitzmann & Gaylord, 2001). Depression and anger are often common responses, especially for women (Aseltine & Kessler, 1993; Kaganoff & Spano, 1995). Adjustment to divorce is complex, and the process takes place over an extended time period (M. A. Fine, 2000).

Many divorced people experience an emotional reaction called the **persistence of attachment:** Although people may no longer love their ex-spouses, they may still feel a remaining bond. After all, the spouse was originally selected because he or she seemed like a good partner. People who are in the process of seeking a divorce may feel simultaneously glad to be out of the relationship and regretful about losing continuing bonds with that person (Kitson, 1992).

Divorce can lead to some positive feelings. For example, mothers often report that they experience greater companionship with their children after a divorce (Gorlick, 1995). Women who felt constrained by an unhappy marriage may also feel relief. As one woman said, "For me, the divorce was not difficult. I had been living in loneliness for years by the time my marriage ended, so that being alone felt uplifting, free" (Hood, 1995, p. 132).

Many women also report that their divorce lets them know they are stronger than they had thought. Some of my own women friends seem to have grown more insightful and stronger after a divorce, and I had wondered whether this apparent strength might be a product of my own wishful thinking. Fortunately, this topic has been carefully examined by Krisanne Bursik (1991a, 1991b). Bursik studied 104 women in the Boston area who had been married at least 5 years and who were separated from their spouses when the study began.

Bursik assessed **ego development,** a kind of psychological growth in which a woman develops a more complex view of herself and of her relationships with other people (Bursik, 1991a). Most adults remain fairly stable in their ego development; they don't fully explore themselves. However, Bursik observed that many women who had been poorly adjusted at the beginning of the study were better adjusted and showed increased ego development one year later. For them, the disruptive effect of the divorce had actually been helpful. By forcing them to introspect about their lives and their strengths, misfortune actually had a long-range positive effect.

Financial Effects of Divorce.   Despite the occasional positive effects of divorce, one consequence is painful: A woman's financial situation is usually worse following a divorce, especially if she has children (Rice, 2001a). In Canada, two-thirds of divorced single mothers and their children live in poverty (Gorlick, 1995). In the United States, 40% to 50% of divorced fathers fail to pay child support (Neft & Levine, 1997; Stacey, 2000).

In summary, divorce can provide an opportunity for women to appreciate their strength and independence. Unfortunately, however, many divorced women find that economic inequities create real-life emergencies for themselves and their children.

SECTION SUMMARY ■

Marriage and Divorce

1. About half of adult North Americans are currently married.

2. Marital satisfaction is high during the newlywed period; it typically drops during the first 20 to 24 years of marriage and then increases after the children have left the home.

3. Both men and women tend to be happier when married, rather than single, and they also tend to live longer.

4. Happy marriages are more common among people who have strong communication skills and conflict-resolution skills and who share equally.

5. Power within a marriage tends to be related to one's salary. Marriages can be categorized as traditional, modern, and egalitarian.

6. Although some Latinas and Latinos emphasize *machismo* and *marianismo* in their marriages, a large percentage of Latinas/os advocate more egalitarian marital patterns. Research with Black families does not support the concept of the Black matriarchy. Asian American families are likely to experience conflicts between traditional values and North American gender roles.

7. Women are more likely than men to complain about their marriage and to initiate divorce.

8. Divorce is almost always stressful, because it creates depression and anger. Some women experience positive effects, such as increased independence and ego development. However, most divorced women experience financial problems that can have serious implications for their well-being.

LESBIANS AND BISEXUAL WOMEN

A **lesbian** is a woman who is psychologically, emotionally, and sexually attracted to other women. Most lesbians prefer the term *lesbian* to the term *homosexual*. They argue that the term *lesbian* acknowledges the emotional components of the relationship, whereas *homosexual* focuses on sexuality. The term *lesbian*—like the term *gay*—is more proud, political, healthy, and positive (Kite, 1994). Some psychologists use the term **sexual minority** to refer to anyone (female or male) who has a same-gender attraction (L. M. Diamond, 2002). Consequently, we can use the phrase *sexual minority* to include lesbians, gay males, bisexual females, and bisexual males. As we'll see in this section, our discussion of sexual orientation focuses on love, intimacy, and affection as well as on sexual feelings.

In Chapter 1, we introduced the term **heterosexism,** or bias against lesbians, gay males, and bisexuals—groups that are not heterosexual. In North American culture, an important consequence of heterosexism is that we judge heterosexual relationships differently from lesbian, gay, and bisexual relationships. Try Demonstration 8.4 to appreciate how heterosexist thinking pervades our culture.

We cannot make definite estimates about the percentage of women who consider themselves lesbians. One reason is that researchers have been more diligent about estimating the number of gay men than the number of lesbian women. Another reason is that social prejudice will cause underreporting (Patterson, 1998; Rothblum, 2000a). A third reason is more complicated: As we will see later in this section, many women consider their sexual orientation to be fluid, changing over the course of a lifetime (L. M. Diamond, 2002; Peplau, 2001). When filling out a questionnaire, these women might not believe that the clear-cut option "lesbian" provides an honest assessment of their sexual orientation. This textbook has emphasized that women and men are not two completely different representations of humanity. Similarly, researchers have found that no clear-cut boundary separates a lesbian sexual orientation from a heterosexual orientation.

With these cautions in mind, let's consider the results of a large-scale survey of English-speaking adults living in the United States. Laumann and his colleagues (1994) found that 1.4% of the women identified themselves as lesbian. However, 4.4% of women in this study reported that they were attracted to people of the same gender, so the estimates clearly depend on the specific way that the question is worded.

An important point is that researchers in psychology and society no longer consider lesbians to be invisible. In fact, while preparing to update this section of the chapter, I gathered 26 books and 72 articles or chapters published in the previous 3 years, and hundreds of additional resources were available.

DEMONSTRATION 8.4 ■■■■■■■■■■■■■■■■■■■

Heterosexist Thinking

Answer each of the following questions, and then explain why each question encourages us to question the heterosexist framework.

1. Suppose that you are walking to class at your college and you see a man and a woman kissing. Do you think, "Why are they flaunting their heterosexuality?"

2. Close your eyes and picture two women kissing each other. Does that kiss seem sexual or affectionate? Now close your eyes and imagine a woman and a man kissing each other. Does your evaluation of that kiss change?

3. Suppose that you have an appointment with a female professor. When you arrive in her office, you notice that she is wearing a wedding ring and has a photo of herself and a man smiling at each other. Do you say to yourself, "Why is she shoving her heterosexuality in my face?"

4. If you are heterosexual, has anyone asked you, "Don't you think that heterosexuality is just a phase you'll outgrow once you are older?"

5. In all the public debates you've heard about sexual orientation, have you ever heard anyone ask any of the following questions:
   a. The divorce rate among heterosexuals is now about 50%. Why don't heterosexuals have more stable love relationships?
   b. Why are heterosexual men so likely to sexually harass or rape women?
   c. What *really* causes heterosexuality?

Sources: Based partly on L. Garnets (1996) and Herek (1996).

In Chapter 2, we examined heterosexism and bias based on sexual orientation; in Chapter 4, we discussed the coming-out experience of adolescent lesbians, and in Chapter 7, we emphasized antilesbian prejudice in the workplace. In upcoming chapters, we will discuss sexuality issues among lesbians (Chapter 9) and the research on lesbian mothers (Chapter 10).

In this section of Chapter 8, we'll first discuss the psychological adjustment of lesbian women. Next we'll explore the fluid nature of sexual orientation and then several characteristics of lesbian relationships. We'll also consider the experiences of lesbian women of color as well as of bisexual women. Our final topic will be potential explanations for sexual orientation.

The Psychological Adjustment of Lesbians

In 1973, the American Psychiatric Association decided that homosexuality should no longer be listed as a disorder in their professional guidebook, the *Diagnostic and Statistical Manual* (Clausen, 1997; Schuklenk et al., 2002). Naturally, however, some therapists still maintain heterosexist attitudes (Peplau & Beals, 2001; Rothblum, 2000b). For example, one lesbian woman reported that a therapist had told her that she "wasn't really gay" but was simply acting out problems related to her father. Fortunately, she then sought a more enlightened therapist whose advice was more helpful (L. Garnets et al., 1991).

A large number of studies have shown that the average lesbian is as well adjusted as the average heterosexual woman (Division 44/Committee on Lesbian, Gay, and Bisexual Concerns, 2000; Peplau & Garnets, 2000a). In a representative study, Rothblum and Factor (2001) compared the mental health of 184 pairs of lesbian women and their heterosexual sisters. The results showed that the two groups were equivalently well adjusted, except that the lesbian women were higher in self-esteem. According to other research, lesbians and heterosexual women are similar on almost all psychological dimensions, except that lesbians score higher on positive characteristics such as "being self-sufficient" and "making decisions easily" (Peplau & Garnets, 2000a).

As our discussion of heterosexism and sexual prejudice emphasized in Chapter 2, many sexual minority individuals are victims of hate crimes. Not surprisingly, lesbians, gays, and bisexuals who have experienced hate crimes are likely to report depression and anxiety (Herek et al., 1999). In other words, hatred has real-life consequences for the well-being of thousands of women and men. Surprisingly, however, lesbian women are not at greater risk for suicide than heterosexual women (Remafedi et al., 1998). In light of the sexual prejudice problem, we should be surprised that lesbians and gay men do *not* have high rates of psychological dysfunction.

Students in my classes often ask whether people who accept their lesbian or gay identity are better adjusted. The research shows that people who accept their lesbian identity have higher self-esteem than those who have not accepted their lesbian identity (J. F. Morris et al., 2001; K. L. Walters & Simoni, 1993). Those who are politically active in the lesbian and gay community may also have better mental health (N. J. Evans & D'Augelli, 1996; Gonsiorek, 1996). Many lesbians create their own communities, and warm, supportive networks develop from the "families" they choose. These communities are especially helpful when lesbians are rejected by their birth families (Cruikshank, 1992; Esterberg, 1996).

The Fluidity of Female Sexual Orientation

For many years, researchers who were interested in the topic of lesbian and gay sexual orientation supported a straightforward model. Specifically, a young person would feel discontent about heterosexual relationships. Then she or he would enter a period of sexual questioning, which would end with the adoption of a lesbian, gay, or bisexual identity. Current researchers realize that this model is too simplistic, because it does not acknowledge the diverse pathways by which sexual orientation develops, especially for women (Baumeister, 2000; Cohler & Galatzer-Levy, 2000; L. M. Diamond, 2002; Peplau, 2001). One problem with the older research is that the sexual minority individuals who had shared their stories were typically openly gay males who were exclusively attracted to other men. Consistent with Theme 3 of this textbook, earlier research focused on sexual minority men rather than on sexual minority women.

As suggested in the introduction to this section (p. 266), sexual orientation is a fluid, changing process rather than a rigid category. Consider, for example, the research of Lisa M. Diamond (1998, 2000, 2002). She began by interviewing 89 women between the ages of 16 and 23 who identified themselves as "nonheterosexual women." Diamond located these women in college courses on sexuality, in college campus groups, and in community events sponsored by lesbian, gay, and bisexual organizations. Diamond continued to interview these women over a period of 5 years. Of the women who had identified themselves as lesbians in the first interview, some described a "classic" development of their lesbian identity, beginning in childhood and continuing in adolescence. However, most of the women in Diamond's study had questioned their sexual identity at some point during that 5-year interval. For instance, 67% of the women changed their orientation at least one time after coming out. Here's a representative quotation from one woman:

> In the past couple of years I've become very comfortable with the fact that there are some men that I will be attracted to, but that any long-term emotional, sexual commitment will be to a woman. I felt comfortable saying to myself "I feel like I'm a lesbian intellectually, but it's okay that I'm still attracted to men physically." But I don't have as much of an emotional connection with men. And [being a lesbian] is a much more important part of my sexuality. (L. M. Diamond, 2002)

Interestingly, many of the women emphasized that they disliked having to fit themselves into someone else's labels or categories.

In this chapter, we have emphasized the variation in women's romantic relationships, consistent with Theme 4. As we've just seen, the current research also suggests that a woman's sexual orientation can vary throughout her lifetime. In the last part of this section on lesbian and bisexual women, we will see the implications of this fluidity for theories of sexual orientation.

Characteristics of Lesbian Relationships

For most North Americans—lesbian, gay male, bisexual, or heterosexual—being in a love relationship is an important determinant of their overall happiness (Peplau et al., 1997). Surveys suggest that between 45% and 80% of lesbians are currently in a steady romantic relationship (Patterson, 1998). In other words, many lesbians consider being part of a couple to be an important part of their life.

Let's now look more closely at several aspects of lesbian relationships. Specifically, how do most lesbian relationships begin? How is equality emphasized in these relationships? How happy are lesbian couples? How do they respond when the relationship breaks up?

The Beginning of a Relationship.   Lesbian women want many of the same qualities in a romantic partner that heterosexual women emphasize. These include characteristics such as dependability and good personality (Peplau & Spalding, 2000). The research suggests that most lesbian couples begin their relationship as friends and then fall in love (Peplau & Spalding, 2000; S. Rose, 2000; Savin-Williams, 2001; Savin-Williams & Diamond, 2000). For many young women, a romantic relationship is a major milestone in the coming-out process of identifying oneself as a lesbian (Schneider, 2001).

An important hallmark of a strong friendship is emotional intimacy. As we'll see, lesbian couples are likely to emphasize emotional closeness. In contrast, physical attractiveness is relatively unimportant as a basis for a lesbian love relationship. In fact, when lesbians place personal ads in newspapers, they rarely emphasize physical characteristics (Peplau & Spalding, 2000; S. Rose et al., 1994).

Equality in Lesbian Relationships.   The balance of power is extremely important in lesbian relationships, and couples are happier if both members of the pair contribute equally to the decision making (Kurdek, 1995b; Peplau et al., 1982). We saw earlier that salary is an important determinant of power for heterosexual couples. However, salary isn't closely related to power among lesbian couples (Kurdek, 1995c; Peplau & Spalding, 2000). One possible explanation for this difference is that money is not as central to a woman's identity as it is to a man's identity.

In Chapter 7, we saw that women do most of the housework in heterosexual marriages, even when both the husband and the wife work full time. As you might expect, lesbian couples are especially likely to emphasize that housework should be divided fairly (Kurdek, 1995c; Oerton, 1998; Peplau & Spalding, 2000).

Satisfaction.   The research on lesbian couples shows that their satisfaction with their relationship is much the same as for heterosexual couples and gay male couples (Caldwell et al., 1981; Kurdek, 1998; Patterson, 1995). Try Demonstration 8.5 before you read further.

Demonstration 8.5 contains some of the questions from a survey, designed by Lawrence Kurdek (1995a), that measures relationship commitment. In this survey, Kurdek's sample of lesbian couples had commitment scores that were similar to the scores of married couples. The results also showed that the lesbian couples were more committed to the relationship than were heterosexual couples who were dating but not living together.

Psychological intimacy is likely to be strong in lesbian couples (Mackey et al., 2000). One woman described this sense of caring and intimacy:

> What has been good is the ongoing caring and respect and the sense that there is somebody there who really cares, who has your best interest, who loves you, who knows you better than anybody, and still likes you . . . and just that knowing, that familiarity, the depth of that knowing, the depth of that connection [make it] so incredibly meaningful. There is something spiritual after awhile. It has a life of its own. This is what is really so comfortable. (Mackey et al., 2000, p. 220)

DEMONSTRATION 8.5 ■ ■ ■ ■ ■ ■ ■ ■ ■ ■ ■ ■ ■ ■ ■ ■ ■ ■ ■

Assessing Commitment to a Relationship

Answer the following questions about a current love relationship or a previous love relationship. Or, if you prefer, think of a couple you know well, and answer the questionnaire from the perspective of one member of that couple. Use a rating scale where 1 = strongly disagree and 5 = strongly agree. These questions are based on a survey by Kurdek (1995a). This is a shorter version. Turn to page 284 to see which relationship dimensions are assessed by these items.

Rating Question

_____ 1. One advantage to my relationship is having someone to count on.

_____ 2. I have to sacrifice a lot to be in my relationship.

_____ 3. My current relationship comes close to matching what I would consider my ideal relationship.

_____ 4. As an alternative to my current relationship, I would like to date someone else.

_____ 5. I've put a lot of energy and effort into my relationship.

_____ 6. It would be difficult to leave my partner because of the emotional pain involved.

_____ 7. Overall, I derive a lot of rewards and advantages from being in my relationship.

_____ 8. Overall, a lot of personal costs are involved in being in my relationship.

_____ 9. My current relationship provides me with an ideal amount of equality.

_____ 10. Overall, alternatives to being in my relationship are appealing.

_____ 11. I have invested a part of myself in my relationship.

_____ 12. It would be difficult to leave my partner because I would still feel attached to him or her.

Source: From Kurdek, L. A. (1995). Assessing multiple determinants of relationship commitment in cohabitating gay, cohabitating lesbian, dating heterosexual, and married heterosexual couples. *Family Relations, 44,* 261–266 (Table 1). Copyright © 1995 by the National Council on Family Relations, 3989 Central Ave. NE, Suite 550, Minneapolis, MN 55421. Reprinted with permission.

Breaking Up. We do not have extensive information about how lesbian partners break up their love relationships. However, the general pattern seems to be similar to the heterosexual breakup pattern (Kurdek, 1995a; Peplau & Beals, 2001). The common reasons for breaking up include feeling emotionally distant from the partner, loneliness, relief from conflict, and differences in interests, background, and attitudes about sex (Kurdek, 1995b; Peplau et al., 1996).

When relationships break up, lesbian women report the same mix of negative and positive emotions that heterosexual women experience (Kurdek, 1991). However, the breakup of a lesbian relationship also differs from heterosexual breakups, especially the breakup of a marriage. For example, many factors prevent heterosexual couples from splitting apart, such as the cost of divorce or joint investments in children and property (Peplau & Spalding, 2000; Peplau et al., 1996). These factors may be less relevant for lesbian couples. In addition, lesbian couples are less likely to have support for their relationship from other family members—a factor that often keeps heterosexual couples together.

Consider another point that lesbian friends have mentioned to me. Lesbians are likely to derive substantial emotional support from their partner, especially because they experience relatively little emotional support from heterosexuals. When their relationship breaks up, there are not many people with whom they can share their sorrow. In addition, their heterosexual friends often consider this loss to be less devastating than the breakup of a heterosexual relationship.

Lesbian Women of Color

Lesbians of color often comment that they face a triple barrier in U.S. society: their ethnicity, their gender, and their sexual orientation (Greene, 1996; J. F. Morris, 2000; J. F. Morris et al., 2001). Lesbians who have immigrated to the United States and Canada from another country face even greater barriers. For example, they may have been persecuted in the country from which they came (Espín, 1996, 1999). Now, these women struggle with cultural differences, and the new culture may have different ideas about lesbians from those in their country of origin.

Many lesbians of color face an extra barrier because their culture has even more traditional views of women than does mainstream European American culture. For example, Beverly Greene (2000a) pointed out that Black churches typically show sexual prejudice toward lesbian and gay individuals. As Alicia Gaspar de Alba (1993) noted, Latina lesbian women do not fit into any of the traditional roles that are part of the stereotypical Latina framework—mother, wife, virgin, or prostitute. The lesbian woman doesn't propagate the race, and she doesn't serve men in either a domestic or a sexual capacity. As a result, she becomes marginalized both within and outside her own culture. Furthermore, other cultures may also be more traditional than European American culture with respect to discussing sexuality. For example, Asian cultures typically believe that sexuality shouldn't be discussed, even with a best friend (C. S. Chan, 1997).

Because some cultures do not discuss sexuality, lesbians are often invisible. For example, Leota Lone Dog (1991) expressed this concern, based on her perspective as a lesbian Native American:

> There's a lot of fear about coming out in our Native American community. . . . It was bad enough to be an Indian—that was lonely enough. But to be gay and Indian, I ask myself, "Where would I ever find another one?" (p. 49)

An additional problem is that many heterosexual people of color believe that only European Americans face the "problem" of having gays and lesbians

(Aguilar–San Juan, 1993; J. F. Morris, 2000). Furthermore, ethnic sexual minorities are more worried than White sexual minorities that their parents will reject them because of their sexual orientation (Dubé et al., 2001). Women of color may be more reluctant than European American women to come out, for example, in the workplace (Hidalgo, 1995).

How do lesbian women of color feel about their own relationships? Peplau and her colleagues (1997) sent questionnaires to 398 Black women throughout the United States who had said they were in a committed romantic relationship with another woman. Three-quarters of the women responded that they were "in love" and felt very close to their romantic partner. They also reported that they were quite satisfied with the relationship; the mean score was 5.3 on a scale where the maximum was 7.0.

In the current era, an increasing number of lesbian women of color can find organizations and community groups that provide support (J. F. Morris, 2000). However, these groups are more likely in urban regions of North America. For example, Mi Ok Bruining (1995) described the Asian Pacific lesbian organization to which she belongs. Mariana Romo-Carmona (1995) explained that Latina lesbians in the New York City area can watch a TV program featuring Latina lesbians, read brochures on health care written in Spanish by Latina lesbians, and march in the Puerto Rican Day parade with a contingent of lesbian and gay Latinas/os. Racism and heterosexism may still be present, but these groups can provide a shared sense of community.

Bisexual Women

Ann Fox recalled her first year in college, when she fell in love with her roommate:

> Since that time, I have loved other women. I have loved women in the same deep and romantic ways that I have loved some of the men in my life. I have loved them as friends, as lovers, and as possible life partners. For me, there has never been a question as to whether my feelings for women were more or less real than my emotional ties to men. They are simply (and complexly) different. I can no more deny the depth of my ability to love people of both genders than I could the fact of being, myself, a woman. (A. Fox, 1991, p. 29)

A **bisexual woman** is a woman who is psychologically, emotionally, and sexually attracted to both women and men (Robin & Hamner, 2000). Consistent with the discussion on pages 268 to 269, a woman is more likely to have had relationships with both women and men than to have had exclusively lesbian relationships throughout her life (L. M. Diamond, 2002; Rust, 2000). As we'll see in the discussion of bisexual identity, most bisexuals are not equally attracted to both women and men at any given moment. We'll also see that bisexuality presents a dilemma for a culture that likes to construct clear-cut categories.

Identity Issues Among Bisexual Women.   Most bisexual women report fluctuations in their romantic interests. For example, a woman with strong heterosexual attractions may, several years later, find that she has equally strong attractions to women (R. L. Pope & Reynolds, 1991).

Most bisexual women report that they felt attracted to men at an earlier age than they felt attracted to women (R. C. Fox, 1996; Weinberg et al., 1994). Weinberg and his colleagues believe that bisexuals actively work to make sense of their sexual interests, that is, to *construct* their bisexuality. Given the heterosexist bias in our culture, these individuals would certainly find it easier to make sense out of their heterosexual desires before they acknowledge any same-gender interests.

Bisexual women differ widely in their romantic experiences. Rust (1995) studied a group of bisexual women who attended conferences or social activities focusing on lesbian and bisexual issues. She found that 40% had been married to a man at some time and that 84% had identified themselves as lesbians at some point in their lives. The nature of the attraction may differ, too, as one woman explains: "I feel a greater physical attraction to men, but a greater spiritual/emotional attraction to women" (Rust, 2000, p. 212). In short, bisexuality creates a fluid identity rather than a clear-cut life pathway (Garber, 1995; Rust, 2000; M. J. K. Williams, 1999).

Although little research has been conducted on the adjustment of bisexual women, they do not seem to have unusual difficulties (R. C. Fox, 1997; LaTorre & Wendenburg, 1983). Also, bisexual women and lesbian women are equally satisfied with their current sexual identity (Rust, 1996b). In other words, bisexual women often think about their sexual identity, but they do not believe that the bisexual process is a painful struggle.

Bisexuals who come from a background of mixed ethnicity often find that their mixed heritage resonates comfortably with their bisexuality. After all, their experience with ethnicity has taught them from an early age that our culture constructs clear-cut ethnic categories. As a result, they are not surprised to encounter our culture's clear-cut categories of sexual orientation (Rust, 2000). For example, here's a quotation from a bisexual woman whose background includes Native American, Jewish, and British ancestors:

> Because I am of mixed ethnicity, I rotate between feeling "left out" of every group and feeling "secretly" qualified for several racial/cultural identities. I notice the same feeling regarding my sexual identity. (Rust, 1996a, pp. 69–70)

Attitudes Toward Bisexual Women.   Bisexual women often report rejection by both the heterosexual and the lesbian communities. Because of sexual prejudice, heterosexuals may condemn bisexuals' same-gender relationships. Heterosexuals also tend to believe that bisexuals are frequently unfaithful to their partners (Peplau & Spalding, 2000). In contrast, lesbians often believe that bisexual women are confused; lesbians sometimes say that sexual prejudice prevents bisexuals from "admitting" that they are lesbians (Herdt, 2001; Rust, 1995; Peplau & Spalding, 2000). As a result, both of these other groups often act as if the bisexual group were invisible (Robin & Hamner, 2000).

In Chapter 2, we emphasized that people like to have precise categories for males and females, fitting everyone neatly into one category or the other. Prejudice against lesbians can be partly traced to the fact that lesbians violate the accepted rules about categories: A person is not supposed to love someone who belongs to the same category. Bisexuals provide an additional frustration for people who like precise categories. After all, bisexuals cannot even be placed into the neat category of lesbians, a group that *clearly* violates the rule about categories. Bisexuals frustrate people who have a low tolerance for ambiguity!

Theoretical Explanations About Sexual Orientation

When we try to explain how lesbians develop their psychological, emotional, and sexual preference for women, we should also consider another question: How do *heterosexual* women develop their psychological, emotional, and sexual preference for men? Unfortunately, theorists rarely mention this question.[1] Because of our culture's heterosexist bias, it is considered both natural and normal for women to be attracted exclusively to men. This assumption implies that lesbianism is considered unnatural and abnormal, and abnormalities require an explanation (Baber, 2000).

In reality, however, heterosexuality is more puzzling. After all, research from many branches of social psychology shows that we prefer people who resemble ourselves, not people who are different. On this basis, we should prefer those of our own gender.

Articles in the popular press proclaim that biological factors can explain the mystery of being lesbian or gay. In reality, we do *not* have strong evidence for a biological explanation for the sexual orientation of lesbians or bisexual women. Fortunately, psychologists who favor sociocultural explanations are now beginning to develop theories about the ways in which social forces and our thought processes may shape our sexual orientations. Let's begin by considering the biological explanations, and then we'll summarize the sociocultural explanations.

Biological Explanations.   To prepare this section on biological explanations, I reviewed dozens of articles and books. Surely, by the twenty-first century, we should have research confirming whether biological factors contribute to women's sexual orientation! In reality, however, researchers who favor biological explanations are much more likely to study gay men than lesbian women. In addition, much of the research examines sexual behavior in nonhuman species (Ellis & Ebertz, 1997) or sexual orientation in individuals exposed to abnormal levels of prenatal hormones (Meyer-Bahlburg et al., 1995). These research areas are too far removed to offer compelling explanations for women's sexual orientation (Byne & Parsons, 1994; Tiefer, 1995a).

Other research examines normal humans to determine whether genetic factors, hormonal factors, or brain structures determine sexual orientation (e.g., Gladue, 1994; Halpern & Cass, 1994; Hershberger, 2001; LeVay, 1991, 1996). Some of the research suggests, for example, that a particular region on the X chromosome may contain genes for homosexuality. However, this research focuses almost exclusively on gay males, not lesbians or bisexuals (Ellis, 1996; L. A. Peplau, personal communication, 1997). Many of these studies also have serious methodological flaws that have been pointed out by other researchers (e.g., Byne, 1994; Byne & Parsons, 1994; Cohler & Galatzer-Levy, 2000; Peplau et al., 1998).

---

[1]One exception is an excellent article by Hyde and Jaffee (2000), which suggests that adolescent women are encouraged toward heterosexuality by means of traditional gender roles and numerous antigay messages.

Let's consider one of the few studies on genetic factors that looked at lesbians rather than gay males. Bailey and his colleagues focused on lesbians who happened to have an identical twin sister (J. M. Bailey et al., 1993). Of these lesbians, 48% had lesbian twin sisters. This is a remarkably high percentage. However, as Ellis (1996) asked, if genetic factors guarantee sexual orientation, why isn't that figure 100%? In addition, these twins grew up in the same environment and had numerous opportunities to discuss sexual orientation with each other. Social factors certainly had some influence on their sexual and romantic lives!

In related research, Pattatucci and Hamer (1995) studied 358 heterosexual, bisexual, and lesbian women and examined the sexual orientation of their family members. Women who were lesbians were significantly more likely than heterosexual women to have female relatives who were lesbian. In one analysis, for example, 6% of lesbian women had a lesbian sister; in contrast, only 1% of heterosexual women had a lesbian sister. Again, however, social factors would have had some influence on the sexual orientation of these family members.

In short, the current research about the biological basis of women's sexual orientation is not convincing, especially because so few studies examine lesbians or bisexual women (Peplau, 2001; Peplau & Garnets, 2000a). We should note, incidentally, that research suggests some support for the role of biological factors in male sexual orientation (Baumeister, 2000; Hershberger, 2001). Clearly, however, the popular press has overemphasized the importance of biological factors in explaining sexual orientation in women.

Sociocultural Explanations.   The recent research and theory suggest that women's sexual orientation is more influenced by sociocultural factors than by biological factors (Baumeister, 2000). Let's consider two complementary theories that explain how these sociocultural factors might operate: (1) the social constructionist approach and (2) the intimate careers approach. As you read about these two approaches, you'll note that they are compatible with each other; we do not need to choose one and reject the other.

The **social constructionist approach** argues that our culture creates sexual categories, which we use to organize our thoughts about our sexuality (Baber, 2000; Bohan, 1996; C. Kitzinger & Wilkinson, 1997). Social constructionists reject an essentialist approach to sexual orientation. In other words, sexual orientation is not a fundamental characteristic of individuals, nor is it a core aspect of their personality acquired either before birth or in early childhood.

The social constructionists propose that, based on their life experiences and cultural messages, most North American women construct heterosexual identities for themselves. Women learn a "script" in which males' sexual needs are most important and in which women are relatively passive (Baber, 2000; Carpenter, 1998). However, some women resist this script; they review their sexual and romantic experiences and decide that they are either lesbian or bisexual.

The social constructionist approach argues that sexuality is both fluid and flexible, consistent with our earlier discussions. For example, women can make a transition from being heterosexual to being lesbian by reevaluating their lives or by reconsidering their political values (C. Kitzinger & Wilkinson, 1997).

To examine the social constructionist approach, Celia Kitzinger and Sue Wilkinson (1997) interviewed 80 women who had strongly identified themselves as heterosexuals for at least 10 years and who, at the time of the study, strongly identified themselves as lesbians. These women reported how they reevaluated their lives in making the transition. For example, one woman said:

> I was looking at myself in the mirror, and I thought, "That woman is a lesbian," and then I allowed myself to notice that it was me I was talking about. And when that happened, I felt whole for the first time, and also absolutely terrified. (p. 197)

However, we need to emphasize an important point: Some lesbians believe that their sexual orientation is truly beyond their conscious control (Golden, 1996). These women had considered themselves different from other females at an early age, usually when they were between 6 and 12 years old.

In short, the social constructionist approach acknowledges that the categories *heterosexual, bisexual,* and *lesbian* are fluid and flexible. This approach also explains how some women consciously choose their sexual category.

A second sociocultural explanation, called the "intimate careers approach," emphasizes the diversity of women's sexual orientations as well as the variation within many women's life course. This approach has been proposed by Letitia Anne Peplau, a prominent researcher in the area of lesbian and gay relationships (Peplau, 2001; Peplau & Garnets, 2000a; Peplau, Spalding et al., 1999). Peplau suggests that we can use people's occupational career development as a metaphor for the way our romantic interests and sexual orientations develop. For instance, think about some of your own friends and the diverse pathways they have taken in developing their career interests. Perhaps one friend is a psychology major, planning to pursue a master's degree in social work. Another friend may be interested in teaching history in high school, and yet another friend is planning to become an electrical engineer.

By adopting the metaphor of occupational careers, the **intimate careers approach** suggests that we humans take a variety of pathways as we develop our intimate relationships. For instance, you may have three female friends; one is exclusively heterosexual, another is exclusively lesbian, and another is bisexual. The intimate careers approach also emphasizes that different people may currently hold the same sexual orientation for a variety of reasons. For example, you may know three women who are lesbians. One woman may have been attracted to women for as long as she can remember. Another woman may have considered herself to be heterosexual throughout her early adulthood; then she developed an intense friendship with another woman, which grew into a lesbian relationship. A third woman may have considered herself heterosexual until she became deeply involved in the women's movement during college; for political reasons, she then decided that she would choose a lesbian identity.

The intimate careers approach is still quite new. Many developmental studies need to be conducted to determine how a woman's sexual identity develops as she forms romantic relationships during adolescence and adulthood.

In reality, then, we don't yet have a satisfying comprehensive theory that considers the wide variety of women's sexual and romantic identities. To construct a theory, we need carefully conducted research that focuses on women who are lesbians and bisexuals. The most comprehensive theory of sexual orientation may actually include a biological predisposition that encourages some women to become lesbian or bisexual. However, social experiences may determine which women will choose lesbian or bisexual identities and which women will choose heterosexual identities (Kauth & Kalichman, 1998). This comprehensive theory would also specify that sexual identities are typically fluid. Sexual orientation is not a clear-cut category but a continuing process of self-discovery.

SECTION SUMMARY ■

Lesbians and Bisexual Women

1. Lesbians are psychologically, emotionally, and sexually attracted to other women; however, our heterosexist culture judges heterosexual relationships differently from other romantic relationships.

2. Research demonstrates that lesbians and heterosexual women are equally well adjusted; lesbians who accept their lesbian identity are typically higher in self-esteem.

3. Research suggests that most lesbians experience a fluid pattern of sexual identity, with some heterosexual interest, rather than a rigid progression toward lesbian identity.

4. The research shows that most lesbian relationships begin with friendship. Lesbian couples are happier when power is evenly divided; lesbian couples and heterosexual couples are equally satisfied with their relationships. The pattern of breaking up is fairly similar for lesbian couples and heterosexual couples.

5. Lesbian women of color are more reluctant than European American lesbians to come out if their ethnic community has conservative values; however, some support groups have been organized for lesbian women of color.

6. Bisexual women illustrate that romantic attractions are often flexible; unfortunately, these women face rejection by both the lesbian and the heterosexual communities.

7. Biological research examines whether genetic factors, hormonal factors, and brain structures determine sexual orientation. However, the research seldom focuses on lesbians or bisexuals; we do not currently have persuasive evidence that biological factors are responsible for women's sexual orientation.

8. Two mutually compatible explanations have been proposed: (a) According to the social constructionist approach, sexual orientation is flexible, and people can reconstruct their identity to make transitions between heterosexual and lesbian orientations; and (b) the intimate careers approach also emphasizes the flexible nature of women's sexual orientation, both in the variety of women's experiences and within each woman's life course.

SINGLE WOMEN

The category "single women" overlaps with many of the groups we have already considered. For example, women who are in dating or cohabiting relationships qualify as single. Women who are separated or divorced are also included. So are lesbians and bisexual women who are not currently married. Widows, whom we will consider in Chapter 14, are also single. In addition, the category of single women includes those who have never married. According to the 2000 U.S. census, 23% of women, 18 years of age and older, had never married (U.S. Census Bureau, 2001b). The comparable figure for Canada is 27% (Status of Women Canada, 2000).

In this section on single women, we will focus on women who have never married, because they are not considered elsewhere in the book. However, the other women mentioned in the previous paragraph share some of the same advantages and disadvantages experienced by these never-married women. Before you read further, try Demonstration 8.6.

DEMONSTRATION 8.6 ■ ■ ■ ■ ■ ■ ■ ■ ■ ■ ■ ■ ■ ■ ■ ■ ■ ■

Attitudes Toward Single Women

Imagine that a friend has invited you to a family picnic with her extended family. She is giving you a brief description of each relative who will be there. For one relative, Melinda Taylor, she says, "I really don't know much about her, but she is in her late 30s and she isn't married."

Try to form a mental image of Melinda Taylor, given this brief description. Compare her with the average woman in her late thirties, using the following list of characteristics. In each case, decide whether Melinda Taylor has *more* of the characteristic (write M), the *same* amount of the characteristic (write S), or *less* of the characteristic (write L).

_____ friendly	_____ bossy
_____ intelligent	_____ lonely
_____ disorganized	_____ attractive
_____ warm	_____ good sense of humor
_____ good conversationalist	_____ unhappy
_____ feminist	_____ politically liberal

Do you see any pattern to your responses?

Characteristics of Single Women

Little research has been conducted on single women, even though they constitute a substantial percentage of adult women (Newtson & Keith, 1997). As you might imagine, single women are more likely than married women to work outside the home ("Facts on Working Women," 1998). Many single women are highly educated, career-oriented individuals. These women often find that being single allows them flexible work hours and geographic mobility (DeFrain & Olson, 1999; Newtson & Keith, 1997).

Many single women have chosen not to marry because they never found an ideal partner. For example, *Time* magazine conducted a survey of 205 never-married women. One question asked, "If you couldn't find the perfect mate, would you marry someone else?" (T. M. Edwards, 2000, p. 48). Only 34% replied that they would choose a less-than-perfect spouse.

Research suggests that single, never-married women receive the same scores as married women on tests measuring psychological distress (Marks, 1996). Single women and married women are also similar in their life span, and both tend to live longer than divorced women (Fincham & Beach, 1999; Friedman et al., 1995). Single women score higher than married women on measures of independence. However, single women score lower than married women on tests of self-acceptance (Marks, 1996).

What about the social relationships of single women? Apparently, there is no typical single woman, just as there is no typical woman who is dating, living with a man, married, or lesbian. Seccombe and Ishii-Kuntz (1994) found that 25% of their sample reported that they never socialized with friends. However, 29% said that they had social activities with friends at least once a week. Consistent with Theme 4 of this book, individual differences among women are large.

How do single women feel about their romantic status? A polling firm sampled people living in New York City who were between the ages of 21 and 40 and were not currently in a serious romantic relationship (Penn & Schoen, 1998). Of the women who identified themselves as heterosexual, 34% were happily single and dating and 27% were happily single and *not* dating. In addition, 30% were looking for a romantic relationship, but only 5% described themselves as "panicking." In summary, single women are generally well adjusted and they are often quite satisfied with their single status.

Attitudes Toward Single Women

What kinds of answers did you provide in Demonstration 8.6? Also, think about the comments aimed at never-married women when you were growing up. Single women are pitied and scorned more than single men are (Waehler, 1996). In some classic research from the 1980s, single women were perceived to be less sociable, less attractive, and less reliable than married women (Etaugh & Foresman, 1983; Etaugh & Riley, 1983). Two decades ago, single people were downgraded on many personal characteristics.

Have attitudes changed in the current era? People seem less likely to use negative terms such as *old maid* or *spinster* when referring to unmarried women. We know that women are more likely to be single in the current era. In 1970, only 10% of 25- to 29-year-old women were unmarried, compared to 39% by 2000 (DeFrain & Olson, 1999; U.S. Census Bureau, 2001b). A chapter about contemporary family patterns comments that this trend in remaining single creates "an increasing recognition that in our society singlehood can be a legitimate, healthy, and happy alternative to marriage" (DeFrain & Olson, 1999, p. 311). However, I've been unable to locate recent surveys on attitudes toward single women. It's clear that researchers have not yet answered many of the interesting questions about women's lives!

Advantages and Disadvantages of Being Single

Among the advantages to being single, women most often mention freedom (DeFrain & Olson, 1999; K. G. Lewis & Moon, 1997). Single people are free to do what they want, according to their own preferences. As one never-married woman remarked:

> I had places to go and things to see. And I wasn't going to be stopped, nobody was going to stop me. It took me a long time to get going, but I made it. (K. R. Allen, 1994, p. 104)

Single women also mention that privacy is an advantage for them. They can be by themselves when they want, without the risk of offending someone. Some also mention that being single allows them to *be* themselves rather than a person who must try to please others (Langford, 1999). By learning to be alone with themselves, many women also say that they have developed a greater level of self-knowledge (Brehm, Miller et al., 2002). In addition, single women mention that they can pursue a greater variety of friendships than would be available if they had married (K. R. Allen, 1989, 1994).

When women are asked about the disadvantages of being single, they frequently mention loneliness (C. M. Anderson & Stewart, 1994; DeFrain & Olson, 1999; T. M. Edwards, 2000). One woman reported, "I am not a widow, but I'm the same as a widow. I'm a woman living alone, going home to an empty house" (K. R. Allen, 1994, p. 104).

Single people sometimes mention that they feel at a disadvantage in communities where couples predominate—a situation that some humorously call the Noah's Ark Syndrome. Our culture seems to believe that it's abnormal for a woman to be alone in a social situation (Watrous & Honeychurch, 1999). Others report that they feel unsafe living alone in urban settings (Chasteen, 1994). Still others resent that they are the objects of pity, and they also resent that friends and relatives are overly concerned that they are not married (K. G. Lewis & Moon, 1997).

However, most single people create their own social networks of friends and relatives. Many of them have a housemate with whom they can share joys, sorrows, and frustrations. One woman described an advantage to her social world, in terms of "having friends that care for you as a person and not as part of a couple" (K. G. Lewis & Moon, 1997, p. 123). These social networks are often innovative. For example, one woman described a system that she called her Ten Top People. These were individuals to whom she could feel free to turn for immediate help or for sharing happiness (M. Adams, 1976). In summary, single women frequently develop alternative support systems for caring and social connection.

Single Women of Color

We noted that little research has been conducted on the general topic of single women. Sadly, single women of color are virtually invisible in the psychology research. This observation is especially ironic because 38% of Black women and 23% of Latina women have never married, in contrast to only 18% of European American women (U.S. Census Bureau, 2001b).

In some ethnic communities, unmarried women serve a valuable function. For example, in Chicana (Mexican American) culture, an unmarried daughter is expected to take care of her elderly parents or to help out with nieces and nephews (Flores-Ortiz, 1998).

The unmarried-daughter role is often expected of Asian American single women as well (Ferguson, 2000; Newtson & Keith, 1997). Additional reasons that Asian American women remain single include an interest in pursuing advanced education and the lack of an appropriate marriage partner (Ferguson, 2000).

Limited research has been conducted with Black women who are single. Supportive friendships often provide invaluable social interactions for single Black women (Mays, 1985). One study focused on the support networks of Black unmarried and married women in Richmond, Virginia (D. R. Brown & Gary, 1985). These women were asked about the number of friends and relatives with whom they maintained close contact. The unmarried respondents emphasized that other family members were extremely important in their lives; roughly two-thirds of the women mentioned kin as their closest relationship. About a quarter of the women mentioned female friends as their major close relationship. Only 6% cited male friends as their closest relationship.

Single Black women also find friends who can provide support for their accomplishments in the workplace. For example, a study of Black professional women uncovered many ways in which these friends could provide encouragement (Denton, 1990). One woman remarked about her friend:

> She makes me feel good about the choices I make. I don't feel recognized or appreciated for my efforts on my job. I know I've done exemplary work . . . but I get no recognition for what I've done. [In this friendship] I get reinforced. She always lets me know I'm talented. (p. 455)

Researchers in past years have failed to provide a rich description of attitudes, social conditions, and behaviors of single women (Condra, 1991). In the next few decades, we may achieve a more complete understanding of the diversity of single women from all ethnic backgrounds.

SECTION SUMMARY ■

Single Women

1. Little research has been conducted on single women; however, single women are fairly similar to married women on various measures of adjustment.

2. Single women vary widely in their social activity.

3. In the past, people have had somewhat negative attitudes toward the social characteristics of single people, but attitudes appear to be growing more positive.

4. Single women value their freedom and their privacy, but they mention that loneliness is a disadvantage; most single women create alternative support systems.

5. Unmarried Latina and Asian women are often expected to take care of family members. Black single women emphasize the importance of family members and friends in providing close relationships and support, both socially and on the job.

■ ■ ■ ■ ■ CHAPTER REVIEW QUESTIONS ■ ■ ■ ■ ■

1. From time to time throughout this book, we have discussed the topic of attractiveness. How is attractiveness important in love relationships?

2. We discussed cross-cultural studies and research with North American women of color at several points in the chapter. Summarize this research with respect to the following topics: (a) the ideal romantic partner, (b) emphasis on friendship in a love relationship, (c) marriage, (d) lesbian women of color, and (e) single women of color.

3. What is evolutionary psychology, how does it explain women's and men's choices for an ideal romantic partner, and why is it inadequate in explaining romantic relationships in the current century? How can the social roles theory account for that research? Finally, why would evolutionary psychology have difficulty accounting for lesbian relationships?

4. The issue of power was discussed several times in this chapter. Summarize the relationship between money and power in marriage, the division of power in the three kinds of marriages, power in Black families, and the importance of balanced power in lesbian relationships.

5. Discuss how this chapter contains many examples of the theme that women differ widely from one another. Be sure to include topics such as patterns of living together, reactions to divorce, sexual orientation, and the social relationships of single women.

6. Discuss gender comparisons that were described throughout this chapter, including the ideal sexual partner, the ideal marriage partner, reactions to breaking up, satisfaction with marriage, and the decision to seek a divorce.

7. We noted that the section on lesbians and bisexual women would be likely to frustrate people who like clear-cut categories. Discuss the fluid nature of sexual orientation, mentioning the research of Lisa Diamond, the experiences of bisexual women, and the two sociocultural theories about sexual orientation.

8. Lesbians, bisexuals, and single women all have lifestyles that differ from the norm. What are people's attitudes toward women in these three groups?

9. Imagine that you are having a conversation with a friend from your high school, whom you know well. This friend says that she thinks that lesbians have more psychological problems than heterosexual women do. She also thinks that lesbian couples are likely to have relationship problems. What information related to her concerns could you provide from this chapter?

10. Suppose that you continue to talk with the high school friend mentioned in Question 9, and the conversation turns to people who have never married. She tells you that she is worried about a mutual friend who doesn't seem to be interested in dating or finding a husband. How would you respond to your friend's concerns?

NEW TERMS

*evolutionary psychology (249)
*social roles explanation (251)
 cohabitation (252)
*traditional marriage (260)
*modern marriage (260)
 egalitarian marriage (261)
*machismo (261)
*marianismo (261)
 Black matriarchy (262)

 persistence of attachment (264)
*ego development (265)
*lesbian (266)
*sexual minority (266)
*heterosexism (266)
*bisexual woman (273)
 social constructionist approach (276)
 intimate careers approach (277)

The terms asterisked in the New Terms section serve as good search terms for InfoTrac College Edition. Go to http://infotrac.thomsonlearning.com and try these added search terms.

RECOMMENDED READINGS

Brown, N. M., & Amatea, E. S. (2000). *Love and intimate relationships: Journeys of the heart.* Philadelphia: Brunner/Mazel. In addition to the topics discussed in the current chapter, Brown and Amatea's textbook also explores communication, conflict, and emotion in love relationships. It also includes extensive quotations from people discussing their romantic experiences.

D'Augelli, A. R., & Patterson, C. J. (Eds.). (2001). *Lesbian, gay, and bisexual identities and youth.* New York: Oxford University Press. This book focuses on adolescents; it provides an excellent overview of numerous topics, such as the biological basis of sexual orientation, the coming-out process, sexual minorities on college campuses, and sexual prejudice.

Peplau, L. A., & Garnets, L. D. (Eds.). (2000b). Women's sexualities: New perspectives on sexual orientation and gender [Special issue]. *Journal of Social Issues, 56*(2). I strongly recommend this resource; the 13 articles are written by prominent researchers in such areas as bisexuality, sexual prejudice, heterosexuality, and the development of sexual orientation.

Winstead, B. A., Derlega, V. J., & Rose, S. (1997). *Gender and close relationships.* Thousand Oaks, CA: Sage. Here's a good overview of love relationships, with chapters on attraction and dating, maintaining a relationship, conflict, and violence.

Worell, J. (Ed.). (2001). *Encyclopedia of women and gender.* San Diego: Academic Press. This two-volume encyclopedia includes about a dozen chapters related to women's love relationships; especially useful chapters examine topics such as divorce, family, lesbian relationships, marriage, power, and midlife transitions.

ANSWERS TO THE DEMONSTRATIONS

Demonstration 8.1: 1. F; 2. F; 3. M; 4. M; 5. F; 6. F; 7. M; 8. F; 9. M; 10. M.

Demonstration 8.5: Kurdek's (1995a) questionnaire is called the Multiple Determinants of Relationship Commitment Inventory, and it assesses six different components of love relationships. On the shortened version in this demonstration, each of six categories is represented with two questions: Rewards (Questions 1 and 7), Costs (Questions 2 and 8), Match to Ideal Comparison (Questions 3 and 9), Alternatives (Questions 4 and 10), Investments (Questions 5 and 11), and Barriers to Leaving the Relationship (Questions 6 and 12). High relationship commitment was operationally defined in terms of high scores on Rewards, Match to Ideal Comparison, Investments, and Barriers to Leaving and low scores on Costs and Alternatives.

ANSWERS TO THE TRUE-FALSE QUESTIONS

1. True (p. 246); 2. True (pp. 249–250); 3. True (p. 254); 4. True (p. 258); 5. False (p. 262); 6. True (p. 264); 7. True (p. 269); 8. False (p. 273); 9. False (pp. 275–276); 10. False (p. 280).

Sexuality

Chuck St. John/PictureQuest

T R U E   O R   F A L S E ?

_____ 1. A small sexual organ called the clitoris plays a major role in women's sexual orgasms.

_____ 2. Women are more likely than men to have several orgasms in sequence.

_____ 3. People consistently judge a sexually active unmarried female more negatively than a sexually active unmarried male.

_____ 4. The majority of parents in the United States say that they want high school sex education courses to discuss birth control.

_____ 5. Most women recall that their first experience of sexual intercourse was pleasant.

_____ 6. A woman who discusses her sexual likes and dislikes with her partner is likely to be more satisfied with her sexual relationships than a woman who does not disclose this information.

_____ 7. When a woman has difficulty reaching orgasm, one common reason is that she is worried about losing control over her emotions.

_____ 8. Researchers know more about male sexuality than about female sexuality.

_____ 9. An adolescent female in the United States is about five times as likely to become pregnant as an adolescent female in France.

_____ 10. When women with an unwanted pregnancy have an abortion, they typically do not experience serious psychological consequences.

On the day I began writing this chapter about sexuality, the headlines of several tabloids caught my eye as I stood in line at the supermarket: "Kathie Lee Turns to New Man. They're Making Beautiful Music Together—and Frank's Furious," proclaimed the *National Enquirer*. "J. Lo Gay Sex Tape Scandal," shouted the *Star*. The so-called women's magazines were equally provocative. *Cosmo* enticed readers with the headline "Sweet Surrender: The One Thing You Must Give Up to Have Utterly Satisfying Sex." Even the relatively sedate *Ladies Home Journal* featured the alluring headline "Bedtime Mystery: Why Does He Like *That*!?!"

Our North American culture is so intrigued with sexuality that we might expect people to be well informed about the topic—but studies suggest otherwise. Mariamne Whatley and Elissa Henken (2000) asked people in Georgia to share some of the "information" they had heard about a variety of sexual topics. They discovered, for instance, that a woman can become pregnant from kissing, from dancing too close to a man, or when having sexual intercourse during her menstrual period (rather than midcycle). Other people reported that when gynecologists have conducted pelvic exams, they have discovered snakes, spiders, or roaches living in women's vaginas. Still others told how they had heard that a tampon, inserted into the vagina, can travel into a woman's stomach. Apparently, people can be seriously misinformed about pregnancy and women's sexual anatomy!

Our chapter begins with some background information about sexuality, although I will assume you know that the vagina is not connected to the stomach. In the second section, we'll discuss sexual attitudes and behavior. We'll briefly describe sexual disorders in the third section, and in the final section, we'll examine the topics of birth control and abortion. (Incidentally, Chapter 11 discusses the related issue of sexually transmitted diseases.)

BACKGROUND ON WOMEN'S SEXUALITY

In most of this chapter, we focus on people's attitudes toward sexuality and on women's sexual behavior. To provide an appropriate context for these topics, we need to address some background questions. What theoretical approaches to sexuality are most prominent in the current era? What parts of a woman's body are especially important in her sexual activities? What sexual responses do women typically experience?

Theoretical Perspectives

Feminist psychologists have pointed out that discussions about sexuality often represent a limited view of the topic (Baber, 2000; Tiefer, 2000; Tolman & Diamond, 2001; J. W. White et al., 2000). For instance, consistent with Theme 3, researchers pay relatively little attention to female sexuality. Instead, researchers frequently consider men's sexual experiences to be the normative standard. This androcentric emphasis is reflected in descriptions of sexuality in textbooks designed for middle school and high school students: The books approach the sex organs from the male perspective. In one textbook, for example, the word *penis* is defined as "the male sexual organ," whereas *vagina* is defined as "receives penis during sexual intercourse" (C. E. Beyer et al., 1996).

Another bias in the discussion of sexuality is that sexual experiences are often viewed from a biological framework, so that hormones, brain structures, and genitals occupy center stage (J. W. White et al., 2000). Furthermore, these biological processes are often assumed to apply universally to all women (Tiefer, 2000). This overemphasis on biology is consistent with the essentialist perspective. As we discussed in Chapter 1, **essentialism** argues that gender is a basic, stable characteristic that resides *within* an individual. According to the essentialist perspective, all women share the same psychological characteristics. Essentialism ignores the widespread individual differences in women's sexual responses, consistent with Theme 4 of this textbook (Baber, 2000). When researchers adopt this essentialist perspective, they often neglect the social and cultural framework, which is especially important because sexuality is so prominent in our popular culture.

In contrast to the essentialist perspective, social constructionism emphasizes that social forces have a major impact on our sexuality. As we discussed in Chapters 1 and 6, **social constructionism** argues that individuals and cultures construct or invent their own versions of reality based on prior experiences, social interactions, and beliefs. For example, in one culture, women may be considered highly sexual, but in another culture, women may be considered uninterested in sexual activity (Fontes, 2001; Tiefer, 2000). According to social constructionists, our cultures even construct the basic sexual vocabulary. For instance, consider the phrase *to have sex*. Most North American women use this term to refer only to sexual intercourse with a man, even if that experience was not sexually pleasurable (Rothblum, 2000a). These women probably would not say that two people "had sex" if their sexual activity was limited to mouth-to-genital stimulation.

Let's briefly discuss women's sexual anatomy and women's sexual responses. Then we will consider women's sexual attitudes and behaviors in greater detail.

Female Sexual Anatomy

Figure 9.1 shows the external sexual organs of an adult female. The specific shapes, sizes, and colors of these organs differ greatly from one woman to the next. Ordinarily, the labia are folded inward, so that they cover the vaginal opening. In this diagram, however, the labia are folded outward to show the locations of the urethral and vaginal openings.

Mons pubis is a Latin phrase referring to the fatty tissue in front of the pubic bone. At puberty, the mons pubis becomes covered with pubic hair. The labia majora are the "large lips," or folds of skin, located just inside a woman's thighs. Located between these two labia majora are the labia minora, or "small lips."

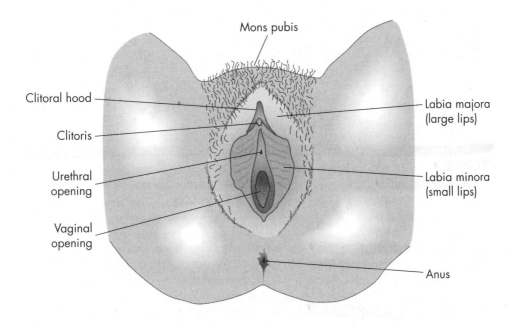

FIGURE 9.1 ■ Female external sexual organs.

Notice that the upper part of the labia region forms the clitoral hood, which covers the clitoris. As we will see later in this section, the **clitoris** (pronounced *klih*-tuh-riss) is a small sensitive organ that plays a central role in women's orgasms. The clitoris has a high density of nerve endings; because the clitoris is so sensitive, women often do not enjoy direct stimulation.

The urethral opening is the part of a woman's body through which urine passes; it is located near the clitoris. Notice that the vaginal opening is located between the urethral opening and the anus. The **vagina** is a flexible canal through which menstrual fluid passes. During heterosexual intercourse, the penis enters the vagina. The vagina also provides a passageway during the normal birth of an infant. At this point, you may wish to return to Figure 4.1, on page 113, to review several important internal organs that are relevant for women's sexuality.

Sexual Responses

You will not be surprised to know that women have a variety of reactions during sexual activity. Emotions and thoughts are extremely important. Certain visual stimuli, sounds, and smells can either increase or decrease arousal (L. L. Alexander et al., 2001; H. Kaplan, 1979). Let's consider the general phases that many women experience during sexual activity, and then we'll discuss some gender comparisons.

General Phases.   William H. Masters and Virginia Johnson (1966) wrote a book, called *Human Sexual Response,* which summarized their research on individuals who readily experienced orgasms during sexual activity. As you can imagine, these findings should not be overgeneralized; sexuality shows much more variety than the neatly ordered sequence of events that Masters and Johnson described (L. L. Alexander et al., 2001; Tiefer, 1995b). Masters and Johnson described four phases, each of which focuses on changes in the genitals. As you read about these phases, keep in mind a caution raised by Wade and Cirese (1991): "The stages are not like the cycles of an automatic washing machine; we are not programmed to move mechanically from one stage to another" (p. 140).

Masters and Johnson called the first phase the excitement phase. During the **excitement phase,** women become sexually aroused by touching and erotic thoughts. During the excitement phase, blood rushes to the genital region, causing **vasocongestion** (pronounced vas-owe-kun-*jess*-chun), or swelling resulting from the accumulation of blood. Vasocongestion causes the clitoris and the labia to enlarge as they fill with blood; it also produces droplets of moisture in the vagina.

During the **plateau phase,** the clitoris shortens in length and draws back under the clitoral hood. The clitoral region is now extremely sensitive. As a result, movement of the clitoral hood, produced either by thrusting of the penis or by other touching, causes stimulation of the clitoris.

During the **orgasmic phase,** the uterus and the outer part of the vagina contract strongly, at intervals roughly a second apart. (Figure 4.1, on page 113, shows the female internal organs, with the uterus located above the vagina.) A woman generally experiences between 3 and 12 of these contractions during an orgasm (Hyde & DeLamater, 2003). Notice, then, that the orgasm—the topic of numerous popular articles, psychological theorizing, and private conversations—usually lasts only a fraction of a minute.

During the **resolution phase,** the sexual organs return to their earlier unstimulated size. The resolution phase may last 30 minutes or more. However, females may have additional orgasms without going directly into the resolution phase.

You'll notice that the clitoris is extremely important when women experience an orgasm (L. L. Alexander et al., 2001). As W. H. Masters and Johnson (1966) observed, orgasms result from stimulation of the clitoris, either from direct touching in the clitoral area or from indirect pressure, for example, from a partner's thrusting penis. Physiologically, the orgasm is the same, no matter what kind of stimulation is used (Hyde & DeLamater, 2003).

Current feminist researchers and theorists emphasize that women's views of sexuality do not focus simply on genitals and orgasms during sexual activity (Conrad & Milburn, 2001; J. W. White et al., 2000). As Naomi McCormick (1994) wrote:

> Cuddling, self-disclosing, even gazing into a partner's eyes are highly valued by women. A feminist vision of sexuality considers whole people, not just their genitals. Intellectual stimulation, the exchange of self-disclosures, and whole body sensuality may feel just as "sexy" as orgasms. (p. 186)

Gender Comparisons in Sexual Responses.   The studies by Masters and Johnson and by more recent researchers allow us to conclude that women and men are reasonably similar in many aspects of their sexual responses. Notice that this conclusion echoes our more general thesis throughout this book: Women and men are not as different as many people think. For example, women and men experience similar phases in their sexual responses. Both men and women experience vasocongestion, and their orgasms are physiologically similar. In addition, women and men have similar psychological reactions to orgasm. Read Demonstration 9.1 and try to guess whether a man or a woman wrote each passage. Vance and Wagner (1977) asked people to guess which descriptions of orgasms were written by women and which were written by men. Most respondents were unable to guess at better than a chance level. Another gender similarity is that women can reach orgasm as quickly as men when the clitoral region is directly stimulated (Tavris & Wade, 1984). We need to emphasize, however, that women typically do not consider "faster" to be "better"!

Several gender differences have also been reported. For instance, women are more likely than men to have multiple orgasms (L. L. Alexander et al., 2001; Crooks & Baur, 2002). Again, however, "more" is not necessarily "better" (Allgeier & Allgeier, 2000). In addition, men ejaculate, expelling semen from the penis; women do not seem to have a comparable process.

In general, then, men and women are reasonably similar in these internal, physiological components of sexuality. In contrast, gender differences are larger in areas influenced by external factors such as culture. For example, we will see

DEMONSTRATION 9.1 ■ ■ ■ ■ ■ ■ ■ ■ ■ ■ ■ ■ ■ ■ ■ ■ ■ ■

Psychological Reactions to Orgasm

Try to guess whether a female or a male wrote each of the following descriptions of an orgasm. Place an F (female) or an M (male) in front of each passage. The answers can be found at the end of the chapter, on page 319.

_____ 1. A sudden feeling of lightheadedness followed by an intense feeling of relief and elation. A rush. Intense muscular spasms of the whole body. Sense of euphoria followed by deep peace and relaxation.

_____ 2. To me, an orgasmic experience is the most satisfying pleasure that I have experienced in relation to any other types of satisfaction or pleasure that I've had, which were nonsexually oriented.

_____ 3. It is like turning a water faucet on. You notice the oncoming flow but it can be turned on or off when desired. You feel the valves open and close and the fluid flow. An orgasm makes your head and body tingle.

_____ 4. A buildup of tension which starts to pulsate very fast, and there is a sudden release from the tension and a desire to sleep.

_____ 5. It is a pleasant, tension-relieving muscular contraction. It relieves physical tension and mental anticipation.

_____ 6. A release of a very high level of tension, but ordinarily tension is unpleasant, whereas the tension before orgasm is far from unpleasant.

_____ 7. An orgasm is a great release of tension with spasmodic reaction at the peak. This is exactly how it feels to me.

_____ 8. A building of tension, sometimes, and frustration until the climax. A _tightening_ inside, palpitating rhythm, explosion, and warmth and peace.

Source: Based on Vance and Wagner (1977, pp. 207–210).

later in the chapter that men and women often hold different beliefs about a culturally transmitted value: whether sexual intercourse is appropriate for a male and a female who are not in a committed relationship.

SECTION SUMMARY ■

Background on Women's Sexuality

1. Feminist psychologists argue that discussions of sexuality have paid relatively little attention to women's perspectives and that the discussions overemphasize biological factors (consistent with essentialism) rather than social and cultural factors (consistent with social constructionism).

2. The clitoris is a sexual organ that plays a major role in women's orgasms.

3. Emotions, thoughts, and sensory stimuli are central to women's sexual responses. Individual differences are large, and sexual responses do not follow a rigid sequence; W. H. Masters and Johnson (1966) described four phases of sexual response: excitement, plateau, orgasm, and resolution.

4. Female orgasms are similar whether they are produced by direct stimulation of the clitoris or by indirect stimulation; current theorists emphasize aspects of sexuality other than genitals and orgasms.

5. Women and men are similar in their sexual responses, their psychological reactions to orgasm, and—with direct clitoral stimulation—their rate of reaching orgasm. However, women are more likely to have multiple orgasms, and men ejaculate during orgasm.

SEXUAL ATTITUDES AND BEHAVIOR

The last few pages briefly outlined the biological side of sexuality—the swelling genitals and the contracting uterus. Let's now turn to the humans who possess these sex organs as we address several questions, such as these: What are people's attitudes about sexuality? How are these attitudes reflected in sex education aimed at young people? What sexual experiences do adults report? Before you read further, however, try Demonstration 9.2 on page 294.

Attitudes About Sexuality

In the early 1900s, most North Americans disapproved of sexual intercourse for an unmarried couple (Brehm, Miller et al., 2002; P. Schwartz & Rutter, 1998). In the current era, nonmarital intercourse is acceptable in some circumstances, such as a committed relationship. For example, in one cross-cultural study, only 12% of Canadian respondents and 29% of U.S. respondents said that sex before

DEMONSTRATION 9.2 ■ ■ ■ ■ ■ ■ ■ ■ ■ ■ ■ ■ ■ ■ ■ ■ ■

Judgments About Sexual Behavior

Use the following scale to answer Questions 1 through 4. Then answer Questions 5 and 6.

1	2	3	4	5	6
Definitely not					Definitely yes

_____ 1. People judge a woman who has had many sex partners more harshly than a man who has had many sex partners.

_____ 2. People have a double standard for sexual behavior, so that it's more acceptable for a man to have many sex partners, compared to a woman who has many sex partners.

_____ 3. Suppose that you have a close female friend who is looking for a casual date. She meets a man whom she finds attractive, but you know that he has had sexual intercourse with at least 10 different women. Should you discourage your friend from going out with this man?

_____ 4. Now, suppose that you have a close male friend who is looking for a casual date. He meets a woman whom he finds attractive, but you know that she has had sexual intercourse with at least 10 different men. Should you discourage your friend from going out with this woman?

5. What labels would you use to describe a woman who has had many sexual partners?

6. What labels would you use to describe a man who has had many sexual partners?

Source: Based on Milhausen and Herold (1999).

marriage is always wrong (Widmer et al., 1998). However, attitudes varied widely across the 24 countries in this study. Less than 5% of respondents in Austria, Germany, Slovenia, and Sweden said that premarital sex was always wrong, in contrast to 35% in Ireland and 60% in the Philippines.

In North America, men typically have more permissive attitudes than women do (Brehm, Miller et al., 2002; N. M. Brown & Amatea, 2000; Hyde & Oliver, 2000). For example, a meta-analysis conducted by Oliver and Hyde (1993) demonstrated that men are significantly more permissive about premarital sex;

the *d* for this gender difference was a substantial 0.81. That is, gender as a *subject variable* is important.

How about gender as a *stimulus variable*? Do people judge a man's sexual behavior differently from a woman's sexual behavior? Before the 1960s, North Americans held a **sexual double standard:** They believed that premarital sex was inappropriate for women but excusable or even appropriate for men. In the present era, the double standard has faded somewhat, but the situation is complicated. Specifically, the likelihood that people will endorse the double standard depends on characteristics of the people who are making the judgment, characteristics of the people being judged, details of the situation, and how the attitudes are assessed (Gentry, 1998; Hatfield & Rapson, 1996; O'Sullivan, 1995). For example, both genders believe that premarital intercourse is equally appropriate for both men and women if a couple is engaged to be married (Hatfield & Rapson, 1996).

Consider a representative study by Robin Milhausen and Edward Herold (1999), who gave questions like those in Demonstration 9.2 to women students at a university in Ontario, Canada. (However, to avoid context effects, the participants in that study saw either Question 3 or Question 4 and either Question 5 or Question 6.) Interestingly, these women believed that *other* people held the double standard. In contrast, they reported that they themselves did not! In other words, they provided answers in the yes range to Questions 1 and 2, but they rated Questions 3 and 4 the same. They also used equally negative words for a promiscuous man and for a promiscuous woman.

In summary, we sometimes find evidence of a double standard, with more tolerant attitudes toward male sexuality. However, present-day North Americans often judge men and women by the same standards.

How does the double standard of sexuality fare in other cultures? Sweden is a country that endorses gender equality in many areas of life, such as work and politics. Consistent with those values, Swedish students are even more likely than U.S. students to judge men and women by the same standards of sexual conduct (Weinberg et al., 1995).

In many cultures, however, a woman who has had nonmarital sex may bring disgrace to her family (Reid & Bing, 2000; Whelehan, 2001). In fact, the double standard is so strong that it has life-threatening consequences for women. For example, in some Asian, Middle Eastern, and Latin American cultures, a man is expected to uphold the family honor by killing a daughter, a sister, or even a mother who is suspected of engaging in "inappropriate" sexual activities (Crooks & Baur, 2002; Eisler, 1996). The same sexual activity would be ignored in a male family member.

Sexual Scripts

A script for a play specifies what people say and do. A **sexual script** is less detailed, but it provides a general description of "appropriate" behavior for women and men in sexual interactions (McCormick, 1994; Tiefer & Kring, 1998). A sexual script describes the cognitive and social features of sexuality, which we learn by growing up in a culture (Kurth et al., 2000). In the twenty-first century, our North American culture provides a sexual script in which men are the initiators of sexual relationships. In contrast, women are expected either to resist or to comply passively with their partner's advances (Baber, 2000; Morokoff, 2000).

People who have traditional values are likely to follow these clear-cut scripts. For example, the woman is supposed to wait for her date to kiss her; she does not initiate kissing. Only one person is in charge in this script-based kind of relationship. Even during marriage, sex is regulated according to the male's erotic schedule (P. Schwartz, 1994).

Some people are not bound by their culture's sexual scripts. P. Schwartz (1994) described several North American married couples who favor more egalitarian relationships. In these relationships, both individuals can initiate sexual activity, and they try to assess their partner's responsiveness. Also, both the man and the woman realize that they can feel free to say, "No, not tonight" without offending their partner. In these egalitarian relationships, women feel more free about expressing their erotic interests.

As we will see in Chapter 13, men sometimes violate the standard sexual script. They may continue to make sexual advances, ignoring their partner's indication that these advances are not welcome. The male may use coercion, for example, by saying that he will break off a relationship if his girlfriend doesn't have sex with him (Brehm, Miller et al., 2002). The most coercive sexual interaction is **rape,** which is sexual intercourse that is forcibly committed, without consent. As we discuss in Chapter 13, a woman can be raped by an acquaintance, a boyfriend, or even a husband, as well as by a stranger.

Sex Education

Take a moment to think about your early ideas, experiences, and attitudes about sexuality. Was sex a topic that produced half-suppressed giggles in the school cafeteria? Did you worry about whether you were too experienced or not experienced enough? Sexuality is an important topic for adolescents and many preadolescents. In this section, we will examine how children learn about sexuality—at home, at school, and from the media.

Parents and Sex Education.   Young women are much more likely to hear about sexuality from their mothers than from their fathers (Baumeister & Twenge, 2002). Furthermore, parents are not likely to talk about pleasurable aspects of sexuality (Conrad & Milburn, 2001; Tolman & Diamond, 2001). As a consequence, certain topics are never discussed. For example, fewer than 1% of students in a college human sexuality course had heard a parent mention the word *clitoris* (Allgeier & Allgeier, 2000). Other women recall hearing mixed messages from their parents, such as "Sex is dirty," and "Save it for someone you love" (K. Wright, 1997).

Individuals who have had a college course in human sexuality are more likely than other similar students to discuss sexuality with their children (B. M. King et al., 1993). These parents may feel more informed and more comfortable about discussing potentially embarrassing concepts. Kathryn Wright (1997), a specialist in adolescent medicine, recommends that parents become well informed and even practice saying words such as *vagina* and *penis,* so that they can approach these conversations more positively.

Some studies have examined parent–child communications among women of color. Latinas often report that sex is a forbidden topic with their parents, who may have conservative ideas about dating (M. Fine et al., 2000; Raffaelli & Ontai, 2001). Black mothers seem to feel more comfortable than Latina or European American mothers in speaking to their daughters about sexuality. For example, one Black adolescent reported discussing contraception with her mother. These conversations were helpful "because she was understanding, she was letting me know if there was anything I needed, that she was there" (J. M. Taylor et al., 1995).

Schools and Sex Education.   What do our school systems say about sexuality? Many sex education programs focus on the reproductive system, or, as some have called it, an "organ recital." Students don't hear about the connections between sexuality and emotions. As a result, sex education in school often has little impact on students' sexual behavior.

In recent years, most schools have required teachers to discuss AIDS (acquired immunodeficiency syndrome). However, these programs often emphasize an oversimplified "just say no" approach (Daniluk & Towill, 2001). This kind of abstinence-only model typically has no effect on sexual activity or the incidence of sexually transmitted diseases (Daniluk & Towill, 2001; Moran, 2000; P. Schwartz & Rutter, 1998).

However, some communities in the United States have developed a comprehensive approach to sexual education. In addition to providing relevant information, this comprehensive model addresses values, attitudes, and emotions; it also provides strategies for making informed choices about sexuality (Daniluk & Towill, 2001). A comprehensive educational program helps students develop the skills and behaviors that encourage them to use the information they receive.

Many schools are now linked with health centers that address adolescent sexuality issues. Students can easily visit these centers, which are often located in the school itself, for information about sexuality as well as for contraceptives and pregnancy tests (D. W. Kaplan, 1995). Research on these comprehensive programs shows that, when contraception is available in the context of an educational program, the services do *not* promote greater sexual activity (K. Wright, 1997).

We often hear reports about parents protesting sex education in the schools. Surprisingly, however, most parents acknowledge that high school sex education classes should take a comprehensive approach (Haffner & Wagoner, 1999; Hyde & DeLamater, 2003). For example, one large-scale U.S. survey reported that 94% of parents wanted the classes to include information about how to deal with pressure to have sex, 90% wanted information on birth control, and 79% wanted information on abortion (Hoff & Greene, 2000).

The Media.   According to a recent survey, many teenagers report that they have learned information about sexual issues from the media: 40% pointed to television and movies, and 35% mentioned magazines (Hoff & Greene, 2000). The average adolescent witnesses about 2,000 sexual acts in the media each year (Sutton et al., 2002). Unfortunately, adolescents are not likely to learn accurate information about sexuality from the media. One study noted that the risks of pregnancy or sexually transmitted diseases are mentioned in less than 0.01%—that's 1 in 10,000—of the sexual portrayals in television or the movies ("Pediatrician Testifies on Impact of Sexuality in Media," 2001). The clear majority of popular programs do not show any consequences—either positive or negative—for sexual activity (Cope-Farrar & Kunkel, 2002).

The nature of these sexual images also raises concerns. In one discussion group, young women reported that they felt they could not attain the perfect look portrayed in the media images of female sexuality. Latina women were especially likely to say that they could not measure up to the European American images (Dello Stritto & Guzmán, 2001). Furthermore, these media images often suggest a combination of innocence and seductiveness (Kilbourne, 1999; P. Schwartz & Rutter, 1998). For instance, one ad shows a young woman dressed in an old-fashioned white dress, but the dress is unbuttoned and pulled down over one shoulder. How can a real-life teenager make sense of this mixed message to be both sexually innocent and sexually active?

Adolescent Sexual Behavior

Adolescent women are likely to have early sexual experiences if they reached puberty before most of their peers (Welsh et al., 2000). Early sexual experience is also related to factors such as poor academic performance, poor parent-child relationships, poverty, and illicit drug use (Crockett et al., 2002; Millstein & Halpern-Felsher, 1998; D. A. Rosenthal et al., 1999).

Ethnicity is also related to adolescent sexual experience. In the United States, for example, Black female adolescents are likely to have their first sexual experience one or two years before European American or Latina female adolescents (Millstein & Halpern-Felsher, 1998; Reid & Bing, 2000). Asian American female adolescents are typically the least likely to have early sexual experiences (C. S. Chan, 2000). In Canada, adolescents born in other countries and emigrating to Canada are much less likely than Canada-born adolescents to have early sexual experiences (Maticka-Tyndale et al., 2001).

Unfortunately, peer pressure encourages some teenagers to become sexually active (R. M. Lerner & Galambos, 1998; Tolman, 1999). These teenagers risk unwanted pregnancies and sexually transmitted diseases—topics we'll examine later in this chapter and in Chapter 11. In other words, biological, psychological, and cultural variables all play an important role (Crockett et al., 2002).

For many adolescents, decisions about sexuality are critically important in defining their values. For instance, one young woman was neither judgmental nor prudish, but she had decided not to be sexually active as a teenager. As she explained:

> I have certain talents and certain gifts, and I owe it to myself to take care of those gifts. I'm not going to just throw it around, throw my body around. And I see that sexuality is part of that. The sexual revolution—I guess we grew up in that—I think a lot of it has cheapened something that isn't cheap. (Kamen, 2000, pp. 87–88)

Romance novels portray idyllic images of young women being blissfully transformed by their first sexual experience. However, most women do not have positive memories of their first intercourse (Conrad & Milburn, 2001; Nicolson, 1997; Tiefer & Kring, 1998). The experience may also be physically painful.

In addition, young women often report that they felt coerced. In fact, they frequently mention that the major reason they consented to intercourse was that they were afraid that their boyfriend would leave them otherwise (K. A. Martin, 1996; P. Schwartz & Rutter, 1998). They are often confused and scared, as if they had lost a part of themselves. K. A. Martin (1996) summarized her interviews: "Girls see sex as boys taking something from them and not as a give-and-take or a two-way interaction that should be enjoyable for both people" (p. 87). Young women who expect a sexual experience to be loving may report disappointment if the romance doesn't continue (Millstein & Halpern-Felsher, 1998).

A description provided by one woman provides a positive contrast to those stories about confusion and loss:

> We were totally in love. We wanted this to be the best experience of our lives. We were at his apartment and we had done everything right. We had talked about it, planned for it, saw this as the highest expression of our joint future. He was very caring, very slow with me. I felt empowered, beautiful. It was a great night. (P. Schwartz & Rutter, 1998)

In summary, young women often learn about sexuality in a less-than-ideal way. As we saw earlier in this section, parents, schools, and the media seldom help young people make informed decisions about sexuality. In addition, many young women's early sexual experiences may not be as romantic and joyous as they had hoped.

Adult Sexual Behavior

Any survey about sexual behavior inevitably runs into roadblocks. How can a survey manage to obtain a random sample of respondents who represent all geographic regions, ethnic groups, and income levels—especially on such a sensitive topic? Probably the most respected U.S. survey of sexual behavior was conducted by sociologist Edward Laumann and his colleagues (1994) at the National Opinion Research Center (NORC). In the NORC survey, 3,432 adults were interviewed; they answered questions about a wide range of topics. The results showed, for example, that 17% of men claimed to have had more than 20 sexual partners during their lifetime, in contrast to 3% of women.

A meta-analysis of 12 earlier studies confirmed a general trend for men to report a somewhat greater number of sexual partners, with a d of 0.25 (Oliver & Hyde, 1993). In all these surveys, men probably overreport their number of sexual partners, whereas women probably underreport—consistent with the sexual double standard (P. Schwartz & Rutter, 1998).

Surveys also show that masturbation is much more common for men than for women (Baumeister et al., 2001; Hyde & Oliver, 2000). Oliver and Hyde (1993) reported a d of 0.96, a value that dwarfs most other gender differences we've discussed in this book. For instance, in the NORC survey, 27% of men and

8% of women reported that they masturbated at least once a week (Laumann et al., 1994). As Baber (2000) noted, it's strange that this risk-free sexual activity is missing from many women's sexual scripts. Perhaps some of the gender differences in masturbation can be traced to the more obvious prominence of the male genitals (Oliver & Hyde, 1993). The gender differences with respect to masturbation may well have some important theoretical significance as well as practical implications for male and female sexuality.

Communication About Sexuality

We mentioned earlier in this section that parents often feel uncomfortable talking about sex with their children. Actually, most couples also feel uncomfortable talking about sex—before, during, or after sexual activity. Most people try to communicate their sexual desire by nonverbal communication, such as kissing or touching. Women are somewhat more likely than men to use indirect verbal messages, such as asking if their male partner has a condom (Hickman & Muehlenhard, 1999). A basic problem, however, is that the meaning of many nonverbal strategies is unclear (Brehm, Miller et al., 2002). When women are uncertain about engaging in sexual activity, they are not likely to communicate this message verbally to a partner. However, that kind of ambivalence is difficult to communicate nonverbally (Brehm, Miller et al., 2002; O'Sullivan & Gaines, 1998). Try imagining how you would convey this ambivalent message nonverbally to a romantic partner, and you can anticipate some communication difficulties.

One important development in the area of sexual communication focuses on women's sexual assertiveness (P. B. Anderson & Struckman-Johnson, 1998). Previous research had suggested that women may hesitate to say no to men's sexual advances because they don't want to hurt their partner's feelings. Therefore, Patricia Morokoff and her colleagues (1997) developed a Sexual Assertiveness Scale for women. Try Demonstration 9.3, which includes some of the questions from the Sexual Assertiveness Scale. Then check the answers at the end of the chapter. Were you fairly accurate in predicting the women's answers? Did this exercise provide any new insights into your own communication patterns with respect to sexual activity?

Another important topic focuses on sexual self-disclosure in dating couples. For instance, E. Sandra Byers and Stephanie Demmons (1999) surveyed Canadian college students who had been dating for at least 3 months. These researchers found that respondents were reluctant to talk with their partner about the sexual activities that they liked or disliked. However, those who self-disclosed more were likely to be more satisfied with the sexual aspects of their relationship. This correlation is consistent with some information from Chapter 8: Married couples are more satisfied with their relationship if they have good communication skills.

Lesbians and Sexuality

Much of the previous discussion focused on heterosexual relationships. Is sexuality substantially different in lesbian relationships? The research suggests that lesbian couples value nongenital physical contact, such as hugging and cuddling

DEMONSTRATION 9.3 ■ ■ ■ ■ ■ ■ ■ ■ ■ ■ ■ ■ ■ ■ ■ ■ ■ ■

The Sexual Assertiveness Scale for Women

The items listed in this demonstration were shown to women students at a large state university in the Northeast. The women were asked to rate each item, using a scale where 1 = disagree strongly and 5 = agree strongly. Your task is to inspect each item and estimate the average rating that the women supplied for that item (e.g., 2.8). When you have finished, check page 319 to see how the women actually responded. (Note: This demonstration is based on Morokoff et al., 1997, but it contains only 6 of the 18 items; the validity of this short version has not been established.)

_____ 1. I let my partner know if I want my partner to touch my genitals.

_____ 2. I wait for my partner to touch my breasts instead of letting my partner know that's what I want.

_____ 3. I give in and kiss if my partner pressures me, even if I already said no.

_____ 4. I refuse to have sex if I don't want to, even if my partner insists.

_____ 5. I have sex without a condom or latex barrier if my partner doesn't like them, even if I want to use one.

_____ 6. I insist on using a condom or latex barrier if I want to, even if my partner doesn't.

Source: From Morokoff, P. J., et al. (1997). Sexual Assertiveness Scale (SAS) for women: Development and validation. _Journal of Personality and Social Psychology, 73,_ 804 (appendix). © 1997 by the American Psychological Association. Reprinted with permission.

(R. L. Klinger, 1996; McCormick, 1994). However, our North American culture tends to define sexual activity in terms of genital stimulation and orgasm. Researchers with that operational definition of sexual activity might conclude that lesbian couples are less sexually active than heterosexual couples or gay male couples (Peplau & Beals, 2001). This conclusion would be especially true for couples who have been together for many years (Hatfield & Rapson, 1996).

According to other research, when lesbians do engage in genital sexual activity, they are more likely than heterosexual women to experience an orgasm. Some possible explanations for this difference are that lesbian couples may communicate more effectively and be more sensitive to each other's preferences. They may also engage in more kissing and caressing than heterosexual couples do (Hatfield & Rapson, 1996; Herbert, 1996).

Laura S. Brown (2000) wrote that lesbians are like the early mapmakers who must construct their own maps about the unknown territories of lesbian sexuality. After all, the well-established maps—or scripts—represent heterosexual territory. An additional challenge is that our culture does not tolerate evidence of sexual affection between two women in public places. I recall a lesbian friend commenting that she feels sad and resentful that she and her partner cannot hold hands or hug each other in public, and kissing would be unthinkable.

Older Women and Sexuality

Women's reproductive systems change somewhat as women grow older. Estrogen production drops rapidly at menopause. As a result, the vagina loses some of its elasticity and may also produce less moisture (S. B. Levine, 1998; P. Schwartz & Rutter, 1998). However, these problems can be at least partly corrected by using supplemental lubricants. Also, women who have been sexually active throughout their lives may not experience a reduction in moisture production (Zeiss, 1998). Furthermore, it's worth questioning a popular belief that a decrease in hormone levels causes a decrease in sexual interest; no persuasive study supports that proposal (Rostosky & Travis, 2000).

Researchers often report that the frequency of genital sexual activity declines as heterosexual and lesbian women grow older (Call et al., 1995; Hyde & DeLamater, 2003; Kehoe, 1989; Laumann et al., 1994). In one study on sexuality in middle-aged women, 15% of the respondents reported that they enjoyed sex less than in the previous year (Mansfield et al., 1998). However, 10% said that they enjoyed sex more. Also, 20% said that they desired more nongenital touching. Notice that this finding is consistent with our observation that sexuality must be defined broadly, beyond a focus on the genitals.

According to Mansfield and her colleagues (1998), older women also emphasized the importance of "sweet warmth and constant tenderness" and "physical closeness and intimacy." One woman wrote, "Touching, hugging, holding, become as or more important than the actual sex act" (p. 297). Most research on older women's sexuality focuses on problems rather than on positive changes (Baber, 2000). Therefore, the study by Mansfield and her colleagues is especially welcome.

Many older women maintain the physiological capability to experience an orgasm as well as an enthusiastic interest in sexual relationships. However, they may no longer have a partner. In addition, some older men may no longer be able to maintain an erection, and they may stop all caressing and sexual activities once intercourse is not possible (Ellison, 2001; S. B. Levine, 1998; L. A. Morris, 1997). In fact, in the NORC survey that we described earlier, 41% of the women in the oldest age category (55–59) reported that they had been sexually inactive during the past year (Laumann et al., 1994).

Another problem is that North Americans seem to think that older women should be asexual. Our culture has constructed images of grandmothers baking cookies in the kitchen, not cavorting around in the bedroom (Regan & Berscheid, 1999; Whelehan, 2001). In some cultures that are generally negative about sexuality, such as the people of Uttar Pradesh in Northern India, older women are expected not to be sexually active. In contrast, in sex-positive cultures, such as the San of Africa or Chinese Taoists, sexuality is considered healthy for the elderly (Whelehan, 2001).

Sexuality seems to be condemned more in older women than in older men. People tolerate a sexually eager old man, and they may even admire him. But they often view a sexually eager old woman with suspicion or disgust. A manu-facturer of lingerie is combating this view with ads of older women in lacy underwear and quotes such as "Time is a purification system that has made me wiser, freer, better, some say sexier. Are those the actions of an enemy?" Yes, I realize that this advertising strategy is not motivated by altruism or feminist convictions. Still, the ads may help to change views of women's sexuality in later life.

SECTION SUMMARY   ▪

Sexual Attitudes and Behavior

1. Most North Americans believe that sex before marriage is acceptable in some circumstances. The double standard about sexuality is no longer widespread in North America, but it is still found in some situations (e.g., people may believe that *other people* endorse the double standard). In some cultures, the double standard seems to have disappeared. In contrast, in some Asian, Middle East-ern, and Latin American cultures, a woman may be killed for suspected sexual activity, whereas a man is allowed sexual freedom.

2. Sexual scripts specify what women and men in a certain culture are supposed to do in sexual interactions; for example, men are supposed to take the initia-tive in sexual activity.

3. Young people typically report that their parents do not discuss pleasurable aspects of sexuality as part of sex education. Sex education programs in schools usually fail to explore the topics most relevant to adolescents, but more comprehensive school programs discuss emotions and decision-making strate-gies; they may also offer contraceptives. The media frequently portray sexual-ity, but they seldom show the consequences of sexual activity.

4. Most women report that their first experience with intercourse was not positive; many say they felt coerced.

5. The research shows that men report more sexual partners than women do and that men are much more likely to report masturbating.

6. Couples seem to experience difficulty communicating about sexual issues; an important component of communication is sexual assertiveness; couples who discuss their preferences about sexual activities are more likely to be satisfied with the sexual aspects of their relationships.

7. Lesbian couples typically value nongenital physical contact; compared to het-erosexual women, they are more likely to experience an orgasm, perhaps because of better communication.

8. Many older women experience subtle changes in their sexual responding; how-ever, lack of a partner is often a more important obstacle to older women's sexual activities.

SEXUAL DISORDERS

A **sexual disorder** is a disturbance in sexual arousal or in sexual responding that causes mental distress (L. L. Alexander et al., 2001; Hyde & DeLamater, 2003). As you might guess, it's difficult to estimate how many women experience these sexual problems. However, one survey, which was based on the NORC study conducted by Laumann and his colleagues (1994), sampled 1,749 sexually active women in the United States. According to their reports, 43% of the women have sexual experiences that are less than ideal (Laumann et al., 1999). Sexual dissatisfaction was especially high among women who experience general depression or recent economic problems as well as among women with relatively little education.

In this section on sexual disorders, we first examine two of the more common sexual problems in women: low sexual desire and female orgasmic disorder. Then we will see how traditional gender roles are partly responsible for sexual problems. Finally, we'll discuss therapy for sexual problems, including some thought-provoking questions raised by feminist theorists and researchers (e.g., Kaschak & Tiefer, 2001; Tiefer, 2001).

Low Sexual Desire

As the name suggests, a woman with **low sexual desire** (also called hypoactive sexual desire disorder) has little interest in sexual activity (Hyde & DeLamater, 2003; LoPiccolo, 2002). For example, one woman had been happily married for 31 years, and she reported that her husband was a gentle and considerate lover. However, she remained entirely passive during lovemaking. In fact, she kept her mind busy creating menus and making shopping lists (D. W. Kaplan, 1995).

A disorder of low sexual desire may be caused by a variety of psychological factors, including a more general problem such as depression (Carlson et al., 1996). A woman who is not satisfied with her romantic relationship may also experience little sexual desire (Hyde & DeLamater, 2003).

Low sexual desire may be the most common sexual problem faced by lesbians (Carlson et al., 1996). In many cases, a lesbian couple may have a harmonious social relationship. However, they no longer have sexual interactions because the more sexually interested member of a lesbian couple is reluctant to pressure her less enthusiastic partner.

Female Orgasmic Disorder

A woman with **female orgasmic disorder** experiences sexual excitement, but she does not reach orgasm (L. L. Alexander et al., 2001). Exactly what constitutes an orgasm problem? Some women want to have an orgasm every time they engage in sexual activity. Others are satisfied if they feel emotionally close to their partner during sexual activity. The diagnosis of female orgasmic disorder should not be applied if a woman is currently satisfied with her situation. For example, suppose that a woman reaches orgasm through clitoral stimulation—but not during intercourse. If she feels satisfied with her sexual experiences, most feminist sex therapists would say that she should not be diagnosed with female orgasmic disorder (Hyde & DeLamater, 2003).

One common cause of female orgasmic disorder is that women who are accustomed to inhibiting their sexual impulses have difficulty overcoming their inhibitions, even in a relationship where sex is approved. Other women have orgasm problems because they are anxious about losing control over their feelings (LoPiccolo, 2002). They may be embarrassed about experiencing such intense pleasure. Still others are easily distracted during sexual activity. They may suddenly focus on a distant noise rather than on the sexual sensations. And many women may not have orgasms because their partners do not provide appropriate sexual stimulation. Unfortunately, female orgasmic disorder is a relatively common sexual problem (Allgeier & Allgeier, 2000; Baber, 2000).

How Gender Roles Contribute to Sexual Disorders

Sexual problems are extremely complex. Their origin may be physical. The problems may also be caused by trauma experienced many years earlier, by psychological factors such as low self-esteem, or by subtle problems in a couple's interactions.

Gender roles, stereotypes, and biases may also contribute to sexual problems. As feminists have pointed out, a heterosexual marriage is typically an unequal playing field, with the man having more power (Tiefer, 1996; Tolman & Diamond, 2001). Various researchers have emphasized that gender roles can create or intensify sexual problems (Baber, 2000; Carlson et al., 1996; Fredrickson & Roberts, 1997; LoPiccolo, 2002; Morokoff, 1998):

1. Women are supposed to be asexual and passive, whereas men are supposed to be sexual and aggressive; many people therefore believe that women shouldn't enjoy sexual activity.
2. The double standard still suggests that males can enjoy some kinds of casual-sex experiences, but females should "save themselves" for marriage.
3. Women are hesitant to appear selfish by requesting the kind of sexual activity they enjoy, such as tender caresses or clitoral stimulation. Stereotypes suggest that women should give rather than request.
4. Because of the emphasis on male sexuality, researchers know how physical illness and drugs affect men's sexual responses. However, they know relatively little about their effects on female sexuality. Consistent with Theme 3 of this book, women are relatively invisible.
5. Male gender roles contribute to sexual problems. Our culture emphasizes the length, strength, and endurance of a man's penis (Zilbergeld, 1999). When a man focuses on these issues, he probably won't be able to *find* the woman's clitoris. He certainly won't worry about whether he is stimulating the clitoris gently, although this concern should be important.
6. Physical attractiveness is emphasized more for females than for males, as we saw in the discussions of adolescence and dating. (We'll encounter this theme again in Chapter 12, on psychological disorders, and in Chapter 14, on older women.) Indeed, many men may prefer to think about women's bodies as

they are airbrushed into perfection in a magazine like *Playboy,* rather than the bodies that belong to the women they know. Gary R. Brooks (1997b) referred to this problem as the "Centerfold Syndrome." Women who feel less than perfectly attractive—that is, almost all women—may worry about their physical appearance. Consequently, many women won't be able to enjoy the sensations of sexual arousal.

Because of these factors, women often believe that they are not supposed to be actively enthusiastic, experienced, or selfish in the area of sexuality. Furthermore, the male penis is viewed as central in sexual interactions. As a result, women are ignored, both in the research and in women's sexual needs.

Therapy for Sexual Disorders

In 1970, Masters and Johnson introduced a kind of sex therapy called sensate focus. **Sensate focus** was designed as a technique to encourage couples to focus on their sensory experience during sexual activity. Partners touch and stroke so that they can discover sensitive areas on their own body and on their partner's body, and they are encouraged to focus on these sensual experiences (LoPiccolo, 2002). Later in the therapy, clitoral masturbation is encouraged for female orgasmic problems. However, couples who focus on sexual sensations may ignore the loving, tender aspects of lovemaking (Tiefer, 1995b). Sensate focus is widely used in sex therapy, even though few studies have been conducted to document its effectiveness (Christensen & Heavey, 1999). It may sometimes be helpful, but it isn't a complete answer.

Many other techniques have been developed by sex therapists (e.g., LoPiccolo, 2002). For example, **cognitive-behavioral therapy** combines behavioral exercises (such as those suggested by W. H. Masters and Johnson, 1970) with therapy techniques that emphasize thought patterns or cognitive factors. One common technique is called **cognitive restructuring;** with this technique, the therapist tries to change people's inappropriately negative thoughts about some aspect of sexuality.

However, all of these traditional approaches to sex therapy may be too limited. Leonore Tiefer (1995b, 1996, 2001), one of the leading feminist sex therapists, points out that sexual problems must be addressed from a broad social perspective rather than by focusing on biological aspects:

> The amount of time devoted to getting the penis hard and the vagina wet vastly outweighs the attention devoted to assessment or education about sexual motives, scripts, pleasure, power, emotionality, sensuality, communication, or connectedness. (Tiefer, 2001, p. 90)

So far, unfortunately, sex therapists have not devised a comprehensive program that addresses inequalities in a relationship while also correcting specific problems in sexual responding. An ideal comprehensive program would also emphasize that human sexuality is much more than swelling sex organs. Tenderness, sensitivity, and communication are also essential.

SECTION SUMMARY ▪

Sexual Disorders

1. When a woman experiences low sexual desire, she has little interest in sexual activity; depression, other psychological problems, and relational issues may contribute to this disorder.

2. A woman who has female orgasmic disorder feels sexual excitement but does not experience orgasm; psychological factors (e.g., anxiety about losing control) and inadequate sexual stimulation are often responsible.

3. Gender roles can contribute to sexual disorders in several ways: (a) Women aren't supposed to be interested in sex; (b) the double standard still operates in some cases; (c) women are hesitant to request their preferred sexual stimulation; (d) male sexuality is emphasized in sexuality research; (e) male gender roles create problems; and (f) physical attractiveness is emphasized for females more than for males.

4. Masters and Johnson's sensate focus therapy may sometimes be helpful, and so may cognitive-behavioral therapy techniques such as cognitive restructuring. However, a feminist perspective emphasizes that these approaches are too narrow; instead, therapy should emphasize a broader perspective that includes gender equality, tenderness, and communication.

BIRTH CONTROL AND ABORTION

Birth control and abortion are highly controversial topics in the current century. For women, decisions about using birth control and terminating a pregnancy are among the most important choices they will make in their lifetime.

The most publicized data about pregnancy in the United States typically focus on teenagers. Unfortunately, U.S. adolescents are more likely to give birth than adolescents in any other industrialized country in the world (Brooks-Gunn et al., 1999; Coley & Chase-Lansdale, 1998). In Table 9.1 on page 308, you can see estimated birth rates for Canada, the United States, and many countries in Western Europe. (We'll discuss the abortion rates in Table 9.1 later in this chapter.)

Figure 9.2 shows estimates of the outcomes for the approximately 1 million teen pregnancies in the United States each year.[1] A young woman who does not experience a miscarriage or a stillbirth must make an extremely important decision: Should she carry the pregnancy to term, or should she seek an abortion?

---

[1]Unfortunately, no comparable analysis is available for the options faced by pregnant teenagers in Canada. However, as Table 9.1 shows, a teenager in Canada is less than half as likely as a U.S. teenager to become pregnant. Also, the abortion rate is somewhat lower in Canada.

TABLE 9.1 ▪ Annual Rate of Adolescent Births (per 1,000 women, ages 15–19) for Canada, the United States, and Countries in Western Europe

Country	Birth Rate	Abortion Rate
Belgium	9	5
Canada	24	21
Denmark	8	14
England and Wales	28	19
France	10	10
Germany	13	4
Ireland	15	4
Italy	7	5
Netherlands	8	4
Northern Ireland	24	5
Norway	14	19
Scotland	27	15
Spain	8	5
Sweden	8	17
United States	54	29

Note: Several countries in Western Europe are missing because data on abortion were not available.

Source: Reproduced with the permission of The Alan Guttmacher Institute from Singh, S., & Darroch, J. E. (2000). Adolescent pregnancy and childbearing: Levels and trends in developed countries. *Family Planning Perspectives, 32,* 14–23 (data selected from Table 2, p. 16).

Should she choose marriage, or should she become a single mother? Should she give her baby up for adoption?

In this section, we will first discuss women's decisions about contraception, and then we'll look at some information about abortion and other alternatives. Because this is a psychology textbook, we will primarily focus on women's experiences. Still, we need to keep in mind that issues such as teen pregnancy have widespread political and economic consequences. For example, one source estimates that teen pregnancy costs the United States $7 billion a year in lost taxes and in costs such as public assistance (Wingert, 1998). Although these costs are noteworthy, we still need to keep them in perspective. For example, in the 1998 fiscal year, the United States spent $627 billion on military expenses, that is, nearly 100 times its expenditure on teen pregnancy.

Birth Control Methods

If a sexually active woman uses no form of birth control whatsoever, she has an 85% chance of becoming pregnant within 1 year (Allgeier & Allgeier, 2000). Table 9.2 describes the major forms of birth control, together with some information about their effectiveness. You'll note that abstinence is the only method of birth control that is 100% effective in preventing pregnancy. In earlier decades,

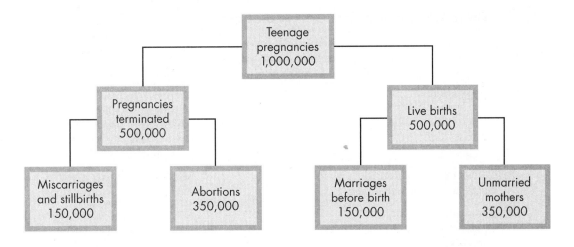

FIGURE 9.2 ■ Estimated outcomes for pregnant U.S. teenagers.
Sources: Based on East and Felice (1996), Luker (1996), and Wingert (1998).

people who recommended abstinence might have been considered prudish. However, in the current era, sexual intercourse presents not only a substantial risk of pregnancy for women but also a significant risk of contracting a deadly disease. As we will discuss in Chapter 11, most of the birth control methods do not reduce the risk of AIDS. Even condoms cannot completely prevent the transmission of this disease. Yes, they make sex *safer,* but not completely safe.

You can see that birth control methods other than abstinence are mostly intended for females. Gender bias may encourage researchers to try to alter female fertility, not male fertility.

Incidentally, Table 9.2 does not list two behavioral birth control methods: (1) withdrawal (removal of the penis before ejaculation) and (2) the rhythm method, also known as natural family planning (intercourse only when a woman is least fertile). These methods are not listed because their effectiveness is unacceptably low: less than 80% (Ballagh, 1998; Hyde & DeLamater, 2003).

However, examining birth control methods is not our primary concern. Instead, we'll focus on the psychological aspects of birth control. Let's consider the personal characteristics related to using birth control, the obstacles that prevent its use, and family planning in developing countries.

Who Uses Birth Control?

Many heterosexual women who are sexually active use either an unreliable birth control method (such as foam, withdrawal, or rhythm) or no contraception at all. Because sexually active heterosexual couples do not always use effective birth control methods, many women have unplanned pregnancies. We emphasized, for example, that approximately 1 million U.S. teenagers become pregnant each

TABLE 9.2 ■ Major Birth Control Methods

Method	Effectiveness When Used Consistently	Possible Side Effects and Disadvantages
Abstinence	100% effective	No physical disadvantages (assuming no sperm contact whatsoever); possible negative emotional reactions (e.g., from peer pressure).
Tubal ligation (severing of female's fallopian tubes)	99% effective	Minor surgical risk; possible negative emotional reactions.
Vasectomy (surgery to prevent passage of male's sperm)	99% effective	Minor surgical risk; possible negative emotional reactions.
Implants (e.g., Norplant) and injections (e.g., Depo-Provera)	99% effective	Menstrual irregularity; occasional surgical difficulty in removing implants; occasional weight gain.
Birth control pills (synthetic hormones, taken by woman)	97–99% effective	Slight risk of blood-clotting disorders, particularly for women over 35 and smokers; other medical side effects possible; must be taken regularly.
Condom (sheath placed on penis)	85–97% effective	Must be applied before intercourse; may decrease pleasure for male.
Diaphragm (placed in vagina) and spermicidal foam or cream	80–95% effective	Must be applied before intercourse; may irritate genital area.
Spermicidal foams, creams, etc.	75–80% effective	Must be applied before intercourse; may irritate genital area.

Note: For more information, consult L. L. Alexander et al. (2001), Allgeier and Allgeier (2000), and Hyde and DeLamater (2003).

year. A study of women of all ages in the United States found that an estimated 57% of all pregnancies were unintended at the time of conception (S. S. Brown & Eisenberg, 1995). In other words, more than half of all U.S. pregnancies are not planned. The comparable figure for Canada is 39% (S. S. Brown & Eisenberg, 1995).

Researchers have tried to identify what kinds of women use birth control, because this information could help to decrease the number of unplanned pregnancies. Here are some relevant demographic factors that are related to women's contraceptive use:

1. *Social class.* Women from the middle and upper socioeconomic classes are more likely to use birth control (Allgeier & Allgeier, 2000; S. S. Brown & Eisenberg, 1995).
2. *Ethnicity.* In the United States, European American women and Latina women are somewhat more likely than Black women to use birth control (Laumann et al., 1994). We do not have comparable data about other ethnic groups.
3. *Level of education.* Women who have had at least some college education are somewhat more likely than other women to use birth control (Becker et al., 1998). However, according to the NORC study, only 52% of women who had at least a master's degree reported that they consistently used contraception (Laumann et al., 1994). In other words, about half of these well-educated women could face an unplanned pregnancy.
4. *Personality characteristics.* Research on adolescents shows that young women are more likely to use contraceptives if they are high in self-esteem and if they dislike taking risks (Becker et al., 1998; N. J. Bell et al., 1999).

Obstacles to Using Birth Control

Why are more than half of all U.S. pregnancies unplanned? The problem is that many obstacles stand in the way of using effective birth control. A woman who avoids pregnancy must have adequate knowledge about contraception. She must also have access to it, and she must be willing to use it on a consistent basis. One U.S. survey showed, for instance, that only 38% of college students reported using a condom the last time they had intercourse (C. D. Fields, 2002). In a Canadian survey of sexually active 18- and 19-year-olds in the general population, only 27% said they had used a condom when they last had intercourse (Statistics Canada, 2000).

In more detail, here are some of the obstacles to using birth control:

1. Parents and educators often avoid discussing birth control with young people because they "don't want to give them any ideas." As a result, many young people are misinformed or have gaps in their knowledge (Murry, 1996).
2. Some young women cannot obtain contraceptive services, so they use less reliable forms of birth control (S. S. Brown & Eisenberg, 1995; M. S. Watson et al., 1996). Other women in the United States have no health insurance, or their health insurance does not cover birth control (Alan Guttmacher Institute, 2001). Researchers estimate that every dollar spent on family planning services saves as much as $18 in health care and welfare costs that would need to be paid for unwanted pregnancies ("The Budget," 1996).
3. Many young women have sexual intercourse without much planning. In a survey of Canadian female college students going to Florida over spring break, 13% reported that they had sex with someone they had just met (Maticka-Tyndale et al., 1998). In a sample of U.S. college students, 26% reported having had intercourse with someone they had met earlier the same night. Casual

sex does not encourage careful planning about contraception strategies (Gavey & McPhillips, 1999; Paul et al., 2000).

4. People may not think rationally about emotional issues connected with sexuality. For example, sexually inexperienced women often believe that they themselves are not likely to become pregnant during intercourse (Brehm, Miller et al., 2002; Whitley & Hern, 1992). A Canadian study revealed other examples of irrational thinking. For example, 75% of adolescent males and females reported that they would always use condoms, yet only 42% of them said that they had used condoms during their last three episodes of sexual intercourse (H. R. L. Richardson et al., 1997).

5. Traditional women believe that if they were to obtain contraception, they would be admitting to themselves that they planned to have intercourse and are therefore not "nice girls" (Luker, 1996). In fact, college students downgrade a woman who is described as providing a condom before sexual intercourse (D. M. Castañeda & Collins, 1998; Hynie et al., 1997).

6. People often believe that birth control devices will interrupt the lovemaking mood, because they are not considered erotic or romantic (Gavey & McPhillips, 1999; Perloff, 2001). Condoms and other contraceptives are seldom mentioned in movies, television, romantic novels, and magazines, as Demonstration 9.4 shows. We can see a woman and a man undressing, groping, groaning, and copulating. The one taboo topic seems to be contraception! Interestingly, women who read romance novels are especially likely to have negative attitudes toward contraception (Diekman et al., 2000).

7. Many young women are pressured to have sexual intercourse, often with a much older man (Coley & Chase-Lansdale, 1998; Luker, 1996). When a 14-year-old female has a partner who is a 21-year-old male, she is unlikely to persuade him to wear a condom.

Earlier in the chapter, we noted that schools must develop more comprehensive sex education programs. Communities need to be sure that adolescents receive appropriate information *before* they become sexually active (Becker et al., 1998). We also need to change people's attitudes toward contraception. People might use contraceptives more often if the women in soap operas were shown

---

DEMONSTRATION 9.4 ■

Contraception as a Taboo Topic

For the next two weeks, keep a record of the number of times you see couples in sexual relationships in the media. Monitor television programs, movies, stories in magazines, and books as well as any other source that seems relevant. In each case, note whether contraceptives are mentioned, shown, or even hinted at.

discussing birth control methods with their gynecologists and if the macho men of the movie screen carefully adjusted their condoms before the steamy love scenes.

Contraception and Family Planning in Developing Countries

In the United States, 74% of couples who are of childbearing age use some kind of contraceptive. The percentage is almost identical for Canada: 73%. How about developing countries throughout the world? The data vary widely. Fewer than 5% of couples use contraceptives in Ethiopia, Angola, and other African countries. In China, however, 83% of couples use contraceptives. The Catholic Church strongly opposes the more reliable forms of birth control. Still, many countries that are predominantly Catholic have very high rates of contraceptive use (Neft & Levine, 1997). These countries include France (81%), Brazil (78%), and Italy (78%).

Some developing countries have instituted family planning programs and contraceptive programs for at-risk young women (e.g., G. Barker et al., 2000). For example, during the 1960s and 1970s, Cuba began a health care campaign that offered free contraceptive devices; 70% of couples now use contraceptives (Neft & Levine, 1997; Stout & Dello Buono, 1996). Iran now requires couples to pass the nation's course in family planning before they can obtain a marriage license (R. Wright, 1998). As a result, 65% of Iranian couples now use contraceptives. In neighboring Iraq, which is also a Muslim country, only 14% of couples use contraceptives (Neft & Levine, 1997).

One of the best predictors of contraceptive use in developing countries is the female literacy rate (Winter, 1996). For example, in India, 31% of high school age girls are in school, and the average adult woman has 3.7 children. The state of Kerala has the same per capita income as the rest of India; however, 93% of high school age girls are in school, and the average adult woman has only 2.0 children (Lott, 2000). When women are well educated, they are likely to take control of their lives and make plans for the future. By limiting their family size, they can increase their economic and personal freedom—and not contribute to the world's overpopulation (P. D. Harvey, 2000). They can also provide better care for the children they already have.

The use of contraceptives throughout the world has been rising steadily (Neft & Levine, 1997). Still, an estimated 120 million married couples throughout the world do not have access to family planning (García-Moreno & Türmen, 1995). When we consider the millions of *unmarried* couples who also have no available family planning, the numbers are staggering. Each of these couples may need to make choices about continuing with a pregnancy, giving the child up for adoption, or having an abortion. Let's now explore the controversial topic of abortion and the alternatives.

Abortion

In 1973, the U.S. Supreme Court's *Roe v. Wade* decision stated that women have the legal right to choose abortion. Before 1973, many abortions were performed illegally, often by untrained individuals in unsanitary conditions. In fact, an estimated 200,000 to 1,200,000 illegal abortions were performed each year in the United States, and about 10,000 women died annually from these illegal abortions (Gorney, 1998).

Before 1973, countless women also attempted to end an unwanted pregnancy themselves. They swallowed poisons such as turpentine, and they tried to stab knitting needles, coat hangers, and other sharp objects through the cervix and into the uterus (Baird-Windle & Bader, 2001; Gorney, 1998).

More recent legal decisions have reduced the power of *Roe v. Wade*. For example, in some states, an abortion can be performed only after a specified waiting period or only in restricted situations (J. A. Baer, 1999; David & Lee, 2001). In both the United States and Canada, health care professionals who perform abortions have been harassed or even murdered by so-called pro-life groups, and abortion clinics have been bombed (Baird-Windle & Bader, 2001; Quindlen, 2001b). In 1998, anti-abortionists murdered gynecologist Barnett Slepian in Amherst, New York, about an hour's drive from my home.

Other techniques are more subtle. For example, a Canadian newspaper reported that Calgary public schools had invited a Christian anti-abortion group to lecture to students and to distribute antichoice pamphlets. Neither students nor their parents had been informed about this visit beforehand (S. Fine, 2001).

It's worth noting that cigarette smoking nearly doubles a woman's chances of having a miscarriage (Ness et al., 1999). However, pro-life groups have not yet harassed the tobacco companies.

Let's emphasize an important point: *No one recommends abortion as a routine form of birth control.* We need to provide more comprehensive education about sexuality so that women do not need to consider the abortion alternative. As you can see from Table 9.1 on page 308, the adolescent abortion rate is higher in the United States and Canada than in all other countries listed. Worldwide, 40 to 50 million abortions are performed each year for women of all ages; about 40% of these abortions are illegal (Allgeier & Allgeier, 2000; P. D. Harvey, 2000; United Nations, 2000). Most of these abortions could have been avoided by using effective birth control methods.

Table 9.3 describes the most common methods of abortion. About one-quarter of all pregnancies in the United States and Canada are terminated by means of a legal abortion (S. S. Brown & Eisenberg, 1995; Statistics Canada, 2000). Compared to women who continue an unwanted pregnancy, pregnant women who seek abortions are more likely to be single women from middle-class or upper-class backgrounds (S. S. Brown & Eisenberg, 1995; L. Phillips, 1998).

Abortion may be a controversial issue, but one aspect of abortion is not controversial: its safety. A woman is about 25 times more likely to die as a result of childbirth than as a result of a legal abortion performed within 9 weeks of conception. As a general rule, women who have abortions performed shortly after conception have fewer complications and recover more quickly than women who had later abortions (Allgeier & Allgeier, 2000). In contrast to this objective information about methods, numbers, and safety, we must now consider the more difficult topics, focusing on the psychological aspects of abortion.

TABLE 9.3 ■ Major Methods of Abortion

Method	When Used	Description
RU-486 (Mifepristone)	Before 7 weeks of pregnancy	This medicine prevents implantation of the fertilized egg; a second medicine induces uterine contractions.
Vacuum aspiration	Before 14 weeks of pregnancy	The cervix is treated with a local anesthetic. Then a vacuum tube is inserted through the cervix into the uterus; suction draws out the tissue.
Dilation and evacuation	13–21 weeks of pregnancy	The cervix is dilated in order to remove the larger volume of tissue; suction draws out the tissue. A general anesthetic is typically used.
Induced abortion	16–24 weeks of pregnancy	Saline or another chemical solution is injected into the uterus, inducing premature labor.

Note: For more information, consult Allgeier and Allgeier (2000), Ginty (2001), Hyde and DeLamater (2003), and Stotland (1998).

Psychological Reactions to an Abortion. Most women report that their primary reaction following an abortion is relief (N. E. Adler & Smith, 1998; David & Lee, 2001; D. H. Miller, 1996). Some women experience sadness, a sense of loss, or other negative feelings. Individual differences in emotional reactions are large, consistent with Theme 4 of this textbook (Major et al., 1998; Russo, 2000). However, studies show that the typical woman who has an abortion suffers no long-term effects, such as problems with anxiety or self-esteem. Women who have had abortions are also no more likely than other women to be admitted to psychiatric hospitals (N. E. Adler & Smith, 1998; David & Lee, 2001; Russo, 2000).

What are some of the factors related to psychological adjustment following an abortion? In general, women who cope most easily are those who have the abortion early in their pregnancy (Allgeier & Allgeier, 2000). An important psychological factor related to adjustment is self-efficacy, or a woman's feeling that she is competent and effective (Cozzarelli, 1993; Major et al., 1998). Another factor is that many women feel that they ought to be ashamed of the abortion, so they keep it a secret; fewer than 25% of teenagers tell their parents (Major & Gramzow, 1999). Not surprisingly, adjustment is better if the woman's friends and relatives can support her decision (N. E. Adler & Smith, 1998; David & Lee,

2001). A medical staff that is helpful and supportive during the abortion procedure also contributes to good adjustment. One woman recalls her experience:

> I elected to have it done with a local anesthetic. I was completely awake for the pro-
> cedure, and it was gentle in every respect. The staff was really crackerjack, and there
> was a nurse with me at all times. The doctor was about as gentle as I could imagine
> him being. And all the follow-up was really nurturing. (De Puy & Dovitch, 1997,
> p. 56)

Follow-up counseling should be available to every woman who has had an
abortion, to assist her in sorting through her emotions (Hatcher & Trussell, 1994;
Kushner, 1997). The counseling should also focus on birth control options and
on the steps that the woman will take to avoid future intercourse, if it is not in
her best interest.

Children Born to Women Who Were Denied Abortions.   In many cases, a woman
wants to obtain an abortion, but circumstances (such as lack of money) prevent
the abortion. As a result, many women will give birth to children who are not
wanted. How do children develop psychologically under these circumstances?
Because abortion has been legal in the United States since 1973, researchers cannot examine this question in this country. However, several studies in other
countries provide some answers. Consider a long-term study conducted with
220 children whose mothers were denied abortions in the former Czechoslova-
kia (David et al., 1988). Each of these children was carefully matched with a
child from a wanted pregnancy, so that the two groups were comparable.

The study showed that, by 9 years of age, the children from unwanted pregnancies had fewer friends and responded poorly to stress, compared to children
from wanted pregnancies. By age 23, the children from unwanted pregnancies
were more likely to report that their mothers were not interested in them. These
children were also likely to receive psychological treatment. In addition, they
had more marital difficulties, drug problems, conflicts at work, and trouble with
the legal system. Ongoing research about these two groups continues to show
numerous problems when these unwanted children are adults, whereas the
wanted children have relatively few problems (David & Lee, 2001).

Other similar studies show that many women who give birth to unwanted
children continue to report negative feelings toward those children many years
later (Barber et al., 1999; Dagg, 1991). These implications for children's lives
should be considered when governments try to make informed decisions about
abortion policies.

Alternatives to Abortion.   Unplanned pregnancies can be resolved by methods
other than abortion. For example, people who oppose abortion often suggest the
alternative of giving the baby up for adoption, and this might be an appropriate
choice for some women. However, adoption may create its own kind of trauma
and pain (David & Lee, 2001). One woman who gave up her daughter for adoption commented two years later:

> I'm sad that I don't see her—the first steps, the first tooth. I'm missing everything,
> missing her discovering life. I love her, I love her to death. If tomorrow they were

to call and say there's a problem, we need a heart, we need something, I'm there. I wouldn't even think twice about it. If that means I have to give my life for her, I'll do it. (Englander, 1997, p. 114)

Another alternative is to deliver the baby and choose the motherhood option. In many cases, an unwanted pregnancy can become a wanted baby by the time of delivery. However, thousands of babies are born each year to mothers who do not want them. This situation can be destructive for both the mother and the child. In the United States, most adolescents who deliver a baby are currently choosing to become single mothers. Unfortunately, most unmarried teenage mothers encounter difficulties in completing school, finding employment, fighting poverty, and facing the biases that unmarried mothers often confront in our society.

We have seen that none of these alternatives—abortion, adoption, or motherhood—is free of problems. Instead, the answer that creates the least psychological pain appears to be pregnancy prevention, so that women do not have to choose among the less-than-optimal alternatives.

SECTION SUMMARY ■

Birth Control and Abortion

1. About 1 million teen pregnancies occur each year in the United States; pregnancy rates are much lower in Canada and Western Europe.

2. Most forms of birth control are intended for the female rather than the male; no method is completely problem free.

3. Many heterosexual, sexually active women do not use reliable birth control methods. Female contraceptive use is related to social class, ethnicity, education, and personality characteristics such as self-esteem and risk taking.

4. Couples avoid using birth control because of inadequate information, unavailable contraceptive services, inadequate planning, irrational thinking, reluctance to admit they are sexually active, and the feeling that birth control devices are not romantic. Also, many women cannot convince their partners to use birth control.

5. Some developing countries have instituted family planning programs, whereas others do not support these programs. Literacy is highly correlated with women's contraceptive use.

6. Before *Roe v. Wade*, thousands of women died each year from illegal abortions; currently, health care providers are being threatened if they perform abortions. Legal abortions are much safer than childbirth.

7. Following an abortion, most women experience a feeling of relief, although some women report sadness; adjustment is best when the abortion occurs early in pregnancy, when the woman feels competent, and when friends and family are supportive.

8. Children born to women who have been denied an abortion are significantly more likely to experience psychological and social difficulties than children from a wanted pregnancy.

9. In general, giving up a child for adoption is not an emotionally satisfactory alternative, and women who choose the motherhood option face many difficulties. Pregnancy prevention is the preferable solution.

■ ■ ■ ■ ■ CHAPTER REVIEW QUESTIONS ■ ■ ■ ■ ■

1. At several points throughout this chapter, we have seen that sexuality has traditionally been male centered. Address this issue, focusing on topics such as (a) theoretical perspectives on sexuality, (b) sexual scripts, and (c) sexual problems. Also, compare how the essentialist perspective and the social constructionist perspective approach sexuality.

2. In many sections of this chapter, we discussed adolescent women. Describe the experiences a young woman might face as she discusses sexuality with her parents, listens to a sex education session in her high school, has her first sexual experience, makes decisions about contraception, and tries to make a decision about an unwanted pregnancy.

3. How are gender roles relevant in (a) the initiation of sexual relationships, (b) sexual activity, (c) sexual problems, (d) therapy for sexual problems, and (e) decisions about contraception and abortion?

4. Review the material on gender comparisons in self-disclosure, which we examined in Chapter 6 (page 193). How might this information be relevant to the section on communication about sexuality in this chapter?

5. Briefly describe the stages of sexual responding, and then discuss gender comparisons in sexual responding. Also discuss gender comparisons with respect to various sexual activities.

6. Describe attitudes about sexuality in the current era. Does the sexual double standard still hold true in the twenty-first century?

7. What information do we have about sexuality among lesbians, including sexual activity and sexual problems? Why would a male-centered approach to sexuality make it difficult to decide what counts as sexual activity in a lesbian relationship? Why is this same problem relevant when we consider older women and sexual activities?

8. Describe the two sexual problems discussed in this chapter. Why might older women be especially likely to experience these problems? Also, summarize the kinds of therapeutic approaches currently used to treat sexual problems.

9. Imagine that you have received a large grant to reduce the number of unwanted pregnancies in the region where you lived as a young teenager. What kinds of programs would you plan, to achieve both immediate and long-term effects?

10. What information do we have about the safety of abortion, the psychological consequences to the woman, and consequences for children whose mothers had been denied an abortion?

NEW TERMS

*essentialism (288)

*social constructionism (288)

*clitoris (290)

*vagina (290)

excitement phase (290)

vasocongestion (290)

plateau phase (290)

orgasmic phase (290)

resolution phase (291)
*sexual double standard (295)
*sexual script (295)
*rape (296)
*sexual disorder (304)

*low sexual desire (304)
 female orgasmic disorder (304)
*sensate focus (306)
*cognitive-behavioral therapy (306)
*cognitive restructuring (306)

 The terms asterisked in the New Terms section serve as good search terms for InfoTrac College Edition. Go to http://infotrac.thomsonlearning.com and try these added search terms.

RECOMMENDED READINGS

Brown, J. D., Steele, J. R., & Walsh-Childers, K. (Eds.). (2002). *Sexual teens, sexual media: Investigating media's influence on adolescent sexuality.* Mahwah, NJ: Erlbaum. Here is an excellent collection of 13 chapters about the kind of material that adolescents learn from the media, including television, magazines, movies, and the Internet.

Hyde, J. S., & DeLamater, J. D. (2003). *Understanding human sexuality* (8th ed.). Boston: McGraw-Hill. Janet Hyde and her husband, John DeLamater, have written a clear, comprehensive, and interesting textbook of sexuality from a feminist perspective.

Kaschak, E., & Tiefer, L. (Eds.). (2001). *A new view of women's sexual problems.* New York: Haworth. Ellyn Kaschak and Leonore Tiefer are two well-known feminist therapists; the chapters in this book explore an approach to sexual problems that emphasizes social constructionism, a female-centered approach to sexuality, and a multicultural perspective.

Kushner, E. (1997). *Experiencing abortion: A weaving of women's words.* New York: Harrington Park Press. To prepare this book, Kushner interviewed 115 women who had abortions; the women's stories describe their decision-making processes as well as the stress, anger, grieving, and acceptance that followed.

Schwartz, P., & Rutter, V. (1998). *The gender of sexuality.* Thousand Oaks, CA: Pine Forge Press. This book provides a brief overview of gender comparisons, sexual relationships, and sexuality in marital relationships.

ANSWERS TO THE DEMONSTRATIONS

Demonstration 9.1: 1. F; 2. M; 3. F; 4. F; 5. M; 6. M; 7. M; 8. F.

Demonstration 9.3: 1. 2.7; 2. 2.7; 3. 4.2; 4. 4.1; 5. 4.6; 6. 4.4. (Note that a woman who is high in sexual assertiveness would provide high ratings for Items 1, 4, and 6; she would provide low ratings for Items 2, 3, and 5. Also note that respondents answered numbers 5 and 6 inconsistently—both having sex without a condom and insisting on a condom.)

ANSWERS TO THE TRUE-FALSE QUESTIONS

1. True (p. 290); 2. True (p. 291); 3. False (p. 295); 4. True (p. 297); 5. False (p. 299); 6. True (p. 300); 7. True (p. 305); 8. True (p. 305); 9. True (p. 308); 10. True (p. 315).

Pregnancy, Childbirth, and Motherhood

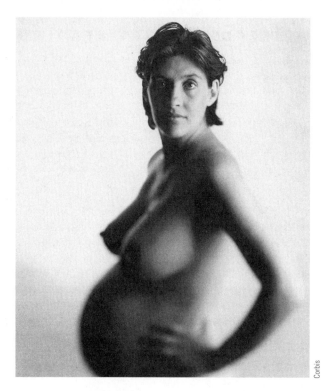

Corbis

T R U E   O R   F A L S E ?

_____ 1. Psychologists have conducted little research on the psychological aspects of pregnancy and childbirth.

_____ 2. A woman can be pregnant and still have a menstrual period.

_____ 3. Pregnancy typically produces a wide range of positive and negative emotions.

_____ 4. Women who are employed more than 45 hours a week are significantly more likely than other women to have difficulties during pregnancy and to have a high rate of premature births.

_____ 5. Cesarean sections account for about one-quarter of all deliveries in North America.

_____ 6. Prepared childbirth is a method of learning about breathing and other techniques so that pain is eliminated during childbirth.

_____ 7. During the first month after childbirth, a mother's dominant emotional response is a feeling of hidden strength and exhilaration.

_____ 8. Children raised by lesbian mothers resemble children raised by heterosexual mothers in characteristics such as intelligence, psychological well-being, and popularity.

_____ 9. Approximately half of North American mothers experience postpartum blues within a few days after the birth of their first child; common symptoms include crying, sadness, and irritability.

_____ 10. Current research shows that people tend to evaluate a woman positively if she chooses not to have children.

Dr. Ingrid Johnston-Robledo is a psychologist who is young, European American, and married. She was also visibly pregnant at the time she wrote a chapter on motherhood (Johnston-Robledo, 2000). She commented on how other people responded to her pregnancy:

> I am greeted by strangers who smile at me with approval. They are seemingly pleased with my choice and ability to fulfill the role of mother. Sometimes these perfect strangers (usually women who have been through this themselves) actually stop me to touch my belly, attempt to figure out the sex of the fetus based on my shape, or ask me plenty of pregnancy-related questions. . . . However, when I am accompanied by my Puerto Rican husband and bicultural toddler, people react to me differently. Their glances are neutral or they appear curious, to put it politely. They may be thinking . . . "they're probably not married" or "look, there she is, pregnant again." The other day a man walked by us and said to his companion as he pointed at us, "See, there it is . . . that's the problem, that's what I'm talking about right there." Were we walking examples of a social ill? (p. 129)

As Johnston-Robledo concluded, the status of a woman's pregnancy often changes, depending on the social context. Interestingly, the importance of pregnancy itself also changes, depending on context. For many women, the sequence of pregnancy, childbirth, and motherhood is a vitally important part of their lives.

The world currently has more than 6 billion inhabitants, each of whom was produced by a woman's pregnancy. Shouldn't the sheer frequency of this personally important event make it a popular topic for psychological research? Surprisingly, the topic of pregnancy is almost invisible in psychology. Issues such as teen pregnancy, unwanted pregnancy, and infertility all attract modest interest. Each year, however, psychologists publish only a handful of studies on normal, intentional pregnancies.

The media provide another context in which the motherhood sequence is invisible. In Chapter 8, we saw that the theme of love dominates music, television, and entertainment. Sexuality—the focus of Chapter 9—is equally prominent. However, pregnancy and childbirth are virtually invisible, consistent with Theme 3, and motherhood is rarely explored in depth.

Let's examine these phases of reproduction in more detail. As you'll see, each phase has important psychological components.

PREGNANCY

What are the major biological components of pregnancy? How do women react to pregnancy, both emotionally and physically? Also, how do other people react to pregnant women? Finally, how do women combine pregnancy with their employment?

The Biology of Pregnancy

Typically, the egg and the sperm unite while the egg is traveling down a fallopian tube. Interestingly, even an act that seems as value free as the joining of the egg and the sperm may be represented in a gender-biased fashion. Specifically, you probably learned from your high school biology textbook that the male sperm *penetrates* the female egg. However, this description is actually a myth, because the egg is much more active during the fertilization process (E. Martin, 2001). In fact, part of the egg reaches out and draws the sperm inward. The egg then penetrates the head of the sperm, distributing the sperm's genetic material throughout the egg (Rabuzzi, 1994).

The fertilized egg continues along the fallopian tube, floats around in the uterus for several days, and then may implant itself in the thick tissue that lines the uterus. If a fertilized egg does not implant itself, then this tissue is sloughed off as menstrual flow—the same menstrual flow that occurs when an egg has not been fertilized. However, if implantation does occur, this tissue provides an ideal environment in which a fertilized egg can develop into a baby.

Shortly after the fertilized egg has implanted itself, the placenta begins to develop. The **placenta,** which is connected to the growing embryo, is an organ that allows oxygen and nutrients to pass from the mother to the embryo. The placenta also helps transport the embryo's waste products back to the mother's system. This amazing organ even manufactures hormones. By the end of her pregnancy, a woman's estrogen and progesterone levels are much higher than they were before her pregnancy (L. L. Alexander et al., 2001).

Typically, a woman first suspects she is pregnant when she has been sexually active and then misses a menstrual period. However, a pregnancy test is necessary to confirm that she is pregnant, because a woman can be pregnant and have a menstrual period or she can miss a menstrual period for reasons other than pregnancy (L. L. Alexander et al., 2001; Allgeier & Allgeier, 2000).

Prenatal care is essential for identifying and treating any complications related to pregnancy as well as for providing relevant information. However, only 65% of pregnant women in developed regions of the world receive prenatal care. In developing countries, that percentage is even lower. In Afghanistan, for instance, only 8% of women have at least one prenatal visit during their pregnancy (United Nations, 2000).

By tradition, pregnancy is divided into three trimesters. Each **trimester** is therefore about 3 months in length. Most women are pregnant for 38 to 42 weeks (L. L. Alexander et al., 2001). Let's now consider how women react both physically and emotionally during these months of pregnancy.

Physical Reactions During Pregnancy

Virtually every organ system in a woman's body is affected by pregnancy, although most of the consequences are relatively minor. Nausea is an especially common symptom during the first trimester. It is often called morning sickness, even though it may occur at any time of the day. Surveys suggest that 70% to 90% of all pregnant women will experience nausea at some point in their pregnancy (Q. Zhou et al., 1999).

Other physical changes during pregnancy include weight gain and protrusion of the abdomen. Many women also report breast tenderness, frequent urination, and fatigue (L. L. Alexander et al., 2001; Carlson et al., 1996).

Several decades ago, pregnancy was regarded as a 9-month sickness, and that view sometimes persists in the current era (Woollett & Marshall, 1997). However, women are increasingly likely to believe that being pregnant is both normal and healthy, although occasionally somewhat uncomfortable and inconvenient.

Our general theme about the wide range of individual differences holds true with pregnancy as with other phases in women's lives. As we noted, some women never experience nausea, but others may be nearly immobilized by nausea and vomiting. Variability is also revealed in women's interest in sexual activity during pregnancy. In one study, 60% of women reported less interest than usual, 20% reported no change, and another 20% actually reported *more* interest in sex (Hofmeyr et al., 1990). In general, however, sexual intercourse is less frequent during pregnancy than before pregnancy (Hyde & DeLamater, 2000; Segraves & Segraves, 2001). However, "pregnant couples" often enjoy other forms of sexual expression.

Emotional Reactions During Pregnancy

> All I seem to think about is the baby. . . . I'm so excited. I'd love to have the baby right now. Somehow this week I feel on top of the world. I love watching my whole tummy move. (Lederman, 1996, p. 35)

> I think I, in a sense, have a prepartum depression—already! . . . Over Easter, when I was home from teaching, it just really hit me how I would be home like that all the time. . . . I was very depressed one day just kind of anticipating it and realizing how much of a change it was going to be, because I had been really active with my teaching, and it had been a pretty major part of my life now for four years. (Lederman, 1996, p. 39)

These quotations from two pregnant women illustrate how individual women respond differently to the same life event, consistent with Theme 4. In pregnancy, the situation is extremely unpredictable, because *each woman* may experience a wide variety of emotions during the 9 months of her pregnancy. For example, those two quotations, although different in emotional tone, could have come from the same woman.

Positive Emotions.   For many women, the news that they are pregnant brings a rush of positive emotions, excitement, and anticipation. Many women report feeling wonder and awe at the thought of having a new, growing person inside their own bodies. Most married women also sense that other people approve of their pregnancy, as we noted at the beginning of the chapter. After all, women are *supposed* to have children.

For many women, pregnancy represents a transition into adulthood. They may describe a sense of purpose and accomplishment about being pregnant (Leifer, 1980). Another positive emotion is the growing sense of attachment that pregnant women feel toward the developing baby (Bergum, 1997; Condon & Corkindale, 1997). One woman reported:

> When I had my first scan, the man explained everything, like this is his leg, this is his foot, little hands, little head. I couldn't see his other leg and asked "Where's his other leg then?" Then they pushed him round and showed me his other leg. It was quite nice. That's when you realize you are having a baby, when you actually see it on the scan. (Woollett & Marshall, 1997, p. 189)

In addition, many pregnant women find pleasure in anticipating the tasks of motherhood and child rearing, which they believe will provide a tremendous source of satisfaction. As we'll see in the section on motherhood, their expectations may be very different from reality.

Negative Emotions.   Unfortunately, many emotions that pregnant women feel are negative, often intensified by their physical reactions of nausea and fatigue. Many women report that their emotions are fragile and continually changing. Depressive feelings, fears, and anxieties are also common (Condon & Corkindale, 1997; L. J. Miller, 2001). Women are especially afraid during the first trimester that they will have a miscarriage (Philipp & Carr, 2001).

As we have mentioned in earlier chapters, women are often evaluated in terms of their attractiveness. Because North American culture values slimness, a woman's self-image may deteriorate as she watches her body grow bigger (Philipp & Carr, 2001). Women often say that they feel fat and ugly during pregnancy. Interestingly, however, these women's romantic partners may feel otherwise. For example, C. P. Cowan and Cowan (1992) questioned married couples who were expecting a baby. They noted that most husbands respond positively:

> Most of the husbands were supportive, and some were truly proud of the changes in their wives' bodies as the pregnancy progressed. They were pleased by what they saw and by what their wives' full bodies signified. Eduardo [one of the fathers in the study] watches his wife maneuver gracefully into a chair during our interview. "The great painters," he says, "tried to show the beauty of a pregnant woman, but when I look at Sonia, I feel they didn't do it justice." (p. 59)

Fortunately, many women are able to overcome our culture's concern about weight. They are excited to see their abdomen swell, to feel the baby move, and to anticipate a healthy pregnancy. Many women are pleased to learn that they can eat slightly more than beforehand, to provide nutrition for the growing baby.

Many women are worried about other physical problems. Some pregnant women are concerned about their health and bodily functions (C. P. Cowan & Cowan, 1992). These anxieties are heightened by the increasing evidence that alcohol, smoking, and a wide variety of drugs can harm the developing fetus (Field, 1998; Streissguth et al., 1999). Incidentally, studies in both the United States and Canada show that many pregnant women try to stop smoking cigarettes during their pregnancy, but it's difficult to break this addiction (N. Edwards & Sims-Jones, 1998; Groff et al., 1997; Ko & Schulken, 1998). Of women who smoked before pregnancy, only 25% to 40% manage to avoid smoking for the full duration of their pregnancy (N. Edwards & Sims-Jones, 1998).

An important part of women's negative reactions to pregnancy is caused by other people beginning to respond differently to them, as we will see in the next section. They are categorized as "pregnant women," that is, women who have no identity aside from the responsibility of a growing baby (Philipp & Carr, 2001). Women may also begin to see themselves in these terms.

In summary, a woman's emotional reaction to pregnancy can range from excitement and anticipation to worry and a loss of identity (Statham et al., 1997). Consistent with Theme 4 of this book, the individual differences can be enormous. For most women, pregnancy is a complex blend of both pleasant and unpleasant reactions.

Naturally, however, a woman's overall response to pregnancy depends on factors such as her physical reactions to pregnancy, whether the pregnancy was planned, her relationship with the baby's father, and her economic status (Barker et al., 2000; Hyde & DeLamater, 2000; Merrick, 1999; Webster et al., 2000). We can understand predominantly negative emotions from an unmarried, pregnant 16-year-old whose boyfriend and family have rejected her and who must work as a waitress to earn an income. We can also understand predominantly positive emotions from a happily married 26-year-old who has hoped for this pregnancy for 2 years and whose family income allows her to buy the stylish "executive" maternity clothes that she can wear to her interesting, fulfilling job.

Attitudes Toward Pregnant Women

Most women experience three major gynecological events: menarche, pregnancy, and menopause. Menarche and menopause are highly private events, to be discussed only with intimate acquaintances. In contrast, pregnancy is public, especially in the last trimester. The quotation at the beginning of the chapter noted that strangers may feel free to pat the stomach of a pregnant woman and offer unsolicited comments to her. These same people would *never* take such liberties with a woman who was not pregnant!

Some classic research by Shelley E. Taylor and Ellen Langer (1977) reported that people tend to avoid standing close to pregnant women. For example, elevator passengers make great efforts to avoid standing near a pregnant woman. Other research suggests that people are especially likely to help a pregnant woman, for example, if she has dropped her keys (Walton et al., 1988). Unfortunately, we don't have recent research in this area. Do people still treat pregnant women differently from women who are not pregnant?

People also tend to infantilize pregnant women. Until recently, a pregnant woman was expected to place herself in the complete care of an obstetrician, who would tell her what to eat and how to live her life (S. Kitzinger, 1995; van Olphen-Fehr, 1998). This kind of treatment would certainly *not* encourage women to be confident, tough, and effective mothers. Theme 2 of this book states that people treat women and men differently. This differential treatment is heightened when a woman is pregnant.

In the current era, most obstetricians are more aware that pregnant women should be treated like intelligent adults who appreciate knowing relevant information. However, the brochures available in their offices often imply that pregnant women worry about trivial issues (Rúdólfsdóttir, 2000). In addition, health care professionals may withhold useful feedback and may fail to explain the reason for certain medical tests (Woollett & Marshall, 1997).

Some years ago, Horgan (1983) reported another measure of people's attitudes toward pregnant women—by visiting department stores. The expensive, high-status stores placed maternity clothes near the lingerie and loungewear. This arrangement suggests an image of femininity, delicacy, luxury, and privacy. In contrast, the less expensive, low-status stores placed maternity clothes near the uniforms and the clothing for overweight women. Here, a pregnant woman is seen as fat, with a job to do. Try Demonstration 10.1, a modification of Horgan's study.

Pregnant Women and Employment

Several decades ago, European American women in the United States and Canada typically stopped working outside the home once they became pregnant. However, Black women have had different expectations. Being a good mother never meant that a woman should stay at home full time (P. H. Collins,

DEMONSTRATION 10.1 ■ ■ ■ ■ ■ ■ ■ ■ ■ ■ ■ ■ ■ ■ ■ ■ ■ ■

Attitudes Toward Pregnant Women, as Illustrated in Department Stores

Select several nearby stores that sell maternity clothes; try to obtain a sample of stores that vary in social status. Visit each store. (You may want to come prepared with a "shopping for a pregnant friend" cover story.) Record where the maternity clothes are placed. Are they near the lingerie, the clothes for overweight women, the uniforms, or someplace else?

Also notice the nature of the clothes themselves. In the 1970s, the clothes were infantile, with ruffles and bows. Clothes are now more like clothing for nonpregnant women. Do the different kinds of stores feature different styles?

Finally, check on the price of the clothing. How much would a pregnant woman's wardrobe be likely to cost, assuming that she will need maternity clothes during the last six months of her pregnancy?

1991). In developing countries, pregnant women are often expected to work in the fields or to perform other physically exhausting tasks, sometimes until labor begins (S. Kitzinger, 1995).

In North America in the current era, many women plan to have both a career and children, especially if the women are college graduates (Hoffnung, 2003). The research shows that pregnant women often continue at their jobs until shortly before their due date (Berryman & Windridge, 1997). However, some physically demanding occupations may be challenging for pregnant women. For example, female doctors who are residents in pediatrics work long hours, and they must also take care of emergency cases about two nights a week. When a sample of pregnant residents was interviewed, roughly one-quarter said that combining work with pregnancy was pleasant. Half reported it was tolerable, and one-quarter found it miserable (Klevan et al., 1990).

Combining a demanding job with pregnancy may sometimes be difficult. However, it does not seem to damage the health of the pregnant woman or the baby. For example, a nationwide questionnaire was sent to all women who had graduated from medical school and were now working as residents (Klebanoff et al., 1990). The questionnaire was also sent to wives of their male classmates, who served as a control group of women who had less time-consuming occupations. The pregnant women who were residents worked almost twice as many hours each week—an average of 70 hours—in contrast to 39 hours for the doctors' wives. However, the women residents were no more likely to have miscarriages, premature births, or low-birth-weight babies. In other words, both pregnant women and their babies are impressively resilient.

SECTION SUMMARY ■

Pregnancy

1. Pregnancy and childbirth receive little attention in psychological research and in the media.

2. At the beginning of pregnancy, the fertilized egg implants itself in the tissue lining the uterus, and the placenta develops shortly afterward.

3. Although individual differences are great, several common physical reactions to pregnancy include nausea, weight gain, and fatigue.

4. The variety of emotional reactions to pregnancy is large. Positive emotions include feelings of excitement and wonder, a sense of purpose, growing attachment, and the anticipated pleasure of motherhood.

5. Negative emotions include fragile emotional stability, concerns about physical appearance, health worries, and concern about the reactions received from others.

6. People may avoid standing near pregnant women or may invade their privacy; pregnant women may also be infantilized.

7. Most women with challenging jobs feel comfortable about combining work with pregnancy, and employment during pregnancy does not endanger the health of the pregnant woman or the baby.

CHILDBIRTH

Women in the United States have an average of 2.0 children, and Canadian women have an average of 1.6 children (United Nations, 2000). In other words, childbirth is a relatively common event in North America. However, this important event is virtually ignored by psychologists. Interesting topics, such as women's emotions during childbirth, are almost invisible. In fact, most of our information must be gathered from nursing journals. Let's consider the biology of childbirth and emotional reactions to childbirth. Then we'll consider some current practices that are likely to improve women's childbirth experiences.

The Biology of Childbirth

Labor for childbirth begins when the uterus starts to contract strongly. The labor period is divided into three stages. During the first stage, the cervix becomes dilated to about 10 cm (4 inches), a process that may last anywhere from a few hours to at least a day.

The second stage of labor lasts from a few minutes to several hours. The contractions, aided by the mother's pushing, move the baby farther down the vagina. Women report feelings of strong pressure and stretching during this stage. The contractions often become extremely painful. Some compare these contractions to the pain of a particularly prolonged bowel movement. Others—but no mothers I know—suggest that contractions are more like a prolonged orgasm (Allgeier & Allgeier, 2000). During the second stage, progesterone levels begin to drop. This stage ends when the baby is born. The photograph on this page illustrates the second stage of labor.

The third stage of labor, which usually lasts less than 20 minutes, is clearly an anticlimax. The placenta separates from the uterine wall, and then it is expelled along with some other tissue that had surrounded the fetus. The levels of estrogen and progesterone drop during this third stage, so that both of them are drastically lower than they were several hours earlier.

Social factors can have a profound effect on the biology of childbirth (Hoyert et al., 2000). In a study conducted in Ireland, for example, pregnant women participated in a program that included customized childbirth classes and a nurse assigned to each woman for the entire childbirth experience (Frigoletto et al., 1995). Labor was 2.7 hours shorter for this group than for a similar group of women who had the standard treatment. Another study in a hospital in the African nation of Botswana reported that women required significantly less pain medication if they had been accompanied by a female relative during labor and

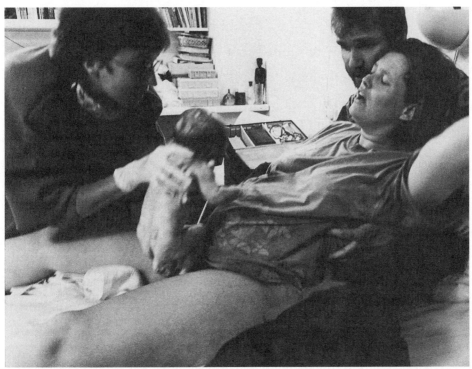

Benelux Press/PictureQuest

PHOTO 10.1 ■ A childbirth scene, showing the end of the second stage of labor.

delivery (Madi et al., 1999). In many cultures—as diverse as Scandinavian countries and Mayan communities in Latin America—childbirth is considered a normal process rather than a medical achievement. In these cultures, women expect to have attendants with them during childbirth (DeLoache & Gottlieb, 2000; Whelehan, 2001).

Currently, about 20% to 25% of all deliveries in the United States and Canada are performed by cesarean section (Allgeier & Allgeier, 2000; Curtin et al., 2000). In a **cesarean section** (or **C-section**), the physician makes an incision through the woman's abdomen and into the uterus to deliver the baby. Some cesarean sections are necessary if a vaginal delivery would be risky, for example, when a woman's uterine contractions are not strong enough (L. L. Alexander et al., 2001). However, many health care critics argue that the rate of C-sections is high because they are more convenient or profitable for the medical staff (Curtin & Kozak, 1998; DiMatteo & Kahn, 1997). With effort, some hospitals have been able to reduce the rate of cesarean sections (Flamm et al., 1998).

In North America, childbirth is relatively safe. In the United States, however, Black women are four times more likely than European American women to die during childbirth (Hoyert et al., 2000). Furthermore, in developing countries, approximately 600,000 women die each year from problems during pregnancy and childbirth (United Nations, 2000). Some of these countries have recently begun formal programs to train midwives in childbirth procedures. This training has reduced the death rate for both the pregnant women and their infants (Buckley, 1997; Otis, 2001).

Emotional Reactions to Childbirth

Women's emotional reactions to the birth of their child can vary as widely as their reactions to pregnancy (Wuitchik et al., 1990). For some women, childbirth can be a peak experience of feeling in tune with the birth. After giving birth, they may express intense joy (Allgeier & Allgeier, 2000). A woman in Hoffnung's (1992) study recalled, years later, her elation when her firstborn arrived:

> I have never had such a high as after he was born! I guess it's the first child; you're so up for the whole thing. I think I could have flown if I had tried. . . . I have never felt that way about anything else at all: not getting married, not my other kids, nothing. (p. 17)

Many women's descriptions of childbirth emphasize the pain, but they may differ in their response to the pain. For example, one woman said:

> I thought of the millions, literally billions of women who have experienced this pain, and if they could experience it, then I can too. That made me feel strong. (Bergum, 1997, p. 50)

Another woman found a different way to cope with the pain:

> I don't think one should focus on the pain, that women should have to experience pain. But in the pain there is an experience of being inward and involved in feeling the pain—not enjoying it but taking hold, enduring, or whatever you do to handle it—and knowing that it is going to produce a child. (Bergum, 1997, p. 41)

Fathers who participate in the birth of their child may also experience intense joy, as in this description offered by a new father:

> I couldn't have imagined the incredibly powerful feelings that engulfed me when I saw Kevin slip out of Tanya. I was right there, and this was my son! All the next day whenever he began to cry or nurse, I was in tears. I'm still transfixed watching him. It's the most amazing experience I ever had. (C. P. Cowan & Cowan, 1992, p. 71)

Alternative Models of Childbirth

Many health care advocates suggest that the childbirth experience can be made more comfortable and emotionally satisfying for women. One of the most widely used approaches, called **prepared childbirth,** features the following elements (L. L. Alexander et al., 2001; Allgeier & Allgeier, 2000; Hyde & DeLamater, 2003):

1. Learning about pregnancy and childbirth in order to reduce fear and dispel myths;
2. Controlled breathing techniques, which distract attention away from the pain of the contractions;
3. Relaxation techniques and muscle-strengthening exercises; and
4. Social support from someone who has also attended classes, usually the baby's father or a close friend of the mother.

People who support prepared childbirth emphasize that this method does not *eliminate* pain; childbirth is still a stressful experience (Hyde & DeLamater, 2003). However, women who have had a helpful coach present during childbirth are significantly more satisfied with the childbirth experience (Dannenbring et al., 1997). Prepared childbirth seems to provide a number of substantial benefits (Hyde & DeLamater, 2003; D. Young, 1982). The mothers report more positive attitudes, less anxiety, and reduced pain. They also require less medication. In addition, the mother's partner can play an active, supportive role during the childbirth experience.

The technology of childbirth has made impressive advances during the past 50 years. Death rates are lower for both mothers and infants. An unfortunate side effect of this high-tech approach, however, is that births in hospitals may focus on expensive equipment, fetal monitoring, and sanitizing every part of the mother rather than on viewing childbirth as an exhilarating experience of warmth, joy, and sharing (Howell-White, 1999; Peterson, 1996; Wolf, 2001).

In contrast to the high-tech approach, the **family-centered approach** in the United States and Canada emphasizes that safe, high-quality health care can be delivered while simultaneously focusing on the woman's sense of individuality and autonomy as well as on the family's psychosocial needs (C. R. Phillips, 2000; "Spotlight on Canada," 2000; D. Young, 1982, 1993). The family-centered approach acknowledges that some high-risk pregnancies may require special technology. However, the vast majority of births are normal. Instead of focusing exclusively on the medical aspects of childbirth, the family-centered approach insists that professionals should realize that childbirth is an important psychological event in which a family is born and new relationships are formed. Mothers, not technology, should be placed at the center of the childbirth experience (Dahlberg et al., 1999; Pincus, 2000).

Some of the changes that have been implemented include the following (Halldórsdóttir & Karlsdóttir, 1996; S. Kitzinger, 1995; Pincus, 2000; van Olphen-Fehr, 1998; D. Young, 1982, 1993):

1. Labor should not be artificially induced simply because it is more convenient for the physician.
2. Women should be encouraged to move around during labor and to sit upright when the child is being delivered, rather than lying flat on the delivery table with their feet in stirrups.
3. Hospital birth practices that have no health benefits should be modified. These include routine enemas, shaving the genital area, and forbidding any food during labor.
4. Anesthetics should not be used unless necessary or desired.
5. A supportive family member or friend should be present.
6. Special birthing rooms and out-of-hospital birth centers typically make the birth experience more pleasant.
7. Health care providers must be empathic individuals who can encourage women's sense of empowerment during childbirth.

The family-centered approach to childbirth emphasizes that the wishes of the mother should be taken seriously. This approach helps redistribute power, so that women in childbirth have more control over their own bodies. Women can make decisions about how they want to give birth rather than being passive and infantilized.

Try Demonstration 10.2 to learn about the childbirth experiences of several women you know. Also, can you detect any changes in childbirth procedures for women with the most recent birth experiences?

SECTION SUMMARY   ■

Childbirth

1. The three stages in labor are (a) dilation of the cervix, (b) childbirth, and (c) expulsion of the placenta. Social factors can influence the duration of labor and the amount of pain medication required.

2. Reactions to childbirth vary widely. Some women report an intensely positive experience; others cope with pain using a variety of approaches.

3. Prepared childbirth emphasizes education, controlled breathing, relaxation, exercise, and social support; this approach generally produces more satisfying childbirth experiences.

4. The family-centered approach to childbirth focuses on providing support to women in labor; it discourages the unnecessary use of high-technology procedures.

DEMONSTRATION 10.2 ■ ■ ■ ■ ■ ■ ■ ■ ■ ■ ■ ■ ■ ■ ■ ■ ■ ■

Comparison of Childbirth Experiences

Locate women who had babies very recently, about 10 years ago, about 20 years ago, and in some year long before you were born. If possible, include your own mother or close relatives in your interview. Ask each of these women to describe her childbirth experience in as much detail as possible. After each woman has finished, you may wish to ask some of the following questions, if they were not already answered:

1. Were you given any medication? If so, do you remember what kind?
2. How long did you stay in the hospital?
3. Did the baby stay with you in the room, or was she or he returned to the nursery after feedings?
4. Was a relative or friend allowed in the room while you were giving birth?
5. When you were in labor, were you encouraged to lie down?
6. Did you have "prepared childbirth"?
7. Do you recall any negative treatment from any of the hospital staff?
8. Were you treated like a competent adult?
9. Do you recall any positive treatment from any of the hospital staff?
10. If you could have changed any one thing about your childbirth experience, what would that have been?

MOTHERHOOD

The word *motherhood* suggests some stereotypes that are well established, although contradictory; we'll consider these stereotypes in the first part of this section. Next we'll see how those stereotypes contrast with reality. We'll also examine the motherhood experience of two groups of women who are outside the mainstream of European American heterosexual mothers; specifically, we'll consider how both women of color and lesbian women experience motherhood. We'll then focus on two issues of concern to women who have just given birth: postpartum depression and breast feeding. The final topics in this chapter focus on the decision about returning to the workplace, the option of deciding not to have children, and the problem of infertility.

Stereotypes About Motherhood

For most people, the word *motherhood* brings forth a rich variety of pleasant emotions such as warmth, strength, protectiveness, nurturance, and self-sacrifice (Ganong & Coleman, 1995). You can easily generate other similar items to complete the list.

According to the stereotype, a pregnant woman is expected to be joyously upbeat, eagerly anticipating the blessed event. Motherhood is portrayed as happy and satisfying, an image that is perpetuated by the media (Coltrane, 1998; Johnston-Robledo, 2000; Maushart, 1999). Furthermore, the motherhood stereotype emphasizes that a woman's ultimate fulfillment is achieved by becoming a mother (Caplan, 1998, 2000, 2001; Villani, 1997).

The motherhood stereotype also specifies that the mother may require only a few moments of adjustment to the new baby, and then she will feel perfectly competent as her "natural" mothering skills take over (Johnston-Robledo, 2000). She is completely devoted to her family, and she shows no concern for her own personal needs (Ex & Janssens, 2000). As you might imagine, many mothers feel guilty when they cannot live up to this standard of perfect mothering (Caplan, 2001; Hrdy, 1999; H. Lerner, 1998).

North American culture is somewhat ambivalent about motherhood, although the negative aspects are generally less prominent. In the media, mothers are sometimes portrayed as being overly concerned or domineering. Mothers' faults are exaggerated, and their positive attributes are ignored. Also, therapists blame the mother, not the father, when children develop a psychological disorder (Caplan, 2000, 2001). You'll recall from Chapter 2 that women in classical mythology and religion are sometimes saints and sometimes villains. Similarly, stereotypes about mothers contain contradictory messages of good and evil (Caplan, 2001).

The Reality of Motherhood

Many lofty phrases are written in tribute to motherhood, but the role is actually accorded low prestige (Caplan, 2000; Hoffnung, 1995). Our society values money, power, and achievement. However, our culture does not associate any of these rewards with taking care of children. In reality, mothers do not receive the appreciation they deserve.

None of the stereotypes captures the rich variety of emotions that mothers actually experience. Columnist Anna Quindlen (2001a) describes this perspective:

> My children have been the making of me as a human being, which does not mean that they have not sometimes been an overwhelming and mind-boggling responsibility. . . . I love my children more than life itself. But just because you love people doesn't mean that taking care of them day in and day out isn't often hard, and sometimes even horrible. (p. 64)

Before you read further, try Demonstration 10.3, which we'll discuss later in this chapter. Let's now explore the reality of motherhood in more detail. We'll first consider a long list of negative factors and then examine the more abstract, but certainly intense, positive factors.

Negative Factors.   A newborn infant certainly creates pressures and stress for the mother. Here are some of the negative factors that women often mention:

1. Fathers help much less with child rearing than mothers had expected. As we noted in Chapter 7, mothers take the major responsibility for child care, including less pleasant tasks such as changing diapers (Johnston-Robledo, 2000; Wolf, 2001).

DEMONSTRATION 10.3 ■ ■ ■ ■ ■ ■ ■ ■ ■ ■ ■ ■ ■ ■ ■ ■ ■ ■ ■

Neonatal Mortality Rate

Look at the list of countries provided, and think about which ones are likely to have a low neonatal mortality rate (i.e., a low rate of an infant dying within the first year of life). Rank these countries, placing a 1 in front of the country that you think would have the lowest rate (among just those countries listed). Place a 2 in front of the country that you think would have the next lowest rate. Continue ranking the 10 countries, placing a 10 in front of the country that you think would have the highest neonatal mortality rate. The answers appear at the end of the chapter.

_____ Australia   _____ Greece

_____ Cuba   _____ Israel

_____ Denmark   _____ Japan

_____ France   _____ Sweden

_____ Germany   _____ United States

Note: These data represent neonatal mortality rates for 1999, the most recent international data that are currently available.

Source: MacDorman et al. (2002).

2. Child care is physically exhausting; fatigue is almost universal in the first weeks after childbirth. Sleep deprivation is also common (S. Kitzinger, 1994; Maushart, 1999). Because infant care takes so much time, new mothers often feel that they can accomplish very little other than taking care of the infant.

3. For several days after childbirth, women report that they feel leaky and dirty, coping with after-birth discharges. They are also likely to feel pain in the vaginal area and in the uterus. Their breasts may ache, and they may also experience pain and discomfort if they have had a cesarean section (S. Kitzinger, 1994).

4. New mothers seldom have training for the tasks of motherhood; they often report feeling incompetent. As a result, they may wonder why no one warned them about the difficulty of child care or how their life would change after the baby was born (Johnston-Robledo, 2000; H. Lerner, 1998).

5. Pregnant women often create a vision of the glowing baby they expect to cuddle in their arms. In reality, babies do not smile until they are about 2 months old; also, many babies are fussy, and they resist cuddling (D. N. Stern & Bruschweiler-Stern, 1998).

6. Because mothering is done at home, mothers of newborns have little contact with other adults (Hays, 1996). Friends and extended family may not be avail-

able to provide support. This kind of isolation further encourages the invisibility of women, already an important issue throughout this book.

7. Women who have been previously employed feel that others judge them negatively as "just a housewife"; they are deprived of other sources of identity (Villani, 1997).

8. Because the woman's attention has shifted to the newborn, her romantic partner may feel neglected. Many mothers comment that their husbands make them feel guilty about not being adequate. The number of fights also increases, especially if the father spends little time taking care of the child (P. Cowan & Cowan, 1998; H. Lerner, 1998; D. N. Stern & Bruschweiler-Stern, 1998).

9. Women feel disappointed in themselves because they do not match the standards of the ideal mother, the completely unselfish and perfect woman. She is our culture's stereotype of motherhood—but no one really lives up to that stereotype (Caplan, 2000; Villani, 1997).

Among all these negative factors is another one—so horrifying that I cannot simply add it to the end of the preceding list. However, the reality is that a large number of children die at an early age. For instance, in Angola, Liberia, Mali, Sierra Leone, and other sub-Saharan African countries, between 20% and 30% of all children die before their fifth birthday (UNICEF, 2002). Some so-called developed countries also have a much higher child death rate than most people expect. The most common measure is called the **infant mortality rate,** which is the annual number of deaths prior to the first birthdays, per 1,000 live births. Check your responses to Demonstration 10.3 against the answers on page 350. Did you guess that the United States has the worst record among the 10 countries on this list? (The infant mortality rate for 1999 was not listed for Canada; however, in 1998, the rate was 5.3, about the same as the rate for Greece in 1999.)

Positive Factors. Motherhood also has its positive side, although these qualities may not predominate early in motherhood. Some women discover that an important positive consequence of motherhood is a sense of their own strength. After all, they have successfully brought a child into this world. As one woman told me, "I discovered that I felt *very* empowered and confident, like, 'Don't mess with *me!* I've given birth!'" (T. Napper, personal communication, 1998). Sadly, we often focus so much on childbirth's negative consequences for women that we fail to explore the life-enhancing consequences.

The major benefits for most mothers are the interactions with their children. One mother in Bergum's (1997) study captures the intensity of this loving interaction with her 3-month-old daughter:

> She smiles at me. She looks me in the eye and smiles to light the world. Supreme harmony reigns as the light dapples through the apple trees.
> There must be traffic on 99th Street but I don't notice. Nothing seems to be going past on the avenue. Betsy and I are far away in this warm world. We are alone and connected and in love with each other.
> It is perhaps the most perfect time in my life. (p. 13)

Parents often point out that children can be fun and interesting, especially when they can look at the world from a new viewpoint, through the eyes of a child. In addition, one mother explained how her children developed an important part of her personality: "My kids have opened up emotions in me that I never knew were possible; they have slowed down my life happily" (Villani, 1997, p. 135). Many women point out that having children helped them to identify and develop their ability to nurture (Bergum, 1997).

Summarizing the comments of many mothers, Hoffnung (1995) wrote:

> The role of mother brings with it benefits as well as limitations. Children affect parents in ways that lead to personal growth, enable reworking of childhood conflicts, build flexibility and empathy, and provide intimate, loving human connections. . . . They expand their caretakers' worlds by their activity levels, their imaginations, and their inherently appealing natures. Although motherhood is not enough to fill an entire life, for most mothers, it is one of the most meaningful experiences in their lives. (p. 174)

If you were to ask a mother of an infant to list the positive and negative qualities of motherhood, the negative list would probably contain more items and more specific details. Most mothers find that the positive side of motherhood is more abstract, more difficult to describe, and yet more intense. The drudgery of dirty diapers is much easier to talk about than the near ecstasy of realizing that this complete human being was once part of her own body, and now this baby breathes and gurgles and hiccups without her help.

Also, shortly after birth, babies develop ways of communicating with other humans. The delights of a baby's first tentative smile are undeniable. An older baby can interact even more engagingly with adults by making appropriate eye contact and conversational noises. Most mothers value the intimate, caring relationships they develop with their children. Motherhood has numerous joyous aspects. Unfortunately, our society has not devised creative ways to diminish the negative aspects so that we can appreciate the joys more completely.

Motherhood and Women of Color

Researchers are beginning to identify how the motherhood experiences of women of color often differ from the European American experience. However, mothers are still relatively invisible, even in the more comprehensive books about women of color.

Two major stereotypes about Black mothers are common in North America (Sparks, 1996, 1998). In one stereotype, the Black welfare mother, the woman is portrayed as being too lazy to work and as having many babies in order to collect welfare payments. This stereotype fails to acknowledge the factors that produce poverty. A second stereotype, the Black superwoman, portrays a woman of incredible strength who sacrifices her own needs for those of her children. In the current era, this stereotypical superwoman may also be highly career focused in the workplace. This stereotype fails to acknowledge how racism may block the options available to Black women. Neither stereotype provides a realistic, positive role model for Black mothers in our culture. And neither stereotype is relevant for the growing number of middle-class Black mothers, who are also typically ignored by social science researchers (Gadsden, 1999).

Several theorists have pointed out the stabilizing influence of extended families in Black culture (East & Felice, 1996; Gadsden, 1999). These networks of grandmothers, aunts, and siblings are especially important among economically poor mothers (P. H. Collins, 1991).

The extended family is also important for Latina/o families. For instance, many immigrants from Latin America move in with relatives who are already established in North America. As a result, young Latina/o children are likely to be cared for by members of their extended family (Leyendecker & Lamb, 1999).

In Chapter 8, we saw that *marianismo* is the belief among Latinas/os that women must be passive and long suffering, giving up their own needs to help their husbands and children (Chin, 1994; Ehlers, 1993; M. Fine et al., 2000). Ginorio and her colleagues (1995) emphasized that real-life Latina mothers have typically been more active, holding substantial power within the family. These researchers also emphasized that these real-life mothers are currently reshaping their roles and becoming more independent, especially as they enter the workforce in increasing numbers.

Some ethnic groups emphasize values in motherhood that would not be central for European American mothers. For example, many North American Indians emphasize the continuity of generations, with grandmothers being central when their daughters give birth (A. Adams, 1995). Consider Theresa, an Aboriginal woman living on the west coast of Canada. Theresa describes how her mother responded to the birth of Theresa's daughter:

> My mother came the day after she was born. She said, "I'm so proud of you. And I'm so happy that now you have a friend for yourself the way I have a friend for myself in you." And that really is how it is. My daughter's been a friend to me for a long time. (Morrison, 1987, p. 32)

Many Asian cultures have special customs for new mothers. For example, after giving birth, mothers in Cambodia stay for one month in a bed placed over a warm fire, to restore the body heat that is believed to be lost during childbirth (Townsend & Rice, 1996). In contrast, in Bali, Indonesia, a mother who has just given birth is considered impure, and she is not allowed to enter any religious temple until about two months after childbirth (Diener, 2000).

Cultural beliefs may conflict with the U.S. medical model when women from Asia emigrate to the United States. For instance, Hmong women who have come to the United States from Southeast Asia are horrified at the prospect of being examined by a male obstetrician when they are pregnant. Other procedures, such as providing a urine sample, may seem terrifying to a Hmong woman, even if they seem routine to European Americans (Symonds, 1996).

As P. H. Collins (1994) pointed out, our knowledge about motherhood will not be helped by claiming that the experiences of women of color are more valid than the experiences of White middle-class women. Instead, Collins emphasized that examining motherhood "from multiple perspectives should uncover rich textures of differences. Shifting the center to accommodate this diversity promises to recontextualize motherhood and point us toward feminist theorizing that embraces differences as an essential part of commonality" (p. 73).

PHOTO 10.2 ■ Numerous studies demonstrate that children raised by lesbian mothers are similar in psychological adjustment to children raised by heterosexual mothers.

Lesbian Mothers

Lesbian mothers are a diverse group. The largest number are women who had a child in a heterosexual relationship and subsequently identified as lesbian. Other lesbians decide to conceive by donor insemination, and still others adopt their children. Some lesbians are single parents; others live with their female partner (Patterson & Chan, 1999).

Many studies have compared the adjustment of children raised in lesbian households and children raised in heterosexual households. These studies show that the children are similar in characteristics such as intelligence, development, self-esteem, psychological well-being, and popularity (Patterson & Chan, 1999; Savin-Williams & Esterberg, 2000; Stacey & Biblarz, 2001). A representative study compared young adults who had been reared as children by either lesbians or heterosexual women. The two groups of young adults were similar in measures of psychological health and feelings about their families (Tasker & Golombok, 1995).

Other research compares the parenting styles of lesbian mothers and heterosexual mothers. The two groups are similar in characteristics such as their enthusiasm about child rearing and their warmth toward children (Patterson, 1998).

My students often ask whether children raised by lesbians have trouble being accepted by the wider community, especially because of the problem of sexual prejudice. Although some children feel uncomfortable talking about their mothers' sexual orientation, most are positive about their mothers' nontraditional relationships (S. M. Johnson & O'Connor, 2001; Patterson & Chan, 1999; Tasker & Golombok, 1997). For example, Katrina is the 17-year-old daughter of a woman who is both a lesbian and a feminist. Katrina points out the advantages she has experienced:

> Having a lesbian mother has enabled me to have a head start on everybody else emotionally, psychologically, intellectually, in every way. I wouldn't know the things that I know, wouldn't be the person I am now, and I wouldn't be as assertive as I am now if I hadn't been brought up by a lesbian mother. My mom has drilled it into me since I was small, that you stand up for yourself, you say what you want, and you don't let any man tell you what to say or do. (Saffron, 1998, p. 36)

As we have seen, the research confirms that children raised by lesbians are well adjusted and that they do not differ substantially from children raised by heterosexuals. In light of these findings, professional organizations have emphasized that the courts should not discriminate against lesbian mothers in custody cases and that lesbians should be allowed to adopt children (e.g., American Academy of Pediatrics, 2002a, 2002b; American Psychological Association, 1995).

Postpartum Disturbances

As we noted earlier, the stereotype about motherhood portrays the new mother as being delighted with both her young infant and her maternal state. Unfortunately, a significant number of women develop psychological disturbances during the **postpartum period,** the 4 to 6 weeks after birth. Take a moment to glance back over the list of nine negative factors on pages 334–336. Imagine that you are a new mother who is exhausted from childbirth and that you are experiencing most of these factors. Also, suppose that your infant is not yet old enough to smile delightfully. Under these stressful circumstances, you can easily imagine how emotional problems could arise (O'Hara et al., 2000).

Two different kinds of postpartum problems occur relatively often. The most common kind of problem is called **postpartum blues** or **maternity blues,** a short-lasting change in mood that usually occurs during the first 10 days after childbirth. Roughly half of new mothers experience postpartum blues, and it is found in many different cultures (Gotlib, 1998; O'Hara & Stuart, 1999; G. E. Robinson & Stewart, 2001). Common symptoms include crying, sadness, insomnia, irritability, anxiety, and feeling overwhelmed (O'Hara & Stuart, 1999; Susman, 1996). Postpartum blues are probably a result of the emotional letdown following the excitement of childbirth, combined with the realistic life changes that a new baby brings (Brockington, 1996). Most women report that the symptoms are gone within a few days, but it is important for women to be well informed about this problem (G. E. Robinson & Stewart, 2001).

Postpartum depression (also called **postnatal depression**) is a more serious disorder, typically involving feelings of extreme sadness, fatigue, despair, loss of interest in enjoyable activities, and loss of interest in the baby. It affects about 10% to 15% of women who have given birth. Postpartum depression usually begins to develop within 6 months after childbirth, and it may last for many months (O'Hara & Stuart, 1999; G. E. Robinson & Stewart, 2001; Wessely, 1998). For example, a woman named Diana reported:

> When I came home from the hospital I had these strange feelings. I would be here during the day and would just vegetate and sometimes I would just lose control and weep. I felt like I didn't have a friend in the world. . . . I couldn't stop crying. (V. Taylor, 1996, p. 26)

Postpartum depression is similar to other kinds of depression that aren't associated with children. In fact, it may be the same as "regular" depression (O'Hara & Stuart, 1999; G. E. Robinson & Stewart, 2001); we'll explore depression in more detail in Chapter 12. As we'll also see in that chapter, most cases of depression can be successfully treated.

Social factors are also important, according to research in the United States, Canada, and Europe. For instance, women who experience major life stress during pregnancy are more likely to develop postpartum depression; as a result, low-income women are at risk (O'Hara & Stuart, 1999; G. E. Robinson & Stewart, 2001; Séguin et al., 1999). Women who lack social support from a partner, relatives, and friends are also likely to develop postpartum depression (G. E. Robinson & Stewart, 2001; Séguin et al., 1999; Wile & Arechigo, 1999). Interestingly, S. Stewart and Jambunathan (1996) found an unusually low rate of postpartum depression among Hmong women who had emigrated from Laos to a community in Wisconsin. They speculated that the psychological health of these women can be traced to the high levels of support they receive from their spouses and family members.

Professionals are beginning to explore the important benefits of social support in preventing postpartum depression. For example, Lavender and Walkinshaw (1998) conducted a well-controlled study with women who were predominantly European American. Half of the women who had just given birth received no special treatment, and half talked with a midwife who offered support and informal counseling. The midwives had no formal training in counseling, and the counseling session lasted between 30 minutes and 2 hours. Three weeks after giving birth, all women completed a standardized measure of depression. The results showed that 55% of the women in the control group received high scores on the depression scale, in contrast to only 9% in the group that had received counseling. If other research finds similar results, then a program of supportive counseling should be a standard procedure following childbirth.

The origins of both postpartum blues and postpartum depression are controversial. We noted that the levels of progesterone and estrogen drop sharply during the last stages of childbirth. The levels of other hormones also change during the weeks following childbirth. Women's popular magazines are likely to emphasize these hormonal factors as a cause of psychological disorders (R. Martinez et al., 2000). However, the relationship between hormonal levels and postpartum disorders is inconsistent and not very strong (V. Hendrick & Altshuler, 1999;

O'Hara & Stuart, 1999; G. E. Robinson & Stewart, 2001). As discussed earlier, however, we know that social factors do play an important role in postpartum disturbances.

Keep in mind that many women do not experience either the blues or depression following the birth of their baby. Earlier in this chapter, we noted that some women experience little discomfort and few psychological problems during pregnancy. In Chapter 4, we pointed out that many women do not have major premenstrual or menstrual symptoms, and we'll see in Chapter 14 that most women pass through menopause without any trauma. In short, women differ widely from one another. The various phases in a woman's reproductive life do not inevitably bring emotional or physical problems.

Breast Feeding

Currently, about 60% of North American mothers breast-feed their newborn infants, and 15% nurse their babies for a whole year (G. E. Robinson & Stewart, 2001; Schafer et al., 1998; Springen, 1998). Mothers who breast-feed are likely to be better educated and to have higher family incomes than mothers who bottle-feed (Humphreys et al., 1998; Schafer et al., 1998). Mothers who are in their twenties or older are also more likely than teenagers to breast-feed (Ineichen et al., 1997). European American and Latina women are more likely than Black mothers to breast-feed their infants (Humphreys et al., 1998). As you might expect, women are more likely to nurse successfully if their friends and the hospital staff members are supportive and encouraging (Humphreys et al., 1998; Tarkka et al., 1998).

Some health care workers have devised programs to encourage mothers to breast-feed. For instance, researchers in Brazil found that mothers who had seen a video about breast feeding were more likely than mothers in a control group to breast-feed until their infants were at least 6 months old (Susin et al., 1999). In other research, low-income mothers were more likely to breast-feed if they had received guidance from women who had successfully breast-fed their own infants (e.g., Ineichen et al., 1997; Schafer et al., 1998). For example, one Black woman described her feelings for her third child, whom she had breast-fed with the help of a counselor:

> Yes, I love all my children and I'm close to them, but there's something special with me and him. It's like he's part of me, and he's still a part of me. I have what he needs. I give it to him, nobody makes it for me. I give it to him. I'm the reason that he's healthy. (Locklin & Naber, 1993, p. 33)

As this mother's remarks suggest, mothers who breast-feed are likely to believe that breast feeding establishes a close bond between mother and baby. They are also pleased that they can satisfy their infant's nutritional needs. These mothers typically report that nursing is a pleasant experience of warmth, sharing, and openness (Lawrence, 1998). In contrast, mothers who bottle-feed their babies are more likely to emphasize that bottle feeding is convenient and trouble free.

The research demonstrates that human milk is better for human infants than is a formula based on cow's milk. After all, evolution has encouraged the development of a liquid that is ideally designed for efficient digestion. Breast milk also protects against allergies, diarrhea, infections, and other diseases (L. L. Alexander et al., 2001; American Academy of Pediatrics, 2001; Lawrence & Lawrence, 1998). Breast feeding also offers some health benefits for mothers, such as reducing the incidence of breast cancer and ovarian cancer (L. L. Alexander et al., 2001; Lawrence, 1998; Lawrence & Lawrence, 1998).

Because of the health benefits, health professionals should try to encourage breast feeding. This precaution is especially valid in developing countries where sanitary conditions make bottle feeding hazardous. However, the health professionals should not make mothers feel inadequate or guilty if they choose to bottle-feed their babies (Blum, 1999; Lawrence & Lawrence, 1998; Maushart, 1999). One researcher echoes our theme of individual differences:

> There is no doubt that, for many women, breast feeding does feel natural and joyous and "empowering." Yet, for [others], breast feeding feels more like hard work for which there is little apparent reward. (Maushart, 1999, p. 150)

Returning to the Workplace After Childbirth

As you might imagine, many mothers are concerned about returning to paid employment after childbirth. For example, Statistics Canada surveyed women who had been employed before the birth of a child. The results showed that 60% of these women returned to the workplace within 6 months after giving birth (Marshall, 1999). According to a U.S. survey, women return to work more quickly if their employers offer them guaranteed jobs after childbirth and if the women have relatively nontraditional attitudes toward parenting (Lyness et al., 1999).

We have seen abundant evidence for Theme 4 throughout this chapter: Throughout pregnancy, childbirth, and motherhood, women differ widely from one another. A major study by Marjorie H. Klein and her colleagues (1998) underscores the importance of individual differences. These researchers surveyed 570 women in 2 Midwestern cities; each woman had recently given birth. Overall, they found that the length of the women's maternity leave—before returning to work—was not correlated with several mental health measures, specifically, depression, anxiety, anger, and self-esteem. However, the researchers conducted a separate analysis for women who considered their employment an important part of their identity. For these women, a longer maternity leave was associated with a *higher* score on the depression measure. For some women, staying home with a baby on an extended maternity leave may actually be harmful if the women really value their work role.

In another part of the same study, M. H. Klein and her colleagues (1998) compared the mental health of three groups of women: homemakers, women employed part time, and women employed full time. One year after childbirth, these three groups of women did not differ on measures of depression, anxiety, anger, or self-esteem. We saw in Chapter 7 that children do not experience problems if they are cared for by someone other than their mother. Similarly, mothers who choose to return to the workplace are no more likely than other mothers to experience mental health problems. In fact, women who are engaged in more than one role (e.g., mother and employee) often have better physical and psychological health than women who have only one role (Barnett & Hyde, 2001).

Deciding Whether to Have Children

As recently as 30 years ago, most married women did not need to make a conscious decision about whether to have a child. Almost all married women who were physically capable of having children did so, with little awareness that they really had a choice. However, attitudes have changed. In the United States, for example, about 20% of women will never have children (Coltrane, 1998). Some of these women may choose not to have children because they are unmarried. Other women may not have children because they, or their partners, are infertile.

In any event, we need to discuss the substantial number of women who prefer not to have children. Let's consider how these "child-free" women are viewed by others. We'll also explore some advantages and disadvantages of deciding not to have children.

Attitudes Toward Women Choosing Not to Have Children.   Many people believe that all women should have children, a viewpoint called **compulsory motherhood** (Coltrane, 1998). A few decades ago, a young woman who did not plan to have children would have been viewed quite negatively. Attitudes toward child-free women are still somewhat negative (Caplan, 2001; Mueller & Yoder, 1999). For example, Demonstration 10.4 is a modified version of a scenario tested by Karla Mueller and Janice Yoder (1997). These researchers found statistically significant differences in the ratings of the women in the two scenarios on all three dimensions included in the demonstration. Table 10.1 shows their results, based on college students in Wisconsin. I suspect that the ratings for the child-free woman would be somewhat more negative in a more general population that includes nonstudents.

Married couples report that they receive advice about the ideal family size from many different people, including their parents, friends, and acquaintances. Couples seem to face a no-win situation (Casey, 1998; Mueller & Yoder, 1999). Child-free couples are informed that they are self-centered and too career oriented. Couples with one child are asked, "Wouldn't your child like a little brother or sister?" Couples with four or more children are told that they cannot give as much attention to their children. Notice, then, that our culture seems to admire only a narrow range of options. A couple may have two or three children; they will be criticized for fewer than two or more than three. Interestingly, however, Mueller and Yoder (1999) found that family size was not correlated with the couples' actual satisfaction. In other words, those with no children were just as happy as those with one, two, three, or more children.

Advantages and Disadvantages of Being Child-Free.   Couples provide many reasons for not wanting to have a child (Casey, 1998; Groat et al., 1997; Ireland, 1993; Megan, 2000):

DEMONSTRATION 10.4 ■ ■ ■ ■ ■ ■ ■ ■ ■ ■ ■ ■ ■ ■ ■ ■ ■ ■

Attitudes Toward Child-Free Women

For this demonstration, you will need some volunteers, ideally, at least five persons for each of the two scenarios described. Read the following paragraph aloud to half of the volunteers, either individually or in a group.

> Kathy and Tom are an attractive couple in their mid-forties. They will be celebrating their twentieth wedding anniversary next year. They met in college and were married the summer after they received their undergraduate degrees. Tom is now a very successful attorney. Kathy, who earned her Ph.D. in social psychology, is a full-time professor at the university. Kathy and Tom have no children. They are completely satisfied with their present family size, because they planned to have no children even before they were married. Because both have nearby relatives, they often have family get-togethers. Kathy and Tom also enjoy many activities and hobbies. Some of their favorites are biking, gardening, and taking small excursions to explore nearby towns and cities.

After reading this paragraph, pass out copies of the rating sheet below and ask volunteers to rate their impression of Kathy.

Follow the same procedure for the other half of the volunteers. However, for the sentence "Kathy and Tom have no children" and the following sentence, substitute this passage: "Kathy and Tom have two children. They are completely satisfied with their present family size, because they planned to have two children even before they were married."

Compare the average responses of the two groups. Is Kathy considered to be more fulfilled if she is described as having two children? Does she have a happier and more rewarding life?

1	2	3	4	5
less fulfilled				more fulfilled

1	2	3	4	5
very unhappy				very happy

1	2	3	4	5
unrewarding life				rewarding life

Source: From Mueller, K. A., & Yoder, J. D. (1997). Gendered norms for family size, employment, and occupation: Are there personal costs for violating them? *Sex Roles, 36,* 211. Reprinted by permission of Kluwer.

1. Parenthood is an irrevocable decision; you can't take children back to the store for a refund.
2. People can spend time with other people's children and be responsible to society, even if they don't have children of their own.

TABLE 10.1 ■ Ratings of a Child-Free Woman and a Woman with Two Children, on Three Different Characteristics

Characteristic	Rating of Woman in Scenario	
	Child-Free Woman	Woman with Two Children
Fulfillment	4.0	4.4
Happiness	3.5	4.3
Rewarding life	3.5	4.2

Note: 5 is the highest level of the attribute.

Source: From Mueller, K. A., & Yoder, J. D. (1997). Gendered norms for family size, employment, and occupation: Are there personal costs for violating them? *Sex Roles, 36,* 216. Reprinted by permission of Kluwer.

3. Raising a child can be extremely expensive, especially for children who will attend college.
4. Some women and men are afraid that they will not be good parents.
5. Some couples realize that they genuinely do not enjoy children.
6. Some couples are reluctant to give up a satisfying and flexible lifestyle for a more child-centered orientation.
7. Children can interfere with educational and vocational plans.
8. Some couples do not want to bring children into a world threatened by nuclear war, terrorism, and other serious global problems.

Still, people who are enthusiastic about parenthood provide many reasons for having children (C. P. Cowan & Cowan, 1992; Gormly et al., 1987; McMahon, 1995):

1. Parenthood is challenging; it offers people the opportunity to be creative and learn about their own potential.
2. Parenthood offers a relationship of love and nurturance with other human beings; children can enrich people's lives.
3. Parents have a unique chance to be responsible for someone's education and training; in raising a child, they can clarify their own values and instill them in their child.
4. Parents can watch their child grow into a socially responsible adult who can help the world become a better place.
5. Some people want to become parents in order to fulfill their relationship with their spouse and to become a "family."
6. Some people have children to "carry on the family line" or to ensure that some part of themselves continues into future generations.
7. Children can be a source of fun, pleasure, and pride.

Infertility

You may know a woman who has wanted to have children, but pregnancy does not seem to be a possibility. One such woman wrote:

How had having a baby, getting pregnant, become such an obsession with me? All I could think was that there must be a mechanism that clicks in once you try to get pregnant that, instead of allowing you to accept that you cannot, compels you to keep trying, no matter what the odds or cost. . . . I never would have suspected, until I tapped into it, just how powerful the desire could be. (Alden, 2000, p. 107)

By the current definition, **infertility** is the failure to conceive after 1 year of sexual intercourse without using contraception (L. L. Alexander et al., 2001; L. Pasch, 2001). About 16% of couples in the United States seek advice about infertility (Scott-Jones, 2001). Most cases of infertility can be traced to a biological cause rather than to a psychological explanation. Infertility is just as likely to be traceable to the male as to the female (L. Pasch, 2001; Scott-Jones, 2001).

Some women manage to reconcile their initial sadness. Consider the conclusion reached by the woman whose words you just read: "It came to me that it really was a choice between two good things—having a child and not having a child. Our life without a child seemed good to me. I caught a glimpse that it was what was right for us, for the best" (Alden, 2000, p. 111). Other women, who had looked forward to children as a central part of their married lives, experience stress and a real sense of loss. However, comparisons of fertile and infertile women show that the two groups do not differ in their marital satisfaction or self-esteem (L. A. Pasch & Dunkel-Schetter, 1997; Stanton & Danoff-Burg, 1995).

Still, the research does suggest that women who are infertile show higher levels of distress and anxiety than fertile women (L. L. Alexander et al., 2001; Stanton & Danoff-Burg, 1995). We need to emphasize an important point: According to theorists, the infertility causes the distress and anxiety. Distress and anxiety do *not* cause infertility. Also, individual differences in psychological reactions to infertility are substantial, consistent with Theme 4 of this book.

One source of psychological strain for a couple that is facing infertility is that they may live with the constant hope, "Maybe next month. . . ." They may see themselves as "not yet pregnant" rather than as permanently childless. As a result, they may feel unsettled, caught between hopefulness and mourning the child they will not have.

Women of color face an additional source of strain when they experience infertility. For example, Ceballo (1999) interviewed married African American women who had tried to become pregnant for many years. These women often struggled with racist health care providers who seemed astonished that a Black woman should be infertile. As these women explained, European Americans seem to believe that infertility is "a White thing," because they believe that Black women should be highly sexualized, promiscuous, and fertile. One woman pointed out how she began to internalize these racist messages; she almost believed that she was "the only Black woman walking the face of the earth that cannot have a baby." Unfortunately, psychologists know little about the impact of infertility on the lives of women of color (L. Pasch, 2001).

Many couples who are concerned about infertility decide to consult health care professionals for an "infertility workup," which includes a medical examination of both partners (L. A. Pasch & Dunkel-Schetter, 1997). About half of couples who seek medical treatment will eventually become parents. They will use one of a wide variety of reproductive technologies, which are often extremely expensive—and the cost is seldom covered by health insurance plans (Cooper & Glazer, 1998; Giudice, 1998).

However, many women will not become pregnant, even after medical treatment, or they may experience miscarriages. Eventually, some will choose to adopt. Others will decide to pursue other interests. A woman who might have focused on the regret of infertility in earlier eras can now shift her emphasis away from what is *not* in her life, so that she can fully appreciate the many positive options available in her future (Alden, 2000).

SECTION SUMMARY ▪

Motherhood

1. The stereotypes about motherhood reveal our ambivalence about mothers: Mothers are warm, nurturant, and happy—but also domineering.

2. Motherhood has a strong negative side, because mothers have more work than they expected; they may feel exhausted, physically uncomfortable, incompetent, unrewarded, isolated, deprived of other sources of identity, and disappointed by their failure to live up to the standards of the ideal mother. In addition, especially in developing countries, a substantial number of children die before their fifth birthday.

3. Motherhood also has a strong positive side; the benefits include a sense of their own strength, pleasurable interactions with the baby, and increased flexibility and empathy as well as abstract, intense joys.

4. Compared to White women, women of color may have different motherhood experiences. Black mothers have to combat the stereotypes of both the Black welfare mother and the Black superwoman; however, they often have the benefit of the extended family; Latinas must combat the values implied by *marianismo*; North American Indians may emphasize the continuity of motherhood; Asian women who have emigrated to the United States may encounter conflicts between their cultural beliefs and U.S. medical practice.

5. Research on lesbian mothers reveals that they do not differ from heterosexual mothers in their parenting skills or the adjustment of their children.

6. About half of new mothers experience the short-lasting depression called postpartum blues; between 10% and 15% experience the more severe postpartum depression.

7. Breast feeding provides benefits for mother-infant bonding as well as for the health of both the infant and the mother.

8. The psychological well-being of mothers of infants is similar for homemakers, women employed part time, and women employed full time; those with multiple roles may even experience benefits to their physical and psychological health.

9. At present, attitudes toward child-free women are somewhat negative; attitudes toward women with large families are also somewhat negative.

10. Child-free couples say that the disadvantages of parenthood include the irrevocability of the decision to have a child, the expense, and the interference with lifestyle and work.

11. Couples who want to have children cite advantages such as the challenge of parenthood, the opportunity to educate children, and the pleasurable aspects of children.

12. Women who are infertile are similar to women with children in terms of their marital satisfaction and self-esteem, but they may be more anxious; many women manage to refocus their lives when infertility seems likely.

▪▪▪▪▪▪▪ CHAPTER REVIEW QUESTIONS ▪▪▪▪▪▪▪

1. At the beginning of the chapter, we emphasized that pregnancy and childbirth are ignored topics, particularly compared to topics such as love and sex. Based on the information in this textbook, why do you think that these topics have such low visibility?

2. This chapter emphasizes ambivalent feelings and thoughts more than any other chapter in the book. Address the issue of ambivalence with respect to six topics: (a) emotional reactions to pregnancy, (b) emotional reactions to childbirth, (c) the reality of motherhood, (d) the decision to have children, (e) returning to the workplace after childbirth, and (f) reactions to infertility.

3. How do people react to pregnant women? How might these reactions contribute to women's emotional responses to pregnancy?

4. Contrast the high-tech approach to childbirth with the family-centered approach. Which of these characteristics would be likely to make women feel more in control of their experience during childbirth?

5. One of the themes of this book has been that stereotypes and reality about women do not always coincide. Address this issue with respect to some of the problems of motherhood.

6. In the chapter on women and work (Chapter 7), we discussed Francine Deutsch's (1999) research on families in which the mother and father take almost equal responsibility for child care. Obviously, men cannot experience pregnancy or childbirth. However, based on the information in this chapter, describe how an ideal father would offer the best possible support during pregnancy and childbirth. What would this father do, once the baby is born, so that the mother's postpartum period is as positive as possible?

7. What are the stereotypes about women of color who are mothers, and how is reality different from these stereotypes? What are the stereotypes and the reality for lesbian mothers?

8. Childbirth educators have made impressive changes in the way childbirth is now approached. However, the stresses of motherhood remain. Imagine that our society valued motherhood enough to fund programs aimed at decreasing the difficulties experienced during the early weeks after a baby is born. First, review those sources of stress. Then describe an ideal program that would include education, assistance, and social support.

9. Psychologists have conducted less research on pregnancy, childbirth, and motherhood than on any other topic in this book. Review this chapter, and suggest possible research projects that could clarify how women experience these three important events in their lives.

10. As we pointed out in this chapter, women in their childbearing years face a no-win situation with respect to decisions about childbearing and employment. Consider the options for three categories of women: (a) married, (b) lesbian, and (c) single. What kinds of prejudices would be aimed at each category of women (e.g., a lesbian who decides to have children and to be employed full-time)? Can any of these women win the complete approval of society?

NEW TERMS

*placenta (322)
*trimester (323)
*cesarean section (C-section) (330)
*prepared childbirth (331)
  family-centered approach (331)
  infant mortality rate (336)
*marianismo (338)

*postpartum period (340)
*postpartum blues (340)
*maternity blues (340)
*postpartum depression (341)
*postnatal depression (341)
*compulsory motherhood (344)
*infertility (347)

 The terms asterisked in the New Terms section serve as good search terms for InfoTrac College Edition. Go to http://infotrac.thomsonlearning.com and try these added search terms.

RECOMMENDED READINGS

Birth: Issues in Perinatal Care. This quarterly journal provides an interdisciplinary perspective on topics that psychologists have generally ignored. The articles examine women's experiences during pregnancy, childbirth, and the postpartum period; they also discuss innovative childbirth programs.

Casey, T. (1998). *Pride and joy: The lives and passions of women without children.* Hillsboro, OR: Beyond Words Publishing. Terri Casey interviewed 25 women who had decided not to have children. These women represent different ethnicities, ages, and professions; readers will appreciate the creative ways in which the women lead fulfilling lives.

Lerner, H. (1998). *The mother dance: How children change your life.* New York: HarperCollins. Harriet Lerner is a well-known feminist psychotherapist; her book describes her personal experiences with motherhood and perspectives on childbirth, stereotypes about mothers, and parenting.

Villani, S. L. (1997). *Motherhood at the crossroads: Meeting the challenge of a changing role.* New York: Plenum Press. This wonderful book examines the myths of motherhood, the frustrations experienced by mothers, and the ways that women resolve their conflicts about motherhood.

Wolf, N. (2001). *Misconceptions.* New York: Doubleday. Naomi Wolf is the author of *The Beauty Myth,* a feminist book about women and attractiveness. This current book traces her personal journey through pregnancy, childbirth, and motherhood. Although the book overemphasizes hormonal factors, it provides interesting insights into the difficulties women face in this important time in their lives.

ANSWERS TO THE DEMONSTRATIONS

Demonstration 10.3:   *Note:* The name of each country is followed by its rank and, in parentheses, its neonatal mortality rate (the number of infant deaths during one year per 1,000 live births). Australia, 7 (5.6); Cuba, 9 (6.4); Denmark, 3 (4.2); France, 4 (4.4); Germany, 5 (4.5); Greece, 6 (5.5); Israel, 8 (5.8); Japan, 1 (3.2); Sweden, 2 (3.4), United States, 10 (7.1).

ANSWERS TO THE TRUE-FALSE QUESTIONS

1. True (p. 322); 2. True (p. 323); 3. True (p. 324); 4. False (p. 327); 5. True (p. 330); 6. False (p. 331); 7. False (pp. 334–336); 8. True (p. 339); 9. True (p. 340); 10. False (p. 344).

Women and Physical Health

C. Darren Modricker/Corbis

T R U E   O R   F A L S E ?

_____ 1. Because women often have unique health problems, medical researchers are more likely to study females than males.

_____ 2. Recent research suggests that men and women are treated similarly with respect to major health problems such as heart disease.

_____ 3. The media have publicized the problem of female genital mutilation for young girls in Africa, the Middle East, and Asia; however, recent investigations have determined that only about 5,000 to 7,000 girls have been hurt by this ceremonial procedure.

_____ 4. When we consider U.S. residents who are in the upper income brackets, White women, White men, Black women, and Black men have fairly similar life expectancies.

_____ 5. Women in the United States are about 10 times more likely to die from heart disease than from breast cancer.

_____ 6. About 20% of U.S. and Canadian women have some form of disability.

_____ 7. A woman who has sex with an HIV-positive man is much more likely to become infected than a man who has sex with an HIV-positive woman.

_____ 8. Aside from AIDS, the other sexually transmitted diseases may be annoying and painful, but they cause no permanent health problems.

_____ 9. In the United States, cigarette smoking is the most common preventable cause of death.

_____ 10. Black women are less likely than White women to smoke cigarettes and to try illegal drugs at some point in their lives.

Sarah is an African American woman who was 70 years old when she was initially diagnosed with breast cancer. In an interview, she talks about her experience with chemotherapy and her doctor's report, four years later, that she is free of cancer. She tells us that her thoughts about cancer still persist: "It's just there, and I can't get it out of my brain, and it's just something that I've just learned to live with. It's just like sometime you wished you could just put your brain under a faucet and just wash the kinks out because it's just sticking there" (Rosenbaum & Roos, 2000, p. 160).

Dr. Susie Kisber is a feminist psychologist who has a neurological disability and a kind of arthritis that requires her to use an electric wheelchair. Dr. Kisber works as a psychotherapist, and she describes a conversation she had with her supervisor. Dr. Kisber had mentioned a client's reaction to her disability, and the supervisor responded, "Well, she probably doesn't even think of you as disabled. I often don't see your chair when I'm talking to you because you are so competent and professional." Dr. Kisber explained, "While I knew he was trying to reassure me and validate my skills, I heard him meaning either 'really disabled people can't or don't work' or 'You're not like _those_ disabled people.

You're just like me. I understand and identify with your experience'" (Kisber, 2001, p. 5).

Both of these women's concerns are included in our chapter on women and physical health, together with information about women's health status, sexually transmitted diseases, and substance abuse. These topics are part of **health psychology,** a field of psychology that looks at the causes of illness, the treatment of illness, illness prevention, and health improvement (Brannon & Feist, 2000; Sarafino, 2002). Why should women's health problems require special attention in a psychology course? In this chapter, we will emphasize three major reasons that health issues are related to the psychology of women and gender.

1. *Gender makes a difference in the kinds of illness that people experience.* One theme of this book is that psychological gender differences are typically small. However, several *biological* gender differences have important consequences for women's health. Some consequences are obvious. For example, women may be diagnosed with cancer of the ovaries and the uterus, but they do not need to worry about developing prostate cancer.

Some consequences are more subtle. For example, the female body has more fat and less fluid than the male body. This gender difference has important consequences for alcohol metabolism. Specifically, women's bodies have less fluid in which the alcohol can be distributed. So, even if a man and a woman weigh the same and consume the same amount of alcohol, the woman will end up with a higher level of alcohol in her blood (J. A. Hamilton & Yonkers, 1996; Haseltine, 1997).

2. *Gender makes a difference in the way a disease is diagnosed and treated.* For example, we'll see that men are more likely than women to be treated for certain heart problems, consistent with Theme 2 of this book. Also, health care providers consider the normative or standard disease symptoms to be those found in males (Benrud & Reddy, 1998). In contrast, the same disease may cause a different set of symptoms in females. For example, AIDS can affect a woman's reproductive system. Ironically, women's disease symptoms are often considered deviations from the norm, consistent with our discussion of the normative male, on page 39 (Porzelius, 2000; Stanton, 1995).

Gender also makes a difference in the way certain diseases are viewed. For example, researchers in previous decades rarely studied osteoporosis, a bone disease found predominantly in women. As Theme 3 emphasizes, topics important to women are often invisible.

However, one cluster of women's health problems *has* received abundant attention: women's reproductive systems (N. G. Johnson, 2001; Stanton, 1995). A physician in the late 1800s captured this perspective: "Woman is a pair of ovaries with a human being attached, where man is a human being furnished with a pair of testes" (cited by Fausto-Sterling, 1985, p. 90).

3. *Illness is an important part of many women's experience.* A textbook on the psychology of women must explore both gender comparisons and the life experiences of women. Sadly, health problems are a major concern for many women, and they become an increasingly central force as women grow older. According to estimates, more than 80% of women who are 55 or older experience at least one chronic health problem (Meyerowitz & Weidner, 1998; Revenson, 2001).

In this chapter, we will explore several important components of women's physical health. In the first section, we examine how gender is related to both health care and health status. In the second section, we will emphasize the theme of variability among women, as we examine the lives of women with disabilities. In the last two sections, we will consider sexually transmitted diseases and substance abuse. The topics in this chapter may initially seem unrelated. However, they all focus on two central issues: How does gender influence people's physical health, and how are women's lives influenced by their health?

THE HEALTH CARE AND HEALTH STATUS OF WOMEN

Theme 2 of this book states that women are treated differently from men. The biases against women in the health care system provide still further evidence for that theme, both in North America and in developing countries. In this section, we will also examine gender comparisons in life expectancy and in general health as well as several diseases that have an important impact on women's lives.

Biases Against Women

The medical profession has consistently been biased against women. Both women physicians and women patients have often been mistreated. A fascinating book by Mary Roth Walsh (1977) features a title based on a 1946 newspaper advertisement: "Doctors Wanted: No Women Need Apply." The book documents the long history of attempts to keep women out of medical schools and medical practice. Even in the current era, women are still underrepresented as chairpersons of academic departments in medical schools and in management positions in health care organizations (Ketenjian, 1999a; Robinson-Walker, 1999).

On the bright side, 48% of first-year U.S. medical students are now female, in contrast to only 9% in 1969 (Barzansky and Etzel, 2002; N. Eisenberg et al., 1989). Now that women constitute such a large percentage of medical students, discrimination will probably decrease.

Nevertheless, the medical profession and the health care system show several biases against women patients. As you read about these biases, keep in mind three cautions: (1) Not every doctor is biased against women, (2) not every female doctor is a feminist, and (3) some male doctors are feminists. What are the biases that operate in health care so that women patients often become second-class citizens?

1. *Women are often neglected in medicine and in medical research.* For example, one study analyzed all illustrations of men and women in medical textbooks, omitting those that focused on reproduction. Men were almost four times as likely as women to be pictured in these illustrations (Mendelsohn et al., 1994). In other words, the male body is normative, and it serves as the standard. With this perspective, medical experts often assume that research conducted on males can be extended to females (Rothbart, 1999).

Furthermore, health care providers' decisions about women's health may be based on research that did not include women. For instance, one major study found that drinking 3 cups of coffee a day did not have an effect on the incidence of heart attacks (T. Adler, 1990). However, the 45,589 participants in the study were all men! Women have been similarly ignored in research on heart disease and on AIDS (Landrine & Klonoff, 2001; Mann, 1999).

Fortunately, this neglect of women has outraged many health care consumers and some legislators. Medical educators are now encouraging medical schools to emphasize women's health as part of the regular curriculum (Porzelius, 2000; Wallis, 1998). Since the early 1990s, the U.S. National Institutes of Health and many other organizations require that funded research must include both women and members of ethnic minorities (N. G. Johnson, 2001; Ruksznis, 1998).

Some health care projects are specifically designed for women. For example, the Women's Health Initiative is currently studying health problems in older women, using a sample of 164,500 women over the age of 50 (Matthews et al., 1997). Thousands of women's health centers have also been established throughout North America ("Women's Health Centers," 1997).

None of these measures will immediately correct the centuries of neglect that health care professionals have shown toward women. However, women's health problems are now more visible. Health care is one area where feminist concerns have had a clear impact on women's lives.

2. *Gender stereotypes are common in medicine.* In Chapter 2, we introduced many of the popular beliefs about men and women. The medical profession remains attached to many of these stereotypes. For example, the advertisements in medical journals seldom show women in a work setting (J. W. Hawkins & Aber, 1993). In addition, many physicians do not consider women's complaints to be as serious as men's complaints. Physicians may believe that women are more emotional than men or that women will not be able to understand information about their medical problems (Chrisler, 2001). Gender stereotypes keep women from receiving appropriate medical treatment.

3. *Medical care provided to women is often irresponsible or inadequate.* Women are sometimes given too much health care, but sometimes they are given too little (Livingston, 1999). Specifically, some surgical procedures are performed too often. We saw in Chapter 10 that cesarean sections are performed too often during childbirth, and we'll see later in this section that hysterectomies are also more common than they need to be. As we noted earlier, women's reproductive systems are emphasized by the medical profession.

In contrast, when we consider diseases that affect both women and men, the women often receive too little health care. For example, women are less likely than men to receive diagnostic testing or surgical treatment for the same severity of coronary heart disease (Gan et al., 2000). The combination of "too much care" and "too little care" means that women often receive inappropriate treatment.

4. *Women are less likely than men in the United States to have adequate insurance.* Specifically, the current U.S. health care system offers the best health care to people who have private insurance provided by employers. Women are at a disadvantage, because they are less likely than men to be employed full time at the high-income jobs that offer the best health insurance benefits (Litt, 1998; S. Miles

& Parker, 1997). In contrast, women are more likely than men to have Medicaid insurance, which offers second-class benefits (Chrisler, 2001; Landrine & Klonoff, 2001). For example, a large-scale study showed that patients with heart disease were twice as likely to receive bypass surgery if they had private insurance rather than Medicaid (Travis et al., 1995). Women of color are especially likely to be second-class citizens with respect to health care (Landrine & Klonoff, 2001).

In summary, the economic inequities we saw in connection with women's employment have widespread consequences. Realistically, health insurance sometimes makes a difference between life and death.

5. *Physician-patient communication patterns often make women feel relatively powerless.* In Chapter 6, we saw that men often interrupt women in ordinary conversations. When the man is a physician and the woman is a patient in a medical setting, the man is even more powerful and the inequity is often worse (Porzelius, 2000; Roter & Hall, 1997). Here is a doctor's conversation with a patient who is nervous about the pain she had previously experienced with an intrauterine device (IUD):

Patient: It won't hurt, will it?

Doctor: Oh, I doubt it.

Patient: I'm taking your word [laugh].

Doctor: I haven't had anybody pass out from one yet.

Patient: The last time/

Doctor: [cuts patient off with a joke, both laugh]

Patient: The last time when I had that Lippes Loop, oh God/

Doctor: [interrupts patient] You won't even know what's going on, we'll just slip that in and you'll be so busy talking and you won't know it.

(A. D. Todd, 1989, p. 47)

By interrupting the patient twice, the doctor never learned that she was concerned about the pain that would persist after the IUD was in place, rather than the pain during insertion.

Physicians' conversational styles may prevent female patients from conveying information and may also impair women's sense of control (Muller, 1990; Porzelius, 2000). Fortunately, some research reports no gender biases in physicians' conversational style, especially when the physician is a woman (Roter & Hall, 1997). Whenever doctors interrupt their patients, they may miss information that would be useful for diagnosis and treatment. In addition, inattentive doctors may mistakenly conclude that a physical disorder is a psychiatric condition, "all in the patient's head" (Klonoff & Landrine, 1997; Litt, 1997).

Health Issues for Women in Developing Countries

In developing countries, women face even more severe biases than in North America. In fact, many women in other countries do not need to be concerned about biased treatment, because they will never even meet a physician, a nurse, or any person trained in health care. When resources are scarce, females are especially likely to suffer. Data gathered in Asia, Africa, and the Middle East demonstrate that parents are significantly more likely to seek medical care for a son than for a daughter. For example, boys in India are more than twice as likely as girls to receive medical treatment (Landrine & Klonoff, 2001). Unfortunately, about two-thirds of the women throughout the world live in poverty (Hunter College Women's Studies Collective, 1995). In many developing countries, only the wealthiest females have access to medical care.

Because women in developing countries usually have inadequate nutrition and health care, they face a relatively high chance of dying as a result of pregnancy or childbirth. For example, a woman living in either Mali or Sierra Leone—two countries in central Africa—stands a 1 in 10 chance of dying during pregnancy or childbirth (United Nations, 2000). The comparable figure for the United States is 1 in about 4,000; for Canada, it's 1 in about 9,000 (Neft & Levine, 1997).

One of the most widely discussed issues related to women's health in some developing countries is female genital mutilation. **Female genital mutilation** involves cutting or removing the female genitals. During this procedure, part or all of the clitoris is removed. In some cultures, the labia minora are also removed, and the labia majora are then stitched together. (See Chapter 9, Figure 9.1, for a review of female external sexual organs.) This more drastic procedure leaves only a tiny opening to allow both urine and menstrual blood to pass out of the body (Neft & Levine, 1997; Toubia, 1995; Whelehan, 2001).

The operation is extremely painful. It can also cause severe blood loss and infections (often leading to death), damage to other organs, and difficulty during childbirth (Neft & Levine, 1997; Thrupkaew, 1999).

Some people use the phrase *female circumcision* to refer to female genital mutilation. However, this term is misleading because it suggests a relatively minor operation similar to male circumcision (cutting off the foreskin from the tip of the penis, without damaging the penis). The male equivalent of the more drastic version of female genital mutilation would require removal of the entire penis and part of the skin surrounding the testicles (Toubia, 1995; Whelehan, 2001).

In about 40 countries throughout the world, more than 100 million girls and women have experienced genital mutilation (American Academy of Pediatrics, 1998; Whelehan, 2001). Most of these women live in Africa, but some live in the Middle East and Asia. Thousands of these women have emigrated to Canada, the United States, and Europe.

The operation is usually performed when the young girl is between the ages of 4 and puberty. The girl is typically held down by female relatives. Meanwhile, an older woman from the village performs the operation, often using an unsterilized razor blade, piece of glass, or sharp rock. According to people in cultures that practice female genital mutilation, this procedure makes the genitals cleaner (Al-Krenawi & Wiesel-Lev, 1999; Neft & Levine, 1997). People also believe that the operation reduces sexual activity outside marriage. Indeed, women's sexual pleasure will be reduced because the clitoris has been removed (Al-Krenawi & Wiesel-Lev, 1999; Neft & Levine, 1997; Thrupkaew, 1999).

The World Health Organization and other prominent health groups have condemned the practice of female genital mutilation. The problem has received worldwide attention, and some countries have banned genital mutilation. Other countries have reduced the percentage of females who experience the procedure, using culturally sensitive educational techniques (El-Bushra, 2000; Thrupkaew, 1999; United Nations, 1999).

Gender Comparisons in Life Expectancy

Let's now shift our focus to a more general question: What is the life expectancy for women and for men? In Canada, the current average life expectancy is 83 years for women and 73 years for men. The comparable figures in the United States are 80 years for women and 73 years for men (Landrine & Klonoff, 1997). In the United States, this gender gap in life expectancy is found in European Americans, Latinas/os, Blacks, Asians, and Native Americans (Costello & Stone, 2001). Furthermore, the gender gap is found in virtually every country in the world, despite the substantial health problems women experience in developing countries.

Social class has a powerful effect on **mortality,** or the death rate. For example, Figure 11.1 shows the likelihood of dying in any given year for both males and females, who are either White or Black, in the United States (Pappas et al., 1993). As you can see, males have higher mortality rates for both ethnic groups. However, at the upper income levels, mortality rates are similar for both genders and both ethnic groups. At these income levels, individuals from all four categories are less likely to live in unsafe environments and to work at risky jobs; they also receive better health care (N. E. Adler & Coriell, 1997; N. E. Adler et al., 1994). These data on social class analyzed only White and Black individuals, and they were gathered about a decade ago. More recent data on social class and mortality would be useful, especially if they include all the major ethnic groups.

But *why* do women live longer? The answer includes both biological and social factors. For example, females' second X chromosome may protect them from some health problems (Landrine & Klonoff, 2001). Gender differences in activities and lifestyles are also likely. For example, men are more likely to die from suicide, homicide, and motor vehicle accidents. Also, more men than women are exposed to dangerous conditions at work, as is the case for coal miners and factory workers (Crose, 1997; Landrine & Klonoff, 2001). As we'll see later in the chapter, North American men are currently more likely to die of AIDS.

In both the United States and Canada, another factor that clearly contributes to women's longevity is that women visit their health care providers more often than men do (Chrisler, 2001; Porzelius, 2000; Statistics Canada, 2000). We saw in earlier chapters that women are somewhat more attuned to emotions and to problems in a relationship. Compared to men, women also may be more sensitive to internal signals that might foreshadow health problems (Chrisler, 2001; Porzelius, 2000). In contrast, the male gender role encourages men to be physically "tough," rarely complaining about minor symptoms. Women may consult physicians during the early stages of a disease, before it becomes fatal.

Gender Comparisons in Overall Health

We have seen that women have an advantage with respect to mortality, or death rate. However, women in both the United States and Canada have a disadvantage with respect to **morbidity,** which is defined as generalized poor health or

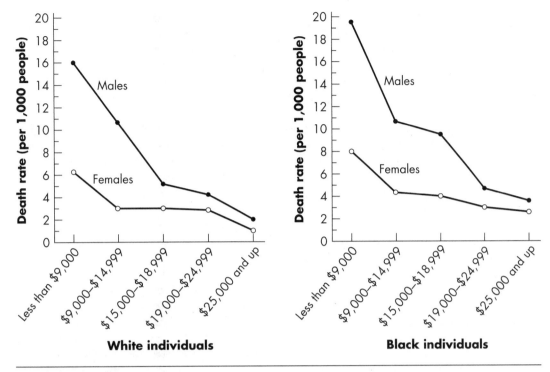

FIGURE 11.1 ■ Annual death rate for male and female Whites and Blacks, as a function of family income.

Source: Pappas et al. (1993).

illness. The research shows that women are more likely than men to have problems such as obesity, anemia, and respiratory illness. Women are also more likely to experience chronic or lifelong illnesses, headaches, and general fatigue (Chrisler, 2001; Furnham & Kirkcaldy, 1997; Statistics Canada, 2000).

Some of this gender difference is easy to explain: 80-year-old women are likely to have health problems related to their age, and most of the 80-year-old men have already died. Some of the difference can probably be traced to the fact that morbidity is usually assessed by self-report (Chrisler, 2001). A woman may be more likely than a man to report that she is bothered by her arthritis.

Some of women's health problems can also be traced to the fact that their incomes are lower than the incomes of men. At least in the United States, economically poor women receive inadequate health care. Economically poor women are also more likely to experience psychological stress, which can intensify the symptoms of many chronic illnesses (Chrisler, 2001). Other explanations for the gender differences in morbidity are not so obvious. For example, women are the primary victims of rape, and women who have been raped are very likely to experience health problems during the years following the attack (Foa, 1998). In addition, an estimated 1.8 million U.S. women each year are victims of abuse from a boyfriend, spouse, or domestic partner (Blumenthal, 1995). Elderly women are also more likely than elderly men to be victims of elder abuse (Whitbourne, 2001). In a variety of ways, then, women are more likely than men to experience illness and poor health.

Heart Disease, Breast Cancer, and Other Specific Health Problems

So far, we have seen that gender makes a difference for both mortality and morbidity. Women live longer, but they experience more illness during their lifetime. Let's now examine several specific diseases and health problems that are important in women's lives. The first problem, heart disease, affects women's lives because it is the most common cause of death, although it is also common in men. The other three problems—cancer of the reproductive system, breast cancer, and osteoporosis—are found either exclusively or more frequently in women. Therefore, these diseases need to be examined in our discussion of women's health.

Heart Disease. Heart disease, also known as **cardiovascular disease,** includes numerous disorders involving the heart and its blood vessels. Heart disease is the major cause of death for U.S. women; it is more deadly than all forms of cancer combined (Travis & Compton, 2001). Each year, heart disease kills about 500,000 women in the United States and about 27,000 women in Canada[1] (L. L. Alexander et al., 2001; Statistics Canada, 2000). Many people think that heart disease is a man's illness, but that myth is not correct. Men experience heart disease an average of 10 years earlier than women do, but women run the same risk by the time they reach 60 years of age (Chrisler, 2001; Woods & Jacobson, 1997). Black women face an especially high risk of heart disease. In fact, Black women are about 30% more likely than White women to die of heart disease (L. L. Alexander et al., 2001).

As we discussed at the beginning of this chapter, men are more likely than women to receive diagnostic testing or surgical treatment for heart disease (Gan et al., 2000). In cardiac rehabilitation programs, researchers are also much more likely to study men than women (Travis & Compton, 2001). As a result, we don't know much about how to prevent women from facing heart problems in the future.

What can people do to help prevent heart disease? Some precautions include a diet that is low in cholesterol and saturated fats, maintenance of a reasonable body weight, and regular exercise (Stampfer et al., 2000; Travis & Compton, 2001). As we'll discuss later in the chapter, women who smoke also run a high risk of heart disease (Stoney, 1998). In general, women who work outside the home are no more likely than other women to experience heart disease (Stoney, 1998).

---

[1] For comparison, it is helpful to know that the U.S. population is roughly nine times that of Canada. Notice that heart disease kills a higher proportion of women in the United States than in Canada.

Several years ago, postmenopausal women were advised to take hormone replacement therapy in order to reduce the likelihood of heart problems. However, we'll see in Chapter 14 that this treatment is no longer recommended. In any event, a sensible diet, exercise, and avoidance of smoking are obvious behavioral precautions that do not have any unfortunate side effects.

Breast Cancer.   At the beginning of this chapter, we noted that gender makes a difference in the way certain diseases are viewed. We've just seen that many people don't associate heart disease with women. The one disease in women that receives widespread publicity is breast cancer. In preparing this chapter, I located numerous recent books about women and breast cancer (e.g., Boehmer, 2000; Hoskins & Haber, 2001; Kasper & Ferguson, 2000; Keitel & Kopala, 2000; Potts, 2000). However, I couldn't find even one book about women and heart disease.

Breast cancer is certainly an important problem that requires extensive medical research, and we all know women who have struggled with this disease. Still, health psychologists are uncertain why both medical researchers and the general public focus on breast cancer more than on other illnesses that are actually more dangerous for women. One likely possibility is that our culture tends to think that breasts are an essential part of being a woman. As a result, a woman who has had a breast removed (or partly removed) is viewed as being less female (Chrisler, 2001; Meyerowitz & Hart, 1995; Saywell, 2000).

Approximately 180,000 women in the United States are diagnosed with breast cancer each year, and about 41,000 U.S. women will die from the disease (Rimer et al., 2001). Also, about 16,000 Canadian women will be diagnosed with breast cancer annually, and about 4,300 Canadian women will die from the disease (Statistics Canada, 2000). However, breast cancer is no longer the most deadly cancer for women. With the high rate of women smoking in the 1990s, it's no surprise that 46,000 U.S. women and 5,500 Canadian women die each year from lung cancer (Carlson et al., 1996; Statistics Canada, 2000).

Perhaps the most personally relevant statistic is that about 1 in 9 women in the United States and Canada will develop breast cancer during the course of her lifetime (K. Phillips et al., 1999; Wymelenberg, 2000). Before you read further, however, try Demonstration 11.1 on page 362.

Regular, systematic breast self-examination seems to be the most important strategy for detecting cancer. Early detection of breast cancer is important because the chances of a cure are very high if the disease is diagnosed at an early stage. If you are a woman who is over the age of 20, you should examine your breasts at least once a month (Keitel & Kopala, 2000). Women who are menstruating should examine their breasts about a week after their menstrual period is over, because breasts are likely to have normal lumps during menstruation. Figure 11.2 on page 363 provides instructions.

Breasts can also be examined using technological methods. For example, a **mammogram** is an X ray of the breast—a picture of breast tissue—taken while the breast tissue is flattened between two plastic plates (L. L. Alexander et al., 2001). Women over the age of 50 should have a screening mammogram every year or two to detect lumps that are too small to detect by self-examination.

DEMONSTRATION 11.1 ■ ■ ■ ■ ■ ■ ■ ■ ■ ■ ■ ■ ■ ■ ■ ■ ■ ■

Thinking About Breast Cancer

Think about and answer the following questions concerning breast cancer and its relevance in your life.

1. When was the last time you heard or saw a discussion of breast cancer? Was the discussion a general one, or did it provide specific information about how to conduct a breast self-examination or where to go for a mammogram?
2. Have you seen any notice about breast self-examination or mammograms (for example, in public buildings or at the student health service)?
3. If a woman in your home community wanted to have a mammogram, do you know where she would go? (If you don't, you can find a nearby location by calling the American Cancer Society at 800-227-2345 or by visiting their Web site at www.cancer.org to find a nearby location.)
4. Think about several women over the age of 50 whom you value. Have you ever discussed breast cancer or mammograms with them? If not, try to figure out how you might raise these issues with them soon, or identify another person who could make certain that these women have had a recent mammogram.

However, it's not yet clear whether women under the age of 50 would benefit from mammograms (Aiken et al., 2001).

Unfortunately, many women over the age of 50 do not have regular mammograms. Women of color have especially low rates for mammogram screening (Royak-Schaler et al., 1997). For example, only about 50% of Asian American women in one study reported having had a mammogram, in contrast to 70% of European American women (Helstrom et al., 1998). Asian American women may be less likely to have mammograms for several reasons. Many do not speak English or do not have health insurance that would cover the cost of the procedure. But perhaps the major reason is that many Asian American women are taught from an early age not to discuss topics related to sexuality, so breast cancer is an especially forbidden topic of conversation (Ketenjian, 1999b).

Latina women are also reluctant to seek mammograms or breast cancer screening by a health care provider. Researchers have discovered that many Latinas believe they do not need screening if they are currently feeling healthy. Many Latinas also believe that it would be indecent for a health care provider to see their unclothed breasts (Borrayo & Jenkins, 2001a, 2001b; Borrayo et al., 2001).

What happens if breast cancer is detected, either through breast self-examination or a screening mammogram? The most common procedure is currently a **lumpectomy,** a surgical procedure that removes the cancerous lump and

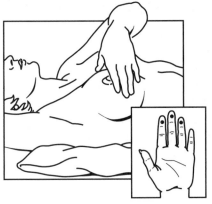

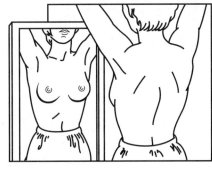

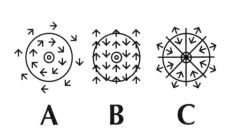

1. Lie down and put a pillow under your right shoulder. Place your right arm behind your head.

2. Use the finger pads of the three middle fingers on your left hand to feel for lumps or thickening. Your finger pads are the top third of each finger.

3. Press hard enough to know how your breast feels. If you're not sure how hard to press, ask your health care provider. Or try to copy the way your health care provider uses the finger pads during a breast exam. Learn what your breast feels like most of the time. A firm ridge in the lower curve of each breast is normal.

4. Move around the breast in a set way. You can choose either the circle (A), the up and down line (B), or the wedge (C). Do it the same way every time. It will help you to make sure that you've gone over the entire breast area, and to remember how your breast feels each month.

5. Now examine your left breast using right hand finger pads.

You might want to check your breasts while standing in front of a mirror right after you do your BSE each month. You might also want to do an extra BSE while you're in the shower. Your soapy hands will glide over the wet skin making it easy to check how your breasts feel.

FIGURE 11.2 ■ Performing a breast self-exam (BSE).

Source: American Cancer Society (2003).

the immediate surrounding breast tissue. Radiation therapy or chemotherapy might also be used (Wymelenberg, 2000).

Naturally, breast surgery and other forms of treatment cause some fear, grief, depression, and anger. As we noted earlier, women's breasts have special signifi- cance in our culture. The treatment cycle can also be both physically painful and difficult, and it is a socially lonely experience (Andersen & Farrar, 2001; Falco, 1998; Hoskins & Haber, 2001). As you might expect, women differ widely in their reactions to breast surgery (Rosenbaum & Roos, 2000; Yurek et al., 2000). In addition, women who have had breast surgery are likely to report major fluctua- tions in their emotions from day to day. For example, Kathlyn Conway (1997) described her reactions after surgery:

> Throughout January, I continue to fluctuate between normal life and desolation. Or perhaps, more accurately, I come to see that normal life holds happy days filled with family, work, and friends interspersed with days when I feel desolate and com- pletely fearful of illness and death. (p. 237)

Fortunately, most women cope well with the stress of surgery and the loss of breast tissue (Andersen & Farrar, 2001; Rowland, 1998). In one study of Black women who were only 2 months postsurgery, 62% reported that they were in very good spirits (Weaver, 1998).

Women often emphasize that the breast cancer experience forced them to clarify their values and to decide where to concentrate their future energies. For example, one woman reported after her surgery, "I'm going to be me. I'm not going to waste time by being someone other than my true self" (McCarthy & Loren, 1997, p. 195). Another commented on her personal transformation: "When you are diagnosed with breast cancer, you become an elder, no matter what your age. Through the events that occur, the decisions you make, the reevaluating and refocusing, you acquire wisdom and strength" (p. 195).

Reproductive System Cancer and Hysterectomies.   Several kinds of cancer often affect women's reproductive systems. These include **cervical cancer** (cancer of the cervix, which is the lower portion of the uterus) and cancer of the endome- trium. Turn back to Figure 4.1, on page 113, to see these structures.

In North America, the death rates from such diseases as cervical cancer are relatively low. A major reason is the effectiveness of a screening test called the Pap smear (Landrine & Klonoff, 2001). The **Pap smear test** involves taking a sample of cells from the cervix to see whether they are normal, precancerous, or cancerous (L. L. Alexander et al., 2001; Falco, 1998). When cervical cancer is detected early, it is highly curable (Burns, 2001; Rimer et al., 2001). Gynecologists recommend that all women who are sexually active or who have reached the age of 18 should have an annual Pap smear. This deadly disease is not limited to older women!

Most European American women have routine Pap smears, but millions of U.S. women without health insurance do not have this test on a regular basis (Landrine & Klonoff, 2001). Cancer of the cervix is much more deadly among women of color, who are less likely to have had this screening test (Helstrom et al., 1998; Rimer et al., 2001). Throughout the world, cancer of the cervix is one of the major causes of death, especially because women in developing countries do not have access to Pap smears (Cannistra & Niloff, 1996).

We noted at the beginning of the chapter that gender influences the way a disease is treated and that women's reproductive systems receive more attention than other health concerns. The best example of this principle is the high rate of hysterectomies in North America. A **hysterectomy** is the surgical removal of a woman's uterus (Hillard, 2001). Some hysterectomies are advisable, for example, when advanced cancer cannot be treated by more limited surgery. However, many surgeons remove a woman's uterus when other less drastic treatments would be effective. As a result, about one-third of all U.S. women can expect to have a hysterectomy at some point in their lifetime ("Alternatives to Hysterectomy," 2001). This rate is much higher than in other developed countries (Angier, 1999). Women need appropriate information about the alternatives before making decisions about whether they should have a hysterectomy.

Some hysterectomies are medically necessary. Also, some women who have had hysterectomies experience only minimal psychological or physical symptoms, consistent with our theme of individual differences (Hillard, 2001). However, the medical community needs to examine its policies on this widespread operation.

Another disorder of the reproductive system has not received the attention it deserves. Cancer of the ovaries has the highest rate of death of all gynecological cancers (L. L. Alexander et al., 2001; Burns, 2001). Unfortunately, no screening test for this disorder has yet been developed that is both reliable and valid. As a result, 80% of ovarian cancers are not discovered until they are in an advanced stage and the cancer has spread to other parts of the body (Falco, 1998). Although women's health issues now receive greater attention than in earlier decades, ovarian cancer is one major disease that requires much more research.

Osteoporosis. In the disorder called **osteoporosis** (pronounced oss-tee-owe-poe-*roe*-siss), the bones become increasingly porous and brittle. Women are twice as likely as men to develop this disorder (T. L. Johnson & Fee, 1997). Osteoporosis is common among older women, especially postmenopausal women. Osteoporosis makes fractures much more likely, even from just tripping and falling in the kitchen. Hip fractures resulting from osteoporosis create major problems, especially because they are likely to cause long-term disability (L. L. Alexander et al., 2001).

Because of the dangerous consequences of osteoporosis, women should be encouraged to do regular weight-bearing exercises, such as walking or jogging. Even young women should be certain to take adequate calcium and vitamin D to build strong bones, and then to continue this precaution throughout their lives (H. D. Nelson, 1998).

Some researchers recommend taking medicines (e.g., raloxifene) that are designed to prevent osteoporosis (L. L. Alexander et al., 2001; Hosking et al., 1998). Until recently, hormone replacement therapy was recommended for postmenopausal women (Delmas et al., 1997). We'll discuss the drawbacks of this approach in Chapter 14, in connection with menopause. Still, exercise and good nutrition are precautions that are easy to implement. They offer only advantages—and no drawbacks—in improving women's health.

SECTION SUMMARY ■

The Health Care and Health Status of Women

1. Health is a crucial issue for women for several reasons: (a) Women experience different illnesses than men, (b) gender influences the way a disease is treated, and (c) illness is an important factor in women's lives.

2. Biases against women include the neglect of women in medicine, the prevalence of gender stereotypes in medicine, inadequate or irresponsible medical care, inadequate health insurance, and problems in the physician-patient relationship.

3. Women in developing countries often experience inadequate nutrition and health care. Female genital mutilation jeopardizes the health of about 100 million girls and women.

4. Women in all ethnic groups live longer than men; the gender differences are especially large for low-income individuals. However, women report more health problems during their lives than men do, so women's morbidity is higher.

5. Heart disease is the most common cause of death in women; precautions such as proper diet and exercise are important.

6. In the United States, about 1 woman in 9 will develop breast cancer in her lifetime, but the chances for survival are high if the cancer is detected soon enough; most women cope remarkably well with breast cancer.

7. Pap smears are effective in detecting early uterine cancer; hysterectomies may be advisable in some cases, but many are performed without sufficient medical justification. Ovarian cancer is an especially deadly disease.

8. Osteoporosis often leads to bone fractures in postmenopausal women.

WOMEN WITH DISABILITIES

We have seen that gender influences people's health, with respect to both health care and specific diseases. Now let's consider how gender is relevant when we consider individuals with disabilities.

One important theme of this book is that women vary widely from one another. We have already examined some factors that create variability: ethnicity, country of residence, social class, sexual orientation, etc. Disability is an additional factor that creates variability. Another theme in this book is that women are relatively invisible. Unfortunately, feminist scholars have typically ignored the topic of women with disabilities; as a consequence, this topic is also relatively invisible (Asch et al., 2001; Bowleg, 1999).

Disability can be defined as a physical or mental impairment that limits a person's ability to perform an activity in the manner considered normal (Asch et al., 2001; Korol & Craig, 2001). In general, the term *person with a disability* is preferable to *disabled person* (Humes et al., 1995). *Person with a disability* emphasizes someone's individuality first and the disability second. In addition, *disability* is generally preferable to *handicap,* which is a more negative term (Wendell, 1997).

By some estimates, 21% of women in the United States and 16% of women in Canada have disabilities (Asch et al., 2001; Bergob, 1995). As you might expect, elderly women are especially likely to have a disability. For instance, consider Canadian women, age 65 and older, who live at home. An estimated 26% of these women live with a disability (Statistics Canada, 2000); the percentage would be still higher if women who live in a nursing home had been included in this statistic.

The variation within the disability category is tremendous. In fact, the term *women with disabilities* is simply a social construct that links together unrelated conditions. In reality, life experiences may be very different for a woman who is blind, a woman who is missing an arm, and a woman who is recovering from a stroke (Asch & Fine, 1992; Asch et al., 2001). Still, many people judge individuals with a disability primarily in terms of that disability. As Y. King (1997) remarked, the popular culture assumes that being disabled is what these individuals *do* and *are:* "She's the one in the wheelchair."

When we consider the topic of disabilities, we need to remind ourselves about a unity between women with disabilities and women without disabilities. Many people do not currently live with a disability. However, everyone could become disabled in a matter of seconds through an accident, a stroke, or a disease. As Lisa Bowleg (1999) pointed out, people who are not disabled should adopt the label "temporarily abled."

Theorists often note that women typically live on the margins of a world in which men occupy the central territory. In many ways, women with disabilities live on the margins of those margins. As a result, they may feel that the culture perceives them to be invisible (Bauer, 2001; Goldstein, 2001; Kisber, 2001). Women of color who have disabilities experience a triple threat, in which they constantly face sexism, racism, and **ableism** (discrimination on the basis of disability). As one woman pointed out, "I am Asian, disabled, and a woman. It's like a triangle. Depending on the issue, one side is up" (K. Martinez & O'Toole, 1991, p. 4).

But how are disabilities related to gender? Why would the life of a woman with a disability be different from the life of a man with a disability? We will see in the following discussions of work and social relationships that disabilities tend to exaggerate the extent to which women and men are treated differently.

Work Patterns of Women with Disabilities

From an early age, women with disabilities face barriers in preparing for a career. For example, many women recall being shortchanged during childhood. Maria, age 15, reported, "My brother has the same hearing problem as I do. Growing up, he was encouraged in school, sports, and to learn to work. I was protected and kept at home" (Asch & Fine, 1992, p. 146). As we discussed in Chapter 3, parents show some tendency to overprotect their daughters. They are even more likely to overprotect daughters with disabilities.

Women with disabilities must overcome additional barriers as they pursue an education. On college campuses, for example, they may be unable to find sign language interpreters, wheelchair-friendly sidewalks, and other support services (Holcomb & Giesen, 1995). These barriers often keep women with disabilities from pursuing further education (Bergob, 1995).

Currently, 28% of U.S. women with a disability are employed; the comparable figure for men is 32%. In other words, the employment rates for these two groups are similar (Asch et al., 2001). However, you'll notice that both genders are much less likely to be employed compared to people without disabilities.

Gender and disability combine in unique ways to form workplace barriers against women with disabilities. Consider Mary Runté, who is unable to use her hands. Her boss had not selected her for a project that interested her. (Only male employees had been selected.) She decided to tell her boss that her skills would be useful to the project team:

> "I don't know," he said, "it wouldn't be fair to the others on the team to have to compensate for you not being able to perform all the assigned tasks. Besides," he added, "it would be embarrassing for you to have to explain to these people that you can't write." . . . When I challenged this manager on the blatant fact that the only "task" I couldn't perform would be taking minutes, and that this task was only assigned to one group member, the recorder, he stated he had assumed this would be the role which the other team members would expect me to fill—"the guys hate taking notes."
>
> As I am a woman, it was assumed I would perform the stereotypical role of secretary if assigned to this team. . . . The glass ceiling for a disabled woman turns her office into a crawl space. (Runté, 1998, p. 102)

As you might imagine, women with disabilities often encounter economic difficulties. For example, women with disabilities have average incomes that are only half of the average income of men with disabilities (Holcomb & Giesen, 1995). Women with disabilities are also unlikely to receive adequate retirement benefits. As we noted at the beginning of this discussion, disabilities tend to exaggerate the differential treatment of women and men. Specifically, disabilities increase the male-female wage gap.

In Chapter 7, we discussed the dilemma faced by lesbians in the workplace: Should they come out of the closet and risk discrimination? Should they try to pass, even though this option requires them to hide an important part of their identity? Women with invisible disabilities face a similar dilemma (Asch et al., 2001). For instance, a woman with multiple sclerosis may not look disabled, but she may tire easily or experience numbness or memory problems. Should she tell her boss and risk patronizing comments or job discrimination? Or should she try to hide her disability, risking exhaustion or criticism for being lazy? In Chapter 7, we examined many biases that employed women face; these problems are intensified for women with disabilities.

Personal Relationships of Women with Disabilities

Throughout the book, we have emphasized how women are judged by their physical attractiveness. By the narrowly rigid standards of attractiveness in North America today, many women with disabilities may be viewed as unattractive (Wendell, 1997). As a consequence, they are likely to be excluded from the social world as well as from some aspects of the employment world (Asch et al., 2001; Rintala et al., 1997). Heterosexual women with disabilities are less likely to date and to marry. Even less is known about the love relationships of lesbian women with disabilities, but the research suggests that they also have limited romantic opportunities (Asch & Fine, 1992).

Ynestra King (1997) described an interesting example of this bias against women with disabilities, with respect to romantic relationships. When she is sitting down, her disability is invisible; when she stands up, it's obvious she has difficulty walking. She commented on the reactions in social settings:

> It is especially noticeable when another individual is flirting and flattering, and has an abrupt change in affect when I stand up. I always make sure that I walk around in front of someone before I accept a date, just to save face for both of us. Once the other person perceives the disability, the switch on the sexual circuit breaker often pops off—the connection is broken. "Chemistry" is over. I have a lifetime of such experiences, and so does every other disabled woman I know. (p. 107)

Many people consider women with disabilities to be asexual (Y. King, 1997). Many North Americans assume that people with physical disabilities are not interested in sex or not capable of engaging in sexual activity (Hyde & DeLamater, 2003). Women with disabilities often complain that they do not receive adequate counseling on sexuality (Asch et al., 2001).

Furthermore, women's own sexual desires are likely to be ignored. A woman who has a spinal disorder described a conversation she had with a gynecologist before her adolescence. She asked whether she would be able to have satisfying sexual relations with a man. He replied, "Don't worry, honey, your vagina will be tight enough to satisfy any man" (Asch et al., 2001, p. 350). Apparently, he did not even consider her own sexual satisfaction!

Nonromantic friendships are also difficult. For instance, women who have friends with disabilities will often avoid certain topics of discussion. These censored areas may include sexuality, dating, and childbearing. Some women with disabilities point out that their friends seem to avoid trying to understand what it's like to live with a disability (Wendell, 1997).

Throughout this book, we have examined how biases can have harmful effects for individuals in a less favored social group. In addition to women, we have seen how people may be mistreated on the basis of ethnic group and sexual orientation. As disability activists increase their publicity, we will become more informed about this additional kind of discrimination.

Women with Disabilities

1. Women with disabilities are diverse, yet they share similar discrimination in a society that is influenced by both sexism and ableism. Disabilities tend to exaggerate the differential treatment of women and men.

2. Women with disabilities may face barriers in education, discrimination on the job, and economic problems.

3. Women with invisible disabilities face a dilemma about whether to reveal their disabilities in the workplace.

4. Women with disabilities are often excluded from the social world of love relationships, sexuality, and friendships.

AIDS AND OTHER SEXUALLY TRANSMITTED DISEASES

Sexually transmitted diseases have major implications for women's health. For instance, thousands of women acquire AIDS each year from their sexual partners. In this section, we will emphasize AIDS. However, we will also briefly look at the consequences for women of five other sexually transmitted diseases: (1) chlamydia, (2) genital herpes, (3) genital warts, (4) gonorrhea, and (5) syphilis.

Women are increasingly at risk for AIDS and other sexually transmitted diseases. In fact, researchers use the phrase "the emerging female face" to characterize these illnesses (S. M. Harvey, 2001). In North America, about 20% of HIV-positive individuals are female. In other parts of the world, AIDS has an even more prevalent female face. In the African countries south of the Sahara desert, an average of 55% of HIV-positive individuals are female. In Botswana, for example, 36% of the entire population is HIV positive; literally hundreds of thousands of women and girls die of AIDS each year (Begley, 2001; "A Devastated Continent," 2000; United Nations, 2000).

Women are much more vulnerable to sexually transmitted diseases than men are. For example, a woman who has sexual intercourse with an HIV-infected man is *eight times* more likely to contract HIV, compared to a man who has sexual intercourse with an HIV-infected woman. One reason for this gender difference is that the concentrations of viruses and bacteria are much greater in semen than in vaginal fluids (Gutiérrez et al., 2000; Ickovics et al., 2001; Statistics Canada, 2000).

Background Information on AIDS

Acquired immunodeficiency syndrome, or **AIDS,** is a viral disease that is spread by infected blood, semen, or vaginal secretions; this disease destroys the body's normal immune system. As of December 2001, an estimated 468,000 U.S.

residents had died of AIDS (Centers for Disease Control, 2002). The outlook is even more grim when we consider the situation worldwide. Currently, an estimated 42 million people throughout the world are HIV positive (World Health Organization, 2002).

Figure 11.3 shows the increasing number of AIDS deaths among U.S. women since 1991. Ethnicity is also related to the likelihood of an AIDS diagnosis. In the United States, the incidence of AIDS is relatively high among Black women, somewhat lower among Latinas, and equally low among Asian American, Native American, and European American women (Wise et al., 2001). In Canada, Black women and Aboriginal (Canadian Indian) women have a higher incidence of AIDS than White or Asian women (Loppie & Gahagan, 2001; Ship & Norton, 2001).

Researchers are now using some culturally sensitive interviewing techniques to discover why ethnicity is related to the incidence of AIDS. For example, earlier research with Latinas showed that they are well informed about AIDS (Landrine, 1995a). So why should they be more likely than European American women to become infected? M. Arguello interviewed young, unmarried Latinas in Los Angeles (cited by Landrine, 1995b). She found that these young women, especially those who belonged to gangs, were engaging in anal intercourse so that they could still be considered virgins when they married several years later.

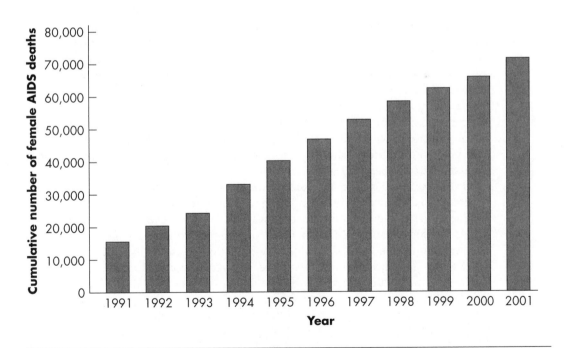

FIGURE 11.3 ■ Cumulative AIDS deaths among females of all ages and all ethnic groups in the United States, 1991–2001.

Source: Centers for Disease Control (2002).

Their Latino boyfriends demanded intercourse, yet Latino men also demand virgins when they marry. Latinas chose anal intercourse as a way to solve the dilemma. Also, the couples did not use condoms during anal intercourse, because condoms were perceived as a birth-control method, not a method for preventing AIDS. This research illustrates the importance of cultural context when we examine issues in the psychology of women.

Let's now consider the medical aspects of AIDS and how the disease is transmitted. Then we'll explore how women cope with AIDS and how the disease can be prevented.

Medical Aspects of AIDS

AIDS is caused by the **human immunodeficiency virus (HIV),** which has the potential to destroy part of the immune system. In particular, HIV invades white blood cells and reproduces itself. HIV then destroys those white blood cells—the very cells that coordinate the immune system's ability to fight infectious diseases (L. L. Alexander et al., 2001).

Many HIV-positive individuals have no symptoms at first, and so they do not realize that they are infected. Most then experience a symptom-free period—perhaps as long as 10 years. They then develop symptoms, such as swollen lymph glands, fatigue, unexplained fevers, weight loss, and diarrhea (L. L. Alexander et al., 2001). Both men and women may have these symptoms if they are HIV positive. However, health care providers are more likely to suspect AIDS in males with these symptoms, so men are more likely to receive early treatment. In addition, women who are HIV positive are likely to develop vaginal infections and cervical cancer. Because the medical community tends to operate from a male-as-normative model, these gynecological symptoms were not included in the original list of diagnostic signs of AIDS (Lorber, 1997; Porzelius, 2000). As a result, many women have not received early treatment.

People who are HIV positive are highly contagious during the initial stages of the infection, even if they have no symptoms (J. A. Kelly, 2001). As a result, HIV-positive individuals are likely to spread the disease to other people without realizing that they are doing so.

It may take as long as 10 years for an HIV infection to develop into AIDS. A diagnosis of AIDS is made when a person's immune level drops below a specified level. At this point, people are seriously ill because of the symptoms mentioned earlier and because other infections have taken advantage of a severely weakened immune system (J. Moore & Smith, 2001; Sarafino, 2002). In particular, women are likely to develop cancer and pneumonia (Carlson et al., 1996). These infections can be particularly deadly for people with AIDS, because their immune system no longer works properly.

New drug therapies have been developed that prolong life for HIV-positive people. However, low-income individuals often have no access to these expensive medications. As we saw in Figure 11.1, social class has an important effect on an individual's health. Research also suggests that women are less likely than men to use these medications, at least partly for financial reasons (J. Moore &

Smith, 2001). As you might suspect, these new drugs are seldom available to or affordable for people in developing countries with the highest rates of HIV infection (J. A. Kelly, 2001).

How AIDS Is Transmitted

Anyone who engages in risky behavior with an infected person can get AIDS. College students report in surveys that they believe they can judge which sexual partners look like they might have HIV infection (S. S. Williams et al., 1992). Unfortunately, *it is impossible to tell whether a person is infected.* Therefore, any contact with blood, semen, or vaginal secretions is potentially dangerous.

Most women are infected with HIV because they used injected drugs or because they had vaginal or anal intercourse with a man who is infected (Ickovics et al., 2001; Statistics Canada, 2000). An important observation is that heterosexual transmission of AIDS occurs much more often in women than in men. This trend is especially likely for Latina women. In fact, only 1% of Latino men in one sample acquired AIDS through heterosexual transmission, in contrast to 42% of Latina women (D. Castañeda, 2000a).

DEMONSTRATION 11.2 ■ ■ ■ ■ ■ ■ ■ ■ ■ ■ ■ ■ ■ ■ ■ ■ ■ ■ ■

Attitudes Toward Condom Use

Imagine a heterosexual woman between the ages of 18 and 35. She is sexually active, and she is not in a long-term relationship. Answer the following questions from the perspective of this woman:

1. How do you feel about condom use in general?
2. When was the last time that you had sexual intercourse?
3. Did you request that your sexual partner use a condom on that occasion?
4. How do you think that this sexual partner feels about using a condom?
5. Do you feel comfortable talking with your sexual partners about using condoms?
6. Do you typically carry a condom with you when you go out on a social occasion?
7. Where do you buy condoms?
8. Is it embarrassing for you to purchase condoms?
9. Suppose that you have been drinking and that you are about to have sexual intercourse. Would you remember to use a condom?
10. Suppose that your sexual partner says that he does not want to use a condom. What would you do?

Source: Based on Perloff (2001).

Gay and bisexual men who have had anal intercourse with men without condom protection are at high risk for becoming infected. However, women who have sex only with women and who do not use injected drugs are at relatively low risk for becoming infected (Dean et al., 2000; J. Moore & Smith, 2001).

Living with AIDS

As you might imagine, HIV-positive individuals are likely to experience depression, anxiety, anger, and fear (J. Moore & Smith, 2001; Porzelius, 2000). One woman living with AIDS described her emotions: "I think I live in a state of numb terror. I'm just scared witless" (Huston, 1997, p. 71).

Many women experience a new perspective on life that is both more hopeful and more tragic. Alicia McWilliams is 36, and she became HIV positive through unprotected sex. She commented:

> I enjoy the simple things in life. I can see the beauty in the sky and the trees. Sometimes I think, "When is my time going to come?" Especially when other people die. Last week I buried a friend. I let people know I'm afraid. Being sick is one of my greatest fears. I know this illness takes people out slow and painfully. (Huston, 1997, p. 17)

People living with AIDS often report that they are stunned by insensitive reactions from other people. For example, doctors may inform patients that they are HIV positive without providing any words of compassion (Gahagan & Loppie, 2001; Huston, 1997). Family members may show no sympathy. A 32-year-old Canadian woman was asked whether her family had been helpful. She replied, "Are you kidding, if I ask my family for help, they say stuff like you did this to yourself and now you want us to clean up after you? I don't talk to them anymore" (Gahagan & Loppie, 2001, p. 119).

However, some women are surprised by the messages of support. For example, Runions (1996) described how she had left a fundamentalist Christian church some years earlier, when her religious beliefs took her in a different direction. When she went public with her personal story about AIDS, many church members wrote to her. "The letters were warm and accepting and forgiving. Bridges that I thought had been damaged beyond repair appeared to have been strengthened by the shock of my illness" (p. 67).

Be sure you have tried Demonstration 11.2 before reading further. This demonstration assesses your attitudes toward using condoms.

Preventing AIDS

At present, we have no cure for AIDS, so the only available alternative is to prevent it. Unfortunately, as the rates of HIV infection rise, people in the United States are becoming less concerned about this health problem (Douglas, 2001). Furthermore, AIDS prevention is difficult, at both the individual and the global level (Dean et al., 2000). Studies also focus on middle-class European American college students rather than on populations at greater risk for HIV/AIDS (S. R.

Jenkins, 2000). Finally, studies usually examine urban populations, ignoring the substantial risk for HIV/AIDS in rural regions (D. Castañeda, 1999).

One problem with AIDS prevention is that most people think, "It can't happen to me!" (Perloff, 2001; Seppa, 1997). Many people also believe that you can eliminate the possibility of AIDS by asking a potential sexual partner about his or her HIV status. However, a study of HIV-positive individuals revealed that 40% of them had not disclosed their HIV status to their sexual partners (Stein et al., 1998). You can probably anticipate another problem. Many people are HIV positive and don't know it. So a woman may be having sex with a man who doesn't realize he is HIV positive or who may not realize that he had sex with an HIV-positive individual two months before. Basically, if a woman decides to have sex, her sexual partner is not only that individual but also all of that individual's former partners . . . and their partners!

Condoms can help to limit the spread of the AIDS epidemic (Jadack, 2001). However, surveys show that only 5% to 26% of women reported that they always used condoms during sexual intercourse (Morokoff, Mays, & Coons, 1997). In Demonstration 11.2, we noted some of the reasons that prevent people from consistently using condoms. In our culture, people are reluctant to discuss condom use with their potential sexual partners (Perloff, 2001).

An important problem with condom use is that women are told that they must protect themselves against AIDS when having intercourse, yet men are the ones who control whether they will use a condom. Power is not equally divided in most sexual relationships, and many women may not feel that they can safely insist that their partner wear a condom (Catania et al., 2001; Gutiérrez et al., 2000; S. R. Jenkins, 2000).

Even regular condom use does *not* guarantee protection against AIDS, because condoms can break or slip off. There is no perfectly safe sex, only *safer* sex. However, a condom is certainly better than no protection at all!

AIDS prevention at the national level must emphasize the use of condoms, even though their use cannot guarantee protection against AIDS. So far, the United States has lagged behind other industrialized countries in encouraging condom use and other AIDS-prevention programs (Hein, 1998).

Any AIDS prevention program must be sensitive to the culture of the individuals served by the program (Sikkema, 1998). For example, Latino men are especially likely to control decisions about condom use during intercourse. A program designed only for Latina women may therefore be unsuccessful (D. Castañeda, 2000a; Raffaelli & Suarez-Al-Adam, 1998). Most programs emphasize developing skills in problem solving and negotiation, as well as the details of condom use (Sikkema, 1998).

Other Sexually Transmitted Diseases

AIDS has attracted far more attention during the current era than all the other sexually transmitted diseases combined. These other diseases are especially important for the psychology of women, however, because women are more likely than men to be infected from a single sexual encounter. Studies in Canada, for example, show that young women are three to seven times more likely than young men to have chlamydia, gonorrhea, or syphilis (Statistics Canada, 2000). Sexually transmitted diseases also produce fewer detectable symptoms in women than in men (Jadack, 2001). In addition, women suffer the most severe long-term consequences of sexually transmitted diseases. For example, many women who do not seek early treatment for these diseases will become infertile, or they may pass the disease on to a newborn (L. L. Alexander et al., 2001; Jadack, 2001). Table 11.1 lists five of these diseases that have particularly important consequences for women's lives. They are **chlamydia** (pronounced klah-*mih*-dee-uh), **genital herpes** (*her*-peas), **genital warts**, **gonorrhea** (gon-uh-*ree*-uh), and **syphilis** (*siff*-ih-liss).

In the twenty-first century, women who are considering a sexual relationship need to worry not only about pregnancy but also about the very real threat of sexually transmitted diseases. Some of these diseases may simply be uncomfortable or painful. However, other diseases may cause recurrent health problems for a woman or potential danger to her infant. Most tragically, a sexual relationship with an individual who has a sexually transmitted disease might literally be deadly.

TABLE 11.1 ■ Sexually Transmitted Diseases (STDs) Other Than AIDS

Disease	Description (for Women)	Consequences
Chlamydia	Most common STD in the U.S.; often no symptoms, but sometimes painful urination and vaginal discharge occur; curable.	Can lead to infertility; can be passed on to newborn during delivery.
Genital herpes	Painful genital blisters, 5 to 9 attacks per year; can be treated but is not currently curable.	Can lead to cervical cancer, which may lead to death. Can be passed on to newborn during delivery.
Genital warts	Caused by the human papilloma virus; small, fleshy, often painless swellings in the genital area; common among college women; can be treated but is not currently curable.	Can lead to cervical cancer, which may lead to death.
Gonorrhea	May produce vaginal discharge and pelvic pain but may not have visible symptoms; usually curable.	Can lead to infertility. Newborns infected during birth may become blind.
Syphilis	Painless sores; may produce rash on the body, but may not have visible symptoms; curable.	Can be passed on to fetus prenatally and to newborn during delivery.

Sources: Based on L. L. Alexander et al. (2001), Cates and Berman (1999), and Jadack (2001).

SECTION SUMMARY ■

AIDS and Other Sexually Transmitted Diseases

1. Acquired immunodeficiency syndrome (AIDS) has killed hundreds of thousands of North Americans; the number of cases among women has risen dramatically in recent years. AIDS is widespread among women in sub-Saharan Africa.

2. AIDS is caused by the human immunodeficiency virus (HIV). People who are HIV positive may be very contagious; however, they may initially have no symptoms, so they often spread the disease.

3. Most women are infected with HIV because they used injected drugs or because they had vaginal or anal intercourse with an infected man.

4. People living with AIDS are likely to be depressed, anxious, angry, and fearful.

5. Currently, AIDS cannot be cured. Sexually active people should know that condoms do not offer complete protection; in addition, because of power inequities, women may feel they cannot safely insist that their partner wear a condom. AIDS prevention programs must be sensitive to the culture of the intended audience.

6. Other sexually transmitted diseases include chlamydia (which can cause infertility and can be passed on to a newborn), genital herpes (which is not curable and can be passed on to a newborn), genital warts (which can cause deadly cervical cancer), gonorrhea (which can lead to infertility), and syphilis (which can be passed on to a newborn).

WOMEN AND SUBSTANCE ABUSE

Substance abuse is an important topic in the psychology of women for the three reasons mentioned at the beginning of the chapter. First, the pattern of substance abuse is somewhat different for women and men, as we'll see shortly. Second, substance abuse is treated differently in men and women. For example, physicians seem to be less effective in identifying problems with alcohol and illegal drugs when the patient is a woman. In addition, the screening tests that are used to identify substance-abuse problems are based on male norms; the tests neglect common female risk factors, such as being a victim of sexual abuse (Wallen, 1998). The final reason that substance abuse is important is that these substances are a common cause of illness and death in women.

Smoking

Cigarette smoking is the largest preventable cause of death in the United States. About 140,000 American women die each year from diseases related to smoking (L. L. Alexander et al., 2001; Rimer et al., 2001). Lung cancer is the best advertised consequence of cigarette smoking. As we mentioned earlier, each year, about 46,000 U.S. women and 5,500 Canadian women die from lung cancer (Carlson et al., 1996; Statistics Canada, 2000). For reasons that are not clear, smoking increases the chance of lung cancer more for women than it does for men (Litt, 1997).

Women who smoke are also more likely than nonsmokers to die of emphysema and other lung diseases, heart disease, and strokes. Smoking also has gynecological consequences. Women who smoke run the risk of cervical cancer, infertility, miscarriages, premature birth, and early menopause (Porzelius, 2000; Rimer et al., 2001). Furthermore, babies born to smokers weigh less than babies born to nonsmokers (Litt, 1997). Older women who smoke also increase their chances of developing osteoporosis (Litt, 1997). You can see why some people say that the tobacco industry is the only business that kills its best customers!

Many nonsmoking women also suffer because of their husband's or partner's smoking habits. For example, women married to men who smoke are significantly more likely to develop lung cancer and heart disease than women married to nonsmokers (L. L. Alexander et al., 2001; Kawachi et al., 1997).

In the United States and Canada, about one-quarter of all females and one-quarter of all males are smokers (Rimer et al., 2001; Statistics Canada, 2000). Ethnicity has a major effect on smoking rates. According to one estimate, for example, the rates in the United States are 33% for Native Americans, 25% for White women, 22% for Black women, 15% for Latina women, and only 8% for Asian American women (Husten, 1998).

Why would young women want to start smoking, given the serious problems associated with smoking? Teenage females often report that they take up smoking in order to control their weight and keep slim (C. S. Pomerleau, Zucker, & Stewart, 2001; Porzelius, 2000; Rimer et al., 2001). Interestingly, only 4% of Black females who are seniors in high school are cigarette smokers (Husten, 1998). This impressively low smoking rate may be partly due to the observation that Black female teenagers are less likely than White female teenagers to be obsessed with their weight and physical appearance (Landrine, 1995b; C. S. Pomerleau et al., 2001). Consider a comment from Edwena, a 15-year-old who describes herself as "a together Black woman":

> Smoking's stupid. People be thinking it looks really cool, but me and my friends just think it's stupid. I play basketball and I sing in the chorus, and so I need to be in good shape, and I need to have a clear voice. That's more important to me than looking so-called cool. Nothing cool about killing yourself. (L. Phillips, 1998, p. 25)

In Chapter 2, we saw that advertisements help perpetuate gender stereotypes, and in Chapter 12 we'll see how ads also contribute to eating disorders in women. Tragically, cigarette ads contribute to the deaths of hundreds of thousands of women by appealing to women's interests in staying slim and looking glamorous. As Kilbourne (1999) said, "Of all the lies that advertising tells us, the ones told in cigarette ads are the most lethal" (p. 180). Demonstration 11.3 asks you to analyze current cigarette ads.

DEMONSTRATION 11.3 ■ ■ ■ ■ ■ ■ ■ ■ ■ ■ ■ ■ ■ ■ ■ ■ ■

Women in Cigarette Ads

Between now and the end of the academic term, try to analyze any ciga-rette advertisements you encounter in the media. (If you discover that your favorite magazine doesn't carry cigarette ads, write a thank-you letter to this magazine!) If you do locate cigarette ads, does even one ad show a woman who is not slender? Are the women in these ads young or old? What ethnic groups are represented? What are they doing in these ads? What message do these ads present about how cigarettes can improve your social life or your enjoyment of life? Kilbourne (1999) pointed out that cigarette ads often portray violent messages, sexual innuendos, and the promise of freedom. Does your sample of these advertisements sup-port this observation?

During the late 1990s, the ads for Virginia Slims showed women engaged in gender-stereotypical behavior (e.g., trying to cram piles of clothing into a suitcase), and they all carried the slogan "It's a Woman Thing!" Somewhat more recently, Virginia Slims tried to lure women of color by showing Black, Asian, and Latina women, accompanied by the slogan "I want to find my voice." Can you identify any similar themes in the ads you inspect?

Alcohol Abuse

A 30-year-old woman, reflecting on her life, wrote the following passage:

> I knew I couldn't be an alcoholic. I had a good job and I drank only wine. I certainly don't look like an alcoholic, whatever that look is. It took a long time for me to admit that I really was dependent on that wine. I needed it every day just to dull the world. (L. L. Alexander et al., 2001, p. 178)

In the section on smoking, we saw that women and men are equally likely to smoke cigarettes. However, men are still more likely than women to be diag-nosed with alcohol abuse. **Alcohol abuse** is defined as a pattern of alcohol use that leads to significant distress or impairment (Kilbey & Burgermeister, 2001). Impairment includes missing work or school, arrests for alcohol-related crimes, or family problems. According to U.S. estimates, about 4% of women and 13% of men are alcohol abusers (Blume, 1998).

Problems Caused by Alcohol. Alcohol directly affects women's health. For example, women who consume at least two drinks a day seem to double their chances of breast cancer, compared to nondrinkers (Wilsnack, 1995; M. D. Wood et al., 2001). Other health consequences of alcohol include liver problems, ulcers, brain damage, high blood pressure, heart attacks, strokes, cognitive problems, and various cancers (M. D. Wood et al., 2001). Children born to alcoholic mothers are likely to have **fetal alcohol syndrome,** which is characterized by facial abnormalities, retarded physical growth, psychological abnormalities, and mental retardation (Streissguth et al., 1999; M. D. Wood et al., 2001).

Alcohol also has indirect effects on women's health. For example, alcohol is a contributing factor in about 19,000 U.S. automobile fatalities each year. Alcohol abuse also increases the number of deaths from workplace injuries, drowning, fires, violent crimes, and suicide (M. D. Wood et al., 2001).

Gender and Alcohol.   Most people think that alcoholism is primarily a male problem (Vogeltanz & Wilsnack, 1997). We just saw that the stereotype is partly correct in the United States, where men are about three times more likely than women to be alcohol abusers (Blume, 1998).

Studies on college campuses also reveal that more males than females abuse alcohol, although the gender difference is not enormous. For example, Wechsler and his colleagues (1994) collected survey data from 17,592 students at 140 representative colleges throughout the United States. One of the most striking findings was the large percentage of students who had engaged in **binge drinking** (defined as five or more drinks in a row for males and four or more drinks in a row for females) during the preceding two weeks. (The researchers specified fewer drinks for women because their body weight is generally lower.) The results showed that 50% of the males and 39% of the females could be categorized as binge drinkers. In addition, binge drinking is less common at women's colleges and at historically Black institutions (Dowdall et al., 1998; Wechsler et al., 1994). Now answer the questions in Demonstration 11.4.

Wechsler and his colleagues (1994) also included items that assessed the behavioral consequences of drinking. Specifically, those who frequently binged were likely to report doing something they later regretted or engaging in unplanned sexual activity.

As we have seen from general surveys, males report greater problems with alcohol abuse. Males are also more likely than females to report that they consumed alcohol at some point during their lives (L. L. Alexander et al., 2001; Kandel, 2000). However, ethnicity has an impact on the size of this gender difference. For example, among European Americans and Native Americans, gender differences are small. In contrast, among Blacks, Latinas/os, and Asian Americans, men are significantly more likely than women to consume alcohol (Windle et al., 1996; Wise et al., 2001). Cultural norms in some ethnic groups specify that women should not consume much alcohol (McCaul, 1998).

In discussing gender and alcohol, we need to expand on a topic mentioned at the beginning of this chapter. Research shows that, when a male and a female with the same body weight consume the same amount of alcohol, the woman will have a significantly higher blood alcohol level (J. A. Hamilton & Yonkers, 1996; Haseltine, 1997). This means that a 150-pound woman who drinks 2 ounces of whiskey will have a higher blood alcohol level than a 150-pound male

DEMONSTRATION 11.4 ■■■■■■■■■■■■■■■■■■■■

Alcohol Consumption and Its Behavioral Consequences

Answer each of the following questions as accurately as possible.

1. Think about your behavior during the last two weeks. How many times have you had four or more drinks in a row if you are female or five or more drinks in a row if you are male? (The operational definition of a "drink" is 12 ounces of beer or a wine cooler, 4 ounces of wine, or 1.25 ounces of liquor.)

2. Since the beginning of this school year, how many times have you personally experienced each of the following problems as a consequence of drinking alcohol?

   a. Had a hangover
   b. Missed a class
   c. Fell behind in schoolwork
   d. Did something you later regretted
   e. Forgot what you did
   f. Argued with friends
   g. Had unplanned sexual activity
   h. Failed to use protection when you had sex
   i. Damaged property
   j. Got into trouble with campus or local police
   k. Got injured or hurt
   l. Required medical treatment for an alcohol overdose

Source: Based on Wechsler et al. (1994).

friend who drinks 2 ounces of the same whiskey. In other words, women need to be more careful than men about limiting their alcohol consumption.

Gender differences are also relevant when people seek treatment for alcohol problems. Families are more likely to deny that female family members have a problem with alcohol (Blume, 1998; Vogeltanz & Wilsnack, 1997). Physicians are also less likely to identify problem drinking in female patients than in male patients (Wilsnack, 1995). In addition, society disapproves more strongly if a woman gets drunk at a party. Women may therefore be more reluctant to admit they have a drinking problem (Vogeltanz & Wilsnack, 1997). Consistent with Theme 2, people react differently to male alcohol abusers than to female alcohol abusers.

Other Substance-Abuse Problems

Smoking and alcohol abuse are the two most common forms of substance abuse, but women also abuse other substances—prescription medicines, for example. Women are more likely than men to use sedatives and tranquilizers (McCaul, 1998; Statistics Canada, 2000; Tapert et al., 1999). These drugs are socially acceptable—after all, a doctor prescribes them! On page 355, for example, we noted that health professionals often give women too much medical attention. In this case, they may be prescribing mind-altering medication to women who don't really need these drugs.

When we consider illicit drugs, however, the picture changes, because men are more likely to use these drugs. For example, a U.S. nationwide survey showed that 42% of men and 30% of women reported using an illegal drug at some time in their life (Kilbey & Burgermeister, 2001). These drugs included marijuana, cocaine, heroin, and LSD. One reason for this gender difference is that females are judged more harshly than males for using these drugs. Also, males are more likely to know someone who sells illegal drugs (Warner et al., 1999). Another trend that would surprise many people is that European American women are more likely than Black or Latina women to have tried illegal drugs at some point in their lives (McCaul, 1998). In contrast to the typical stereotype, a young woman who is experimenting with drugs is likely to be a young European American female from a relatively wealthy family (Alderman & Friedman, 1995).

Women may also metabolize illegal drugs differently than men do, but little research has been conducted on this topic. In addition, few substance-abuse programs are designed to help women (S. Hall, 1998; Kandall, 1999; Litt, 1997). Once again, women at risk for health problems are invisible, and their health needs are often ignored.

In this chapter, we have examined several health issues that are central to women's lives. We began by considering general health care issues, showing that women are often second-class citizens in the United States. Women in developing countries face the risks of poor health care, complications during pregnancy, and female genital mutilation. We also saw that women with disabilities experience exaggerated discrimination. In addition, women in the current era are increasingly likely to contract AIDS and other sexually transmitted diseases. Finally, many women have problems with smoking, alcohol, and illegal substances. Feminist concerns have increased the visibility of women's health problems, but many of these health problems still remain to be solved.

SECTION SUMMARY ■

Women and Substance Abuse

1. In the current era, women and men are equally likely to smoke cigarettes, a problem that has widespread consequences for women's health.

2. Women are less likely than men to be alcohol abusers, but female abusers face the risks of health problems for themselves and fetal alcohol syndrome for their children.

3. People are more likely to ignore alcohol problems in females than in males.

4. Women are more likely than men to use prescription drugs, whereas men are more likely than women to use illegal drugs.

▪▪▪▪▪ CHAPTER REVIEW QUESTIONS ▪▪▪▪▪

1. At the beginning of this chapter, we examined gender comparisons in mortality, morbidity, and use of the health care system. Summarize this information, and describe how these factors may be interrelated.

2. One of the themes of this book is that men and women are treated differently. Apply this theme to the following topics: (a) biases against women in health care, (b) women with disabilities, (c) diagnosis of specific diseases, and (d) substance abuse.

3. What are some of the specific health problems that women are likely to face, and how can women reduce the chances of developing these life-threatening diseases? What are other serious problems for women who smoke or abuse alcohol?

4. What is a disability, and how do women with disabilities differ from one another? In what ways does the life of a woman with a disability differ from the life of a woman who is not disabled?

5. What is AIDS, how is it transmitted, and why should sexually active women be concerned about this disease? Name and briefly describe five other sexually transmitted diseases.

6. Some people argue that the sexually transmitted diseases are biologically sexist; that is, they hurt women more than they hurt men. Provide some examples to support this statement. How does this statement also apply to alcohol abuse?

7. Imagine that you are counseling a high school female about preventing AIDS, avoiding smoking, and preventing alcohol abuse. What arguments would you use?

8. How is social class relevant when we consider health care, mortality, the life expectancy for people with AIDS, and substance abuse? How is ethnicity relevant when we consider women in developing countries, women's life expectancy, AIDS, and substance abuse?

9. Explain why gender comparisons are complicated when we consider the topic of substance abuse. Before you had read the section on substance abuse, what did you believe about gender comparisons in this area?

10. One theme of this book is that women are relatively invisible. Relate this theme to topics such as the general research on women's health and the specific research on women with disabilities and on women with substance-abuse problems. In what areas are women unusually *visible*?

NEW TERMS

*health psychology (353)
*female genital mutilation (357)
*mortality (358)

*morbidity (358)
*cardiovascular disease (360)
*mammogram (361)

*lumpectomy (364)
*cervical cancer (364)
*Pap smear test (364)
*hysterectomy (365)
*osteoporosis (365)
*disability (367)
*ableism (367)
*acquired immunodeficiency syndrome
 (AIDS) (370)

*human immunodeficiency virus (HIV) (372)
*chlamydia (376)
*genital herpes (376)
*genital warts (376)
*gonorrhea (376)
*syphilis (376)
*alcohol abuse (379)
*fetal alcohol syndrome (380)
*binge drinking (380)

 The terms asterisked in the New Terms section serve as good search terms for InfoTrac College Edition. Go to http://infotrac.thomsonlearning.com and try these added search terms.

RECOMMENDED READINGS

Alexander, L. L., LaRosa, J. H., & Bader, H. (2001). *New dimensions in women's health* (2nd ed.). Boston, MA: Jones and Bartlett. Here's an excellent textbook about women's health that is comprehensive, clearly written, and interesting; special features include Web site listings, self-assessment exercises, and first-person narratives.

Baum, A., Revenson, T. A., & Singer, J. E. (Eds.). (2001). *Handbook of health psychology.* Mahwah, NJ: Erlbaum. In addition to excellent general discussions about health issues, some chapters especially relevant to women focus on women's health promotion, cultural diversity, AIDS and sexually transmitted diseases, and substance abuse.

Davis, L. J. (Ed.). (1997). *The disability studies reader.* New York: Routledge. Here's an excellent introduction to the interdisciplinary area of disability studies, with essays from historical, biological, psychological, and literary perspectives.

Stotland, N. L., & Stewart, D. E. (Eds.). (2001). *Psychological aspects of women's health care* (2nd ed.). Washington, DC: American Psychiatric Press. You'll find this book especially useful if you would like more information about breast cancer, gynecological disorders, and HIV/AIDS.

Women and HIV/AIDS. (2001, Summer/Fall). *Lwes cahiers de la femme* [Canadian Woman Studies], *21*(2). This excellent special issue focuses on general issues about women and AIDS, preventing AIDS, and living with AIDS.

Worell, J. (Ed.). (2001). *Encyclopedia of women and gender.* San Diego: Academic Press. I strongly recommend this two-volume encyclopedia, because it includes numerous chapters relevant to women and health. Some particularly informative chapters focus on health care, disabilities, sexually transmitted diseases, and substance abuse.

ANSWERS TO THE TRUE-FALSE QUESTIONS

1. False (p. 355); 2. False (p. 355); 3. False (p. 357); 4. True (pp. 358–359); 5. True (pp. 360–361); 6. True (p. 367); 7. True (p. 370); 8. False (p. 376); 9. True (p. 377); 10. True (p. 378, p. 382).

Women and Psychological Disorders

Creasource/PictureQuest

T R U E   O R   F A L S E ?

———————— 1. Men are more likely than women to have a psychological disorder that is characterized by lying, aggressiveness, and other antisocial behavior.

———————— 2. Women in the United States and Canada are two to three times more likely than men to experience major depression; however, in other cultures, the gender differences are minimal.

———————— 3. In the United States and Canada, men are more likely than women to attempt suicide and also to die from suicide.

———————— 4. When a distressing event has happened, women are more likely than men to think about their emotions and about the causes and consequences of that event.

———————— 5. People with anorexia nervosa are underweight, and they experience several physical problems; however, they are otherwise fairly well adjusted.

———————— 6. People with bulimia nervosa are typically overweight because of their binge-eating episodes.

———————— 7. Contrary to popular opinion, media images do not seem to encourage eating disorders.

———————— 8. Black women are typically more satisfied with their bodies than European American women are.

———————— 9. People of color are less likely than European Americans to use mental health services.

———————— 10. Feminist therapy emphasizes that power should be fairly evenly distributed between the therapist and the client.

Brenda is a woman in her thirties who has struggled with depression. She described how she has felt when struggling with intense depression:

It was really hard to get out of bed in the morning. I just wanted to hide under the covers and not talk to anyone. I didn't feel much like eating and I lost a lot of weight. Nothing seemed fun anymore. I was tired all the time, yet I wasn't sleeping well at night. But I knew that I had to keep going because I've got kids and a job. It just felt so impossible, like nothing was going to change or get better. (National Institute of Mental Health, 2002, p. 3)

Jennifer, 17 years old, has an eating disorder. She described an early phase of this disorder:

I was just under five feet, six inches and weighed 76 pounds. My hair was falling out and my skin was dry and flaky. People stared at me. Some said I looked like a victim of a concentration camp. I took these comments as compliments. I thought these people were jealous of my body, envied me for how much weight I had lost. Their comments reassured me—confirmed that I was doing a good job restricting my calories. I was successful. (Shandler, 1999, p. 24)

Like many people throughout the world, these two women are experiencing **psychological disorders;** they have emotions, thoughts, and behaviors that are typically maladaptive, distressing to themselves, and different from the social norm (Barlow & Durand, 2002). As we'll see in this chapter, women are more likely than men to suffer from depression and eating disorders. They are also more likely to seek therapy for these problems.

Men are more likely than women to experience other problems. We saw in Chapter 11 that men are currently more likely than women to abuse alcohol and other drugs. Men are also about three times more likely than women to have **antisocial personality disorder,** which is characterized by a variety of behaviors that clearly violate the rights of other people; these behaviors include excessive lying, impulsiveness, and aggressiveness (American Psychiatric Association, 2000; Skodol, 2000; Wyche, 2001). People with this disorder also believe that they are perfectly well adjusted and that the rest of the world has a problem.

If we compile overall tallies—and include all individuals with substance-abuse problems and antisocial personality disorder—then the incidence of psychological disorders in women and men is roughly similar (Russo & Green, 1993). Keep in mind, however, that the specific types of disorders may differ.

In this chapter, we will focus on two categories of disorders that are more common among women than men: depression and eating disorders. Then we will investigate both traditional and nontraditional approaches to treating psychological disorders.

DEPRESSION

Brenda, the woman who was introduced at the beginning of this chapter, is suffering from depression. A person with **major depressive disorder** has frequent episodes of hopelessness and low self-esteem; this person seldom finds pleasure in any activities (American Psychiatric Association, 2000; Whiffen, 2001).

In North America, women are two to three times more likely than men to experience depression during their lifetime (American Psychiatric Association, 2000; Nolen-Hoeksema, 2001; Whiffen, 2001). Interestingly, no consistent gender differences in depression are found among young children. However, around the time of puberty, females begin reporting more depressive symptoms than males. This gender difference continues throughout the life span (Lapointe & Marcotte, 2000; Nolen-Hoeksema & Girgus, 1995).

Gender differences in depression rates hold for White, Black, and Latina women in the United States (Russo & Green, 1993). Research in Canada shows gender differences for people from all ethnic backgrounds, including British, European, and Asian ethnicities (K. L. Dion & Giordano, 1990; Franks & Faux, 1990). Finally, cross-cultural studies report that women are more likely than men to experience depression in countries as varied as Sweden, Lebanon, South Korea, Germany, Uganda, and New Zealand (Culbertson, 1997; Frodi & Ahnlund, 1995; Whiffen, 2001). Let's consider some of the characteristics of depression and then examine some explanations for the higher incidence of depression in women.

Characteristics of Depression

Depression is a disorder that includes the following emotional, cognitive, behavioral, and physical symptoms (American Psychiatric Association, 2000; Whiffen, 2001; Whooley & Simon, 2000; Worell & Remer, 2003):

1. *Emotional symptoms:* feeling sad, gloomy, tearful, guilty, apathetic, irritable, and unable to experience pleasure.
2. *Cognitive symptoms:* thoughts of inadequacy, worthlessness, helplessness, self-blame, and pessimism; these depressed thoughts interfere with normal functioning, so that the individual has trouble concentrating and making decisions.
3. *Behavioral symptoms:* decreased ability to do ordinary work, neglected personal appearance, decreased social contacts, and sleep disturbance. Many depressed individuals attempt suicide. In the United States and Canada, women are more likely than men to think about suicide and also to attempt suicide. However, men are more likely to die from suicide. They typically use more lethal methods (such as firearms) when they try to kill themselves (Canetto, 2001b; Canetto & Lester, 1995; Canetto & Sakinofsky, 1998).
4. *Physical symptoms:* illnesses such as indigestion, headaches, dizzy spells, fatigue, and generalized pain. Weight gain or weight loss is also common.

We should emphasize that most people have occasional episodes of extreme sadness. For example, this sadness is considered normal when a close friend or family member dies. However, these symptoms normally do not continue many years after the loss. Women with major depression struggle with persistent depression, without relief. They are also likely to have other problems discussed in this book, such as substance abuse and eating disorders (Craighead & Vajk, 1998; Joiner & Blalock, 1995). These additional problems, in turn, make the depression even more intense.

There is no "typical" depressed woman. However, some characteristics tend to be associated with depression. For example, a woman is more likely to be depressed if she has several young children in the home or if her income is low (Fishel, 1995; Whiffen, 2001). As you might imagine, women who are unhappily married are more likely than happily married women to be depressed (Culp & Beach, 1998; Fincham et al., 1997; Sperberg & Stabb, 1998).

Personality characteristics are also important. Women who are depressed are especially likely to experience low self-esteem, a low sense of personal accomplishment, traditional feminine gender typing, and/or little sense of control over their own lives (L. Allen et al., 1996; Russo et al., 1993; Thornton & Leo, 1992).

Explanations for the Gender Difference in Depression

What are some of the explanations for the prevalence of depression among women? Let's begin with some explanations that were once thought to be important but no longer seem relevant. Then we will examine a much longer list of factors that do contribute to the gender differences in depression.

Factors No Longer Considered Relevant. Several decades ago, many theorists believed that gender differences in biological factors could explain why women are more likely than men to be depressed. For example, perhaps the gender differences could be directly traced to biochemical components, hormonal fluctuations, or some genetic factor associated with having two X chromosomes. However, careful reviews of the literature suggest that biological factors cannot explain the greater prevalence of depression in women (Fivush & Buckner, 2000; Sprock & Yoder, 1997; Worell & Remer, 2003).[1]

Maybe you've thought about another potential explanation. In Chapter 11, we pointed out that women are more likely than men to seek medical help. Is it possible that women and men are equally depressed but that women are simply more likely to seek help from a therapist? To answer this question, researchers have examined the incidence of depression in the general population, rather than the incidence in the groups of people who consult therapists. Even in the general population, women are much more likely than men to be depressed (Gater et al., 1998; R. C. Kessler, 2000; Sprock & Yoder, 1997).

Let's now consider some of the explanations that are currently thought to account for the gender differences in depression. As we frequently observe in psychology, human behavior is so complex that a single explanation is usually inadequate (Matlin, 1999). *All* the following factors probably help to explain why the rate of depression is so much higher in women than in men.

Diagnostic Biases in Therapists.   The research suggests that therapists tend to *overdiagnose* depression in women (Sprock & Yoder, 1997). That is, therapists are more likely to supply a diagnosis of major depression in women, compared to men with similar psychological symptoms. At the same time, therapists tend to *underdiagnose* depression in men (Sprock & Yoder, 1997; Whiffen, 2001). That is, therapists are guided by their stereotypes about men being "tough," so they are reluctant to conclude that men have depression. In addition, men may try to disguise their depression by drinking excessively, so therapists may miss the appropriate diagnosis of depression ("Mood Disorders," 1998; Wolk & Weissman, 1995). Therapists' bias helps to explain why women are more likely to be diagnosed with depression. However, a large number of other factors also contribute to the very real gender difference in depression.

General Discrimination Against Women.   Several forms of discrimination seem to increase the incidence of depression in women (Burt & Hendrick, 1997; Jack, 1999b; Landrine & Klonoff, 1997). In earlier chapters, we noted that women experience general discrimination and that their accomplishments are often devalued relative to those of men. As Klonoff and her colleagues (2000) discovered, female students who frequently experience sexist treatment are especially likely to report symptoms of depression.

Furthermore, in Chapter 7, we showed that women are less likely to be hired and promoted in the workplace. In many cases, women's work is also less

---

[1] Researchers have established that biological factors can predispose individuals to develop depression. However, males and females are similarly affected by these biological factors. For example, women are no more likely than men to have a genetic background associated with depression.

rewarding and prestigious. According to B. Silverstein and A. D. Lynch (1998), depression is especially likely when women face barriers in their careers and when their achievements do not seem to be valued. Discrimination against women—in everyday life and in the workplace—leads women to feel that they have relatively little control over their lives (Nolen-Hoeksema et al., 1999).

Poverty.   Throughout this book, we have emphasized how social class influences psychological and physical well-being. In addition, people with economic problems are especially likely to have high levels of depression (Jayakody & Stauffer, 2000; Simonds, 2001; Woods et al., 1999). We can understand why an unemployed woman who is trying to support three young children—with no assistance from a husband who has deserted the family—should experience depression. In fact, the real question may be why many women who have economic problems are resilient rather than depressed (J. L. Todd & Worell, 2000).

Housework.   Women who choose a traditional role as a full-time homemaker often find that their work is unstimulating and undervalued. This focus on caring for others may lead to depression (Simonds, 2001). On the other hand, women who work outside the home often have the equivalent of two jobs. We saw in Chapter 7 that most women thrive when they are employed. However, some women who become overwhelmed with housework, in addition to a job, may develop depression (Nolen-Hoeksema, 2001; Simonds, 2001; X. Wu & DeMaris, 1996).

To examine the relationship between housework and depression, Golding (1990) surveyed more than 1,000 Mexican American and European American women in the Los Angeles area. For both groups of women, the amount of housework contributed to household strain, which in turn was related to depressive symptoms. In short, gender inequities in housework may contribute to the higher rate of depression among women.

Emphasis on Physical Appearance.   Beginning in adolescence, some young women become excessively concerned about their physical appearance. As we'll see in the section on eating disorders, adolescent females often resent the weight they gain during puberty. They may find their changing body shape especially unappealing in an era when female fashion models are so painfully thin. This dissatisfaction may contribute to depression (Fredrickson & Roberts, 1997; Whiffen, 2001). At this point, try Demonstration 12.1 before you read further.

Violence.   As we will emphasize in Chapter 13, many females are the targets of violence. Some girls are sexually abused during childhood. Some women face sexual harassment at school and at work. They may be physically abused by their boyfriends or husbands. One review of the research discovered that about half of battered women experience depression (Golding, 1999a). Furthermore, a large number of women are raped, either by men they know or by men who are strangers. The stress of violence clearly contributes to depression (Nolen-Hoeksema, 2001; Ullman & Breclin, 2002; Whiffen, 2001).

DEMONSTRATION 12.1 ■ ■ ■ ■ ■ ■ ■ ■ ■ ■ ■ ■ ■ ■ ■ ■ ■ ■ ■

Responses to Depression

Suppose that you are in a depressed mood because of a recent personal event (e.g., an unexpectedly low grade on an exam, the breakup of a love relationship, or a quarrel with a close friend or relative). Check which of the following activities you are likely to engage in when you are depressed.

_____ 1. Working on a hobby that takes concentration

_____ 2. Writing in a diary about how you are feeling

_____ 3. Getting away from everyone else to try to sort out your emotions

_____ 4. Doing something with your friends

_____ 5. Getting drunk

_____ 6. Telling friends about how depressed you are

_____ 7. Punching something

_____ 8. Engaging in sports

_____ 9. Writing a letter to someone describing your emotions

_____ 10. Engaging in reckless behavior (e.g., driving 10 miles over the speed limit)

_____ 11. Listening to music

_____ 12. Making a list of the reasons you are sad or depressed

When you have finished, count up how many of your responses fall into the first group: Items 2, 3, 6, 9, 11, and 12. Then count up the number that fall into the second group: Items 1, 4, 5, 7, 8, and 10. The results are discussed in the text.

Source: Based on Nolen-Hoeksema (1990).

A 30-year-old Latina teacher wrote the following account about how an acquaintance rape continues to affect her:

I wake up three or four mornings a week in a state of terror. . . . My last dream reminded me of a bad experience I had in college when my date drove to an isolated part of town, held me down, and threatened to beat me up unless I had sex with him. I tried to get away, but couldn't. I gave up fighting. But my reactions don't make sense. That experience was 10 years ago, and I didn't react much at the time. . . . I didn't tell anyone until last week when I called the crisis line. I feel like I am going crazy. I just don't usually get this overpowered by things. (Worell & Remer, 2003, p. 204)

Not surprisingly, women are likely to feel depressed and anxious during the months after they have been raped. Once again, the real question may be why so many women who are victims of violence manage to escape the symptoms of depression.

Women's Relationships.   Men are more likely than women to say that their spouses understand them and bring out their best qualities (McGrath et al., 1990). In other words, women typically give more social support than they receive in a marital relationship. Women are also more likely than men to feel responsible for making sure that the relationship is going well (O'Mahen et al., 2001). They may believe that they ought to be more unselfish in a relationship rather than expressing their own personal preferences (Jack, 1999b).

In addition, many women become overly involved in the problems of their friends and family members. We saw in Chapter 6 that women sometimes have closer relationships with their friends than men do. Some theorists (e.g., J. V. Jordan, 1997) have emphasized that these intimate friendships are a source of empowerment and strength for women. However, other theorists and researchers have argued that women may become so involved with others' problems that they actually neglect their own needs (Fritz & Helgeson, 1998; Helgeson & Fritz, 1998; Westkott, 1997; Whiffen, 2001).

Responses to Depression.   So far, we have noted that a number of factors make depression more likely in women than in men. Therapists may overdiagnose depression in women. In addition, many factors—general discrimination, poverty, housework, concern about physical appearance, violence, and interpersonal relationships—predispose women to depression.

Another major factor also encourages depression: Women often respond differently than men when they are experiencing a depressed mood. Demonstration 12.1 focused on responses to depression.

Susan Nolen-Hoeksema is the major researcher on responses to depression. She proposed that, when women are depressed, they are more likely than men to turn inward and focus on their symptoms. They contemplate the possible causes and consequences of their emotions, an approach called a **ruminative style** of response. For example, they worry about how tired they are, and they keep thinking about all the things that are wrong in their life (Nolen-Hoeksema & Jackson, 2001). Research confirms that women are significantly more likely than men to use ruminative strategies when they are depressed (Nolen-Hoeksema, 1990; Nolen-Hoeksema & Jackson, 2001; Nolen-Hoeksema et al., 1999; Tamres et al., 2002).

Furthermore, Nolen-Hoeksema proposed that rumination prolongs and intensifies a bad mood. Rumination tends to create a negative bias in people's thinking, so that predominantly pessimistic ideas come to mind. People are more likely to blame themselves and to feel helpless. This pessimistic style increases the likelihood of more long-term, serious depression. We also saw in the previous section that women often worry about other people's problems. Women who tend to ruminate about all these problems often make their depressed mood even worse.

Now look at your responses to Demonstration 12.1. Naturally, no 12-item questionnaire can provide an accurate assessment of your style of responding to depression. However, if you checked more items in the first group, you may tend to have a ruminative style. In contrast, if you checked more items in the second group, you are probably more likely to distract yourself when you are depressed. (Incidentally, if you checked Item 1, 4, or 8, your distracting style may help lift you out of a depressed mood. However, if you checked Item 5 or 10, you should be concerned that your response style could endanger yourself and others.)

What should you do if you have a ruminative style? The next time you are depressed, think briefly about the problem and then do some activity that takes your mind away from your emotions. Wait until your depressed mood has lifted somewhat. Then you can begin to analyze the situation that made you depressed. When you are less depressed, you will be able to think more clearly about how to solve the problem and how to gain control over the situation. However, if your depression persists, you should seek help from a therapist.

Conclusions About Gender and Depression.   Therapists may be able to help women readjust their ruminative style. But look at the other sources of gender difference, such as poverty, workload, and violence. These problems of our society cannot be typically addressed by therapists working one on one with their clients. People who are genuinely concerned about depression in women must pressure elected officials and join organizations that publicize these issues. If social inequities created the depression problem, then we must work to change these inequities. As Susan Nolen-Hoeksema and her colleagues (1999) wrote:

> Helping women achieve a greater sense of control over their circumstances and engage in problem solving rather than ruminating should be useful. Changing the social circumstances that many women face so that they do not have so much to ruminate about is equally important. (p. 1071)

Hare-Mustin and Marecek (1997) argued that many current psychologists and psychiatrists place too much emphasis on biological factors, which reside inside each person. Those professionals de-emphasize society's contributions. When they treat depression, they simply prescribe an antidepressant such as Prozac rather than address the problems in society. This shifting focus parallels the increasingly conservative politics in the United States. For example, we saw in Chapter 7 that the U.S. government's policy on welfare has changed. This policy suggests that poverty is now the people's problem—in reality, women's own problem—rather than a societal problem that the government should try to correct. In contrast, feminist psychologists emphasize a different strategy: To address psychological problems, we must acknowledge that these problems occur in a social context and are intertwined with the other gender inequities discussed throughout this textbook.

SECTION SUMMARY ■

Depression

1. Women are more likely than men to suffer from depression and eating disorders; men are more likely to have problems with substance abuse and antisocial personality disorder.

2. Depression is two to three times more common in women than in men; this gender difference has been reported in a variety of ethnic groups in North America and also in many other countries.

3. Depression includes feelings of sadness and apathy, thoughts of inadequacy and pessimism, decreased performance, a potential for suicide attempts, and physical complaints.

4. Depression is more likely if a woman has young children in the home, a low income, an unhappy marriage, and low self-esteem.

5. The gender differences in depression cannot be explained by differences in biological predisposition or by women's being more likely to seek therapy.

6. Some likely explanations for gender differences in depression include therapists' diagnostic biases, general discrimination, poverty, housework, emphasis on physical appearance, violence, personal relationships, and ruminative responses to depression. Attempts to reduce depression in women must emphasize societal problems.

EATING DISORDERS AND RELATED PROBLEMS

Frances M. Berg (2000) began her book on eating disorders with a thought-provoking quotation:

> The number one wish of brilliant, ambitious young women is not to save the rain forests or succeed in a career, but to lose weight. . . . Why do modern women in the most affluent countries in the world live like starving people in a [developing country]? Why do they choose to be weak, apathetic and unable to fully contribute to their families, their careers, and their communities? Why, when instead they could be strong, capable, and caring women? (p. 15)

The truth is that most women in North America are preoccupied with their weight. Many women may not have one of the life-threatening disorders we will discuss shortly. However, their thoughts are often drawn away from social pleasures and professional concerns because they focus on their physical appearance and dieting. In reality, symptoms of disordered eating occur on a continuum of severity (Piran, 2001; Striegel-Moore & Cachelin, 1999; Tyrka et al., 2000). Anorexia nervosa and bulimia nervosa are at the most extreme end of that continuum. Still, many other females have varying degrees of body image problems, so that their disorders can be placed on the less extreme portion of that continuum.

In this section, we'll first consider anorexia nervosa, bulimia nervosa, and binge-eating disorder. Then we'll address the more general question of our culture's emphasis on being slim. Our final topic will be the related issues of being overweight and dieting. We need to emphasize in advance that being overweight is *not* a psychological disorder. However, the emphases on slimness and dieting combined with the fear of being overweight are major factors in creating eating disorders.

Anorexia Nervosa

At the beginning of this chapter, you read about a young woman who has anorexia nervosa. A person with **anorexia nervosa** has an extreme fear of becoming obese and also refuses to maintain an adequate body weight, defined as 85% of expected weight (American Psychiatric Association, 2000; Sokol & Gray, 1998). People with this disorder overestimate their body weight (Andreasen & Black, 2001). For example, one young woman with anorexia nervosa weighed only 100 pounds, yet she said:

> I look in the mirror and see myself as grotesquely fat—a real blimp. My legs and arms are really fat and I can't stand what I see. I know that others say I am too thin, but I can see myself and I have to deal with this my way. (L. L. Alexander et al., 2001, p. 64)

Approximately 90% of those with anorexia nervosa are female, and the disorder strikes between 0.5% and 4% of adolescent females. The typical age range for the onset of anorexia nervosa is 14–18 years, although concern about weight often begins many years earlier (American Psychiatric Association, 2000; National Institute of Mental Health, 2001; Sokol & Gray, 1998).

Anorexia nervosa starts in a variety of ways. Some women with anorexia were initially slightly overweight. Then a comment from someone or even a query as innocent as "Are you gaining weight?" prompts them to begin a severe dieting program. Other women with anorexia trace the beginning of their disorder to a stressful life event, such as moving to a new school, or to a traumatic event, such as sexual abuse (American Psychiatric Association, 2000; Zerbe, 1999). Many who develop this disorder tend to be overly perfectionistic and eager to please other people (R. A. Gordon, 2000; Levenkron, 2000; Polivy & Herman, 2002).

One important medical consequence of anorexia nervosa is **amenorrhea,** or the cessation of menstrual periods. Other frequent medical consequences include heart, lung, kidney, and gastrointestinal disorders. In fact, virtually every organ in the body is affected (American Psychiatric Association, 2000; D. E. Stewart & Robinson, 2001; Zerbe, 1999). For example, researchers have reported changes in brain structures among young women with anorexia (Katzman et al., 1997). Another common problem is osteoporosis, the bone disorder we discussed in Chapter 11. Osteoporosis afflicts women with anorexia because of their low estrogen levels and inadequate nutrition (R. A. Gordon, 2000).

Anorexia nervosa is considered serious because between 5% and 10% of people with anorexia die (American Psychiatric Association, 2000; M. Siegel et al., 1997; Steinhausen, 1995). Unfortunately, treatment for this disorder is difficult, especially because many people with anorexia also meet the criteria for major depression. About 40% of individuals with anorexia will recover, and about 35%

will show some improvement. Recovery is especially likely if treatment begins during the early stages of anorexia (Sokol & Gray, 1998).

Anorexia nervosa illustrates the potentially life-threatening consequences of our culture's preoccupation with thinness. One father told me about his daughter, who was struggling with anorexia: "She'd rather be dead than fat."

Bulimia Nervosa

A person with **bulimia nervosa** is able to maintain a normal body weight (unlike a person with anorexia nervosa); however, she or he has frequent episodes of binge eating and typically uses inappropriate methods to prevent weight gain. Binge eating means consuming huge amounts of food, typically 2,000 to 3,000 calories at a time (L. L. Alexander et al., 2001; American Psychiatric Association, 2000; Kreipe & Birndorf, 2000). The binge-eating episodes are typically secretive. People with bulimia nervosa then try to compensate for this huge food intake by vomiting or using laxatives (National Institute of Mental Health, 2001). In between binges, they may diet or exercise excessively. Like people with anorexia, those with bulimia are obsessed about food, eating, and physical appearance. For example, a 20-year-old college student with bulimia nervosa described her situation:

> How did I get so weird? My life revolves around eating and ridding myself of food. My days are a waste. . . . There hasn't been a day when I haven't been tormented by the frustration I create for myself about where, when, and what I shall eat.
>
> I have potential that if released could do amazing things. But it's trapped inside me. I am a suffering, driven, and depressed person. I remember myself as an involved, bright, laughing girl. . . . But somehow I began to change. That sparkly person disappeared. Who I was became how I looked. Finally, all that mattered was my weight.
>
> Freedom for me is having no concern for how I look or what I eat. Probably the stupidest, most shallow definition of freedom ever written. (Pipher, 1995, p. 39)

At least 90% of individuals with bulimia nervosa are female, and the disorder is especially common on college campuses. Between 1% and 5% of adolescent and young adult females develop bulimia (Heffernan, 1998; National Institute of Mental Health, 2001; Piran, 2001). However, recognizing the presence of bulimia is difficult because people with bulimia typically maintain a normal body weight (M. Siegel et al., 1997). They do not stand out in a crowd.

The medical consequences of bulimia nervosa include gastrointestinal, heart, liver, and metabolism problems (L. L. Alexander et al., 2001; Andreasen & Black, 2001; Kreipe & Birndorf, 2000). Bulimia nervosa is typically not as life threatening as anorexia nervosa. However, bulimia is difficult to treat effectively and it is associated with serious medical and psychological problems (R. A. Gordon, 2000; Tobin, 2000).

Binge-Eating Disorder

Psychologists and psychiatrists have recently proposed a third kind of eating disorder, although it has not yet been studied as thoroughly as anorexia nervosa and bulimia nervosa. People with **binge-eating disorder** have frequent episodes of binge eating (at least two episodes each week for at least 6 weeks), during which they consume huge amounts of food, and they feel that they cannot control these binges. Afterward, they typically feel disgusted with themselves and depressed. Unlike people with bulimia nervosa, they do not use inappropriate methods, such as vomiting or using laxatives, to compensate for the binges (American Psychiatric Association, 2000; R. A. Gordon, 2000; Zerbe, 1999). As a result, those with binge-eating disorder are typically overweight.

Between 0.7% and 4% of the general population suffers from binge-eating disorder. About 60% of these individuals are female. In other words, the majority are female, but the gender ratio is much less skewed toward females than the gender ratio for anorexia nervosa or bulimia nervosa (American Psychiatric Association, 2000; R. A. Gordon, 2000). The research also suggests that people with binge-eating disorder do not value thinness as much as people with the other two eating disorders. Researchers are currently trying to identify risk factors and personal characteristics associated with binge-eating disorder (R. A. Gordon, 2000).

Let's briefly review the three kinds of eating disorders, and then we'll consider some cultural factors related to these disorders.

1. People with *anorexia nervosa* refuse to maintain appropriate body weight, so they are dangerously thin.
2. People with *bulimia nervosa* maintain normal body weight, but they have frequent episodes of binge eating; they typically use inappropriate methods to prevent weight gain.
3. People with *binge-eating disorder* have frequent episodes of binge eating, but they do not use inappropriate methods to prevent weight gain; they are typically overweight.

The Culture of Slimness

Most North American females are concerned that they are overweight, a tendency called the **culture of slimness** (J. K. Thompson et al., 1999). Let's explore components of this issue in more detail, because they help to explain the behavior of those with eating disorders and of those with less extreme concerns about slimness. We'll explore media images, discrimination against overweight people, and women's general dissatisfaction with their bodies. Finally, we'll focus on how women of color view their bodies.

Media Images.   Kate Dillon (2000) recalled her earlier experience in fashion modeling. She was 5'11" and weighed only 125 pounds, yet she was instructed to lose 10 to 20 pounds. In fact, the women in fashion magazines often look anorexic. Women who seek treatment for eating disorders frequently recall that the models in fashion magazines were an important motivational force in encouraging their pursuit of slimness (R. A. Gordon, 2000; M. P. Levine & Smolak, 1996; Smolak & Striegel-Moore, 2001).

Research demonstrates that the media emphasize weight consciousness and dieting. For example, Malkin and her colleagues (1999) analyzed the covers of popular women's magazines; 78% of them contained messages about weight loss or other aspects of physical appearance. In contrast, not one of the covers of popular men's magazines contained these messages.

Other research on the media assesses how these images influence women's views of their bodies. For instance, studies in both Canada and the United States show that young women who frequently read fashion magazines are likely to be especially dissatisfied with their own bodies (Hofschire & Greenberg, 2002; Morry & Staska, 2001). In several experiments, women felt worse about their bodies after they had seen photographs or television advertisements featuring slender fashion models rather than neutral images (Henderson-King et al., 2001; Lavine et al., 1999; Posavac et al., 1998).

Discrimination Against Overweight Women. Our society is biased against women who are overweight. For example, most people would hesitate before making a racist comment, but they would not hesitate before making a comment about an overweight woman (Crandall et al., 2001; J. M. Price, 2002). Women who are overweight also receive lower salaries than slender women, and they experience other forms of job discrimination. They are less likely to be viewed as sexually attractive and less likely to marry (W. C. Goodman, 1995; Regan, 1996; Wing & Klem, 1997). Furthermore, consistent with Theme 2 of this book, people discriminate more strongly against overweight women than against overweight men (J. M. Price, 2002).

Adults are not alone in downgrading overweight individuals. Even first-graders report that they would prefer to be friends with a slender child rather than a heavier one. Beginning at an early age, then, children may be biased against their overweight peers (J. K. Thompson et al., 1999). In fact, children may have even more rigid ideas about ideal body weight than adults do (Rand & Resnick, 2000; Rand & Wright, 2000). Children's physical attractiveness can have widespread consequences for the way they are treated by other people (Langlois et al., 2000).

Females' Dissatisfaction with Their Bodies.   In our culture, the ideal is the emaciated women who inhabit fashion magazines. As a result, many females feel unhappy about their bodies (F. M. Berg, 2000). For instance, in one survey of 803 adult women from throughout the United States, roughly one-half were dissatisfied with their body weight, hips, and stomach (Cash & Henry, 1995). In addition, normal-weight women rated themselves as heavier than they really are (McCreary & Sadava, 2001). Furthermore, college women typically believe that other women are thinner than they themselves are (C. A. Sanderson et al., 2002). As a result, women often spend time worrying unnecessarily about their weight.

Research on children in elementary school now shows widespread concern about being fat and about dieting (Flannery-Schroeder & Chrisler, 1996; Grogan, 1999; Smolak & Levine, 2001). As early as 5 years of age, girls who are overweight are more likely to have negative self-concepts compared to normal-weight girls (Davison & Birch, 2001).

Also, our current culture encourages young women to evaluate how their bodies appear in the eyes of other people (McKinley, 1998, 1999). Women's current dissatisfaction with their bodies produces unhappiness. It also focuses their attention on relatively superficial characteristics and on themselves rather than on meaningful interactions with other people (Brumberg, 1997).

All females are not uniformly preoccupied with physical appearance. Compared to heterosexual women, lesbian women are generally more satisfied with their bodies (Bergeron & Senn, 1998; Guille & Chrisler, 1999; Rothblum, 2002). In addition, women who have feminist attitudes toward physical attractiveness or toward male-female relationships are typically happier with their bodies than women with more traditional values (Cash et al., 1997; Dionne et al., 1995). Also, lower-class European American women are less worried about slimness than are European American women from middle and upper income brackets (Bowen et al., 1999). One further variable that is sometimes related to body dissatisfaction is ethnicity. Let's now turn our attention to the way that women of color regard these body image issues.

Women of Color, Body Image, and Slimness.   For many years, the research on body image focused on European American populations (Smolak & Levine, 2001). Fortunately, several studies now provide some information about women of color.

In general, Black women are more satisfied with their body image than are European American women. Black women also believe that an average-weight woman is more attractive than a too-thin woman (Bowen et al., 1999; Cash & Henry, 1995; Smolak & Striegel-Moore, 2001; Wise et al., 2001). Interestingly, Black males also prefer average-weight women, whereas White males prefer thinner women (S. H. Thompson et al., 1996). A 34-year-old Black woman interviewed by Bowen and her colleagues (1999) commented:

> At work, where there are only a few of us Black women, I feel pretty fat. At home, with my friends, I don't think about it hardly at all. I guess it's because I'm closer to the middle of my Black friends' weight range. (p. 292)

However, the European American admiration for thinness now seems to be spreading to Black individuals. We may soon see an increase in eating disorders among Black women (Polivy & Herman, 2002).

The research on Latina women reveals some contradictions. Some research suggests that Latinas are less preoccupied with slimness, but other research reports that Latinas and European American women have similar levels of body dissatisfaction (Bowen et al., 1999; Cash & Henry, 1995). One reason for the inconclusive findings is the diversity within each ethnic group. For example, women from the Dominican Republic may not emphasize slimness. In contrast, women raised in upper-class Argentinean families may value slimness even more than European American women do (B. Thompson, 1994; J. K. Thompson et al., 1999). Factors such as social class, country of origin, and current place of residence undoubtedly influence how Latina women view their bodies. Another important factor is probably acculturation. Latina women who have adopted mainstream values while living in the United States and Canada tend to adopt our culture's ideas about slimness (Cachelin et al., 2000; Geller & Thomas, 1998).

The research on Asian Americans reveals some similar trends. For example, South Asian college women are more likely to be ashamed of their bodies—after viewing slender models wearing revealing clothing—if they were born and raised in the United States rather than in South Asia (Chand, 2002). In another study, eating disorders were more common among Asian women who had lived a long time in the United States than among Asian women who were recent immigrants (Cachelin et al., 2000). Still, eating disorders are more common in college women who are European American rather than Asian American (L. B. Mintz & Kashubeck, 1999).

Being Overweight and Dieting

A variety of different measures have been used to assess whether an individual is overweight. Depending on the specific measure, between 33% and 55% of the adult population in the United States is overweight (Cogan & Ernsberger, 1999). *Being overweight is not classified as a mental disorder.* However, we need to discuss the issue of being overweight because it is a central topic in many women's lives. In addition, the fear of becoming overweight is a major factor in anorexia nervosa and bulimia nervosa.

Research demonstrates that people who eat foods that are high in fat—and who also do not exercise sufficiently—are likely to face greater health risks than other people. In addition, overweight people are more likely than other people to have high blood pressure and heart disease and to be at a greater risk for cancer (J. M. Price, 2002; Wing & Polley, 2001). Earlier in this section, we pointed out that overweight people face another cluster of problems through social and professional discrimination.

Unfortunately, losing extra weight is a major challenge. Some people take up smoking to suppress their appetites. However, we saw in Chapter 11 that smoking has enormous health risks. Also, people are at risk for heart problems if they repeatedly lose and regain weight (Ernsberger & Koletsky, 1999).

Approximately 40% of U.S. women (compared with 20% of men) are currently dieting to lose weight (F. M. Berg, 1999). According to one estimate, U.S. residents can now choose from more than 17,000 different diet plans and products (Hesse-Biber, 1998). However, these options are often expensive. In addition, many of them are ineffective because people regain the lost weight (J. M. Price, 2002; Zerbe, 1999). Think about this: If any of these programs were truly effective, why are there so many other programs on the market?

Ironically, dieting can often lead to weight gain. Dieting causes a change in metabolism. The dieter can survive on increasingly smaller portions of food. A "normal" food intake therefore causes weight gain. In addition, dieters may become so focused on food that they are tempted to binge (Polivy & McFarlane, 1998). For these reasons, many clinicians suggest that clients should be encouraged to accept themselves, avoid further weight gain, not focus on reaching a specific weight, and exercise moderately (W. C. Miller, 1999; Wing & Polley, 2001).

In this section, we have looked at four groups of people who are highly concerned about their weight:

1. People with anorexia try to lose weight, and they succeed, sometimes with fatal consequences.
2. People with bulimia fluctuate between gorging and dieting; their weight is usually normal, but their eating habits produce numerous other problems.
3. People with binge-eating disorder have frequent episodes of eating large amounts of food; they are typically overweight.
4. People who are overweight may try to lose weight, typically without success.

Think how the guilt and anxiety that all four groups associate with eating might be reduced if more women were encouraged to accept their bodies.

We all need to focus less on weight issues, and we need to encourage the media not to show so many anorexic female actors and models. Something is clearly wrong when normal-weight women begin dieting! Fortunately, consumer activism can influence the media. For instance, a group concerned about eating disorders wrote letters to the Hershey Food Corporation, protesting their advertisement for chocolates that said, "You can never be too rich or too thin." Hershey actually removed the ad (J. K. Thompson & Heinberg, 1999). Imagine, too, how much more positive we might feel if the women in the media had bodies that showed as much variety as the bodies we see in real life. And wouldn't it be wonderful to glance at the covers of magazines in the grocery store and *not* see guilt-inducing articles titled "Finally—An Answer to Problem Thighs" or "How To Lose 15 Pounds in Just One Month!"? Now that you are familiar with the issues related to eating disorders, try Demonstration 12.2.

DEMONSTRATION 12.2 ■■■■■■■■■■■■■■■■■■■■

Analyzing Your Own Attitudes Toward Body Size

Answer each of the questions in this demonstration using the following scale:

1	2	3	4	5
Never				Frequently

_____ 1. I comment about my own weight to other people.

_____ 2. I compliment other people if they seem to have lost weight.

_____ 3. If someone has gained weight, I avoid commenting about this.

_____ 4. I make jokes about people who are overweight.

_____ 5. I encourage people to feel good about their bodies, even if they do not meet the cultural norms for being slender.

_____ 6. When looking at a magazine, I admire the most slender people in the photographs.

_____ 7. When someone makes a joke about fat people, I express my disapproval.

_____ 8. I eat relatively little food, so that I can keep thinner than average.

_____ 9. I compliment other people when they show self-control in their eating habits.

_____ 10. When looking at a magazine, I'm concerned that the photographs may be encouraging eating disorders.

Now calculate your score: Add together your ratings for Items 1, 2, 4, 6, 8, and 9. From this sum, subtract your ratings for Items 3, 5, 7, and 10. If your total score is low, congratulations! You have a positive attitude toward body size diversity.

Source: Based on F. M. Berg (2000).

SECTION SUMMARY ■

Eating Disorders and Related Problems

1. Many females have varying degrees of body image problems. Anorexia nervosa and bulimia nervosa are at the extreme end of the continuum.

2. People with anorexia nervosa have an extreme fear of becoming overweight, and they do not maintain an appropriate body weight; the problem is especially prominent among adolescent women. They have numerous health problems, which may have fatal consequences.

3. People with bulimia nervosa binge frequently, but they maintain a normal weight because they vomit or use other methods to prevent weight gain. They typically have many health problems.

4. People with binge-eating disorder have frequent large-scale binges, but they do not use inappropriate methods to maintain a normal weight.

5. The media present images of exaggerated slimness, and these images make women dissatisfied with their bodies; both adults and children discriminate against overweight people.

6. Many women are dissatisfied with their bodies, although body dissatisfaction depends on factors such as feminist attitudes, sexual orientation, and ethnicity.

7. Being overweight is not a psychological disorder, but it has potential health and social consequences; dieting can be both difficult and potentially dangerous.

8. Two recommended strategies are consumer activism and an acceptance of a greater range of body sizes.

TREATING PSYCHOLOGICAL DISORDERS IN WOMEN

So far, we have discussed two categories of psychological disorders that are more common in women than in men: depressive disorders and eating disorders. If a woman seeks help for psychological problems such as these, she will probably receive psychotherapy and/or drug treatment.

Psychotherapy is a process in which a therapist aims to treat psychological problems most often through verbal interactions. Professionals offer more than 400 different kinds of psychotherapy (Garfield, 1995). Severely disturbed individuals who receive therapy are typically treated in hospitals or other psychiatric facilities. Others may receive psychotherapy for many years, but they can still function while living at home. Still others choose psychotherapy to help them during brief periods of stress in their lives.

Drug therapy treats psychological disorders by means of medication. In recent years, new drugs have been developed to help people cope with some psychological disorders. When used in conjunction with psychotherapy, these drugs may be useful. However, drugs are sometimes prescribed inappropriately. We'll briefly discuss drug therapy in this section, although we'll emphasize psychotherapy as an approach to treating psychological disorders.

Let's first consider how sexism may influence psychotherapy, and then we will discuss psychotherapy with lesbians and bisexuals, as well as psychotherapy with women of color. Our final two sections will examine traditional approaches to psychotherapy and feminist therapy.

Psychotherapy and Sexism

Gender and Misdiagnosis.   Earlier in this chapter, we noted the potential for sexism in diagnosing psychological disorders. Specifically, therapists may overdiagnose depression in women and underdiagnose depression in men (Sprock & Yoder, 1997).

Sexism also encourages another kind of misdiagnosis. We saw in Chapter 11 that many health care professionals respond less to medical problems in women than in men. A related concern is that a woman's physical disorder may be misdiagnosed as a psychological problem (Di Caccavo & Reid, 1998; R. Martin et al., 1998). For example, an overactive thyroid gland often produces severe anxiety. Health care professionals may refer women who have this problem to a psychotherapist rather than to a medical specialist (Klonoff & Landrine, 1997; Lerman, 1996).

The Treatment of Women in Therapy.   Gender bias may lead to misdiagnosis, and gender bias may lead to inappropriate treatment in therapy. For example, therapists may view men as more competent than women in work settings (Gilbert & Scher, 1999). Therapists may also evaluate clients in terms of how well their behavior fits the gender stereotypes specified for women and men. In addition, therapists may blame women for events beyond their control. In treating a woman who has been sexually abused, for instance, they may ask her what she did to encourage the attack. In summary, therapists may be influenced by the same kinds of gender stereotypes and discriminatory behavior that operate throughout our culture.

In the United States, another problem for women in therapy is that women's insurance may cover a relatively small portion of the costs for mental health care (Travis & Compton, 2001). Women also earn less than men, so they cannot afford some of the options for psychotherapy that many men are likely to have (Gilbert & Rader, 2001).

Sexual Relationships Between Therapists and Clients.   One of the principles of ethical conduct for psychologists and psychiatrists states that therapists must not disrupt their professional relationships with clients by engaging in sexual intimacy with them. Nonetheless, some therapists break this rule. According to surveys, about 4% of male therapists and 1% of female therapists have had sexual relationships with their clients (K. Pope, 2001). As you can imagine, a woman who has been sexually exploited by a therapist is likely to feel guilty, angry, and emotionally fragile. She will also have an increased risk for suicide (Gilbert & Rader, 2001; K. Pope, 2001).

We need to emphasize that most psychotherapists are ethical people who understand that sexual relationships with clients are forbidden (Gilbert & Scher, 1999; K. Pope, 2001). Still, anyone who feels uneasy about a therapist's sexual advances should try to discuss the issue with the therapist. If this option is not possible, the client should seek a different therapist and consider reporting the offender to a licensing board (Bohmer, 2000; Gilbert & Scher, 1999).

Sexual relationships with clients are especially damaging because they demonstrate a violation of trust. They are also damaging because they represent situations in which a person with power takes advantage of someone who is relatively powerless and vulnerable (Bohmer, 2000). We examine similar power inequities in Chapter 13, where we'll discuss sexual harassment, rape, and battering.

Psychotherapy with Lesbian and Bisexual Women

Lesbian and bisexual women should feel valued and respected when they visit a therapist. Therefore, therapists must be well informed about the research on sexual orientation and the importance of love relationships. Therapists must also recognize that most lesbian and bisexual women experience **sexual prejudice,** a negative attitude toward individuals because of their sexual orientation. They must also be aware that lesbian and bisexual women of color may experience different forms of sexual prejudice in their own ethnic communities (Greene, 2000b; Morrow, 2000). In addition, therapists must be knowledgeable about community resources and support groups that are available for lesbian and bisexual clients (Division 44/Committee on Lesbian, Gay, and Bisexual Concerns, 2000; Reynolds & Hanjorgiris, 2000; Schreier & Werden, 2000).

Therapists must also be aware of **heterosexism,** which is bias against lesbians, gay males, and bisexuals or any group that is not exclusively heterosexual. For example, heterosexual therapists must avoid the heterosexist assumption that a client's lesbian relationship is somehow less important than another client's heterosexual relationship (Gilbert & Rader, 2001; Tozer & McClanahan, 1999). Feminists believe that women should not be treated as second-class citizens in comparison to men. Feminists also believe that lesbians and bisexual women should not be treated as second-class citizens in comparison to heterosexual women. Now let's consider psychotherapy with women of color, who are also frequently treated as second-class citizens in comparison to European American women.

Psychotherapy with Women of Color

The United States and Canada are rapidly becoming two of the most ethnically diverse countries in the world. In the United States, for example, 98 million people (out of a total population of 278 million) say that they are Latina/o, Black, Asian, or Native American (U.S. Census Bureau, 2001b). In Canada, 3 million people (out of a total population of 31 million) consider their ethnic origins to be Asian, Aboriginal, Caribbean, African, or Latin American (Statistics Canada, 2001c). As a result, North American therapists need to be sensitive to ethnic group differences in values and beliefs (C. C. I. Hall, 1997).

One basic problem is that people of color are not as likely as European Americans to use mental health services. Some of the reasons for this under-usage include (1) shame in talking about personal problems to strangers; (2) suspicion about therapists, especially European American therapists; (3) language and economic barriers; (4) reluctance to recognize that help is necessary; and (5) culturally based preferences for talking with female relatives or using other interventions, such as prayer (Chin, 1998; Dinges & Cherry, 1995; Kakaiya, 2000).

Some members of an ethnic group will be able to see a therapist from their own background. For example, Espín (1997) described her own work as a Latina therapist, helping a Latina client who had experienced domestic violence. Espín's condemnation of this abuse was far more credible than if the same message had come from a European American therapist.

However, most members of ethnic minority groups will not be able to choose therapists from their own background. Only about 5% of U.S. therapists belong to ethnic minority groups (C. C. I. Hall, 1997). As a result, most people of color must consult therapists whose life experiences may be very different from their own. For instance, those therapists would not be familiar with the continuing racism faced by people of color (Comas-Díaz, 2000).

You can probably anticipate another advantage of clients being matched with therapists from their own ethnic background. Most European American therapists are not fluent in a language other than English, so language can be a major barrier. To make the situation more vivid, if your own first language isn't Spanish, imagine describing your psychological problems to someone who speaks only Spanish. Your Spanish may be fluent enough to discuss the weather, but could you describe to a Latina therapist precisely how and why you feel depressed? Could you accurately capture the subtleties of your binge-eating disorder? In addition, many terms—such as *depression* and *eating disorder*—may not even exist in some women's vocabularies.

Let's consider some of the important issues that arise in therapy for four different ethnic groups of women: Latinas, Blacks, Asian Americans, and Native Americans. Then we'll discuss some general therapeutic issues for women of color.

Latinas.   In earlier chapters, we noted that Latina/o culture emphasizes gender roles in terms of *machismo* for men and *marianismo* for women (W. M. L. Lee, 1999). Latina mothers usually emphasize that their daughters must remain virgins until marriage, when they must cater to their husband's sexual needs (Espín, 1997). Young girls also learn to play the role of "little wives" to the males in the family. Especially in working-class homes, women may learn that they are second-class citizens (Gilbert & Scher, 1999).

Furthermore, some Latinas have come to North America as refugees from a country besieged by war and turmoil. For example, government repression in El Salvador during the 1980s resulted in more than 75,000 deaths, as well as numerous rapes, tortures, "disappearances," and other human rights abuses.

A woman who escaped from El Salvador may have seen her daughter raped and tortured and her neighbors slaughtered (Guarnaccia, 1997). Living through such traumatic circumstances often creates long-lasting stress-related disorders and other psychological problems. Well-meaning therapists, even if they are fluent in Spanish, may be unprepared to provide therapy for women who have lived through political upheaval.

Black Women.   Black women are likely to experience a kind of stress that is qualitatively different from the stress experienced by middle-class European American women. Specifically, Black women may report stressful factors such as extreme poverty, inadequate housing, and neighborhood crime (Adebimpe, 1997; W. M. L. Lee, 1999; Wyche, 2001).

However, Black women may have an advantage over European American women because their heterosexual relationships are often more evenly balanced with respect to power (McAdoo, 1993). Still, they are at a disadvantage if they seek help from a European American therapist who accepts the myth of the Black matriarchy (R. L. Taylor, 2000; see Chapter 8). Therapists should also resist the myth that all Black women are strong and resilient (Greene, 1994; Reid, 2000). That perspective would encourage therapists to believe that their Black female clients do not really require care for themselves.

Asian American Women.   Although individual differences are substantial, many Asian American families are strongly influenced by the traditional perspective that the male should be the powerful member of the household. These families often expect women to play a passive, subordinate role (W. M. L. Lee, 1999). Younger, more educated women are likely to experience conflict when they sense that they have been unfairly treated by family members. These women are especially likely to have problems with parents and male partners who have traditional orientations (True, 1990).

Also, therapists who are not familiar with an Asian culture may misinterpret some interactions. For example, they may believe that a quiet Asian American woman is reserved because of her cultural values or her lack of fluency in English. However, she may actually be experiencing major depression (Root, 1998; Uba, 1994).

Many researchers have tried to determine why Asian Americans are especially reluctant to use mental health services. They have concluded that Asian Americans are just as likely as European Americans to have mental health problems (Atkinson et al., 1993; Uba, 1994). However, an important cultural value in many Asian groups is to maintain the honor of the family and to avoid any possibility of bringing shame to one's relatives. Psychological problems are judged especially harshly. As a result, a woman who enters psychotherapy is basically admitting that she has failed (W. M. L. Lee, 1999; Uba, 1994; Wang, 1994).

Several Asian American mental health centers are trying outreach programs, using culturally sensitive techniques. These centers have been reasonably successful in increasing the number of community residents who seek therapy (Root, 1998; True, 1995).

Native Americans.   Among Native American and Canadian Aboriginal (Canadian Indian) women, two major mental health problems are the high rates of alcoholism and depression (LaFromboise et al., 1995; Waldram, 1997). Many theorists trace these problems to earlier governmental programs in both the United States and Canada (W. M. L. Lee, 1999). For example, in Canada, many Aboriginal children were taken from their families and placed in residential schools, where they were punished for speaking their own language. These programs encouraged children to assimilate into the European-focused mainstream in Canada and undermined the influence of the tribal elders. Currently, unemployment and poverty are widespread in many Native communities. The combination of all these factors is partly responsible for the high suicide rate. For example, the suicide rate among Canadian Aboriginal women is much higher than for other Canadian women (Statistics Canada, 2000; Waldram, 1997).

Eidell Wasserman is a European American therapist who was hired as a therapist for a reservation in Arizona. She reported that Native Americans may be suspicious of European Americans because of a long history of harmful interactions (Wasserman, 1994). She found that one of her most powerful therapeutic tools was to enlist the support of community members. In addition, she helped to train members of the Native community to work as mental health paraprofessionals.

General Strategies for Therapy with Women of Color.   Many therapists have suggested methods for European Americans who want to increase their skills in helping women of color. Many of these suggestions have been incorporated into graduate training programs (Chin, 1998; Enns, 1997; Greene et al., 1997; C. C. I. Hall, 1997; Mohamed & Smith, 1999; Sparks & Park, 2000; Wyche, 2001). As you'll see, many of these recommendations apply to *all* clients, not just women of color.

1. Search the client's history for strengths that can facilitate the counseling process.
2. Show empathy, caring, respect, and appreciation for your client.
3. Learn about the history, experiences, religion, family dynamics, and cultural values of the client's ethnic group as well as about the discrimination this ethnic group has faced. However, be aware of the diversity within any cultural group.
4. Keep in mind that each ethnic category includes many cultures that can differ substantially from one another. For example, the category "African Caribbean women" includes both Jamaican women and Haitian women; however, these two cultures are quite different from each other.
5. Be aware that some immigrants and other people of color might want to become more acculturated into the European American mainstream but that others want to connect more strongly with their own culture.
6. Communicate to the client that racism may have played a significant role in her life; however, do not use racial oppression to explain all of a client's problems.

7. Hire bilingual staff members and paraprofessionals from the relevant ethnic communities; enlist other community professionals (e.g., school teachers) to help identify relevant problems in the community.
8. Consider offering workshops that target women from a specific ethnic group.

Traditional Therapies and Women

Therapists approach their work from a variety of theoretical viewpoints. A therapist's viewpoint influences attitudes toward women, the techniques used in therapy, and the goals of therapy. We'll discuss two traditional psychotherapy orientations: the psychodynamic approach and the cognitive-behavioral approach. We'll also consider drug therapy in this section.

Psychodynamic Approach. **Psychodynamic therapy** refers to a variety of approaches descended from Sigmund Freud's psychoanalytic theories, proposed in the early 1900s. During treatment, classic psychoanalysis requires the "patient" to free-associate, saying any thoughts that come to mind; the therapist's task is to interpret these thoughts (Andreasen & Black, 2001; Arlow, 2000). Like Freud, current psychodynamic therapists focus on unconscious and unresolved conflicts stemming from childhood. However, psychodynamic therapists now emphasize social interactions more than Freud did (Westen, 1998).

We need to discuss Freud's theory in connection with therapy, because it has had an important long-term effect on psychotherapy. Furthermore, no other writer has influenced our culture's views on women as strongly as Freud did (Appignanesi & Forrester, 1992; Bornstein, 2001). Interestingly, Freud himself admitted that his theories about women were the weakest part of his work (Slipp, 1993). However, this caution is seldom mentioned when supporters discuss Freudian theory.

Here are some components of Freud's approach that present problems for individuals who are concerned about women's mental health (Abel, 1995; Caplan, 2000; Chodorow, 1994; Saguaro, 2000; Slipp, 1993):

1. In Freudian theory, the masculine is the norm for humans, and the feminine is less important.
2. Freud argued that women show **masochism** (pronounced *mass*-owe-kism), or pleasure derived from pain—a perspective that does not encourage modern-day therapists to treat battered women appropriately.
3. According to Freudian theory, women's lack of a penis leads them to experience more shame and envy than men; women realize that they are inferior to men. Freud also argued that women develop a less mature sense of justice, because they do not fully resolve childhood conflicts.
4. Freud's approach argues that penis envy can be partially resolved by having a baby. If a woman decides not to have children, she would be judged to have a psychological disorder.
5. Mothers are the caretakers of young children. The Freudian approach blames mothers for the psychological problems that children experience, but it does not praise the positive aspects of mothers' interactions with their children.
6. Freud did not address issues such as social class or ethnicity, although variables like these have an important impact on women's experiences.

A major part of psychodynamic therapy sessions focuses on childhood relationships and unconscious forces—factors that presumably help therapists understand current psychological problems. This emphasis on the unconscious is not inherently biased against women. However, most feminist critics argue that the six points we just outlined would not encourage women to become more positive about themselves or more psychologically healthy.

Many modern psychodynamic theorists have redefined some of the classic Freudian concepts. You may want to read further about these more feminist approaches (M. J. Buhle, 1998; Chodorow, 1999, 2000; Y. M. Jenkins, 2000; J. V. Jordan, 1998; J. B. Miller & Stiver, 1997; Saguaro, 2000).

Cognitive-Behavioral Approach. **Cognitive-behavioral therapy** argues that psychological problems arise from inappropriate thinking (cognitive factors) and inappropriate learning (behavioral factors). This approach encourages clients to try new behaviors (W. C. Sanderson & McGinn, 2001). For example, a woman who is depressed and lonely might be encouraged to initiate—within the next week—at least five social interactions (Andreasen & Black, 2001; DeRubeis et al., 2001). The cognitive-behavioral approach also asks clients to question any irrational thought patterns they may have. For instance, suppose that a woman is depressed because she feels she is not socially skilled. A therapist may help the woman to see alternative viewpoints, such as "Just because my friend ate lunch with someone else today, it doesn't mean that I'm a loser." Well-controlled research demonstrates that cognitive-behavioral therapy (CBT) is effective in reducing depression (Craighead et al., 2002; W. C. Sanderson & McGinn, 2001; Worell & Remer, 2003).

Cognitive-behavioral therapy is frequently used to treat eating disorders (e.g., Agras et al., 2000; J. R. Grant & Cash, 1995). Well-controlled research on bulimia nervosa shows that CBT is more effective than antidepressant medication, which is the standard drug therapy for bulimia nervosa (C. T. Wilson & Fairburn, 2002). For example, a cognitive-behavioral therapist may help a client develop behavioral strategies to reduce compulsive eating. The therapist may also work with the client to reword negative statements (e.g., "My thighs are disgusting") into more neutral forms (e.g., "My thighs are the heaviest part of me").

Many cognitive-behavioral principles can be combined with feminist therapy (Worell & Remer, 2003). As we will discuss shortly, however, most cognitive-behavioral therapists work to change clients' own individual behaviors and inappropriate thoughts (Enns, 1997). They typically do not discuss with the client the more general problem of society's widespread gender biases.

Drug Therapy. As noted earlier, drug therapies treat psychological disorders by using medication. Our focus in this chapter is on psychotherapy, but other resources offer additional information about drug therapy (e.g., Andreasen & Black, 2001; Brawman-Mintzer & Yonkers, 2001; Weissman, 2001).

Women are more likely than men to use sedatives, tranquilizers, and antidepressants (McCaul, 1998; Simoni-Wastila, 1998; Travis & Compton, 2001). However, women may be more likely than men to experience the kinds of psychological disorders for which these medications are appropriate. Unfortunately, current research has not examined whether physicians may be overprescribing drugs for their female clients.

In the current era, drug therapy is an important component of treating most serious psychological disorders (Thase et al., 2000; Zerbe, 1999). In many cases, drugs can allow severely disturbed clients to be more receptive to therapy. However, the physician must carefully select the drug and discuss it with the client. Unfortunately, doctors frequently prescribe drug therapy without presenting alternative options ("Treatment of Depression," 2001). Physicians and therapists must also monitor the side effects of any medications. Furthermore, therapists would strongly argue that any client with a disorder serious enough to be treated with drug therapy should receive psychotherapy as well. Before reading further, be sure to try Demonstration 12.3.

DEMONSTRATION 12.3 ■ ■ ■ ■ ■ ■ ■ ■ ■ ■ ■ ■ ■ ■ ■ ■ ■ ■

Preferences About Therapists

Imagine that you have graduated from college and that a personal problem has developed for which you would like to consult a therapist. You feel that the problem is not a major one. However, you would like to sort out your thoughts and emotions on this particular problem by talking with a psychotherapist. The following list describes characteristics and approaches that therapists may have. Place a check mark in front of each characteristic that you would look for in a therapist. When you are done, check page 415 to see how to interpret your responses.

_____ 1. I want my therapist to avoid using sexist language.

_____ 2. I would like my therapist to help me think about forces in our society that might be contributing to my problem.

_____ 3. I would like my therapist to believe that the client and the therapist should have reasonably similar power in a therapy situation.

_____ 4. My therapist should avoid encouraging me to act in a more gender-stereotyped fashion.

_____ 5. I want my therapist to be well informed about the research on women and gender.

_____ 6. I think that therapists should reveal relevant information about their own experiences, if the situation is appropriate.

_____ 7. I want my therapist to address relevant issues other than gender in our therapy sessions—issues such as age, social class, ethnicity, disability, and sexual orientation.

_____ 8. My therapist should encourage me to develop relationships in which the two individuals are fairly similar in their power.

_____ 9. I want my therapist to avoid interacting with me in a gender-stereotyped fashion.

Source: Based on Enns (1997).

Feminist Therapy

We have examined how the psychodynamic approach, the cognitive-behavioral approach, and drug therapy can be used in treating psychological disorders. However, the women's movement has created an awareness that psychotherapy must be sensitive to gender issues.

Most therapists probably believe that therapy should be nonsexist, even if they don't always act in a gender-fair fashion. According to the principles of **nonsexist therapy,** women and men should be treated similarly rather than in a gender-stereotyped fashion (Worell & Johnson, 2001; Worell & Remer, 2003). The nonsexist therapy approach argues that therapists should be informed about the recent research on the psychology of women and about the pervasiveness of sexism in our society. Therapists should also avoid sexist language and gender-biased testing instruments (Enns, 1997). However, nonsexist therapy does not specifically examine broader political issues such as social inequalities (Worell & Remer, 2003). In contrast, feminist therapy goes beyond nonsexist therapy in order to address these social inequalities. Demonstration 12.3 highlighted some of the differences between nonsexist therapy and feminist therapy.

Feminist therapy has three important components: (1) Clients should be treated in a nonsexist fashion; (2) social inequalities have been responsible for shaping women's behavior, so the personal is political; and (3) the distribution of power between the client and the therapist should be as egalitarian as possible (Gilbert & Scher, 1999; Worell & Johnson, 2001). Feminist therapy provides a philosophical approach rather than a specific set of techniques (Ballou & West, 2000; Marecek, 2001b).

In recent years, interest in feminist therapy has blossomed. Numerous books and other resources describe both the theory and the practice of feminist psychotherapy (e.g., Enns, 1997; Gilbert & Scher, 1999; Marecek, 2001b; Worell & Johnson, 2001; Worell & Remer, 2003). Let's consider how feminist therapy addresses two central issues: social forces and power in the relationship.

Several principles of feminist therapy point out how social forces operate to devalue women (Albee, 1996; Ballou & West, 2000; Brabeck & Ting, 2000; Enns, 1997; Gilbert & Scher, 1999; Marecek, 2001b; L. B. Silverstein & Goodrich, 2001; Worell & Johnson, 2001; Worell & Remer, 2003). Let's examine these important principles:

1. Feminist therapists believe that women are less powerful than men in our culture, and so women have been assigned an inferior status. Women's major problems are not internal, personal deficiencies; instead, the problems are primarily societal ones, such as sexism and racism.
2. Women and men should have equal power in their social relationships.
3. Society should be changed to be less sexist; women should not be encouraged to adjust to a sexist society by being quieter and more obedient.
4. We must focus on women's strengths, not on characteristics that are presumed to be their deficits. Women can use these strengths to help define and solve problems.
5. We must work to change those institutions that devalue women, including governmental organizations, the justice system, educational systems, and the structure of the family.

6. Inequalities with respect to ethnicity, age, sexual orientation, social class, and disabilities should also be addressed; gender is not the only important inequality.

Another crucial component of feminist therapy focuses on power issues within the therapeutic relationship. In most traditional psychotherapy sessions, therapists have much more power than clients. In contrast, feminist therapy emphasizes more egalitarian interactions (Enns, 1997; Gilbert & Scher, 1999; Mahalik et al., 2000; Marecek, 2001b; Simi & Mahalik, 1997; Wyche & Rice, 1997). Here are some of the ways that power can be balanced in feminist therapy:

1. Whenever possible, the therapist should try to enhance the client's power in the therapeutic relationship. After all, if women clients are placed in subordinate roles in therapy, the situation simply mirrors women's inferior status in society.
2. Throughout therapy, clients are encouraged to become more self-confident and independent and to develop skills to help themselves; therapists are educators who help clients discover and enhance their own strengths.
3. The therapist believes that the client—rather than the therapist—is her own best expert on herself.
4. When appropriate, feminist therapists may share information about their own life experiences, further reducing the power differential. However, a therapist's primary tasks are listening and thinking, not talking.

Feminist therapy appears to be a powerful tool in encouraging clients to analyze their psychological problems and to develop their personal strengths. However, we have relatively little current research that examines the effectiveness of feminist therapy. We do know that female clients who consider themselves feminists are more satisfied when their therapist is a feminist (Marecek, 2001b). In other research, clients rated themselves higher on a scale of personal and social power, following therapy sessions with a feminist therapist (Worell & Johnson, 2001).

Ideally, all therapists should respect the value of women and should encourage egalitarian relationships. However, a recent study examined a sample of male therapists; only about one-quarter of them considered themselves feminist therapists (Szymanski et al., 2002). Fortunately, several male therapists have written books outlining how feminist therapy can be useful when working with male clients (G. R. Brooks, 1998; W. S. Pollack & Levant, 1998). Therapists are supposed to focus on improving the psychological well-being of human beings. Isn't it puzzling that many therapists are not more concerned about females having an equal right to be psychologically healthy?

SECTION SUMMARY ■

Treating Psychological Disorders in Women

1. Gender stereotypes may encourage some therapists to misdiagnose some psychological disorders, to misdiagnose some physical illnesses as psychological disorders, and to treat clients in a gender-biased fashion.

2. One clearly harmful violation of ethical conduct is a sexual relationship between a therapist and a client.

3. In treating lesbians and bisexual clients, therapists must be aware of problems caused by sexual prejudice and heterosexism.

4. People of color are less likely than European Americans to use mental health services. Therapists must be aware of characteristics of diverse ethnic groups that may be relevant in therapy.

5. Therapists can increase their skills in helping women of color by a variety of methods, including searching the client's history for her personal strengths, being aware that the client may not share some of the values typically found in her culture, realizing that each ethnic group includes a variety of specific cultures, and learning more about the client's ethnic group.

6. The classic psychodynamic therapy is based on Freudian theory, an approach that emphasizes childhood experiences and unconscious conflict. This gender-biased approach considers women to be masochistic and relatively immature. Mothers are blamed for their children's psychological problems.

7. Cognitive-behavioral therapy emphasizes restructuring inappropriate thoughts and changing behaviors; it is effective in treating depression, eating disorders, and other psychological problems.

8. Drug therapy may sometimes be helpful, but it must be used with caution.

9. Nonsexist therapy treats women and men similarly, and it attempts to avoid gender-stereotyped behavior.

10. Feminist therapy proposes that (a) nonsexist therapy must be practiced, (b) social inequalities have helped shape women's behavior, and (c) power should be more equally divided between the therapist and the client.

■ ■ ■ ■ ■ ■ **CHAPTER REVIEW QUESTIONS** ■ ■ ■ ■ ■ ■

1. What are the characteristics of major depressive disorder? What personal characteristics are most likely to be related to depression? Based on these characteristics, describe a woman who would be *unlikely* to experience depression.

2. What two factors are no longer considered relevant when we try to account for the fact that women are more likely than men to develop depression? What factors seem to be important in explaining this gender difference? In this second list, note how each factor could be related to cultural and societal forces.

3. Discuss anorexia nervosa and bulimia nervosa. Describe typical characteristics of these eating disorders as well as their medical consequences. Explain why women with these two eating disorders would also be likely to experience depression. How does binge-eating disorder differ from these other two problems?

4. Describe the "culture of slimness." How might this emphasis help produce eating disorders? What kind of women would be most likely to resist this cultural norm?

5. Discuss the information on ethnicity and body image. Then summarize the material on the unique concerns that women of color bring to a psychotherapy session. Why must therapists emphasize individual differences within every ethnic group?

6. Describe why the issues of being overweight and dieting present problems that are difficult to solve with respect to the advisability of losing weight and the challenge of permanent weight loss.

7. Based on what you have read in this chapter, why does the classical approach of Sigmund Freud present major problems for those who favor a nonsexist or feminist approach to therapy?

8. Imagine that you are a feminist therapist working with a female client who is severely depressed. Imagine someone who would fit this description, and point out how you would use selected principles of feminist therapy to facilitate her recovery.

9. Many therapists favor an eclectic approach to the treatment of psychological disorders, in which they combine elements of several approaches. If you were a therapist, how could you combine elements of cognitive-behavioral therapy and feminist therapy?

10. In this chapter, we have emphasized psychological disorders. Some theorists point out that psychologists should place more emphasis on how individuals can achieve positive mental health rather than just avoiding disorders. Based on the information in this chapter, describe the characteristics of an individual who is mentally healthy.

NEW TERMS

*psychological disorders (387)
*antisocial personality disorder (387)
*major depressive disorder (387)
 ruminative style (392)
*anorexia nervosa (395)
*amenorrhea (395)
*bulimia nervosa (396)
*binge-eating disorder (396)
 culture of slimness (397)

*psychotherapy (402)
*drug therapy (402)
*sexual prejudice (404)
*heterosexism (404)
*psychodynamic therapy (408)
*masochism (408)
 cognitive-behavioral therapy (409)
 nonsexist therapy (411)
*feminist therapy (411)

The terms asterisked in the New Terms section serve as good search terms for InfoTrac College Edition. Go to http://infotrac.thomsonlearning.com and try these added search terms.

RECOMMENDED READINGS

Nathan, P. E., & Gorman, J. M. (Eds.). (2002). *A guide to treatments that work* (2nd ed.). New York: Oxford University Press. This general resource examines the published research about how a variety of psychological disorders can be treated with psychotherapy and drug therapy; although this book does not address feminist therapy, it will be useful to people who want to learn more about a variety of psychological problems.

Simonds, S. L. (2001). *Depression and women: An integrative treatment approach.* New York: Springer. I recommend this clearly written overview of the complexity of women's experiences with depression.

Thompson, J. K., & Smolak, L. (Eds.). (2001). *Body image, eating disorders, and obesity in youth: Assessment, prevention, and treatment.* Washington, DC: American Psychological Association.

Here's an excellent resource that focuses on risk factors for eating disorders as well as on the assessment, prevention, and treatment of these disorders.

Unger, R. K. (Ed.). (2001). *Handbook of the psychology of women and gender.* New York: Wiley. This superb handbook has 27 chapters focusing on the psychology of women; three chapters that are especially relevant to the current topic include those on feminist clinical psychology,

feminist therapy, and counseling women of color.

Worell, J., & Remer, P. P. (2003). *Feminist perspectives in therapy: Empowering diverse women* (2nd ed.). New York: Wiley. I strongly recommend this interesting book, because it emphasizes feminist and multicultural perspectives. It includes informative chapters on topics such as depression, surviving abuse, and feminist ethics.

ANSWERS TO THE DEMONSTRATIONS

Interpreting Demonstration 12.3: Look at your answers to Demonstration 12.3, and count how many of the following items you endorsed: Items 1, 4, 5, and 9. If you checked most of these, you tend to appreciate a nonsexist therapy approach. Now count how many of the following items you endorsed: Items 2, 3, 6, 7, and 8. Add this second number to the previous total to get a grand total. If your score is close to 9, you tend to appreciate a feminist therapy approach, in addition to nonsexist therapy.

ANSWERS TO THE TRUE-FALSE QUESTIONS

1. True (p. 387); 2. False (p. 387); 3. False (p. 388); 4. True (p. 392); 5. False (p. 395); 6. False (p. 396); 7. False (pp. 397–398); 8. True (p. 399); 9. True (p. 405); 10. True (p. 412).

Violence Against Women

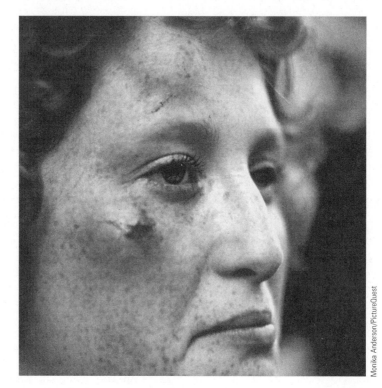

Monika Anderson/PictureQuest

T R U E   O R   F A L S E ?

_____ 1. In order for a remark to be labeled "sexual harassment" from the legal standpoint, the person making the remark must specify that some sort of sexual favor is requested.

_____ 2. According to surveys, about half of female physicians say that they have been sexually harassed.

_____ 3. Women who have been sexually harassed say that the harassment was moderately unpleasant but it had no long-lasting emotional effects.

_____ 4. An estimated 15% to 30% of North American women will be victims of a rape during their lifetime.

_____ 5. More than twice as many women as men report that they are afraid of walking alone at night.

_____ 6. Some women report that the aftereffects of rape last at least a year following the attack.

_____ 7. According to research, virtually all mentally stable men say that they would never consider raping a woman.

_____ 8. The term *abuse of women* refers to both psychological abuse and physical abuse.

_____ 9. Unemployment increases the likelihood of partner abuse.

_____ 10. Most abusive relationships improve spontaneously, but therapy is recommended when the abuse is severe or long-lasting.

A European American professional woman in her thirties met some friends one evening after work. A well-dressed man began a conversation with her and later asked if he could call her sometime. She gave him a business card, which listed only her work address and phone number. When he called later that week, she agreed to meet him for dinner at a restaurant. However, he then began to choose what she would have for her meal; he also stated that any woman he dated must dress and act in a certain way. Realizing that he was overly domineering, she quietly excused herself to go to the women's room and then left the restaurant. Soon afterward, the man discovered her home address, forced his way into her apartment, and beat her. She then obtained a restraining order to keep him away. However, he returned and beat her a second time, even more violently (S. M. Shaw & Lee, 2001).

This woman's story describes abuse, one of the topics of this chapter. Sexual harassment, rape, and the abuse of women may initially seem to have little in common. However, they share important similarities. For instance, all three involve some form of violence—either physical or emotional.

In all three situations, men typically possess more power than women. Sexual harassers are usually persons with power at work or in an academic setting. In rape and abusive situations, men typically have more physical power.

An additional similarity focuses on entitlement, a concept we examined in Chapter 7, on women and work (p. 219). In our culture, many men have a sense of **entitlement;** based on their membership in the male social group, they believe they have a right to certain "privileges" and rewards when they interact with women (Baumeister et al., 2002; Marin & Russo, 1999). For instance, a high-ranking executive assumes he has the right to fondle his secretary. A male college student may feel little guilt about raping his girlfriend. The man described at the beginning of this chapter believes he is entitled to select his female companion's meal—and to batter her if she tries to avoid him (S. M. Shaw & Lee, 2001).

Furthermore, in all three kinds of victimization, women are left feeling even less powerful after the violence. They have been forced to accept unwanted sexual attention, or their bodies have been violated or beaten. Powerlessness is yet another variation on one of the themes of this book: Women are often treated differently from men.

Unfortunately, women seldom regain power by reporting the violence committed against them. Legal procedures are often embarrassing and humiliating; they invade a woman's right to privacy even further. All these acts of violence encourage women to become more silent and more invisible. The relative invisibility of women is a theme we have emphasized repeatedly throughout this book.

Another similarity across all three situations is that people often blame the victim (J. W. White et al., 2001). A woman is sexually harassed because "those tight pants invite it." A woman is raped because she "asked for it" by her seductive behavior. A woman is beaten because "she probably did something to make her husband angry." In contrast, the aggressor is often perceived as behaving "like any normal male." Although attitudes are changing, the aggressor may receive little blame for the violence.

Finally, all three kinds of violence have their origins in the customary gender-role socialization that has operated since childhood (O'Neil & Nadeau, 1999; J. W. White et al., 2001). Men are "supposed to be" aggressive, dominant, and controlling. Women are "supposed to be" unaggressive, submissive, and yielding. Early in life, children also begin to absorb the messages about entitlement and unequal power in male-female relationships. In a sense, sexual harassment, rape, and the abuse of women all represent a tragic exaggeration of traditional gender roles.

SEXUAL HARASSMENT

Sexual harassment refers to unwanted gender-related behavior, such as sexual coercion, offensive sexual attention, and hostile behaviors that focus on gender (Fitzgerald et al., 2001). Most sexual harassment situations occur in either a work setting or a school setting.

The American legal system now prohibits two kinds of sexual harassment. In the first kind, called **quid pro quo harassment,** an individual with power in an organization makes it clear that someone with less power must submit to sexual advances in order to keep a job, get a good grade in a course, receive a promotion, and so forth (Paludi & Barickman, 1998).

The second kind of sexual harassment, called **hostile environment,** applies to a situation in which the atmosphere in a school or work setting is so intimidating and offensive that a student or an employee cannot work effectively (Fitzgerald et al., 2001; Paludi & Barickman, 1998). Before you read further, try Demonstration 13.1, an exercise designed to help you appreciate the characteristics of sexual harassment.

DEMONSTRATION 13.1 ■ ■ ■ ■ ■ ■ ■ ■ ■ ■ ■ ■ ■ ■ ■ ■ ■ ■ ■

Making Judgments About Sexual Harassment

Read each of the following four stories. If you believe that a story describes an incident of sexual harassment, write "yes" in front of the item number. If the story does not seem to describe sexual harassment, write "no." Then, for each story, try to guess what percentage of students at a Northeastern urban university judged the story to represent sexual harassment. (The sample was 50% female, and the study was conducted in 2002.)

1. Dr. X, a male professor, approaches Mary after class and says the following: "Mary, I noticed your new haircut, and it really looks nice." Mary replies, "Thanks, Dr. X." Dr. X says, "No, I mean it *really* looks great . . . or maybe I mean that *you* look great." As she walks off to class, Mary says, "I really have to get to class now, Dr. X."

2. Jill is working with a man named Dr. Q on an independent study. Their work involves meeting together once a week. At their last meeting, the following conversation took place. Dr. Q said, "You know, Jill, we've been meeting for three weeks now, and I can't help but notice how nice you look in those jeans you wear to class. I was wondering why you don't wear them when we meet together. I thought you knew how much they turned me on." Jill did not verbally respond; she simply left the room.

3. Ann got on the elevator on her way to class. As usual, the elevator became crowded, and she was forced to move to the back. Feeling that the person next to her was staring at her, Ann looked up to see who it was. She recognized it was Dr. U from her morning class, and he was eyeing her body up and down and grinning. The elevator doors opened and Ann quickly got out.

4. Ellen is taking a class with Dr. Y. Dr. Y has repeatedly asked Ellen to meet him for coffee or lunch. Ellen has repeatedly declined all his offers. Dr. Y called her at home last night and said, "Ellen, I know you keep refusing to have lunch with me, and I'm calling to find out why and hopefully to change your mind. I'm a nice guy, and all I want to do is spend some time with you so that we can get to know each other better." Ellen told him to stop calling her and hung up the phone.

These stories are based on the vignettes from a study by Dr. Krisanne Bursik (2002). Turn to page 455 at the end of this chapter to compare the percentages you provided with the percentage of students in Bursik's study who judged each story as representing sexual harassment.

Source: From Bursik, K. (2002). Perception of sexual harassment in an academic context. *Sex Roles,* 27, 401–412. Reprinted by permission of Kluwer.

Let's consider several examples of sexual harassment so that we can appreciate the variety of problems in this area.

1. *Quid pro quo sexual coercion.* Deborah, an office manager at a small company, was being bothered by Bill, the marketing manager, who continually described to her his unsatisfying sex life with his wife. He persisted, despite her objections. During a corporate restructuring, Bill became president of the company. In their first meeting, Bill told Deborah, "Either we engage in a sexual relationship, or I no longer need an office manager." Fortunately, Deborah filed a sexual harassment charge and won (Bravo & Cassedy, 1999).

2. *Hostile environment in the workplace.* In a study of Black female firefighters, more than 90% said that they had experienced unwanted sexual teasing, jokes, and remarks on the job (J. D. Yoder & Aniakudo, 1996). The women also reported that their male coworkers played pranks, such as pouring syrup into their firefighting boots and bursting in while they were using the toilet. Many also reported that their male coworkers created a hostile work environment by shunning them. One woman who had been a firefighter for 7 years said that some of the men still refuse to talk to her. It's likely that sexism and racism combined to create an especially hostile environment for these women.

3. *Hostile environment in an academic setting.* Psychologist Keri Heitner (1998) recalls her experience as a graduate student. As she walked down a hallway in the psychology building, one of her male professors approached her and asked, "After classes tonight, why don't you come to my apartment, so that I can make a nude drawing of you?" Fortunately, Heitner had the presence of mind to ask him to repeat the question and then replied, "That's what I thought you said, and if you ever ask me anything like that again, I'm going to the department chair" (p. 14).

Most of this section on sexual harassment examines how males sexually harass females they perceive to be heterosexual. Keep in mind, however, that lesbian women might be sexually harassed, for example, by males or by other women in positions of power. Males can also be sexually harassed by women or by other men. However, in the most common situation, a male is harassing a female (Kurth et al., 2000; Paludi, 2000).

You may read reports about females being harassed by their male classmates, beginning in elementary school and continuing through college; women are also harassed by their peers in the workplace (Bravo & Cassedy, 1999; Duffy et al., 2003; Rozee, 2000a; M. Walsh et al., 2003). In addition, women are also harassed in public settings by whistles, catcalls, and sexually explicit comments. These forms of harassment are certainly worrisome. In this chapter, however, we will focus on two situations in which a female is being harassed by a male with higher status: (1) professors harassing students in college settings and (2) supervisors harassing employees in work settings. Both situations raise particular problems because they involve power inequities and reasonably long-term relationships between the woman and the harasser.

Why Is Sexual Harassment an Important Issue?

Sexual harassment is important for several reasons (L. L. Alexander et al., 2001; Bravo & Cassedy, 1999; B. Murray, 1998; L. Phillips, 1998; Reese & Lindenberg, 1999):

1. Sexual harassment emphasizes that men typically have more power than women in our society.
2. Sexual demands are often coercive because women are offered economic or academic advantages if they comply and harmful consequences if they say no.
3. Sexual harassment dehumanizes women and treats them in a sexist fashion; women are seen primarily as sexual beings rather than as intelligent and skilled employees or students.
4. Women are often forced to be silent victims because of fear and the need to continue either in the workplace or at school.
5. If sexual harassment occurs in a public setting, without condemnation from supervisors, many onlookers will conclude that sexist behavior is acceptable.

Factors associated with sexual harassment can also have more subtle consequences. For instance, men who are likely to sexually harass women have been shown to treat women in a relatively domineering fashion and to spend relatively little time talking with them. Women may feel uncomfortable in these interactions, and their academic and work performance may suffer as a consequence (Driscoll et al., 1998; J. D. Murphy et al., 1999).

How Often Does Sexual Harassment Occur?

It is extremely difficult to estimate how often sexual harassment occurs. The boundaries of sexual harassment are often unclear. Also, people are reluctant to use the label "sexual harassment," even when they have experienced clear-cut harassment (Reese & Lindenberg, 1999; Shepela & Levesque, 1998). Furthermore, many cases go unreported (Fitzgerald et al., 2001; Wenniger & Conroy, 2001).

Reports of sexual harassment on college campuses suggest that between 20% and 40% of undergraduate women have been harassed (C. C. Cochran et al., 1997; V. C. Rabinowitz, 1996; Sandler & Shoop, 1997). Women in graduate programs are typically more likely to experience sexual harassment. For example, in a U.S. survey of 4,501 female physicians, 48% reported that they had experienced gender-based harassment (E. Frank et al., 1998).

The incidence of sexual harassment in the workplace varies widely, depending on the employment setting. Women employed in traditionally male occupations are especially likely to experience sexual harassment (Bondurant & White, 1996; Fitzgerald et al., 2001). For instance, women in the military frequently report sexual teasing, unwanted touching, and pressure for sexual favors. According to one survey, 76% of women in the military said that they had experienced sexual harassment during the previous 12 months (J. D. Yoder, 2001).

Sexual harassment is not limited to North America. Reports come from countries such as the Czech Republic, England, Pakistan, India, China, and Hong Kong (Bauerova, 2000; D. K.-S. Chan et al., 1999; Fitzgerald et al., 2001; Hodges, 2000; Kishwar, 1999; M. Zhou, 1994). In all the cultures examined so far, one universal finding is that only a small percentage of women choose to report the sexual harassment (Fitzgerald et al., 2001).

Women's Reactions to Sexual Harassment

Sexual harassment is not simply a minor inconvenience to women; it can change their lives. If a woman refuses her boss's sexual advances, she may receive a negative job evaluation, a demotion, or a transfer to another job. She may be fired or pressured into quitting (Kurth et al., 2000; Paludi & Barickman, 1998). A woman who has been harassed in an academic setting may drop out of school or miss classes taught by the harasser (Duffy et al., 2002; Paludi & Barickman, 1998). The victim still suffers, even if she is no longer in the harasser's classroom. As one student reported, "Although there are still people there whom I trust and learn from, I am angry and insecure every time I'm in that building" (Paludi et al., 1995, p. 178).

How do women respond emotionally to sexual harassment? Most women experience anxiety, fear, self-doubt, embarrassment, and depression. They may also feel ashamed, as if they were somehow responsible for the harassment (Bravo & Cassedy, 1999; Paludi & Barickman, 1998; Quina, 1996; Woodzicka & LaFrance, 2001). In contrast, women are not as likely to feel responsible when they are victims of crimes such as robbery. Understandably, women who have been sexually harassed may become less self-confident about their academic or occupational abilities (Duffy et al., 2002; Rozee, 2000a; Satterfield & Muehlenhard, 1997). Common physical reactions include headaches, eating disorders, and sleep disturbances (Paludi & Barickman, 1998).

Attitudes About Sexual Harassment

Susan Bordo (1998) recalled her experience with sexual harassment when she was a graduate student. One of her professors had laughingly said, "It's time for class, dear," patting her on the rear as they stood in the open doorway of a classroom filled with other students. When she described the episode to some of her close male friends, they acted casual about the harassment. As they replied, "Well, what did you expect? You don't exactly dress like a nun!" (p. B6).

Men are usually more accepting of sexual harassment than women are, at least in North American research (Burian et al., 1998; Cleveland et al., 2000; LaRocca & Kromrey, 1999; Reese & Lindenberg, 1999). However, the characteristics of the situation are more important than the rater's gender in determining attitudes toward sexual harassment (Gutek & O'Connor, 1995). For example, Bursik (1992, 2002) conducted two studies—a decade apart. She found no gender differences when college students classified the stories you saw in Demonstration 13.1. Notice from the data on page 455 that most of these students considered the situation described in Scenario 2 to be sexual harassment. However, only about half the students thought that the other situations illustrated sexual harassment. Were your own reactions consistent with this pattern?

What to Do About Sexual Harassment

Individual Action.   What can an individual woman do when she has been sexually harassed? Here are some recommendations for students who are concerned about harassment in an academic setting (L. L. Alexander et al., 2001; Paludi, 2000; Quina, 1996):

1. Become familiar with your campus's policy on sexual harassment, and know which officials are responsible for complaints.
2. If a professor's behavior seems questionable, review the situation objectively with someone you trust.
3. Sexual harassment frequently increases when the person being harassed simply tries to disregard it. If the problem persists, consider telling the harasser directly that his sexual harassment makes you feel uncomfortable. Another possible strategy is to send a typewritten letter to the harasser. Give a factual account of the events, describe your objections to the incident, and state clearly that you want the actions to stop (Paludi & Barickman, 1998). Sign your full name to the letter. Many harassment policies cannot be legally applied unless the harasser has been informed that the behavior is unwanted and inappropriate.
4. Keep records of all occurrences, and keep copies of all correspondence.
5. If the problem persists, report it to the appropriate officials on campus. An institution that takes no action is responsible if another act of harassment occurs after an incident is reported.
6. Join a feminist group on campus, or help to start one. A strong support group can encourage real empowerment, reduce the chances that other students will experience sexual harassment, and help to change campus policy on this important issue. Some women have also reported that people who might not identify themselves as feminists may also provide assistance.

These six suggestions can also be adapted for the workplace; employed women can take similar steps to avoid and eliminate sexual harassment. If a harasser persists, threats of exposure to a superior may be necessary. Employees may need to file a formal complaint with a superior, a union official, or a personnel officer. Competent legal advice may also be necessary. Fortunately, a U.S. Supreme Court decision states that employers may be held financially liable when supervisors harass employees, even when the companies are not aware of the misconduct (Fitzgerald et al., 2001).

A woman who files a sexual harassment charge may find that her complaint is treated seriously and compassionately. Unfortunately, however, she may encounter an unsympathetic response from college administrators or company officials (Reese & Lindenberg, 1999). She might be told that the event was simply a misunderstanding or that the harasser is so competent and valuable that this "minor" incident should be forgotten. Many women report feeling completely isolated and alienated during this experience.

Students in women's studies courses often protest that nothing about sexual harassment seems fair. This viewpoint is absolutely correct. A woman shouldn't have to suffer the pain and embarrassment of sexual harassment, see the quality of her work decline, and then—in many cases—find that administrators, supervisors, and the legal system do not support her.

How Men Can Help.   Men who care about women and women's issues can be part of the solution (Zalk, 1996). First, they themselves must avoid behaviors that might be perceived as sexual harassment. In addition, men should speak up when they see another man sexually harassing someone. Harassers may be more likely to stop if other males point out that they are offended by sexual harassment (Langelan, 1993).

If you are a male reading this book, think about what steps you might take if you hear that a woman is being sexually harassed by one of your male friends. It's difficult to tell a male friend that a woman may not enjoy his comments about her body. However, if you do not comment, your silence may be interpreted as approval. You can also offer compassion and support to a female friend who tells you that she has been sexually harassed.

Society's Response to the Harassment Problem.   Individual women and men need to take action against sexual harassment. However, to stop sexual harassment more effectively, *institutions* must be firmly committed to fighting the problem. In a survey of women in the military, only 25% said that their commanding officer had spoken against sexual harassment and wanted it stopped (Firestone & Harris, 2003). Clearly, most officers were not firmly committed to stopping sexual harassment.

Universities and corporations need to develop clear policies about sexual harassment (Paludi, 2000; Reese & Lindenberg, 1999; Wenniger & Conroy, 2001). They should also publicize these policies and hold workshops—with top administrators in attendance—on sexual harassment issues. Students and employees should receive information about procedures to follow if they believe they have been sexually harassed.

Public opinion also needs to be changed. People must be informed that women should not be blamed when they are victims of sexual harassment. The public must also become more aware that sexual harassment limits women's rights and opportunities in academic and work settings. Men need to realize that women often do not appreciate uninvited sexual attention. In addition, behavior that a man regards as flirtation may feel more like sexual harassment to a woman. Some men who harass may not be aware that they are creating a problem. Others may believe that they have a sanction to harass because of good-natured responses from other men.

However, the real answer lies in the unequal distribution of power between men and women (Langelan, 1993). If we really want to eliminate sexual harassment, we must go beyond the level of trying to convince individual harassers to alter their behavior. Instead, we need to change the uneven distribution of power that encourages sexual harassment.

SECTION SUMMARY   ▪

Sexual Harassment

1. Sexual harassment, rape, and abuse of women all focus on violence and power inequalities—situations in which men feel entitled to certain privileges. All of these behaviors make women feel less powerful and less visible, and women are also blamed for causing the violence. These three forms of violence are also related to gender-role socialization.

2. Two kinds of sexual harassment are (a) quid pro quo harassment and (b) harassment that creates a hostile environment.

3. Sexual harassment is an important issue because (a) it emphasizes violence and gender inequalities, (b) it is coercive and dehumanizing, (c) it may force women to be silent victims, and (d) it may encourage onlookers to believe that sexist behavior is acceptable.

4. Sexual harassment occurs fairly often in academia and in the workplace; it is especially frequent for women in traditionally male occupations.

5. Women who have been sexually harassed often quit jobs or leave school; they may experience anxiety, fear, embarrassment, depression, shame, and reduced self-confidence.

6. Men typically have more tolerant attitudes toward sexual harassment than women do.

7. When we consider how to reduce sexual harassment, we must emphasize not only the individual actions of women and men but also the policies of universities and corporations, as well as the more general issue of the unequal distribution of power in society.

RAPE

Rape can be defined as sexual penetration—without the individual's consent—obtained by force or by threat of physical harm, or when the victim is incapable of giving consent (Bachar & Koss, 2001; S. M. Shaw & Lee, 2001). A broader term, **sexual assault,** includes sexual touching and other forms of unwanted sexual contact, which may be accompanied by psychological pressure and coercion or by physical threats (L. L. Alexander et al., 2001). For example, a man may say, "If you really loved me, you'd let me," or he may threaten to leave the relationship if the woman does not comply. The legal definition of rape may be used in a court case. However, the inclusiveness of the term *sexual assault* helps us understand the many ways in which men have power over women's lives.

Some rapes are committed by strangers. However, we'll emphasize in this section that a rapist is more likely to be an acquaintance. In other words, women who are worried about rape need to be especially concerned about someone they already know rather than a stranger.

A rapist may even be a woman's husband. By some estimates, between 10% and 15% of wives have been raped by a husband or an ex-husband (L. A. Morris, 1997). Unfortunately, only 17 countries in the world currently consider marital rape a crime (Women in Action, 2001).

Tragically, rape is found in virtually every culture and in most civilizations throughout history, not just in contemporary North America (Bachar & Koss, 2001; Zillman, 1998). In recent years, invading soldiers have systematically raped women in countries such as Bangladesh, Cyprus, Peru, Somalia, and Uganda (Agathangelou, 2000; Neft & Levine, 1997). In one of the most tragic episodes, Serbian forces in the former Yugoslavia raped countless thousands of Muslim women in an attempt to drive Muslims from their homeland (Nikolic-Ristanovic, 2000; Sharratt & Kaschak, 1999). Rape is therefore a weapon of war as well as a sexual attack on individual women (Agathangelou, 2000).

Other examples of rape have been less publicized. Consider the young men at a coed boarding school in Kenya. The male students had called for a strike against the school's headmaster. When their female classmates refused to strike, the young men attacked, raping 71 young women and killing 19 others. The deputy principal—a woman—announced, "The boys never meant any harm against the girls. They just wanted to rape" (Francisco, 1999, p. 1).

How Often Does Rape Occur?

As you can imagine, estimating the incidence of rape is difficult. One problem is that surveys differ in their definitions of rape and sexual assault. Another problem is that women are reluctant to indicate on a survey that they have been raped (Koss, 1992). Furthermore, only a fraction of rape victims report the crime to the police. In the United States, for instance, only about 5% to 20% of victims report the rape, depending on the group that is surveyed (Bachar & Koss, 2001; Boeschen et al., 1998; S. M. Shaw & Lee, 2001; J. W. White et al., 2001). In the United States, women report about 90,000 rapes to the police each year (U.S. Census Bureau, 2001b)—certainly an underestimate of the true number of rapes. Current estimates in both the United States and Canada suggest that between 15% and 30% of women will be victims of rape at some point during their lives (J. A. Humphrey & White, 2000; L. A. Morris, 1997; Muehlenhard et al., 1997; Tjaden & Thoennes, 1998). The data clearly demonstrate that rape is a real problem for women in North America.

In other countries, the percentage of women who report a rape is even lower. In South Korea, for example, fewer than 2% of rape victims contact the police (United Nations, 1995). Extremely low reporting is understandable in countries such as Pakistan, where a woman who has been raped may find herself charged with adultery. The judicial system can then impose unspeakably harsh sentences, such as death by stoning for illegal sexual relations (Neft & Levine, 1997). Meanwhile, the rapist is usually not punished because the law requires several eyewitnesses to convict a rapist.

DEMONSTRATION 13.2 ■ ■ ■ ■ ■ ■ ■ ■ ■ ■ ■ ■ ■ ■ ■ ■ ■ ■

Knowledge About Rape

For each of the following statements about rape, check the space that represents your response. The correct answers are listed on page 455.

	True	False
1. Women who have had sexual relationships with a man often try to protect their reputation by claiming they have been raped.	____	____
2. Women cannot always prevent being raped by resisting their attackers.	____	____
3. Men rape because they experience uncontrollable sexual urges.	____	____
4. Most women secretly want to be raped.	____	____
5. Most rapes are not reported to the police.	____	____
6. A woman who is sexually experienced will not really be damaged by rape.	____	____
7. Women who dress in a sexually seductive way provoke rape.	____	____
8. Most reported sexual assaults actually were true cases of sexual assaults.	____	____
9. Sexual assaults usually occur away from a woman's home—in isolated areas.	____	____
10. You can tell whether someone is a rapist by his appearance or general behavior.	____	____

Source: Based partly on Worell and Remer (1992, pp. 195–196).

Before you read further, try Demonstration 13.2 to assess your knowledge about rape. Then you can check the answers at the end of the chapter.

Acquaintance Rape

Psychologists and other researchers are increasingly aware that a rapist is not likely to be a stranger attacking in a dark alley. Instead, a rapist may be your chemistry lab partner, your sister's boyfriend, a business acquaintance, or the boy next door. **Acquaintance rape** can be defined as "unlawful sexual intercourse accomplished by force or fear with a person known to the victim who is not related by blood or marriage" (Wallace, 1999, p. 313). Let's consider some important aspects of acquaintance rape as well as attitudes toward this kind of sexual assault.

Surveys suggest that about 15% of women will experience acquaintance rape. An additional 35% to 40% of women will experience some other form of sexual assault from an acquaintance (J. W. White & Kowalski, 1998).

Women who have been forced—against their will—to have sex with a person they know are often unsure whether they have been raped (Wallace, 1999). Researchers in Canada and the United States have studied groups of women who had been assaulted by an acquaintance and whose experience met the legal definition for rape. Among these women, only about 40% classified the assault as rape (Kahn & Andreoli Mathie, 2000; Shimp & Chartier, 1998). In other words, most of these women had indeed been raped, yet they did not apply that term to the assault.

What kind of conditions are associated with acquaintance rape? By some estimates, at least half of rapes are associated with the use of alcohol by either the perpetrator or the victim (Abbey, 2002; Christopher, 2001; Marchell & Cummings, 2001). Alcohol clearly impairs people's ability to make appropriate decisions (Abbey et al., 2000). For instance, women who have been drinking may be more likely to judge a sexually aggressive situation as being relatively safe (Testa & Livingston, 1999).

You may also have read about a drug called Rohypnol, sometimes called roofie or the date rape drug. Rohypnol can be mixed with alcohol to increase the sensation of drunkenness (L. L. Alexander et al., 2001; Gorin, 2000; Zorza, 2001). Both the United States and Canada have reported many cases in which Rohypnol or some similar drug has been slipped into a woman's drink. The effect is like an alcohol blackout; the woman typically has no recall of any events that occurred after she passed out, even a rape attack. Obviously, a drug-induced rape can have a devastating effect on a woman.

Other researchers have tried to determine what kind of setting is associated with acquaintance rape. For example, certain conditions at fraternity parties increase the risk of rape. Specifically, rape is more common when the men attending the parties engage in hostility and conversations that degrade women (Boswell & Spade, 1999; S. E. Humphrey & Kahn, 2000).

Some cases of acquaintance rape can probably be traced to a particular kind of miscommunication. Specifically, research by Antonia Abbey and her colleagues has demonstrated that men are more likely than women to perceive other people as being seductive (Abbey et al., 2000, 2001). For example, Saundra may smile pleasantly when talking with Ted. To her, this nonverbal behavior is intended to convey platonic friendship. Nevertheless, Ted may interpret her behavior as a sexual invitation.

In general, research has confirmed the tendency for men to interpret behavior in a more sexual manner than women do (Edmondson & Conger, 1995; Patton & Mannison, 1995). Furthermore, sexually aggressive men are especially likely to misinterpret neutral behavior (V. Anderson et al., 2002; Bondurant & Donat, 1999). Unfortunately, however, this research has often been misconstrued

(M. Crawford, 1995). For example, the popular media often blame women for sending the wrong messages rather than acknowledging that men misinterpret the messages.

The findings on miscommunication have practical implications for both women and men. First, women should be aware that their friendliness may be misperceived by men. Second, men must learn that friendly verbal and nonverbal messages from a woman may simply mean "I like you" or "I enjoy talking with you." A smile and extended eye contact do not necessarily mean "I want to have a sexual relationship with you."

Fear of Rape

In the previous sections, we focused on women who had been raped. However, we also need to consider that all women suffer because of the threat of rape (Beneke, 1997; Rozee, 2000a). Young girls and elderly women can be raped, and many women are raped in the "safety" of their own homes—the one location where they are supposed to feel most secure. All women are vulnerable. One woman reported a routine that might sound familiar:

> When I get into the car, I always check the back seat to make sure that there is no one lurking around. I always have my keys in my hand, so that when I get to the car, I can stick the key into the door. . . . And I lock the doors right away. (Stanko, 1993, p. 159)

Surveys in both the United States and Canada confirm this perceived danger and fear of rape (M. B. Harris & Miller, 2000). For instance, about 40% of women report that they feel unsafe when they are out alone at night, in contrast to only about 15% of men (M. D. Schwartz & DeKeseredy, 1997; Statistics Canada, 2000; L. E. Taylor, 1995). Furthermore, men are often astonished to learn about the large number of safety measures that women employ (Rozee, 2000a).

Fear of rape controls women's behavior and restricts what they can do, no matter where they live. I teach at a college that is located in a small village in upstate New York farmland. Nevertheless, if my female students are alone at night, they do not feel safe. Sadly, the fear of rape drastically reduces women's sense of freedom (Rozee, 2000a).

A survey of women at a Midwestern university documented that they take many precautions to avoid being raped by a stranger. However, they take significantly fewer precautions to avoid being raped by an acquaintance, even though they correctly acknowledge that acquaintance rape is more common than stranger rape (Hickman & Muehlenhard, 1997).

We need to examine several important aspects of rape: women's reactions to rape, attitudes and myths about rape, child sexual abuse, and rape prevention.

Women's Reactions to Rape

Women experience many diverse reactions during a rape attack. Naturally, a woman's responses may depend on the nature of the attack, whether she knows the assailant, the threat of danger, her stage in life, and other circumstances.

However, almost all women who have been raped report that they were terrified, repulsed, confused, overwhelmed, and anxious during the time they were being raped (Lloyd & Emery, 2000). Many women say that they had felt their life was in danger (Raitt & Zeedyk, 2000; Ullman, 2000).

During the rape, some women report that they feel detachment from their own body (Pierce-Baker, 1998; Raine, 1998). One woman described her reaction to an acquaintance rape:

> The experience moved from heavy petting to forced intercourse. I realized that a fly on the wall watching would have seen two people making love. But inside I was horrified and remembered thinking to myself that this can't be happening to me. I felt like throwing-up, and I shriveled up inside of myself, so that the outside of my body and the parts he was touching were just a shell. (Funderburk, 2001, p. 263)

Short-Term Adjustment.   Women report a wide range of feelings during the first few weeks after a rape. Some women have an expressive style. They show their feelings of fear, anger, and anxiety by crying and being restless and tense (Kahn & Andreoli Mathie, 2000; Lloyd & Emery, 2000). Others have a controlled style; they hide their feelings with a calm, composed, and subdued external appearance.

Once again, we must emphasize our theme of individual differences. For example, M. Fine (1997a) described a 24-year-old mother who had just experienced a brutal gang rape. She showed little concern for her own physical and mental health and chose not to take legal action. As she told the staff members in the hospital emergency room:

> Prosecute? No, I just want to get home. While I'm pickin' some guy out of some line, who knows who's messin' around with my momma and my baby. (p. 152)

Most rape victims feel helpless and devalued. Women frequently feel guilty as well, and they blame themselves for the rape (Funderburk, 2001; Kahn & Andreoli Mathie, 2000; Lloyd & Emery, 2000). For instance, one woman who had been raped by an acquaintance said, "I never thought of it as date rape until very recently. I just always thought of it as my fault that I let things get out of hand" (Lloyd & Emery, 2000, p. 119). Self-blame is a particularly troublesome reaction because, in nearly all cases, the woman did nothing to precipitate the assault.

Immediately following a rape, a woman may experience physical symptoms in addition to psychological effects. She may be sore and bruised. She may also experience gynecological symptoms, such as vaginal discharge and generalized pain. Realistically, a woman who has been raped needs to worry about whether her attacker infected her with AIDS and other sexually transmitted diseases—in addition to the possibility of pregnancy (Golding, 1996; W. S. Rogers & Rogers, 2001). However, many women are too upset or too ashamed to seek medical attention.

A woman who has been raped must also decide whether to report the crime to the police. Women often decide not to make an official report because "it wouldn't do any good." They believe that the criminal justice system won't handle the case effectively, that officials won't believe them, and that they might be embarrassed by the verifying procedure. These fears may be realistic. The legal system often harasses and frightens women who have been raped, often minimizes their anguish, and often blames victims rather than supporting them (Raitt & Zeedyk, 2000; Rhode, 1997). In recent years, however, a growing number of women have reported that they were treated with compassion and respect.

Long-Term Adjustment. The effects of a rape do not disappear suddenly. The physical and mental aftereffects may last for years. Common physical health problems include pelvic pain, excessive menstrual bleeding, vaginal infections, gastrointestinal problems, and headaches (Golding, 1999b, 1999c; Golding et al., 1998; C. M. West et al., 2000). Excessive weight loss, eating disorders, substance abuse, and sexual dysfunction are also common (Funderburk, 2001; Laws & Golding, 1996).

Many rape victims also meet the criteria for a psychological disorder called **posttraumatic stress disorder (PTSD),** a pattern of symptoms such as intense fear, heightened anxiety, and emotional numbing that follow a traumatic event (American Psychiatric Association, 2000; Foa, 1998; Funderburk, 2001). A woman experiencing PTSD following a rape may report that she keeps reexperiencing the rape, either in nightmares or in thoughts intruding during daily activities. Her memories of the rape may seem vivid and emotionally intense. One large-scale study reported that 32% of rape victims met the criteria for PTSD during the period following the rape. In addition, 12% still experienced PTSD at least one year afterward (Foa, 1998). Once again, however, individual differences are striking. For instance, many women experience a decrease in psychological symptoms within 3 months of the assault, but some women will continue to have symptoms for several years (Warshaw, 2001).

Many women seek professional psychotherapy to reduce persistent symptoms. Controlled studies have shown that several kinds of psychotherapy are effective. Many current approaches use components of the cognitive-behavioral approach (see p. 409 in Chapter 12). For example, the therapist may ask the client to gradually confront the painful memories. Then the therapist helps her manage the anxieties that arise as she creates a mental image of the traumatic event (Foa, 1998; Meadows & Foa, 1999). Group counseling can also be beneficial because women can share their concerns with others who have survived similar experiences (Funderburk, 2001).

Women who are raped can often manage to transform their terrifying experience in a way that makes them stronger, more determined, and more resilient. Many survivors choose to speak out against violence, for example, at a forum on a college campus. As Funderburk (2001) wrote:

> Besides being a therapeutic experience in its own right, speaking out helps transform self-blame to anger and can galvanize the campus to making a commitment to social change through education and awareness. (p. 278)

Attitudes About Rape

Before you read further, try Demonstration 13.3 on page 432, which examines your own perspectives on rape.

Women who are raped are often doubly victimized, first by the assailant and later by the attitudes of other people. The victim may find that her own family

DEMONSTRATION 13.3 ■ ■ ■ ■ ■ ■ ■ ■ ■ ■ ■ ■ ■ ■ ■ ■ ■ ■

Assigning Responsibility for Rape

Read the first scenario in this demonstration. Then decide who is responsible for the occurrence of the rape, John or Jane. If you believe that John is entirely responsible, assign a value of 100% to the John column and 0% to the Jane column. If they are both equally responsible, assign a value of 50% to each one. If Jane is entirely responsible, assign a value of 0% to the John column and 100% to the Jane column. Use any values between 0% and 100%, as long as the two values sum to 100. To make the situations comparable, assume that both John and Jane are college students in all five scenarios. After completing the first scenario, read and evaluate each subsequent one.

John   Jane

_____ _____ 1. Jane is walking back to her dorm from the library at 9 p.m., taking a route that everyone considers safe. As she passes the science building, John leaps out, knocks her down, drags her to an unlit area, and rapes her.

_____ _____ 2. Jane is at a party, where she meets a pleasant-looking student named John. After dancing for a while, he suggests they go outside to cool off. No one else is outside. John knocks her down, drags her to an unlit area, and rapes her.

_____ _____ 3. Jane is at a party, and she is wearing a very short skirt. She meets a pleasant-looking student named John. After dancing for a while, he suggests they go outside to cool off. No one else is outside. John knocks her down, drags her to an unlit area, and rapes her.

_____ _____ 4. Jane is on a first date with John, whom she knows slightly from her history class. After the movies, they go out for an elegant late-night meal. They decide to split the cost of both the movies and the meal. In the car on the way home, John stops in a secluded area. Jane tries to escape once she realizes what is happening, but John is much larger than she is, and he pins her down and rapes her.

_____ _____ 5. Jane is on a first date with John, whom she knows slightly from her history class. After the movies, they go out for an elegant late-night meal. John pays for the cost of both the movies and the meal. In the car on the way home, John stops in a secluded area. Jane tries to escape once she realizes what is happening, but John is much larger than she is, and he pins her down and rapes her.

and friends, the court system, and society all tend to blame her and treat her negatively because of something that was not her fault. These responses are particularly damaging at a time when she needs help and compassion.

The legal system's treatment of rape is mostly beyond the scope of this book. However, we hear numerous reports of injustice and mistreatment. For example, a judge in Massachusetts explained why he had given a rapist a light sentence: "It's not like [the victim] was tortured or chopped up." A New York City judge recommended leniency for a man who had forcibly sodomized a retarded woman, because "there was no violence here" (Rhode, 1997, p. 122).

People differ in their attitudes about rape. For example, people with traditional gender roles or conservative viewpoints are more likely to blame rape victims for an assault (B. E. Johnson et al., 1997; A. J. Lambert & Raichle, 2000; Simonson & Subich, 1999).

In addition, men are usually more likely than women to blame rape victims for the assault (G. Cowan & Quinton, 1997; Haworth-Hoeppner, 1998; A. J. Lambert & Raichle, 2000; Workman & Freeburg, 1999). For example, Alan J. Lambert and Katherine Raichle (2000) asked students at a Midwestern university to read a date rape scenario in which students named Bill and Donna began talking at a party and then go to her apartment. They undress; Donna says she does not want to have sex, yet Bill continues, despite her continuous pleading. Participants were asked how much they thought each person could be blamed for what happened. As Figure 13.1 shows, both female and male participants thought that

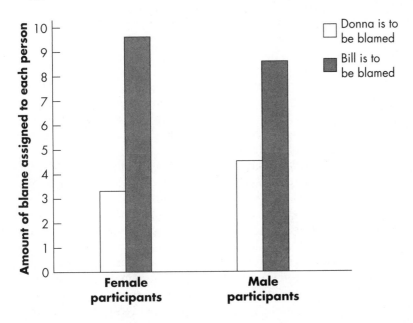

FIGURE 13.1 ■ Responses to an acquaintance rape scenario, as a function of the participant's gender. (Note: 0 = not at all to be blamed; 10 = very much to be blamed.)

Source: Based on A. J. Lambert and Raichle (2000).

Bill was more to blame than Donna. However, you can see that males assigned a greater proportion of the total blame to Donna.

People's attitudes about rape also depend on the circumstances surrounding the assault. For instance, people are much more likely to blame the rapist in a case of stranger rape than in a case of acquaintance rape (L. A. Morris, 1997; Wallace, 1999). Compare your answers to the first and second scenario in Demonstration 13.3. In the first scenario, did you assign all (or almost all) of the blame to John? Did you shift the blame somewhat when Jane had known John for perhaps 30 minutes? People are also reluctant to use the word *rape* to describe an assault in which two individuals know each other (Hannon et al., 1996).

Now look at your response for the third scenario, in which Jane was wearing a short skirt. People are likely to hold a woman more responsible for a rape if she is wearing a short skirt rather than more conservative clothing (Workman & Freeburg, 1999).

Now see whether your assignment of blame differed for Scenarios 4 and 5. In general, people are more likely to hold a woman responsible for a rape if the man paid for the date (L. A. Morris, 1997; Parrot, 1999). Let's say that the evening cost $90. In Scenario 4, they therefore each paid $45. In Scenario 5, John paid $90. If John pays $45 extra, does he have the right to rape Jane?

Myths About Rape

The attitudes toward rape that we have just examined are partially shaped by numerous myths about rape, rapists, and rape victims. As you might imagine, these rape myths can intensify the anguish of a woman who has been raped. Here are five of the more common myths:

Myth 1: Rapists are strangers, that is, people unknown to the victim. We don't know precisely the percentage of rapes committed by strangers, especially because women are less likely to report a rape that was committed by someone they know. However, as we have emphasized in this chapter, rapes are frequently committed by acquaintances and by relatives.

Myth 2: Only deviant men would consider raping a woman. Many people believe the myth that only men with serious psychological disorders would think about raping someone (B. E. Johnson et al., 1997; Rozee, 2000b). This myth is not correct. For example, Osland and her colleagues (1996) gave a questionnaire about rape to undergraduate males at a small Midwestern college affiliated with a Protestant church. We might expect males at this kind of college to be especially repulsed by thoughts of sexual violence. However, 34% of them reported some likelihood to engage in rape or forced sex—similar to the percentages reported by males at other colleges (Rozee, 2000b). These results certainly do not imply that every college male is a potential rapist. However, the high percentage who would consider rape—in some circumstances—suggests that the inclination to rape is not limited to a few deviant men.

Myth 3: Women ask to be raped; they could avoid rape if they wanted to. Some people believe that women invite rape (Hinck & Thomas, 1999; Worell & Remer, 2003). According to one study, for example, 17% of undergraduates agreed with the statement that women provoke rape (B. E. Johnson et al., 1997). Rape is the crime that is most likely to be blamed on the victim (J. W. White & Sorenson, 1992). In addition, many advertisements glamorize rape. For example, one perfume ad that appeared in several teen magazines portrayed a very young woman along with the message, "Apply generously to your neck so he can smell the scent as you shake your head 'no'" (Kilbourne, 1999, p. 213). Although the reasons are not clear, women of color are especially likely to be blamed for being raped (A. I. Castañeda, 1998; M. Fine & Carney, 2001; A. Smith, 2001).

Myth 4: Women routinely lie about rape. In a few rare cases, rape charges against a man are later found to be false. However, the percentage of false reports is very low. In the United States, for example, about 1% to 2% of women's reports of rapes are estimated to be false—about the same as the incidence of false reports for other violent crimes (C. A. Ward, 1995). Unfortunately, many people partly believe this rape myth. For example, Hinck and Thomas (1999) studied rape myths among college students. One item on the questionnaire was "Women frequently call rape falsely" (p. 821). On a scale where a rating of 1 indicated complete acceptance of the myth and 6 indicated complete rejection of the myth, the male average was only 3.9 and the female average was only 4.5.

Myth 5: Pornography provides a "safety valve" or catharsis that makes men less likely to rape. According to this catharsis myth, rape would decrease if pornography were more widely available. However, researchers have discovered no support for this myth (R. J. Harris, 1994; B. A. Scott, 2000). Instead, pornography that emphasizes violence can indeed be harmful.

Consider a study by Malamuth (1998) in which men were asked whether they had ever been sexually aggressive toward a woman. Malamuth also assessed these men with respect to three risk factors, which he called hostile masculinity, promiscuity, and pornography consumption. The results showed that 72% of the men who were high in hostility, high in promiscuity, and high in pornography consumption reported at least one case of sexual aggression. In contrast, 44% of the men who were high in hostility, high in promiscuity, and *low* in pornography consumption reported sexual aggression. Although we need to be cautious about confounding variables, men who frequently viewed pornography had a 64% higher risk of sexual aggression in this sample. (Incidentally, "only" 11% of men who were low on all three variables reported sexual aggression.)

Pornography is clearly a complex social, moral, and legal issue (Koss, 1999; Russell, 1998; B. A. Scott, 2000). Many men can view pornography without behaving violently toward women. However, pornography is not simply an innocent entertainment.

Child Sexual Abuse

So far, we have focused on the sexual abuse of teenage and adult women. We also need to discuss child sexual abuse, which is one of the most devastating forms of sexual violence. For example, Katherine Brady (1993)—now a middle-aged woman—recalled how her father sexually abused her from the ages of 8 to 18. He showed her pornographic photos as "teaching tools" before engaging in fellatio and sexual intercourse. He also played sexual games with her, for example, pretending that he was wiring her breasts together. The issue of child sexual abuse reminds us that adult women are not the only victims of violence; even young children are vulnerable.

Child sexual abuse is particularly cruel because, in most cases, children are abused by relatives, neighbors, and caretakers. The irony is that the abusers are the very individuals who should be protecting them, nurturing them, and acting in their best interests.

Definitions of child sexual abuse vary. Some definitions specify physical contact between the perpetrator and the child, and some do not. However, according to a typical definition, **child sexual abuse** is sexual activities with a child under circumstances that can harm the child's health or welfare (Wallace, 1999).

The incidence of child sexual abuse depends on whether we use a broad or a limited definition of the term. Estimations are also difficult because only a fraction of the cases are reported. Even so, estimates suggest that about 20% to 25% of all females had experienced child sexual abuse by the time they were 18 years old (L. Phillips, 1998; Wallace, 1999).

Incest is a particular kind of child sexual abuse; again, definitions vary. One accepted definition is that **incest** refers to sexual relations between blood relatives (Wallace, 1999). Unfortunately, a large proportion of child sexual abuse incidents, including rape, are committed by relatives (L. Phillips, 1998; J. W. White et al., 2001).

The Consequences of Child Sexual Abuse.   Sexual abuse can have a profound impact on a child, both immediately and over the long term. The immediate psychological consequences of child sexual abuse include fear, anger, depression, and guilt. Nightmares and other sleep disturbances are also common. As you might expect, many victims also stop trusting other people (Wallace, 1999). The long-term consequences of child sexual abuse may include posttraumatic stress disorder (discussed on page 431), depression, substance abuse, eating disorders, and risky sexual behavior (Laws, 1998; Saywitz et al., 2000; Wallace, 1999). In addition, a girl who has been raped may have lifelong problems with her reproductive system (Laws, 1998).

Ethnicity has an important impact on a child's reaction to sexual abuse (Fontes, 1995). For example, many Asian cultures emphasize loyalty to parents and to other adults, and sexual issues are not discussed (Okamura et al., 1995; Root, 1998). As a result, child sexual abuse is seldom reported to authorities, and the child is often blamed for somehow attracting the adult's sexual attention.

The Recovered-Memory/False-Memory Controversy.   The topic of child sexual abuse has created a major debate among psychologists. This topic has important implications for women's lives. When children have been sexually abused, some psychologists argue that children may forget their memory of that experience, perhaps recovering that memory when a later event triggers recall (the **recovered-memory perspective**). Other psychologists argue that many of these "recovered memories" are actually incorrect memories or constructed stories about events that never really happened (the **false-memory perspective**). This controversy has produced hundreds of articles, chapters, and books (e.g., D. P. Brown et al.,

1998; de Rivera, 2000; Enns, 2000; Freyd, 1996; Freyd & DePrince, 2001; Loftus & Guyer, 2002a, 2002b; Stoler et al., 2001; L. M. Williams & Banyard, 1999).

One major problem is that we cannot easily determine whether a memory of childhood abuse is accurate. Children are abused in private settings without witnesses. Also, in order to resolve the recovered-memory/false-memory controversy, psychologists cannot ethically conduct genuinely realistic research about child sexual abuse. We know from research on eyewitness testimony that people can be convinced to create a false memory for an event that never really happened. For example, researchers working with adults can plant a "memory" of a fictitious childhood event, such as spilling punch at a wedding. In follow-up interviews, these adults may claim that the event really did occur (Hyman et al., 1995; Loftus, 1997). However, we cannot generalize from the creation of bland false memories such as these to the creation of traumatic memories about sexual abuse (Freyd & Quina, 2000).

In the current era, psychologists in both the United States and Canada have begun to adopt a position that acknowledges the complexity of the issues. They argue that both the recovered-memory and the false-memory positions are at least partly correct (e.g., Kimball, 1999; Matlin, 2002; Prout & Dobson, 1998). Here are some general points:

1. In many cases, children can provide accurate testimonies about how they have been abused sexually (for instance, by a stranger), and they resist "remembering" false information that someone presented to them (Bidrose & Goodman, 2000; G. S. Goodman et al., 2001).

2. In some cases, people who have truly experienced childhood sexual abuse may forget about the abuse for many decades, and they suddenly recover that memory; this recovered memory is especially likely when the abuser was a close relative or other trusted adult (Freyd, 1996; Schacter, 1996; Schacter et al., 1999).

3. In some other cases, misinformation about child sexual abuse can be implanted by a therapist, a relative, or another person, and an individual mistakenly "remembers" it; this false memory is especially likely when the misinformation is plausible and when it focuses on relatively trivial details (Pezdek, 2001; Stoler et al., 2001). Unfortunately, however, some individuals can "remember" an elaborate history of child abuse that did not actually happen (Loftus & Guyer, 2002a, 2002b; Tavris, 2002).

In any event, the ongoing recovered-memory/false-memory debate should not distract us from our central concerns. Childhood sexual abuse is a critically important problem in our society because children are frequently betrayed by close caregivers who use power inappropriately (Freyd, 1996, 1997; Herman, 2000).

Rape Prevention

We've examined several important characteristics of rape; what can people do to prevent it? Rape prevention is an issue both for individual women and for our entire society. Table 13.1, which lists some precautions that individual women

TABLE 13.1 ■ Safety Precautions to Avoid a Rape Confrontation with a Stranger

Note: Read the section on individuals' prevention of rape by strangers (page 439) before you look at the following information.

General Precautions

1. Before an emergency arises, locate the nearest Rape Crisis Center (or the appropriate organization on your college campus) to obtain material on rape prevention.
2. Make certain that your consumption of alcohol or other drugs does not endanger your alertness; women who use drugs or alcohol before a rape attack experience more severe sexual abuse and bodily injury.
3. Take a self-defense course; learn the vulnerable body parts of a potential attacker.
4. If you are attacked, do not be afraid to be rude. Instead, yell loudly and throw any available object at the attacker.

Precautions at Home

1. Make certain to use secure locks on doors and windows.
2. Ask repairmen and delivery men for identification before opening the door; do not let strangers inside your home to use your phone.
3. If you live in an apartment, don't enter the elevator with a strange man and don't enter a deserted basement or laundry room; insist that the apartment manager keep hallways, entrances, and grounds well lit.

Precautions on the Street

1. Do not hitchhike. (Unfortunately, hitchhiking is notoriously dangerous.)
2. When you are walking, walk purposefully and assertively; be alert to your surroundings.
3. Avoid being alone on the streets or on campus late at night; if you cannot avoid being alone, carry a whistle that will make a loud noise, or a "practical" weapon such as an umbrella, a pen, or keys.
4. If you are being followed by a car, quickly turn around and then walk in the opposite direction to the nearest open store or neighbor.

Precautions in Cars and on Buses or Subways

1. Keep car doors locked, even when you are riding.
2. Keep your gas tank filled and the car in good working order. If you have car trouble, raise the hood; if a male offers to help, ask him to call the police.
3. If you are being followed, don't pull into your driveway; drive to the nearest police or fire station and honk your horn.
4. At bus or subway stations, stay in well-lit sections, near change booths or near a group of people.

Sources: Based on L. L. Alexander et al. (2001), Crooks and Baur (2002), Parrot (1999), Rozee (2000b), and Ullman and Knight (1993).

can take, is culled from much longer lists in several resources. More than 1,100 different rape-prevention strategies have been listed, and the advice is often confusing and conflicting (Corcoran & Mahlstedt, 1999; Fischhoff, 1992). Furthermore, no magic formula can prevent rape, although some strategies may reduce the dangers. Let's consider separately how women can help prevent rape by strangers and by acquaintances. Then we'll discuss how society can work to prevent rape.

Individuals' Prevention of Rape by Strangers.   Two major issues arise in connection with what individual women can do to avoid rape. The first issue can be called the blame-the-victim problem. Notice that many of the items in Table 13.1 will force women to limit their own freedom. Women should not hitchhike or walk in unlighted areas. Why should women—the potential victims—be the ones who have to restrict their behavior? This complaint cannot be answered satisfactorily (Corcoran & Mahlstedt, 1999; Rozee, 2000b). The situation definitely *is* unjust. However, the reality is that women are less likely to be raped if they take these precautions. This injustice also emphasizes that the real solutions would require changes in society, rather than modifying only your own behavior.

The second issue about rape prevention at the individual level is whether a woman should attempt to physically resist an attacker. The studies show that women *reduce* their chances of being raped when they try to block their assailants physically, push them, or incapacitate them (Allison & Wrightsman, 1993; Fischhoff, 1992; Parrot, 1996; Rozee, 2000b). Notice, then, that the most effective techniques are those that are assertive and stereotypically masculine rather than stereotypically feminine (Parrot, 1999).

Resources on rape avoidance also recommend training in self-defense, especially because self-defense affords women greater empowerment and personal competence (Crooks & Baur, 2002; Hammerle, 1997). In a rape situation, women must quickly assess the specific situation, as well as their own physical strength, before deciding whether to resist. However, as Parrot (1996) pointed out, "Even if a woman does not employ any of these prevention strategies and the result is rape, it is never the fault of the victim" (p. 224). The person who commits the rape is responsible; we must not blame the victim.

Individuals' Prevention of Acquaintance Rape.   Women may feel comforted to think that they can protect themselves from rape by locking their doors and avoiding late-night walks in dangerous areas. But how will those precautions protect women from being raped by someone they know?

Unfortunately, women must use a different set of strategies to protect themselves from an acquaintance (Carroll & Jackson, 1996). One precaution is to avoid a relationship with a man who talks negatively about women in general or with a domineering man who insults you and ignores what you say. These men are likely to ignore your refusals if you say you do not want to have sex (Crooks & Baur, 2002).

Some precautions on dating safety may sound obvious, but they can decrease the chances of acquaintance rape. When you are just getting to know someone, go to public places with a group of people. If possible, drive yourself to the location. Limit your alcohol intake, and make sure that no one can slip a drug into your drink. Also, take some time to think how you would respond if a situation becomes threatening. What would your options be? Throughout a relationship, communicate with your dating partner about any sexual activities that seem appropriate or inappropriate (Abbey, 2002).

In the previous section, we discussed effective ways of preventing rape by strangers. When the attacker is an acquaintance, he may respond to verbal assertiveness. For example, a woman can shout, "Stop it! This is rape, and I'm calling the police!" (Parrot, 1996, p. 226). An attacker may stop if you try to appeal to him on a human level. Screaming or running away may also be effective.

In an ideal world, women can trust their dates, their classmates, and their friends. In the real world, the clear majority of men would not rape an acquaintance. However, some do, and women must be prepared for this possibility.

Society's Prevention of Rape.   An individual might be able to avoid being raped by following certain precautions. However, many rapists will simply seek another victim. In addition, solutions at the individual level mean that women will continue to live in fear of being raped. To prevent rape, we need to take a broader approach, encouraging people to value women and men equally. We must acknowledge that a violent society—which often devalues women—will tend to encourage rape (Corcoran & Mahlstedt, 1999; G. C. N. Hall & Barongan, 1997). Our list starts with concrete suggestions and then considers some problems that require more fundamental changes (Abbey, 2002; R. Campbell & Salem, 1999; Corcoran & Mahlstedt, 1999; DeKeseredy & Schwartz, 1998; Rozee, 2000b; M. D. Schwartz & DeKeseredy, 1997):

1. Professionals who work with children need to be alert for evidence of child sexual abuse; in many states, people who work with children are required to complete relevant training programs.
2. Hospitals and medical providers should be sensitive to the emotional and physical needs of girls and women who have been raped.
3. Rape victims should be encouraged to report rape. Anonymous telephone counseling services and legal assistance should be easily available and widely publicized.
4. Laws must be reformed so that the legal process is less stressful and more supportive for the victims.
5. Education about rape needs to be improved, beginning in junior high or high school. Students need this information when they are young, because they have already formed their attitudes toward rape by the time they reach college. Rape-prevention programs must emphasize that men *can* control their sexual impulses and that women are not to be blamed for rape. The programs should also be a mandatory part of orientation for first-year college students, especially because women face a high risk of rape during the first weeks of college. Carefully designed programs can change people's knowledge and attitudes about rape (B. Fouts & Knapp, 2001; Lonsway & Kothari, 2000; Pinzone-Glover et al., 1998).

6. Men's groups must become more involved in rape prevention (Binder, 2001). On some college campuses, fraternities will join together with campus women's groups to organize a rape awareness day or a "Take Back the Night" rally. One campus designed an educational seminar for fraternity members. Afterward, one fraternity man described how he now felt alarmed when he saw a woman in a potentially dangerous situation: "I don't look or talk to any man the same anymore. I find it hard to have fun at my fraternity events" (Mahlstedt & Corcoran, 1999, p. 315). Unfortunately, however, this kind of collaborative activism is rare. Men and men's organizations need to remember this important quotation: "If you're not part of the solution, you're part of the problem."

7. Violence must be less glorified in the media. The violence in films and on television is widely recognized, yet the situation has not improved dramatically in recent years (Rozee, 2000b; Scharrer, 1998). We must emphasize that violent "entertainment" encourages aggression against women.

8. Ultimately, our society must direct more attention toward the needs of women. As we've emphasized throughout this book, women are relatively underpaid, powerless, and invisible. Their needs are often trivialized and ignored. Every woman should be able to feel that her body is safe from attack and that she has the same freedom of movement that men have. Our culture must not tolerate violence toward women.

SECTION SUMMARY ■

Rape

1. Rape is found in almost all cultures throughout the world; between 15% and 30% of women in the United States and Canada will become victims of rape during their lifetime.

2. Frequently, women who have been raped by an acquaintance will not consider the assault to be a "real" rape. Acquaintance rape is associated with alcohol and other drugs and with a setting that is hostile toward women. Some instances of acquaintance rape can be traced to misinterpretations of sexual interest.

3. Because of the threat of rape, many women feel unsafe, and they restrict their activities.

4. Women who have been raped report that, during the assault, they felt terrified, confused, and anxious. Afterward, victims often feel helpless and devalued; they may also blame themselves for the rape.

5. Long-term consequences for a rape victim may include posttraumatic stress disorder and physical health problems, although individual differences are prominent.

6. A woman who has been raped may be blamed by her family, the court system, and the general public; attitudes about rape depend on factors such as gender, gender-role beliefs, and whether the woman was raped by a stranger or by an acquaintance.

7. Some myths about rape are not based on fact: Rapists are strangers; only deviant men would consider rape; women ask to be raped; women lie about rape; and pornography reduces the incidence of rape.

8. Child sexual abuse has both immediate and long-term effects on mental and physical health; some memories of child sexual abuse can be forgotten and then recovered later, but some adults can construct false memories of abuse that did not occur.

9. Safety precautions that prevent rape by a stranger typically limit women's freedom at home and in public places; it is important not to blame the victim of a rape attack.

10. Safety precautions for avoiding rape by an acquaintance include avoiding men who downgrade women; dating in groups at the beginning of a relationship; being verbally assertive; and appealing to an acquaintance on a human level.

11. Ultimately, the number of rapes can be reduced only by greater societal attention to women's needs. The issues include reforming the medical, counseling, legal, and educational resources for rape victims. Violence must be less glorified in the media, and women's issues must receive more attention.

THE ABUSE OF WOMEN

Dr. Christine Dotterer, a successful family physician, described how her husband abused her over a period of 19 years:

> In some ways my situation was classic. He would hit and punch me, and then would want to make up, usually with sex. There were stretches of time when things seemed pretty good, and the fact that he had bruised me two months earlier seemed to vanish. It's true that he actively discouraged my having friends—he didn't want me even to talk on the phone. But I thought that I just wasn't good at making friends, not that he might want me to be isolated. (Dotterer, 1992, p. 49)

Dr. Dotterer finally left this abusive relationship, after she saw her husband beat up her son. As in many other cases of domestic violence, this couple was European American, well educated, and middle class. The abuse of women is found in every social group on our continent.

I will use the term *abuse of women* to include the kind of aggression that Christine Dotterer experienced from her husband. In contrast, the term *domestic violence* implies that the man and the woman are living together. Therefore, this term seems to exclude the kind of violence often found in dating relationships, including high school and college students (DeKeseredy & Schwartz, 1998; Lloyd & Emery, 2000; Ryan et al., 1999). The term *domestic violence* and the related term *battered women* also imply *physical* abuse (McHugh & Bartoszek, 2000; J. W. White et al., 2001). However, women who have been abused often report that the psychological abuse is the most destructive component of the abusive experience (K. D. O'Leary & Maiuro, 2001; L. E. A. Walker, 2000).

The **abuse of women** includes intentional acts that injure a woman; these acts may be physical, psychological, or sexual. (We explored sexual abuse in the discussion of acquaintance rape in the previous section.)

Physical abuse can include hitting, kicking, burning, pushing, choking, and use of a weapon. Emotional abuse can include humiliation, name calling, degradation, intimidation, extreme jealousy, and refusal to speak (L. L. Alexander et al., 2001; Wallace, 1999). Another form of emotional abuse focuses on finances, for example, when a man withholds money or takes money away from his wife (Arriaga & Oskamp, 1999).

Because of space limitations, in this section, we will focus on male violence against females. The research demonstrates that females may abuse males. However, the evidence is clear that women experience much more severe abuse from their male partners than men do from their female partners (Christopher & Lloyd, 2000; DeKeseredy & Schwartz, 1998; Jiwani, 2000). In addition, we will not examine abuse in lesbian relationships; this topic is discussed in other resources (e.g., McHugh & Bartoszek, 2000; Renzetti, 1998; J. W. White et al., 2001). Before you read further, try Demonstration 13.4.

DEMONSTRATION 13.4 ■ ■ ■ ■ ■ ■ ■ ■ ■ ■ ■ ■ ■ ■ ■ ■ ■ ■ ■

Thinking About Your Own Romantic Relationship

As you can imagine, no simple questionnaire can assess whether a relationship shows signs of abuse. However, look at the following questions and see whether they may apply, either to a current relationship or to a previous relationship.

Does your partner:

Make fun of you or make demeaning comments when other people are present?

Tell you that everything is your fault?

Check up on you at work or other locations, to make certain that you are at the place where you said you'd be?

Make you feel unsafe in the current relationship?

Make you feel that he (or she) would explode if you did the wrong thing?

Act very jealous about your romantic relationship with another person?

Try to keep you from developing nonromantic friendships with other people?

Try to make you do things you don't want to do?

Criticize you frequently?

Decide what you will wear, eat, or buy—when you have expressed a preference for something else?

Threaten to hurt you?

Intentionally hurt you physically?

Sources: Lloyd and Emery (2000), S. M. Shaw and Lee (2001), and Warshaw (2001).

How Often Does the Abuse of Women Occur?

Earlier in this chapter, we discussed the difficulty of estimating how many women experience sexual harassment and rape. According to a traditional taboo, women must not let others know that they have been abused; this silence prevents us from obtaining accurate data about violence in intimate relationships (Jiwani, 2000). According to estimates, however, about 25% of women in the United States will experience abuse during their lifetime (L. L. Alexander et al., 2001; Christopher & Lloyd, 2000). Looking at the statistics another way, 3,000,000 U.S. women are abused each year (L. E. A. Walker, 2001; J. W. White et al., 2001). The data for women in Canada are similar; about 25% to 30% of married or formerly married women reported that they had been abused (Statistics Canada, 1993, 2000; L. E. Taylor, 1995).

Furthermore, between 30% and 55% of women who are seen in U.S. hospital emergency departments have injuries related to domestic violence (Litt, 1997; Warshaw, 2001). Even pregnancy does not protect women from abuse. Each year, between 15% and 20% of all pregnant women experience physical or sexual abuse (Eisenstat & Bancroft, 1999; Sternberg & Lamb, 1999; Warshaw, 2001).

As we mentioned at the beginning of this section, abuse is also common in dating relationships. For example, DeKeseredy and Schwartz (1998) reported the results from a large-scale survey of Canadian university students. The survey revealed that 31% of the women had been pushed, grabbed, or shoved by someone they were dating. Psychological abuse was even more common: 65% of the women said they had been degraded in front of friends or family and 65% had experienced insults or swearing.

The problem of partner abuse is not limited to North America. The rate of abuse in European countries is similar to the North American rate (Neft & Levine, 1997; United Nations, 1995). Data gathered in Asia, Latin America, and Africa reveal even higher rates of abuse (e.g., Ellsberg et al., 1999; Pickup, 2001). In many countries, more than half of adult women reported that they had been physically assaulted by a partner. For example, an interviewer asked a man in South Korea if he had beaten his wife. He replied:

> I was married at 28, and I'm 52 now. How could I have been married all these years and not beaten my wife? . . . For me, it's better to release that anger and get it over with. Otherwise, I just get sick inside. (Kristof, 1996, p. 17A)

Notice, however, that this man never considered whether the abuse was also better for his wife.

The Dynamics of Abuse

Most women are not abused continually. A cyclical pattern of abuse is more common, although certainly not universal (S. A. Anderson & Schlossberg, 1999; L. E. A. Walker, 2000, 2001; Wallace, 1999). This **abuse cycle** typically has three phases: (1) the tension building phase, (2) the acute battering phase, and (3) the loving phase.

In the tension building phase, the physical abuse is relatively minor, but verbal outbursts and threats increase the tension. The woman often tries to calm her partner. She may try to keep his abuse from escalating by anticipating his whims. However, tension keeps building.

When tension builds too high, the abuser responds with an acute battering incident, the hallmark of the second phase. The woman may experience extreme physical abuse. Even a trivial event can trigger a battering incident (Lloyd & Emery, 2000). For example, one wealthy professional man broke his wife's jaw when he discovered that one of the potted plants in his mansion had not been watered sufficiently (Stahly, 2000).

In the third phase, the batterer usually becomes charming and loving. He apologizes and promises that he will never be violent again. He begs for forgiveness and makes the woman feel guilty if she is considering leaving the relationship. This may be a pleasant and flattering, although confusing, phase of the relationship. In fact, the woman may be encouraged to forget the tension, uncertainty, and pain of the earlier two phases. Indeed, the man may be genuinely repentant at this point in the cycle. Unfortunately, the cycle usually repeats itself, often with increasingly severe abuse and a shorter loving phase (L. E. A. Walker, 2000).

Women's Reactions to Abuse

As you might expect, women typically react to abuse with fear, terror, and mistrust. Women who have been abused may be hyperalert, searching for signs that their partner may be ready to strike again (Christopher & Lloyd, 2000; Wallace, 1999). Women may alter their own behavior, in the hope of preventing future outbursts. However, these adjustments are often ineffective. The abuser will simply find another reason to be violent.

Women who have been abused may feel anxious and low in self-esteem (Ali & Toner, 2001; Stahly, 2000; Warshaw, 2001). More than half of abused women develop depression. An estimated 25% to 40% of women may attempt suicide after experiencing abuse (L. L. Alexander et al., 2001; Litt, 1997).

Abused women also experience many problems with their physical health. They may suffer from bruises, cuts, burns, and broken bones as a direct result of an assault; abusers may even prevent women from seeking medical care. Many months afterward, women may still experience headaches, sleep disturbances, extreme fatigue, abdominal pain, pelvic pain, gynecological problems, and other chronic disorders (Ali & Toner, 2001; Koss et al., 2001; Warshaw, 2001). Naturally, these physical problems may intensify their psychological problems.

Characteristics Associated with Abusive Relationships

Researchers have identified several factors related to the abuse of women. For example, some family characteristics may be associated with abuse. In addition, certain personal attributes are especially common among men who abuse their partners.

Family Variables Associated with Abuse.   Abuse of women is somewhat more common among low-income families, although the relationship between abuse and social class is complex (Christopher & Lloyd, 2000; Weitzman, 2000; J. W. White et al., 2001). For example, police may receive more domestic violence calls from the poorer areas of a city. However, middle-class and upper-class women may simply be less likely to call for police help. Also, remember that women on university campuses are likely to experience physical violence, even though most students come from families with relatively high incomes (DeKeseredy & Schwartz, 1998). In other words, no social class is immune (L. E. A. Walker, 2000).

The relationship between ethnicity and family violence is also complex. Many analyses do not take social class into account, and we have just seen that social class is somewhat related to patterns of abuse. In general, White women and Latina women are similar in the severity and frequency of abuse; abuse may be slightly higher for Black women and Native American women (Hamby, 2002; E. Klein et al., 1997; Tjaden & Thoennes, 1998; C. M. West, 1998; J. W. White et al., 2001).

The number of *reported* cases of domestic abuse is relatively low in Asian American communities (E. Klein et al., 1997). One reason may be that Asian American families are extremely reluctant to let anyone outside the immediate family know about domestic problems (Ho, 1997; Lum, 1998; McHugh & Bartoszek, 2000). Many Asian cultures believe that women should accept their suffering and endure their hardships, and this value system discourages women from reporting domestic violence (Ho, 1997; C. G. Tran & Des Jardins, 2000).

Personal Characteristics of Male Abusers.   One of the most commonly reported characteristics of male abusers is that they feel they are entitled to hurt their partners. From their egocentric perspective, their own needs come first (Birns, 1999). A good example of this male entitlement perspective is the Korean man who felt he was better off releasing his anger by beating his wife (p. 444). Abusers are also likely to believe that the male should be the head of the family, along with other traditional concepts about gender roles (Wallace, 1999; J. W. White et al., 2001). Furthermore, abusers are more likely than nonabusers to have witnessed family violence during childhood (McHugh & Bartoszek, 2000; Ryan et al., 1999; L. E. A. Walker, 2000). Not surprisingly, abusers have more positive attitudes toward physical and verbal aggression, compared to men who are not abusers (Bookwala et al., 1992).

Batterers are often described as being charming con artists. Their apparent sincerity can often fool unsuspecting people: "How could such a delightful, devoted husband possibly beat his wife?" In fact, a relatively large number of batterers meet the psychiatric diagnosis of antisocial personality disorder (Christopher & Lloyd, 2000; Wallace, 1999). People with **antisocial personality disorder** have complete disregard for the lives of other people; they also display a variety of antisocial behaviors, including lying, impulsiveness, and aggressiveness (American Psychiatric Association, 2000). Men with this disorder show little concern for the welfare of others. However, they may appear charming to people who know them only superficially. Of course, many men who batter do not have antisocial personality disorder. Instead, they have learned our culture's emphasis on male entitlement.

Situational factors also increase the likelihood of partner abuse. For example, men who are unemployed have a relatively high rate of domestic violence (E. Klein et al., 1997; Marin & Russo, 1999). Men whose friends endorse the abuse of women are also more likely to be aggressive (DeKeseredy & Schwartz, 1998).

Research also suggests that males who have a drinking problem are more likely to abuse women physically (Christopher & Lloyd, 2000; J. W. White et al., 2001). It's possible that alcohol plays an important role because it affects judgment and other cognitive processes. However, many men simply use alcohol as an excuse for their violence. A typical explanation may be, "I don't know what got into me. It must have been the alcohol." Males who use drugs, such as cocaine, are also likely to be abusers (Grisso et al., 1999).

Attitudes About the Abuse of Women

The research on attitudes toward partner abuse suggests that we can be cautiously optimistic. An increasing number of North Americans believe that domestic violence is a serious crime. In the United States, for example, all 50 states have passed statutes to protect abused women (A. R. Roberts, 1996a). As feminists, we should not be premature in claiming that the problem is nearly solved. The abuse of women is still an extremely important topic. However, we should be pleased when feminist educational efforts combine with the media and legal reform to change societal attitudes (A. R. Roberts, 1996a).

In earlier chapters, we pointed out the negative impact that the media can have on such issues as gender stereotypes and body images. However, North American research suggests that the media had a generally positive impact on knowledge about domestic violence during the 1990s. For example, 93% of U.S. residents in a nationwide survey said that they had learned from media coverage that domestic violence is a serious problem. Furthermore, 91% reported that family and friends should learn more about how to help victims of domestic violence (E. Klein et al., 1997).

In many countries throughout the world, the media continue to reinforce the traditional myths about the abuse of women. However, some feminist groups have had surprising success in encouraging the media to provide accurate information about domestic violence. For instance, television news and newspaper coverage have been helpful in countries such as Georgia (which was formerly part of the Soviet Union), Cambodia, and Indonesia (Pickup, 2001).

According to North American research conducted in recent years, people typically acknowledge that the abuse of women is wrong (Drout, 1997; Locke & Richman, 1999). Women usually have more negative attitudes than men do (E. Klein et al., 1997; Locke & Richman, 1999; Straus et al., 1997). Gender roles are also important. Specifically, people with traditional attitudes toward women are likely to sympathize with a man who has abused his wife. In contrast, people with nontraditional attitudes are likely to blame the man (D. L. R. Graham & Rawlings, 1999; Willis et al., 1996).

Although the public is more likely than in previous eras to condemn the abuse of women, we still have a long distance to cover before the abuse of women is treated with sufficient seriousness. For example, a man who is convicted of domestic violence in Wyoming can expect up to a 2-year jail sentence and a $2,000 fine. In contrast, a man who is convicted of stealing a horse can expect up to a 10-year jail sentence and a $10,000 fine (K. LaFrance, 1998).

Myths About the Abuse of Women

We have already discussed the evidence against several commonly accepted myths about the abuse of women. For example, we have considered research that contradicts the following myths:

1. Abuse is relatively rare.
2. Men experience as much abuse as women.
3. Abuse is limited to the lower social classes.
4. Abuse is much more common among ethnic minority groups.

Let's examine some other myths. In each case, think about how the myth can lead people to blame women for being battered.

Myth 1: Abused women enjoy being beaten. Early theorists reasoned that women who remain in violent relationships enjoy the trauma of being abused. A portion of the general population still holds this belief (E. Klein et al., 1997). However, we have no evidence for this myth (A. R. Roberts, 1996b; L. E. A. Walker, 2000). Women do not enjoy being abused, just as women do not enjoy being raped.

Myth 2: Abused women deserve to be beaten. According to this myth, when a woman oversteps the boundaries of a proper wife, she ought to be beaten. In other words, the blame for this abuse lies in the woman's behavior, not in the man's response. A student in my psychology of women course related an incident in which she had described a wife-abuse case to a group of friends. Specifically, a man had seriously injured his wife because dinner was not ready as soon as he came home from work. A male friend in this student's group, whom my student had previously considered enlightened, responded, "Yes, but she really should have prepared dinner on time."

Myth 3: Abused women could easily leave, if they really wanted to. This myth ignores both the interpersonal and the practical factors that prevent a woman from leaving. She may feel some love for the abusing man, because he is often decent. Also, as we noted earlier, many abusers become generous and kind in the days following a violent episode. An abused woman may sincerely believe that her husband is basically a good man who can be reformed.

Many abused women also face practical barriers. A woman may have no place to go, no money, and no way of escaping (McHugh et al., 1993). Another practical concern is that an abusing husband often becomes even more violent once a woman decides to leave (Birns, 1999; Jacobson & Gottman, 1998). In fact, a woman is at greater risk of being killed or seriously injured during the 2 years after a separation than she was during the years the couple lived in the same home.

How Abused Women Take Action

An abused woman may remain in the relationship or, like most abused women, she may decide to pursue one of several options. Consider the case of 18-year-old Felicia, who decided to confide in her social worker at the health clinic. Felicia explained why she took this important step:

> I told her because she always listened. She didn't blame me—for being pregnant or for him beating on me. It was a relief, because no one else believed it was happening. I told her because I was sick of it. But it was hard. It hurt a lot to talk about it. It made it real. But deep down inside, I was a really hurt person. When I told her, she believed it. What helped was a lot of counseling and a lot of friends telling me I was not a bad person. I had to hear it a lot of times, LOTS OF TIMES, but then I heard it. (B. Levy, 1993, p. 82)

To some extent, women's strategies for handling abuse depend on their family background. For example, some families emphasize persevering in unpleasant situations and hiding domestic problems (Ho, 1997). These women may therefore be less likely to try to escape from an abusive relationship.

Let's discuss several options for women who have been abused: They can seek therapy, they can leave, or they can go to a battered women's shelter.

Therapy.   An abusive relationship seldom improves spontaneously. In fact, as we noted earlier, violence frequently escalates in a relationship. Women often seek the services of therapists. In earlier eras, therapists frequently adopted a blame-the-victim approach. Fortunately, therapists are becoming more aware that society's attitudes can encourage the abuse of women.

Psychotherapy for abused women is influenced by the principles of feminist therapy (see pages 411–412). An important focus is to help women think about themselves with compassion rather than with criticism. Like other forms of women-centered therapy, this model empowers women to pursue their own goals, rather than simply focusing on other people's needs (Ali & Toner, 2001). Group therapy is often helpful for abused women, because they can see that other women have similar problems.

Consider the feminist therapy approach that Rinfret-Raynor and Cantin (1997) used in working with French Canadian women who were abused. The therapists informed the women about their legal rights, helped them explore community resources, and conducted both individual and group therapy. A major message throughout therapy was that the abuser is responsible for the violence, not the victim. The therapists also worked to increase the women's self-esteem and sense of independence. Compared to women who had received standard nonsexist therapy, the women who had received feminist therapy experienced a greater decrease in physical violence.

In general, therapists believe that a man and a woman in a physically abusive relationship must not enter couples therapy together. If both meet at the same time with the therapist, the woman may say something during the session that the man will use as an excuse for battering when they return home (Christensen & Jacobson, 2000). Limited success is possible in couples without any recent physical abuse, when the man willingly chooses to pursue therapy. The therapist can encourage the man to realize that the abuse is his personal responsibility; he also learns alternative methods to resolve arguments. Meanwhile, a woman who has been abused may receive feminist therapy with the goals of self-empowerment and greater understanding of domestic violence (P. D. Brown & O'Leary, 1997; Hamby, 1998; Philpot et al., 1997).

Deciding to Leave a Relationship.   Many women decide that abuse is too high a price to pay for the advantages of remaining in a relationship. Many women reach a crisis point after a particularly violent episode (Lloyd & Emery, 2000). Consider the following example:

> With Virginia, the day of reckoning came while James was cleaning his gun. It had no bullets in it, but when he pointed it at her after it was clean, she did not know it was empty. He said, "Do you realize how easy it would be for me to accidentally use this on you some day?" He was in a relatively good mood, or so it seemed. Somehow, his concrete threat, said in a joking manner, crystallized the danger she was in, better than all the serious threats he had made in a bad mood. She took those earlier threats seriously, but she remembers thinking, "Even when he's happy, he still likes to torment me." At the moment he pointed the gun at her, Virginia began her countdown to escape. (Jacobson & Gottman, 1998, p. 139)

Other women begin planning to leave after they have been attacked in front of their children, after their partner breaks a promise about stopping the abuse, or after talking with a supportive friend (Giles-Sims, 1983; Jacobson & Gottman, 1998). Many women, however, are likely to experience increased violence once they leave their husband; husbands may interpret the departure as a threat to their own power.

Unfortunately, people are so intrigued by the question, "Why do battered women stay?" that they forget to ask more important questions. Some of these questions include "Why are violent men allowed to stay?" and "How can our society make it clear that emotional and physical abuse is not acceptable?"

Shelters for Battered Women.   Shelters offer a temporary place where an abused woman can go for safety, support, and information about social services available in the community. Many shelters also offer counseling services. Staff members can help women make their own decisions about their future options (Birns, 1999; Sattler, 2000; L. E. A. Walker, 2001). In these shelters, many women become aware that the abuse problem is a social issue and that victims must not be blamed for the abuse (Sattler, 2000).

Canada currently has about 500 shelters that address the issue of domestic violence (Statistics Canada, 2000). The United States—with about 9 times the population of Canada—currently has about 2,000 shelters (L. E. A. Walker, 2001). Many North American women become homeless rather than continuing to live with a violent partner (K.-L. Miller & Du Mont, 2000). Outside North America, few shelters are available for women trying to escape a violent partner (Pickup, 2001).

Unfortunately, these shelters operate on extremely limited budgets, and we need hundreds of additional shelters throughout North America. Thousands of women are turned away each year from shelters that are filled to capacity (L. E. A. Walker, 2001). These women must return to their homes, where they risk being beaten once again. Ironically, the U.S. government is projecting an $804 billion budget for national defense for fiscal year 2004, not including the Iraq War (War Resisters League, 2003). Meanwhile, our government is decreasing its funding for battered women's shelters, which must struggle to locate funding from individuals and organizations in the community (C. Mazzotta, personal communication, 2003).

Society's Response to the Problem of Abuse

In recent years, the criminal justice system and the general public have become much more aware that abuse is a serious problem. Still, government policies have no consistent plan for providing shelters, services, and assistance for abused women or for requiring counseling for the men who abuse them. Government officials and agencies must publicize the fact that abuse of any kind is unacceptable. This educational publicity should be just as vigorous as the antidrug and anti–drunk driving campaigns (Koshland, 1994; Websdale, 1998). As Lenore E. A. Walker (2000) pointed out, "Domestic violence cannot be considered a private family matter. Its painful repercussions extend into the general community" (p. 218).

Police training must also be improved. One woman, living in rural Kentucky, had been abused many times by her husband. She described how the local police officers treated her: "They always acted like smart alecks. Laughed at me all the time" (Websdale, 1998, p. 97). Clearly, police officers must be required to complete training about domestic violence issues (Minow, 1999; Pickup, 2001; Ptacek, 1999). Program directors of battered women's shelters should be invited to provide additional information about the abuse of women (A. R. Roberts, 1996a).

Community organizations are often silent about the issue of abused women. Imagine what could happen if church groups, parent-teacher associations, and service organizations (such as the Rotary Club and the Kiwanis) were to sponsor a program on domestic violence. These organizations often set the moral tone for a community, and they could send a strong message that abuse of women cannot be tolerated.

One optimistic development is that medical organizations are gradually paying more attention to the issue of the abuse of women. Earlier research (summarized by Koss et al., 2001) demonstrated that health care providers who saw battered women in the emergency department seldom asked whether they were experiencing domestic violence. However, many physicians are now being trained to screen all women by asking a question such as "We're concerned about the health effects of domestic abuse, so we now ask a few questions of all our patients" (Eisenstat & Bancroft, 1999, p. 889; Minow, 1999). Training materials are also being developed. For instance, the Massachusetts Medical Society and Stanford University School of Medicine have developed an interactive set of CD-ROMs and videos designed to train physicians to recognize and help women who have been abused. Physicians should be less likely to ignore the evidence of abuse now that a new norm of concern is being established.

Concern about the abuse of women is emerging even more slowly in developing countries. For instance, most countries in the world do not offer legal protection for women who have been abused (R. J. R. Levesque, 2001). Still, some of the efforts are encouraging. On a recent trip to Nicaragua, I found several resources on violence against women. One brochure, developed for church groups in Nicaragua, debunked common myths, such as that women deserve to be mistreated, that abuse is God's will, and that abuse is limited to the lower class (M. West & Fernández, 1997). A brief handbook has also been developed to educate health care workers about the problem of the abuse of women (Ellsberg et al., 1998).

Ultimately, however, any attempt to solve the problem of abuse must acknowledge that the power imbalance in intimate relationships reflects the power imbalance in our society (Pickup, 2001; Whalen, 1996). As Jacobson and Gottman (1998) pointed out, men who abuse women have been socialized to expect to have power over women. In addition, our culture trains some men to control their intimate partners through physical and emotional abuse. Television programs, music videos, and other media reinforce the images of men's violence toward women (M. Rich et al., 1998). We can help to counteract these attitudes by encouraging the media to provide less violent entertainment. We can also encourage schools to address the issue of abuse at an early age, beginning in elementary school and continuing through college (DeKeseredy & Schwartz, 1998; Giordano, 2001). We must work toward a world in which violence is not directed at women as a group in order to keep them powerless. Instead, our intimate relationships should be based on "social equality, mutual trust, and caring" (Whalen, 1996, p. 112).

SECTION SUMMARY ▪

The Abuse of Women

1. About one-quarter of women in the United States and Canada will experience abuse during their lifetime; abuse is also common in dating relationships; abuse is even more likely in some other countries.

2. A common pattern is an abuse cycle, which begins with verbal outbursts and moderate physical abuse; then, tension builds toward an acute battering incident, followed by a period of calm and repentance.

3. Women who have been abused may feel afraid, anxious, and depressed, and they experience many physical health problems.

4. Abuse is somewhat correlated with social class, and its relationship with ethnicity is complex; male abusers have a sense of entitlement, and they are often charming con artists; unemployment is a risk factor.

5. North Americans consider domestic violence a more serious issue than they did in an earlier era; both gender and gender roles are related to attitudes about domestic violence.

6. Myths about abused women that are not supported by the research are that abused women are masochists, that they deserve to be beaten, and that they could easily leave the relationship.

7. Therapy for an abused woman focuses on reducing self-criticism and increasing self-esteem; women often decide to leave an abusive relationship after reaching a specific crisis point; shelters are helpful, but they are poorly funded and temporary.

8. Government policies have no uniform provisions about shelters or services for abused women; health care providers now have better training about abuse issues.

9. As in other issues of violence, the problem of battered women cannot be resolved without seeking social equality at the societal level.

■■■■■■ CHAPTER REVIEW QUESTIONS ■■■■■■

1. Throughout this chapter, we emphasized that people often blame the victims for events that are beyond their control. Describe how this process operates in sexual harassment, rape, and the abuse of women.

2. As we noted in the introduction to this chapter, a culture that values men more than women encourages some men to feel that they are entitled to certain privileges. Explain how this sense of entitlement is relevant in sexual harassment, rape, and the abuse of women.

3. How do women react to sexual harassment? Contrast these reactions with women's reactions to rape and abuse. How would you explain the similarities and differences?

4. In this chapter, we examined attitudes about sexual harassment, rape, and abuse. Identify any similarities that apply to all three topics. Also, comment on gender comparisons in these attitudes and the relationship between gender roles and these attitudes.

5. What are the two general categories of sexual harassment? Give at least one example for each category, based on the recent media or on reports from friends. How do these examples illustrate why sexual harassment is an important issue? (Consult pp. 418–421 if necessary.)

6. Summarize the information about acquaintance rape and child sexual abuse. What does this information tell us about the balance of power and sexual violence in close personal relationships?

7. What are some of the common myths about sexual harassment, rape, and abuse? What do all these myths reveal about society's attitudes toward men and women?

8. Imagine that you have been appointed to a national committee to address the problems of sexual harassment, rape, and abuse. What recommendations would you make for government policy, the legal system, universities, business institutions, the media, and educational programs? Feel free to list items other than those mentioned in this chapter.

9. According to Theme 3, women are less visible than men in many important areas; topics important in women's lives are also considered relatively unimportant. How often had you heard about the topics of sexual harassment, rape, and abuse before the course for which you are reading this book? What are some factors that encourage these three topics to be relatively invisible?

10. Think about a high school female whom you know well. Imagine that she is about to go

off to college. What kind of information can you supply from this chapter that would be helpful for her to know, with respect to violence against women? Now think about a high school male whom you know. If he were preparing to go to college, what information would you provide—both with respect to his avoiding violence against women and his role in supporting women who have experienced violence? (Better still, figure out how you can have an actual conversation about these topics with those individuals!)

NEW TERMS

entitlement (418)
*sexual harassment (418)
*quid pro quo harassment (418)
*hostile environment (418)
*rape (425)
*sexual assault (425)
*acquaintance rape (427)
*posttraumatic stress disorder (PTSD) (431)

*child sexual abuse (436)
*incest (436)
recovered-memory perspective (436)
false-memory perspective (436)
*abuse of women (443)
*abuse cycle (444)
*antisocial personality disorder (446)

The terms asterisked in the New Terms section serve as good search terms for InfoTrac College Edition. Go to http://infotrac.thomsonlearning.com and try these added search terms.

RECOMMENDED READINGS

Bravo, E., & Cassedy, E. (1999). *The 9 to 5 guide to combating sexual harassment.* Milwaukee: 9 to 5 Working Women Education Fund. This resource explores sexual harassment in the workplace, including topics such as myths about sexual harassment, legal aspects, and practical advice.

Chrisler, J. C., Golden, C., & Rozee, P. D. (Eds.). (2000). *Lectures on the psychology of women* (2nd ed.). Boston: McGraw-Hill. This wonderful resource book includes 24 chapters on topics relevant to women's lives; the chapters on fear of rape, pornography, battered women, and sexual harassment are particularly relevant to the current chapter.

Lloyd, S. A., & Emery, B. C. (2000). *The dark side of courtship: Physical and sexual aggression.* Thousand Oaks, CA: Sage. Here's an excellent overview of two topics in this chapter: rape and the abuse of women. I especially appreci-

ate the way that the authors blend interview material with the research findings.

Ottens, A. J., & Hotelling, K. (Eds.). (2001). *Sexual violence on campus: Policies, programs, and perspectives.* New York: Springer. I recommend this book to students and faculty members who want to address the issues of rape and the abuse of women in a college setting. The book includes chapters on topics such as assault prevention in the fraternity and sorority community, drug-facilitated rape, and relationship violence among cohabiting students.

Pickup, F. (2001). *Ending violence against women: A challenge for development and humanitarian work.* Oxford, England: Oxfam. Anyone interested in the worldwide problems of violence should read this book; it conveys both the depth of violence throughout the world and the creativity that people have used in addressing these issues.

ANSWERS TO THE DEMONSTRATIONS

Demonstration 13.1: The percentages of students who considered each scenario to be sexual harassment were: Scenario 1, 44%; Scenario 2, 87%; Scenario 3, 54%; and Scenario 4, 47%.

Demonstration 13.2: 1. False; 2. True; 3. False; 4. False; 5. True; 6. False; 7. False; 8. True; 9. False; 10. False.

ANSWERS TO THE TRUE-FALSE QUESTIONS

1. False (pp. 418–419); 2. True (p. 421); 3. False (p. 422); 4. True (p. 426); 5. True (p. 429); 6. True (p. 431); 7. False (p. 434); 8. True (p. 443); 9. True (p. 447); 10. False (p. 449).

Women and Older Adulthood

Al Behrman, AP/Wide World Photos

T R U E   O R   F A L S E ?

_____ 1. Because most researchers are middle-aged or older, journals publish about twice as much research on this period as on childhood and adolescence combined.

_____ 2. People are consistently more negative when they are judging elderly women than when they are judging elderly men.

_____ 3. Compared to elderly women in North America, elderly women in other cultures consistently have much less power.

_____ 4. Women typically have fewer retirement problems than men do.

_____ 5. Although young men earn significantly more than young women, the incomes for retired men and women are roughly equal.

_____ 6. When asked to describe a "middle-aged menopausal woman," people are significantly more negative than when describing a "middle-aged woman."

_____ 7. Because of hormonal changes, menopause often produces psychological symptoms such as depression and irritability.

_____ 8. Most women experience moderate depression when their children leave home.

_____ 9. European American grandmothers are more likely than Black and Native American grandmothers to think they should provide advice to their grandchildren.

_____ 10. Because of a variety of health and social problems, elderly women are typically less satisfied with their lives, compared to younger women.

In January, 1999—at the age of 89—Doris Haddock began an amazing journey, walking from California to Washington, D.C. Her mission was to tell U.S. voters that we must reform the way that political campaigns are financed. At present, wealthy individuals and corporations donate large contributions so that politicians will vote "appropriately." Ms. Haddock, also known as Granny D, had been a reformer for most of her life, and she figured out how to reach citizens across the country. She describes how she was greeted in small towns, how a fraternity along the route made her a "Sweetheart of Sigma Chi," how a motorcycle gang accompanied her for part of the route, and how she cross-country skied for 100 miles after a heavy snowstorm. The photo on p. 456 shows Granny D. in November 1999 in Kentucky, with the city of Cincinnati in the background. She ended her trip on the steps of the Capitol building, with a rousing speech to senators and congressional representatives that included this message:

> The people I met along my way have given me messages to deliver here. The messages are many, written with old and young hands of every color, and yet the messages are the same. They are this: Shame on you, senators and congressmen, who have turned this headquarters of a great and self-governing people into a bawdy

house. . . . If I have offended you speaking this way on your front steps, that is as it should be; you have offended America and you have dishonored the best things it stands for. . . . [The people] are ready for real leaders, unselfish and principled leaders who will prove their worth by voting for meaningful reform. (D. Haddock, 2001, pp. 248–250)

Throughout this textbook, we have emphasized the contrast between people's stereotypes about women and the reality of women's lives. This contrast is also obvious when we examine the lives of older women. We seldom see media coverage of this group. (More evidence of our theme of invisible women!) Furthermore, the rare media images of elderly women convey the message that they are powerless and unproductive. Doris Haddock's journey—and other examples throughout this chapter—provide a contrast to those media stereotypes.

In this chapter, we will consider women in middle age and in old age, two life periods that are not defined by any clear-cut age spans. However, one fairly standard guideline is that middle age begins at about 40 and that old age begins at about 65 (Etaugh & Bridges, 2001; Nadien & Denmark, 1999).

For many years, psychological research has ignored older people, especially older women, consistent with our invisibility theme (Canetto, 2001a; Holden, 1997). Feminist research has also paid little attention to older women (Calasanti & Slevin, 2001); articles on women over 40 seldom appear in prominent journals such as *Psychology of Women Quarterly* and *Sex Roles.* This neglect is especially shameful because the average life span for a woman in North America and Europe is about 80 years (Kinsella, 2000). In other words, about half of a woman's life has been largely ignored.

The absence of information is also unfortunate because North America has so many elderly women. In 2000, the United States had 20.6 million women and 14.4 million men over the age of 65—roughly 43% more women than men (U.S. Census Bureau, 2001b). The comparable figures for Canada in 1999 were 2.2 million women and 1.6 million men over age 65, or 37% more women than men (Statistics Canada, 2000). As an increasing number of women live into their seventies, eighties, and older, we need to emphasize the issues of older women.

A further problem is that researchers and theorists explore only a small portion of women's lives. For example, a computer search of the psychology literature under the topic of "women and retirement" showed only 82 articles published between January 1998 and August 2002. A similar search under the topic "menopause" revealed 455 citations during the same time span. Most women probably spend more time planning and thinking about their retirement, yet this topic is relatively invisible.

Both psychology and women's studies are now beginning to demonstrate concern about the needs and experiences of older women (Sinnott & Shifren, 2001). For instance, we have already explored many components of older women's lives. Specifically, in Chapter 8 we discussed long-lasting romantic relationships, and in Chapter 9 we looked at sexuality and aging. In Chapter 11, we explored some issues relevant to older women's health, including elder abuse, heart disease, osteoporosis, reproductive system cancer, and breast cancer. In this chapter, we'll focus on four additional topics: (1) attitudes toward older women, (2) retirement and economic issues, (3) menopause, and (4) social aspects of older women's lives.

ATTITUDES TOWARD OLDER WOMEN

Ageism is a bias based on age, most often a bias against elderly people (Calasanti & Slevin, 2001). Common examples of ageism include negative emotions, attitudes, myths, stereotypes, and discrimination—as well as attempts to avoid interacting with elderly people (Braithwaite, 2002; Kite & Wagner, 2002; Whitbourne & Sneed, 2002). We already mentioned one example of ageism: that researchers generally avoid studying elderly people. Another example of ageism is that many physicians believe that elderly individuals complain too much about relatively minor medical problems (Jorgensen, 2001; Zebrowitz & Montepare, 2000). Physicians also treat elderly patients with less respect, compared to younger patients (Pasupathi & Löckenhoff, 2002).

Ageism is an ironic bias, because the elderly constitute the only stigmatized social group that we all will join eventually—unless we happen to die early! Furthermore, if our ageism prevents us from interacting with elderly people, we won't realize that many ageist assumptions are not correct (Cuddy & Fiske, 2002).

We'll begin this section on attitudes by considering how the media treat older women. Then we'll examine whether women are more likely than men to experience ageism—the double standard of aging. Finally, we'll see that elderly women may be treated more positively in some other cultures.

The Media

Try Demonstration 14.1 to discover how older women are represented on television. When you finally find a TV show that features older women, most of those women will be concerned about cookie recipes or holiday decorations rather than issues of greater significance. We all know spirited, accomplished older

---

DEMONSTRATION 14.1 ■

Older Women on Television

Between now and the end of this academic term, keep a record of the way older women are portrayed on television. This record should include both middle-aged women and elderly women. Be sure to include several kinds of programs (soap operas, game shows, situation comedies, shows during prime time, and Saturday morning cartoons) as well as advertisements. Pay attention to the number of older women and how they are shown. Are they working outside the home? Do they have interests, hobbies, and important concerns, or are they mainly busy being nurturant? Are they portrayed as intelligent or absent-minded? Do they enjoy the friendship of other women—the way that real older women do? Do they seem "real," or are they represented in a stereotypical fashion?

women in real life. However, your inspection of television's older women may not reveal many women of that caliber. Many of you who are reading this book are older women, and you may have noticed that women like yourself are invisible in the media.

A glance through magazines reveals the same message: Older women are essentially invisible. For instance, an investigation of advertisements in *Time* and *Newsweek* revealed that only 2% of the ads featured women who appeared to be older than 65, in contrast to 6% of the ads showing men older than 65 (McConatha et al., 1999). Most of the ads in this study displayed women in gender-stereotypical roles, such as an older woman serving dinner to her family. In the fashion magazines, older women are featured primarily in advertisements for age-concealing products. These ads are designed to make older women feel inadequate (Calasanti & Slevin, 2001; Etaugh & Bridges, 2001; Whitbourne, 1996). To hide signs of age, the ads say, women should dye their hair and have face-lifts. One surgical procedure removes fat from a woman's thighs or buttocks and injects it into her lips, to restore a youthful fullness. Just imagine! You could be the first on your block to wear your hips on your lips!

Older women do not fare better in the movies. For instance, women over the age of 39 accounted for only 27% of the best actress Academy Award winners, whereas men over 39 accounted for 67% of the best actor Academy Award winners (Markson & Taylor, 1993). Furthermore, older women are more likely than younger women to be portrayed as unfriendly, evil, unattractive, and not very intelligent (Bazzini et al., 1997).

This pervasive bias against older women has not been limited to recent decades. Images of evil elderly women have been common throughout Western literature, storytelling, and fairy tales (Mangum, 1999; Rostosky & Travis, 2000). Children dress up as "wicked old witches" for Halloween, but have you ever seen a costume for a wicked old *man*? You've heard many mother-in-law jokes; how about *father*-in-law jokes? We shouldn't be surprised, then, when older women themselves show ageism. Sadly, they may indeed be biased against people their own age (B. R. Levy & Banaji, 2002; Shear, 2001; Whitbourne & Sneed, 2002).

The Double Standard of Aging

As we've seen, North Americans typically have negative views about the aging process. Some theorists have proposed that people judge elderly women even more harshly than elderly men, a discrepancy called the **double standard of aging** (Zebrowitz & Montepare, 2000). For example, people tend to think that wrinkles in a man's face reveal character and maturity. However, wrinkles in a woman's face send a far different message. After all, the ideal woman's face should be unblemished and show no signs of previous experiences or emotions!

Does the research provide evidence for the double standard of aging? This is a difficult question to answer because our stereotypes about older men and women are complicated. As you'll see, these stereotypes depend on factors such as the age and occupation of the individuals we are judging, the particular attribute we are judging, and how the judgments are measured (Canetto, 2001a;

Kite & Wagner, 2002; Pasupathi et al., 1995). Let's consider two areas in which the double standard of aging has been tested: (1) personal and social characteristics and (2) love relationships.

Personal and Social Characteristics.   A classic study by Mary E. Kite and her colleagues (1991) emphasized the complicated nature of the double standard of aging. In general, Kite's results suggested that young adults are more ageist than sexist. For example, the young adults in this study made a major distinction between their reactions to 35-year-olds and their reactions to 65-year-olds. However, they didn't consider 65-year-old women much different from 65-year-old men. In fact, the young adults in this study saw both elderly women and elderly men as generous, family oriented, and friendly but focused more on the past than on the future and troubled by health problems.

Still, the participants in this study did make some distinctions between the elderly women and men. A 65-year-old man was more likely to be considered intelligent and wise. In contrast, a 65-year-old woman was more likely to be considered active in the community, a grandparent, and—consistent with our earlier discussion—wrinkled.

Using a different method, Hummert and her colleagues (1997) found more clear-cut evidence of a generalized double standard of aging. These researchers carefully assembled photographs of men and women representing different age groups. Let's consider specifically the part of this study in which the photographs being judged (the targets) had neutral facial expressions and were of people in either their sixties or their seventies. The participants in this study included men and women whose ages ranged from 18 through 96. They were asked to place each photograph next to one of six cards that described either a positive stereotype (e.g., a person who was lively, sociable, and interesting) or a negative stereotype (e.g., a person who was depressed, afraid, and lonely).

Figure 14.1 shows the average number of positive stereotypes that the participants selected. (The participants' age did not have a major impact on judgments, so Figure 14.1 combines the judgments of all participants.) As you can see, people selected a far smaller number of positive stereotypes for the older group of women than for all of the other three groups.

How do women visualize themselves during the aging process? Quirouette and Pushkar (1999) studied Canadian college-educated women between the ages of 45 and 65. They found that most women were optimistic and confident about their own future aging. They anticipated stability rather than change during their own future aging. Perhaps it's difficult for these women to believe that they themselves could become elderly.

Love Relationships.   In general, people uphold a double standard of aging with respect to love relationships. Specifically, older men are considered appropriate romantic partners, but older women are not. Consistent with our earlier observations about movies, older women are rarely shown in romantic relationships. For example, when I was writing this section, the newest James Bond movie, *Die Another Day*, featured 49-year-old Pierce Brosnan and 34-year-old Halle Berry. The 15-year discrepancy in their ages is fairly standard. Not surprisingly, people

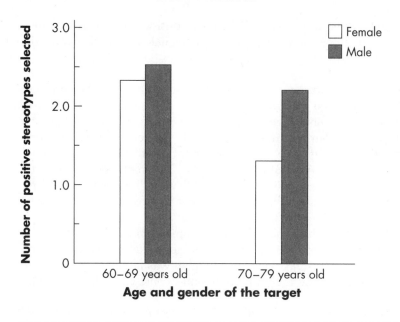

FIGURE 14.1 ■ Average number of positive stereotypes selected, as a function of target age and target gender. (Note: Maximum positive score = 3.0.)
Source: Based on Hummert et al. (1997).

often think that a marriage is not likely to succeed when a wife is much older than the husband (G. Cowan, 1984).

Lesbians also report that people react negatively when one partner is much older than the other. A 41-year-old woman wrote:

> I set about telling my friends that I am a lesbian and, at the same time, that I love a 63-year-old woman. The questions, stated or implied: Am I looking for a mother? Is she looking for some security in her old age? Is lesbian love, then, really asexual? (Macdonald & Rich, 2001, p. 11)

The double standard of aging also applies to sexuality, because aging women are often dismissed as being undesirable sex partners (Blieszner, 1998; R. H. Jacobs, 1997). As we noted in Chapter 9, people admire an old man's interest in sexuality, but they condemn the same interest shown by an old woman. Older women therefore face a particular disadvantage with respect to sexuality. Not only are they considered to look sexually unattractive and wrinkled, but they are also expected to show minimal interest in sexuality.

In this discussion, we've seen that the double standard of aging operates in some circumstances, although it is not universal (Kite & Wagner, 2002). Specifically, this double standard is most powerful when people judge two clusters of characteristics: (1) intelligence and competence and (2) physical attractiveness and romantic potential. Notice that the double standard of aging is, in fact, a variant of Theme 2 of this book: People react differently to women than they do to men. However, the differential treatment often increases as men and women grow older. As you might imagine, young women tend to be more anxious than young men about the prospect of growing older (Cummings et al., 2000).

Cross-Cultural Views of Older Women

In this book, we have often focused on women in North America. However, when we explore other cultures, we can find useful alternative models for viewing older women. In many of these cultures, a woman's power within the family increases as she grows older (Uba, 1994). For example, in some subcultures in African countries such as Nigeria and Kenya, elderly women are quite powerful (Calasanti & Slevin, 2001).

In some cultures, older women have direct power. For example, in many Latina/o cultures, elderly people are believed to have inner strength and a sense of mastery, so that they serve as a resource for younger people (Paz, 1993). In India, the elderly control family wealth and power, they arrange marriages, and they counsel younger people (Naidoo, 1990).

These positive attitudes in other cultures can certainly make older women feel valued. These attitudes also have important implications for cognitive functioning. For example, elderly women show little memory decline in cultures with positive attitudes toward the elderly, such as China (B. R. Levy & Langer, 1994). In contrast, people in the mainstream U.S. and Canadian cultures do not expect elderly women to be very intelligent. These expectations may indirectly encourage elderly women to perform less well on a variety of cognitive tasks (Gilleard & Higgs, 2000).

This section on attitudes toward elderly women may prompt you to introspect about the aging process. Do you hold any attitudes that are inappropriately negative? Think about some of the characteristics of the older women you admire, such as their wisdom, sense of humor, warmth, and competence. Try to incorporate these characteristics into your general viewpoint about older women. Can you think of specific ways in which your revised viewpoint can modify your response to the next older woman you meet?

SECTION SUMMARY ▪

Attitudes Toward Older Women

1. Ageism is a bias against elderly people.

2. The media underrepresent and misrepresent elderly women in magazine advertisements and in the movies.

3. The double standard of aging proposes that people judge older women more harshly than they do older men. The research on personality and social characteristics does not consistently support this concept, but it does typically show that people believe older men are more intelligent than older women.

4. The double standard of aging seems to apply when people assess romantic relationships and sexual attractiveness; elderly men are considered more appropriate as a romantic partner, compared to elderly women.

5. In some cultures outside North America, older women's power increases as they grow older.

OLDER WOMEN, RETIREMENT, AND ECONOMIC ISSUES

Think about the topic of women and retirement for a moment. Have you ever read a short story or a book about a woman retiring from her job? Have you seen many television shows or movies on this issue? Women are missing from the popular lore about retirement—and from the research (Dailey, 1998; Flippen & Tienda, 2000; Gilleard & Higgs, 2000). For example, an article in a Canadian publication is titled "Working Past Age 65"; however, the study included only males (M. Walsh, 1999). Once again, we have evidence for the relative invisibility of women. However, this invisibility may change now that so many women are working outside the home. For example, in 2000, about two-thirds of U.S. women between the ages of 45 and 64 were employed (U.S. Census Bureau, 2001b). The media typically lag behind reality, but maybe we'll soon see a movie that includes a retirement party for a woman!

In contrast to retirement, the issue of poverty among elderly women has received some publicity, and we also hear women's personal stories. For example, one 70-year-old Vermont woman was diagnosed with both breast cancer and osteoporosis. Her company's retirement plan does not include prescription coverage, and she spends about $1,800 a year on medication. This expense is more than 10% of her annual income (Butler, 2002). Women with inadequate retirement funds must often struggle to pay for basic living expenses. Let's now consider these interrelated topics: retirement and economic issues.

Planning for Retirement

Women retire for a number of reasons, such as personal health problems and the appeal of free time (Burtless & Quinn, 2001; Etaugh & Bridges, 2001). Many women retire early to take care of relatives with health problems (Flippen & Tienda, 2000; Kim & Moen, 2001b).

One worrisome gender difference is that women are less likely than men to seek information about retirement benefits before they retire (Dailey, 1998; Kim & Moen, 2001a, 2001b). One important reason is that married women assume that their husbands will be responsible for financial planning (Onyx & Benton, 1999). This avoidance may be a major problem because, as we'll soon see, they receive much lower retirement benefits than men do.

Adjusting to Retirement

Consistent with Theme 4 of this book, women differ widely in their reactions to retirement (Calasanti, 1996; V. E. Richardson, 1999). Many women welcome retirement as an opportunity to relax, pursue new interests, and enjoy social interactions. However, most of the research suggests that women may experience more retirement problems than men. Women may also need more time to adapt to retirement (Kim & Moen, 2001a, 2001b; V. E. Richardson, 1999). One reason for these gender differences is that many women have lower incomes, so they often have financial problems (Calasanti & Slevin, 2001; S. D. Phillips & Imhoff, 1997). Another reason is that retired women perform more housework than their retired husbands (S. T. Charles & Carstensen, 2002; Gilleard & Higgs, 2000; Szinovacz, 2000), and few women are inspired by housework. As one woman commented, "When a married couple retire, the women seem to spend most of the time doing housework etc., whereas men *do* retire" (Skucha & Bernard, 2000, p. 32).

When professional women retire, they frequently report that they miss their professional identity. One physician described how much she had enjoyed her career, so that retirement represented some losses:

> I was probably still in grade school when I decided to be a doctor. And to say I'm going to put aside this very gratifying way that I spend my days . . . I'm going to turn my back on everything that I've learned, all the experience I've accumulated. I'm setting aside all those years of study and of training. (C. A. Price, 2000, p. 90)

As you can imagine, a woman's adjustment during retirement is influenced by her reasons for retirement. If a woman retires because she wants more time for herself, she will probably adjust well to retirement. In contrast, if a woman retires because she needs to care for a sick relative, she will probably not enjoy her retirement (Onyx & Benton, 1999; V. E. Richardson, 1999). Significant life events, such as divorce or the death of family members, also influence a woman's adjustment to retirement. However, when married couples have been retired for at least 2 years, both women and men are happier with their lives and their marriages, compared with couples who have not yet retired (Kim & Moen, 2001a; Moen et al., 2001).

We still have many unanswered questions about women and retirement. For example, how can we encourage women to learn more about their retirement benefits? What successful strategies do married women use to negotiate a more equal sharing of housework during retirement? How can women best maintain their social connections from work? And what kinds of activities are most likely to enhance a woman's satisfaction with retirement?

Economic Issues

At present, about one-quarter of elderly European American women in the United States live in poverty. For U.S. women over the age of 65, the average income is about $11,000, compared to $19,168 for men (Crenshaw, 2002).

Economic problems are even more widespread for women of color. For example, more than half of Black and Latina elderly women are living in poverty (Canetto, 2001a; Carstensen, 1998; Cox, 2001). U.S. women also receive lower Social Security benefits than men do (Carstensen, 1998; Hatch, 2000). Poverty is also an issue for older Canadian women. For Canadians over the age of 65, the average income for women is about $16,000, compared to $26,000 for men (Canadian dollars) (Statistics Canada, 2000).

The other major source of income for elderly women is private pension plans. These are also based on earned income, and most women are not employed in jobs with pension plans. In Canada, only 52% of older female employees have a pension plan, compared to 76% of older male employees (Statistics Canada, 2000). The comparable figures for the United States are 56% for older women and 64% for older men (L. Shaw & Hill, 2001). In the United States, African American women are especially unlikely to have a pension plan (Canetto, 2001a).

Here are some other reasons that women have lower incomes than men during old age (Belsky, 2001; Flippen & Tienda, 2000; Gotwals & Stewart, 2002; Hardy & Shuey, 2000):

1. Employed women receive lower salaries than men; the wage gap means that women's lifetime earnings are an average of $250,000 less than men's (Butler, 2002). Therefore, women are less likely to set aside retirement funds during their employment years, and less money also goes toward their Social Security benefits.
2. Middle-aged women are more likely than middle-aged men to have lost a job before retirement.
3. Women are not compensated for their unpaid work in the home.
4. Many women are displaced homemakers who worked in the home and then became divorced or widowed; as a result, they have limited financial resources. For widows, the family finances may have been depleted by the husband's health care expenses.
5. Women live longer, so their annual income from savings is much lower than men's annual income.
6. As we saw in Chapter 11, women are more likely to have chronic illnesses, and the expense of treatment further decreases their usable income.

Naturally, we need to remind ourselves about individual differences. On the average, elderly women do indeed have lower incomes than elderly men, but some women are relatively well-off financially. Furthermore, research with U.S. residents suggests that, beyond the income necessary to buy the essentials, extra income does not typically buy happiness (Myers, 2000). Still, we cannot ignore the substantial number of women whose lives are altered by poverty. However, as we will see in the final section of this chapter, many elderly women lead lives that are satisfying and emotionally rich.

SECTION SUMMARY ■

Older Women, Retirement, and Economic Issues

1. The issue of women's retirement is relatively invisible in both the media and the psychological research, although the issue of economically poor elderly women has received some attention.

2. Women are less likely than men to seek information about retirement.

3. Although individual differences are large, women are likely to experience more adjustment problems in retirement than men do, especially if they retire to care for a sick relative.

4. Many elderly women in the United States and Canada live in poverty; they are likely to have lower incomes than men because of such factors as lower salaries when they were employed, lower retirement benefits, lower annual income from savings, and chronic illness.

MENOPAUSE

So far, our study of older adulthood has examined two topics that are central in the life experiences of older women: (1) how other people react to them and represent them in the media and (2) how older women experience retirement and economic issues. Let's turn our attention to the one topic that has generated the most media attention for older women: menopause. As we'll see, most older women do not consider the experience of menopause centrally important in their lives.

As women grow older, their ovaries gradually produce less estrogen and progesterone, so the smooth sequence of the menstrual cycle is disrupted. Eventually, the hormone levels dip too low to produce shedding of the endometrial lining of the uterus. As a result, women no longer menstruate on a regular basis (L. L. Alexander et al., 2001; L. R. Gannon, 1999). A woman enters **menopause** when she has stopped having menstrual periods for one year. Most women experience menopause between the ages of 45 and 55, with 51 being the most common age (L. L. Alexander et al., 2001).

A decade ago, menopause was rarely discussed in the media, but it has become a much more popular topic (L. R. Gannon, 1999). It's interesting that numerous books on menopause have been published since 1990, yet only one book on women and retirement has made it to the bookshelves in that same time period (Dailey, 1998). Perhaps our culture's current fascination with the biological basis of behavior is partly responsible (Buchanan et al., 2001; Rostosky & Travis, 2000). The popularity of menopause issues may also reflect our culture's emphasis on women's reproductive roles. Finally, if we *really* paid attention to issues such as women's retirement, the problem would require costly, societally based remedies (N. H. DeCourville, personal communication, 1999).

Let's consider four components of menopause. We'll begin with the physical symptoms and next discuss hormone replacement therapy. We'll then consider attitudes toward menopause, ending with a discussion of women's psychological reactions to menopause.

Physical Changes During Menopause

Several common physical symptoms accompany menopause. The best-known symptom is the **hot flash,** a sensation of heat coming from within the body and usually affecting the chest, neck, and head (L. R. Gannon, 1999). For most women, hot flashes are accompanied by heavy perspiration, and severe hot flashes often disrupt sleep (Hyde & DeLamater, 2003; Sommer, 2001).

About 75% to 85% of women in the United States experience hot flashes during menopause. However, only 10% to 20% of women consider them bothersome enough to need treatment (L. L. Alexander et al., 2001). Furthermore, the intensity of hot flashes decreases over time (Sherwin, 2001; Sommer, 2001).

Other physical changes during menopause may include osteoporosis (which we discussed in Chapter 11), decreased vaginal secretions, thinning of the vaginal tissues, headaches, urinary symptoms, and fatigue (L. L. Alexander et al., 2001; Sommer, 2001). This list of physical symptoms sounds frightening, but few women experience all symptoms. Throughout this book, we have emphasized individual differences in gynecological issues such as menarche, menstrual pain, premenstrual syndrome, pregnancy, and childbirth. Women's reactions to the physical changes of menopause show similar variation (Buchanan et al., 2001; P. Rich & Mervyn, 1999), providing additional evidence for Theme 4 of this book.

Hormone Replacement Therapy

Should women take hormones after menopause? This question may sound innocent. For the past decade, however, it has been a confusing and controversial issue. The problem is that hormones certainly relieve many of the physical symptoms of menopause, and they could potentially offer additional health benefits. However, they also have potential disadvantages. The question is especially important because most women in North America will be postmenopausal for more than one-third of their lives. Consequently, women need to make decisions that have long-term consequences.

Let me try to summarize the issues as of 2002, although the recommendations may change as results come in from several ongoing research projects. The original **estrogen replacement therapy** uses estrogen by itself, which effectively relieves symptoms such as hot flashes and genital changes; it also helps prevent osteoporosis.

A known problem with estrogen replacement therapy, however, is that it increases the risk of uterine cancer (L. L. Alexander et al., 2001). For women who have had a hysterectomy (and therefore do not have a uterus), estrogen replacement therapy has often been recommended, especially because estrogen was originally thought to reduce the risk of heart disease. The research on estrogen replacement therapy is still continuing, and we probably will not know the outcome for several years (Writing Group for the Women's Health Initiative Investigators, 2002).

However, most women undergoing menopause still have an intact uterus, so estrogen by itself could be harmful. Therefore, for many years, health care providers often recommended that these women use **hormone replacement therapy,** a term that usually refers to estrogen supplemented by progestin. Progestin is also a hormone, and it seems to reduce the risk of uterine cancer (L. L. Alexander et al., 2001; "HRT 2000," 2000). Several years ago, health care providers often recommended hormone replacement therapy, because the combination of these two hormones was believed to reduce the risk of heart disease (e.g., V. C. Jordan, 1998; Matthews et al., 1997). Early studies also showed that hormone replacement therapy was associated with a substantially lower risk of death, although its relationship with breast cancer was not clear (Bush & Whiteman, 1999; Colditz et al., 1995; Grodstein et al., 1997; Sellers et al., 1997).

Based on the research conducted during the 1990s, many women began using hormone replacement therapy. However, people concerned about women's health were waiting to hear the results of several long-term research projects. One of the largest of these projects is the Women's Health Initiative study, which included more than 16,000 women who had an intact uterus. In this carefully designed study, half of the women were given hormone replacement therapy (with both estrogen and progestin). The other half were in the control group; they were given a placebo, a pill with no active ingredients.

In May 2002, the Women's Health Initiative researchers suddenly halted the study—more than 3 years before the scheduled completion date. They had examined the results and had discovered that the estrogen-progestin combination did not prevent heart disease; in fact, it slightly increased the risk of heart attacks, strokes, and blood clots. It also slightly increased the risk of breast cancer. The combination did reduce the risk of hip fractures and of cancers of the colon and rectum, but not enough to offset the increase in the other risks (Writing Group for the Women's Health Initiative Investigators, 2002). Naturally, this discovery about hormone replacement therapy left millions of North American women angry. Why hadn't researchers conducted the appropriate studies? Why hadn't the drug companies discovered the potentially harmful effects of this hormone combination? At present, women are encouraged to eat nutritious food, exercise appropriately—and be cautious about the claims from drug companies.

Attitudes Toward Menopause

You can assess your friends' attitudes toward menopause by trying Demonstration 14.2. Menopause is no longer a taboo subject, but my students in their twenties report that they rarely discuss menopause with their friends.

Unfortunately, menopause has had a long history of being represented negatively in the medical literature (L. R. Gannon, 1999; Rostosky & Travis, 2000; Woods, 1999). The popular media echo this negative view of menopause. These sources suggest that a woman who is experiencing menopause is plagued by

DEMONSTRATION 14.2 ■ ■ ■ ■ ■ ■ ■ ■ ■ ■ ■ ■ ■ ■ ■ ■ ■ ■

Attitudes Toward Menopause

For this demonstration, you will need to locate at least six friends to participate in a brief study on what people of all ages think about typical people during their middle-aged years. Test at least two people in each of the three conditions.

Tell the people in the first group, "Please list items that you associate with men in the age range of 45 to 55 years. You can list words that describe their personality, appearance, attitudes, interests, emotions, and behaviors." After a couple of minutes, tell them to go back over those items and give a rating to indicate how positive or negative each characteristic is. Instruct them to use a rating scale where 1 is very negative, 3 is neutral, and 5 is very positive.

Repeat these instructions with people in two additional groups. For the second group, substitute the phrase "women in the age range of 45 to 55 years." For the third group, substitute the phrase "menopausal women in the age range of 45 to 55 years."

After you have tested everyone, calculate an "average rating" for each of the three middle-aged groups. Do your three groups differ?

Source: Based on Marcus-Newhall et al. (2001, p. 704).

intense mood swings. According to this view, a menopausal woman's wildly fluctuating hormones force her to be grouchy, highly anxious, and depressed (e.g., Futterman & Jones, 1998). An examination of the popular print media revealed 350 negative descriptions and only 27 positive descriptions of menopausal symptoms (L. R. Gannon, 1999).

Another problem is that the media often provide worst-case scenarios. For example, a director of a menopause clinic complained about the phone calls he receives from reporters. They typically ask him to describe the most severe menopausal symptoms rather than the norm (Azar, 1994). As a consequence, the media contribute to the public's negative attitudes toward menopause. The media also perpetuate another related myth: that menopausal women are no longer interested in sexual activity. In Chapter 9, though, we noted that women who have sexual partners typically remain sexually active during old age.

Given the negative representation of menopause in both medicine and the media, you won't be surprised to learn that the general public has similar negative attitudes. For example, Amy Marcus-Newhall and her colleagues (2001) asked people to list words that they would associate with each of three middle-aged groups of people. (Demonstration 14.2 is based on this study.) Then people evaluated each term on a rating scale. Attitudes toward 45- to 55-year-old menopausal women were significantly more negative than attitudes toward 45- to 55-year-old women (with no mention of menopause) and 45- to 55-year-old men. For example, they believed that menopausal women would be significantly less likely than members of the other two groups to have hobbies or to look attractive and significantly more likely to express negative emotions. In Demonstration 14.2, do your friends show this same trend?

Psychological Reactions to Menopause

At the beginning of this chapter, we emphasized that attitudes toward elderly women are often negative; they do not accurately describe the characteristics of real-world elderly women. Similarly, we find that attitudes toward menopause do not accurately describe women's actual experiences during menopause (Hvas, 2001; Sommer et al., 1999). For instance, a survey of physicians from one community revealed that 21% thought that menopause was a major health problem. In contrast, not one of the 120 menopausal women from that same community thought that menopause was a major health problem (DeLorey, 1992).

Some women report psychological symptoms such as depression, irritability, and mood swings. However, we have no evidence that menopause—by itself—causes these symptoms (L. L. Alexander et al., 2001; Sommer, 2001; Zerbe, 1999). In this chapter, we have already pointed out a number of depressing factors in the lives of older women, including attitudes toward older women and women's economic status. Women also experience health problems, divorce, and death of relatives and friends. All these stressful factors are more important than menopause itself in determining the psychological status of middle-aged women (L. R. Gannon, 1999; Sommer 2001).

Most women do not report major psychological reactions to menopause (L. R. Gannon, 1999; P. Rich & Mervyn, 1999; G. Robinson, 2002; Sommer et al., 1999; Woods, 1999). For example, a 50-year-old woman provides her perspective on menopause: "I was well into my menopause before I realized what was happening. My symptoms were so minor and rather vague. I didn't understand all the hype about symptoms" (L. L. Alexander et al., 2001, p. 398). Other women regard menopause as a life event that encourages them to evaluate their lives and decide whether they want to change directions (P. Rich & Mervyn, 1999; Zerbe, 1999).

Interestingly, women who have actually gone through natural menopause have significantly *less* negative attitudes toward menopause than do younger women. As part of a larger study, L. Gannon and Ekstrom (1993) asked women about their attitudes toward menopause in relation to their more general attitudes toward aging. Figure 14.2 shows the results for women who were postmenopausal, for women who were premenopausal but over the age of 35, and for women under the age of 35. As you can see, women who have experienced menopause generally consider it mildly negative—not as negative as it was judged by the two groups that had no personal knowledge of menopause.

In Chapter 4, we explored the concept of menstrual joy, or the idea that women can find some pleasure in menstruation. Some women have experiences that we could call menopausal joy. For example, Lotte Hvas (2001) asked Danish

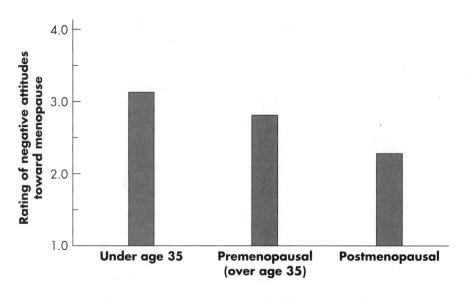

FIGURE 14.2 ■ Negative attitudes toward menopause, as a function of age and menopausal experience. (Note: 1 = neutral; 5 = most negative.)

Source: From Gannon, L., & Ekstrom, B. (1993). Attitudes toward menopause: The influence of sociocultural paradigms. *Psychology of Women Quarterly, 17,* 275–288 (Figure 1, p. 283).

women to describe their experiences with menopause. About half described at least one positive component. For instance, a 51-year-old woman said:

> Physically I have obtained a great strength passing the menopause—my sexual life has become more fun—I know for sure what I want—I look forward to becoming a grandmother soon, I am about to change my job, and I look forward to it. (Hvas, 2001, p. 14)

In general, however, the potentially positive aspects of menopause are ignored in both the medical world and the media (Sherwin, 2001).

Some researchers are beginning to explore how women of color experience menopause. For example, Barbara Sommer and her colleagues (1999) analyzed telephone interviews that had been conducted with more than 16,000 middle-aged women throughout the United States. Ethnic group differences were small but statistically significant. African American women had the most positive attitudes; European American and Latina women were intermediate; and Asian American women were least positive. Studies have also shown that other factors may influence attitudes toward menopause among women of color. For instance, immigrant Korean and Filipina women report that menopause is a relatively minor problem compared to the significant challenges these women face in adjusting to a new culture (J. A. Berg & Lipson, 1999; Im & Meleis, 2000).

Women from cultures outside North America may have relatively positive views, especially if older women are valued in the culture (G. Robinson, 2002). For example, Lamb (2000) studied women in a town in the West Bengal region of India. Young women and older women uniformly described menopause in positive terms, because menopause meant that they were free of the hassles of menstruation and that they could participate in religious ceremonies that are forbidden to menstruating women. Alternative viewpoints such as this one help us to understand how each culture constructs menopause according to its own values. Multicultural and cross-cultural perspectives also provide us with some positive alternatives.

SECTION SUMMARY ■

Menopause

1. Menopause, or the cessation of menstrual periods, is now a relatively popular topic in the media.

2. Common physical symptoms of menopause include hot flashes, osteoporosis, genital changes, headaches, and fatigue.

3. Hormone replacement therapy is a controversial topic. At present, it does not seem to provide substantial health benefits and probably has drawbacks.

4. Menopause has been represented negatively in both medicine and the media, and women who are not yet menopausal are more negative about it than women who are postmenopausal.

5. Contrary to folklore, menopause does not cause psychological symptoms such as depression and irritability. Women often have some positive reactions to menopause. Small ethnic group differences have been reported in the United States, and women in other parts of the world may have relatively positive reactions to menopause.

SOCIAL ASPECTS OF OLDER WOMEN'S LIVES

In this chapter, we have considered how society views older women, as well as women's experiences as they pass through menopause and retire from the work force. Now let's examine the changing social world of older women. How do their family relationships evolve as they grow older? How do women respond to the death of a spouse or other romantic partner? How do the experiences of women of color compare with the experiences of European American women? How happy are women with their lives—and how do they alter their lives if they are not satisfied?

Family Relationships

In Chapter 8, on love relationships, we explored one family role that is important for many women: being a wife. In that chapter, we examined some characteristics of happy, long-term relationships. We also looked at lesbian and bisexual relationships, which are central in the lives of many women. Let's now explore other important family roles for many older women—their roles as mothers, daughters, and grandmothers. These relationships have become more complex in recent decades because of increasing cohabitation, divorce, and remarriage (K. R. Allen et al., 1999, 2000; Bedford & Blieszner, 2000b).

Older Women as Mothers.   Much of the earlier research and theory on middle-aged women focused on the **empty nest,** or the period after children are no longer living at home. Notice that the name *empty nest* implies that a woman's role focuses completely on being a mother. Years ago, researchers were eager to demonstrate that mothers felt depressed when children left home.

In reality, however, the research reveals the same wide variety of responses that our other discussions of women's lives have uncovered (Theme 4). In general, though, the current research confirms that middle-aged mothers whose children have left home tend to be about as happy as or even slightly happier than middle-aged mothers who have at least one child at home (Antonucci et al., 2001; Calasanti & Slevin, 2001; Johnston-Robledo, 2000). Keep in mind, too, that most mothers are still concerned about their children, even when those children no longer live at home.

My college-age students are often dismayed to learn that their mothers may be somewhat happier after the children leave home. Please do not conclude that women are overjoyed with their children's departure. Mothers may indeed be saddened. However, serious depression is rare. Instead, mothers learn to reshape their lives around new interests and activities as their daughters and sons move into adulthood (Johnston-Robledo, 2000).

Older Women as Daughters.   We usually think of adult women's roles as mothers and grandmothers. However, adult women are often daughters, as well.

Most of the research on the daughter role focuses on adult women who take care of elderly parents. The term **sandwich generation** refers to middle-aged people, especially women, who find themselves responsible for both their children and their parents. Most researchers estimate that daughters are about three times as likely as sons to become caretakers for an elderly parent who is in poor health (Canetto, 2001a; Etaugh & Bridges, 2001; Huyck, 1999). In addition, compared to sons, daughters typically report that caregiving causes more stress (Blieszner & Wingfield, 2000). Because women spend much more time on these tasks than men do, taking care of the elderly is really a women's issue.

Many of the resources on women's caregiving roles emphasize that the tasks are unpleasant and burdensome for middle-aged daughters, and indeed there are often substantial negative aspects (Fingerman, 2001; Kerson, 2001; M. P. Lawton et al., 2000). However, recent studies have found that many daughters willingly accept this responsibility, especially because they feel that their parents had raised them with so much love and generosity (Antonucci et al., 2001; R. Leonard, 1999; Whitbourne, 2001). They also feel satisfied to know that their parents have received good care (Martire & Schulz, 2001; Stephens & Franks, 1999). For instance, a colleague described how she commuted 800 miles each way to care for her severely ill mother—while working toward tenure at her university.

Indeed, she had experienced incredible strain. On one occasion, in the intensive care unit, she held her mother's hand with her right hand as her mother fought pneumonia. Simultaneously, with her left hand, this woman typed a psychology exam that was later faxed to a colleague teaching the course for her. The additional responsibilities did have an impact on her academic career. However, as she wrote:

> I considered myself blessed to have been able to give so much to my mother and to provide her hospice care in her home. She died in my arms. Yes it was stressful. Yes it was difficult. And, yes, I had these positive feelings—as well as negative feelings— at the time I was doing this. But I have no regrets and would do it again without thinking about it. (L. Skinner, personal communication, 1999)

A small number of researchers have begun to explore other aspects of the relationship between grown children and their parents—beyond the caretaking role (Fingerman, 2001; Roberto et al., 1999). Unfortunately, however, the media generally ignore the social interactions between middle-aged people and their parents. Aside from an occasional brief reference, how often have you seen or read about a relationship between an adult woman and her mother in which they were interacting as adults?

Older Women as Grandmothers.   According to one of the traditional stereotypes, grandmothers are jolly white-haired old ladies who bestow cookies and affection on their grandchildren. According to another stereotype, grandmothers are frail and helpless (Denmark, 2002; L. Morgan & Kunkel, 2001). Neither of these stereotypes captures the wide variety of capabilities, interests, and personality characteristics that are typical of real grandmothers (Barer, 2001).

Most women are grandmothers for about half of their lives (Kivett, 1996). However, once again, we have relatively little recent research on this role. In one study of individuals over the age of 85, only about 20% of the grandparents saw a grandchild more often than once a week (C. L. Johnson & Barer, 1997).

What do grandmothers do when they interact with their grandchildren? In terms of activities, they are likely to babysit and drop by for visits, often playing games, reading books, sharing family history, and enjoying conversations when they visit. They are also likely to impart advice to grandchildren about doing what is morally right and socially appropriate (L. Morgan & Kunkel, 2001; J. P. Scott, 1997). However, our theme of individual differences is evident in patterns of grandmothering. Some women argue that good grandparents should not interfere with their grandchildren's upbringing, but others feel it is their duty to advise (Kornhaber, 1996; Roberto et al., 1999; Whitbourne, 2001). In Black and Native American families, grandmothers may be expected to play an especially important advisory role (Trotman & Brody, 2002).

Widowhood and the Death of Life Partners

For married women, the death of a spouse is typically one of the most traumatic and stressful events of their lives. Women are more likely to become widows than men are to become widowers. Several factors explain this discrepancy. For example, women live longer, they typically marry men older than themselves, and they are less likely to remarry (Bradsher, 1997; Canetto, 2001a). As a result, the U.S. census shows 3.4 times as many widows as widowers over the age of 65 (U.S. Census Bureau, 2001b). The ratio in other regions of the world is even more extreme. For instance, Africa has about seven times as many widows as widowers (United Nations, 2000).

When a woman's husband dies, she faces the pain, grief, and mourning that accompany bereavement. Loneliness is one of the major problems for widows (Bedford & Blieszner, 2000a; Chambers, 2000; van den Hoonaard, 1999). Many women have never lived alone; they went directly from the home of their parents into the home in which they lived with their husbands. Widows also report that they often feel awkward in social situations where most people are with a spouse.

Most of the recent gender comparisons in bereavement patterns show that men are more likely than women to experience depression (Bonanno & Kaltman, 1999; Canetto, 2001a; S. T. Charles & Carstensen, 2002; Stroebe et al., 2001). However, when a spouse dies, both women and men are likely to experience loneliness, grief, stress, and health problems.

We know relatively little about the grieving process for other life partners. For example, I located a full-length book on gay male widowers (Shernoff, 1997) but only two journal articles relevant to lesbian bereavement. Shenk and Fullmer (1996) described a lesbian couple in their eighties who had lived together for 15 years in a small Midwestern town. Hilda wrote about her bereavement after the death of her partner, Maurine:

> I sit to remember, to wish, and then to realize that life has to be different. I know life has to be different, and I am now picking up the happy thoughts from the past and going on. (p. 85)

Unfortunately, our culture's heterosexism is likely to deny lesbians the kind of social support that is typically offered to women whose husbands have died. For instance, one woman teaching in a small rural school was afraid she would lose her job if she revealed her grief after the death of her partner (Deevey, 2000). They had spent years concealing their romantic relationship, and now she could not publicly express her sorrow.

We find enormous individual differences in bereavement, as in all important transitions in women's lives (Black & Rubinstein, 2000; Feldman, 1999; Nolen-Hoeksema & Larson, 1999). Many women are deeply depressed, long after the death of a romantic partner. As one 49-year-old woman wrote:

> We were never apart for our married life. We saw each other every day for 27 years. . . . He thought of us first. He was a good person with ordinary faults. There is no sense to it. It still irritates and hurts me. This should be our time together. (Nolen-Hoeksema & Larson, 1999, p. 52)

Many women eventually discover a hidden strength that aids their recovery. For example, a 48-year-old woman wrote:

> I think that when you lose a loved one, it's a rebirth for yourself. You can't always dwell on the loss of the loved one. You have to look forward to what you are going

to do with your life now. . . . Every day's a little learning experience for myself, of doing new things and learning new things as a single person. (Nolen-Hoeksema & Larson, 1999, p. 149)

Older Women of Color

Women of color are far more likely than European American women to face the economic difficulties we discussed earlier. We noted earlier that Black and Latina elderly women are twice as likely as European American elderly women to live in poverty (Canetto, 2001a; Carstensen, 1998; Cox, 2001). Consequently, many elderly women of color face a daily struggle in paying for housing, health care, transportation, and even enough food to eat. However, older women of color also benefit from an advantage: They are more likely than European American women to have an extended family living nearby who can provide assistance and support (Armstrong, 2001; Bedford & Blieszner, 2000a; Trotman, 2002).

Two different stereotypes are used to characterize elderly Black women (Ralston, 1997; Trotman, 2002). One portrays them as victims of poverty and urban decay; the other portrays them as superhuman individuals who surmount obstacles through hard work and a good heart. Neither portrayal captures the complexity of their actual lives.

In general, elderly Black women are likely to be active in selected community organizations such as a church (Armstrong, 2001; Conway-Turner, 1999). In addition, Black women are often closely involved in the lives of their grandchildren (Barer, 2001; Conway-Turner, 1999; Harm, 2001; McWright, 2002). These women give their grandchildren social support, monitor their activities, discipline them, and encourage them to achieve. However, many Black grandmothers report resentment about becoming the primary caretaker for grandchildren, especially if they only recently finished rearing their own children (Barer, 2001; Baydar & Brooks-Gunn, 1998; Calasanti & Slevin, 2001; Harm, 2001).

We have little research on Latinas (Facio, 1997). Like Black grandmothers, Latina grandmothers are treated with respect, and they typically enjoy their social role. However, they often describe the role as "confining" or "limiting," especially if they are expected to take on child-care responsibilities (Facio, 1997; Harm, 2001). A study of Puerto Rican women currently living in the United States emphasized that elderly women are expected to provide help to children and grandchildren (Sánchez-Ayéndez, 1993). In return, elderly women are expected to *seek* help when they need it. It's worth noting, too, that Black and Latina women are somewhat less likely than European American women to experience the empty nest effect (Facio, 1997).

When we look at elderly Asian American women, we see additional evidence of diversity within ethnic groups. For example, an elderly woman from India may be a retired physician. In contrast, fewer than 20% of elderly women from Laos have completed high school (Kagawa-Singer et al., 1997). In general, however, elderly Asians are more likely than elders in any other ethnic group to live with their children (Armstrong, 2001; Conway-Turner, 1999). Research with both Vietnamese refugees and South Asian immigrants concluded that elderly women who lived with their family had better social adjustment than those who lived in different households (Guglani et al., 2000; T. V. Tran, 1991).

Elderly Native American women are the least visible group in the psychology research. One important variable that determines the life patterns of these elderly women is whether they live in an urban or a rural setting. About half of elderly Native Americans live in cities, where they are dispersed throughout the general urban population. Little is known about these urban elderly women (Armstrong, 2001; R. John et al., 1997). The remaining half live in rural areas or on reservations, where they typically assume the roles of grandmother, caregiver, educator, and wisdom keeper (Conway-Turner, 1999; R. John et al., 1997).

A study of Apache grandmothers living on a reservation in Arizona emphasized the strong bond between grandmothers and their grandchildren (Bahr, 1994). Apache children are more likely than European American children to live with their grandparents because parents often leave the reservation to seek employment in an urban setting. Most grandmothers in this study reported that they felt great satisfaction in caring for their grandchildren. These grandmothers are expected to be wise, energetic, and resourceful, especially in transmitting their cultural heritage to their grandchildren. In turn, young Native Americans are more likely than young European Americans to believe that they have a responsibility to take care of the elderly (Gardiner et al., 1998).

Throughout this chapter, we have discussed the invisibility of older women. Older women of color are even less visible. Psychologists may glance briefly at elderly women of color, but we typically lack the crucial information that would provide a clear picture of their lives and experiences.

Satisfaction with Life

If you browse through some of the topics discussed in this book, you'll see that many older women have every right to be unhappy. In Chapter 11, we examined physical problems such as breast cancer and osteoporosis, which are relatively common among older women. We also saw in that chapter that some elderly women are abused by their younger relatives. In the current chapter, we have seen that women may be unhappy about retiring. Many worry about the health of their parents. Many will mourn the loss of a spouse or a close companion. Many older women, especially women of color, are likely to face economic crises. Even women who do not have any of these problems are likely to experience negative reactions from others because they live in a culture that rejects older women's wrinkles and other signs of age.

In reality, however, most middle-aged and elderly women are reasonably satisfied with their lives (Keyes & Ryff, 1998; Magai, 2001; Whitbourne & Sneed, 2002). For example, Neill and Kahn (1999) found that elderly widows gave themselves an average rating of 19 on a life satisfaction scale where the most negative score was 0 and the most positive was 26. Furthermore, older women are actually less likely than younger women to be depressed (L. R. Gannon, 1999; Myers, 2000).

Several factors help explain why most elderly women are reasonably happy. Specifically, they have learned how to cope effectively with negative emotions and how to spend time on activities that are enjoyable. They have also adjusted their goals so that they are more realistic. In addition, they can maintain a positive view of themselves, even when faced with disappointments (Magai, 2001; Whitbourne & Sneed, 2002).

Remember the theme of individual variation, emphasized throughout this book. In particular, women vary in the ways they achieve happiness. Researchers have found that women do not share a ready-made blueprint for happiness (C. L. Johnson & Barer, 1997). One woman might find happiness through her husband and children, whereas another might be equally happy with a less traditional lifestyle.

Rewriting Our Life Stories

Many young women think they know exactly where their lives are heading, and many women's lives do reveal a pattern of continuity and predictability. However, many women find that their lives take an unexpected route. For example, Vickers and Thomas (1993) interviewed women between the ages of 40 and 60. Most reported that they had begun to rethink and reshape their lives.

Other research confirms that most middle-aged women welcome new challenges and are more confident than they were in earlier years (Babladelis, 1999; Edelstein, 1999; A. J. Stewart et al., 2001). Furthermore, middle-aged women who have worked outside the home report that the women's movement had helped them feel more powerful and self-confident (Agronick & Duncan, 1998). Yes, some middle-aged women say that—several years earlier—they had regrets about their life path. However, if they had made life changes and rewritten their life stories, they were more satisfied than those who continued to live with their regrets (A. J. Stewart & Vandewater, 1999).

Several books have explored the way women make choices and changes. Some titles capture how women can choose to pursue new life directions: *The Art of Midlife* (Edelstein, 1999), *The Last Gift of Time* (Heilbrun, 1997), *On Women Turning 70: Honoring the Voices of Wisdom* (Rountree, 1999), *Getting Over Getting Older* (Pogrebin, 1996), *Tangled Lives: Daughters, Mothers, and the Crucible of Aging* (L. B. Rubin, 2000), and—my favorite title—*No More Frogs, No More Princes: Women Making Creative Choices at Midlife* (Vickers & Thomas, 1993).

The interviews in these books emphasize that, as women grow older, they can play by new rules. At the age of 46, Linda N. Edelstein (1999) faced the possibility of cancer, but the tumor turned out to be benign. She reported that the incident forced her to question what she really wanted and how she should pursue these dreams. As she wrote, "The sadness and hopelessness some women experience in the middle years does not come from trying and failing, but from not trying" (p. 195).

We need to emphasize, however, that older women in the United States would be more likely to create positive, productive life stories if our society—especially our government—truly valued these women. In a country of such enormous wealth, none of these women should have to struggle to obtain adequate food, housing, and health care. For the last demonstration of this chapter, try Demonstration 14.3, when you have a convenient opportunity.

DEMONSTRATION 14.3 ■■■■■■■■■■■■■■■■■■■■■■■■

The Life Stories of Older Women

The instructions for this demonstration are more open-ended than for the previous demonstrations. Think of a woman you know fairly well who is at least 40 years old. Ask if you might interview her at a convenient time. Before the interview, select some of the questions given in this demonstration, keeping in mind that a few questions may be too personal. Also, construct several other questions based on the information in this chapter. Before you begin the interview, be sure to emphasize that she can choose not to answer any question you give her.

Sample Questions

1. What was the happiest time in your life?
2. When you were 20, did you think that your life would take you along the pathway you have been going?
3. Was there anything you would have done differently if you had the chance to relive part of your life?
4. Has your self-confidence changed since you were 20 or 30?
5. If you were 20 years old, living in today's world, what kind of choices would you make?
6. (If relevant) When your children left home, what kinds of emotional reactions did you have?
7. (If relevant) When you retired from your job, what kinds of emotional reactions did you have?
8. Do you feel that you are still searching for a sense of who you are?
9. Do you feel that people treat you differently because of your age and your gender?
10. Is there a question about your life that I somehow didn't ask—one that is personally interesting to you?

Sources: Questions based on Babladelis (1999), A. J. Stewart and Vandewater (1999), and A. J. Stewart et al. (2001).

Final Words

To conclude this chapter, I asked a 69-year-old friend to reflect about her life and about old age. At the age of 58, Anne Hardy and her husband, Duane, decided to leave their comfortable community in Rochester, New York, to work in the South for several organizations that are concerned with civil rights and social justice. She wrote about this period in her life:

> When our children were through college and on their own, our feeling was that it was time to close out the marketplace phase of our lives. We never had the empty-

nest feeling. It was, instead, a kind of liberation, a time to move into a new phase. Just as marriage had been a new phase, followed by parenthood, this was another.

The caring, the sharing of concerns, the readiness to be of help to each other when necessary, would continue with our children, unchanged by the fact that we were no longer living under one roof, but we were ready to move on, just as they were. We had both done a great deal of volunteer work in our free time for many years, and now we had the opportunity to do it full-time. Our needs are modest, we were able to accept subsistence salaries until we were able to "retire" on Social Security, at which time we continued to work full-time but no longer drew salaries.

. . . I am very conscious that my life hasn't been "typical," if there is such a thing. I've had many advantages denied to others. We have had fairly low income at times but were never really poor and certainly never hungry; my health has, for the most part, been good; we have loving, caring children; and best of all, I've had, in my husband, a superb companion and best friend. With today's economic stresses and disrupted families, I doubt it's a norm.

After 10 years of work in the South, Anne and her husband, Duane, retired and moved back north. Anne still continued to work for organizations such as the Women's International League for Peace and Freedom and the U.S.-China People's Friendship Association. She commented on this transition:

"Retirement" has many advantages. It's possible to be involved in many activities, yet not be pressured by them. We set our own schedules. We're free of regimentation. If something interesting to do comes up, we can do that and shift other commitments around. It's a more flexible, less rigid, less scheduled life.

At the age of 69, I still don't feel "old," although chronologically, I'm not "young." I think one ages—given reasonable health—as one has been gradually aging in all the years before, very much depending on the quality of life one has built. My interests haven't changed, except that we have the added joy of six grandchildren in our lives. Elderly people are as diverse as young people. Differences between them remain; previous likes and dislikes remain, for the most part. I am still me, "old" or not, though I feel that I have become more understanding, less judgmental, more open to new experiences, still trying to grow as a person.

We have begun to experience the loss of relatives and friends, and chronic and serious illnesses are beginning to appear among our associates. It's sad, of course, but it has the positive side of drawing us closer to those of our families and friends who are still in our lives, makes us more loving, more willing to overlook small irritants, more giving. . . .

There are serious concerns and hopes about the future, naturally, both in regard to personal matters such as health and loss of close ones, and in regard to national and international events. . . . I have lost much of my sense that we can influence the course of events; I have increasingly stronger conviction that we are in the hands of multinationals and conglomerates, of Eisenhower's "military-industrial complex." That feeling can be an immobilizing one. But to do nothing is to go along with what's happening. I know it's a cliché, but the future is *now*. This is the only world any of us has, and if we don't like it, or if we are worried about the direction it's going, we have to work to change it. "This is the way it is" is something we can't settle for. We have to work toward being able to say, "That is the way it *was*, and we have helped to improve it." I console myself a bit with the recollection that 40 years ago, when we debated whether we should bring children into the world, I had the same concerns— and we're all still here!

A Fundamentalist relative asked me recently what I felt about eternity. I answered that for me eternity is being created daily in what I do, how I live vis-à-vis other human beings, what kinds of values I gave and continue to give our children so that they in turn would have good values to pass on to their world and their children.

SECTION SUMMARY ■

Social Aspects of Older Women's Lives

1. Some women experience the empty nest effect, but research shows that most women are relatively happy after their children leave home.

2. During middle age, daughters are more likely than sons to become caregivers for elderly parents; the negative components of this caregiver role have been emphasized in the research, but many women identify positive components.

3. Women differ widely in their grandmothering styles; for example, many feel that they should avoid interfering, but others believe that they should give advice to grandchildren.

4. Most married women find that the death of a spouse is traumatic, and loneliness is a frequent problem. When lesbians lose a life partner, they may have the added burden of needing to conceal their grief.

5. Older women of color are especially likely to experience poverty, yet they are more likely than older European American women to have the support of an extended family.

6. Elderly Black women are likely to be active in community organizations and to take responsibility for rearing grandchildren. Elderly Latinas are expected to help with children and grandchildren and to seek help when they need it. Elderly Asian women are more likely than women from other ethnic groups to live with their children. Elderly Native American women are expected to have close relationships with their grandchildren and to share their cultural heritage with these children.

7. Older women seem to be as satisfied with their lives as younger women, despite health, financial, and personal problems.

8. Many women rethink their lives during middle age or later, and they make choices that take them in new directions.

▪▪▪▪▪▪ CHAPTER REVIEW QUESTIONS ▪▪▪▪▪▪

1. One of the themes of this book is that women tend to be relatively invisible, and this tendency is especially true for older women. Discuss this theme, pointing out how older women have not received enough attention in the following areas: (a) representation in the media, (b) research on retirement, and (c) the lives of elderly women of color. Then add to the list any other areas of older women's lives that seem important and were not covered in this chapter.

2. What is the double standard of aging? When does it seem most likely to operate, and when does it not apply?

3. From what you know about retirement, describe a woman who is likely to adjust well to retirement. Then describe a woman who is likely to adjust poorly to retirement.

4. Describe the economic situation of elderly women, and list as many factors as you can recall that account for the gender differences in income for elderly men and women.

5. Think about the women you know who have retired from their paid employment. How do their lives match the information on retirement that was discussed in this chapter, with respect to the timing of their retirement, their financial resources during later adulthood, and their adjustment to retirement?

6. What are some of the physical symptoms of menopause? Imagine that a middle-aged friend is now experiencing menopause, and she is considering hormone replacement ther-apy. How would you describe the pros and cons of both estrogen replacement and estrogen-progestin replacement?

7. What psychological reactions do women have to menopause? How do the attitudes of pre-menopausal women compare with women's actual experiences?

8. Research in the psychology of women often focuses too heavily on the experiences of European American middle-class women. What did you learn in this chapter about the lives of elderly women of color, economically disadvantaged women, and women in other cultures? In the section "Rewriting Our Life Stories," we noted that a number of books describe how older women can make life changes and take risks. What groups of older women are *least* likely to have these options?

9. The theme of individual differences has been prominent throughout this book. However, some researchers argue that individual differences increase throughout our lives. Look at the topics in the outline on page 456 and describe the nature of those individual differences, where relevant.

10. In this chapter, we have discussed many legitimate reasons why older women might be dissatisfied with their lives. List as many of these as you can. Then suggest reasons why many older women are reasonably satisfied, adding your own insights to the information in this chapter.

NEW TERMS

*ageism (459)
double standard of aging (460)
*menopause (467)
*hot flash (468)

*estrogen replacement therapy (468)
*hormone replacement therapy (469)
*empty nest (474)
*sandwich generation (474)

The terms asterisked in the New Terms section serve as good search terms for InfoTrac College Edition. Go to http://infotrac.thomsonlearning.com and try these added search terms.

RECOMMENDED READINGS

Calasanti, T. M., & Slevin, K. F. (2001). *Gender, social inequalities, and aging.* Walnut Creek, CA: AltaMira Press. Written by two sociologists, this book is especially strong on topics such as gender inequalities, retirement, and caregiving.

Dailey, N. (1998). *When baby boom women retire.* Westport, CT: Praeger. In this book, Nancy Dailey summarizes her careful research, which argues that the majority of women born between 1946 and 1964 will have financial trouble during retirement.

Fingerman, K. L. (2001). *Aging mothers and their adult daughters: A study in mixed emotions.* New York: Springer. I strongly recommend this book for anyone interested in the research on the subtleties of mother-daughter relationships.

Garner, J. D., & Mercer, S. O. (Eds.). (2001). *Women as they age* (2nd ed.). New York: Haworth. This interesting book primarily emphasizes the social components of older women's lives.

Nelson, T. D. (Ed.). (2002). *Ageism: Stereotyping and prejudice against older persons.* Cambridge, MA: MIT Press. Here is the definitive book on age biases, including general attitudes, ageism in the workplace, reducing ageism, and well-being in the elderly. Most studies do not examine whether ageism is different for males and females, so this book is useful if you are searching for interesting research topics that could be related to gender.

Whitbourne, S. K. (2001). *Adult development and aging: Biopsychosocial perspectives.* New York: Wiley. I'd recommend this book for anyone who wants a good general perspective on aging processes. Whitbourne includes chapters on such topics as cognitive processes, retirement, social relationships, and personality.

ANSWERS TO THE TRUE-FALSE QUESTIONS

1. False (p. 458); 2. False (pp. 460–461); 3. False (p. 463); 4. False (p. 465); 5. False (pp. 465–466); 6. True (pp. 470–471); 7. False (p. 471); 8. False (p. 474); 9. False (p. 475); 10. False (p. 478).

Moving Onward . . .

AFP/Corbis

T R U E O R F A L S E ?

_____ 1. In Iran, more than half of the students entering the universities are female.

_____ 2. Most college courses in the psychology of women were taught for the first time during the 1960s, even before the rebirth of the women's movement.

_____ 3. Females now constitute the majority of students enrolled in North American psychology Ph.D. programs.

_____ 4. When women from some ethnic groups become feminist activists, the men in their ethnic community often tell them that this activism is a threat to ethnic unity.

_____ 5. One of the basic beliefs of the Promise Keepers—and others who support the religious approach to the men's movement—is that men must take back their roles as family leaders and women should be followers.

_____ 6. The media often claim that women now have the same advantages that men do and that feminism is the source of women's dissatisfaction.

_____ 7. According to qualitative research, students say that their women's studies courses have increased their feminist identity; however, quantitative research shows that women's studies courses do not have a significant effect.

_____ 8. The first wave of the North American feminist movement began in the 1920s, as a result of women winning the right to vote.

_____ 9. The number of feminist groups in North America has actually decreased during the last decade.

_____ 10. By the year 2000, women had been heads of state in more than 30 countries, and groups throughout the world had created thousands of projects to benefit women and girls.

Y ou have now read 14 chapters about the lives of females, from their prenatal development through old age. As you struggle to assimilate all the diverse statistics, research studies, theories, and personal testimonies, you may be asking one central question: How are women doing as we move further into the new millennium?

To answer this question, let's consider some representative information— both uplifting and depressing—on the lives of women in the current era:

- Women now receive 43% of all Ph.D. degrees in the United States ("The Nation: Students," 2001).
- In Multan, Pakistan, a tribal council was distressed that an 11-year-old boy had been walking with a girl from another tribe. To punish the boy's "crime," the council ordered that his 18-year-old *sister* be sentenced to gang rape. Four men raped her repeatedly (E. Goodman, 2002).
- In Iran, a country just to the west of Pakistan, 52% of the students entering the universities are female (Mir-Hosseini, 2001).

- The United Nation's Convention on the Elimination of All Forms of Discrimination Against Women has been ratified by 170 countries throughout the world; this document condemns female genital mutilation, selling women for prostitution, and domestic abuse. However, several countries have refused to sign the document, including Somalia, Sudan, Iran, and . . . the United States (E. Goodman, 2002).

As these examples suggest, women's lives have improved considerably in some areas, yet the progress is often slow. We'll begin this chapter by discussing the future of the discipline we call the psychology of women. Then we'll examine how feminism is constructed for women of color. Our third section explores several different components of the men's movement. We'll then consider some discouraging trends, specifically, a perceived tendency to interpret feminism too rigidly and the far more worrisome backlash against women's progress. Our final section examines some encouraging trends, such as women's studies courses, the women's movement, and activism.

THE FUTURE OF THE DISCIPLINE OF THE PSYCHOLOGY OF WOMEN

As we noted in Chapter 1, the discipline of the psychology of women is relatively young. Most college courses with that title were offered for the first time in the 1970s or 1980s. People who teach courses in the psychology of women or the psychology of gender often emphasize the strong connection we immediately felt with this emerging discipline (e.g., Deaux, 2001a; Hyde, 2001). For example, Letitia Anne Peplau said, "Feminist perspectives helped me understand my own life experiences and relationships in new and more insightful ways. . . . Feminist activism sought to improve the lives of women and to work toward a more just society that places a high value on women as well as men" (Peplau, 1994, p. 44).

Hundreds of professors throughout North America share this passion for teaching and studying the psychology of women. Two concerns related to the future of our discipline are (1) the increasing number of women entering psychology and (2) the issue of developing a more inclusive psychology of women.

The Increasing Number of Women in Psychology

Most undergraduates in psychology are female: 70% in the United States, for example (Kyle & Williams, 2000). Females also outnumber males in North American psychology graduate programs. For instance, women constitute 70% of the full-time students in psychology Ph.D. programs in Canada (Boatswain et al., 2001). The current gender ratio for psychology faculty members still favors males, however, with only 37% of the full-time U.S. psychology faculty being female (Kyle & Williams, 2000). Fortunately, that percentage will increase when the current female graduate school students become faculty members.

The increasing number of women in psychology does not necessarily *guarantee* a strong feminist discipline. For example, a group of psychologists was asked to identify the most eminent psychologists of the twentieth century; only 3 of the top 80 were women (Haggbloom et al., 2002). Furthermore, as we have seen throughout this book, women and men often hold similar stereotypes about gender. However, the increasing number of women entering psychology has certainly contributed to the growing support for feminist theory and research.

Developing a More Inclusive Psychology of Women

In constructing the new discipline of psychology of women, we hoped to create a new perspective that values women's and men's lives equally. An ongoing problem, however, has been that the psychology of women has typically focused on educated, heterosexual, middle-class European American females (Espín, 1994; Sgoutas, 2001; J. D. Yoder & Kahn, 1993). After all, the psychologists—as well as the college women they typically study—are most likely to be educated, heterosexual, middle-class European American women (Enns, 1997).

In recent years, some scholars have moved away from the traditional population of European American females to examine other populations (e.g., J. James & Sharpley-Whiting, 2000; Kafka, 2000; Landrine, 1995a; Peplau, DeBro et al., 1999; Saldívar-Hull, 2000). However, much of the current research on women of color, lesbian women, or lower-class women is limited to a comparison between the normative group and the "nonstandard" group. This group-comparisons approach often keeps European American women at the center. Every other group is then a "special case," located on the periphery (Morawski & Bayer, 1995; J. D. Yoder & Kahn, 1993).

Another problem with a group-comparisons approach is that psychologists often select topics for research in which the ethnic group that is not European American is suspected to be deficient. For example, as I searched for studies on Native Americans and Canadian Aboriginals, I kept finding research on alcoholism and suicide. Why couldn't I find a similar abundance of research on topics such as romantic relationships during adolescence or the experience of motherhood?

Unfortunately, too, psychologists seldom explore areas in which people of color successfully negotiate a problem. We could all learn from research in Chapter 14, which demonstrated that they are likely to be active in community organizations. How do these organizations provide support networks that may assist low-income women?

In summary, the psychology of women must not repeat the errors made by earlier generations of psychologists when they ignored women. Consistent with Theme 4, we need to appreciate—and, in fact, celebrate—the diversity of females included within the category called "women." In the next section, we'll focus on a related topic: How women of color respond to the feminist movement.

SECTION SUMMARY ▪

The Future of the Discipline of the Psychology of Women

1. The psychology of women is a relatively new discipline; most people in this area are committed to its continued growth.

2. The percentage of women in psychology has been increasing markedly; however, women still constitute a relatively small proportion of the highly influential psychologists, and not all female psychologists are feminists. Still, this trend contributes to the support for feminist theory and research.

3. The discipline needs to explore the diversity of backgrounds that women represent, rather than centering on educated, heterosexual, middle-class European American females.

WOMEN OF COLOR AND THE FEMINIST MOVEMENT

A Black feminist scholar, bell hooks, recalled a lecture she had given in a crowded auditorium, in which she described how feminism had changed her life. A Black female student then rose to give an impassioned speech against feminism. The student said that feminism addressed the needs of White women only, with whom she had nothing in common (hooks, 1993, 1994).

Many Black women do not feel connected with feminism. Some Black women report that their life experiences are too different from the life experiences of White women, who are more economically privileged (P. H. Collins, 1995). Black women also complain that they feel no connection with White women who are racist (hooks, 2000b, 2001; Tong, 1998). In addition, Black women may be reluctant to criticize Black men, who already experience negative reactions from White individuals (S. A. Jackson, 1998; Rosen, 2000).

Many Black women engage in feminist activities, but they do not label themselves feminists (J. James, 1999). For instance, S. A. Jackson (1998) interviewed Black women who were active in a variety of organizations in which Black women held leadership roles. One woman saw herself as a feminist, which she defined as someone who "works on issues to promote the interests of women" (p. 41). However, most of the other participants in the study avoided calling themselves feminists. Many participants were also unclear about the definition of the term, or they had mixed feelings about feminism. As you can imagine, many women from other ethnic groups also share these perspectives.

Most U.S. students learn something about Black history and the civil rights movement in high school. However, unless you live in the western United States, you are less likely to hear about the Chicana/o movement, which addresses the concerns of Mexican Americans. When women began to participate in the Chicana/o movement in recent decades, they started to question their traditional roles and protested that this movement ignored women's issues (Saldívar-Hull, 2000). They also acknowledged that Chicana feminism would need to address both race and class, in addition to gender (Garcia, 1991; Moraga, 1993). However, Chicano males have often misinterpreted the Chicana feminist movement as a threat to the political unity of the Chicana/o movement (Garcia, 1995). In fact, Chicano male activists may label them *vendidas*, or "sellouts." A Chicana feminist might also be accused of "acting like a White woman" (Kafka, 2000; E. Martínez, 1995). However, many college courses in Chicana/o studies now acknowledge the contributions of Chicana women (Blea, 1997; Saldívar-Hull, 2000).

Asian American women face different challenges in identifying with the feminist movement. In general, Asian cultures require women to be relatively passive, invisible, and supportive of men (Root, 1995). Asian women may prefer to achieve social change by using indirect methods rather than more confrontational approaches (Ang, 2001). When Asian American women do express feminist perspectives, they are likely to be criticized by community members. These critics accuse them of diluting the resources in the Asian American community and destroying the working relationships between Asian women and men (Chow, 1991).

Furthermore, many women with an Asian background are not familiar with the feminist movement (J. Lee, 2001). Pramila Aggarwal (1990) described how she discovered a way to discuss feminist issues with Indian immigrant women in Canada. Aggarwal, a bilingual student, had been hired to teach English to Punjabi women who were working in a garment factory in Toronto. During these English classes, Aggarwal discovered that the women were interested in women's issues, such as the division of labor in the home and sexual harassment in the workplace. From this experience, she concluded that feminist organizing requires being sensitive to the specific needs of women, rather than imposing one's own personal viewpoint.

In summary, women of color may identify feminist issues in their lives. However, they are often reluctant to label themselves feminists. They may find it difficult to become feminist activists because activism is not consistent with their culture or because the males in their culture might believe that feminism threatens the efforts to unify their ethnic group. In addition, they may feel that feminist groups that are organized by European Americans may not be sensitive to the concerns of women of color.

Fortunately, however, the situation is gradually changing, and women from every ethnic group are now writing about how feminism can transform the lives of women of color (Eng, 1999; Kirk & Okazawa-Rey, 2001). Furthermore, many women of color have formed activist organizations. One directory lists 200 organizations, including groups for women of color who have survived breast cancer, college alumnae with a Philippine heritage, Black women's history, and women artists of color (Women of Color Resource Center, 2000).

SECTION SUMMARY ■

Women of Color and the Feminist Movement

1. Many Black women do not feel connected with feminism, because their lives are too different from the lives of European American women and because they are reluctant to criticize Black men.

2. Similarly, Chicana feminists may be accused of undermining the Chicana/o movement; college courses are now being offered on Chicana issues.

3. Asian American women may find that feminist activism is not consistent with the traditional role of women in their culture; critics may accuse Asian feminists of undermining the unity in their community.

4. In the current era, an increasing number of women of color are writing about feminism and creating activist organizations.

THE MEN'S MOVEMENT

Beginning in the mid-1970s, some men began examining the masculine gender role and its implications for men's lives. These investigations inspired a new academic field, called men's studies. **Men's studies** is a collection of scholarly activities, such as teaching courses and conducting research, that focus on men's lives. Men's studies often emphasizes gender-role socialization, gender-role conflict, and the issue of sexism (J. A. Doyle, 1995; Sweet, 2000). A variety of books present more details on men's studies (e.g., E. R. Barton, 2000a; S. V. Cochran & Rabinowitz, 2000; A. G. Johnson, 1997; Kilmartin, 2000; M. S. Kimmel, 2000; M. S. Kimmel & Messner, 1998; Levant, 1996; L. A. Morris, 1997; F. E. Rabinowitz & Cochran, 2002).

Just as there is no unitary women's movement, we also find no unitary, single-focus men's movement. Three strands within the men's movement are commonly mentioned: (1) the profeminists, (2) the mythopoetic movement, and (3) the religiously oriented approach. Students who are learning about the psychology of women need to know that some men's groups serve as allies, whereas others may be antagonists.

The **profeminists** want to eliminate the destructive aspects of gender, such as gender stereotypes, gender inequalities, and gender-related violence (Kilmartin, 2000; Rhode, 1997). The profeminist movement is the strand of the men's movement that grew out of the feminist movement. Most people who teach men's studies in colleges and universities would probably call themselves profeminists (Rhode, 1997).

Within psychology, the most visible profeminist group is called the Society for the Psychological Study of Men and Masculinity (SPSMM, Division 51 of the American Psychological Association). As their mission statement states:

> SPSMM promotes the critical study of how gender shapes and constricts men's lives, and is committed to an enhancement of men's capacity to experience their full human potential. SPSMM endeavors to erode constraining definitions of masculinity which historically have inhibited men's development, their capacity to form meaningful relationships, and have contributed to the oppression of other people. ("SPSMM Mission Statement," 2002, p. 17)

In 2002, for example, SPSMM sponsored a variety of presentations at the annual meeting of the American Psychological Association. Several relevant topics included gender-role conflict in adolescent males, men in relationships, and masculinity in multicultural perspectives.

DEMONSTRATION 15.1 ■ ■ ■ ■ ■ ■ ■ ■ ■ ■ ■ ■ ■ ■ ■ ■ ■ ■ ■

Identifying Allies

As we note in the text, allies are people who provide support to groups other than their own group. Begin this demonstration by thinking of several males you know personally who are likely to provide support to females. (If you are male, you may be able to include yourself in this list.) Write down each man's name and then list some specific things that this individual did to support girls and women. Then repeat this exercise by thinking about White people who are likely to provide support to people of color; identify their specific contributions. Continue this process with several other social groups who frequently experience biased treatment (e.g., gays and lesbians, immigrants, people with disabilities).

As individuals, profeminist men can serve as **allies,** people who provide support to groups other than their own (Roades & Mio, 2000). Try Demonstration 15.1 to explore this concept in more detail. Profeminist men can also work together to organize public actions. For example, in Toronto, the Metro Men Against Violence began wearing white ribbons after the murder of 14 women at École Polytechnique in Montreal in 1989,[1] and they continued to hold meetings to examine issues related to male violence (Lees, 1992). A group called Black Men for the Eradication of Sexism has brought young Black men in Atlanta together to examine gender issues (Rosado-Majors, 1998).

Whereas the profeminist men focus on how traditional gender roles hurt both men and women, the mythopoetic men focus on how these gender roles hurt themselves. Men who favor the **mythopoetic approach** believe that modern men should use myths and poetry to develop their own spiritual growth (E. R. Barton, 2000b; Bliss, 1995; Sweet, 2000). To achieve this growth, men join all-male gatherings in order to work through their psychological difficulties, focus on male role models, and gain a mature masculine quality.

Many men in the mythopoetic movement express somewhat feminist views, with an emphasis on gender justice (E. R. Barton, 2000b). However, profeminists point out that the majority of the men at these all-male mythopoetic gatherings are middle-class, middle-aged European American heterosexual men. They represent the most powerful cohort in North America; compared to most other men, they have the greater economic resources and have benefited more than any other group in our society (A. G. Johnson, 1997; Kilmartin, 2000; S. R. Wilson & Mankowski, 2000).

---

[1] In 1989, a man named Marc Lepin entered a classroom in the engineering school at École Polytechnique and forced the female students to line up along a wall. Shouting "You are all feminists," he shot them all. He then tracked down other women in the building, killing a total of 14 women.

The religiously oriented approach to the men's movement has become more visible during the current era. The **religious approach** argues that men should take back their roles as head of the household so that they can become leaders in their family, church, and community (Levant, 2001; Metzger, 2002; Rhode, 1997). As a result, women should accept the role of being followers. If these basic principles don't sound alarming, try replacing the sexism with racist equivalents: "Whites should take back their roles as masters, and Blacks should accept the role of being slaves."

Among the religious approaches, the most prominent is the Promise Keepers. This organization claims that close to 5 million men had attended its regional rallies by 1997 (Metzger, 2002). At these huge rallies, the messages are strongly traditional, and men are told to be assertive about taking back their natural role. Another example of the religious approach was the Million Man March, a gathering of Black men in Washington, D.C., in 1995. Women were explicitly banned from participating in the march; they were ordered to stay at home and pray (Rhode, 1997).

The Promise Keepers, the organizers of the Million Man March, and other religiously based forms of the men's movement may voice some admirable statements, such as encouraging men to become more actively involved in nurturing their children (L. B. Silverstein et al., 1999). However, we must carefully examine their principles, because these groups typically want to reduce the rights of women.

How do college students react to these different men's groups? Rickabaugh (1994) asked undergraduates at a California university to read descriptions of several men, each representing a different strand of the men's movement. Both men and women gave the highest rating to the profeminist man. The profeminist man was perceived as both nurturant and competent—a finding that should be encouraging to profeminist male students who are reading this book!

SECTION SUMMARY ■

The Men's Movement

1. Men's studies includes scholarly activities, such as teaching courses and conducting research, that focus on men's lives.

2. Three major strands within the men's movement are (a) the profeminists, (b) the mythopoetic approach, and (c) the religious approach.

SOME DISCOURAGING TRENDS

In the first section of this chapter, we focused on the future of the psychology of women as a discipline, a topic that raises some optimism. Our discussions about women of color and the men's movement provided a mixture of optimism and pessimism. Now we'll turn to the bad news: two current trends that have the potential to undermine feminism and the advancement of women. The first problem is a tendency toward a rigid interpretation of feminism. The second, more worrisome problem is the backlash against feminism and women's issues.

The Rigid Interpretation of Feminism

Students, researchers, and the general public sometimes perceive feminism as a set of rigid rules rather than as a source of inspiration. Students sometimes ask whether feminists can wear makeup and shave their legs or whether feminists can stay home full time raising their young children (Mandle, 2000; Peplau, 1994). Unfortunately, many people have misunderstood feminism. They believe—erroneously—that feminism specifies a set of rigid regulations and that women must obtain a perfect score on some test to qualify as feminists. However, feminist principles actually argue that we should respect women and their life choices and that we should also examine the societal forces influencing those choices (Stange, 2002).

Another issue concerns feminists' ideas about men. In general, feminists feel positive about most men, although a few may feel that men have done too much harm to women to deserve positive feelings. However, the media suggest that all feminists are male-bashers (Rhode, 1997; W. S. Rogers & Rogers, 2001).

How did feminism acquire the reputation that supporters must pass rigid tests and display antagonism toward men? In general, the media have created these highly exaggerated impressions. They apparently believe that a more reasonable depiction of feminism won't sell magazines or attract an audience (Kilbourne, 1999). Consider this example of media exaggeration. In 1968, a group of feminists placed false eyelashes, dishcloths, and bras into a "Freedom Trash Can." The media began calling feminists "bra burners," even though no bra was ever burned (Berkeley, 1999; W. S. Rogers & Rogers, 2001).

A happily married, 50-year-old mother in California commented on the media's distortion of feminism:

> I think women of all ages have trouble with the word "feminism" because it is defined for them by white males in positions of authority. . . . The connotations that feminists are strident, aggressive, dissatisfied, non-feminine women who want to deny safe, loving, secure homes to truly feminine women are advanced and embellished upon endlessly. . . . It is a fine scare tactic. (Langer, 1996, p. 246)

In reality, there is no single, unified version of feminism. For example, feminists disagree among themselves about a variety of important issues. Some of these issues include whether women should be encouraged to join the military, whether pornography should be regulated, and whether capitalism encourages gender discrimination (W. S. Rogers & Rogers, 2001; Tobias, 1997). Feminism also continues to grow and evolve in many directions (Berkeley, 1999; W. S. Rogers & Rogers, 2001; Steenbergen, 2001). For example, ecofeminism is a relatively new kind of feminism that moves beyond humans' oppression of other humans (Tong, 1998; Winter, 1996). **Ecofeminists** oppose the way humans destroy other animals and natural resources, as well as each other.

One of the best ways to illustrate the diversity of views within feminism is to listen to the voices of women who call themselves feminists. For example, one of my personal heroes is Bella Abzug, a member of Congress who died in 1998. When asked for her views on feminism, she replied, "I'm proud to be a lifelong one. It's as natural as breathing, feeling, and thinking. Never go back, never apologize, and never forget we're half the human race" (Aronson, 1997, p. 43). Actor and producer Cybill Shepherd objects to women who "don't use the word 'feminist' when they are all benefiting from the great feminists who struggled and suffered and worked to give us everything women now enjoy—including the right to vote, to bring a lawsuit, the right to custody in divorce—everything. I feel it is my responsibility to use that word because of all the sacrifices women have made" (Aronson, 1997, p. 43).

To complete this section on the diversity among feminists, try Demonstration 15.2.

The Backlash Against Feminism

A stream of antifeminist messages keeps flowing from the popular media in North America, in a blatant backlash against feminism (F. Davis, 1999; Steenbergen, 2001). For example, the right-wing televangelist Pat Robertson has said, "Feminists encourage women to leave their husbands, kill their children, practice witchcraft, become lesbians, and destroy capitalism" (cited by Baumgardner & Richards, 2000, p. 61). According to other commentators, women and men are now being treated equally and feminists should just stop whining. The media and other aspects of popular culture also try to persuade women that feminism has caused them dissatisfaction. The media often minimize women's accomplishments or ignore press conferences in which feminists discuss important

---

DEMONSTRATION 15.2 ■ ■ ■ ■ ■ ■ ■ ■ ■ ■ ■ ■ ■ ■ ■ ■ ■ ■

Diversity of Views About Feminism

At the top of several pieces of paper, write these instructions: "Please define feminism in your own words, and describe how feminism is relevant or irrelevant in your life." Distribute one page to each of several friends, and ask them to provide a written reply. (You may wish to specify that they can omit their names from the sheets or use other precautions so that their replies are anonymous.) Among those who have positive views of feminism, can you identify a variety of perspectives? (Check page 6 to remind yourself about various kinds of feminism.) Those who express negative views can help you understand a topic in the next section of this chapter: the backlash against feminism.

issues (Faludi, 1991, 1995). This backlash undercuts the progress that the women's movement has made in recent years. The backlash also keeps women from improving their own lives and the lives of other women.

The media especially enjoy featuring women who claim that feminism has gone astray. Christina Hoff Sommers (1994) in the United States is a media favorite who likes to criticize women's studies programs as being unscholarly. In Canada, Donna LaFramboise (1996) claims that feminism is now dominated by an arrogant lunatic fringe. Fortunately, however, academically challenging women's studies courses are thriving on college campuses, and feminist projects can now be found throughout the world, as we will see in the final section of this book.

SECTION SUMMARY ■

Some Discouraging Trends

1. Some people believe that feminism consists of a set of rigid rules and that it dictates that women must be antagonistic toward men; in reality, feminism represents a diversity of viewpoints.

2. The popular media are filled with backlash messages, which wildly distort the goals of feminism and attack women's studies programs.

SOME HELPFUL TRENDS

Despite the discouraging trends we have just examined, women's lives have gradually improved in recent decades. The progress is slower than many of us had naïvely imagined in the 1970s. We also notice a tendency to take two steps forward and then one step backward. However, in this textbook we have noted greater public awareness of such issues as women in the workplace, the gender-biased distribution of housework, and violence against women. Three forces that have helped to improve women's lives are (1) women's studies courses, (2) the women's movement in North America, and (3) the women's movement at the international level. The final part of this section explores how you can become an activist, helping to solve the problems we have discussed in this book.

Women's Studies Courses

Thousands of women's studies courses are offered at colleges and universities throughout the United States and Canada. The National Women's Studies Association currently estimates that there are about 800 women's studies programs in the United States (L. Younger, personal communication, 2002). Women's studies is now well established, especially because it enrolls more college students than any other interdisciplinary field (Buhle, 2000; S. M. Shaw & Lee, 2001).

Students often comment that they gain a new perspective from women's studies courses (Guy-Sheftall, 1996; J. G. James, 1999). For example, a Chicana student from Wisconsin commented on her women's studies course:

I am a Chicana; not only must I deal with racism but I must also live in a sexist world. I come from a family with strong conservative views compared to other families in the U.S. . . . Machismo is very prominent and sometimes cannot be seen but it is there. I never really thought about important feminist issues in high school. But I always knew that women were oppressed in our society. I saw it in my own home. It was not until I broke away from home that I began to think about my identity. I must say that my first real exposure to feminist ideas was when I left home for college. It is here where I am learning and trying to understand feminist ideas. (Rhoades, 1999, p. 68)

A graduate of San Diego State emphasized the importance of the knowledge she gained from women's studies:

My greatest reward for studying Women's Studies is that it has given credence to my convictions. It has given me a language/vocabulary to describe the many injustices I have felt as a woman. Before Women's Studies I knew that I didn't like the way I was treated; now I am able to define it. I was able to back up the many arguments I have found myself in with "facts" such as court cases, studies, and statistics. (Luebke & Reilly, 1995, p. 58)

Research using quantitative methods confirms that these courses have an important impact on students' lives. For instance, women enrolled in women's studies courses are significantly more likely than similar women enrolled in other courses to develop a more nontraditional attitude toward gender roles and a strong feminist identity after taking the course (Gerstmann & Kramer, 1997; K. L. Harris et al., 1999; Stake & Hoffmann, 2001; J. F. Wilson, 1997). Also, women's studies courses are more likely than other courses to encourage activism related to women's issues (Stake & Hoffmann, 2001). In addition, these courses enhance self-confidence and a sense of control over one's life (K. L. Harris et al., 1999; Stake & Hoffmann, 2000). Finally, students emphasize that their women's studies courses encourage critical thinking (Stake & Hoffmann, 2000).

Michelle Fine (2001), an especially creative feminist psychologist, documented the impact of women's studies in an unusual setting: Bedford Women's Prison in New York state. In this program, the women read novels by Alice Walker and discussed postmodern philosophy. Even the correction officers were astonished at the transformation. As one officer reported, "Before, at night, they would fight or bite each other. Now they are reading!"

In summary, students report that their women's studies courses are thought-provoking and informative. These courses also change students' attitudes, self-confidence, and political actions.

The Women's Movement in North America

The first wave of the feminist movement in North America was inspired by the antislavery movement of the 1830s. Women such as Susan B. Anthony and Elizabeth Cady Stanton learned how to organize a political movement, and they saw clear links between freedom for slaves and freedom for women (Kravetz & Marecek, 2001). However, their concerns were not answered for almost a century. For instance, U.S. women did not win the right to vote until August 26, 1920, when the Nineteenth Amendment to the U.S. Constitution was passed.

The current women's movement emerged from the general discontent of the 1960s. Women were active in the civil rights movement and in protesting the war in Vietnam. As in the previous century, this focus on issues of social justice made women more aware that they were second-class citizens (Tobias, 1997). The National Organization for Women (NOW) was founded in 1966, and it is still the largest women's rights organization in the United States (Kravetz & Marecek, 2001).

The scope of current feminist organizations is astonishing. Some groups, such as NOW, have a general focus that addresses issues such as violence against women, reproductive rights, and workplace issues. Other groups emphasize a more specific issue, for example, the abuse of women, antimilitarism, women's health, reproductive rights, welfare issues, urban schools, women of color, older women, lesbian and bisexual concerns, immigration issues, or community problems (Freedman, 2002; Kravetz & Marecek, 2001; Naples, 1998). Also, feminist communities have created a variety of feminist-run businesses. These include feminist therapy groups, feminist bookstores, theater groups, vacation resorts, and spirituality groups.

In summary, the North American feminist movement has grown and diversified considerably in recent decades. Fortunately, too, feminists in the United States and Canada now emphasize a global approach: Women face discrimination in every country, and we must work to change this problem (Berkeley, 1999).

The Women's Movement Worldwide

In New Zealand, women won the right to vote in 1893. Australia, Canada, and many European countries followed within the next three decades. As of 1999, women still could not vote in Kuwait. Women have been heads of state in more than 30 countries—among them, India, Haiti, Turkey, Iceland, Bolivia, and Canada—but not the United States (Neft & Levine, 1997).

Women throughout the world have been somewhat active in official government positions, but their grass-roots actions have been more impressive. Consider the Mothers of the Plaza de Mayo, a group of women whose children "disappeared" during the military dictatorship in Argentina between 1976 and 1983. (More than 30,000 people were killed during this era; many of them were young people who were secretly murdered because they had opposed the government.) The government had forbidden all public demonstrations, yet these mothers risked their lives by gathering at the Plaza de Mayo in Buenos Aires every Thursday, holding large photos of their missing children. Their bravery ultimately helped end that terrifying regime, and it helped women in countries such as El Salvador and Guatemala to become activists (Brabeck & Rogers, 2000; E. B. Kimmel & Kazanis, 1995).

Consider another representative project, which the Undugu Society developed to help street children in Kenya, a country in the eastern portion of central Africa. For many years, the Undugu Society successfully helped young boys who had been working during the day on the busy streets of Nairobi. However, the young girls were not visible during the day, because they worked as prostitutes at night. The Society has recently established the Undugu Girls Center about 30 miles away from the city. At this center, the street girls can attend school, participate in discussion groups, and plan a new future for themselves (G. Barker et al., 2000).

Throughout the world, groups of women are working to improve women's lives. We now have rich resources describing women's activism (e.g., DeLamotte et al., 1997; Grewal & Kaplan, 2002; Porter & Judd, 1999; Sweetman, 2000; Walter, 2001). Women's studies courses are now being taught in countries such as Japan, Latvia, Ghana, and Turkey (Howe, 2001b; L. White, 2001).

A superb group called The Global Fund for Women (2002) provides small grants for projects developed by women in countries throughout the world. By 2002, the Fund had donated $25 million to more than 2,000 groups in 159 countries. Here is just a small sample from a recent list of its projects:

- In Dhaka, Bangladesh, for a women's center that improves living conditions for women who work in sweatshops.
- In Zagreb, Croatia, for a group that maintains a lesbian helpline.
- In Beijing, China, for a group that raises awareness about violence against women and women's rights.
- In Suleimani, Iraq, to a group that takes action against honor killings, in which a woman can be killed by a male member of her family if she has been raped.

Women in developing countries share many of the same perspectives and concerns that women in North America and Europe express. However, women in these countries must also overcome basic survival problems. Some of the subtler points of North American feminism may seem irrelevant to a woman in India who knows that she must give her son more food than her daughter so that he can grow strong. These points may also seem irrelevant for a woman in Burma who must work under harsh conditions for 4 cents an hour, making sneakers for a prestigious American company (Selinger, 1998).

Helping to Change the Future: Becoming an Activist

So far, in this section on some hopeful trends in women's issues we have examined women's studies courses, the women's movement in North America, and the women's movement worldwide. In most psychology courses, students remain passive as they read about the future of a discipline. This time it's different: *You* can be part of the hopeful trend—if you're not already involved—rather than assuming that someone else will do the work. Here are just a few of the many options:

- Subscribe to a feminist magazine, such as *Ms. Magazine.* It will inform you about political activities that you may want to support, and the articles will keep you thinking about feminist issues.
- Talk with friends and relatives about feminist issues. In our everyday conversations, we need to make many decisions. If someone makes a sexist or a racist remark, we can take a small activist step by deciding not to join in the laughter (A. G. Johnson, 2001).

- Serve as a mentor to a girl or a younger woman. For example, a student in my psychology of women class last year traveled with her mother, her aunt, and her 10-year-old cousin to the Women's Rights Museum in Seneca Falls, New York—the site of first-wave feminists' early activism. Her cousin was both impressed to learn about the early history of the women's movement and outraged to learn that women still earn much less than men (K. DePorter, personal communication, 2002).

- Help fight the backlash against women. When you see an advertisement that represents women negatively, find the company's address through the Internet. Then write them to express your dissatisfaction. Also, when you see a positive ad, send a compliment to the company.

- Be a "critical consumer" when you read or listen to reports about women in the media. Review the research biases listed in Figure 1.3, and ask yourself whether the conclusions in the report seem justified. If you'd like to express your discontent—or possibly your approval!—call in to a radio show or write a letter to the editor of a newspaper or magazine. Remember: You now have more information about women's lives than most other individuals, so you can inform other people about these perspectives.

- Join a women's group on campus or in your community—or help to start one. Work with the group to make certain that diversity issues are an integral part of your mission.

Remember: No one individual can attack all the problems that women face, and change does not happen overnight (Baumgardner & Richards, 2000). Take comfort in small victories, and share these victories with other people. Also, keep in mind a bumper sticker that quotes advice from anthropologist Margaret Mead: "Never doubt that a small group of thoughtful, committed citizens can change the world; indeed it's the only thing that ever has."

SECTION SUMMARY ▪

Some Helpful Trends

1. Qualitative and quantitative research on women's studies courses demonstrates that these courses can change people's attitudes and self-confidence and that they can also encourage activism.

2. The first wave of the feminist movement in North America arose out of the anti-slavery movement and culminated in the passage of the Nineteenth Amendment to the U.S. Constitution.

3. The current feminist movement arose out of other social protests of the 1960s; feminist groups in the current era address numerous different issues concerned with women.

4. Women have achieved some positions of leadership throughout the world; the accomplishments of grass-roots women's organizations are even more impressive.

5. Students can use a variety of methods to become activists who will help to change women's lives.

■ ■ ■ ■ ■ ■ **CHAPTER REVIEW QUESTIONS** ■ ■ ■ ■ ■ ■

1. What are the trends with respect to the gender ratio in psychology? What is the current gender ratio for psychology faculty and psychology majors at your own college or university? Why might the changing gender ratio help the women's movement, and why might it be less effective than expected?

2. People concerned about the psychology of women have emphasized that the discipline should include more information about women of color. Why does a problem arise if researchers use the group-comparisons approach when they study ethnicity?

3. In one section of this chapter, we focused on women of color and feminism, and we mentioned that most students have little exposure to research on ethnic groups other than Blacks. Before you took any courses on the psychology of women (or the psychology of gender), describe the information you learned in high school or college about ethnicity. What have you learned outside class, in the popular media? Did any of this information examine women of color?

4. Why do women of color face special challenges in identifying with the feminist movement? Why would men of color want to oppose women from their ethnic group who would like to be active feminists?

5. Describe the three basic strands within the men's movement. Which would be likely to support the growth of the women's movement? Which would oppose it? Which might consider it irrelevant? Do you see any evidence of the men's movement in your community?

6. Describe the backlash against feminism, and explain why this factor could encourage the rigid interpretation of feminism. What evidence of the backlash have you seen in the media in recent weeks?

7. Briefly trace the history of the women's movement in North America. What issues concerned the early activists? Then comment on the women's movement worldwide. What kinds of concerns have been addressed?

8. In several parts of this chapter, we examined attitudes toward feminist issues. Why do you think that people in North America and throughout the world are reluctant to call themselves feminists?

(These final two questions require you to review the entire textbook.)

9. In this chapter, we focused on the positive and negative trends with respect to women and gender. To help yourself review this book, go back through the 15 chapters. Note which specific developments are moving in a positive direction and which are moving in a negative direction.

10. You will need to set aside several hours for this final task: On separate pieces of paper, list each of the four themes of this book. Then skim through each of the 15 chapters and note any mention of the themes on the appropriate piece of paper. (You can determine whether your lists are complete by checking the entries for Themes 1, 2, 3, and 4 in the subject index.) After you have completed that task, try to synthesize the material within each of the four themes.

NEW TERMS

*men's studies (491)
profeminists (491)
*allies (492)

mythopoetic approach (492)
religious approach (493)
*ecofeminists (495)

 The terms asterisked in the New Terms section serve as good search terms for InfoTrac College Edition. Go to http://infotrac.thomsonlearning.com and try these added search terms.

RECOMMENDED READINGS

Kilmartin, C. (2000). *The masculine self* (2nd ed.). Boston: McGraw-Hill. I recommend this excellent textbook, which provides a concise, primarily profeminist summary of the research on the psychology of men.

Kirk, G., & Okazawa-Rey, M. (2001). *Women's lives: Multicultural perspectives* (2nd ed.). Mountain View, CA: Mayfield. This textbook is designed for an introductory course in women's studies; it includes many articles about international issues as well as suggestions about how students can become activists.

Storm, C., & Gurevich, M. (Eds.). (2001). Looking forward, looking back: Women in psychology [Special issue]. *Canadian Psychology/Psychologie canadienne, 42*(4). The special issue of this journal, which is published by the Canadian Psychological Association, contains seven articles about the history of feminist psychology in Canada, as well as its current status; to my knowledge, the American Psychological Association has not yet published a similar document.

Walter, L. (2001). *Women's rights: A global view.* Westport, CT: Greenwood. Anyone interested in the status of women outside North America will appreciate this book, which contains a chapter on women in each of 15 countries. The chapters include an introductory overview, a description of a typical woman's life in that country, and a summary of the history and current situation for women.

ANSWERS TO THE TRUE-FALSE QUESTIONS

1. True (p. 486); 2. False (p. 487); 3. True (p. 487); 4. True (pp. 489–490); 5. True (p. 493); 6. True (pp. 495–496); 7. False (p. 497); 8. False (p. 497); 9. False (p. 498); 10. True (p. 498).

References

AAUW Educational Foundation. (1992). *How schools shortchange girls.* Washington, DC: Author.

Abbey, A. (2002). Alcohol-related sexual assault: A common problem among college students. *Journal of Studies on Alcohol, 14* (Suppl.), 118–128.

Abbey, A., Zawacki, T., & McAuslan, P. (2000). Alcohol's effects on sexual perception. *Journal of Studies on Alcohol, 61,* 688–697.

Abbey, A., et al. (2001). Attitudinal, experiential, and situational predictors of sexual assault perpetration. *Journal of Interpersonal Violence, 16,* 784–807.

Abel, E. (1995). Race, class, and psychoanalysis? Opening questions. In N. Tuana & R. Tong (Eds.), *Feminism and philosophy* (pp. 508–525). Boulder, CO: Westview Press.

Abele, A. E. (2000). A dual-impact model of gender and career-related processes. In T. Eckes & H. M. Traytner (Eds.), *The developmental social psychology of gender* (pp. 361–388). Mahwah, NJ: Erlbaum.

Aboud, F. E., & Fenwick, V. (1999). Exploring and evaluating school-based interventions to reduce prejudice. *Journal of Social Issues, 55,* 767–786.

Adair, L. S., & Gordon-Larsen, P. (2001). Maturational timing and overweight prevalence in U.S. adolescent girls. *American Journal of Public Health, 91,* 642–644.

Adams, A. (1995). Maternal bonds: Recent literature on mothering. *Signs, 20,* 414–427.

Adams, M. (1976). *Single blessedness.* New York: Basic Books.

Adams, S., Juebli, J., Boyle, P. A., & Fivush, R. (1995). Gender differences in parent-child conversations about past emotions: A longitudinal investigation. *Sex Roles, 33,* 309–323.

Adebimpe, V. R. (1997). Mental illness among African Americans. In I. Al-Issa & M. Tousignant (Eds.), *Ethnicity, immigration, and psychopathology* (pp. 95–118). New York: Plenum.

Ader, D. N., & Johnson, S. B. (1994). Sample description, reporting, and analysis of sex in psychological research: A look at APA and APA division journals in 1990. *American Psychologist, 49,* 216–218.

Adler, N. E., & Coriell, M. (1997). Socioeconomic status and women's health. In S. J. Gallant, G. P. Keita, & R. Royak-Schaler (Eds.), *Health care for women: Psychological, social, and behavioral influences* (pp. 11–23). Washington, DC: American Psychological Association.

Adler, N. E., & Smith, L. B. (1998). Abortion. In E. A. Blechman & K. D. Brownell (Eds.), *Behavioral medicine and women: A comprehensive handbook* (pp. 510–514). New York: Guilford.

Adler, N. E., et al. (1994). Socioeconomic status and health. *American Psychologist, 49,* 15–24.

Adler, T. (1990, December). NIH opens office on women's issues. *APA Monitor,* p. 5.

Agathangelou, A. M. (2000, Winter). Nationalist narratives and (dis)appearing women. *Canadian Woman Studies/Les cahiers de la femme, 19,* 12–27.

Aggarwal, P. (1990). English classes for immigrant women: A feminist organizing tool. *Fireweed, 30,* 95–100.

Agras, W. S., et al. (2000). Outcome predictors for the cognitive-behavioral treatment of bulimia nervosa: Data from a multisite study. *American Journal of Psychiatry, 157,* 1302–1308.

Agronick, G. S., & Duncan, L. E. (1998). Personality and social change: Individual differences, life path, and importance attributed to the women's movement. *Journal of Personality and Social Psychology, 74,* 1545–1555.

Aguilar–San Juan, K. (1993). Landmarks in literature by Asian American lesbians. *Signs, 18,* 936–943.

Aguirre, A., Jr. (2000). *Women and minority faculty in the academic workplace.* San Francisco: Jossey-Bass.

Aiken, L. S., Gerend, M. A., & Jackson, K. M. (2001). Subjective risk and health protective behavior: Cancer screening and cancer prevention. In A. Baum, T. A. Revenson, & J. E. Singer (Eds.), *Handbook of health psychology* (pp. 727–746). Mahwah, NJ: Erlbaum.

Alan Guttmacher Institute. (2001). *Can more progress be made? Teenage sexual and reproductive behavior in developed countries: Executive Summary.* New York: Author.

Albee, G. W. (1996). The psychological origins of the White male patriarchy. *Journal of Primary Prevention, 17,* 75–97.

Albelda, R., & Tilly, C. (1997). *Glass ceilings and bottomless pits: Women's work, women's poverty.* Boston: South End Press.

Alden, P. B. (2000). Crossing the moon. In R. Ratner (Ed.), *Bearing life: Women's writings on childlessness* (pp. 106–111). New York: Feminist Press.

Alderman, E. M., & Friedman, S. B. (1995). Behavioral problems of affluent youths. *Pediatric Annals, 24,* 186–191.

Alexander, L. L., & LaRosa, J. H. (1994). *New dimensions in women's health.* Boston: Jones and Bartlett.

Alexander, L. L., LaRosa, J. H., & Bader, H. (2001). *New dimensions in women's health* (2nd ed.). Boston: Jones and Bartlett.

Alexander, S. H. (1999). Messages to women on love and marriage from women's magazines. In M. Meyers (Ed.), *Mediated women: Representations in popular culture* (pp. 25–37). Cresskill, NJ: Hampton Press.

Algoe, S. B., Buswell, B. N., & DeLamater, J. D. (2000). Gender and job status as contextual cues for the interpretation of facial expression of emotion. *Sex Roles, 42,* 183–208.

Ali, A., & Toner, B. B. (2001). Emotional abuse of women. In J. Worell (Ed.), *Encyclopedia of women and gender* (pp. 379–390). San Diego: Academic Press.

Al-Krenawi, A., & Wiesel-Lev, R. (1999). Attitudes toward and perceived psychosocial impact of female circumcision as practiced among the Bedouin-Arabs of the Negev. *Family Processes, 38,* 431–443.

Allen, B. P. (1995). Gender stereotypes are not accurate: A replication of Martin (1987) using diagnostic vs. self-report and behavioral criteria. *Sex Roles, 32,* 583–600.

Allen, K. R. (1989). *Single women/family ties: Life histories of older women.* Newbury Park, CA: Sage.

Allen, K. R. (1994). Feminist reflections on lifelong single women. In D. L. Sollie & L. A. Leslie (Eds.), *Gender, families, and close relationships: Feminist research journeys* (pp. 97–119). Thousand Oaks, CA: Sage.

Allen, K. R., Blieszner, R., & Roberto, K. A. (2000). Families in the middle and later years: A review and critique of research in the 1990s. *Journal of Marriage and the Family, 62,* 911–926.

Allen, K. R., et al. (1999). Older adults and their children: Family patterns of structural diversity. *Family Relations, 48,* 151–157.

Allen, L., et al. (1996). Acculturation and depression among Latina urban girls. In B. J. R. Leadbeater & N. Way (Eds.), *Urban girls: Resisting stereotypes, creating identities* (pp. 337–352). New York: New York University Press.

Allgeier, E. R., & Allgeier, A. R. (2000). *Sexual interactions* (5th ed.). Boston: Houghton Mifflin.

Allison, J. A., & Wrightsman, L. S. (1993). *Rape: The misunderstood crime.* Newbury Park, CA: Sage.

Almey, M. (1995). Labour force characteristics. In Statistics Canada (Ed.), *Women in Canada: A statistical report* (3rd ed.). Ottawa, Canada: Author.

Alternatives to hysterectomy. (2001, April). *Harvard Women's Health Watch,* pp. 5–7.

Amato, P. R., & Rogers, S. J. (1997). A longitudinal study of marital problems and subsequent divorce. *Journal of Marriage and the Family, 59,* 612–624.

American Academy of Pediatrics. (1998). Female genital mutilation. *Pediatrics, 102,* 153–156.

American Academy of Pediatrics. (2001). WIC Program. *Pediatrics, 108,* 1216–1217.

American Academy of Pediatrics. (2002a). Coparent or second-parent adoption by same-sex parents. *Pediatrics, 109,* 339–340.

American Academy of Pediatrics. (2002b). Technical report: Coparent or second-parent adoption by same-sex parents. *Pediatrics, 109,* 341–344.

American Cancer Society. (2003). *Breast cancer: Early detection.* Retrieved January 7, 2003, from http://documents.cancer.org/6114.00

American Institutes for Research. (1998). *Gender gaps: Where schools still fail our children.* Washington, DC: American Association of University Women Educational Foundation.

American Psychiatric Association. (2000). *Diagnostic and statistical manual of mental disorders* (DSM-IV-TR; 4th ed.). Washington, DC: American Psychiatric Press.

American Psychological Association. (1990). Ethical principles of psychologists. *American Psychologist, 45,* 390–395.

American Psychological Association. (1995). *Lesbian and gay parenting: A resource for psychologists.* Washington, DC: Author.

American Psychological Association. (2001). *Publication manual of the American Psychological Association* (5th ed.). Washington, DC: Author.

Amnesty International. (2002, September). *Amina Lawal must not face death by stoning.* Retrieved September 18, 2002, from http://www.mertonai.org/amina/

Anastasopoulos, V., & Desmarais, S. (2000). *Deciding whether to self-label as a feminist: Examining the effects of attitudes.* Paper presented at the annual convention of the Canadian Psychological Association.

Andersen, B. L., & Farrar, W. B. (2001). Breast disorders and breast cancer. In N. L. Stotland & D. E. Stewart (Eds.), *Psychological aspects of women's health care* (2nd ed., pp. 457–475). Washington, DC: American Psychiatric Press.

Anderson, C. M., & Stewart, S. (1994). *Flying solo: Single women in midlife.* New York: W. W. Norton.

Anderson, K. J., & Leaper, C. (1998). Meta-analyses of gender effects on conversational interruption: Who, what, when, where, and how. *Sex Roles, 39,* 225–252.

Anderson, P. B., & Struckman-Johnson, C. (Eds.). (1998). *Sexually aggressive women: Current perspectives and controversies.* New York: Guilford.

Anderson, S. A., & Schlossberg, M. C. (1999). Systems perspectives on battering: The importance of context and pattern. In M. Harway & J. M. O'Neil (Eds.), *What causes men's violence against women?* (pp. 137–152). Thousand Oaks, CA: Sage.

Anderson, V., Simpson-Taylor, D., & Herrmann, D. (2002). *Rules about rape.* Unpublished manuscript, Indiana State University, Terre Haute.

Anderson, W. (2001, Spring). International news: Pakistani women victims of abuse. *International Psychology Reporter,* pp. 9–18.

Andreasen, N. C., & Black, D. W. (2001). *Introductory textbook of psychiatry* (3rd ed.). Washington, DC: American Psychiatric Publishing.

Andriote, J. (1998, February). The 1998 survey. *Working Woman,* pp. 24–45.

Ang, I. (2001). I'm a feminist but . . . 'Other' women and postnational feminism. In K. Bhavnani (Ed.), *Feminism and 'race'* (pp. 394–409). Oxford, England: Oxford University Press.

Angier, N. (1999). *Woman: An intimate geography.* Boston: Houghton Mifflin.

Antill, J. K., Goodnow, J. J., Russell, G., & Cotton, S. (1996). The influence of parents and family context on children's involvement in household tasks. *Sex Roles, 34,* 215–236.

Antonucci, T. C., Akiyama, H., & Merline, A. (2001). Dynamics of social relationships in midlife. In M. E. Lachman (Ed.), *Handbook of midlife development* (pp. 571–598). New York: Wiley.

Appignanesi, L., & Forrester, J. (1992). *Freud's women.* New York: Basic Books.

Apter, T. (1995). *Secret paths: Women in the new midlife.* New York: Norton.

Archer, J. (1996). Comparing women and men: What is being compared and why? *American Psychologist, 51,* 153–154.

Aries, E. (1996). *Men and women in interaction: Reconsidering the differences.* New York: Oxford University Press.

Aries, E. (1998). Gender differences in interaction. In D. J. Canary & K. Dindia (Eds.), *Sex differences and similarities in communication* (pp. 65–81). Mahwah, NJ: Erlbaum.

Arlow, J. A. (2000). Psychoanalysis. In R. J. Corsini & D. Wedding (Eds.), *Current psychotherapies* (6th ed., pp. 16–53). Itasca, IL: F. E. Peacock Publishers.

Armstrong, M. J. (2001). Ethnic minority women as they age. In J. D. Garner & S. O. Mercer (Eds.), *Women as they age* (2nd ed., pp. 97–111). New York: Haworth.

Arnold, K. D., Noble, K. D., & Subotnik, R. F. (1996). Perspectives on female talent development. In K. D. Arnold, K. D. Noble, & R. F. Subotnik (Eds.), *Remarkable women: Perspectives on female talent development* (pp. 1–19). Cresskill, NJ: Hampton Press.

Aronson, A. (1997, September/October). Yes I am a feminist and . . . *Ms. Magazine,* pp. 42–49.

Arriaga, X. B., & Oskamp, S. (1999). The nature, correlates, and consequences of violence in intimate relationships. In X. B. Arriaga & S. Oskamp (Eds.), *Violence in intimate relationships* (pp. 3–16). Thousand Oaks, CA: Sage.

Asch, A., & Fine, M. (1992). Beyond pedestals: Revisiting the lives of women with disabilities. In M. Fine (Ed.), *Disruptive voices: The possibilities of feminist research* (pp. 139–171). Ann Arbor, MI: University of Michigan Press.

Asch, A., Perkins, T. S., Fine, M., & Rousso, H. (2001). Disabilities and women: Deconstructing myths and reconstructing realities. In J. Worell (Ed.), *Encyclopedia of women and gender* (pp. 345–354). San Diego: Academic Press.

Asch-Goodkin, J. (1994, April). Women in pediatrics. *Contemporary Pediatrics*, pp. 54–67.

Aseltine, R. H., Jr., & Kessler, R. C. (1993). Marital disruption and depression in a community sample. *Journal of Health and Social Behavior, 34*, 237–251.

Astin, H. S., & Lindholm, J. A. (2001). Academic aspirations and degree attainment of women. In J. Worell (Ed.), *Encyclopedia of women and gender* (pp. 15–27). San Diego: Academic Press.

Atkinson, D. R., Morten, G., & Sue, D. W. (1993). *Counseling American minorities: A cross-cultural perspective* (4th ed.). Dubuque, IA: Brown & Benchmark.

Auster, C. J., & Ohm, S. C. (2000). Masculinity and femininity in contemporary American society: A reevaluation using the Bem Sex-Role Inventory. *Sex Roles, 43*, 499–528.

Austria, A. M. (2000, August). *Faculty allies: The need for heterosexuals to address homophobia.* Paper presented at the Convention of the American Psychological Association, Washington, DC.

Aven, F. F., Parker, B., & McEvoy, G. M. (1993). Gender and attitudinal commitment to organizations: A meta-analysis. *Journal of Business Research, 26*, 63–73.

Azar, B. (1994, May). Women are barraged by media on "the change." *APA Monitor*, pp. 24–25.

Baber, K. M. (2000). Women's sexualities. In M. Biaggio & M. Hersen (Eds.), *Issues in the psychology of women* (pp. 145–171). New York: Kluwer Academic/Plenum.

Babladelis, G. (1999). Autonomy in the middle years. In M. B. Nadien & F. L. Denmark (Eds.), *Females and autonomy: A life-span perspective* (pp. 101–129). Boston: Allyn & Bacon.

Baca Zinn, M., & Wells, B. (2000). Diversity within Latino families: New lessons for family social science. In D. H. Demo, K. R. Allen, & M. A. Fine (Eds.), *Handbook of family diversity* (pp. 252–273). New York: Oxford University Press.

Bachar, K., & Koss, M. (2001). Rape. In J. Worell (Ed.), *Encyclopedia of women and gender* (pp. 893–903). San Diego: Academic Press.

Baer, J. (1999). Gender differences. In M. A. Runco & S. R. Pritzker (Eds.), *Encyclopedia of creativity* (Vol. 1, pp. 753–758). San Diego: Academic Press.

Baer, J. A. (1999). *Our lives before the law.* Princeton, NJ: Princeton University Press.

Bahr, K. S. (1994). The strengths of Apache grandmothers: Observations on commitment, culture, and caretaking. *Journal of Comparative Family Studies, 25*, 233–248.

Bailey, J. M., Pillard, R. C., Neale, M. C., & Agyei, Y. (1993). Heritable factors influence sexual orientation in women. *Archives of General Psychiatry, 50*, 217–223.

Bailey, K. R. (1993). *The girls are the ones with the pointy nails: An exploration of children's conceptions of gender.* London, Canada: Althouse Press.

Bains, A. (1998, February). Thirty-eight cents a shirt. *Toronto Life*, pp. 41–50.

Baird-Windle, P., & Bader, E. J. (2001). *Targets of hatred: Anti-abortion terrorism.* New York: Palgrave.

Baker, L. C. (1996). Differences in earnings between male and female physicians. *New England Journal of Medicine, 334*, 960–964.

Ballagh, S. A. (1998). Contraception. In E. A. Blechman & K. D. Brownell (Eds.), *Behavioral medicine and women* (pp. 506–514). New York: Guilford.

Ballou, M., & West, C. (2000). Feminist therapy approaches. In M. Biaggio & M. Hersen (Eds.), *Issues in the psychology of women* (pp. 273–297). New York: Kluwer Academic/Plenum.

Banaji, M. R., & Hardin, C. D. (1996). Automatic stereotyping. *Psychological Science, 7*, 136–141.

Barbee, A. P., et al. (1993). Effects of gender role expectations on the social support process. *Journal of Social Issues, 49*, 175–190.

Barber, J. S., Axinn, W. G., & Thornton, A. (1999). Unwanted childbearing, health, and mother-child relationships. *Journal of Health and Social Behavior, 40*, 231–257.

Barer, B. M. (2001). The "grands and greats" of very old black grandmothers. *Journal of Aging Studies, 15*, 1–11.

Bargad, A., & Hyde, J. S. (1991). A study of feminist identity development in women. *Psychology of Women Quarterly, 15*, 181–201.

Barker, G., Knaul, F., Cassaniga, N., & Schrader, A. (2000). *Urban girls: Empowerment in especially difficult circumstances.* London: Intermediate Technology Publications.

Barker, M. A. (1996). Remedying gender-based wage discrimination: The comparable worth approach. In P. J. Dubeck & K. Borman (Eds.), *Women and work: A handbook* (pp. 375–382). New York: Garland.

Barlow, D. H., & Durand, V. M. (2002). *Abnormal psychology* (3rd ed.). Belmont, CA: Wadsworth.

Barnett, R. C. (1997). How paradigms shape the stories we tell: Paradigm shifts in gender and health. *Journal of Social Issues, 53,* 351–368.

Barnett, R. C. (2001). Work-family balance. In J. Worell (Ed.), *Encyclopedia of women and gender* (pp. 1181–1190). San Diego: Academic Press.

Barnett, R. C., & Hyde, J. S. (2001). Women, men, work, and family: An expansionist theory. *American Psychologist, 56,* 781–796.

Barnett, R. C., & Rivers, C. (1996). *She works, he works.* San Francisco: Harper.

Barone, D. F., Maddux, J. E., & Snyder, C. R. (1997). *Social cognitive psychology: History and current domains.* New York: Plenum.

Barton, C., & Nazombei, E. (2000). Women's labour and economic globalisation: A participatory workshop created by Alternative Women in Development. In C. Sweetman (Ed.), *Gender in the 21st century.* Oxford, England: Oxfam.

Barton, E. R. (Ed.). (2000a). *Mythopoetic perspectives of men's healing work.* Westport, CT: Bergin & Garvey.

Barton, E. R. (2000b). Parallels between mythopoetic men's work/men's peer mutual support group and selected feminist theories. In E. R. Barton (Ed.), *Mythopoetic perspectives of men's healing work* (pp. 3–20). Westport, CT: Bergin & Garvey.

Bartsch, R. A., Burnett, T., Diller, T. R., & Rankin-Williams, E. (2000). Gender representation in television commercials: Updating an update. *Sex Roles, 43,* 735–743.

Barusch, A. S. (1994). *Older women in poverty: Private lives and public policies.* New York: Springer.

Barzansky, B., & Etzel, S. I. (2002). Educational programs in U.S. medical schools, 2001–2002. *Journal of the American Medical Association, 288,* 1067–1072.

Basow, S. A. (1998). Student evaluations: The role of gender bias and teaching styles. In L. H. Collins, J. C. Crisler, & K. Quina (Eds.), *Career strategies for women in academe: Arming Athena* (pp. 135–156). Thousand Oaks, CA: Sage.

Basow, S. A. (2000). Gender dynamics in the classroom. In J. C. Chrisler, C. Golden, & P. D. Rozee (Eds.), *Lectures on the psychology of women* (pp. 37–46). Boston: McGraw-Hill.

Basow, S. A. (2001). Androcentrism. In J. Worell (Ed.), *Encyclopedia of women and gender* (pp. 125–135). San Diego: Academic Press.

Basow, S. A., & Johnson, K. (2000). Predictors of homophobia in female college students. *Sex Roles, 42,* 391–404.

Basow, S. A., & Rubin, L. R. (1999). Gender influences on adolescent development. In N. G. Johnson, M. C. Roberts, & J. Worell (Eds.), *Beyond appearance: A new look at adolescent girls* (pp. 25–52). Washington, DC: American Psychological Association.

Bate, B., & Bowker, J. (1997). *Communication and the sexes* (2nd ed.). Prospect Heights, IL: Wavelength Press.

Bauer, A. M. (2001). "Tell them we're girls": The invisibility of girls with disabilities. In P. O'Reilly, E. M. Penn, & K. deMarrais (Eds.), *Educating young adolescent girls* (pp. 29–45). Mahwah, NJ: Erlbaum.

Bauerova, L. (2000, January 9). Sex harassment ubiquitous in Central Europe. *San Jose Mercury News,* p. A16.

Baum, A., Revenson, T. A., & Singer, J. E. (Eds.). (2001). *Handbook of health psychology.* Mahwah, NJ: Erlbaum.

Baumeister, R. F. (2000). Gender differences in erotic plasticity: The female sex drive as socially flexible and responsive. *Psychological Bulletin, 126,* 347–374.

Baumeister, R. F., Catanese, K. R., & Vohs, K. D. (2001). Is there a gender difference in strength of sex drive? Theoretical views, conceptual distinctions, and a review of relevant evidence. *Personality and Social Psychology Review, 5,* 242–273.

Baumeister, R. F., Catanese, K. R., & Wallace, H. M. (2002). Conquest by force: A narcissistic reactance theory of rape and sexual coercion. *Review of General Psychology, 6,* 92–135.

Baumeister, R. F., & Twenge, J. M. (2002). Cultural suppression of female sexuality. *Review of General Psychology, 6,* 166–203.

Baumgardner, J., & Richards, A. (2000). *Manifesta: Young women, feminism, and the future.* New York: Farrar, Straus and Giroux.

Baydar, N., & Brooks-Gunn, J. (1998). Profiles of grandmothers who help care for their grandchildren in the United States. *Family Relations, 47,* 385–393.

Bazzini, D. G., et al. (1997). The aging woman in popular film: Underrepresented, unattractive, unfriendly, and unintelligent. *Sex Roles, 36,* 531–543.

Beach, S. (2001, August/September). Census takers. *Ms. Magazine,* p. 30.

Beall, A. E. (1993). A social constructionist view of gender. In A. E. Beall & R. J. Sternberg (Eds.), *The psychology of gender* (pp. 127–147). New York: Guilford.

Beaton, A. M., & Tougas, F. (1997). The representation of women in management: The more, the merrier? *Personality and Social Psychology Bulletin, 23,* 773–782.

Beatty, W. W., & Bruellman, J. A. (1987). Absence of gender differences in memory for map learning. *Bulletin of the Psychonomic Society, 25,* 238–239.

Becker, E., Rankin, E., & Rickel, A. U. (1998). *High-risk sexual behavior: Interventions with vulnerable populations.* New York: Plenum.

Beckman, L. J., Harvey, S. M., Satre, S. J., & Walker, M. A. (1999). Cultural beliefs about social influence strategies of Mexican immigrant women and their heterosexual partners. *Sex Roles, 40,* 871–892.

Bedford, V. H., & Blieszner, R. (2000a). Older adults and their families. In D. H. Demo, K. R. Allen, & M. A. Fine (Eds.), *Handbook of family diversity* (pp. 216–232). New York: Oxford University Press.

Bedford, V. H., & Blieszner, R. (2000b). Personal relationships in later life families. In R. M. Milardo & S. Duck (Eds.), *Families as relationships* (pp. 157–174). Chichester, England: Wiley.

Begley, S. (2001, June 11). AIDS at 20. *Newsweek,* pp. 34–40.

Belansky, E. S., & Boggiano, A. K. (1994). Predicting helping behaviors: The role of gender and instrumental/expressive self-schemata. *Sex Roles, 30,* 647–661.

Belansky, E. S., Clements, P., & Eccles, J. S. (1992, March). *Adolescence: A crossroads for gender-role transcendence or gender-role intensification.* Paper presented at the Meeting of the Society for Research on Adolescence, Washington, DC.

Belknap, P., & Leonard, W. M., II. (1991). A conceptual replication and extension of Erving Goffman's study of gender advertisements. *Sex Roles, 25,* 103–118.

Bell, A. R. (1990). Separate people: Speaking of Creek men and women. *American Anthropologist, 92,* 332–345.

Bell, D., & Klein, R. (1996). Beware: Radical feminists speak, read, write, organise, enjoy life, and never forget. In R. Bell & R. Klein (Eds.), *Radically speaking: Feminism reclaimed* (pp. xvii–xxx). North Melbourne, Australia: Spinifex.

Bell, N. J., O'Neal, K. K., Feng, D., & Schoenrock, C. J. (1999). Gender and sexual risk. *Sex Roles, 41,* 313–332.

Bellamy, C. (2000). *The state of the world's children 2000.* New York: United Nations Children's Fund.

Belle, D. (1997, Summer). Poverty facts test. *Association for Women in Psychology Newsletter,* p. 1.

Beller, M., & Gafni, N. (2000). Can item format (multiple choice vs. open-ended) account for gender differences in mathematics achievement? *Sex Roles, 42,* 1–21.

Bellinger, D. C., & Gleason, J. B. (1982). Sex differences in parental directives to young children. *Sex Roles, 8,* 1123–1139.

Belsky, J. (2001). Aging. In J. Worell (Ed.), *Encyclopedia of women and gender* (pp. 95–107). San Diego: Academic Press.

Bem, S. L. (1974). The measurement of psychological androgyny. *Journal of Consulting and Clinical Psychology, 42,* 155–162.

Bem, S. L. (1977). On the utility of alternative procedures for assessing psychological androgyny. *Journal of Consulting and Clinical Psychology, 45,* 196–205.

Bem, S. L. (1981). Gender schema theory: A cognitive account of sex typing. *Psychological Review, 88,* 354–364.

Bem, S. L. (1983). Gender schema theory and its implications for child development: Raising gender-aschematic children in a gender-schematic society. *Signs, 8,* 598–616.

Bem, S. L. (1985). Androgyny and gender schema theory: A conceptual and empirical integration. In T. B. Sonderegger (Ed.), *Nebraska Symposium on Motivation, 1984: Psychology and gender* (pp. 179–226). Lincoln, NE: University of Nebraska Press.

Bem, S. L. (1993). *The lenses of gender: Transforming the debate on sexual inequality.* New Haven, CT: Yale University Press.

Bem, S. L. (1995). Dismantling gender polarization and compulsory heterosexuality: Should we turn the volume down or up? *Journal of Sex Research, 32,* 329–334.

Bem, S. L. (1996). Transforming the debate on sexual inequality: From biological difference to institutionalized androcentrism. In J. C. Chrisler, C. Golden, & P. D. Rozee (Eds.), *Lectures on the psychology of women* (pp. 9–21). New York: McGraw-Hill.

Bem, S. L. (1998). *An unconventional family.* New Haven, CT: Yale University Press.

Benbow, C. P. (1988). Sex differences in mathematical reasoning ability in intellectually talented preadolescents: Their nature, effects, and possible causes. *Behavioral and Brain Sciences, 11,* 169–232.

Benbow, C. P., & Stanley, J. C. (1980). Sex differences in mathematical ability: Fact or artifact? *Science, 210,* 1262–1264.

Benbow, C. P., et al. (2000). Sex differences in mathematical reasoning ability at age 13: Their status 20 years later. *Psychological Science, 11,* 474–480.

Beneke, T. (1997). Men on rape. In M. B. Zinn, P. Hondagneu-Sotelo, & M. A. Messner (Eds.), *Through the prism of difference: Readings on sex and gender* (pp. 130–135). Boston: Allyn & Bacon.

Benjamin, L. T., Jr., & Shields, S. A. (1990). Foreword. In H. L. Hollingworth, *Leta Stetter Hollingworth: A biography* (pp. ix–xviii). Bolton, MA: Anker Publishing.

Benokraitis, N. V. (1997a). Sex discrimination in the 21st century. In N. V. Benokraitis (Ed.), *Subtle sexism: Current practice and prospects for change* (pp. 5–33). Thousand Oaks, CA: Sage.

Benokraitis, N. V. (1997b). *Subtle sexism: Current practice and prospects for change.* Thousand Oaks, CA: Sage.

Benokraitis, N. V. (1998). Working in the ivory basement: Subtle sex discrimination in higher education. In L. H. Collins, J. C. Chrisler, & K. Quina (Eds.), *Career strategies for women in academe: Arming Athena* (pp. 3–43). Thousand Oaks, CA: Sage.

Benokraitis, N. V., & Feagin, J. R. (1994). *Modern sexism: Blatant, subtle, and covert discrimination* (2nd ed.). Englewood Cliffs, NJ: Prentice Hall.

Benrud, L. M., & Reddy, D. M. (1998). Differential explanations of illness in women and men. *Sex Roles, 38,* 375–386.

Berg, F. M. (1999). Health risks associated with weight loss and obesity treatment programs. *Journal of Social Issues, 55,* 277–297.

Berg, F. M. (2000). *Women afraid to eat: Breaking free in today's weight-obsessed world.* Hettinger, ND: Healthy Weight Network.

Berg, J. A., & Lipson, J. G. (1999). Information sources, menopause beliefs, and health complaints of midlife Filipinas. *Health Care for Women International, 20,* 81–92.

Berg, J. H., Stephen, W. G., & Dodson, M. (1981). Attributional modesty in women. *Psychology of Women Quarterly, 5,* 711–727.

Bergeron, S. M., & Senn, C. Y. (1998). Body image and sociocultural norms: A comparison of heterosexual and lesbian women. *Psychology of Women Quarterly, 22,* 385–401.

Bergob, M. (1995). Women with disabilities. In Statistics Canada (Ed.), *Women in Canada: A statistical report* (3rd ed., pp. 163–166). Ottawa, Canada: Author.

Bergum, V. (1997). *A child on her mind: The experience of becoming a mother.* Westport, CT: Bergin & Garvey.

Berkeley, K. C. (1999). *The women's liberation movement in America.* Westport, CT: Greenwood Press.

Berman, P. W. (1980). Are women more responsive than men to the young? A review of developmental and situational variables. *Psychological Bulletin, 88,* 668–695.

Berryman, J. C., & Windridge, K. C. (1997). Maternal age and employment in pregnancy and after childbirth. *Journal of Reproductive and Infant Psychology, 15,* 287–302.

Berzon, B. (1996). *Setting them straight.* New York: Penguin.

Best, D. L., & Williams, J. E. (1993). A cross-cultural viewpoint. In A. E. Beall & R. J. Sternberg (Eds.), *The psychology of gender* (pp. 215–248). New York: Guilford.

Bettencourt, B. A., & Miller, N. (1996). Gender differences in aggression as a function of provocation: A meta-analysis. *Psychological Bulletin, 119,* 422–447.

Betz, N. E. (1993). Women's career development. In F. L. Denmark & M. A. Paludi (Eds.), *Psychology of women: A handbook of issues and theories* (pp. 627–684). Westport, CT: Greenwood Press.

Betz, N. E. (1994). Basic issues and concepts in career counseling for women. In W. B. Walsh & S. H. Osipow (Eds.), *Career counseling for women* (pp. 1–41). Hillsdale, NJ: Erlbaum.

Betz, N. E. (1997). What stops women and minorities from choosing and completing majors in science and engineering? In D. Johnson (Ed.), *Minorities and girls in school: Effects on achievement and performance* (pp. 105–140). Thousand Oaks, CA: Sage.

Betz, N. E., & Fitzgerald, L. F. (1987). *The career psychology of women.* Orlando: Academic Press.

Beyer, C. E., et al. (1996). Gender representation in illustrations, text, and topic areas in sexuality education curricula. *Journal of School Health, 66,* 361–364.

Beyer, S. (1998). Gender differences in self-perception and negative recall biases. *Sex Roles, 38,* 103–133.

Beyer, S. (1998/1999). Gender differences in causal attribution by college students of performance on course examinations. *Current Psychology: Developmental, Learning, Personality, Social, 17,* 346–358.

Beyer, S. (1999a). The accuracy of academic gender stereotypes. *Sex Roles, 40,* 787–813.

Beyer, S. (1999b). Gender differences in the accuracy of grade expectancies and evaluation. *Sex Roles, 41,* 279–296.

Beyer, S., & Bowden, E. M. (1997). Gender differences in self-perceptions: Convergent evidence from three measures of accuracy and bias. *Personality and Social Psychology Bulletin, 23,* 157–172.

Bianchi, S. M., Milkie, M. A., Sayer, L. C., & Robinson, J. P. (2000). Is anyone doing the housework? Trends in the gender division of household labor. *Social Forces, 79,* 191–228.

Bidrose, S., & Goodman, G. S. (2000). Testimony and evidence: A scientific case study of memory for child sexual abuse. *Applied Cognitive Psychology, 14,* 197–213.

Biehl, M., et al. (1997). Matsumoto's and Ekman's Japanese and Caucasian Facial Expressions of Emotion (JACFEE): Reliability data and cross-national differences. *Journal of Nonverbal Behavior, 21,* 3–21.

Biernat, M., & Wortman, C. B. (1991). Sharing of home responsibilities between professionally employed women and their husbands. *Journal of Personality and Social Psychology, 60,* 844–860.

Bigler, R. S. (1995). The role of classification skill in moderating environmental influences on children's gender stereotyping: A study of the functional use of gender in the classroom. *Child Development, 66,* 1072–1087.

Bigler, R. S. (1999a). Psychological interventions designed to counter sexism in children: Empirical limitations and theoretical foundations. In W. B. Swann Jr., J. H. Langlois, & L. A. Gilbert (Eds.), *Sexism and stereotypes in modern society* (pp. 129–151). Washington, DC: American Psychological Association.

Bigler, R. S. (1999b). The use of multicultural curricula and materials to counter racism in children. *Journal of Social Issues, 55,* 687–705.

Binder, R. (2001). Changing a culture: Sexual assault prevention in the fraternity and sorority community. In A. J. Ottens & K. Hotelling (Eds.), *Sexual violence on campus: Policies, programs, and perspectives* (pp. 120–140). New York: Springer.

Bing, J. M., & Bergvall, V. L. (1998). The question of questions: Beyond binary thinking. In J. Coates (Ed.), *Language and gender: A reader* (pp. 495–510). Malden, MA: Blackwell.

Bird, C. E. (1999). Gender, household labor, and psychological distress: The impact of the amount and division of housework. *Journal of Health and Social Behavior, 40,* 32–45.

Bird, S. E. (1999). Tales of difference: Representations of American Indian women in popular film and television. In M. Meyers (Ed.), *Mediated women: Representations in popular culture* (pp. 91–109). Cresskill, NJ: Hampton Press.

Birns, B. (1999). Battered wives: Causes, effects, and social change. In C. Forden, A. E. Hunter, & B. Birns (Eds.), *Readings in the psychology of women: Dimensions of the female experience* (pp. 280–288). Boston: Allyn & Bacon.

Björkqvist, K. (1994). Sex differences in physical, verbal, and indirect aggression: A review of recent research. *Sex Roles, 30,* 177–188.

Black, H. K., & Rubinstein, R. L. (2000). *Old souls: Aged women, poverty, and the experience of God.* New York: Aldine de Gruyter.

Blakemore, J. E. O. (1998). The influence of gender and parental attitudes on preschool children's interest in babies: Observations in natural settings. *Sex Roles, 38,* 73–94.

Blank, R., & Slipp, S. (1994). *Voices of diversity: Real people talk about problems and solutions in a workplace where everyone is not alike.* New York: American Management Association.

Blau, G., & Tatum, D. (2000). Correlates of perceived gender discrimination for female versus male medical technologists. *Sex Roles, 43,* 105–118.

Blea, I. I. (1997). *U.S. Chicanas and Latinas within a global context.* Westport, CT: Praeger.

Blieszner, R. (1998). *Feminist perspectives on old women's lives and ageism in society.* Paper presented at Virginia Polytechnic Institute, Blacksburg.

Blieszner, R., & Wingfield, N. P. (2000). Adulthood. In A. E. Kazdin (Ed.), *Encyclopedia of psychology* (Vol. 6, pp. 55–61). New York: Oxford University Press.

Bliss, S. (1995). Mythopoetic men's movements. In M. S. Kimmel (Ed.), *The politics of manhood* (pp. 292–307). Philadelphia: Temple University Press.

Blum, L. M. (1999). *At the breast.* Boston: Beacon Press.

Blume, S. B. (1998, March). Alcoholism in women. *Harvard Mental Health Letter,* pp. 5–7.

Blumenthal, S. J. (1995). Improving women's mental and physical health: Federal initiative and programs. *Review of Psychiatry, 14,* 181–204.

Boatswain, S., et al. (2001). Canadian feminist psychology: Where are we now? *Canadian Psychology/Psychologie canadienne, 42,* 276–285.

Bobo, M., Hildreth, B. L., & Durodoye, B. (1998). Changing patterns in career choices among African-American, Hispanic, and Anglo children. *Professional School Counseling, 1,* 37–42.

Boehmer, U. (2000). *The personal and the political: Women's activism in response to the breast cancer and AIDS epidemics.* Albany, NY: State University of New York Press.

Boeschen, L. E., Sales, B. D., & Koss, M. P. (1998). Rape trauma experts in the courtroom. *Psychology and Law, 4,* 414–432.

Bohan, J. S. (1992). Prologue: Re-viewing psychology, re-placing women: An end searching for a means. In J. S. Bohan (Ed.), *Seldom seen, rarely heard: Women's place in psychology* (pp. 9–53). Boulder, CO: Westview Press.

Bohan, J. S. (1993). Regarding gender: Essentialism, constructionism, and feminist psychology. *Psychology of Women Quarterly, 17,* 5–21.

Bohan, J. S. (1996). *Psychology and sexual orientation: Coming to terms.* New York: Routledge.

Bohan, J. S. (1997, August). *The psychology of women, the women of psychology: Recurring questions, persistent themes.* Paper presented at the annual convention of the American Psychological Association, Chicago.

Bohmer, C. (2000). *The wages of seeking help: Sexual exploitation by professionals.* Westport, CT: Praeger.

Bonanno, G. A., & Kaltman, S. (1999). Toward an integrative perspective on bereavement. *Psychological Bulletin, 125,* 760–776.

Bondurant, B., & Donat, P. L. N. (1999). Perceptions of women's sexual interest and acquaintance rape. *Psychology of Women Quarterly, 23,* 691–705.

Bondurant, B., & White, J. W. (1996). Men who sexually harass: An embedded perspective. In D. K. Shrier (Ed.), *Sexual harassment in the workplace and academia: Psychiatric issues* (pp. 59–78). Washington, DC: American Psychiatric Press.

Bonebright, T. L., Thompson, J. L., & Leger, D. W. (1996). Gender stereotypes in the expression and perception of vocal affect. *Sex Roles, 34,* 429–445.

Bookwala, J., Frieze, I. H., Smith, C., & Ryan, K. (1992). Predictors of dating violence: A multivariate analysis. *Violence and Victims, 7,* 297–311.

Boot, T. (1999). Black or African American: What's in a name? In Y. Alaniz & N. Wong (Eds.), *Voices of color* (pp. 69–72). Seattle: Red Letter Press.

Bordo, S. (1998, May 1). Sexual harassment is about bullying, not sex. *Chronicle of Higher Education,* p. B6.

Bornstein, R. F. (2001). The impending death of psychoanalysis. *Psychoanalytic Psychology, 18,* 3–20.

Borrayo, E. A., Guarnaccia, C. A., & Mahoney, M. J. (2001). Prediction of breast cancer screening behavior among older women of Mexican descent: Applicability of theoretical models. *Revista International de Psicología Clínica y de la Salud/ International Journal of Clinical and Health Psychology, 1,* 73–90.

Borrayo, E. A., & Jenkins, S. R. (2001a). Feeling healthy: So why should Mexican-descent women screen for breast cancer? *Qualitative Health Research, 11,* 812–823.

Borrayo, E. A., & Jenkins, S. R. (2001b). Feeling indecent: Breast cancer screening resistance of Mexican-descent women. *Journal of Health Psychology, 6,* 537–550.

Boston, L. B., Chambers, S., Canetto, S. S., & Slinkard, B. (2001, August). *That kind of woman: Stereotypical representations in computer magazine advertising.* Paper presented at the annual meeting of the American Psychological Association, San Francisco.

Boswell, A. A., & Spade, J. Z. (1999). Fraternities and collegiate rape culture: Why are some fraternities more dangerous places for women? In L. A. Peplau et al. (Eds.), *Gender, culture, and ethnicity: Current research about women and men* (pp. 269–283). Mountain View, CA: Mayfield.

Bowen, D. J., Tomoyasu, N., & Cauce, A. M. (1999). The triple threat: A discussion of gender, class, and race differences in weight. In L. A. Peplau et al. (Eds.), *Gender, culture, and ethnicity: Current research about women and men* (pp. 291–306). Mountain View, CA: Mayfield.

Bowleg, L. (1999). "When I look at you, I don't see race" and other diverse tales from the introduction to women's studies classroom. In B. S. Winkler & C. DiPalma (Eds.), *Teaching introduction to women's studies: Expectations and strategies* (pp. 111–122). Westport, CT: Bergin & Garvey.

Boyatzis, C. J., & Eades, J. (1999). Gender differences in preschoolers' and kindergartners' artistic production and preference. *Sex Roles, 41,* 627–638.

Boyatzis, C. J., Mallis, M., & Leon, I. (1999). Effects of game type on children's gender-based peer preferences: A naturalistic observational study. *Sex Roles, 40,* 93–105.

Boyd, C. (1997). "Just like one of the boys": Tactics of women taxi drivers. In P. Greenhill & D. Tye (Eds.), *Undisciplined women: Tradition and culture in Canada* (pp. 213–222). Montreal: McGill-Queen's University Press.

Brabant, S., & Mooney, L. A. (1997). Sex role stereotyping in the Sunday comics: A twenty year update. *Sex Roles, 37,* 269–281.

Brabeck, M. M. (1996). The moral self, values, and circles of belonging. In K. F. Wyche & F. J. Crosby (Eds.), *Women's ethnicities: Journeys through psychology* (pp. 145–165). Boulder, CO: Westview Press.

Brabeck, M. M., & Rogers, L. (2000). Human rights as a moral issue: Lessons for moral educators from human rights work. *Journal of Moral Education, 29,* 167–182.

Brabeck, M. M., & Satiani, A. (2001). Feminist ethics and moral psychology. In J. Worell (Ed.), *Encyclopedia of women and gender* (pp. 439–446). San Diego: Academic Press.

Brabeck, M. M., & Ting, K. (2000). Feminist ethics: Lenses for examining ethical psychological practice. In M. M. Brabeck (Ed.), *Practicing feminist ethics in psychology* (pp. 17–35). Washington, DC: American Psychological Association.

Bradsher, J. E. (1997). Older women and widowhood. In J. M. Coyle (Ed.), *Handbook on women and aging* (pp. 418–429). Westport, CT: Greenwood Press.

Brady, K. (1993). Testimony on pornography and incest. In D. E. H. Russell (Ed.), *Making violence sexy: Feminist views on pornography* (pp. 43–45). New York: Teachers College Press.

Brady, K. L., & Eisler, R. M. (1995). Gender bias in the college classroom: A critical review of the literature and implications for future research. *Journal of Research and Development in Education, 29,* 9–19.

Brady, K. L., & Eisler, R. M. (1999). Sex and gender in the college classroom: A quantitative analysis of faculty-student interactions and perceptions. *Journal of Educational Psychology, 91,* 127–145.

Braithwaite, V. (2002). Reducing ageism. In T. Nelson (Ed.), *Ageism: Stereotyping and prejudice against older persons* (pp. 311–337). Cambridge, MA: MIT Press.

Brannon, L., & Feist, J. (2000). *Health psychology: An introduction to behavior and health* (4th ed.). Belmont, CA: Wadsworth.

Brant, C. R., Mynatt, C. R., & Doherty, M. E. (1999). Judgments about sexism: A policy capturing approach. *Sex Roles, 41,* 347–374.

Bravo, E., & Cassedy, E. (1999). *The 9 to 5 guide to combating sexual harassment.* Milwaukee: 9 to 5 Working Women Education Fund.

Brawman-Mintzer, O., & Yonkers, K. A. (2001). Psychopharmacology in women. In N. L. Stotland & D. E. Stewart (Eds.) *Psychological aspects of women's health care* (2nd ed., pp. 401–420). Washington, DC: American Psychiatric Press.

Brayfield, A. A. (1992). Employment resources and housework in Canada. *Journal of Marriage and the Family, 54,* 19–30.

Breedlove, S. M. (1994). Sexual differentiation of the human nervous system. *Annual Review of Psychology, 45,* 389–418.

Brehm, S. S., Kassin, S., & Fein, S. (2002). *Social psychology* (5th ed.). Boston: Houghton Mifflin.

Brehm, S. S., Miller, R. S., Perlman, D., & Campbell, S. M. (2002). *Intimate relationships* (3rd ed.). Boston: McGraw-Hill.

Bridge, M. J. (1994). *Arriving on the scene: Women's growing presence in the news.* New York: Women, Men and Media.

Bridges, J. S. (1993). Pink or blue: Gender-stereotypic perceptions of infants as conveyed by birth congratulations cards. *Psychology of Women Quarterly, 17,* 193–205.

Bridges, J. S., & Etaugh, C. (1994). Black and White college women's perceptions of early maternal employment. *Psychology of Women Quarterly, 18,* 427–431.

Bridges, J. S., & Etaugh, C. (1995). College students' perceptions of mothers: Effects of maternal employment-childrearing pattern and motive for employment. *Sex Roles, 32,* 735–751.

Bridges, J. S., & Etaugh, C. (1996). Black and White college women's maternal employment outcome expectations and their desired timing of maternal employment. *Sex Roles, 35,* 543–562.

Briere, J., & Lanktree, C. (1983). Sex-role related effects of sex bias in language. *Sex Roles, 9,* 625–632.

Briton, N. J., & Hall, J. A. (1995). Beliefs about female and male nonverbal communication. *Sex Roles, 32,* 79–90.

Brockington, I. (1996). *Motherhood and mental health.* Oxford, England: Oxford University Press.

Brody, L. R. (1999). *Gender, emotion, and the family.* Cambridge, MA: Harvard University Press.

Brody, L. R., & Hall, J. A. (1993). Gender and emotion. In M. Lewis & J. M. Haviland (Eds.), *Handbook of emotions* (pp. 447–460). New York: Guilford.

Bronstein, P. A., Briones, M., Brooks, T., & Cowan, B. (1996). Gender and family factors as predictors of late adolescent emotional expressiveness and adjustment: A longitudinal study. *Sex Roles, 34,* 739–765.

Bronstein, P. A., & Farnsworth, L. (1998). Gender differences in faculty experiences of interpersonal climate and processes for advancement. *Research in Higher Education, 39,* 557–572.

Bronstein, P. A., & Quina, K. (1988). Perspectives on gender balance and cultural diversity in the teaching of psychology. In P. A. Bronstein & K. Quina (Eds.), *Teaching a psychology of people: Resources for gender and sociocultural awareness* (pp. 3–11). Washington, DC: American Psychological Association.

Brooks, C. I. (1987). Superiority of women in statistics achievement. *Teaching of Psychology, 14,* 45.

Brooks, G. R. (1997a). The centerfold syndrome. In R. F. Levant & G. R. Brooks (Eds.), *Men and sex: New psychological perspectives* (pp. 28–57). New York: Wiley.

Brooks, G. R. (1997b, Spring). Our voice can make a difference. *Society for the Psychological Study of Men and Masculinity Bulletin,* pp. 1–3.

Brooks, G. R. (1998). *A new psychotherapy for traditional men.* San Francisco: Jossey-Bass.

Brooks-Gunn, J., Han, W., & Waldfogel, J. (2002). Maternal employment and child cognitive outcomes in the first three years of life: The NICHD Study of Early Child Care. *Child Development, 73,* 1052–1072.

Brooks-Gunn, J., Schley, S., & Hardy, J. (1999). Marriage and the baby carriage: Historical change and intergenerational continuity in early parenthood. In L. J. Crockett & R. K. Silbereisen (Eds.), *Negotiating adolescence in times of social change.* New York: Cambridge University Press.

Brown, B. B., Dolcini, M. M., & Leventhal, A. (1997). Transformations in peer relationships at adolescence: Implications for health-related behavior. In J. Schulenberg, J. L. Maggs, & K. Hurrelmann (Eds.), *Health risks and developmental transitions during adolescence* (pp. 161–189). New York: Cambridge University Press.

Brown, D. P., Scheflin, A. W., & Hammond, D. C. (1998). *Memory, trauma treatment, and the law.* New York: Norton.

Brown, D. R., & Gary, L. E. (1985). Social support network differentials among married and non-married Black females. *Psychology of Women Quarterly, 9,* 229–241.

Brown, E. B. (1990). African-American women's quilting: A framework for conceptualizing and teaching African-American women's history. In M. M. Malson, E. Mudimbe-Boyi, J. F. O'Barr, & M. Wyer (Eds.), *Black women in America* (pp. 9–18). Chicago: University of Chicago Press.

Brown, J. D., Steele, J. R., & Walsh-Childers, K. (Eds.). (2002). *Sexual teens, sexual media: Investigating media's influence on adolescent sexuality.* Mahwah, NJ: Erlbaum.

Brown, L. M. (1998). *Raising their voices: The politics of girls' anger.* Cambridge, MA: Harvard University Press.

Brown, L. M., Way, N., & Duff, J. L. (1999). The others in my I: Adolescent girls' friendships and peer relations. In N. G. Johnson, M. C. Roberts, & J. Worell (Eds.), *Beyond appearance: A new look at adolescent girls* (pp. 205–225). Washington, DC: American Psychological Association.

Brown, L. S. (2000). Dangerousness, impotence, silence, and invisibility: Heterosexism in the construction of women's sexuality. In C. B. Travis & J. W. White (Eds.), *Sexuality, society, and feminism* (pp. 273–297). Washington, DC: American Psychological Association.

Brown, N. M., & Amatea, E. S. (2000). *Love and intimate relationships: Journeys of the heart.* Philadelphia: Brunner/Mazel.

Brown, P. D., & O'Leary, K. D. (1997). Wife abuse in intact couples. In G. K. Kantor & J. L. Jasinski (Eds.), *Out of the darkness: Contemporary perspectives on family violence* (pp. 194–207). Thousand Oaks, CA: Sage.

Brown, S. S., & Eisenberg, L. (1995). *The best intentions: Unintended pregnancy and the well-being of children and families.* Washington, DC: National Academy Press.

Browne, B. A. (1997). Gender and beliefs about work force discrimination in the United States and Australia. *Journal of Social Psychology, 137,* 107–116.

Brownlow, S., Jacobi, T., & Rogers, M. (2000). Science anxiety as a function of gender and experience. *Sex Roles, 42,* 119–131.

Brownlow, S., Whitener, R., & Rupert, J. M. (1998). "I'll take gender differences for $1000!": Domain-specific intellectual success on "Jeopardy." *Sex Roles, 38,* 269–285.

Brownmiller, S. (1999). *In our time: Memoir of a revolution.* New York: Dial Press.

Bruining, M. O. (1995). A few thoughts from a Korean, adopted, lesbian, writer/poet, and social worker. *Journal of Gay and Lesbian Social Services, 3,* 61–66.

Brumberg, J. J. (1997). *The body project: An intimate history of American girls.* New York: Random House.

Brunsdon, C., D'Acci, J., & Spigel, L. (Eds.). (1997). *Feminist television criticism reader.* New York: Oxford University Press.

Brush, L. D. (1998). Gender, work, who cares?! Production, reproduction, industrialization, and business as usual. In M. M. Ferree, J. Lorber, & B. B. Hess (Eds.), *Revisioning gender* (pp. 161–189). Thousand Oaks, CA: Sage.

Buchanan, M. C., Villagran, M. M., & Ragan, S. L. (2001). Women, menopause, and (Ms.)information: Communication about the climacteric. *Health Communication, 14,* 99–119.

Buckley, S. (1997, October 20). A matter of life and death. *Washington Post National Weekly Edition,* pp. 6–8.

The budget. (1996, February 12). *Family Planning Advocates Legislative Update,* p. 1.

Buhle, J. (2000). Introduction. In F. Howe (Ed.), *Testimony from thirty founding mothers* (pp. xv–xxvi). New York: Feminist Press.

Buhle, M. J. (1998). *Feminism and its discontents.* Cambridge, MA: Harvard University Press.

Bullock, H. E., Wyche, K. F., & Williams, W. R. (2001). Media images of the poor. *Journal of Social Issues, 57,* 229–246.

Bureau of Labor Statistics. (2001a). *Current population survey data for 2000 by detailed occupation and sex.* Retrieved December 24, 2001, from ftp://ftp.bls.gov/pub/special.requests/lf.aat11.txt

Bureau of Labor Statistics. (2001b). *Employment characteristics of families summary.* Retrieved December 27, 2001, from http://www.bls.gov/news.release/famee.txt

Bureau of Labor Statistics. (2001c). *Employment status of the civilian noninstitutional population 16 years and over by sex.* Retrieved December 12, 2001, from ftp://ftp.bls.gov/pub/special.requests/1f/aat2.txt

Bureau of Labor Statistics. (2001d, August). *Highlights of women's earnings in 2000* (Report 952). Washington, DC: Author.

Burgoon, M., & Klingle, R. S. (1998). Gender differences in being influential and/or influenced: A challenge to prior explanations. In D. J. Canary & K. Dindia (Eds.), *Sex differences and similarities in communication.* Mahwah, NJ: Erlbaum.

Burian, B. K., Yanico, B. J., & Martinez, C. R., Jr. (1998). Group gender composition effects on judgments of sexual harassment. *Psychology of Women Quarterly, 22,* 465–480.

Burke, R. J. (1999). Workaholism in organizations: Gender differences. *Sex Roles, 41,* 333–345.

Burn, S. M. (1996). *The social psychology of gender.* New York: McGraw-Hill.

Burn, S. M., Aboud, R., & Moyles, C. (2000). The relationship between gender, social identity, and support for feminism. *Sex Roles, 42,* 1081–1089.

Burnham, L. (1994). Race and gender: The limits of analogy. In E. Tobach & B. Rosoff (Eds.), *Challenging racism and sexism: Alternatives to genetic explanations* (pp. 143–162). New York: Feminist Press.

Burnham, L., & Gustafson, K. (2000). *Working hard, staying poor.* Berkeley, CA: Women of Color Center.

Burns, L. H. (2001). Gynecologic oncology. In N. L. Stotland & D. E. Stewart (Eds.), *Psychological aspects of women's health care* (pp. 307–329). Washington, DC: American Psychiatric Press.

Bursik, K. (1991a). Adaptation to divorce and ego development in adult women. *Journal of Personality and Social Psychology, 60,* 300–306.

Bursik, K. (1991b). Correlations of women's adjustment during the separation and divorce process. *Journal of Divorce and Remarriage, 14,* 137–162.

Bursik, K. (1992). Perceptions of sexual harassment in an academic context. *Sex Roles, 27,* 401–412.

Bursik, K. (1998). Moving beyond gender differences: Gender role comparisons of manifest dream content. *Sex Roles, 38,* 203–214.

Bursik, K. (2000, August). *Gender, gender role, and ego level: Individual differences in feminism.* Paper presented at the annual convention of the American Psychological Association, Washington, DC.

Bursik, K. (2002). *Then and now: Perceptions of sexual harassment in an academic context.* Paper presented at the annual meeting of the Eastern Psychological Association, Boston, MA.

Burt, V. V., & Hendrick, V. C. (1997). *Concise guide to women's mental health.* Washington, DC: American Psychiatric Press.

Burtless, G., & Quinn, J. F. (2001). Retirement trends and policies to encourage work among older Americans. In P. B. Budetti, R. V. Burkhauser, J. M. Gregory, & H. A. Hunt (Eds.), *Ensuring health and income security for an aging workforce* (pp. 375–415). Kalamazoo, MI: W. E. Upjohn Institute for Employment Research.

Bush, T. L., & Whiteman, M. K. (1999). Hormone replacement therapy and risk of breast cancer. *Journal of the American Medical Association, 281,* 2140–2141.

Buss, A. H., & Perry, M. (1992). The aggression questionnaire. *Journal of Personality and Social Psychology, 63,* 452–459.

Buss, D. M. (1994). *The evolution of desire: Strategies of human mating.* New York: Basic Books.

Buss, D. M. (1995). Psychological sex differences: Origins through sexual selection. *American Psychologist, 50,* 164–168.

Buss, D. M. (1998). The psychology of human mate selection: Exploring the complexity of the strategic repertoire. In C. Crawford & D. L. Krebs (Eds.), *Handbook of evolutionary psychology: Ideas, issues, and applications* (pp. 405–429). Mahwah, NJ: Erlbaum.

Buss, D. M., & Schmitt, D. P. (1993). Sexual strategies theory: An evolutionary perspective on human mating. *Psychological Review, 100,* 204–232.

Bussey, K., & Bandura, A. (1999). Social cognitive theory of gender development and differentiation. *Psychological Review, 106,* 676–713.

Butler, A. (2002). *The state of older women in America.* Washington, DC: Older Women's League.

Buttner, E. H., & McEnally, M. (1996). The interactive effect of influence tactic, applicant gender, and type of job on hiring recommendations. *Sex Roles, 34,* 581–591.

Byers, E. S., & Demmons, S. (1999). Sexual satisfaction and sexual self-disclosure within dating relationships. *Journal of Sex Research, 36,* 180–189.

Bylsma, W. H., & Major, B. (1992). Two routes to eliminating gender differences in personal entitlement: Social comparisons and performance evaluations. *Psychology of Women Quarterly, 16,* 193–200.

Byne, W. (1994, May). The biological evidence challenged. *Scientific American,* pp. 50–55.

Byne, W., & Parsons, B. (1994, February). Biology and human sexual orientation. *Harvard Mental Health Newsletter,* pp. 5–7.

Cachelin, F. M., Veisel, C., Barzegarnazari, E., & Striegel-Moore, R. H. (2000). Disordered eating, acculturation, and treatment-seeking in a community sample of Hispanic, Asian, Black, and White women. *Psychology of Women Quarterly, 24,* 244–253.

Cahan, S., & Ganor, Y. (1995). Cognitive gender differences among Israeli children. *Sex Roles, 32,* 469–484.

Calasanti, T. M. (1996). Gender and life satisfaction in retirement: An assessment of the male model. *Journal of Gerontology: Social Sciences, 51B,* 518–529.

Calasanti, T. M., & Slevin, K. F. (2001). *Gender, social inequalities, and aging.* Walnut Creek, CA: AltaMira Press.

Caldera, Y. M., & Sciaraffa, M. A. (1998). Parent-toddler play with feminine toys: Are all dolls the same? *Sex Roles, 39,* 657–668.

Caldwell, M. A., Finn, S., & Marecek, J. (1981). Sex-role identity, sex-role behavior, and satisfaction in heterosexual, lesbian, and gay male couples. *Psychology of Women Quarterly, 5,* 488–494.

Call, V., Sprecher, S., & Schwartz, P. (1995). The incidence and frequency of marital sex in a national sample. *Journal of Marriage and the Family, 57,* 639–652.

Callan, J. E. (2001) Gender development: Psychoanalytic perspectives. In J. Worell (Ed.), *Encyclopedia of women and gender* (pp. 523–536). San Diego: Academic Press.

Cameron, D., McAlinden, F., & O'Leary, K. (1993). Lakoff in context: The social and linguistic functions of tag questions. In S. Jackson (Ed.), *Women's studies: Essential readings* (pp. 421–426). New York: New York University Press.

Campbell, C. R., & Henry, J. W. (1999). Gender differences in self-attributions: Relationship of gender to attributional consistency, style, and expectations for performance in a college course. *Sex Roles, 41,* 95–104.

Campbell, R., & Salem, D. A. (1999). Concept mapping as a feminist research method: Examining the community response to rape. *Psychology of Women Quarterly, 23,* 65–89.

Campenni, C. E. (1999). Gender stereotyping of children's toys: A comparison of parents and nonparents. *Sex Roles, 40,* 121–138.

Canary, D. J., & Dindia, K. (Eds.). (1998). *Sex differences and similarities in communication.* Mahwah, NJ: Erlbaum.

Canary, D. J., & Emmers-Sommer, T. M. (1997). *Sex and gender differences in personal relationships.* New York: Guilford.

Canetto, S. S. (2001a). Older adult women: Issues, resources, and challenges. In R. K. Unger (Ed.), *Handbook of the psychology of women and gender* (pp. 183–197). New York: Wiley.

Canetto, S. S. (2001b). Suicidal behavior in girls. In M. Forman-Brunell (Ed.), *Girlhood in America: An encyclopedia* (pp. 616–621). Santa Barbara, CA: ABC-CLIO.

Canetto, S. S., & Lester, D. (1995). Women and suicidal behavior: Issues and dilemmas. In S. S. Canetto & D. Lester (Eds.), *Women and suicidal behavior* (pp. 3–8). New York: Springer.

Canetto, S. S., & Sakinofsky, I. (1998). The gender paradox in suicide. *Suicide and Life-Threatening Behavior, 28,* 1–23.

Cann, A. (1993). Evaluative expectations and the gender schema: Is failed inconsistency better? *Sex Roles, 28,* 667–678.

Cannistra, S. A., & Niloff, J. M. (1996). Cancer of the uterine cervix. *New England Journal of Medicine, 334,* 1030–1038.

Caplan, P. J. (1998). Mother-blaming. In M. Ladd-Taylor & L. Umansky (Eds.), *"Bad" mothers: The politics of blame in twentieth-century America* (pp. 127–144). New York: New York University Press.

Caplan, P. J. (2000). *The new don't blame mother: Mending the mother-daughter relationship.* New York: Routledge.

Caplan, P. J. (2001). Motherhood: Its changing face. In J. Worell (Ed.), *Encyclopedia of women and gender* (pp. 783–794). San Diego: Academic Press.

Caplan, P. J., & Caplan, J. B. (1999). *Thinking critically about research on sex and gender* (2nd ed.). New York: Longman.

Caplan, P. J., Crawford, M., Hyde, J. S., & Richardson, J. T. E. (Eds.). (1997). *Gender differences in human cognition.* New York: Oxford University Press.

Carli, L. L. (1990). Gender, language, and influence. *Journal of Personality and Social Psychology, 59,* 941–951.

Carli, L. L. (1998). Coping with adversity. In L. H. Collins, J. C. Chrisler, & K. Quina (Eds.), *Career strategies for women in academe* (pp. 275–297). Thousand Oaks, CA: Sage.

Carli, L. L. (1999). Gender, interpersonal power, and social influence. *Journal of Social Issues, 55,* 81–99.

Carli, L. L. (2001). Gender and social influence. *Journal of Social Issues, 57,* 725–741.

Carli, L. L., & Bukatko, D. (2000). Gender, communication and social influence: A developmental perspective. In T. Eckes & H. M. Trautner. (Eds.), *The developmental social psychology of gender* (pp. 295–331). Mahwah, NJ: Erlbaum.

Carli, L. L., LaFleur, S. J., & Loeber, C. C. (1995). Nonverbal behavior, gender, and influence. *Journal of Personality and Social Psychology, 68,* 1030–1041.

Carlo, G., Raffaeli, M., Laible, D. J., & Meyer, K. A. (1999). Why are girls less physically aggressive than boys? Personality and parenting mediators of physical aggression. *Sex Roles, 40,* 711–729.

Carlson, K. J., Eisenstat, S. A., & Ziporyn, T. (1996). *The Harvard guide to women's health.* Cambridge, MA: Harvard University Press.

Carothers, B. J., & Allen, J. B. (1999). Relationships of employment status, gender role, insult, and gender with use of influence tactics. *Sex Roles, 41,* 375–387.

Carpenter, L. M. (1998). From girls into women: Scripts for sexuality and romance in *Seventeen* magazine. *Journal of Sex Research, 35,* 158–168.

Carroll, K., & Jackson, T. L. (1996). Rape education and prevention training. In T. L. Jackson (Ed.), *Acquaintance rape: Assessment, treatment, and prevention* (pp. 177–213). Sarasota, FL: Professional Resource Press.

Carroll, R. (1997). *Sugar in the raw.* New York: Random House.

Carstensen, L. L. (1998, March/April). Everything old is new again. *Stanford Today,* pp. 46–50.

Carter, J., Lane, C., & Kite, M. (1991, August). *Which sex is more likeable? It depends on the subtype.* Paper presented at the annual meeting of the American Psychological Society, Washington, DC.

Casey, T. (1998). *Pride and joy: The lives and passions of women without children.* Hillsboro, OR: Beyond Words Publishing.

Cash, T. F., Ancis, J. R., & Strachan, M. D. (1997). Gender attitudes, feminist identity, and body images among college women. *Sex Roles, 36,* 433–447.

Cash, T. F., & Henry, P. E. (1995). Women's body images: The results of a national survey in the U.S.A. *Sex Roles, 33,* 19–28.

Cassell, J., & Jenkins, H. (Eds.). (1998). *From Barbie to Mortal Kombat: Gender and computer games.* Cambridge, MA: MIT Press.

Castañeda, A. I. (1998). History and the politics of violence against women. In C. Trujillo (Ed.), *Living Chicana theory* (pp. 310–319). Berkeley, CA: Third Woman Press.

Castañeda, D. (1996). Gender issues among Latinas. In J. C. Chrisler, C. Golden, & P. D. Rozee (Eds.), *Lectures on the psychology of women* (pp. 166–181). New York: McGraw-Hill.

Castañeda, D. (1999). Community-based health promotion and community health advisors. In M. O. Loustaunau & M. Sanchez-Bane (Eds.), *Life, death, and in-between on the U.S.-Mexico border: Así es la vida* (pp. 113–130). Westport, CT: Bergin & Garvey.

Castañeda, D. (2000a). The close relationship context and HIV/AIDS risk reduction among Mexican Americans. *Sex Roles, 42,* 551–580.

Castañeda, D. (2000b). Gender issues among Latinas. In J. E. Chrisler, C. Golden, & P. D. Rozee

(Eds.), *Lectures on the psychology of women* (2nd ed., pp. 192–207). Boston: McGraw-Hill.

Castañeda, D. M., & Collins, B. E. (1998). The effects of gender, ethnicity, and a close relationship theme on perceptions of persons introducing a condom. *Sex Roles, 39,* 369–390.

Catania, J. A., et al. (2001). Frontiers in the behavioral epidemiology of HIV/STDs. In A. Baum, T. A. Revenson, & J. E. Singer (Eds.), *Handbook of health psychology* (pp. 777–799). Mahwah, NJ: Erlbaum.

Cates, W., Jr., & Berman, S. M. (1999). Prevention of sexually transmitted diseases other than human immunodeficiency virus. In A. J. Goreczny & M. Hersen (Eds.), *Handbook of pediatric and adolescent health psychology* (pp. 361–370). Boston: Allyn & Bacon.

Catsambis, S. (1999). The path to math: Gender and racial-ethnic differences in mathematics participation from middle school to high school. In L. A. Peplau, S. C. DeBro, R. C. Veniegas, & P. L. Taylor (Eds.), *Gender, culture, and ethnicity: Current research about women and men* (pp. 102–120). Mountain View, CA: Mayfield.

Ceballo, R. (1999). "The only Black woman walking the face of the earth who cannot have a baby?" In M. Romero & A. Stewart (Eds.), *Women's untold stories: Outside the master narrative.* New York: Routledge.

Center for Gender Equality. (2000). *Give voice to equality* [Brochure]. New York: Author.

Centers for Disease Control. (2002, September 23). *HIV/AIDS Surveillance Report 13.* Retrieved January 8, 2003, from the Centers for Disease Control Web site: http://www.cdc.gov/hiv/stats/hasrlink .htm

Chambers, P. (2000). Widowhood in later life. In M. Bernard, J. Phillips, L. Machin, & V. H. Davies (Eds.), *Women ageing: Changing identities, challenging myths* (pp. 127–147). London: Routledge.

Chan, C. S. (1997). Don't ask, don't tell, don't know: The formation of a homosexual identity and sexual expression among Asian American lesbians. In B. Greene (Ed.), *Ethnic and cultural diversity among lesbians and gay men* (pp. 240–248). Thousand Oaks, CA: Sage.

Chan, C. S. (2000). Asian American women and adolescent girls: Sexuality and sexual expression. In J. C. Chrisler, C. Golden, & P. D. Rozee (Eds.), *Lectures on the psychology of women* (2nd ed., pp. 148–177). Boston: McGraw-Hill.

Chan, D. K.-S., Tang, C. S., & Chan, W. (1999). Sexual harassment: A preliminary analysis of its effects on Hong Kong Chinese women in the workplace and academia. *Psychology of Women Quarterly, 23,* 661–672.

Chance, C., & Fiese, B. H. (1999). Gender-stereotyped lessons about emotion in family narratives. *Narrative Inquiry, 9,* 243–255.

Chand, A. E. (2002). *The influence of national culture on self-objectification and body shame.* Unpublished master's thesis, New School University, New York.

Charles, N., et al. (2001, December 10). Beyond the call. *People Magazine,* pp. 88–107.

Charles, S. T., & Carstensen, L. L. (2002). Marriage in old age. In M. Yalom & L. L. Carstensen (Eds.), *Inside the American couple* (pp. 236–254). Berkeley, CA: University of California Press.

Chasteen, A. L. (1994). "The world around me": The environment and single women. *Sex Roles, 31,* 309–328.

Chesler, P. (1976). *Women, money, and power.* New York: Bantam Books.

Chin, J. L. (1994). Psychodynamic approaches. In L. Comas-Díaz & B. Greene (Eds.), *Women of color* (pp. 194–222). New York: Guilford.

Chin, J. L. (1998). Mental health services and treatment. In L. C. Lee & N. W. S. Zane (Eds.), *Handbook of Asian American psychology* (pp. 485–504). Thousand Oaks, CA: Sage.

Chipman, S. F. (1996). Female participation in the study of mathematics: The U.S. situation. In G. Hanna (Ed.), *Towards gender equity in mathematics education.* Norwell, MA: Kluwer.

Chiu, C. (1998). Do professional women have lower job satisfaction than professional men? Lawyers as a case study. *Sex Roles, 38,* 521–537.

Chodorow, N. J. (1994). *Femininities, masculinities, sexualities: Freud and beyond.* Lexington, KY: University Press of Kentucky.

Chodorow, N. J. (1999). *The power of feelings: Personal meaning in psychoanalysis, gender, and culture.* New Haven, CT: Yale University Press.

Chodorow, N. J. (2000). The psychodynamics of the family. In S. Saguaro (Ed.), *Psychoanalysis and woman: A reader* (pp. 108–127). New York: New York University Press.

Choo, P., Levine, T., & Hatfield, E. (1996). Gender, love schemas, and reactions to romantic breakups. *Journal of Social Behavior and Personality, 11,* 143–160.

Chow, E. N. (1991). The development of feminist consciousness among Asian American women. In J. Lorber & S. A. Farrell (Eds.), *The social construction of gender* (pp. 255–268). Newbury Park, CA: Sage.

Chow, E. N. (1994). Asian American women at work. In M. Baca Zinn & B. T. Dill (Eds.), *Women of color in U.S. society* (pp. 203–227). Philadelphia: Temple University Press.

Chrisler, J. C. (1996). PMS as a culture-bound syndrome. In J. C. Chrisler, C. Golden, & P. D. Rozee (Eds.), *Lectures on the psychology of women* (pp. 106–121). New York: McGraw-Hill.

Chrisler, J. C. (2000). PMS as a culture-bound syndrome. In J. C. Chrisler, C. Golden, & P. D. Rozee (Eds.), *Lectures on the psychology of women* (2nd ed., pp. 96–110). Boston: McGraw-Hill.

Chrisler, J. C. (2001). Gendered bodies and physical health. In R. K. Unger (Ed.), *Handbook of the psychology of women and gender* (pp. 289–301). New York: Wiley.

Chrisler, J. C. (2002). Hormone hostages: The cultural legacy of PMS as a legal defense. In L. H. Collins, J. C. Chrisler, & M. R. Dunlap (Eds.), *Charting a new course for feminist psychology.* Westport, CT: Praeger.

Chrisler, J. C., Golden, C., & Rozee, P. D. (Eds.). (2000). *Lectures on the psychology of women* (2nd ed.). Boston: McGraw-Hill.

Chrisler, J. C., Johnston, I. K., Champagne, N. M., & Preston, K. E. (1994). Menstrual joy: The construct and its consequences. *Psychology of Women Quarterly, 18,* 375–387.

Chrisler, J. C., & Levy, K. B. (1990). The media construct a menstrual monster: A content analysis of PMS articles in the popular press. *Women and Health, 16,* 89–104.

Christensen, A., & Heavey, C. L. (1999). Intervention for couples. *Annual Review of Psychology, 50,* 165–190.

Christensen, A., & Jacobson, N. S. (2000). *Reconcilable differences.* New York: Guilford.

Christopher, F. S. (2001). *To dance the dance: A symbolic interactional exploration of premarital sexuality.* Mahwah, NJ: Erlbaum.

Christopher, F. S., & Lloyd, S. A. (2000). Physical and sexual aggression in relationships. In C. Hendrick & S. S. Hendrick (Eds.), *Close relationships* (pp. 331–356). Thousand Oaks, CA: Sage.

Clark, J., & Zehr, D. (1993). Other women can: Discrepant performance predictions for self and same-sex other. *Journal of College Student Development, 34,* 31–35.

Clark, R., Lennon, R., & Morris, L. (1993). Of Caldecotts and Kings: Gendered images in recent American children's books by Black and non-Black illustrators. *Gender and Society, 7,* 227–245.

Clark, R. A. (1993). Men's and women's self-confidence in persuasive, comforting, and justificatory communicative tasks. *Sex Roles, 28,* 553–567.

Clark, R. A. (1998). A comparison of topics and objectives in a cross section of young men's and women's everyday conversations. In D. J. Canary & K. Dindia (Eds.), *Sex differences and similarities in communication* (pp. 303–319). Mahwah, NJ: Erlbaum.

Clarkberg, M., Stolzenberg, R. M., & Waite, L. J. (1995). Attitudes, values, and entrance into cohabitational versus marital unions. *Social Forces, 74,* 609–634.

Clausen, J. (1997). *Beyond gay or straight: Understanding sexual orientation.* Philadelphia: Chelsea House.

Clayton, S. D., & Crosby, F. J. (1992). *Justice, gender, and affirmative action.* Ann Arbor, MI: University of Michigan Press.

Cleveland, J. N., Stockdale, M., & Murphy, K. R. (2000). *Women and men in organizations.* Mahwah, NJ: Erlbaum.

Clinchy, B. M., & Norem, J. K. (Eds.). (1998). *The gender and psychology reader.* New York: New York University Press.

Clopton, N. A., & Sorell, G. T. (1993). Gender differences in moral reasoning: Stable or situational? *Psychology of Women Quarterly, 17,* 85–101.

Cobb, R. J., Davila, J., & Bradbury, T. N. (2001). Attachment security and marital satisfaction: The role of positive perceptions and social support. *Personality and Social Psychology Bulletin, 27,* 1131–1143.

Cochran, C. C., Frazier, P. A., & Olson, A. M. (1997). Predictors of responses to unwanted sexual attention. *Psychology of Women Quarterly, 21,* 207–226.

Cochran, S. V., & Rabinowitz, F. E. (2000). *Men and depression.* San Diego: Academic Press.

Coffin, F. (1997). Drywall rocker and taper. In M. Martin (Ed.), *Hard-hatted women: Life on the job* (pp. 63–70). Seattle: Seal Press.

Cogan, J. C., & Ernsberger, P. (1999). Dieting, weight, and health: Reconceptualizing research and policy. *Journal of Social Issues, 55,* 187–205.

Cohen, J. (1969). *Statistical power analysis for the behavioral sciences.* New York: Academic Press.

Cohen, J., et al. (1996). *Girls in the middle: Working to succeed in school.* Washington, DC: American Association of University Women.

Cohler, B. J., & Galatzer-Levy, R. M. (2000). *The course of gay and lesbian lives: Social and psychoana-*

lytic perspectives. Chicago: University of Chicago Press.

Cohn, S. (2000). *Race and gender discrimination at work.* Boulder, CO: Westview Press.

Colapinto, J. (2000). *As nature made him: The boy who was raised as a girl.* New York: HarperCollins.

Colditz, G. A., et al. (1995). The use of estrogens and progestins and the risk of breast cancer in postmenopausal women. *New England Journal of Medicine, 332,* 1589–1593.

Coleman, M. (1996). Barriers to career progress for women in education: The perceptions of female headteachers. *Educational Research, 38,* 317–332.

Colen, S. (1997). "With respect and feelings": Voices of West Indian child care and domestic workers in New York City. In M. Crawford & R. Unger (Eds.), *In our own words: Readings on the psychology of women and gender* (pp. 199–218). New York: McGraw-Hill.

Coley, R. L., & Chase-Lansdale, P. L. (1998). Adolescent pregnancy and parenthood. *American Psychologist, 53,* 152–166.

Collaer, M. L., & Hines, M. (1995). Human behavioral sex differences: A role for gonadal hormones during early development? *Psychological Bulletin, 118,* 55–107.

Collins, L. H., Chrisler, J. C., & Quina, K. (Eds.). (1998). *Career strategies for women in academe.* Thousand Oaks, CA: Sage.

Collins, P. H. (1990). *Black feminist thought: Knowledge, consciousness, and the politics of empowerment.* Boston: Unwin Hyman.

Collins, P. H. (1991). The meaning of motherhood in Black culture and Black mother-daughter relationships. In P. Bell-Scott et al. (Eds.), *Double stitch: Black women write about mothers and daughters* (pp. 42–60). Boston: Beacon Press.

Collins, P. H. (1994). Shifting the center: Race, class, and feminist theorizing about motherhood. In D. Bassin, M. Honey, & M. M. Kaplan (Eds.), *Representations of motherhood* (pp. 56–74). New Haven, CT: Yale University Press.

Collins, P. H. (1995). The social construction of Black feminist thought. In N. Tuana & R. Tong (Eds.), *Feminism and philosophy* (pp. 526–547). Boulder, CO: Westview Press.

Collins, P. H. (2000). *Black feminist thought: Knowledge, consciousness, and the politics of empowerment* (2nd ed.). New York: Routledge.

Collins, W. A., & L. A. Sroufe (1999). Capacity for intimate relationships: A developmental construction. In W. Furman, B. B. Brown, & C. Feiring (Eds.), *The development of romantic relationships in adolescence* (pp. 125–147). New York: Cambridge University Press.

Collison, M. N.-K. (2000, February 3). The "other Asians." *Black Issues in Higher Education,* pp. 20–24.

Coltrane, S. (1998). *Gender and families.* Thousand Oaks, CA: Pine Forge Press.

Coltrane, S., & Adams, M. (1997a). Children and gender. In T. Arendell (Ed.), *Parenting: Contemporary issues and challenges.* Newbury Park, CA: Sage.

Coltrane, S., & Adams, M. (1997b). Work-family imagery and gender stereotypes: Television and the reproduction of difference. *Journal of Vocational Behavior, 50,* 323–347.

Coltrane, S., & Adams, M. (2001a). Men, women, and housework. In D. Vannoy (Ed.), *Gender mosaics: Social perspectives* (pp. 145–154). New York: Roxbury.

Coltrane, S., & Adams, M. (2001b). Men's family work: Child-centered fathering and the sharing of domestic labor. In R. Hertz & N. L. Marshall (Eds.), *Working families: The transformation of the American home* (pp. 72–99). Berkeley: University of California Press.

Coltrane, S., & Messineo, M. (2000). The perpetuation of subtle prejudice: Race and gender imagery in 1990s television advertising. *Sex Roles, 42,* 363–389.

Comas-Díaz, L. (2000). An ethnopolitical approach to working with people of color. *American Psychologist, 55,* 1319–1325.

Comas-Díaz, L., & Greene, B. (1994). Women of color with professional status. In L. Comas-Díaz & B. Greene (Eds.), *Women of color: Integrating ethnic and gender identities in psychotherapy* (pp. 347–388). New York: Guilford.

Committee on Women in Psychology. (1998). *Surviving and thriving in academia: A guide for women and ethnic minorities.* Washington, DC: American Psychological Association.

Condon, J. T., & Corkindale, C. (1997). The correlates of antenatal attachment in pregnant women. *British Journal of Medical Psychology, 70,* 359–372.

Condra, M. B. (1991). The social environment of older, unmarried persons [Review of the book *The unmarried in later life*]. *Contemporary Psychology, 36,* 146–147.

Condry, J. C., & Condry, S. (1976). Sex differences: A study of the eye of the beholder. *Child Development, 47,* 812–819.

Conkright, L., Flannagan, D., & Dykes, J. (2000). Effects of pronoun type and gender role consistency on children's recall and interpretation of stories. *Sex Roles, 43*, 481–497.

Conley, F. K. (1998). *Walking out on the boys.* New York: Farrar, Straus & Giroux.

Conrad, S., & Milburn, M. (2001). *Sexual intelligence.* New York: Crown.

Conway, K. (1997). *Ordinary life: A memoir of illness.* New York: Freeman.

Conway, M., Pizzamiglio, M. T., & Mount, L. (1996). Status, communality, and agency: Implications for stereotypes of gender and other groups. *Journal of Personality and Social Psychology, 71*, 25–38.

Conway-Turner, K. (1999). Older women of color: A feminist exploration of the intersections of personal, familial, and community life. In J. D. Garner (Ed.), *Fundamentals of feminist gerontology* (pp. 115–130). New York: Haworth.

Coontz, S. (1997). *The way we really are: Coming to terms with America's changing families.* New York: Basic Books.

Cooper, S. L., & Glazer, E. S. (1998). *Choosing assisted reproduction.* Indianapolis: Perspectives Press.

Cope-Farrar, K. M., & Kunkel, D. (2002). Sexual messages in teens' favorite prime-time television programs. In J. D. Brown, J. R. Steele, & K. Walsh-Childers (Eds.), *Sexual teens, sexual media* (pp. 59–78). Mahwah, NJ: Erlbaum.

Corcoran, C. B., & Mahlstedt, D. (1999). Preventing sexual assault on campus: A feminist perspective. In C. Forden, A. E. Hunter, & B. Birns (Eds.), *Readings in the psychology of women* (pp. 289–299). Boston: Allyn & Bacon.

Cortés, C. E. (1997). Chicanas in film: History of an image. In C. E. Rodríguez (Ed.), *Latin looks: Images of Latinas and Latinos in the U.S. media* (pp. 121–141). Boulder, CO: Westview Press.

Cortese, A. J. (1999). *Provocateur: Images of women and minorities in advertising.* Oxford, England: Rowman & Littlefield.

Cosgrove, L. (2000). Crying out loud: Understanding women's emotional distress as both lived experience and social construction. *Feminism and Psychology, 10*, 247–267.

Cosgrove, L., & Riddle, B. (2001a). *Constructions of femininity and experiences of menstrual distress.* Paper presented at the Society for Menstrual Cycle Research, Avon, CT.

Cosgrove, L., & Riddle, B. (2001b, August). *Libidinal and bleeding bodies: Deconstructing menstrual cycle research.* Presented at the annual meeting of the American Psychological Association, San Francisco.

Costello, C. B., & Stone, A. J. (2001). *The American woman 2001–2002.* New York: Norton.

Cota, A. A., Reid, A., & Dion, K. L. (1991). Construct validity of a diagnostic ratio measure of gender stereotypes. *Sex Roles, 25*, 225–235.

Cowan, C. P., & Cowan, P. A. (1992). *When partners become parents: The big life change for couples.* New York: Basic Books.

Cowan, G. (1984). The double standard in age discrepant relationships. *Sex Roles, 11*, 17–24.

Cowan, G., & Hoffman, C. D. (1986). Gender stereotyping in young children: Evidence to support a concept-learning approach. *Sex Roles, 14*, 11–22.

Cowan, G., & Quinton, W. J. (1997). Cognitive style and attitudinal correlates of the Perceived Causes of Rape Scale. *Psychology of Women Quarterly, 21*, 227–245.

Cowan, P., & Cowan, C. P. (1998). New families: Modern couples as new pioneers. In M. A. Mason, A. Skolnick, & S. D. Sugarman (Eds.), *All our families* (pp. 169–192). New York: Oxford University Press.

Cox, M. (2001, February/March). Zero balance. *Ms. Magazine*, pp. 56–59.

Cozzarelli, C. (1993). Personality and self-efficacy as predictors of coping with abortion. *Journal of Personality and Social Psychology, 65*, 1224–1236.

Crabb, P. B., & Bielawski, D. (1994). The social representation of material culture and gender in children's books. *Sex Roles, 30*, 69–79.

Craighead, W. E., Hart, A. B., Craighead, L. W., & Ilardi, S. S. (2002). Psychosocial treatments for major depressive disorder. In P. E. Nathan & J. Gorman (Eds.), *A guide to treatments that work* (2nd ed., pp. 245–261). New York: Oxford University Press.

Craighead, W. E., & Vajk, F. C. (1998). Depression and comorbid disorders. In E. A. Blechman & K. D. Brownell (Eds.), *Behavioral medicine and women: A comprehensive handbook* (pp. 757–763). New York: Guilford.

Crandall, C. S., Tsang, J., Goldman, S., & Pennington, J. T. (1999). Newsworthy moral dilemmas: Justice, caring, and gender. *Sex Roles, 40*, 187–209.

Crandall, C. S., et al. (2001). An attribution-value model of prejudice: Anti-fat attitudes in six nations. *Personality and Social Psychology Bulletin, 27*, 30–37.

Crawford, M. (1995). *Talking difference: On gender and language.* Thousand Oaks, CA: Sage.

Crawford, M. (2001). Gender and language. In R. K. Unger (Ed.), *Handbook of the psychology of women and gender* (pp. 228–244). New York: Wiley.

Crawford, M., & Chaffin, R. (1997). The meanings of difference: Cognition in social and cultural context. In P. J. Caplan, M. Crawford, J. S. Hyde, & J. T. E. Richardson (Eds.), *Gender differences in human cognition* (pp. 81–130). New York: Oxford University Press.

Crawford, M., Chaffin, R., & Fitton, L. (1995). Cognition in social context. *Learning and Individual Differences, 7,* 341–362.

Crawford, M., & MacLeod, M. (1990). Gender in the college classroom: An assessment of the "chilly climate" for women. *Sex Roles, 23,* 101–122.

Crenshaw, A. B. (2002, June 2). Her next step? Growing numbers of American women face retirement financially insecure. *Washington Post,* pp. H1, H3.

Crick, N. R., & Bigbee, M. A. (1998). Relational and overt forms of peer victimization: A multi-informant approach. *Journal of Consulting and Clinical Psychology, 66,* 337–347.

Crick, N. R., Casas, J. F., & Mosher, M. (1997). Relational and overt aggression in preschool. *Developmental Psychology, 33,* 579–588.

Crick, N. R., & Rose, A. J. (2000). Toward a gender-balanced approach to the study of social-emotional development: A look at relational aggression. In P. M. Miller & E. K. Scholnick (Eds.), *Toward a feminist developmental psychology* (pp. 153–168). New York: Routledge.

Crockett, L. J., Raffaeli, M., & Moilanen, K. 2002. Adolescent sexuality: Behavior and meaning. In G. R. Adams & M. Berzonsky (Eds.), *Blackwell handbook of adolescence.* Oxford, England: Blackwell.

Crombie, G. (1983). Women's attribution patterns and their relation to achievement: An examination of within-sex differences. *Sex Roles, 9,* 1171–1182.

Cronin, C., & Jreisat, S. (1995). Effects of modeling on the use of nonsexist language among high school freshpersons and seniors. *Sex Roles, 33,* 819–830.

Crooks, R., & Baur, K. (2002). *Our sexuality* (8th ed.). Pacific Grove, CA: Wadsworth.

Crosby, F. J. (1982). *Relative deprivation and working women.* New York: Oxford University Press.

Crosby, F. J., & Cordova, D. I. (2000). Words worth of wisdom: Toward an understanding of affirmative action. In F. J. Crosby & C. VanDeVeer (Eds.), *Sex, race, and merit: Debating affirmative action in education and employment* (pp. 13–20). Ann Arbor, MI: University of Michigan Press.

Crose, R. (1997). *Why women live longer than men.* San Francisco: Jossey-Bass.

Cross, S. E. (2001). Training the scientists and engineers of tomorrow: A person-situation approach. *Journal of Applied Social Psychology, 31,* 296–323.

Cross, S. E., & Madson, L. (1997a). Elaboration of models of the self: Reply to Baumeister and Sommer (1997) and Martin and Ruble (1997). *Psychological Bulletin, 122,* 51–55.

Cross, S. E., & Madson, L. (1997b). Models of the self: Self-construals and gender. *Psychological Bulletin, 122,* 5–37.

Cross, S. E., & Vick, N. V. (2001). The interdependent self-construal and social support: The case of persistence in engineering. *Personality and Social Psychology Bulletin, 27,* 820–832.

Crowley, K., Callanan, M. A., Tenenbaum, H. R., & Allen, E. (2001). Parents explain more often to boys than to girls during shared scientific thinking. *Psychological Science, 12,* 258–261.

Cruikshank, M. (1992). *The gay and lesbian liberation movement.* New York: Routledge.

Cuddy, A. J. C., & Fiske, S. T. (2002). Doddering, but dear: Process, content, and function in stereotyping of older persons. In T. D. Nelson (Ed.), *Ageism: Stereotyping and prejudice against older persons* (pp. 3–26). Cambridge, MA: MIT Press.

Culbertson, F. M. (1997). Depression and gender: An international review. *American Psychologist, 52,* 25–31.

Cull, P. (1997). Carpenter. In M. Martin (Ed.), *Hard-hatted women: Life on the job* (pp. 45–54). Seattle: Seal Press.

Culp, L. N., & Beach, S. R. H. (1998). Marriage and depressive symptoms: The role and bases of self-esteem differ by gender. *Psychology of Women Quarterly, 22,* 647–663.

Cummings, S. M., Kropf, N., & DeWeaver, K. L. (2000). Knowledge of and attitudes toward aging among non-elders: Gender and race differences. *Journal of Women & Aging, 12,* 77–91.

Currie, D. H. (1999). *Girl talk: Adolescent magazines and their readers.* Toronto: University of Toronto Press.

Curtin, S. C., & Kozak, L. J. (1998). Decline in U.S. cesarean delivery appears to stall. *Birth, 25,* 259–262.

Curtin, S. C., Kozak, L. J., & Gregory, K. D. (2000). U.S. Cesarean and VBAC rates stalled in the mid-1990s. *Birth, 27,* 54–60.

Dabul, A. J., & Russo, N. F. (1998). Rethinking psychological theory to encompass issues of gender and ethnicity: Focus on achievement. In B. M. Clinchy (Ed.), *The gender and psychology reader* (pp. 754–768). New York: New York University Press.

Dagg, P. K. B. (1991). The psychological sequelae of therapeutic abortions: Denied and completed. *American Journal of Psychiatry, 148,* 578–585.

Dahlberg, K., Berg, M., & Lundgren, I. (1999). Commentary: Studying maternal experiences of childbirth. *Birth, 26,* 215–225.

Dailey, N. (1998). *When baby boom women retire.* Westport, CT: Praeger.

Daly, F. Y. (2001). Perspectives of Native American women on race and gender. In G. Kirk & M. Okazawa-Rey (Eds.), *Women's lives: Multicultural perspectives* (2nd ed., pp. 60–68). Mountain View, CA: Mayfield.

Daniluk, J. C., & Towill, K. (2001). Sexuality education: What is it, who gets it, and does it work? In J. Worell (Ed.), *Encyclopedia of women and gender* (pp. 1023–1031). San Diego: Academic Press.

Dannenbring, D., Stevens, M. J., & House, A. E. (1997). Predictors of childbirth pain and maternal satisfaction. *Journal of Behavioral Medicine, 20,* 127–142.

Dasgupta, S. D. (1998). Gender roles and cultural continuity in the Asian Indian immigrant community in the U.S. *Sex Roles, 38,* 953–974.

Daubman, K. A., Heatherington, L., & Ahn, A. (1992). Gender and the self-presentation of academic achievement. *Sex Roles, 27,* 187–204.

D'Augelli, A. R., & Patterson, C. J. (Eds.). (2001). *Lesbian, gay, and bisexual identities and youth.* New York: Oxford University Press.

Davey, F. H. (1998). Young women's expected and preferred patterns of employment and child care. *Sex Roles, 38,* 95–102.

David, H. P., Dytrych, Z., Matějček, Z., & Schüller, V. (Eds.). (1988). *Born unwanted: Developmental effects of denied abortion.* New York: Springer.

David, H. P., & Lee, E. (2001). Abortion and its health effects. In J. Worell (Ed.), *Encyclopedia of women and gender* (pp. 1–14). San Diego: Academic Press.

Davidson, M. J., & Fielden, S. (1999). Stress and the working woman. In G. N. Powell (Ed.), *Handbook of gender and work* (pp. 413–426). Thousand Oaks, CA: Sage.

Davis, F. (1999). *Moving the mountain: The women's movement in America since 1960.* Urbana, IL: University of Illinois Press.

Davis, L. J. (Ed.). (1997). *The disability studies reader.* New York: Routledge.

Davis, S. K., & Chavez, V. (1995). Hispanic househusbands. In A. M. Padillo (Ed.), *Hispanic psychology: Critical issues in theory and research* (pp. 257–270). Thousand Oaks, CA: Sage.

Davison, K. K., & Birch, L. L. (2001). Weight status, parent reaction, and self-concept in five-year-old girls. *Pediatrics, 107,* 46–53.

Dayhoff, S. A. (1983). Sexist language and person perceptions: Evaluation of candidates from newspaper·articles. *Sex Roles, 9,* 543–555.

Dean, L., et al. (2000). Lesbian, gay, bisexual, and transgender health: Findings and concerns. *Journal of the Gay and Lesbian Medical Association, 4,* 101–151.

Dean-Jones, L. A. (1994). *Women's bodies in classical Greek science.* New York: Oxford University Press.

Deaux, K. (1979). Self-evaluation of male and female managers. *Sex Roles, 5,* 571–580.

Deaux, K. (1995). How basic can you be? The evolution of research on gender stereotypes. *Journal of Social Issues, 51,* 11–20.

Deaux, K. (1999). An overview of research on gender: Four themes from 3 decades. In W. B. Swann Jr., J. H. Langlois, & L. A. Gilbert (Eds.), *Sexism and stereotypes in modern society: The gender science of Janet Taylor Spence* (pp. 11–33). Washington, DC: American Psychological Association.

Deaux, K. (2001a). Autobiographical perspectives. In A. N. O'Connell (Ed.), *Models of achievement: Reflections of eminent women in psychology* (Vol. 3, pp. 202–218). Mahwah, NJ: Erlbaum.

Deaux, K. (2001b). Social identity. In J. Worell (Ed.), *Encyclopedia of women and gender.* San Diego: Academic Press.

Deaux, K., & Major, B. (1987). Putting gender into context: An interactive model of gender-related behavior. *Psychological Review, 94,* 369–389.

de Beauvoir, S. (1961). *The second sex.* New York: Bantam Books.

Debold E., Brown, L. M., Weseen, S., & Brookins, G. K. (1999). Cultivating hardiness zones for adolescent girls: A reconceptualization of resilience in relationships with caring adults. In N. Johnson, M. C. Roberts, & J. Worell (Eds.), *Beyond appearance: A new look at adolescent girls* (pp. 181–

204). Washington, DC: American Psychological Association.

Deevey, S. (2000). Cultural variation in lesbian bereavement experiences in Ohio. *Journal of the Gay and Lesbian Medical Association, 4*, 9–17.

DeFrain, J., & Olson, D. H. (1999). Contemporary family patterns and relationships. In M. Sussman, S. K. Steinmetz, & G. W. Peterson (Eds.), *Handbook of marriage and the family* (2nd ed., pp. 309–326). New York: Plenum.

DeKeseredy, W. S., & Schwartz, M. D. (1998). *Woman abuse on campus: Results from the Canadian National Survey.* Thousand Oaks, CA: Sage.

DeLamotte, E., Meeker, N., & O'Barr, J. (Eds.). (1997). *Women imagine change.* New York: Routledge.

Delaney, C. (2000). Making babies in a Turkish village. In J. DeLoache & A. Gottlieb (Eds.), *A world of babies: Imagined childcare guides for seven societies* (pp. 117–144). New York: Cambridge University Press.

Delaney, J., Lupton, M. J., & Toth, E. (1988). *The curse: A cultural history of menstruation* (2nd ed.). Urbana, IL: University of Illinois Press.

De las Fuentes, C., & Vasquez, M. J. T. (1999). Immigrant adolescent girls of color: Facing American challenges. In N. G. Johnson, M. C. Roberts, & J. Worell (Eds.), *Beyond appearance: A new look at adolescent girls* (pp. 131–150). Washington, DC: American Psychological Association.

Delk, J. L., Madden, R. B., Livingston, M., & Ryan, T. T. (1986). Adult perceptions of the infant as a function of gender labeling and observer gender. *Sex Roles, 15*, 527–534.

Dello Stritto, M. E., & Guzmán, B. L. (2001, Spring). Media images of female sexuality: The impact on women's psychological health. *Community Psychologist*, p. 30.

Delmas, P. D., et al. (1997). Effects of raloxifene on bone mineral density, serum cholesterol concentration, and uterine endometrium in postmenopausal women. *New England Journal of Medicine, 337*, 1641–1647.

DeLoache, J., & Gottlieb, A. (Eds.). (2000). *A world of babies.* New York: Cambridge University Press.

DeLorey, C. (1992). Differing perspectives of menopause: An attribution theory approach. In A. J. Dan & L. L. Lewis (Eds.), *Menstrual health in women's lives* (pp. 198–205). Urbana, IL: University of Illinois Press.

Demarest, J., & Glinos, F. (1992). Gender and sex-role differences in young adult reactions towards "newborns" in a pretend situation. *Psychological Reports, 71*, 727–737.

Denham, S. A. (1998). *Emotional development in young children.* New York: Guilford.

Denmark, F. L. (2002, March). *Myths of aging.* Paper presented at the annual convention of the Southeastern Psychological Association.

Denton, T. C. (1990). Bonding and supportive relationships among black professional women: Rituals of restoration. *Journal of Organizational Behavior, 11*, 447–457.

De Puy, C., & Dovitch, D. (1997). *The healing choice: Your guide to emotional recovery after an abortion.* New York: Simon & Schuster.

de Rivera, J. (2000). Sound advice in muddied water [Review of the book *Recollections of sexual abuse: Treatment principles and guidelines*]. *Contemporary Psychology, 45*, 212–215.

DeRubeis, R. J., Tang, T. Z., & Beck, A. T. (2001). Cognitive therapy. In K. S. Dobson (Ed.), *Handbook of cognitive-behavioral therapies* (2nd ed., pp. 349–392). New York: Guilford.

Desmarais, S., & Curtis, J. (1997a). Gender and perceived pay entitlement: Testing for effects of experience with income. *Journal of Personality and Social Psychology, 72*, 141–150.

Desmarais, S., & Curtis, J. (1997b). Gender differences in pay histories and views on pay entitlement among university students. *Sex Roles, 37*, 623–642.

Desmarais, S., & Curtis, J. (2001). Gender and perceived income entitlement among full-time workers: Analysis for Canadian national samples, 1984 and 1994. *Basic and Applied Social Psychology, 23*, 157–168.

Desrochers, S. (1995). What types of men are most attractive and most repulsive to women? *Sex Roles, 32*, 375–391.

Deutsch, F. M. (1999). *Halving it all: How equally shared parenting works.* Cambridge, MA: Harvard University Press.

Deutsch, F. M. (2001). Equally shared parenting. *Current Directions in Psychological Science, 10*, 25–28.

Deutsch, F. M., & Saxon, S. E. (1998a). The double standard of praise and criticism for mothers and fathers. *Psychology of Women Quarterly, 22*, 665–683.

Deutsch, F. M., & Saxon, S. E. (1998b). Traditional ideologies, nontraditional lives. *Sex Roles, 38*, 331–362.

A devastated continent. (2000, January 1). *Newsweek,* p. 41.

Devereaux, M. S. (1993, Autumn). Time use of Canadians in 1992. *Canadian Social Trends,* pp. 13–35.

De Wolff, A. (2000, Fall). The face of globalization: Women working poor in Canada. *Canadian Woman Studies/Les cahiers de la femme,* pp. 54–59.

DeZolt, D. M., & Hull, S. H. (2001). Classroom and school climate. In J. Worell (Ed.), *Encyclopedia of women and gender* (pp. 257–264). San Diego: Academic Press.

Dhruvarajan, V. (1992). Conjugal power among first generation Hindu Asian Indians in a Canadian city. *International Journal of Sociology of the Family, 22,* 1–33.

Diamond, L. M. (1998). Development of sexual orientation among adolescent and young adult women. *Developmental Psychology, 34,* 1085–1095.

Diamond, L. M. (2000). Sexual identity, attractions, and behavior among young sexual-minority women over a 2-year period. *Developmental Psychology, 36,* 241–250.

Diamond, L. M. (2002). What we got wrong about sexual identity development: Unexpected findings from a longitudinal study of young women. In A. Omoto & H. Kurtzman (Eds.), *Recent research on sexual orientation.* Washington, DC: American Psychological Association.

Diamond, L. M., Savin-Williams, R. C., & Dubé, E. M. (1999). Sex, dating, passionate friendships, and romance: Intimate peer relations among lesbian, gay, and bisexual adolescents. In W. Furman, C. Feiring, & B. B. Brown (Eds.), *Contemporary perspectives on adolescent romantic relationships.* New York: Oxford University Press.

Diamond, M. (1996). Prenatal predisposition and the clinical management of some pediatric conditions. *Journal of Sex and Marital Therapy, 22,* 139–147.

Diamond, M., & Sigmundson, H. K. (1999). Sex reassignment at birth. In S. J. Ceci & S. M. Williams (Eds.), *The nature-nurture debate* (pp. 57–75). Malden, MA: Blackwell.

Di Caccavo, A., & Reid, F. (1998). The influence of attitudes toward male and female patients on treatment decisions in general practice. *Sex Roles, 38,* 613–629.

Diekman, A. B., & Eagly, A. H. (2000). Stereotypes as dynamic constructs: Women and men of the past, present, and future. *Personality and Social Psychology Bulletin, 26,* 1171–1188.

Diekman, A. B., McDonald, M., & Gardner, W. L. (2000). Love means never having to be careful: The relationship between reading romance novels and safe sex behavior. *Psychology of Women Quarterly, 24,* 179–188.

Diener, M. (2000). Gift from the gods: A Balinese guide to early child rearing. In J. DeLoache & A. Gottlieb (Eds.), *A world of babies: Imagined child-care guides for seven societies* (pp. 91–116). New York: Cambridge University Press.

Dietz, T. L. (1998). An examination of violence and gender role portrayals in video games: Implications for gender socialization and aggressive behavior. *Sex Roles, 38,* 425–442.

Dillon, K. (2000). Sizing myself up: Tales of a plus-size model. In O. Edut (Ed.), *Body outlaws: Young women write about body image and identity* (pp. 232–239). Seattle: Seal Press.

DiMatteo, M. R., & Kahn, K. L. (1997). Psychosocial aspects of childbirth. In S. J. Gallant, G. P. Keita, & R. Royak-Schaler (Eds.), *Health care for women: Psychological, social, and behavioral influences* (pp. 175–186). Washington, DC: American Psychological Association.

Dindia, K., & Allen, M. (1992). Sex differences in self-disclosure: A meta-analysis. *Psychological Bulletin, 112,* 106–124.

Dinges, N. G., & Cherry, D. (1995). Symptom expression and the use of mental health services among American ethnic minorities. In J. F. Aponte, R. Y. Rivers, & J. Wohl (Eds.), *Psychological interventions and cultural diversity* (pp. 40–56). Boston: Allyn & Bacon.

Dion, K. K., & Dion, K. L. (1998). Individualistic and collectivistic perspectives on gender and the cultural context of love and intimacy. In D. L. Anselmi & A. L. Law (Eds.), *Questions of gender* (pp. 520–531). New York: McGraw-Hill.

Dion, K. K., & Dion, K. L. (2001a). Gender and cultural adaptation in immigrant families. *Journal of Social Issues, 57,* 511–521.

Dion, K. K., & Dion, K. L. (2001b). Gender and relationships. In R. K. Unger (Ed.), *Handbook of the psychology of women and gender* (pp. 256–271). New York: Wiley.

Dion, K. L., & Dion, K. K. (1993). Gender and ethnocultural comparisons in styles of love. *Psychology of Women Quarterly, 17,* 463–473.

Dion, K. L., & Giordano, C. (1990). Ethnicity and sex as correlates of depression symptoms in a Canadian university sample. *International Journal of Social Psychiatry, 36,* 30–41.

Dionne, M., et al. (1995). Feminist ideology as a predictor of body dissatisfaction in women. *Sex Roles, 33,* 277–287.

Division 44/Committee on Lesbian, Gay, and Bisexual Concerns. (2000). Guidelines for psychotherapy with lesbian, gay, and bisexual clients. *American Psychologist, 55,* 1440–1451.

Dodd, E. H., Giuliano, T. A., Boutell, J. M., & Moran, B. A. (2001). Respected or rejected: Perceptions of women who confront sexist remarks. *Sex Roles, 45,* 567–577.

Dodson, J. E. (1997). Conceptualizations of African American families. In H. P. McAdoo (Ed.), *Black families* (3rd ed., pp. 67–82). Thousand Oaks, CA: Sage.

Dodson, L. (1998). *Don't call us out of name.* Boston: Beacon Press.

Donovan, P. (2000, March). Game designed with girls in mind. *UUP Voice,* p. 11.

Doosje, B., Rojahn, K., & Fischer, A. (1999). Partner preferences as a function of gender, age, political orientation, and level of education. *Sex Roles, 40,* 45–60.

Dotterer, C. S. (1992, April 27). Physician tells of her struggle to leave abusive husband. *American Medical News,* p. 49.

Douglas, E. (2001, July/August). HIV/AIDS: A new report from CDC, the response from Congress, and psychology's role in the solution. *Psychological Science Agenda,* p. 12.

Dow, B. J. (1996). *Prime-time feminism.* Philadelphia: University of Pennsylvania Press.

Dowdall, G. W., Crawford, M., & Wechsler, H. (1998). Binge drinking among American college women. *Psychology of Women Quarterly, 22,* 705–715.

Dowling, C. (2000). *The frailty myth: Women approaching physical equality.* New York: Random House.

Doyle, J. A. (1995). *The male experience* (3rd ed.). Madison, WI: Brown & Benchmark.

Doyle, M. (1995). *The A–Z of non-sexist language.* London: The Women's Press.

Dreger, A. D. (1998). *Hermaphrodites and the medical invention of sex.* Cambridge, MA: Harvard University Press.

Driscoll, D. M., Kelly, J. R., & Henderson, W. L. (1998). Can perceivers identify likelihood to sexually harass? *Sex Roles, 38,* 557–588.

Drolet, M. (2001, December). The male-female wage gap. *Perspectives on Labour and Income,* pp. 5–13.

Drout, C. E. (1997). Professionals' and students' perceptions of abuse among married and unmarried cohabiting couples. *Journal of Social Behavior and Personality, 12,* 965–978.

Dryden, C. (1999). *Being married, doing gender.* London: Routledge.

Dubé, E. M., Savin-Williams, R. C., & Diamond, L. M. (2001). Intimacy development, gender, and ethnicity among sexual-minority youths. In A. R. D'Augelli & C. J. Patterson (Eds.), *Lesbian, gay, and bisexual identities and youth* (pp. 129–152). New York: Oxford University Press.

Duck, S., & Wright, P. H. (1993). Reexamining gender differences in same-gender friendships: A close look at two kinds of data. *Sex Roles, 28,* 709–727.

Duffy, J., Gunther, G., & Walters, L. (1997). Gender and mathematical problem solving. *Sex Roles, 37,* 477–494.

Duffy, J., Wareham, S., & Walsh, M. (2003). *Psychological consequences for high school students of having been sexually harassed.* Manuscript submitted for publication.

Duffy, J., Warren, K., & Walsh, M. (2001). Classroom interactions: Gender of teacher, gender of student, and classroom subject. *Sex Roles, 45,* 579–593.

Dugger, K. (1996). Social location and gender-role attitudes: A comparison of Black and White women. In E. N. Chow, D. Wilkinson, & M. B. Zinn (Eds.), *Race, class, and gender: Common bonds, different voices* (pp. 32–51). Thousand Oaks, CA: Sage.

Du Mont, J., & Parnis, D. (1999, Spring/Summer). Judging women: The pernicious effects of rape mythology. *Canadian Woman Studies/Les cahiers de la femme, 19,* 102–109.

Duncan, G. J., & Brooks-Gunn, J. (1997). Income effects across the life span: Integration and interpretation. In G. J. Duncan & J. Brooks-Gunn (Eds.), *Consequences of growing up poor* (pp. 596–610). New York: Russell Sage Foundation.

Dunn, D. (1996). Gender and earnings. In P. J. Dubeck & K. Borman (Eds.), *Women and work: A handbook* (pp. 61–63). New York: Garland.

Dunning, D., & Sherman, D. A. (1997). Stereotypes and tacit inference. *Journal of Personality and Social Psychology, 73,* 459–471.

Durkin, K., & Nugent, B. (1998). Kindergarten children's gender-role expectations for television actors. *Sex Roles, 38,* 387–402.

Eagly, A. H. (2001). Social role theory of sex differences and similarities. In J. Worell (Ed.), *Encyclopedia of women and gender* (pp. 1069–1078). San Diego: Academic Press.

Eagly, A. H. (In press). Prejudice: Toward a more inclusive understanding. In A. Eagly, R. M. Baron, & V. L. Hamilton (Eds.), *The social psychology of group identity and social conflict: Theory, application, and practice.* Washington, DC: American Psychological Association.

Eagly, A. H., & Crowley, M. (1986). Gender and helping behavior: A meta-analytic review of the social psychological literature. *Psychological Bulletin, 100,* 283–308.

Eagly, A. H., & Diekman, A. B. (2003). *The malleability of sex differences in response to changing social roles.* In L. G. Aspinwall & U. M. Staudinger (Eds.), *A psychology of human strengths.* Washington, DC: American Psychological Association.

Eagly, A. H., & Johannesen-Schmidt, M. C. (2001). The leadership styles of women and men. *Journal of Social Issues, 57,* 781–797.

Eagly, A. H., & Johnson, B. T. (1990). Gender and leadership style: A meta-analysis. *Psychological Bulletin, 108,* 233–256.

Eagly, A. H., & Karau, S. J. (1991). Gender and the emergence of leaders: A meta-analysis. *Journal of Personality and Social Psychology, 60,* 685–710.

Eagly, A. H., Karau, S. J., & Makhijani, M. G. (1995). Gender and the effectiveness of leaders: A meta-analysis. *Psychological Bulletin, 117,* 125–145.

Eagly, A. H., Makhijani, M. G., & Klonsky, B. G. (1992). Gender and the evaluation of leaders: A meta-analysis. *Psychological Bulletin, 111,* 3–22.

Eagly, A. H., Makhijani, M. G., & Klonsky, B. G. (1995). Gender and the effectiveness of leaders: A meta-analysis. *Psychological Bulletin, 117,* 125–145.

Eagly, A. H., & Mladinic, A. (1994). Are people prejudiced against women? Some answers from research on attitudes, gender stereotypes, and judgments of competence. In W. Stroebe & M. Hewstone (Eds.), *European Review of Social Psychology.* New York: Wiley.

Eagly, A. H., Mladinic, A., & Otto, S. (1991). Are women evaluated more favorably than men? An analysis of attitudes, beliefs, and emotions. *Psychology of Women Quarterly, 15,* 203–216.

Eagly, A. H., & Wood, W. (1991). Explaining sex differences in social behavior: A meta-analytic perspective. *Personality and Social Psychology Bulletin, 17,* 306–315.

Eagly, A. H., & Wood, W. (1999). The origins of sex differences in human behavior: Evolved dispositions versus social roles. *American Psychologist, 54,* 408–423.

Eagly, A. H., Wood, W., & Diekman, A. (2000). Social role theory of sex differences and similarities: A current appraisal. In T. Eckes & H. M. Trautner (Eds.), *The developmental social psychology of gender.* Mahwah, NJ: Erlbaum.

East, P. L., & Felice, M. E. (1996). *Adolescent pregnancy and parenting: Findings from a racially diverse sample.* Mahwah, NJ: Erlbaum.

Eberhardt, J. L., & Fiske, S. T. (1998). Affirmative action in theory and practice: Issues of power, ambiguity, and gender versus race. In D. L. Anselmi & A. L. Law (Eds.), *Questions of gender: Perspectives and paradoxes* (pp. 629–641). New York: McGraw-Hill.

Eccles, J. S. (1987). Gender roles and women's achievement-related decisions. *Psychology of Women Quarterly, 11,* 135–172.

Eccles, J. S. (1994). Understanding women's educational and occupational choices. *Psychology of Women Quarterly, 18,* 585–609.

Eccles, J. S. (1997). User-friendly science and mathematics: Can it interest girls and minorities in breaking through the middle school wall? In D. Johnson (Ed.), *Minorities and girls in school: Effects on achievement and performance* (pp. 65–104). Thousand Oaks, CA: Sage.

Eccles, J. S. (2001). Achievement. In J. Worell (Ed.), *Encyclopedia of women and gender* (pp. 43–53). San Diego: Academic Press.

Eccles, J. S., Adler, T., & Meece, J. L. (1984). Sex differences in achievement: A test of alternate theories. *Journal of Personality and Social Psychology, 46,* 26–43.

Eccles, J. S., Barber, B., & Jozefowicz, D. (1999). Linking gender to educational, occupational, and recreational choices: Applying the Eccles et al. model of achievement-related choices. In W. B. Swann Jr., J. H. Langlois, & L. A. Gilbert (Eds.), *Sexism and stereotypes in modern society* (pp. 153–192). Washington, DC: American Psychological Association.

Eccles, J. S., Jacobs, J. E., & Harold, R. D. (1990). Gender-role stereotypes, expectancy effects, and parents' socialization of gender differences. *Journal of Social Issues, 46,* 183–201.

Eccles, J. S., Wigfield, A., & Schiefele, U. (1998). Motivation to succeed. In W. Damon (Series Ed.) & N. Eisenberg (Volume Ed.), *Handbook of child psychology: Vol. 4. Social, emotional, and personality development* (pp. 1017–1095). New York: Wiley.

Eccles, J. S., et al. (1999). Self-evaluations of competence, task values, and self-esteem. In N. G. Johnson, M. C. Roberts, & J. Worell (Eds.), *Beyond appearance: A new look at adolescent girls* (pp. 53–83). Washington, DC: American Psychological Association.

Eccles, J. S., et al. (2000). Gender-roles socialization in the family: A longitudinal approach. In T. Eckes & H. M. Trautner (Eds.), *The developmental social psychology of gender* (pp. 333–360). Mahwah, NJ: Erlbaum.

Eccles (Parsons), J. S., Adler, T. F., & Kaczala, C. M. (1982). Socialization of achievement attitudes and beliefs: Parental influences. *Child Development, 53,* 310–321.

Eckes, T., & Trautner, H. M. (Eds.). (2000a). *The developmental social psychology of gender.* Mahwah, NJ: Erlbaum.

Eckes, T., & Trautner, H. M. (2000b). Developmental social psychology of gender: An integrative framework. In T. Eckes & H. M. Trautner (Eds.), *The developmental social psychology of gender* (pp. 3–32). Mahwah, NJ: Erlbaum.

Edelstein, L. N. (1999). *The art of midlife.* Westport, CT: Bergin & Garvey.

Edmondson, C. B., & Conger, J. C. (1995). The impact of mode of presentation on gender differences in social perception. *Sex Roles, 32,* 169–183.

Edwards, C. P., Knoche, L., & Kumuru, A. (2001). Play patterns and gender. In J. Worell (Ed.), *Encyclopedia of women and gender.* San Diego: Academic Press.

Edwards, N., & Sim-Jones, N. (1998). Smoking and smoking relapse during pregnancy and postpartum: Results of a qualitative study. *Birth, 25,* 94–100.

Edwards, T. M. (2000, August 28). Flying solo. *Time,* pp. 47–53.

Ehlers, T. B. (1993). Debunking marianismo: Economic vulnerability and survival strategies among Guatemalan wives. In M. Womack & J. Martl (Eds.), *The other fifty percent* (pp. 303–319). Prospect Heights, IL: Waveland Press.

Ehrenreich, B. (2001). *Nickel and dimed: On (not) getting by in America.* New York: Metropolitan Books.

Eisenberg, C. (1989). The changing demography of the medical profession. *New England Journal of Medicine, 321,* 1540–1544.

Eisenberg, N., Fabes, R., & Shea, C. (1989). Gender differences in empathy and prosocial moral reasoning: Empirical investigations. In M. M. Brabeck (Ed.), *Who cares? Theory, research, and educational implications of the ethic of care* (pp. 127–143). New York: Praeger.

Eisenberg, N., & Lennon, R. (1983). Sex differences in empathy and related capacities. *Psychological Bulletin, 94,* 100–131.

Eisenberg, N., Martin, C. L., & Fabes, R. A. (1996). Gender development and gender effects. In D. C. Berliner & R. C. Calfee (Eds.), *Handbook of educational psychology* (pp. 358–396). New York: Macmillan.

Eisenberg, S. (1998). *We'll call you if we need you: Experiences of women working construction.* Ithaca, NY: Cornell University Press.

Eisenstat, S. A., & Bancroft, L. (1999). Domestic violence. *New England Journal of Medicine, 341,* 886–892.

Eisler, R. (1996). *Sacred pleasure: Sex, myth, and the politics of the body.* New York: HarperCollins.

El-Bushra, J. (2000). Rethinking gender and development practice for the twenty-first century. In C. Sweetman (Ed.), *Gender in the 21st century* (pp. 55–62). Oxford, England: Oxfam.

Eliason, M. J. (1995). Accounts of sexual identity formation in heterosexual students. *Sex Roles, 32,* 821–834.

Ellis, L. (1996). Theories of homosexuality. In R. C. Savin-Williams & K. Cohen (Eds.), *The lives of lesbians, gays, and bisexuals: Children to adults* (pp. 11–34). Fort Worth, TX: Harcourt Brace.

Ellis, L., & Ebertz, L. (Eds.). (1997). *Sexual orientation: Toward biological understanding.* Westport, CT: Praeger.

Ellison, C. R. (2001). A research inquiry into some American women's sexual concerns and problems. In E. Kaschak & L. Tiefer (Eds.), *A new view of women's sexual problems* (pp. 147–159). New York: Haworth.

Ellsberg, M., et al. (1998). *¿Cómo atender a las mujeres que viven situaciones de violencia doméstica?* [How to attend to women who live in violent domestic situations.] Managua, Nicaragua: Arco Producciones.

Ellsberg, M., et al. (1999). Domestic violence and emotional distress among Nicaraguan women. Results from a population-based study. *American Psychologist, 54,* 30–36.

Elton, S. (2000, February/March). Canada update. *Ms. Magazine,* p. 27.

Emans, S. J. (1997). Menarche and beyond: Do eating and exercise make a difference? *Pediatric Annals, 26,* S137–S141.

Eng, P. (1999). *Warrior lessons.* New York: Simon & Schuster.

England, P. (1992). *Comparable worth: Theories and evidence.* New York: Aldine de Gruyter.

Englander, A. (1997). *Dear Diary, I'm pregnant.* Toronto: Annick Press.

Enns, C. Z. (1997). *Feminist theories and feminist psychotherapies.* New York: Haworth.

Enns, C. Z. (2000). The politics and psychology of false memory syndrome. In J. C. Chrisler, C. Golden, & P. D. Rozee (Eds.), *Lectures on the psychology of women* (2nd ed., pp. 322–338). Boston: McGraw-Hill.

Enns, C. Z., & Sinacore, A. (2001). Feminist theories. In J. Worell (Ed.), *Encyclopedia of women and gender* (pp. 469–480). San Diego: Academic Press.

Erchick, D. B. (2001). Developing mathematical voice: Women reflecting on the adolescent years. In P. O'Reilly, E. M. Penn, & K. deMarrais (Eds.), *Educating young adolescent girls.* Mahwah, NJ: Erlbaum.

Erel, O., Oberman, Y., & Yirmiya, N. (2000). Maternal versus nonmaternal care and seven domains of children's development. *Psychological Bulletin, 126,* 727–747.

Erkut, S., Fields, J. P., Sing, R., & Marx, F. (1996). Diversity in girls' experiences: Feeling good about who you are. In B. J. R. Leadbeater & N. Way (Eds.), *Urban girls: Resisting stereotypes, creating identities* (pp. 53–64). New York: New York University Press.

Erkut, S., Marx, F., & Fields, J. P. (2001). A delicate balance: How teachers can support middle school girls' confidence and competence. In P. O'Reilly, E. M. Penn, & K. deMarrais (Eds.), *Educating young adolescent girls* (pp. 83–101). Mahwah, NJ: Erlbaum.

Erkut, S., Marx, F., Fields, J. P., & Sing, R. (1999). Raising confident and competent girls: One size does not fit all. In L. A. Peplau, S. C. DeBro, R. C. Veniegas, & P. L. Taylor (Eds.), *Gender, culture, and ethnicity: Current research about women and men* (pp. 83–101). Mountain View, CA: Mayfield.

Ernsberger, P., & Koletsky, R. J. (1999). Biomedical rationale for a wellness approach to obesity: An alternative to a focus on weight loss. *Journal of Social Issues, 55,* 221–260.

Espín, O. M. (1994). Feminist approaches. In L. Comas-Díaz & B. Greene (Eds.), *Women of color: Integrating ethnic and gender identities in psychotherapy* (pp. 265–286). New York: Guilford.

Espín, O. M. (1996). Immigrant and refugee lesbians. In E. D. Rothblum & L. A. Bond (Eds.), *Preventing heterosexism and homophobia* (pp. 174–183). Thousand Oaks, CA: Sage.

Espín, O. M. (1997). *Latina realities: Essays on healing, migration, and sexuality.* Boulder, CO: Westview Press.

Espín, O. M. (1999). *Women crossing boundaries: A psychology of immigration and transformations of sexuality.* New York: Routledge.

Espinosa, P. (1997, October 3). The rich tapestry of Hispanic America is virtually invisible on commercial TV. *Chronicle of Higher Education,* p. B7.

Esterberg, K. G. (1996). Gay cultures, gay communities: The social organization of lesbians, gay men, and bisexuals. In R. C. Savin-Williams & K. Cohen (Eds.), *The lives of lesbians, gays, and bisexuals: Children to adults* (pp. 375–392). Fort Worth, TX: Harcourt Brace.

Etaugh, C. A. (1993). Maternal employment: Effects on children. In J. Frankel (Ed.), *Employed mothers and the family context* (pp. 68–88). New York: Springer.

Etaugh, C. A., & Bridges, J. S. (2001). Midlife transitions. In J. Worell (Ed.), *Encyclopedia of women and aging* (pp. 759–769). San Diego: Academic Press.

Etaugh, C. A., & Foresman, E. (1983). Evaluations of competence as a function of sex and marital status. *Sex Roles, 9,* 759–765.

Etaugh, C. A., & Hoehn, S. (1995). Perceiving women: Effects of marital, parental, and occupational sex-typing variables. *Perceptual and Motor Skills, 80,* 320–322.

Etaugh, C. A., & Liss, M. B. (1992). Home, school, and playroom: Training grounds for adult gender roles. *Sex Roles, 26,* 129–147.

Etaugh, C. A., & Riley, S. (1983). Evaluating competence of women and men: Effects of marital and parental status and occupational sex-typing. *Sex Roles, 9,* 943–952.

Ethier, K., & Deaux, K. (1990). Hispanics in ivy: Assessing identity and perceived threat. *Sex Roles, 22,* 427–460.

Etzkowitz, H., Kemelgor, C., & Uzzi, B. (2000). *Athena unbound: The advancement of women in science and technology.* New York: Cambridge University Press.

Evans, L., & Davies, K. (2000). No sissy boys here: A content analysis of the representation of masculinity in elementary school reading textbooks. *Sex Roles, 42,* 255–270.

Evans, N. J., & D'Augelli, A. R. (1996). Lesbians, gay men, and bisexual people in college. In R. C. Savin-Williams & K. Cohen (Eds.), *The lives of lesbians, gays, and bisexuals: Children to adults* (pp. 201–226). Fort Worth, TX: Harcourt Brace.

Evelyn, J. (2000, August 3). Double standard reform. *Black Issues in Higher Education*, p. 6.

Ex, C. T. G. M., & Janssens, J. M. A. M. (1998). Maternal influences on daughters' gender role attitudes. *Sex Roles, 38,* 171–186.

Ex, C. T. G. M., & Janssens, J. M. A. M. (2000). Young females' images of motherhood. *Sex Roles, 43,* 865–890.

Fabes, R., & Martin, C. L. (2000). *Exploring child development: Transactions and transformations.* Boston: Allyn & Bacon.

Facio, E. (1997). Chicanas and aging: Toward definitions of womanhood. In J. M. Coyle (Ed.), *Handbook on women and aging* (pp. 335–350). Westport, CT: Greenwood Press.

Facteau, J. D., & Dobbins, G. H. (1996). Sex bias in performance evaluations. In P. J. Dubeck & K. Borman (Eds.), *Women and work: A handbook* (pp. 334–338). New York: Garland.

Facts on working women. (1998). In R. Breden (Ed.). *Perspectives: Women's studies* (pp. 3–6). Boulder, CO: Coursewise.

Fagot, B. I. (1978). The influence of sex of child on parental reactions to toddler children. *Child Development, 49,* 459–465.

Fagot, B. I. (1995). Psychological and cognitive determinants of early gender-role development. *Annual Review of Sex Research, 6,* 1–31.

Fagot, B. I., & Leinbach, M. D. (1995). Gender knowledge in egalitarian and traditional families. *Sex Roles, 32,* 513–526.

Fagot, B. I., & Rodgers, C. (1998). Gender identity. In H. Friedman (Ed.), *Encyclopedia of mental health* (Vol. 2, pp. 267–276). San Diego: Academic Press.

Fagot, B. I., Rodgers, C. S., & Leinbach, M. D. (2000). Theories of gender socialization. In T. Eckes & H. M. Trautner (Eds.), *The developmental social psychology of gender* (pp. 65–89). Mahwah, NJ: Erlbaum.

Falco, K. (1998). *Reclaiming our lives after breast and gynecologic cancer.* Northvale, NJ: Jason Aronson.

Faludi, S. (1991). *Backlash: The undeclared war against American women.* New York: Crown.

Faludi, S. (1995, March/April). "I'm not a feminist, but I play one on TV." *Ms. Magazine,* pp. 31–39.

Fausto-Sterling, A. (1985). *Myths of gender: Biological theories about women and men.* New York: Basic Books.

Fausto-Sterling, A. (1993, March/April). The five sexes: Why male and female are not enough. *The Sciences,* pp. 20–24.

Fausto-Sterling, A. (2000). *Sexing the body: Gender politics and the construction of sexuality.* New York: Basic Books.

Favreau, O. E. (1993). Do the *N*'s justify the means? Null hypothesis testing applied to sex and other differences. *Canadian Psychology/Psychologie canadienne, 34,* 64–78.

Favreau, O. E. (1997). Sex and gender comparisons: Does null hypothesis testing create a false dichotomy? *Feminism and Psychology, 7,* 63–81.

Favreau, O. E., & Everett, J. C. (1996). A tale of two tails. *American Psychologist, 51,* 268–269.

Feingold, A. (1988). Cognitive gender differences are disappearing. *American Psychologist, 43,* 95–103.

Feingold, A. (1993). Cognitive gender differences: A developmental perspective. *Sex Roles, 29,* 91–112.

Feingold, A. (1994). Gender differences in personality: A meta-analysis. *Psychological Bulletin, 116,* 429–456.

Feiring, C. (1996). Concepts of romance in 15-year-old adolescents. *Journal of Research on Adolescents, 6,* 181–200.

Feiring, C. (1998). Gender identity and the development of romantic relationships in adolescence. In W. Furman, B. B. Brown, & C. Feiring (Eds.), *Contemporary perspectives in adolescent romantic relationships.* Cambridge, England: Cambridge University Press.

Feiring, C. (1999a). Gender identity and the development of romantic relationships in adolescence. In W. Furman, B. B. Brown, & C. Feiring (Eds.), *The development of romantic relationships in adolescence* (pp. 211–232). New York: Cambridge University Press.

Feiring, C. (1999b). Other-sex friendship networks and the development of romantic relationships in adolescence. *Journal of Youth and Adolescence, 28,* 495–512.

Feldman, S. (1999). "No more dinners, only lunches": Older widowed women relating to the world. In M. Poole & S. Feldman (Eds.), *A certain age: Women growing older* (pp. 165–181). St. Leonards, New South Wales, Australia: Allen & Unwin.

Ferguson, S. J. (2000). Challenging traditional marriage: Never married Chinese American and Japanese American women. *Gender and Society, 14,* 136–159.

Fernald, J. L. (1995). Interpersonal heterosexism. In B. Lott & D. Maluso (Eds.), *The social psychology of interpersonal discrimination* (pp. 80–117). New York: Guilford.

Ferree, M. M. (1994). Negotiating household roles and responsibilities: Resistance, conflict, and change. In M. R. Stevenson (Ed.), *Gender roles through the life span* (pp. 203–221). Muncie, IN: Ball State University Press.

Fiala, S. E., Giuliano, T. A., Remlinger, N. M., & Braithwaite, L. C. (1999). *Journal of Applied Social Psychology, 29,* 2164–2176.

Field, T. (1998). Maternal cocaine use and fetal development. In E. A. Blechman & K. D. Brownell (Eds.), *Behavioral medicine and women: A comprehensive handbook* (pp. 27–30). New York: Guilford.

Fields, C. D. (2002, January 31). Sexual responsibility on campus. *Black Issues in Higher Education,* pp. 18–24.

Fields, J., & Casper, L. M. (2001). *America's families and living arrangements: Population characteristics* (Current Population Reports, P20-537). Washington, DC: U.S. Census Bureau.

Fiese, B. H., & Skillman, G. (2000). Gender differences in family stories: Moderating influence of parent gender role and child gender. *Sex Roles, 43,* 267–283.

Figert, A. E. (1996). *Women and the ownership of PMS: The structuring of a psychiatric disorder.* New York: Aldine de Gruyter.

Fincham, F. D., & Beach, S. R. H. (1999). Conflict in marriage: Implications for working with couples. *Annual Review of Psychology, 50,* 47–77.

Fincham, F. D., & Bradbury, T. N. (1990). *The psychology of marriage: Basic issues and applications.* New York: Guilford.

Fincham, F. D., & Bradbury, T. N. (1992). Assessing attributions in marriage: The relationship attribution measure. *Journal of Personality and Social Psychology, 62,* 457–468.

Fincham, F. D., et al. (1997). Marital satisfaction and depression: Different causal relationships for men and women? *Psychological Science, 8,* 351–357.

Fine, M. (1997a). Coping with rape: Critical perspectives on consciousness. In M. Crawford & R. Unger (Ed.), *In our own words: Readings on the psychology of women and gender* (pp. 152–164). New York: McGraw-Hill.

Fine, M. (1997b). *Off White: Readings on race, power, and society.* New York: Routledge.

Fine, M. (2001, August). *The presence of an absence.* Paper presented at the annual convention of the American Psychological Association, San Francisco.

Fine, M., & Carney, S. (2001). Women, gender, and the law: Toward a feminist rethinking of responsibility. In R. K. Unger (Ed.), *Handbook of the psychology of women and gender* (pp. 388–409). New York: Wiley.

Fine, M., Roberts, R., & Weis, L. (2000). Refusing the betrayal: Latinas redefining gender, sexuality, culture and resistance. *Review of Education/Psychology/Cultural Studies, 22,* 87–119.

Fine, M. A. (2000). Divorce and single parenting. In C. Hendrick & S. S. Hendrick (Eds.), *Close relationships* (pp. 138–152). Thousand Oaks, CA: Sage.

Fine, S. (2001, May 8). Anti-abortion lectures incense school parents. *Toronto Globe and Mail,* pp. A1, A4.

Fingerman, K. L. (2001). *Aging mothers and their adult daughters: A study in mixed emotions.* New York: Springer.

Finlay, B., & Love, G. D. (1998). Gender differences in reasoning about military intervention. *Psychology of Women Quarterly, 22,* 481–485.

Firestone, J. M., & Harris, R. J. (2003). Personal responses to structural problems: Organizational climate and sexual harassment in the U.S. military, 1988 and 1995. *Gender, Work, and Organization, 10.*

Fischhoff, B. (1992). Giving advice: Decision theory perspectives on sexual assault. *American Psychologist, 47,* 577–588.

Fischman, G. E. (2000). *Imagining teachers: Rethinking gender dynamics in teacher education.* Lanham, MD: Rowman & Littlefield.

Fishel, A. H. (1995). Mental health. In C. I. Fogel & N. F. Woods (Eds.), *Women's health care: A comprehensive handbook* (pp. 323–362). Thousand Oaks, CA: Sage.

Fisher-Thompson, D. (1990). Adult sex-typing of children's toys. *Sex Roles, 23,* 291–303.

Fisher-Thompson, D. (1993). Adult toy purchases for children: Factors affecting sex-typed toy selection. *Journal of Applied Developmental Psychology, 14,* 385–406.

Fisher-Thompson, D., & Burke, T. A. (1998). Experimenter influences and children's cross-gender behavior. *Sex Roles, 39,* 669–684.

Fisher-Thompson, D., Sausa, A. D., & Wright, T. E. (1995). Toy selection for children: Personality and toy request influences. *Sex Roles, 33,* 239–255.

Fiske, S. T. (1993). Social cognition and social perception. *Annual Review of Psychology, 44,* 155–194.

Fiske, S. T., Lin, M., & Neuberg, S. L. (1999). The continuum model ten years later. In S. Chaiken & Y. Trope (Eds.), *Dual-process theories in social psychology* (pp. 231–254). New York: Guilford.

Fiske, S. T., & Stevens, L. E. (1993). What's so special about sex? Gender stereotyping and discrimination. In S. Oskamp & M. Costanzo (Eds.), *Gender issues in contemporary society* (pp. 173–196). Newbury Park, CA: Sage.

Fiske, S. T., et al. (1991). Social science research on trial: Use of sex stereotyping research in *Price Waterhouse v. Hopkins. American Psychologist, 46,* 1049–1060.

Fiske, S. T., et al. (1993). Accuracy and objectivity on behalf of the APA. *American Psychologist, 48,* 55–56.

Fitch, R. H., Cowell, P. E., & Denenberg, V. H. (1998). The female phenotype: Nature's default? *Developmental Neuropsychology, 14,* 213–231.

Fitzgerald, L. F., Collinsworth, L. L., & Harned, M. S. (2001). Sexual harassment. In J. Worell (Ed.), *Encyclopedia of women and gender* (pp. 991–1004). San Diego: Academic Press.

Fitzgerald, L. F., & Rounds, J. (1994). Women and work: Theory encounters reality. In W. B. Walsh & S. H. Osipow (Eds.), *Career counseling for women* (pp. 327–353). Hillsdale, NJ: Erlbaum.

Fivush, R. (1989). Exploring sex differences in the emotional content of mother-child conversations about the past. *Sex Roles, 20,* 675–691.

Fivush, R., Brotman, M. A., Buckner, J. P., & Goodman, S. H. (2000). Gender differences in parent-child emotion narratives. *Sex Roles, 42,* 233–253.

Fivush, R., & Buckner, J. P. (2000). Gender, sadness, and depression: The development of emotional focus through gendered discourse. In A. H. Fischer (Ed.), *Gender and emotion: Social psychological perspectives* (pp. 232–253). Cambridge, England: Cambridge University Press.

Flamm, B. L., Berwick, D. M., & Kabcenell, A. (1998). Reducing cesarean section rates safely: Lessons from a "breakthrough series" collaborative. *Birth, 25,* 117–127.

Flanders, L. (1997). *Real majority, media minority.* Monroe, ME: Common Courage Press.

Flannagan, D., & Perese, S. (1998). Emotional references in mother-daughter and mother-son dyads' conversations about school. *Sex Roles, 39,* 353–367.

Flannery-Schroeder, E. C., & Chrisler, J. C. (1996). Body esteem, eating attitudes, and gender-role orientation in three age groups of children: *Current Psychology, 15,* 235–248.

Flippen, C., & Tienda, M. (2000). Pathways to retirement: Patterns of labor force participation and labor market exit among the pre-retirement population by race, Hispanic origin, and sex. *Journal of Gerontology: Social Sciences, 55B,* S14–S27.

Flores, L. Y., & O'Brien, K. M. (2002). The career development of Mexican American adolescent women: A test of social cognitive career theory. *Journal of Counseling Psychology, 49,* 14–27.

Flores-Ortiz, Y. G. (1998). Voices from the couch: The co-creation of a Chicana psychology. In C. Trujillo (Ed.), *Living Chicana theory* (pp. 102–122). Berkeley, CA: Third Woman Press.

Foa, E. B. (1998). Rape and posttraumatic stress disorder. In K. A. Blechman & K. D. Brownell (Eds.), *Behavioral medicine and women: A comprehensive handbook* (pp. 742–746). New York: Guilford.

Foertsch, J., & Gernsbacher, M. A. (1997). In search of gender neutrality: Is singular *they* a cognitively efficient substitute for generic *he? Psychological Science, 8,* 106–111.

Fontes, L. A. (Ed.). (1995). *Sexual abuse in nine North American cultures.* Thousand Oaks, CA: Sage.

Fontes, L. A. (2001). The new view and Latina sexualities: *Pero no soy una máquina!* In E. Kaschak & L. Tiefer (Eds.), *A new view of women's sexual problems* (pp. 33–37). New York: Haworth.

Ford, T. (1999). *Becoming multicultural: Personal and social construction through critical teaching.* New York: Falmer Press.

Foubert, J. D., & Sholley, B. K. (1996). Effects of gender role, and individualized trust on self-disclosure. *Journal of Social Behavior and Personality, 11,* 277–288.

Fouts, B., & Knapp, J. (2001). A sexual assault education and risk reduction workshop for college freshmen. In A. J. Ottens & K. Hotelling (Eds.), *Sexual violence on campus: Policies, programs, and perspectives* (pp. 98–119). New York: Springer.

Fouts, G., & Burggraf, K. (1999). Television situation comedies: Female body images and verbal reinforcements. *Sex Roles, 40,* 473–481.

Fox, A. (1991). Development of a bisexual identity: Understanding the process. In L. Hutchins & L. Kaahumanu (Eds.), *Bi any other name: Bisexual people speak out.* Boston: Alyson Publications.

Fox, R. C. (1996). Bisexuality in perspective: A review of theory and research. In B. A. Firestein (Ed.), *Bisexuality: The psychology and politics of an invisible minority* (pp. 3–50). Thousand Oaks, CA: Sage.

Fox, R. C. (1997). Understanding bisexuality. *Society for the Psychological Study of Men and Masculinity Bulletin, 2*(4), 13–14.

Fox, R. F. (2000). *Harvesting minds: How TV commercials control kids.* Westport, CT: Praeger.

Francisco, P. W. (1999). *Telling: A memoir of rape and recovery.* New York: HarperCollins.

Frank, A. (1972). *The diary of a young girl.* New York: Pocket Books.

Frank, E., Brogan, D., & Schiffman, M. (1998). Prevalence and correlates of harassment among U.S. women physicians. *Archives of Internal Medicine, 158,* 352–358.

Franks, F., & Faux, S. A. (1990). Depression, stress, mastery, and social resources in four ethnocultural women's groups. *Research in Nursing and Health, 13,* 283–292.

Fraser, L. (1997, July/August). Fear of fat: Why images of overweight women are taboo. *Extra!,* pp. 22–23.

Fredrickson, B. L., & Roberts, T. (1997). Objectification theory: Toward understanding women's lived experiences and mental health. *Psychology of Women Quarterly, 21,* 173–206.

Freed, A. F. (1996). Language and gender research in an experimental setting. In V. L. Bergvall, J. M. Bing, & A. F. Freed (Eds.), *Rethinking language and gender research: Theory and Practice* (pp. 54–76). New York: Longman.

Freedman, E. B. (2002). *No turning back: The history of feminism and the future of women.* New York: Ballantine.

French, M. (1992). *The war against women.* New York: Summit Books.

Frey, C., & Hoppe-Graff, S. (1994). Serious and playful aggression in Brazilian girls and boys. *Sex Roles, 30,* 249–268.

Freyd, J. J. (1996). *Betrayal trauma: The logic of forgetting childhood abuse.* Cambridge, MA: Harvard University Press.

Freyd, J. J. (1997). Violations of power, adaptive blindness, and betrayal trauma theory. *Feminism and Psychology, 7,* 22–32.

Freyd, J. J., & DePrince, A. P. (Eds.). (2001). *Trauma and cognitive science.* New York: Haworth.

Freyd, J. J., & Quina, K. (2000). Feminist ethics in the practice of science: The contested memory controversy as an example. In M. M. Brabeck (Ed.), *Practicing feminist ethics in psychology* (pp. 101–

123). Washington, DC: American Psychological Association.

Fried-Buchalter, S. (1997). Fear of success, fear of failure, and the imposter phenomenon among male and female marketing managers. *Sex Roles, 37,* 847–859.

Friedman, H. S., et al. (1995). Psychosocial and behavioral predictors of longevity. *American Psychologist, 50,* 69–78.

Frieze, I. H., & McHugh, M. C. (Eds.). (1997). Measuring beliefs about appropriate roles for women and men [Special issue]. *Psychology of Women Quarterly, 21*(1).

Frigoletto, F. D., Jr., et al. (1995). A clinical trial of active management of labor. *New England Journal of Medicine, 333,* 745–750.

Fritz, H. L., & Helgeson, V. S. (1998). Distinctions of unmitigated communion from communion: Self-neglect and overinvolvement with others. *Journal of Personality and Social Psychology, 75,* 121–140.

Frodi, A., & Ahnlund, K. (1995). *Gender differences in the vulnerability to depression.* Paper presented at the annual convention of the Eastern Psychological Association, Boston.

Frodi, A., Macaulay, J., & Thome, P. R. (1977). Are women always less aggressive than men? A review of the experimental literature. *Psychological Bulletin, 84,* 634–660.

Frome, P. M., & Eccles, J. S. (1998). Parents' influence on children's achievement-related perceptions. *Journal of Personality and Social Psychology, 74,* 435–452.

Funder, D. C. (2001). Personality. *Annual Review of Psychology, 52,* 197–221.

Funderburk, J. R. (2001). Group counseling for survivors of sexual assault. In A. J. Ottens & K. Hotelling (Eds.), *Sexual violence on campus: Policies, programs, and perspectives* (pp. 254–282). New York: Springer.

Funk, J. B., & Buchman, D. D. (1996). Children's perceptions of gender differences in social approval for playing electronic games. *Sex Roles, 35,* 219–231.

Furman, W., Brown, B. B., & Feiring, C. (Eds.). (1999). *The development of romantic relationships in adolescence.* New York: Cambridge University Press.

Furnham, A. (2000). Parents' estimates of their own and their children's multiple intelligences. *British Journal of Developmental Psychology, 18,* 583–594.

Furnham, A., Abramsky, S., & Gunter, B. (1997). A cross-cultural content analysis of children's television advertisements. *Sex Roles, 37,* 91–99.

Furnham, A., & Kirkcaldy, B. (1997). Age and sex differences in health beliefs and behaviours. *Psychological Reports, 80,* 63–66.

Furnham, A., & Mak, T. (1999). Sex-role stereotyping in television commercials: A review and comparison of fourteen studies done on five continents over 25 years. *Sex Roles, 41,* 413–437.

Furnham, A., Mak, T., & Tanidjojo, L. (2000). An Asian perspective on the portrayal of men and women in television advertisements: Studies from Hong Kong and Indonesian television. *Journal of Applied Social Psychology, 30,* 2341–2364.

Furnham, A., Rakow, T., Sarmany-Schuller, I., & De Fruyt, F. (1999). European differences in self-perceived multiple intelligences. *European Psychologist, 4,* 131–138.

Furnham, A., & Rawles, R. (1995). Sex differences in the estimation of intelligence. *Journal of Social Behavior and Personality, 10,* 741–748.

Furnham, A., & Singh, A. (1986). Memory for information about sex differences. *Sex Roles, 15,* 479–486.

Furnham, A., & Skae, E. (1997). Changes in the stereotypical portrayal of men and women in British television advertisements. *European Psychologist, 2,* 44–51.

Furnham, A., & Thomson, L. (1999). Gender role stereotyping in advertisements on two British radio stations. *Sex Roles, 40,* 153–165.

Furumoto, L. (1996, August). *Reflections on gender and the character of American psychology.* Paper presented at the annual convention of the American Psychological Association, Toronto, Canada.

Futterman, L. A., & Jones, J. E. (1998). *The PMS and perimenopause sourcebook.* Los Angeles: Lowell House.

Gadsden, V. L. (1999). Black families in intergenerational and cultural perspective. In M. E. Lamb (Ed.), *Parenting and child development in "nontraditional" families* (pp. 221–246). Mahwah, NJ: Erlbaum.

Gaeddert, W. P. (1987). The relationship of gender, gender-related traits, and achievement orientation to achievement attributions: A study of subject-selected accomplishments. *Journal of Personality, 55,* 687–710.

Gahagan, J., & Loppie, C. (2001, Summer/Fall). Counting pills or counting on pills? What HIV+ women have to say about antiretroviral therapy. *Canadian Woman Studies/Les cahiers de la femme, 21,* 118–123.

Galea, L. A. M., & Kimura, D. (1993). Sex differences in route-learning. *Personality and Individual Differences, 14,* 53–65.

Galinsky, E., & Bond, J. T. (1996). Work and family: The experiences of mothers and fathers in the U.S. labor force. In C. Costello & B. K. Krimgold (Eds.), *The American woman, 1996–97: Women and work.* New York: W. W. Norton.

Gallaher, P. E. (1992). Individual differences in nonverbal behavior: Dimensions of style. *Journal of Personality and Social Psychology, 63,* 133–145.

Gan, S. C., et al. (2000). Treatment of acute myocardial infarction and 30-day mortality among women and men. *New England Journal of Medicine, 343,* 8–15.

Gannon, L., & Ekstrom, B. (1993). Attitudes toward menopause: The influence of sociocultural paradigms. *Psychology of Women Quarterly, 17,* 275–288.

Gannon, L. R. (1999). *Women and aging: Transcending the myths.* New York: Routledge.

Ganong, L. H., & Coleman, M. (1995). The content of mother stereotypes. *Sex Roles, 32,* 495–512.

Ganong, L. H., & Coleman, M. (1999). *Changing families, changing responsibilities: Family obligations following divorce and remarriage.* Mahwah, NJ: Erlbaum.

Garber, M. (1995). *Vice versa: Bisexuality and the eroticism of everyday life.* New York: Simon & Schuster.

Garcia, A. M. (1991). The development of Chicana feminist discourse, 1970–1980. In J. Lorber & S. A. Farrell (Eds.), *The social construction of gender* (pp. 269–287). Newbury Park, CA: Sage.

Garcia, A. M. (1995). The development of Chicana feminist discourse, 1970–1980. In A. S. López (Ed.), *Latina issues* (pp. 359–380). New York: Garland.

García-Moreno, C., & Türmen, T. (1995). International perspectives on women's reproductive health. *Science, 269,* 790–792.

Gardiner, H. W., Mutter, J. D., & Kosmitzki, C. (1998). *Lives across cultures: Cross-cultural human development.* Boston: Allyn & Bacon.

Gardner, W., & Wilcox, B. L. (1993). Political intervention in scientific peer review: Research on adolescent sexual behavior. *American Psychologist, 48,* 972–983.

Garfield, S. L. (1995). *Psychotherapy: An eclectic-integrative approach* (2nd ed.). New York: Wiley.

Garner, J. D., & Mercer, S. O. (Eds.). (2001). *Women as they age* (2nd ed.). New York: Haworth.

Garner, P. W., & Estep, K. M. (2001). Empathy and emotional expressivity. In J. Worell (Ed.), *Encyclopedia of women and gender* (pp. 391–402). San Diego: Academic Press.

Garnets, L. (1996). Life as a lesbian: What does gender have to do with it? In J. C. Chrisler, C. Golden, & P. D. Rozee (Eds.), *Lectures on the psychology of women* (pp. 136–151). New York: McGraw-Hill.

Garnets, L., et al. (1991). Issues in psychotherapy with lesbians and gay men: A survey of psychologists. *American Psychologist, 46,* 964–972.

Garnets, L. D., & Peplau, L. A. (2000). Understanding women's sexualities and sexual orientations: An introduction. *Journal of Social Issues, 56,* 181–192.

Garrod, A., Smulyan, L., Powers, S., & Kilkenny, R. (1992). *Adolescent portraits.* Boston: Allyn & Bacon.

Garst, J., & Bodenhausen, G. V. (1997). Advertising's effects on men's gender role attitudes. *Sex Roles, 36,* 551–572.

Gash, H., & Morgan, M. (1993). School-based modifications of children's gender-related beliefs. *Journal of Applied Developmental Psychology, 14,* 277–287.

Gaspar de Alba, A. (1993). Tortillerismo: Work by Chicana lesbians. *Signs, 18,* 956–963.

Gastil, J. (1990). Generic pronouns and sexist language: The oxymoronic character of masculine generics. *Sex Roles, 23,* 629–643.

Gater, R., et al. (1998). Sex differences in the prevalence and detection of depressive and anxiety disorders in general health care settings. *Archives of General Psychiatry, 55,* 405–413.

Gauthier, J. (1994, Fall). Women's health research. *Psynopsis,* p. 10.

Gavey, N., & McPhillips, K. (1999). Subject to romance: Heterosexual passivity as an obstacle to women initiating condom use. *Psychology of Women Quarterly, 23,* 349–367.

Geary, D. C. (1995). Sexual selection and sex differences in spatial cognition. *Learning and Individual Differences, 7,* 289–301.

Geary, D. C. (1998). *Male, female: The evolution of human sex differences.* Washington, DC: American Psychological Association.

Geller, G., & Thomas, C. D. (1998, May). *A review of eating disorders among immigrant women.* Paper presented at the annual convention of the Canadian Psychological Association, Edmonton, Alberta, Canada.

Gender affects educational learning styles, researchers confirm. (1995, October). *Women in Higher Education,* p. 7.

Gender-specific pain relief. (1993, July 11). *Los Angeles Daily News,* p. C1.

Gentry, M. (1998). The sexual double standard: The influence of number of relationships and level of sexual activity on judgments of women and men. *Psychology of Women Quarterly, 22,* 505–511.

George, D., Carroll, P., Kersnick, R., & Calderon, K. (1998). Gender-related patterns of helping among friends. *Psychology of Women Quarterly, 22,* 685–704.

Gerber, G. L. (2001). *Women and men police officers: Status, gender, and personality.* Westport, CT: Praeger.

Gerbner, G. (1997). Gender and age in prime-time television. In S. Kirschner & D. A. Kirschner (Eds.), *Perspectives on psychology and the media* (pp. 69–94). Washington, DC: American Psychological Association.

Gergen, M. (2001). Social constructionist theory. In J. Worell (Ed.), *Encyclopedia of women and gender* (pp. 1043–1058). San Diego: Academic Press.

Gerrard, L. (1999). Feminist research in computers and composition. In K. Blair & P. Takayoshi (Eds.), *Feminist cyberscapes: Mapping gendered academic spaces* (pp. 377–400). Stamford, CT: Ablex.

Gerstmann, E. A., & Kramer, D. A. (1997). Feminist identity development: Psychometric analyses of two feminist identity scales. *Sex Roles, 36,* 327–348.

Gibbon, M. (1999). *Feminist perspectives on language.* London: Longman.

Gibbons, J. L. (2000). Gender development in cross-cultural perspective. In T. Eckes & H. M. Trautner (Eds.), *The developmental social psychology of gender* (pp. 389–415). Mahwah, NJ: Erlbaum.

Gibbons, J. L., Brusi-Figueroa, R., & Fisher, S. L. (1997). Gender-related ideals of Puerto Rican adolescents: Gender and school context. *Journal of Early Adolescence, 17,* 349–370.

Gibbons, J. L., Hamby, B. A., & Dennis, W. D. (1997). Researching gender-role ideologies internationally and cross-culturally. *Psychology of Women Quarterly, 21,* 151–170.

Gibbons, J. L., Richter, R. R., Wiley, D. C., & Stiles, D. A. (1996). Adolescents' opposite-sex ideal in four countries. *Journal of Social Psychology, 136,* 531–537.

Gibbons, J. L., Stiles, D. A., & Shkodriani, G. M. (1991). Adolescents' attitudes toward family and gender roles: An international comparison. *Sex Roles, 25,* 625–643.

Gilbert, L. A., & Rader, J. (2001). Counseling and psychotherapy: Gender, race/ethnicity, and sexuality. In J. Worell (Ed.), *Encyclopedia of women and gender* (pp. 265–277). San Diego: Academic Press.

Gilbert, L. A., & Scher, M. (1999). *Gender and sex in counseling and psychotherapy.* Boston: Allyn & Bacon.

Giles-Sims, J. (1983). *Wife battering: A systems theory approach.* New York: Guilford.

Gilleard, C., & Higgs, P. (2000). *Cultures of ageing: Self, citizen, and the body.* Harlow, England: Prentice Hall.

Gilligan, C. (1982). *In a different voice.* Cambridge, MA: Harvard University Press.

Gilligan, C. (1990). Preface. In C. Gilligan, N. P. Lyons, & T. J. Hanmer (Eds.), *Making connections* (pp. 6–29). Cambridge, MA: Harvard University Press.

Ginorio, A. B., Gutiérrez, L., Cauce, A. M., & Acosta, M. (1995). Psychological issues for Latinas. In H. Landrine (Ed.), *Bringing cultural diversity to feminist psychology: Theory, research, and practice* (pp. 241–263). Washington, DC: American Psychological Association.

Ginty, M. M. (2001, February/March). What you need to know about RU-486. *Ms. Magazine,* pp. 72–79.

Giordano, F. (2001). Helping co-habiting college students manage angry feelings to prevent relationship violence. In A. J. Ottens & K. Hotelling (Eds.), *Sexual violence on campus* (pp. 162–189). New York: Springer.

Girvan, S. (2000). *Canadian global almanac 2001.* Toronto: Macmillan Canada.

Giudice, L. C. (1998). Reproductive technologies. In E. A. Blechman & K. D. Brownell (Eds.), *Behavioral medicine and women: A comprehensive handbook* (pp. 515–519). New York: Guilford.

Gladue, B. A. (1994). The biopsychology of sexual orientation. *Current Directions in Psychological Science, 3,* 150–154.

Gleiser, M. (1998). The glass wall. In A. M. Pattatucci (Ed.), *Women in science* (pp. 204–218). Thousand Oaks, CA: Sage.

Glenn, D. (2002, June 21). What the data actually show about welfare reform. *Chronicle of Higher Education,* p. A14.

Glick, P. (1991). Trait-based and sex-based discrimination in occupational prestige, occupational salary, and hiring. *Sex Roles, 25,* 351–378.

Glick, P., & Fiske, S. T. (1996). The Ambivalent Sexism Inventory: Differentiating hostile and benevolent sexism. *Journal of Personality and Social Psychology, 70,* 491–512.

Glick, P., & Fiske, S. T. (1997). Hostile and benevolent sexism: Measuring ambivalent sexist attitudes toward women. *Psychology of Women Quarterly, 21,* 119–135.

Glick, P., & Fiske, S. T. (1998). Gender, power dynamics, and social interaction. In M. M. Ferree, J. Lorber, & B. B. Hess (Eds.), *Revisioning gender* (pp. 365–398). Thousand Oaks, CA: Sage.

Glick, P., & Fiske, S. T. (1999). Sexism and other "isms": Independence, status, and the ambivalent content of stereotypes. In W. B. Swann Jr., J. H. Langlois, & L. A. Gilbert (Eds.), *Sexism and stereotypes in modern society: The gender science of Janet Taylor Spence* (pp. 193–221). Washington, DC: American Psychological Association.

Glick, P., & Fiske, S. T. (2001a). An ambivalent alliance: Hostile and benevolent sexism as complementary justifications for gender inequality. *American Psychologist, 56,* 109–118.

Glick, P., & Fiske, S. T. (2001b). Ambivalent sexism. *Advances in Experimental Social Psychology, 33,* 115–188.

Glick, P., Wilk, K., & Perreault, M. (1995). Images of occupations: Components of gender and status in occupational stereotypes. *Sex Roles, 32,* 565–582.

Glick, P., et al. (2000). Beyond prejudice as simple antipathy: Hostile and benevolent sexism across cultures. *Journal of Personality and Social Psychology, 79,* 763–775.

Global Fund for Women (2002, September). *About the Global Fund.* Retrieved September 6, 2002, from http://www.globalfundforwomen.org

Gold, A. G. (2001). New light in new times? Women's songs on schooling girls in rural Rajasthan. *Manushi, 123,* 27–35.

Goldberg, P. A. (1968). Are women prejudiced against women? *Transaction, 5,* 28–30.

Golden, C. (1996). What's in a name? Sexual self-identification among women. In R. C. Savin-Williams & K. M. Cohen (Eds.), *The lives of lesbians, gays, and bisexuals* (pp. 229–249). Fort Worth, TX: Harcourt Brace.

Golden, C. (1998, December). Separate and unequal [Review of the book *The two sexes: Growing up apart, coming together*]. *Women's Review of Books, 16,* pp. 24–25.

Golden, C. (2000). The intersexed and the transgendered: Rethinking sex/gender. In J. C. Chrisler,

C. Golden, & P. D. Rozee (Eds.), *Lectures on the psychology of women* (2nd ed., pp. 80–95). Boston: McGraw-Hill.

Golding, J. M. (1990). Division of household labor, strain, and depressive symptoms among Mexican Americans and non-Hispanic Whites. *Psychology of Women Quarterly, 14,* 103–117.

Golding, J. M. (1996). Sexual assault history and women's reproductive and sexual health. *Psychology of Women Quarterly, 14,* 103–117.

Golding, J. M. (1999a). Intimate partner violence as a risk factor for mental disorders: A meta-analysis. *Journal of Family Violence, 14,* 99–132.

Golding, J. M. (1999b). Sexual assault history and headache. *Journal of Nervous and Mental Disease, 187,* 624–629.

Golding, J. M., (1999c). Sexual-assault history and long-term physical health problems: Evidence from clinical and population epidemiology. *Current Directions in Psychological Science, 8,* 191–194.

Golding, J. M., Wilsnack, S. C., & Learman, L. A. (1998). Prevalence of sexual assault history among women with common gynecological symptoms. *American Journal of Obstetrics and Gynecology, 179,* 1013–1019.

Goldstein, L. A. (2001, Fall). "And you can quote me on that." *Michigan Today,* pp. 10–11.

Golombok, S., & Fivush, R. (1994). *Gender development.* New York: Cambridge University Press.

Golub, S. (1992). *Periods: From menarche to menopause.* Newbury Park, CA: Sage.

Gonsiorek, J. C. (1996). Mental health and sexual orientation. In R. C. Savin-Williams & K. M. Cohen (Eds.), *The lives of lesbians, gays, and bisexuals: Children to adults* (pp. 462–478). Fort Worth, TX: Harcourt Brace.

Goodman, E. (2002, July 29). Women: A treaty worth signing. *Liberal Opinion Week,* p. 27.

Goodman, G. S., et al. (2001). Effects of past abuse experiences on children's eyewitness memory. *Law and Human Behavior, 25,* 269–298.

Goodman, W. C. (1995). *The invisible woman: Confronting weight prejudice in America.* Carlsbad, CA: Gürze Books.

Gordon, M. (1993, Fall). Sexual slang and gender. *Women and Language, 16,* 16–21.

Gordon, R. (1998). "Girls cannot think as boys do": Socializing children through the Zimbabwean school system. In C. Sweetman (Ed.), *Gender, education, and training* (pp. 53–58). Oxford, England: Oxfam.

Gordon, R. A. (2000). *Eating disorders* (2nd ed.). Oxford, England: Blackwell.

Gorin, T. (2000, Fall). Rohypnol: How the hype tricks women. *Canadian Woman Studies/Les cahiers de la femme, 20,* 92–96.

Gorlick, C. A. (1995). Divorce: Options available, constraints forced, pathways taken. In N. Mandell & A. Duffy (Eds.), *Canadian families: Diversity, conflict, and change* (pp. 211–234). Toronto: Harcourt Brace Canada.

Gormly, A. V., Gormly, J. B., & Weiss, H. (1987). Motivations for parenthood among young adult college students. *Sex Roles, 16,* 31–39.

Gorney, C. (1998). *Articles of faith: A frontline history of the abortion wars.* New York: Simon & Schuster.

Gose, B. (1998, April 24). The feminization of veterinary medicine. *Chronicle of Higher Education,* pp. A55–A56.

Gotlib, I. H. (1998). Postpartum depression. In E. A. Blechman & K. D. Brownell (Eds.), *Behavioral medicine and women: A comprehensive handbook* (pp. 489–494). New York: Guilford.

Gottheil, M., Steinberg, R., & Granger, L. (1999). An exploration of clinicians' diagnostic approaches to premenstrual symptomatology. *Canadian Journal of Behavioural Sciences, 31,* 254–262.

Gotwals, A. E., & Stewart, E. (2002). *Social Security privatization: A false promise for women.* Washington, DC: Older Women's League.

Gourevitch, P. (1999, February 22). A husband for Dil. *New Yorker,* pp. 78–102.

Graber, J. A., & Brooks-Gunn, J. (1998). Puberty. In E. A. Blechman & K. D. Brownell (Eds.), *Behavioral medicine and women* (pp. 51–58). New York: Guilford.

Graber, J. A., & Brooks-Gunn, J. (1999). "Sometimes I think that you don't like me": How mothers and daughters negotiate the transition into adolescence. In M. J. Cox & J. Brooks-Gunn (Eds.), *Conflict and cohesion in families: Causes and consequences* (pp. 207–242). Mahwah, NJ: Erlbaum.

Graham, D. L. R., & Rawlings, E. I. (1999). Observers' blaming of battered wives: Who, what, and why? In M. A. Paludi (Ed.), *The psychology of sexual victimization* (pp. 55–94). Westport, CT: Greenwood.

Graham, S. (1997). "Most of the subjects were White and middle class": Trends in published research on African Americans in selected APA journals. In L. A. Peplau & S. E. Taylor (Eds.), *Sociocultural perspectives in social psychology: Current readings* (pp. 52–71). Upper Saddle River, NJ: Prentice Hall.

Grant, J. R., & Cash, T. F. (1995). Cognitive-behavioral body image therapy: Comparative efficacy of group and modest-contact treatments. *Behavior Therapy, 26,* 69–84.

Grant, L. (1994). Helpers, enforcers, and go-betweens: Black females in elementary school classrooms. In M. Baca Zinn & B. T. Dill (Eds.), *Women of color in U.S. society* (pp. 43–63). Philadelphia: Temple University Press.

Gray, J. (1992). *Men are from Mars, women are from Venus.* New York: HarperCollins.

Green, B. L., & Kenrick, D. T. (1994). The attractiveness of gender-typed traits at different relationship levels: Androgynous characteristics may be desirable after all. *Personality and Social Psychology Bulletin, 20,* 244–253.

Greene, B. (1994). Diversity and difference: The issue of race in feminist therapy. In M. P. Mirkin (Ed.), *Women in context: Toward a feminist reconstruction of psychotherapy* (pp. 333–351). New York: Guilford.

Greene, B. (1996). Lesbians and gay men of color: The legacy of ethnosexual mythologies in heterosexism. In E. D. Rothblum & L. A. Bond (Eds.), *Preventing heterosexism and homophobia* (pp. 59–70). Thousand Oaks, CA: Sage.

Greene, B. (2000a). African American lesbian and bisexual women. *Journal of Social Issues, 56,* 239–249.

Greene, B. (2000b). African American lesbian and bisexual women in feminist-psychodynamic psychotherapies. In L. C. Jackson & B. Greene (Eds.), *Psychotherapy with African American women* (pp. 82–125). New York: Guilford.

Greene, B., et al. (1997). Diversity: Advancing an inclusive feminist psychology. In J. Worell & N. G. Johnson (Eds.), *Shaping the future of feminist psychology* (pp. 173–202). Washington, DC: American Psychological Association.

Grewal, I., & Kaplan, C. (2002). *An introduction to women's studies.* Boston: McGraw-Hill.

Grieco, H. (1999, Fall). Media institute sets sights on feminist network. *National NOW Times,* p. 3.

Grisso, J. A., et al. (1999). Violent injuries among women in an urban area. *New England Journal of Medicine, 341,* 1899–1905.

Groat, H. T., et al. (1997). Attitudes toward childbearing among young parents. *Journal of Marriage and the Family, 59,* 568–581.

Grodstein, F., et al. (1997). Postmenopausal hormone therapy and mortality. *New England Journal of Medicine, 336,* 1769–1775.

Groff, J. Y., Mullen, P. D., Mongoven, M., & Burau, K. (1997). Prenatal weight gain patterns and infant birthweight associated with maternal smoking. *Birth, 24,* 234–239.

Grogan, S. (1999). *Body image: Understanding body dissatisfaction in men, women, and children.* New York: Routledge.

Grote, N. K., & Frieze, I. H. (1994). The measurement of friendship-based love in intimate relationships. *Personal Relationships, 1,* 275–300.

Gruber, S. (1999). "I, a Mestiza, continually walk out of one culture into another": Alba's story. In K. Blair & P. Takayoshi (Eds.), *Feminist cyberspaces: Mapping gendered academic spaces* (pp. 105–132). Stamford, CT: Ablex.

Grusec, J. E., & Lytton, H. (1988). *Social development.* New York: Springer.

Guarnaccia, P. J. (1997). Social stress and psychological distress among Latinos in the United States. In I. Al-Issa & M. Tousignant (Eds.), *Ethnicity, immigration, and psychopathology* (pp. 71–94). New York: Plenum.

Guglani, S., Coleman, P. G., & Sonuga-Barke, J. S. (2000). Mental health of elderly Asians in Britain: A comparison of Hindus from nuclear and extended families of differing cultural identities. *International Journal of Geriatric Psychiatry, 15,* 1046–1053.

Guille, C., & Chrisler, J. C. (1999). Does feminism serve a protective function against eating disorders? *Journal of Lesbian Studies, 3,* 141–148.

Guinier, L., Fine, M., & Balin, J. (1997). *Becoming gentlemen: Women, law school, and institutional change.* Boston: Beacon Press.

Gunter, B., & McAleer, J. (1997). *Children and television* (2nd ed.). London: Routledge.

Gupta, S. R. (1999). Forged by fire: Indian-American women reflect on their marriages, divorces, and on rebuilding lives. In S. R. Gupta (Ed.), *Emerging voices: South Asian American women redefine self, family, and community* (pp. 193–221). Walnut Creek, CA: AltaMira Press.

Gur, R. C., et al. (1995). Sex differences in regional cerebral glucose metabolism during a resting state. *Science, 267,* 528–530.

Gur, R. C., et al. (1999). Sex differences in brain gray and white matter in healthy young adults: Correlations with cognitive performance. *Journal of Neuroscience, 19,* 4065–4072.

Gutek, B. A. (2001). Working environments. In J. Worell (Ed.), *Encyclopedia of women and gender* (pp. 1191–1204). San Diego: Academic Press.

Gutek, B. A., & O'Connor, M. (1995). The empirical basis for the reasonable woman standard. *Journal of Social Issues, 51,* 151–166.

Guthrie, R. V. (1998). *Even the rat was white: A historical view of psychology* (2nd ed.). Boston: Allyn & Bacon.

Gutiérrez, L., Oh, H. J., & Gillmore, M. R. (2000). Toward an understanding of (em)power(ment) for HIV/AIDS prevention with adolescent women. *Sex Roles, 42,* 581–611.

Guy-Sheftall, B. (1996). *Women's studies: A retrospective.* New York: Ford Foundation.

Haddock, D. (2001). *Granny D: Walking across America in my ninetieth year.* New York: Villard Books.

Haddock, G., & Zanna, M. P. (1994). Preferring "housewives" to "feminists": Categorization and the favorability of attitudes toward women. *Psychology of Women Quarterly, 18,* 25–52.

Haffner, D. W., & Wagoner, J. (1999, August/September). Vast majority of Americans support sexuality education. *SIECUS Report, 27,* 22–23.

Hafter, D. M. (1979). An overview of women's history. In M. Richmond-Abbott (Ed.), *The American woman* (pp. 1–27). New York: Holt, Rinehart & Winston.

Haggbloom, S. J., et al. (2002). The 100 most eminent psychologists of the 20th century. *Review of General Psychology, 6,* 139–152.

Haley, H. (2001, June). *Crisscrossing gender lines and color lines: A test of the subordinate male target hypothesis.* Paper presented at the meeting of the American Psychological Society, Toronto, Ontario.

Hall, C. C. I. (1997). Cultural malpractice: The growing obsolescence of psychology with the changing U.S. population. *American Psychologist, 52,* 642–651.

Hall, C. C. I., & Crum, M. J. (1994). Women and "body-isms" in television beer commercials. *Sex Roles, 31,* 329–337.

Hall, D. R., & Zhao, J. Z. (1995). Cohabitation and divorce in Canada: Testing the selectivity hypothesis. *Journal of Marriage and the Family, 57,* 421–427.

Hall, G. C. N., & Barongan, C. (1997). Prevention of sexual aggression: Sociocultural risk and protective factors. *American Psychologist, 52,* 5–14.

Hall, G. S. (1906). The question of coeducation. *Munsey's Magazine,* 588–592.

Hall, J. A. (1984). *Nonverbal sex differences: Communication accuracy and expressive style.* Baltimore: Johns Hopkins University Press.

Hall, J. A. (1987). On explaining gender differences: The case of nonverbal communication. In P. Shaver & C. Hendrick (Eds.), *Sex and gender* (pp. 177–200). Newbury Park, CA: Sage.

Hall, J. A. (1998). How big are nonverbal sex differences? The case of smiling and sensitivity to nonverbal cues. In D. J. Canary & K. Dindia (Eds.), *Sex differences and similarities in communication* (pp. 155–177). Mahwah, NJ: Erlbaum.

Hall, J. A., & Carter, J. D. (1999). Gender-stereotype accuracy as an individual difference. *Journal of Personality and Social Psychology, 77,* 350–359.

Hall, J. A., Carter, J. D., & Horgan, T. G. (2000). Gender differences in nonverbal communication of emotion. In A. H. Fischer (Ed.), *Gender and emotion: Social psychological perspectives* (pp. 97–117). New York: Cambridge University Press.

Hall, J. A., & Halberstadt, A. G. (1986). Smiling and gazing. In J. S. Hyde & M. C. Linn (Eds.), *The psychology of gender: Advances through meta-analysis* (pp. 136–158). Baltimore: Johns Hopkins University Press.

Hall, J. A., & Halberstadt, A. G. (1994). "Subordination" and sensitivity to nonverbal cues: A study of working women. *Sex Roles, 31,* 149–165.

Hall, J. A., & Halberstadt, A. G. (1997). Subordination and nonverbal sensitivity: A hypothesis in search of support. In M. R. Walsh (Ed.), *Women, men, and gender: Ongoing debates* (pp. 120–133). New Haven, CT: Yale University Press.

Hall, J. A., Halberstadt, A. G., & O'Brien, C. E. (1997). "Subordination" and nonverbal sensitivity: A study and synthesis of findings based on trait measures. *Sex Roles, 37,* 295–317.

Hall, R. L. (2000). Sweating it out: The good news and the bad news about women and sport. In J. C. Chrisler, C. Golden, & P. D. Rozee (Eds.), *Lectures on the psychology of women* (2nd ed., pp. 48–63). Boston: McGraw-Hill.

Hall, R. M., & Sandler, B. R. (1982). *The classroom climate: A chilly one for women? Project on the Status and Education of Women.* Washington, DC: Association of American Colleges.

Hall, S. (1998). Drug abuse treatment. In E. A. Blechman & K. D. Brownell (Eds.), *Behavioral medicine and women: A comprehensive handbook* (pp. 420–424). New York: Guilford.

Halldórsdóttir, S., & Karlsdóttir, S. I. (1996). Empowerment or discouragement: Women's experience of caring and uncaring encounters during childbirth. *Health Care for Women International, 17,* 361–379.

Hallingby, L. (1993, January/February). "Sesame Street" still no kid treat. *New Directions for Women,* p. 13.

Halpern, D. F. (1985). The influence of sex-role stereotypes on prose recall. *Sex Roles, 12,* 363–375.

Halpern, D. F. (1997). Sex differences in intelligence: Implications for education. *American Psychologist, 52,* 1091–1102.

Halpern, D. F. (2000). *Sex differences in cognitive abilities* (3rd ed.). Mahwah, NJ: Erlbaum.

Halpern, D. F. (2001). Sex difference research: Cognitive abilities. In J. Worell (Ed.), *The encyclopedia of women and gender* (pp. 963–971). San Diego: Academic Press.

Halpern, D. F., & Cass, M. (1994). Laterality, sexual orientation, and immune system functioning: Is there a relationship? *International Journal of Neuroscience, 77,* 167–180.

Halpern, D. F., & Tan, U. (2001). Stereotypes and steroids: Using a psychobiosocial model to understand cognitive sex differences. *Brain and Cognition, 45,* 392–414.

Hamby, S. L. (1998). Partner violence: Prevention and intervention. In J. L. Jasinski & L. M. Williams (Eds.), *Partner violence* (pp. 210–258). Thousand Oaks, CA: Sage.

Hamby, S. L. (2002). The importance of community in a feminist analysis of domestic violence among American Indians. In A. E. Hunter & C. Forden (Eds.), *Readings in the psychology of gender* (pp. 209–226). Boston, MA: Allyn & Bacon.

Hamilton, D. L., & Sherman, J. W. (1994). Stereotypes. In R. S. Wyers Jr. & T. K. Srull (Eds.), *Handbook of social cognition* (2nd ed., Vol. 2, pp. 1–68). Hillsdale, NJ: Erlbaum.

Hamilton, D. L., Sherman, S. J., & Ruvolo, C. M. (1990). Stereotype-based expectancies: Effects on information processing and social behavior. *Journal of Social Issues, 46,* 35–60.

Hamilton, J. A., & Yonkers, K. A. (1996). Sex differences in pharmacokinetics of psychotropic medication. In M. F. Jensvold, U. Habreich, & J. A. Hamilton (Eds.), *Psychopharmacology and women: Sex, gender, and hormones* (pp. 11–42). Washington, DC: American Psychiatric Press.

Hamilton, M. C. (1991a). Masculine bias in the attribution of personhood: People = male, male = people. *Psychology of Women Quarterly, 15,* 393–402.

Hamilton, M. C. (1991b). *Preference for sons or daughters and the sex role characteristics of the potential parents.* Paper presented at the annual meeting of the Association for Women in Psychology, Hartford, CT.

Hamilton, M. C. (2001). Sex-related difference research: Personality. In J. Worell (Ed.), *Encyclopedia of women and gender* (pp. 973–981). San Diego: Academic Press.

Hammerle, G. (1997). Challenging sexual stereotypes: An interview with Charlene L. Muehlenhard. *Teaching of Psychology, 24,* 64–68.

Hannon, R., et al. (1996). College students' judgments regarding sexual aggression during a date. *Sex Roles, 35,* 765–780.

Hanson, S. L., & Johnson, E. P. (2000). Expecting the unexpected: A comparative study of African-American women's experiences in science during the high school years. *Journal of Women and Minorities in Science and Engineering, 6,* 265–294.

Hardie, E. A. (1997). Prevalence and predictors of cyclic and noncyclic affective change. *Psychology of Women Quarterly, 21,* 299–314.

Hardy, M. A., & Shuey, K. (2000). Pension decisions in a changing economy: Gender, structure, and choice. *Journal of Gerontology: Social Sciences, 55B,* S271–S277.

Hare-Mustin, R. T., & Marecek, J. (1994). Asking the right questions: Feminist psychology and sex differences. *Feminism and Psychology, 4,* 531–537.

Hare-Mustin, R. T., & Marecek, J. (1997). Abnormal and clinical psychology: Some critical perspectives. In D. Fox & I. Prilleltensky (Eds.), *Abnormal and clinical psychology: Some critical perspectives* (pp. 105–120). London: Sage.

Harm, N. J. (2001). Grandmothers raising grandchildren: Parenting the second time around. In J. D. Garner & S. O. Mercer (Eds.), *Women as they age* (2nd ed., pp. 131–146). New York: Haworth.

Harris, K. L., Melaas, K., & Rodacker, E. (1999). The impact of women's studies courses on college students in the 1990s. *Sex Roles, 40,* 969–977.

Harris, M. B., & Knight-Bohnhoff, K. (1996). Gender and aggression II: Personal aggressiveness. *Sex Roles, 35,* 27–42.

Harris, M. B., & Miller, K. C. (2000). Gender and perceptions of danger. *Sex Roles, 43,* 843–863.

Harris, M. G. (1994). Cholas, Mexican-American girls, and gangs. *Sex Roles, 30,* 289–301.

Harris, R. J. (1994). The impact of sexually explicit media. In J. Bryant & D. Zillmann (Eds.), *Media effects: Advances in theory and research* (pp. 247–272). Hillsdale, NJ: Erlbaum.

Harris, R. J., & Firestone, J. M. (1998). Changes in predictors of gender role ideologies among women: A multivariate analysis. *Sex Roles, 38,* 239–252.

Hartup, W. W. (1999). Foreword. In W. Furman, B. B. Brown, & C. Feiring (Eds.), *The development of romantic relationships in adolescence* (pp. xi–xv). New York: Cambridge University Press.

Harvey, E. (1999). Short-term and long-term effects of early parental employment on children of the National Longitudinal Survey of Youth. *Developmental Psychology, 35,* 445–459.

Harvey, J. A., & Hansen, C. E. (1999). Gender role of male therapists in both professional and personal life. *Sex Roles, 41,* 105–113.

Harvey, P. D. (2000). *Let every child be wanted.* Westport, CT: Auburn House.

Harvey, S. M. (2001, Autumn). Preventing HIV/STDs and unintended pregnancies: A decade of challenges. *Population and Environmental Psychology Bulletin,* pp. 1–6.

Harville, M. L., & Rienzi, B. M. (2000). Equal worth and gracious submission: Judeo-Christian attitudes toward employed women. *Psychology of Women Quarterly, 24,* 145–147.

Hase, M. (2001). Student resistance and nationalism in the classroom: Some reflections on globalizing the curriculum. *Feminist Teacher, 13,* 90–107.

Haseltine, F. P. (1997). Conclusion. In F. P. Haseltine & B. G. Jacobson (Eds.), *Women's health research: A medical and policy primer* (pp. 331–336). Washington, DC: Health Press.

Haskell, M. (1997). *Holding my own in no man's land: Women and men and film and feminists.* New York: Oxford University Press.

Haslett, B. J., Geis, F. L., & Carter, M. R. (1992). *The organizational woman: Power and paradox.* Norwood, NJ: Ablex.

Hatch, L. R. (2000). *Beyond gender differences: Adaptation to aging in life course perspective.* Amityville, NY: Baywood.

Hatcher, R. A., & Trussell, J. (1994). Contraceptive implants and teenage pregnancy. *New England Journal of Medicine, 331,* 1229–1230.

Hatfield, E., & Rapson, R. L. (1993). *Love, sex, and intimacy: Their psychology, biology, and history.* New York: HarperCollins.

Hatfield, E., & Rapson, R. L. (1996). *Love and sex: Cross-cultural perspectives.* Boston: Allyn & Bacon.

Hatfield, E., & Sprecher, S. (1995). Men's and women's preferences in marital partners in the United States, Russia, and Japan. *Journal of Cross-Cultural Psychology, 26,* 728–750.

Hawkins, B. D. (1994, November 3). An evening with Gwendolyn Brooks. *Black Issues in Higher Education,* pp. 16–21.

Hawkins, B. D. (1996, July 11). Gender gap. *Black Issues in Higher Education,* pp. 20–22.

Hawkins, J. W., & Aber, C. S. (1988). The content of advertisements in medical journals: Distorting the image of women. *Women and Health, 14,* 43–59.

Hawkins, J. W., & Aber, C. S. (1993). Women in advertisements in medical journals. *Sex Roles, 28,* 233–242.

Haworth-Hoeppner, S. (1998). What's gender got to do with it: Perceptions of sexual coercion in a university community. *Sex Roles, 38,* 757–779.

Hays, S. (1996). *The cultural contradictions of motherhood.* New Haven, CT: Yale University Press.

Headlee, S., & Elfin, M. (1996). *The cost of being female.* New York: Praeger.

Heatherington, L., Burns, A. B., & Gustafson, T. B. (1998). When another stumbles: Gender and self-presentation to vulnerable others. *Sex Roles, 38,* 889–913.

Heatherington, L., et al. (1993). Two investigations of "female modesty" in achievement situations. *Sex Roles, 29,* 739–754.

Hecht, M. A., & LaFrance, M. (1998). License or obligation to smile: The effect of power and sex on amount and type of smiling. *Personality and Social Psychology Bulletin, 24,* 1332–1342.

Hedges, L., & Nowell, A. (1995). Sex differences in mental test scores, variability, and numbers of high-scoring individuals. *Science, 269,* 41–45.

Heffernan, K. (1998). Bulimia nervosa. In E. A. Blechman & K. D. Brownell (Eds.), *Behavioral medicine and women: A comprehensive handbook* (pp. 358–363). New York: Guilford.

Heilbrun, C. G. (1997). *The last gift of time: Life beyond sixty.* New York: Dial Press.

Heilman, M. E. (2001). Description and prescription: How gender stereotypes prevent women's ascent up the organizational ladder. *Journal of Social Issues, 57,* 657–674.

Hein, K. (1998). Aligning science with politics and policy in HIV prevention. *Science, 280,* 1905–1906.

Heitner, K. (1998, Summer). Backtalk. *Division 35 Newsletter,* p. 14.

Helgeson, V. S., & Fritz, H. L. (1998). Distinctions of unmitigated communion from communion: Self-neglect and overinvolvement with others. *Personality and Social Psychology Review, 75,* 121–140.

Helstrom, A. W., Coffey, C., & Jorgannathan, P. (1998). Asian-American women's health. In A. Blechman & K. D. Brownell (Eds.), *Behavioral medicine and women: A comprehensive handbook* (pp. 826–832). New York: Guilford.

Helwig, A. A. (1998). Gender-role stereotyping: Testing theory with a longitudinal sample. *Sex Roles, 38,* 403–423.

Henderson-King, D., Henderson-King, E., & Hoffman, L. (2001). Media images and women's self-evaluations: Social context and importance of attractiveness as moderators. *Personality and Social Psychology Bulletin, 27,* 1407–1416.

Hendrick, C., & Hendrick, S. (1996). Gender and the experience of heterosexual love. In J. T. Wood (Ed.), *Gendered relationships* (pp. 131–148). Mountain View, CA: Mayfield.

Hendrick, V., & Altshuler, L. L. (1999). Biological determinants of postpartum depression. In L. J. Miller (Ed.), *Postpartum mood disorders* (pp. 65–82). Washington, DC: American Psychiatric Press.

Henley, N. M. (1985). Psychology and gender. *Signs, 11,* 101–119.

Henley, N. M., et al. (1998). Developing a scale to measure the diversity of feminist attitudes. *Psychology of Women Quarterly, 22,* 317–348.

Henrie, R. L., Aron, R. H., Nelson, B. D., & Poole, D. A. (1997). Gender-related knowledge variations within geography. *Sex Roles, 36,* 605–623.

Herbert, S. E. (1996). Lesbian sexuality. In R. P. Cabaj & T. S. Stein (Eds.), *Textbook of homosexuality and mental health* (pp. 723–742). Washington DC: American Psychiatric Press.

Herdt, G. (2001). Social change, sexual diversity, and tolerance for bisexuality in the United States. In A. R. D'Augelli & C. J. Patterson (Eds.), *Lesbian, gay, and bisexual identities and youth* (pp. 267–283). New York: Oxford University Press.

Herek, G. M. (1994). Heterosexism, hate crimes, and the law. In M. Costanzo & S. Oskamp (Eds.), *Violence and the law* (pp. 89–112). Thousand Oaks, CA: Sage.

Herek, G. M. (1996). Why tell if you're not asked? Self-disclosure, intergroup contact, and heterosexuals' attitudes toward lesbians and gay men. In G. M. Herek, J. B. Jobe, & R. M. Carney (Eds.), *Out in force: Sexual orientation and the military* (pp. 197–225). Chicago: University of Chicago Press.

Herek, G. M. (2000). Sexual prejudice and gender: Do heterosexuals' attitudes toward lesbians and gay men differ? *Journal of Social Issues, 56,* 251–266.

Herek, G. M., & Capitanio, J. P. (1999). Sex differences in how heterosexuals think about lesbians and gay men: Evidence from survey context effects. *Journal of Sex Research, 36,* 348–360.

Herek, G. M., Gillis, J. R., & Cogan, J. C. (1999). Psychological sequelae of hate-crime victimization among lesbian, gay, and bisexual adults. *Journal of Consulting and Clinical Psychology, 67,* 945–951.

Herek, G. M., Gillis, J. R., Cogan, J. C., & Glunt, E. K. (1997). Hate crime victimization among lesbian, gay, and bisexual adults: Prevalence, psychological correlates, and methodological issues. *Journal of Interpersonal Violence, 12,* 195–215.

Herek, G. M., Kimmel, D. C., Amaro, H., & Melton, G. B. (1991). Avoiding heterosexist bias in psychological research. *American Psychologist, 46,* 957–963.

Herlitz, A., Airaksinen, E., & Nordström, E. (1999). Sex differences in episodic memory: The impact of verbal and visuospatial ability. *Neuropsychology, 13,* 590–597.

Herlitz, A., Nilsson, L., & Bäckman, L. (1997). Gender differences in episodic memory. *Memory and Cognition, 25,* 801–811.

Herman, J. L. (2000). *Father-daughter incest.* Cambridge, MA: Harvard University Press.

Herrmann, D. J., Crawford, M., & Holdsworth, M. (1992). Gender-linked differences in everyday memory performance. *British Journal of Psychology, 83,* 221–231.

Hershberger, S. L. (2001). Biological factors in the development of sexual orientation. In A. R. D'Augelli & C. J. Patterson (Eds.), *Lesbian, gay, and bisexual identities and youth* (pp. 27–51). New York: Oxford University Press.

Hesse-Biber, S. (1998). Am I thin enough yet? In P. S. Rothenberg (Ed.), *Race, class, and gender in the United States: An integrated study* (4th ed., pp. 489–497). New York: St. Martin's Press.

Hesse-Biber, S., & Carter, G. L. (2000). *Working women in America: Split dreams.* New York: Oxford University Press.

Hickman, S. E., & Muehlenhard, C. L. (1997). College women's fears and precautionary behaviors relating to acquaintance rape and stranger rape. *Psychology of Women Quarterly, 21,* 527–547.

Hickman, S. E., & Muehlenhard, C. L. (1999). "By the semi-mystical appearance of a condom": How young women and men communicate sexual consent in heterosexual situations. *Journal of Sex Research, 36,* 258–272.

Hidalgo, H. (1995). The norms of conduct in social service agencies: A threat to the mental health of Puerto Rican lesbians. *Journal of Gay and Lesbian Social Services, 3,* 23–41.

Higginbotham, A. (1996, March/April). Teen mags: How to get a guy, drop 20 pounds, and lose your self-esteem. *Ms. Magazine,* pp. 84–87.

Hillard, P. J. A. (2001). Gynecologic disorders and surgery. In N. L. Stotland & D. E. Stewart (Eds.), *Psychological aspects of women's health care* (2nd ed., pp. 277–305). Washington, DC: American Psychiatric Press.

Hilton, J. L., & von Hippel, W. (1996). Stereotypes. *Annual Review of Psychology, 47,* 237–271.

Hinck, S. S., & Thomas, R. W. (1999). Rape myth acceptance in college students: How far have we come? *Sex Roles, 40,* 815–832.

Hines, N. J., & Fry, D. P. (1994). Indirect modes of aggression among women of Buenos Aires, Argentina. *Sex Roles, 30,* 213–236.

Ho, C. K. (1997). An analysis of domestic violence in Asian American communities: A multicultural approach to counseling. In K. P. Monteiro (Ed.), *Ethnicity and psychology* (pp. 138–152). Dubuque, IA: Kendall/Hunt.

Hochschild, A. R. (1997). *The time bind.* New York: Henry Holt.

Hodges, L. (2000, June 1). Any complaints, students? Go and tell the Queen. *The Independent,* pp. 2–3.

Hoff, T., & Greene, L. (2000). *Sex education in America.* Menlo Park, CA: Henry J. Kaiser Family Foundation.

Hoffman, L. W. (2000). Maternal employment: Effects of social context. In R. D. Taylor and M. C. Wang (Eds.), *Resilience across contexts: Family, work, culture, and community* (pp. 147–176). Mahwah, NJ: Erlbaum.

Hoffman, L. W., & Kloska, D. D. (1995). Parents' gender-based attitudes toward marital roles and child rearing: Development and validation of new measures. *Sex Roles, 32,* 273–295.

Hoffman, L. W., & Youngblade, L. M. (1999). *Mothers at work: Effects on children's well-being.* New York: Cambridge University Press.

Hoffman, P. H., & Hale-Benson, J. (1987). Self-esteem of Black middle-class women who choose to work inside or outside the home. *Journal of Multicultural Counseling and Development, 15,* 71–80.

Hoffnung, M. (1992). *What's a mother to do? Conversations on work and family.* Pasadena, CA: Trilogy.

Hoffnung, M. (1993). *College women's expectations for work and family.* Poster presented at the annual meeting of the Association for Women in Psychology, Atlanta, GA.

Hoffnung, M. (1995). Motherhood: Contemporary conflict for women. In J. Freeman (Ed.), *Women: A feminist perspective* (pp. 162–181). Mountain View, CA: Mayfield.

Hoffnung, M. (1999, Spring). Women's changing attitudes toward work and family: College to five years after. *Women and Work, 1,* 27–39.

Hoffnung, M. (2000, March). *Motherhood and career: Changes in college women's thoughts over time.* Paper presented at the annual meeting of the Eastern Psychological Association, Baltimore.

Hoffnung, M. (2003). Studying women's lives: College to seven years after. In E. S. Adler & R. Clark (Eds.), *How it's done: An invitation to social research* (pp. 74–78). Pacific Grove, CA: Wadsworth.

Hofmeyr, G. J., Marcos, E. F., & Butchart, A. M. (1990). Pregnant women's perceptions of themselves: A survey. *Birth, 17,* 205–206.

Hofschire, L. J., & Greenberg, B. S. (2002). Media's impact on adolescents' body dissatisfaction. In J. D. Brown, J. R. Steele, & K. Walsh-Childers (Eds.), *Sexual teens, sexual media: Investigating media's influence on adolescent sexuality* (pp. 125–149). Mahwah, NJ: Erlbaum.

Holcomb, L. P., & Giesen, C. B. (1995). Coping with challenges: College experiences of older women and women with disabilities. In J. C. Chrisler & A. H. Hemstreet (Eds.), *Variations on a theme: Diversity and the psychology of women* (pp. 175–199). Albany, NY: State University of New York Press.

Holden, S. L. (1997, September). *Older women in undergraduate introductory psychology textbooks.* Paper presented at the annual meeting of the American Psychological Association, Chicago.

Holland, D. C., & Eisenhart, M. A. (1990). *Educated in romance: Women, achievement, and college culture.* Chicago: University of Chicago Press.

Hollingworth, L. S. (1914). *Functional periodicity: An experimental study of mental and motor abilities of women during menstruation* (Contributions to Education No. 69, pp. v–14, 86–101). New York: Teachers College, Columbia University.

Holmes, J. (1998). Women's talk: The question of sociolinguistic universals. In J. Coates (Ed.), *Language and gender: A reader* (pp. 461–483). Malden, MA: Blackwell.

Holms, V. L., & Esses, L. M. (1988). Factors influencing Canadian high school girls' career motivation. *Psychology of Women Quarterly, 12,* 313–328.

Holt, C. L., & Ellis, J. B. (1998). Assessing the current validity of the Bem Sex-Role Inventory. *Sex Roles, 39,* 929–941.

Hondagneu-Sotelo, P. (1997). Working "without papers" in the United States: Toward the integration of legal status in frameworks of race, class, and gender. In E. Higginbotham & M. Romero (Eds.), *Women and work: Exploring race, ethnicity, and class* (pp. 101–125). Thousand Oaks, CA: Sage.

Hood, A. (1995). It's a wonderful divorce. In P. Kaganoff & S. Spano (Eds.), *Women and divorce* (pp. 119–133). New York: Harcourt Brace.

hooks, b. (1993, October). Confronting sexism in Black life: The struggle continues. *Z Magazine,* pp. 36–39.

hooks, b. (1994, July 13). Black students who reject feminism. *Chronicle of Higher Education,* p. A44.

hooks, b. (2000a). *Feminism is for everybody: Passionate politics.* Cambridge, MA: South End Press.

hooks, b. (2000b). *Feminist theory: From margin to center.* Cambridge, MA: South End Press.

hooks, b. (2000c, November 17). Learning in the shadow of race and class. *Chronicle of Higher Education,* pp. B14–B15.

hooks, b. (2001). Revolutionary feminism: An antiracist agenda. In S. M. Shaw & J. Lee (Eds.), *Women's voices, feminist visions* (pp. 33–36). Mountain View, CA: Mayfield.

Horgan, D. (1983). The pregnant woman's place and where to find it. *Sex Roles, 9,* 333–339.

Horner, M. S. (1968). *Sex differences in achievement motivation and performance in competitive and noncompetitive situations.* Unpublished doctoral dissertation, University of Michigan, Ann Arbor.

Horner, M. S. (1978). The measurement and behavioral implications of fear of success in women. In J. W. Atkinson & J. O. Raynor (Eds.), *Personality, motivation, and achievement* (pp. 41–70). Washington, DC: Hemisphere.

Hosking, D., et al. (1998). Prevention of bone loss with alendronate in postmenopausal women under 60 years of age. *New England Journal of Medicine, 338,* 485–491.

Hoskins, C. N., & Haber, J. (2001). *Breast cancer: Journey to recovery.* New York: Springer.

Hosoda, M., & Stone, D. L. (2000). Current gender stereotypes and their evaluative content. *Perceptual and Motor Skills, 90,* 1283–1294.

Houston, B. (1989). Prolegomena to future caring. In M. M. Brabeck (Ed.), *Who cares? Theory, research, and educational implications of the ethic of care* (pp. 84–100). New York: Praeger.

Howard, J. A., & Hollander, J. (1997). *Gendered situations, gendered selves.* Thousand Oaks, CA: Sage.

Howe, F. (2001a). *The politics of women's studies: Testimony from thirty founding mothers.* New York: Feminist Press.

Howe, F. (2001b). "Promises to keep": Trends in women's studies worldwide. In S. Ruth (Ed.), *Issues in feminism* (5th ed.). Mountain View, CA: Mayfield.

Howell-White, S. (1999). *Birth alternatives: How women select childbirth care.* Westport, CT: Greenwood Press.

Hoyert, D. L., Daniel, I., & Tully, P. (2000). Maternal mortality, United States and Canada, 1982–1997. *Birth, 27,* 4–11.

Hoynes, W. (1999, September/October). The cost of survival. *Extra!,* pp. 11–23.

Hrdy, S. B. (1999). *Mother nature: A history of mothers, infants, and natural selection.* New York: Random House.

HRT 2000: Pause for thought. (2000, April). *Women's Health Watch,* pp. 1–3.

Humes, C. W., Szymanski, E. M., & Hohenshil, T. H. (1995). Roles of counseling in enabling persons with disabilities. In R. R. Atkinson & G. Hackett (Eds.), *Counseling diverse populations* (pp. 155–166). Madison, WI: Brown & Benchmark.

Humm, M. (1995). *The dictionary of feminist theory* (2nd ed.). Columbus, OH: Ohio State University.

Hummert, M. L., Garstka, T. A., & Shaner, J. L. (1997). Stereotyping of older adults: The role of target facial cues and perceiver characteristics. *Psychology and Aging, 12,* 107–114.

Humphrey, J. A., & White, J. W. (2000). Women's vulnerability to sexual assault from adolescence to young adulthood. *Journal of Adolescent Health, 27,* 419–424.

Humphrey, S. E., & Kahn, A. S. (2000). Fraternities, athletic teams, and rape: Importance of identification with a risky group. *Journal of Interpersonal Violence, 15,* 1313–1322.

Humphreys, A., Thompson, N. J., & Miner, K. P. (1998). Intention to breastfeed in low-income pregnant women: The role of social support and previous experience. *Birth, 25,* 169–174.

Huntemmann, N., & Morgan, M. (2001). Mass media and identity development. In D. G. Singer & J. L.

Singer (Eds.). *Handbook on children and the media* (pp. 309–322). Thousand Oaks, CA: Sage.

Hunter College Women's Studies Collective. (1995). *Women's realities, women's choices* (2nd ed.). New York: Oxford University Press.

Hurtz, W., & Durkin, K. (1997). Gender role stereotyping in Australian radio commercials. *Sex Roles, 36,* 103–114.

Husten, C. G. (1998). Cigarette smoking. In E. A. Blechman & K. D. Brownell (Eds.), *Behavioral medicine and women: A comprehensive handbook* (pp. 425–430). New York: Guilford.

Huston, R. (1997). *A positive life: Portraits of women living with HIV.* Philadelphia: Running Press.

Huttenlocher, J., et al. (1991). Early vocabulary growth: Relation to language input and gender. *Developmental Psychology, 27,* 236–248.

Huyck, M. H. (1999). Gender roles and gender identity in midlife. In S. L. Willis & J. D. Reid (Eds.), *Life in the middle* (pp. 209–232). San Diego: Academic Press.

Hvas, L. (2001). Positive aspects of menopause: A qualitative study. *Maturitas, 39,* 11–17.

Hyde, J. S. (1981). How large are cognitive gender differences? A meta-analysis using w^2 and d. *American Psychologist, 36,* 892–901.

Hyde, J. S. (1996a). Gender and cognition: A commentary on current research. *Learning and Individual Differences, 8,* 33–38.

Hyde, J. S. (1996b). Where are the gender differences? Where are the gender similarities? In D. M. Buss & N. M. Malamuth (Eds.), *Sex, power, conflict: Evolutionary and feminist perspectives* (pp. 107–118). New York: Oxford University Press.

Hyde, J. S. (2001). Autobiographical perspectives. In A. N. O'Connell (Ed.), *Models of achievement: Reflections of eminent women in psychology* (Vol. 3, pp. 308–327). Mahwah, NJ: Erlbaum.

Hyde, J. S., & DeLamater, J. (2000). Sexuality during pregnancy and the year postpartum. In C. B. Travis & J. W. White (Eds.), *Sexuality, society, and feminism* (pp. 167–180). Washington, DC: American Psychological Association.

Hyde, J. S., & DeLamater, J. D. (2003). *Understanding human sexuality* (8th ed.). Boston: McGraw-Hill.

Hyde, J. S., Fennema, E., Ryan, M., Frost, L. A., & Hopp, C. (1990). Gender comparisons of mathematics attitudes and affect: A meta-analysis. *Psychology of Women Quarterly, 14,* 299–324.

Hyde, J. S., & Jaffee, S. R. (2000). Becoming a heterosexual adult: The experiences of young women. *Journal of Social Issues, 56,* 283–296.

Hyde, J. S., & Kling, K. C. (2001). Women, motivation, and achievement. *Psychology of Women Quarterly, 25,* 364–378.

Hyde, J. S., & Linn, M. C. (1988). Gender differences in verbal ability: A meta-analysis. *Psychological Bulletin, 104,* 53–69.

Hyde, J. S., & McKinley, N. M. (1997). Gender differences in cognition: Results from meta-analyses. In P. J. Caplan, M. Crawford, J. S. Hyde, & J. T. E. Richardson (Eds.), *Gender differences in human cognition* (pp. 30–51). New York: Oxford University Press.

Hyde, J. S., & Mezulis, A. H. (2001). Gender difference research. In J. Worell (Ed.), *Encyclopedia of women and gender* (pp. 551–559). San Diego: Academic Press.

Hyde, J. S., & Oliver, M. B. (2000). Gender differences in sexuality: Results from meta-analysis. In C. B. Travis & J. W. White (Eds.), *Sexuality, society, and feminism* (pp. 57–77). Washington, DC: American Psychological Association.

Hyde, J. S., & Plant, E. A. (1995). Magnitude of psychological gender differences: Another side to the story. *American Psychologist, 50,* 159–161.

Hyman, I. E., Jr., Husband, T. H., & Billings, F. J. (1995). False memories of childhood experiences. *Applied Cognitive Psychology, 9,* 181–197.

Hynie, M., Lydon, J. E., & Taradash, A. (1997). Commitment, intimacy, and women's perceptions of premarital sex and contraceptive readiness. *Psychology of Women Quarterly, 21,* 447–464.

"IA matrimonial classifieds." (2001, October 26). *India Abroad,* pp. 44–46.

Ickovics, J. R., Thayaparan, B., & Ethier, K. A. (2001). Women and AIDS: A contextual analysis. In A. Baum, T. A. Revenson, & J. E. Singer (Eds.), *Handbook of health psychology* (pp. 817–840). Mahwah, NJ: Erlbaum.

Idle, T., Wood, E., & Desmarais, S. (1993). Gender role socialization in toy play situations: Mothers and fathers with their sons and daughters. *Sex Roles, 28,* 679–691.

Im, E., & Meleis, A. I. (2000). Meanings of menopause to Korean immigrant women. *Western Journal of Nursing Research, 22,* 84–102.

Ineichen, B., Pierce, M., & Lawrenson, R. (1997). Teenage mothers as breastfeeders: Attitudes and behavior. *Journal of Adolescence, 20,* 505–509.

Intons-Peterson, M. J., & Reddel, M. (1984). What do people ask about a neonate? *Developmental Psychology, 20,* 358–359.

Ireland, M. S. (1993). *Reconceiving women: Separating motherhood from female identity.* New York: Guilford.

Ivins, M. (1997, September 27). Teen mothers lack good role models. *Liberal Opinion Week,* p. 12.

Ivy, D. K., et al. (1995). The lawyer, the babysitter, and the student: Inclusive language usage and instruction. *Women and Language, 18,* 13–21.

Jack, D. C. (1999a). *Behind the mask: Destruction and creativity in women's aggression.* Cambridge, MA: Harvard University Press.

Jack, D. C. (1999b). Silencing the self: Inner dialogues and outer realities. In T. Joiner & J. C. Coyne (Eds.), *The interactional nature of depression* (pp. 221–246). Washington, DC: American Psychological Association.

Jacklin, C. N., & Baker, L. A. (1993). Early gender development. In S. Oskamp & M. Costanzo (Eds.), *Gender issues in contemporary society* (pp. 41–57). Newbury Park, CA: Sage.

Jacklin, C. N., & Maccoby, E. E. (1983). Issues of gender differentiation. In M. D. Levine, W. B. Carey, A. C. Crocker, & R. T. Gross (Eds.), *Developmental-behavioral pediatrics* (pp. 175–184). Philadelphia: Saunders.

Jacklin, C. N., & Reynolds, C. (1993). Gender and childhood socialization. In A. E. Beall & R. J. Sternberg (Eds.), *The psychology of gender* (pp. 197–214). New York: Guilford.

Jackson, A. P., Brooks-Gunn, J., Huang, C., & Glassman, M. (2000). Single mothers in low-wage jobs: Financial strain, parenting, and preschoolers' outcomes. *Child Development, 71,* 1409–1423.

Jackson, D. Z. (1998, April 27). Women on welfare need education: Why deny them? *Liberal Opinion,* p. 1.

Jackson, L. A., Fleury, R. E., Girvin, J. L., & Gerard, D. A. (1995). The numbers game: Gender and attention to numerical information. *Sex Roles, 33,* 559–568.

Jackson, L. A., Fleury, R. E., & Lewandowski, D. A. (1996). Feminism: Definitions, support, and correlates of support among female and male college students. *Sex Roles, 34,* 687–693.

Jackson, S. A. (1998). "Something about the word": African American women and feminism. In K. M. Blee (Ed.), *No middle ground: Women and radical protest* (pp. 38–50). New York: New York University Press.

Jacobs, J. A. (1995). Women's entry into management: Trends in earnings, authority, and values among salaried managers. In J. A. Jacobs (Ed.), *Gender inequality at work* (pp. 152–177). Thousand Oaks, CA: Sage.

Jacobs, R. H. (1997). *Be an outrageous older woman.* New York: HarperCollins.

Jacobson, N. S., & Gottman, J. M. (1998). *When men batter women.* New York: Simon & Schuster.

Jadack, R. A. (2001). Sexually transmitted infections and their consequences. In J. Worell (Ed.), *Encyclopedia of women and gender* (pp. 1033–1041). San Diego: Academic Press.

Jaffee, S., & Hyde, J. S. (2000). Gender differences in moral orientation: A meta-analysis. *Psychological Bulletin, 126,* 703–726.

Jaffee, S., et al. (1999). The view from down here: Feminist graduate students consider innovative methodologies. *Psychology of Women Quarterly, 23,* 423–430.

James, E. M. (1994, August). *Helen Thompson Woolley: Forgotten pioneer of the psychology of women.* Paper presented at the annual convention of the American Psychological Association, Los Angeles, CA.

James, J. (1999). *Shadowboxing: Representations of Black feminist politics.* New York: St. Martin's Press.

James, J., & Sharpley-Whiting, T. D. (Eds.). (2000). *The Black feminist reader.* Malden, MA: Blackwell.

James, J. B. (1997). What are the social issues involved in focusing on *difference* in the study of gender? *Journal of Social Issues, 53,* 213–232.

James, J. G. (1999). The contributions of women's studies programs. In S. N. Davis, M. Crawford, & J. Sebrechts (Eds.), *Coming into her own* (pp. 23–36). San Francisco: Jossey-Bass.

Janz, T. A., & Pyke, S. W. (2000). A scale to assess student perceptions of academic climates. *Canadian Journal of Higher Education, 30,* 89–122.

Jay, T. (2000). *Why we curse.* Philadelphia: John Benjamins.

Jayakody, R., & Stauffer, D. (2000). Mental health problems among single mothers: Implications for work and welfare reform. *Journal of Social Issues, 56,* 617–634.

Jenkins, S. R. (2000). Introduction to the special issue: Defining gender, relationships, and power. *Sex Roles, 42,* 467–493.

Jenkins, Y. M. (2000). The Stone Center theoretical approach revisited: Applications for African American women. In L. C. Jackson & B. Greene (Eds.), *Psychotherapy with African American women* (pp. 62–81). New York: Guilford.

Jennings, J., Geis, L., & Brown, V. (1980). Influence of television commercials on women's self-confidence and independent judgments. *Journal of Personality and Social Psychology, 38,* 203–210.

Jensen-Campbell, L. A., Graziano, W. G., & West, S. G. (1995). Dominance, prosocial orientation, and female preferences: Do nice guys really finish last? *Journal of Personality and Social Psychology, 68,* 427–440.

Jensvold, M. E., & Dan, C. E. (2001). Psychological aspects of the menstrual cycle. In N. L. Stotland & D. E. Stewart (Eds.), *Psychological aspects of women's health care* (pp. 177–203). Washington, DC: American Psychiatric Press.

Jiwani, Y. (2000, Fall). The 1999 general social survey on spousal violence: An analysis. *Canadian Woman Studies/Les cahiers de la femme, 20,* 34–40.

Johannesen-Schmidt, M. C., & Eagly, A. H. (2002). Another look at sex differences in preferred mate characteristics: The effects of endorsing the traditional female gender role. *Psychology of Women Quarterly, 26,* 322–328.

John, D., & Shelton, B. A. (1997). The production of gender among Black and White women and men: The case of household labor. *Sex Roles, 36,* 171–193.

John, R., Blanchard, P. H., & Hennessy, C. H. (1997). Hidden lives: Aging and contemporary American Indian women. In J. M. Coyle (Ed.), *Handbook on women and aging* (pp. 290–315). Westport, CT: Greenwood Press.

Johnson, A. G. (1997). *The gender knot: Unraveling our patriarchal legacy.* Philadelphia: Temple University Press.

Johnson, A. G. (2001). *Privilege, power, and differences.* Mountain View, CA: Mayfield.

Johnson, B. E., Kuck, D. L., & Schander, P. R. (1997). Rape myth acceptance and sociodemographic characteristics: A multidimensional analysis. *Sex Roles, 36,* 693–707.

Johnson, C. (1994). Gender, legitimate authority, and leader-subordinate conversations. *American Sociological Review, 59,* 122–135.

Johnson, C. L., & Barer, B. M. (1997). *Life beyond 85 years: The aura of survivorship.* New York: Springer.

Johnson, J. D., Adams, M. S., Ashburn, L., & Reed, W. (1995). Differential gender effects of exposure to rap music on African American adolescents' acceptance of teen dating violence. *Sex Roles, 33,* 597–605.

Johnson, L. B. (1997). Three decades of Black family empirical research: Challenges for the 21st century. In H. P. McAdoo (Ed.), *Black families* (3rd ed., pp. 94–113). Thousand Oaks, CA: Sage.

Johnson, M. E., & Dowling-Guyer, S. (1996). Effects of inclusive vs. exclusive language on evaluations of the counselor. *Sex Roles, 34,* 407–418.

Johnson, N. G. (2001, October). Changing outcomes in women's health. *APA Monitor,* p. 5.

Johnson, S. M., & O'Connor, E. (2001). *For lesbian parents: Your guide to helping your family grow up happy, healthy, and proud.* New York: Guilford.

Johnson, S. R. (1995). Menstruation. In M. W. O'Hara, et al. (Eds.), *Psychological aspects of women's reproductive health* (pp. 3–25). New York: Springer.

Johnson, T. L., & Fee, E. (1997). Women's health research: An introduction. In F. P. Haseltine & B. G. Jacobson (Eds.), *Women's health research: A medical and policy primer* (pp. 3–26). Washington, DC: Health Press International.

Johnston-Robledo, I. (2000). From postpartum depression to the empty nest syndrome: The motherhood mystique revisited. In J. C. Chrisler, C. Golden, & P. D. Rozee (Eds.), *Lectures on the psychology of women* (2nd ed., pp. 128–147). Boston: McGraw-Hill.

Joiner, T. E., Jr., & Blalock, J. A. (1995). Gender differences in depression: The role of anxiety and generalized negative affect. *Sex Roles, 33,* 91–108.

Jones, M. (1991). Gender stereotyping in advertisements. *Teaching of Psychology, 18,* 231–233.

Jordan, J. V. (1997). The relational model is a source of empowerment for women. In M. R. Walsh (Ed.), *Women, men, and gender: Ongoing debates* (pp. 373–379). New Haven, CT: Yale University Press.

Jordan, J. V. (1998). Empathy, mutuality, and therapeutic change: Clinical implications of a relational model. In B. M. Clinchy & J. K. Norem (Eds.), *The gender and psychology reader* (pp. 543–548). New York: New York University Press.

Jordan, V. C. (1998, October). Designer estrogens. *Scientific American,* pp. 60–67.

Jorgensen, L. A. B. (2001). Public policy effects on the health care of older women: Who is in charge? In J. D. G. Garner & S. O. Mercer (Eds.), *Women as they age* (2nd ed., pp. 195–214). New York: Haworth.

Jussim, L., et al. (2000). Stigma and self-fulfilling prophecies. In T. F. Heatherton, R. E. Kleck, M. R. Hebl, & J. G. Hull (Eds.), *The social psychology of stigma* (pp. 374–418). New York: Guilford.

Kafka, P. (2000). *(Out)classed women: Contemporary Chicana writers on inequitable gendered power relations.* Westport, CT: Greenwood Press.

Kaganoff, P., & Spano, S. (Eds.). (1995). *Women and divorce.* New York: Harcourt Brace.

Kagawa-Singer, M., Hikoyeda, N., & Tanjasiri, S. P. (1997). Aging, chronic conditions, and physical disabilities in Asian and Pacific Islander Americans. In K. S. Markides & M. R. Miranda (Eds.), *Minorities, aging, and health* (pp. 149–180). Thousand Oaks, CA: Sage.

Kahn, A. S., & Andreoli Mathie, V. (2000). Understanding the unacknowledged rape victim. In C. B. Travis & J. W. White (Eds.), *Sexuality, society, and feminism* (pp. 377–403). Washington, DC: American Psychological Association.

Kahn, A. S., & Yoder, J. D. (1989). The psychology of women and conservatism. *Psychology of Women Quarterly, 13,* 417–432.

Kail, R. V., Jr., Carter, P., & Pellegrino, J. (1979). The locus of sex differences in spatial ability. *Perception and Psychophysics, 26,* 182–186.

Kakaiya, D. (2000). Identity development and conflicts among Indian immigrant women. In J. L. Chin (Ed.), *Relationships among Asian American Women* (pp. 133–149). Washington, DC: American Psychological Association.

Kalichman, S. C. (1989). The effects of stimulus context on paper-and-pencil spatial task performance. *Journal of General Psychology, 116,* 133–139.

Kalick, S. M., Zebrowitz, L. A., Langlois, J. H., & Johnson, R. M. (1998). Does human face attractiveness honestly advertise health? *Psychological Science, 9,* 8–13.

Kamen, P. (2000). *Her way: Young women remake the sexual revolution.* New York: New York University Press.

Kandall, S. R. (1999). Women and drug addiction. In G. Null & B. Seaman (Eds.), *For women only: Your guide to health empowerment* (pp. 677–679). New York: Seven Stories Press.

Kandel, D. B. (2000). Gender differences in the epidemiology of substance dependence in the United States. In E. Frank (Ed.), *Gender and its effects on psychopathology* (pp. 231–252). Washington, DC: American Psychiatric Press.

Kantrowitz, B. (1987, February 16). Kids and contraceptives. *Newsweek,* pp. 54–65.

Kaplan, A. G., Gleason, N., & Klein, R. (1991). Women's self development in late adolescence. In J. V. Jordan et al. (Eds.), *Women's growth in con-*nection: *Writings from the Stone Center* (pp. 122–140). New York: Guilford.

Kaplan, D. W. (1995, April). School-based health centers: Primary care in high school. *Pediatric Annals, 24,* 192–200.

Kaplan, H. (1979). *Disorders of sexual desire.* New York: Brunner/Mazel.

Kaplan, J., & Aronson, D. (1994, Spring). The numbers gap. *Teaching Tolerance,* pp. 21–27.

Karniol, R., Gabay, R., Ochion, Y., & Harari, Y. (1998). Is gender or gender-role orientation a better predictor of empathy in adolescence? *Sex Roles, 39,* 45–59.

Karraker, K. H., Vogel, D. A., & Lake, M. A. (1995). Parents' gender-stereotyped perceptions of newborns: The eye of the beholder revisited. *Sex Roles, 33,* 687–701.

Kaschak, E., & Tiefer, L. (Eds.). (2001). *A new view of women's sexual problems.* New York: Haworth.

Kasper, A. S., & Ferguson, S. J. (2000). *Breast cancer: Society shapes an epidemic.* New York: St. Martin's Press.

Kasser, T., & Sharma, Y. S. (1999). Reproductive freedom, educational equality, and females' preferences for resource-acquisition characteristics in mates. *Psychological Science, 10,* 374–377.

Kastberg, S. M., & Miller, D. G. (1996). Of blue collars and ivory towers: Women from blue-collar backgrounds in higher education. In K. Arnold, K. D. Noble, & R. F. Subotnik (Eds.), *Remarkable women: Perspectives on female talent development* (pp. 49–67). Creskill, NJ: Hampton Press.

Kato, N. R. (1999). Asian Americans defy "model minority" myth. In Y. Alaniz & N. Wong (Eds.), *Voices of color* (pp. 150–153). Seattle: Red Letter Press.

Katz, D. (1987). Sex discrimination in hiring: The influence of organizational climate and need for approval on decision making behavior. *Psychology of Women Quarterly, 11,* 11–20.

Katz, P. A. (1987). Variations in family constellation: Effects on gender schemata. In L. S. Liben & M. L. Signorella (Eds.), *Children's gender schemata* (pp. 39–56). San Francisco: Jossey-Bass.

Katz, P. A. (1996). Raising feminists, *Psychology of Women Quarterly, 20,* 323–340.

Katz, P. A., Boggiano, A., & Silvern, L. (1993). Theories of female personality. In F. L. Denmark & M. A. Paludi (Eds.), *Psychology of women: A handbook of issues and theories* (pp. 247–280). Westport, CT: Greenwood Press.

Katz, P. A., & Kofkin, J. A. (1997). Race, gender, and young children. In S. Luthar, J. A. Baruck, D. Cicchetti, & J. Weisz (Eds.), *Developmental psychopathology: Perspectives on adjustment, risk, and disorder* (pp. 51–74). New York: Cambridge University Press.

Katzman, D. K., et al. (1997). A longitudinal magnetic resonance imaging study of brain changes in adolescents with anorexia nervosa. *Archives of Pediatric and Adolescent Medicine, 151,* 793–797.

Kaufman, G. (1999). The portrayal of men's family roles in television commercials. *Sex Roles, 41,* 439–458.

Kaufman, J. (1999). Adolescent females' perception of autonomy and control. In M. B. Nadien & F. L. Denmark (Eds.), *Females and autonomy* (pp. 43–72). Boston: Allyn & Bacon.

Kauth, M. R., & Kalichman, S. C. (1998). Sexual orientation and development: An interactive approach. In D. L. Anselmi & A. L. Law (Eds.), *Questions of gender: Perspectives and paradoxes* (pp. 329–344). New York: McGraw-Hill.

Kawachi, I., et al. (1997). A prospective study of passive smoking and coronary heart disease. *Circulation, 95,* 2374–2379.

Kearns, J. R., & Christopherson, V. A. (1992). Mexican-American women's perceptions of menopause. In A. J. Dan & L. L. Lewis (Eds.), *Menstrual health in women's lives* (pp. 191–197). Urbana, IL: University of Illinois Press.

Kehoe, M. (1989). *Lesbians over 60 speak for themselves.* New York: Harrington Park Press.

Keitel, M. A., & Kopala, M. (2000). *Counseling women with breast cancer.* Thousand Oaks, CA: Sage.

Kelly, J. A. (2001). Safer sex behaviors. In J. Worell (Ed.), *Encyclopedia of women and gender* (pp. 933–939). San Diego: Academic Press.

Kelly, J. R., & Hutson-Comeaux, S. L. (2000). The appropriateness of emotional expression in women and men: The double-bind of emotion. *Journal of Social Behavior and Personality, 15,* 515–528.

Kelly, K., & Jordan, L. (1990). Effects of academic achievement and gender on academic and social self-concept: A replication study. *Journal of Counseling and Development, 69,* 173–177.

Kerpelman, J. L., & Schvaneveldt, P. L. (1999). Young adults' anticipated identity importance of career, marital, and parental roles: Comparisons of men and women with different role balance orientations. *Sex Roles, 41,* 189–217.

Kerr, B. (1994). *Smart girls two: A new psychology of girls, women, and giftedness.* Dayton, OH: Ohio Psychology Press.

Kerson, T. S. (2001). Social work practice with women as they age. In J. D. Garner & S. O. Mercer (Eds.), *Women as they age* (2nd ed., pp. 69–84). New York: Haworth.

Kessler, R. C. (2000). Gender differences in major depression: Epidemiological findings. In E. Frank (Ed.), *Gender and its effects on psychopathology* (pp. 61–84). Washington, DC: American Psychiatric Press.

Kessler, S. J. (1998). *Lessons from the intersexed.* Piscataway, NJ: Rutgers University Press.

Ketenjian, T. (1999a). Interview of Alice Wolfson. In G. Null & B. Seaman (Eds.), *For women only: Your guide to health empowerment* (pp. 1495–1499). New York: Seven Stories Press.

Ketenjian, T. (1999b). Interview of Patsy Mink. In G. Null & B. Seaman (Eds.), *For women only: Your guide to health empowerment* (pp. 1042–1045). New York: Seven Stories Press.

Keyes, C. L. M., & Ryff, C. D. (1998). Generativity in adult lives: Social structural contours and quality of life consequences. In D. P. McAdams & E. de St. Aubin (Eds.), *Generativity and adult development: How and why we care for the next generation* (pp. 227–263). Washington, DC: American Psychological Association.

Kilbey, M. M., & Burgermeister, D. (2001). Substance abuse. In J. Worell (Ed.), *Encyclopedia of women and gender* (pp. 1113–1127). San Diego: Academic Press.

Kilbourne, J. (1999). *Deadly persuasion.* New York: Free Press.

Kilmartin, C. (2000). *The masculine self* (2nd ed.). Boston: McGraw-Hill.

Kim, J. E., & Moen, P. (2001a). Is retirement good or bad for subjective well-being? *Current Directions in Psychological Science, 10,* 83–86.

Kim, J. E., & Moen, P. (2001b). Moving into retirement: Preparation and transitions in late midlife. In M. E. Lachman (Ed.), *Handbook of midlife development* (pp. 487–527). New York: Wiley.

Kimball, M. M. (1989). A new perspective on women's math achievement. *Psychological Bulletin, 105,* 198–214.

Kimball, M. M. (1995). *Feminist visions of gender similarities and differences.* Binghamton, NY: Haworth.

Kimball, M. M. (1999). Acknowledging truth and fantasy: Freud and the recovered memory debate. In M. Rivera (Ed.), *Fragment by fragment: Feminist perspectives on memory and child sexual abuse* (pp. 21–42). Charlottetown, PEI, Canada: gynergy books.

Kimmel, E. B., & Kazanis, B. W. (1995). Explorations of the unrecognized spirituality of women's communion. *Women and Therapy, 6*, 215–227.

Kimmel, M. S. (2000). *The gendered society.* New York: Oxford University Press.

Kimmel, M. S., & Messner, M. A. (Eds.). (1998). *Men's lives* (4th ed.). Boston: Allyn & Bacon.

Kimura, D. (1987). Are men's and women's brains really different? *Canadian Psychology/Psychologie canadienne, 28*, 133–147.

Kimura, D. (1992, September). Sex differences in the brain. *Scientific American, 267*, 118–125.

Kimura, D. (1999). *Sex and cognition.* Cambridge, MA: MIT Press.

King, B. M., Parisi, L. S., & O'Dwyer, K. R. (1993). College sexuality between former students and their children. *Journal of Sex Education and Therapy, 19*, 285–293.

King, Y. (1997). The other body: Reflections on difference, disability, and identity politics. In M. Crawford & R. Unger (Eds.), *In our own words: Readings on the psychology of women and gender* (pp. 107–111). New York: McGraw-Hill.

Kinsella, K. (2000). Demographic dimensions of global aging. *Journal of Family Issues, 21*, 541–558.

Kirk, G., & Okazawa-Rey, M. (2001). *Women's lives: Multicultural perspectives* (2nd ed.). Mountain View, CA: Mayfield.

Kisber, S. (2001, Spring). Reflections on my experience as a disabled feminist psychologist. *Association for Women in Psychology Newsletter*, pp. 4–5.

Kishwar, M. (1995). When daughters are unwanted: Sex determination tests in India. *Manushi, 86*, 15–22.

Kishwar, M. (1999). *Off the beaten track: Rethinking gender justice for Indian women.* New Delhi: Oxford University Press.

Kite, M. E. (1994). When perceptions meet reality: Individual differences in reactions to lesbians and gay men. In B. Greene & G. M. Herek (Eds.), *Contemporary perspectives on gay and lesbian psychology* (pp. 25–53). Newbury Park, CA: Sage.

Kite, M. E. (1996). Age, gender, and occupational label: A test of social role theory. *Psychology of Women Quarterly, 20*, 361–374.

Kite, M. E., & Balogh, D. W. (1997). Warming trends: Improving the chilly campus climate. In N. V. Benokraitis (Ed.), *Subtle sexism: Current practice and prospects for change* (pp. 264–278). Thousand Oaks, CA: Sage.

Kite, M. E., & Branscombe, N. R. (1998). *Evaluation of subtypes of women and men.* Unpublished manuscript.

Kite, M. E., & Deaux, K. (1986). Attitudes toward homosexuality: Assessment and behavioral consequences. *Basic and Applied Social Psychology, 7*, 137–162.

Kite, M. E., Deaux, K., & Miele, M. (1991). Stereotypes of young and old: Does age outweigh gender? *Psychology and Aging, 6*, 19–27.

Kite, M. E., & Wagner, L. S. (2002). Attitudes toward older adults. In T. Nelson (Ed.), *Ageism: Stereotyping and prejudice against older persons* (pp. 129–161). Cambridge, MA: MIT Press.

Kite, M. E., & Whitley, B. E., Jr. (1996). Sex differences in attitudes toward homosexual persons, behaviors, and civil rights: A meta-analysis. *Personality and Social Psychology Bulletin, 22*, 336–353.

Kite, M. E., & Whitley, B. E., Jr. (1998). Do heterosexual women and men differ in their attitudes toward homosexuality? A conceptual and methodological analysis. In G. M. Herek (Ed.), *Stigma, prejudice, and violence against lesbians and gay men.* Thousand Oaks, CA: Sage.

Kitson, G. C. (1992). *Portrait of divorce: Adjustment to marital breakdown.* New York: Guilford.

Kitzinger, C., & Wilkinson, S. (1997). Transitions from heterosexuality to lesbianism: The discursive production of lesbian identities. In M. R. Walsh (Ed.), *Women, men, and gender: Ongoing debates* (pp. 188–203). New Haven, CT: Yale University Press.

Kitzinger, S. (1994). *The year after childbirth: Surviving and enjoying the first year of motherhood.* New York: Scribner's.

Kitzinger, S. (1995). *Ourselves as mothers: The universal experience of motherhood.* Reading, MA: Addison-Wesley.

Kitzmann, K. M., & Gaylord, N. K. (2001). Divorce and child custody. In J. Worell (Ed.), *Encyclopedia of women and gender* (pp. 355–367). San Diego: Academic Press.

Kivett, V. R. (1996). The saliency of the grandmother-granddaughter relationship: Predictors of association. *Journal of Women and Aging, 8*, 25–39.

Klebanoff, M. A., Shiono, P. H., & Rhoads, G. G. (1990). Outcomes of pregnancy in a national sample of resident physicians. *New England Journal of Medicine, 323*, 1040–1045.

Klebanov, P. K., & Jemmott, J. B., III. (1992). Effects of expectations and bodily sensations on self-reports of premenstrual symptoms. *Psychology of Women Quarterly, 16,* 289–310.

Klein, E., Campbell, J., Soler, E., & Ghez, M. (1997). *Ending domestic violence: Changing public perceptions/ Halting the epidemic.* Thousand Oaks, CA: Sage.

Klein, M. H., Hyde, J. S., Essex, M. J., & Clark, R. (1998). Maternity leave, role quality, work involvement, and mental health one year after delivery. *Psychology of Women Quarterly, 22,* 239–266.

Klevan, J. L., Weiss, J. C., & Dabrow, S. M. (1990). Pregnancy during pediatric residency. *American Journal of Diseases of Children, 144,* 767–777.

Kling, K. C., & Hyde, J. S. (2001). Self-esteem. In J. Worell (Ed.), *Encyclopedia of women and gender.* San Diego: Academic Press.

Kling, K. C., Hyde, J. S., Showers, C., & Buswell, B. (1999). Gender differences in self-esteem: A meta-analysis. *Psychological Bulletin, 125,* 470–500.

Klinger, R. L. (1996). Lesbian couples. In R. P. Cabaj & T. S. Stein (Eds.), *Textbook of homosexuality and mental health* (pp. 339–352). Washington DC: American Psychiatric Press.

Klonis, S., Endo, J., Cosby, F., & Worell, J. (1997). Feminism as life raft. *Psychology of Women Quarterly, 21,* 333–345.

Klonoff, E. A., & Landrine, H. (1997). *Preventing misdiagnosis of women: A guide to physical disorders that have psychiatric symptoms.* Thousand Oaks, CA: Sage.

Klonoff, E. A., Landrine, H., & Campbell, R. (2000). Sexist discrimination may account for well-known gender differences in psychiatric symptoms. *Psychology of Women Quarterly, 24,* 93–99.

Knight, G. P., Fabes, R. A., & Higgins, D. A. (1996). Concerns about drawing causal inferences from meta-analyses: An example in the study of gender differences in aggression. *Psychological Bulletin, 119,* 410–421.

Knight, J. L., & Giuliano, T. A. (2001). He's a Laker; she's a "looker": The consequences of gender-stereotypical portrayals of male and female athletes by the print media. *Sex Roles, 45,* 217–229.

Knox, M., Funk, J., Elliott, R., & Bush, E. G. (2000). Gender differences in adolescents' possible selves. *Youth and Society, 31,* 287–309.

Ko, M., & Schulken, E. D. (1998). Factors related to smoking cessation and relapse among pregnant smokers. *American Journal of Health Behavior, 22,* 83–89.

Kohlberg, L. (1966). A cognitive-developmental analysis of children's sex-role concepts and attitudes. In E. E. Maccoby (Ed.), *The development of sex differences* (pp. 82–173). Stanford, CA: Stanford University Press.

Kohlberg, L. (1981). *The philosophy of moral development: Essays on moral development* (Vols. 1 & 2). San Francisco: Harper & Row.

Kohlberg, L. (1984). *Essays on moral development: Vol. 2. The psychology of moral development.* San Francisco: Freeman.

Kohlberg, L., & Ullian, D. Z. (1974). Stages in the development of psychosexual concepts and attitudes. In R. C. Friedman, R. M. Richart, & R. L. Van de Wiele (Eds.), *Sex differences in behavior* (pp. 209–222). New York: Wiley.

Koivula, N. (1999). Gender stereotyping in televised media sport coverage. *Sex Roles, 41,* 589–604.

Kolbe, R. H., & Albanese, P. J. (1996). Man to man: A content analysis of sole-male images in male-audience magazines. *Journal of Advertising, 25,* 1–20.

Kolbe, R. H., & Albanese, P. J. (1997). The functional integration of sole-male images into magazine advertisements. *Sex Roles, 36,* 813–836.

Kolpin, V. W., & Singell, L. D., Jr. (1996). The gender composition and scholarly performance of economic departments: A test for employment discrimination. *Industrial and Labor Relations Review, 49,* 408–423.

Konrad, A. M., & Linnehan, F. (1999). Affirmative action: History, effects, and attitudes. In G. N. Powell (Ed.), *Handbook of gender and work* (pp. 429–452). Thousand Oaks, CA: Sage.

Konrad, A. M., & Pfeffer, J. (1991). Understanding the hiring of women and minorities in educational institutions. *Sociology of Education, 64,* 141–157.

Kornhaber, A. (1996). *Contemporary grandparenting.* Thousand Oaks, CA: Sage.

Korol, C. T., & Craig, K. D. (2001). Pain from the perspectives of health psychology and culture. In S. S. Kazarian & D. R. Evans (Eds.), *Handbook of cultural health psychology* (pp. 241–265). San Diego: Academic Press.

Kortenhaus, C. M., & Demarest, J. (1993). Gender role stereotyping in children's literature: An update. *Sex Roles, 28,* 219–232.

Koshland, D. E., Jr. (1994). The spousal abuse problem. *Science, 265,* 455.

Koski, L. R., & Shaver, P. R. (1997). Attachment and relationship satisfaction across the lifespan. In R. J. Sternberg & M. Hojjat (Eds.), *Satisfaction in close relationships* (pp. 26–55). New York: Guilford.

Koss, M. P. (1992). The underdetection of rape: Methodological choices influence incidence estimates. *Journal of Social Issues, 48,* 61–75.

Koss, M. P. (1999). A field trip with an expert in pornography [Review of the book *Dangerous relationships: Pornography, misogyny, and rape*]. *Contemporary Psychology, 44,* 493–495.

Koss, M. P., Ingram, M., & Pepper, S. L. (2001). Male partner violence: Relevance to health care providers. In A. Baum, T. A. Revenson, & J. E. Singer (Eds.), *Handbook of health psychology* (pp. 541–557). Mahwah, NJ: Erlbaum.

Kowalski, R. (2000). Including gender, race, and ethnicity in psychology content courses. *Teaching of Psychology, 27,* 18–24.

Kowalski, R. M. (Ed.). (2001). *Behaving badly: Aversive behaviors in interpersonal relationships.* Washington, DC: American Psychological Association.

Kravetz, D., & Marecek, J. (2001). The feminist movement. In J. Worell (Ed.), *Encyclopedia of women and gender* (pp. 457–468). San Diego: Academic Press.

Kreipe, R. E., & Birndorf, S. A. (2000). Eating disorders in adolescents and young adults. *Medical Clinics of North America, 84,* 1027–1049.

Kring, A. M., & Gordon, A. H. (1998). Sex differences in emotion: Expression, experience, and physiology. *Journal of Personality and Social Psychology, 7,* 686–703.

Krishman, A., & Sweeney, C. J. (1998). Gender differences in fear of success imagery and other achievement-related background variables among medical students. *Sex Roles, 39,* 299–310.

Kristof, N. D. (1996, December 9). Wife-beating still common practice in much of Korea. *San Jose Mercury News,* p. 17A.

Kunda, Z. (1999). *Social cognition: Making sense of people.* Cambridge, MA: MIT Press.

Kunda, Z., & Sherman-Williams, B. (1993). Stereotypes and the construal of individuating information. *Personality and Social Psychology Bulletin, 19,* 90–99.

Kunkel, A. W., & Burleson, B. R. (1998). Social support and the emotional lives of men and women: An assessment of the different cultures perspective. In D. J. Canary & K. Dindia (Eds.), *Sex differences and similarities in communication* (pp. 101–125). Mahwah, NJ: Erlbaum.

Kurdek, L. A. (1991). The dissolution of gay and lesbian couples. *Journal of Social and Personal Relationships, 8,* 265–278.

Kurdek, L. A. (1995a). Assessing multiple determinants of relationship commitment in cohabiting gay, cohabiting lesbian, dating heterosexual, and married heterosexual couples. *Family Relations, 44,* 261–266.

Kurdek, L. A. (1995b). Developmental changes in relationship quality in gay and lesbian cohabiting couples. *Developmental Psychology, 31,* 86–94.

Kurdek, L. A. (1995c). Lesbian and gay couples. In A. R. D'Augelli & C. J. Patterson (Eds.), *Lesbian, gay, and bisexual identities over the lifespan: Psychological perspectives* (pp. 243–261). New York: Oxford University Press.

Kurdek, L. A. (1998). Relational outcomes and their predictors: Longitudinal evidence from heterosexual married, gay cohabiting, and lesbian cohabiting couples. *Journal of Marriage and the Family, 60,* 553–568.

Kurth, S. B., Spiller, B. B., & Travis, C. B. (2000). Consent, power, and sexual scripts: Deconstructing sexual harassment. In C. B. Travis & J. W. White (Eds.), *Sexuality, society, and feminism* (pp. 323–354). Washington, DC: American Psychological Association.

Kushner, E. (1997). *Experiencing abortion: A weaving of women's words.* New York: Harrington Park Press.

Kwa, L. (1994). Adolescent females' perceptions of competence: What is defined as healthy and achieving. In J. Gallivan, S. D. Crozier, & V. M. Lalande (Eds.), *Women, girls, and achievement* (pp. 121–132). North York, Canada: Captus University Publications.

Kyle, T. M., & Williams, S. (2000, April). *1998–1999 APA survey of undergraduate departments of psychology.* Washington, DC: American Psychological Association.

LaFramboise, D. (1996). *The princess at the window: A new gender morality.* Toronto: Penguin Books.

LaFrance, K. (1998, May 4). Livestock afforded more protection than an abused spouse. *Liberal Opinion,* p. 14.

LaFrance, M., & Hecht, M. A. (2000). Gender and smiling: A meta-analysis. In A. H. Fischer (Ed.), *Gender and emotion* (pp. 118–142). Cambridge, England: Cambridge University Press.

LaFrance, M., & Henley, N. M. (1997). On oppressing hypotheses: Or, differences in nonverbal sensitivity revisited. In M. R. Walsh (Ed.), *Women, men, and gender: Ongoing debates* (pp. 104–119). New Haven, CT: Yale University Press.

LaFromboise, T. D., Heyle, A. M., & Ozer, E. J. (1990). Changing and diverse roles of women in American Indian cultures. *Sex Roles, 22,* 455–476.

LaFromboise, T. D., et al. (1995). American Indian women and psychology. In H. Landrine (Ed.), *Bringing cultural diversity to feminist psychology: Theory, research, and practice* (pp. 197–239). Washington, DC: American Psychological Association.

Lakoff, R. T. (1990). *Talking power: The politics of language in our lives.* New York: Basic Books.

LaMar, L., & Kite, M. E. (1996, August). *Sex differences in attitudes toward gay men and lesbians: A multidimensional perspective.* Paper presented at the annual convention of the American Psychological Association, Toronto, Canada.

Lamb, S. (2000). *White saris and sweet mangoes: Aging, gender, and body in North India.* Berkeley, CA: University of California Press.

Lambert, A. J., & Raichle, K. (2000). The role of political ideology in mediating judgments of blame in rape victims and their assailants: A test of the just world, personal responsibility, and legitimization hypothesis. *Personality and Social Psychology Bulletin, 26,* 853–863.

Lambert, J. C. (2000, May 2). Self-made? Male myth. *City Newspaper,* p. 6.

Lamke, L. K., Sollie, D. L., Durbin, R. G., & Fitzpatrick, J. A. (1994). Masculinity, femininity, and relationship satisfaction: The mediating role of interpersonal competence. *Journal of Social and Personal Relationships, 11,* 535–554.

Lance, L. M. (1998). Gender differences in heterosexual dating: A content analysis of personal ads. *Journal of Men's Studies, 6,* 297–305.

Landrine, H. (Ed.). (1995a). *Bringing cultural diversity to feminist psychology: Theory, research, and practice.* Washington, DC: American Psychological Association.

Landrine, H. (1995b). Introduction: Cultural diversity, contextualism, and feminist psychology. In H. Landrine (Ed.), *Bringing cultural diversity to feminist psychology: Theory, research, and practice* (pp. 1–20). Washington, DC: American Psychological Association.

Landrine, H., & Klonoff, E. A. (1997). *Discrimination against women: Prevalence, consequences, remedies.* Thousand Oaks, CA: Sage.

Landrine, H., & Klonoff, E. A. (2001). Health and health care: How gender makes women sick. In J. Worell (Ed.), *Encyclopedia of women and gender* (pp. 577–592). San Diego: Academic Press.

Landry, B. (2000). *Black working wives.* Berkeley: University of California Press.

Langelan, M. J. (1993). *Back off! How to confront and stop sexual harassment and harassers.* New York: Simon & Schuster.

Langer, C. L. (1996). *A feminist critique: How feminism has changed American society, culture, and how we live from the 1940s to the present.* New York: HarperCollins.

Langford, W. (1999). *Revolutions of the heart: Gender, power and the delusions of love.* London: Routledge.

Langlois, J. H., et al. (2000). Maxims or myths of beauty? A meta-analytic and theoretical review. *Psychological Bulletin, 126,* 390–423.

Lanis, K., & Covell, K. (1995). Images of women in advertisements: Effects on attitudes related to sexual aggression. *Sex Roles, 32,* 639–649.

Lapointe, V., & Marcotte, D. (2000). Gender-typed characteristics and coping strategies of depressed adolescents. *European Review of Applied Psychology, 50,* 451–460.

LaRocca, M. A., & Kromrey, J. D. (1999). The perception of sexual harassment in higher education: Impact of gender and attractiveness. *Sex Roles, 40,* 921–940.

Larson, R. W., Clore, G. L., & Wood, G. A. (1999). The emotions of romantic relationships: Do they wreak havoc on adolescents? In W. Furman, B. D. Brown, & C. Feiring (Eds.), *The development of romantic relationships in adolescence.* New York: Cambridge University Press.

LaTorre, R. A., & Wendenburg, K. (1983). Psychological characteristics of bisexual, heterosexual, and homosexual women. *Journal of Homosexuality, 9,* 87–97.

Laumann, E. O., Gagnon, J. H., Michael, R. T., & Michaels, S. (1994). *The social organization of sexuality: Sexual practices in the United States.* Chicago: University of Chicago Press.

Laumann, E. O., Paik, A., & Rosen, R. C. (1999). Sexual dysfunction in the United States: Prevalence and predictors. *Journal of the American Medical Association, 281,* 537–544.

Lavender, T., & Walkinshaw, S. A. (1998). Can midwives reduce postpartum psychological morbidity? A randomized trial. *Birth, 25,* 215–219.

Lavine, H., Sweeney, D., & Wagner, S. H. (1999). Depicting women as sex objects in television advertising: Effects on body dissatisfaction. *Personality and Social Psychology Bulletin, 25,* 1049–1058.

Lawler, A. (1999). Tenured women battle to make it less lonely at the top. *Science, 286,* 1272–1278.

Lawrence, R. A. (1998). Breastfeeding. In E. A. Blechman & K. D. Brownell (Eds.), *Behavioral medicine and women: A comprehensive handbook* (pp. 495–500). New York: Guilford.

Lawrence, R. A., & Lawrence, R. M. (1998). *Breast-feeding: A guide for the medical profession*. St. Louis, MO: Mosby.

Laws, A. (1998). Sexual abuse. In E. A. Blechman & K. D. Brownell (Eds.), *Behavioral medicine and women: A comprehensive handbook* (pp. 470–474). New York: Guilford.

Laws, A., & Golding, J. M. (1996). Sexual assault history and eating disorder symptoms among White, Hispanic, and African-American women and men. *American Journal of Public Health, 86,* 579–582.

Lawton, C. A. (1996). Strategies for indoor wayfinding: The role of orientation. *Journal of Environmental Psychology, 16,* 137–145.

Lawton, C. A., Charleston, S. I., & Zieles, A. S. (1996). Individual and gender-related differences in indoor wayfinding. *Environment and Behavior, 28,* 204–219.

Lawton, C. A., & Morrin, K. A. (1999). Gender differences in pointing accuracy in computer-simulated 3D mazes. *Sex Roles, 40,* 73–92.

Lawton, M. P., Moss, M., Hoffman, C., & Perkinson, M. (2000). Two transitions in daughters' caregiving careers. *The Gerontologist, 40,* 437–447.

Leadbeater, B. J. R., Way, N., & Raden, A. (1996). *Why not marry your baby's father? Answers from African American and Hispanic adolescent mothers.* (pp. 193–209). New York: New York University Press.

Leaper, C. (2000). The social construction and socialization of gender during development. In P. H. Miller & E. K. Scholnick (Eds.), *Toward a feminist developmental psychology* (pp. 129–152). New York: Routledge.

Leaper, C., Anderson, K. J., & Sanders, P. (1998). Moderators of gender effects on parents' talk to their children: A meta-analysis. *Developmental Psychology, 34,* 3–27.

Leaper, C., & Valin, D. (1996). Predictors of Mexican American mothers' and fathers' attitudes toward gender equality. *Hispanic Journal of Behavioral Sciences, 18,* 343–355.

Lederman, R. P. (1996). *Psychosocial adaptation in pregnancy* (2nd ed.). New York: Springer.

Lee, J. (2001). Beyond bean counting. In S. M. Shaw & J. Lee (Eds.), *Women's voices, feminist visions* (pp. 36–39). Mountain View, CA: Mayfield.

Lee, J., & Sasser-Coen, J. (1996). *Blood stories: Menarche and the politics of the female body in contemporary U.S. society.* New York: Routledge.

Lee, W. M. L. (1999). *An introduction to multicultural counseling.* Philadelphia: Taylor & Francis.

Lees, D. (1992, December). The war against men. *Toronto Life,* pp. 45, 104.

Leifer, M. (1980). *Psychological effects of motherhood.* New York: Praeger.

Leonard, A. S. (1994, July 25). Fired for being gay. *The New Yorker,* p. 6.

Leonard, D. K., & Jiang, J. (1999). Gender bias and the college predictions of the SAT's: A cry of despair. *Research in Higher Education, 40,* 375–407.

Leonard, R. (1999). Unpaid work, grasshopper accusations, and the threat to social capital. In J. Onyx, R. Leonard, & R. Reed (Eds.), *Revisioning aging: Empowerment of older women* (pp. 77–92). New York: Peter Lang.

Lepowsky, M. (1998). Women, men, and aggression in an egalitarian society. In D. L. Anselmi & A. L. Law (Eds.), *Questions of gender* (pp. 170–179). New York: McGraw-Hill.

Lerman, H. (1996). *Pigeonholing women's misery.* New York: Basic Books.

Lerner, H. (1989). *Women in therapy.* New York: Harper & Row.

Lerner, H. (1998). *The mother dance: How children change your life.* New York: HarperCollins.

Lerner, R. M., & Galambos, N. L. (1998). Adolescent development: Challenges and opportunities for research, programs, and policies. *Annual Review of Psychology, 49,* 413–446.

Levant, R. F. (1996). *Masculinity reconstructed: Changing the rules of manhood.* New York: Plume.

Levant, R. F. (2001). Men and masculinity. In J. Worell (Ed.), *Encyclopedia of women and gender* (pp. 717–727). San Diego: Academic Press.

Levant, R. F., & Majors, R. G. (1997). Masculinity ideology among African American and European American college women and men. *Journal of Gender, Culture, and Health, 2,* 33–43.

Levant, R. F., Majors, R. G., & Kelley, M. L. (1998). Masculinity ideology among young African American and European American women and men in different regions of the United States. *Cultural Diversity and Mental Health, 4,* 227–236.

Levant, R. F., & Pollack, W. S. (Eds.). (1995). *A new psychology of men.* New York: Basic Books.

LeVay, S. (1991). A difference in hypothalamic structure between heterosexual and homosexual men. *Science, 253,* 1034–1037.

LeVay, S. (1996). *The use and abuse of research into homosexuality.* Cambridge, MA: MIT Press.

Leve, L. D., & Fagot, B. I. (1997). Gender-role social-ization and discipline processes in one- and two-parent families. *Sex Roles, 36,* 1–21.

Levenkron, S. (2000). *Anatomy of anorexia.* New York: Norton.

Levenson, R. W., Carstensen, L. L., & Gottman, J. M. (1994). The influence of age and gender on affect, physiology, and their interrelations: A study of long-term marriages. *Journal of Personality and Social Psychology, 67,* 56–68.

Levering, M. (1994). Women, the state, and religion today in the People's Republic of China. In A. Sharma (Ed.), *Today's woman in world religions* (pp. 171–224). Albany, NY: State University of New York Press.

Levesque, M. J., & Lowe, C. A. (1999). Face-ism as a determinant of interpersonal perceptions: The influence of context on facial prominence effects. *Sex Roles, 41,* 241–259.

Levesque, R. J. R. (2001). *Culture and family violence.* Washington, DC: American Psychological Association.

Levine, F., & Le De Simone, L. (1991). The effects of experimenter gender on pain report in male and female subjects. *Pain, 44,* 69–72.

Levine, M. P., & Smolak, L. (1996). Media as a con-text for the development of disordered eating. In L. Smolak, M. P. Levine, & R. Striegel-Moore (Eds.), *The developmental psychopathology of eating disorders* (pp. 235–257). Mahwah, NJ: Erlbaum.

Levine, S. B. (1998). *Sexuality in mid-life.* New York: Plenum.

Levstik, L. S. (2001). Daily acts of ordinary courage: Gender-equitable practice in the social studies classroom. In P. O'Reilly, E. M. Penn, & K. de-Marrais (Ed.), *Educating young adolescent girls* (pp. 189–211). Mahwah, NJ: Erlbaum.

Levy, B. (1993). *In love and in danger.* Seattle: Seal Press.

Levy, B. R., & Banaji, M. R. (2002). Implicit ageism. In T. Nelson (Ed.), *Ageism: Stereotyping and preju-dice against older persons* (pp. 49–75). Cambridge, MA: MIT Press.

Levy, B. R., & Langer, E. (1994). Aging free from negative stereotypes: Successful memory in China and among the American deaf. *Journal of Person-ality and Social Psychology, 66,* 989–997.

Levy, G. D., & Fivush, R. (1993). Scripts and gender: A new approach for examining gender-role devel-opment. *Developmental Review, 13,* 126–146.

Levy, G. D., Sadovsky, A. L., & Troseth, G. L. (2000). Aspects of young children's perceptions of gender-type occupations. *Sex Roles, 42,* 993–1006.

Lewis, C., Scully, D., & Condor, S. (1992). Sex stereo-typing of infants: A re-examination. *Journal of Reproductive and Infant Psychology, 10,* 53–63.

Lewis, K. G., & Moon, S. (1997). Always single and single again women: A qualitative study. *Journal of Marital and Family Therapy, 23,* 115–134.

Leyendecker, B., & Lamb, M. E. (1999). Latino fami-lies. In M. E. Lamb (Ed.), *Parenting and child de-velopment in "nontraditional" families* (pp. 247–262). Mahwah, NJ: Erlbaum.

Li, A. K. F., & Adamson, G. (1995). Motivational patterns related to gifted students' learning of mathematics, science, and English: An examina-tion of gender differences. *Journal for the Educa-tion of the Gifted, 18,* 284–297.

Lightdale, J. R., & Prentice, D. A. (1994). Rethinking sex differences in aggression: Aggressive behav-ior in the absence of social roles. *Personality and Social Psychology Bulletin, 20,* 34–44.

Lim, I.-S. (1997). Korean immigrant women's chal-lenge to gender inequality at home: The inter-play of economic resources, gender, and family. *Gender and Society, 11,* 31–51.

Lin, C. A. (1998). Uses of sex appeal in prime-time television commercials. *Sex Roles, 38,* 461–475.

Lindsey, L. L. (1996). Full-time homemaker as un-paid laborer. In P. J. Dubeck & K. Borman (Eds.), *Women and work: A handbook* (pp. 98–99). New York: Garland Press.

Linn, M. C., & Kessel, C. (1995, April). *Participation in mathematics courses and careers: Climate, grades, and entrance examination scores.* Paper presented at the annual meeting of the American Educa-tional Research Association, San Francisco.

Linn, M. C., & Petersen, A. C. (1985). Emergence and characterization of sex differences in spatial ability: A meta-analysis. *Child Development, 56,* 1479–1498.

Linn, M. C., & Petersen, A. C. (1986). A meta-analysis of gender differences in spatial ability: Implica-tions for mathematics and science achievement. In J. S. Hyde & M. C. Linn (Eds.), *The psychology of gender: Advances through meta-analysis* (pp. 67–101). Baltimore: Johns Hopkins University Press.

Lips, H. M. (2001). Power: Social and interpersonal aspects. In J. Worell (Ed.), *Encyclopedia of women and gender* (pp. 847–858). San Diego: Academic Press.

Liss, M., Hoffner, C., & Crawford, M. (2000). What do feminists believe? *Psychology of Women Quar-terly, 24,* 279–284.

Liss, M., O'Connor, C., Morosky, E., & Crawford, M. (2001). What makes a feminist? Predictors and correlates of feminist social identity in college women. *Psychology of Women Quarterly, 25,* 124–133.

Litt, I. F. (1997). *Taking our pulse: The health of America's women.* Stanford, CA: Stanford University Press.

Litt, I. F. (1998). Health issues for women in the 1990s. In D. L. Anselmi & A. L. Law (Eds.), *Questions of gender: Perspectives and paradoxes* (pp. 690–701). New York: McGraw-Hill.

Livingston, M. (1999). How to think about women's health. In C. Forden, A. E. Hunter, & B. Birns (Eds.), *Readings in the psychology of women: Dimensions of the female experience* (pp. 244–253). Boston: Allyn & Bacon.

Lloyd, S. A., & Emery, B. C. (2000). *The dark side of courtship: Physical and sexual aggression.* Thousand Oaks, CA: Sage.

Lobel, T. E., et al. (2000). Gender schema and social judgments: A developmental study of children from Hong Kong. *Sex Roles, 43,* 19–42.

Locke, L. M., & Richman, C. L. (1999). Attitudes toward domestic violence: Race and gender issues. *Sex Roles, 40,* 227–247.

Locklin, M. P., & Naber, S. J. (1993). Does breastfeeding empower women? Insights from a select group of educated, low-income, minority women. *Birth, 20,* 30–35.

Loftus, E. F. (1997, September). Creating false memories. *Scientific American,* pp. 71–75.

Loftus, E. F., & Guyer, M. J. (2002a, May/June). Who abused Jane Doe? (Part 1). *Skeptical Inquirer,* pp. 24–32.

Loftus, E. F., & Guyer, M. J. (2002b, July/August). Who abused Jane Doe? (Part 2). *Skeptical Inquirer,* pp. 37–40.

Lone Dog, Leota. (1991). Coming out as a Native American. In B. Sang, J. Warshow, & A. J. Smith (Eds.), *Lesbians at midlife: The creative transition* (pp. 49–53). San Francisco: Spinsters Ink.

Lonsway, K. A., & Kothari, C. (2000). First year campus acquaintance rape education: Evaluating the impact of a mandatory intervention. *Psychology of Women Quarterly, 24,* 220–232.

LoPiccolo, J. (2002). Integrative sex therapy: A postmodern model. In J. Lebow (Ed.), *Comprehensive handbook of psychotherapy* (Vol. 4). New York: Wiley.

Loppie, C., & Gahagan, J. (2001, Summer/Fall). Stacked against us: HIV/AIDS statistics and women. *Canadian Woman Studies/Les cahiers de la femme, 21,* 6–9.

Lorber, J. (1994). *Paradoxes of gender.* New Haven, CT: Yale University Press.

Lorber, J. (1997). *Gender and the social construction of illness.* Thousand Oaks, CA: Sage.

Loring-Meier, S., & Halpern, D. F. (1999). Sex differences in visuospatial working memory: Components of cognitive processing. *Psychonomic Bulletin and Review, 6,* 464–471.

Lott, B. (1987). Sexist discrimination as distancing behavior: I. A laboratory demonstration. *Psychology of Women Quarterly, 11,* 47–58.

Lott, B. (1989). Sexist discrimination as distancing behavior: II. Primetime television. *Psychology of Women Quarterly, 13,* 341–355.

Lott, B. (1996). Politics or science? The question of gender sameness/difference. *American Psychologist, 51,* 155–156.

Lott, B. (2000). Global connections: The significance of women's poverty. In J. C. Chrisler, C. Golden, & Rozee, P. D. (Eds.), *Lectures on the psychology of women* (2nd ed., pp. 27–36). Boston: McGraw-Hill.

Lott, B., Lott, A. J., & Fernald, J. L. (1990). Individual differences in distancing responses to women on a photo choice task. *Sex Roles, 22,* 97–110.

Lott, B., & Maluso, D. (1993). The social learning of gender. In A. E. Beall & R. J. Sternberg (Eds.), *The psychology of gender* (pp. 99–123). New York: Guilford.

Lott, B., & Maluso, D. (1995). Introduction: Framing the questions. In B. Lott & D. Maluso (Eds.), *The social psychology of interpersonal discrimination* (pp. 1–11). New York: Guilford.

Lott, B., & Maluso, D. (2001). Gender development: Social learning. In J. Worell (Ed.), *Encyclopedia of women and gender* (pp. 537–549). San Diego: Academic Press.

Lott, B., & Saxon, S. (2002). The influence of ethnicity, social class, and context on judgments about U.S. women. *Journal of Social Psychology, 142,* 481–499.

Lottes, I. L., & Kuriloff, P. J. (1994). The impact of college experiences on political and social attitudes. *Sex Roles, 31,* 31–54.

Lubin, A. (1999, March 24). Commenting on the news. *New York Teacher,* p. 9.

Luebke, B. F., & Reilly, M. E. (1995). *Women's studies graduates: The first generation.* New York: Teachers College Press.

Luker, K. (1996). *Dubious conceptions: The politics of teenage pregnancy.* Cambridge, MA: Harvard University Press.

Lum, J. L. (1998). Family violence. In L. C. Lee & N. W. S. Zane (Eds.), *Handbook of Asian American psychology* (pp. 505–525). Thousand Oaks, CA: Sage.

Lundeberg, M. A., Fox, P. W., Brown, A. C., & Elbedour, S. (2000). Cultural influences on confidence: Country and gender. *Journal of Educational Psychology, 92,* 152–159.

Lykes, M. B., & Qin, D. (2001). Individualism and collectivism. In J. Worell (Ed.), *Encyclopedia of women and gender* (pp. 625–643). San Diego: Academic Press.

Lyness, K. S., & Judiesch, M. K. (1999). Are women more likely to be hired or promoted into management positions? *Journal of Vocational Behavior, 53,* 158–173.

Lyness, K. S., Thompson, C. A., Francesco, A. M., & Judiesch, M. K. (1999). Work and pregnancy: Individual and organizational factors influencing organizational commitment, timing of maternity leave, and return to work. *Sex Roles, 41,* 485–508.

Lyness, K. S., & Thompson, D. E. (1997). Above the glass ceiling? A comparison of matched samples of female and male executives. *Journal of Applied Psychology, 82,* 359–375.

Lyness, K. S., & Thompson, D. E. (2000). Climbing the corporate ladder: Do female and male executives follow the same route? *Journal of Applied Psychology, 85,* 86–101.

Lyons, N. P. (1990). Listening to voices we have not heard. In C. Gilligan, N. P. Lyons, & T. J. Hanmer (Eds.), *Making connections* (pp. 30–72). Cambridge, MA: Harvard University Press.

Lytton, H., & Romney, D. M. (1991). Parents' differential socialization of boys and girls: A meta-analysis. *Psychological Bulletin, 109,* 267–296.

Maccoby, E. E. (1998). *The two sexes: Growing up apart, coming together.* Cambridge, MA: Harvard University Press.

Maccoby, E. E., & Jacklin, C. N. (1974). *The psychology of sex differences.* Stanford, CA: Stanford University Press.

Macdonald, B., & Rich, C. (2001). *Look me in the eye: Old women, aging, and ageism* (expanded ed.). Denver, CO: Spinsters Ink.

MacDorman, M. F., Minino, A. M., Strobino, D. M., & Guyer, B. (2002). Annual summary of vital statistics: 2001. *Pediatrics, 110,* 1037–1052.

MacKay, N. J., & Covell, K. (1997). The impact of women in advertisements on attitudes toward women. *Sex Roles, 36,* 573–583.

Mackey, R. A., Diemer, M. A., & O'Brien, B. A. (2000). Psychological intimacy in the lasting relationships of heterosexual and same-gender couples. *Sex Roles, 43,* 201–227.

Mackie, M. (1991). *Gender relations in Canada: Further explorations.* Toronto: Butterworths.

Macrae, C. N., & Bodenhausen, G. V. (2000). Social cognition: Thinking categorically about others. *Annual Review of Psychology, 51,* 93–120.

Macrae, C. N., Milne, A. B., & Bodenhausen, G. V. (1994). Stereotypes as energy-saving devices: A peek inside the cognitive toolbox. *Journal of Personality and Social Psychology, 66,* 37–47.

Madden, M. E., & Hyde, J. S. (1998). Integrating gender and ethnicity into psychology courses. *Psychology of Women Quarterly, 22,* 1–12.

Madi, B. C., Sandall, J., Bennett, R., & MacLeod, C. (1999). Effects of female relative support in labor: A randomized controlled trial. *Birth, 26,* 4–8.

Madsen, S. S. (1998, July 31). A welfare mother in academe. *Chronicle of Higher Education,* p. A44.

Magai, C. (2001). Emotions over the life span. In J. E. Birren & K. W. Schaie (Eds.), *Handbook of the psychology of aging* (5th ed., pp. 399–426). San Diego: Academic Press.

Mahalik, J. R., Van Ormer, E. A., & Simi, N. L. (2000). Ethical issues in using self-disclosure in feminist therapy. In M. M. Brabeck (Ed.), *Practicing feminist ethics in psychology* (pp. 189–201). Washington, DC: American Psychological Association.

Mahlstedt, D., & Corcoran, C. B. (1999). Preventing dating violence. In S. N. Davis, M. Crawford, & J. Sebrechts (Eds.), *Coming into her own: Educational success in girls and women* (pp. 311–327). San Francisco: Jossey-Bass.

Major, B., Barr, L., Zubek, J., & Babey, S. H. (1999). Gender and self-esteem: A meta-analysis. In W. B. Swann Jr., J. H. Langlois, & L. A. Gilbert (Eds.), *Sexism and stereotypes in modern society* (pp. 223–253). Washington, DC: American Psychological Association.

Major, B., & Gramzow, R. H. (1999). Abortion as stigma: Cognitive and emotional implications of concealment. *Journal of Personality and Social Psychology, 77,* 735–745.

Major, B., et al. (1998). Personal resilience, cognitive appraisals, and coping: An integrative model of adjustment to abortion. *Journal of Personality and Social Psychology, 74,* 735–752.

Malamuth, N. M. (1998). The confluence model as an organizing framework for research on sexually aggressive men: Risk moderators, imagined aggression, and pornography consumption. In R. G. Geen & E. Donnerstein (Eds.), *Human aggression: Theories, research, and implications for social policy* (pp. 229–245). San Diego: Academic Press.

Malkin, A. R., Wornian, K., & Chrisler, J. C. (1999). Women and weight: Gendered messages on magazine covers. *Sex Roles, 40,* 647–655.

Mandle, J. D. (2000). *Can we wear our pearls and still be feminists?* Columbia MO: University of Missouri Press.

Mangum, T. (1999). Little women: The aging female character in nineteenth-century British children's literature. In K. Woodward (Ed.), *Figuring age: Women, bodies, generations* (pp. 59–87). Bloomington, IN: Indiana University Press.

Mann, C. (1999). Women's health research blossoms. In G. Null & B. Seaman (Eds.), *For women only: Your guide to health empowerment* (pp. 1404–1411). New York: Seven Stories Press.

Mansfield, P. K., Koch, P. B., & Voda, A. M. (1998). Qualities midlife women desire in their sexual relationships and their changing sexual response. *Psychology of Women Quarterly, 22,* 285–303.

Maquila workers attacked for organizing a union. (2001, August). *U.S./Labor Education in the Americas Project,* pp. 1–3.

Marchell, T., & Cummings, N. (2001). Alcohol and sexual violence among college students. In A. J. Ottens & K. Hotelling (Eds.), *Sexual violence on campus* (pp. 30–52). New York: Springer.

Marcus-Newhall, A., Thompson, S., & Thomas, C. (2001). Examining a gender stereotype: Menopausal women. *Journal of Applied Social Psychology, 31,* 698–719.

Marecek, J. (2001a). After the facts: Psychology and the study of gender. *Canadian Psychology/Psychologie canadienne, 42,* 254–267.

Marecek, J. (2001b). Disorderly constructs: Feminist frameworks for clinical psychology. In R. K. Unger (Ed.), *Handbook of women and gender* (pp. 303–329). New York: Wiley.

Marin, A. J., & Russo, N. F. (1999). Feminist perspectives on male violence against women. In M. Harway & J. M. O'Neil (Eds.), *What causes men's violence against women?* (pp. 18–35). Thousand Oaks, CA: Sage.

Marketing Services Group Inc. (2000). *College mailing list directory.* Wilmington, MA: Author.

Marks, N. F. (1996). Flying solo at midlife: Gender, marital status, and psychological well-being. *Journal of Marriage and the Family, 58,* 917–932.

Markson, E. W., & Taylor, C. A. (1993). Real versus reel world: Older women and the Academy Awards. *Women and Therapy, 14,* 157–172.

Marleau, J. D., & Saucier, J.-F. (2002). Preference for a first-born boy in Western societies. *Journal of Biosocial Science, 34,* 13–27.

Marshall, K. (1999, Autumn). Employment after childbirth. *Perspectives,* pp. 18–22.

Marston, W. (1998, March). Seeing red, feeling blue? Cramps! Bloating! Breakouts! *Jump,* pp. 107–109.

Martell, R. F. (1991). Sex bias at work: The effects of attentional and memory demands on performance ratings of men and women. *Journal of Applied Social Psychology, 21,* 1939–1960.

Martell, R. F. (1996a). Sex discrimination at work. In P. J. Dubeck & K. Borman (Eds.), *Women and work: A handbook* (pp. 329–332). New York: Garland.

Martell, R. F. (1996b). What mediates gender bias in work behavior ratings? *Sex Roles, 35,* 153–169.

Martell, R. F., Parker, C., Emrich, C. G., & Crawford, M. S. (1998). Sex stereotyping in the executive suite: "Much ado about something." *Journal of Social Behavior and Personality, 13,* 127–138.

Martin, C. L. (1987). A ratio measure of sex stereotyping. *Journal of Personality and Social Psychology, 52,* 489–499.

Martin, C. L., & Dinella, L. M. (2001). Gender development: Gender schema theory. In J. Worell (Ed.), *Encyclopedia of women and gender* (pp. 507–521). San Diego: Academic Press.

Martin, C. L., & Ruble, D. N. (1997). A developmental perspective on self-construals and sex differences: Comment on Cross and Madson (1997). *Psychological Bulletin, 122,* 45–50.

Martin, E. (2001). The egg and the sperm: How science has constructed a romance based on stereotypical male-female roles. In S. Ruth (Ed.), *Issues in feminism* (5th ed., pp. 473–482). Mountain View, CA: Mayfield.

Martin, K. A. (1996). *Puberty, sexuality, and the self: Boys and girls at adolescence.* New York: Routledge.

Martin, P. Y., & Collinson, D. L. (1998). Gender and sexuality in organizations. In M. M. Ferree, J. Lorber, & B. B. Hess (Eds.), *Revisioning gender* (pp. 285–310). Thousand Oaks, CA: Sage.

Martin, R., Gordon, E. E. I., & Lounsbury, P. (1998). Gender disparities in the attribution of cardiac-related symptoms: Contribution of common sense models of illness. *Health Psychology, 17,* 346–357.

Martínez, E. (1995). In pursuit of Latina liberation. *Signs: Journal of Women in Culture and Society, 20,* 1019–1028.

Martínez, E. (1997, Spring). Unite and overcome! *Teaching Tolerance*, pp. 11–15.

Martínez, K., & O'Toole, C. J. (1991, January/February). Disabled women of color face triple threat. *New Directions for Women*, p. 4.

Martínez, R., Johnston-Robledo, I., Ulsh, H. M., & Chrisler, J. C. (2000). Singing "the baby blues": A content analysis of popular press articles about postpartum affective disturbances. *Women and Health, 31*, 37–56.

Martire, L. M., & Schulz, R. (2001). Informal caregiving to older adults: Health effects of providing and receiving care. In A. Baum, T. A. Revenson, & J. E. Singer (Eds.), *Handbook of health psychology* (pp. 477–493). Mahwah, NJ: Erlbaum.

Marx, D. M., & Roman, J. S. (2002). Female role models: Protecting women's math test performance. *Personality and Social Psychology Bulletin, 28*, 1183–1193.

Marx, J. (1995). Snaring the genes that divide the sexes for mammals. *Science, 269*, 1824–1825.

Massoth, N. A. (1997). Editorial: It's not comical. *Society for the Psychological Study of Men and Masculinity Bulletin, 3*(1), 2.

Masters, M. S., & Sanders, B. (1993). Is the gender difference in mental rotation disappearing? *Behavior Genetics, 23*, 337–341.

Masters, W. H., & Johnson, V. E. (1966). *Human sexual response.* Boston: Little, Brown.

Masters, W. H., & Johnson, V. E. (1970). *Human sexual inadequacy.* Boston: Little, Brown.

Mathews, J. (1994, July 25). Different strokes for different genders. *Washington Post National Weekly Edition*, p. 22.

Maticka-Tyndale, E., Herold, E. S., & Mewhinney, D. (1998). Casual sex on spring break: Intentions and behaviors of Canadian students. *Journal of Sex Research, 35*, 254–264.

Maticka-Tyndale, E., McKay, A., & Barrett, M. (2001, November). *Teenage sexual and reproductive behavior in developed countries: Country report for Canada.* New York: Alan Guttmacher Institute.

Matlin, M. W. (1999). *Psychology* (3rd ed.). Fort Worth, TX: Harcourt Brace.

Matlin, M. W. (2000). *The psychology of women* (4th ed.). Fort Worth, TX: Harcourt College.

Matlin, M. W. (2002). *Cognition* (5th ed.). Fort Worth, TX: Harcourt.

Matthews, K. A., et al. (1997). Women's Health Initiative: Why now? What is it? What's new? *American Psychologist, 52*, 101–116.

Maushart, S. (1999). *The mask of motherhood.* New York: New Press.

Mayerson, C. (1996). *Goin' to the chapel: Dreams of love, realities of marriage.* New York: Basic Books.

Mays, V. M. (1985). Black women working together: Diversity in same-sex relationships. *Women's Studies International Forum, 8*, 67–71.

Mazzarella, S. R. (1999). The "superbowl of all dates": Teenage girl magazines and the commodification of the perfect prom. In S. R. Mazzarella & N. O. Pecora (Eds.), *Growing up girls: Popular culture and the construction of identity* (pp. 97–110). New York: Peter Lang.

McAdoo, J. L. (1993). Decision making and marital satisfaction in African American families. In H. P. McAdoo (Ed.), *Family ethnicity: Strength in diversity* (pp. 109–119). Newbury Park, CA: Sage.

McCarthy, P., & Loren, J. A. (1997). *Breast cancer? Let me check my schedule!* Boulder, CO: Westview Press.

McCaul, M. E. (1998). Drug abuse. In E. A. Blechman & K. D. Brownell (Eds.), *Behavioral medicine and women: A comprehensive textbook* (pp. 414–424). New York: Guilford.

McClintock, M. K., & Herdt, G. (1996). Rethinking puberty: The development of sexual attraction. *Current Directions in Psychological Science, 5*, 178–183.

McClure, E. B. (2000). A meta-analytic review of sex differences in facial expression processing and their development in infants, children, and adolescence. *Psychological Bulletin, 126*, 424–453.

McConatha, J. T., Schnell, F., & McKenna, A. (1999). Descriptions of older adults as depicted in magazine advertisements. *Psychological Reports, 85*, 1051–1056.

McCormick, N. B. (1994). *Sexual salvation: Affirming women's sexual rights and pleasures.* Westport, CT: Praeger.

McCreary, D. R., & Sadava, S. W. (2001). Gender differences in relationships among perceived attractiveness, life satisfaction, and health in adults as a function of Body Mass Index and perceived weight. *Psychology of Men and Masculinity, 2*, 108–116.

McDonald, S. M. (1989). Sex bias in the representation of male and female characters in children's picture books. *Journal of Genetic Psychology, 150*, 389–401.

McDougall, J., DeWit, D. J., & Ebanks, C. E. (1999). Parental preferences for sex of children in Canada. *Sex Roles, 41*, 615–626.

McGill, A. L. (1993). Selection of a causal background: Role of expectation versus feature mutability. *Journal of Personality and Social Psychology, 64*, 701–707.

McGrath, E., Keita, G. P., Strickland, B. R., & Russo, N. F. (Eds.). (1990). *Women and depression.* Washington, DC: American Psychological Association.

McGuinness, C. (1998). Cognition. In K. Trew & J. Kremer (Eds.), *Gender and psychology* (pp. 66–81). London: Arnold Publishers.

McHugh, M. C., & Bartoszek, T. A. R. (2000). Intimate violence. In M. Biaggio & M. Hersen (Eds.), *Issues in the psychology of women* (pp. 115–142). New York: Kluwer Academic/Plenum.

McHugh, M. C., & Cosgrove, L. (1998). Research for women: Feminist methods. In D. M. Ashcraft (Ed.), *Women's work: A survey of scholarship by and about women* (pp. 19–43). New York: Haworth.

McHugh, M. C., Frieze, I. H., & Browne, A. (1993). Research on battered women and their assailants. In F. L. Denmark & M. A. Paludi (Eds.), *Psychology of women: A handbook of issues and theories* (pp. 513–552). Westport, CT: Greenwood Press.

McIlwee, J. S., & Robinson, J. G. (1992). *Women in engineering: Gender, power, and workplace culture.* Albany, NY: State University of New York Press.

McIntosh, P. (1998). White privilege: Unpacking the invisible knapsack. In P. S. Rothenberg (Ed.), *Race, class, and gender in the United States: An integrated study* (4th ed., pp. 165–169). New York: St. Martin's Press.

McKinley, N. M. (1998). Gender differences in undergraduates' body esteem: The mediating effect of objectified body consciousness and actual/ideal weight discrepancy. *Sex Roles, 39*, 113–123.

McKinley, N. M. (1999). Women and objectified body consciousness: Mothers' and daughters' body experience in cultural, developmental, and familial context. *Developmental Psychology, 35*, 760–769.

McMahon, M. (1995). *Engendering motherhood: Identity and self-transformation in women's lives.* New York: Guilford.

McNamara, E. (2001, April 30). A sad site: Abuse for sale. *Liberal Opinion Week,* p. 7.

McNulty, J. K., & Karney, B. R. (2001). Attributions in marriage: Integrating specific and global evaluations of a relationship. *Personality and Social Psychology Bulletin, 27*, 943–955.

McWright, L. (2002). African American grandmothers' and grandfathers' influence in the value socialization of grandchildren. In H. P. McAdoo (Ed.), *Black children* (2nd ed., pp. 27–44). Thousand Oaks, CA: Sage.

Meadows, E. A., & Foa, E. B. (1999). Cognitive-behavioral treatment of traumatized adults. In P. A. Saigh & J. D. Bremner (Eds.), *Posttraumatic stress disorder* (pp. 376–390). Boston: Allyn & Bacon.

Mednick, M. T., & Thomas, V. (1993). Women and the psychology of achievement: A view from the eighties. In F. L. Denmark & M. A. Paludi (Eds.), *Psychology of women: A handbook of issues and theories* (pp. 585–626). Westport, CT: Greenwood Press.

Megan, C. E. (2000, November). Childless by choice. *Ms. Magazine,* pp. 43–46.

Meinz, E. J., & Salthouse, T. A. (1998). Is age kinder to females than to males? *Psychonomic Bulletin and Review, 5*, 56–70.

Mendelsohn, K. D. et al. (1994). Sex and gender bias in anatomy and physical diagnosis text illustrations. *Journal of the American Medical Association, 272*, 1267–1270.

Merrick, E. (1999). "Like chewing gravel": On the experience of analyzing qualitative research findings using a feminist epistemology. *Psychology of Women Quarterly, 23*, 47–57.

Merritt, R. D., & Kok, C. J. (1995). Attribution of gender to a gender-unspecified individual: An evaluation of the people = male hypothesis. *Sex Roles, 33*, 145–157.

Merskin, D. (1999). Adolescence, advertising, and the ideology of menstruation. *Sex Roles, 40*, 941–957.

Metzger, T. (2002, June 19–25). The Cross and the Y chromosome: Promise Keepers storm Rochester. *City Newspaper,* pp. 10–12.

Meyer-Bahlburg, H. F. L., et al. (1995). Prenatal estrogens and the development of homosexual orientation. *Developmental Psychology, 31*, 12–21.

Meyerowitz, B. E., & Hart, S. (1995). Women and cancer: Have assumptions about women limited our research agenda? In A. L. Stanton & S. L. Gallant (Eds.), *The psychology of women's health: Progress and challenges in research and application* (pp. 51–84). Washington, DC: American Psychological Association.

Meyerowitz, B. E., & Weidner, G. (1998). Section editors' overview. In E. A. Blechman & K. D. Brownell (Eds.), *Behavioral medicine and women: A comprehensive handbook* (pp. 537–545). New York: Guilford.

Meyers, M. (Ed.). (1999). *Mediated woman: Representations in popular culture.* Cresskill, NJ: Hampton Press.

Milar, K. S. (2000). The first generation of women psychologists and the psychology of women. *American Psychologist, 55,* 616–619.

Miles, C. (1935). Sex in social psychology. In C. Murchinson (Ed.), *Handbook of social psychology* (pp. 699–704). Worcester, MA: Clark University Press.

Miles, S., & Parker, K. (1997). Men, women, and health insurance. *New England Journal of Medicine, 336,* 218–221.

Milhausen, R. R., & Herold, E. S. (1999). Does the sexual double standard exist? Perceptions of university women. *Journal of Sex Research, 36,* 361–368.

Milkie, M. A. (1999). Social comparisons, reflected appraisals, and mass media: The impact of pervasive beauty images on Black and White girls' self-concepts. *Social Psychology Quarterly, 62,* 190–210.

Millard, J. E., & Grant, P. R. (2001). *Stereotypes of women in magazines: Content analysis of advertisements and fashion photographs.* Paper presented at the annual meeting of the Canadian Psychological Association, St. Foy, Quebec, Canada.

Miller, C., Swift, K., & Maggio, R. (1997, September/October). Liberating language. *Ms. Magazine,* pp. 50–54.

Miller, D. H. (1996). A matter of consequence: Abortion rhetoric and media messages. In R. L. Parrott & C. M. Condit (Eds.), *Evaluating women's health messages: A resource book* (pp. 33–47). Thousand Oaks, CA: Sage.

Miller, D. T., Taylor, B., & Buck, M. L. (1991). Gender gaps: Who needs to be explained? *Journal of Personality and Social Psychology, 61,* 5–12.

Miller, E. J., Smith, J. E., & Trembath, D. L. (2000). The "skinny" on body size requests in personal ads. *Sex Roles, 43,* 129–141.

Miller, J., & Chamberlin, M. (2000). Women are teachers, men are professors: A study of student perceptions. *Teaching Sociology, 28,* 283–298.

Miller, J. B., & Stiver, I. P. (1997). *The healing connection: How women form relationships in therapy and life.* Boston: Beacon Press.

Miller, K.-L., & Du Mont, J. (2000, Fall). Countless abused women: Homeless and inadequately housed. *Canadian Woman Studies/Les cahiers de la femme, 20,* 115–122.

Miller, L. C., Putcha-Bhagavatula, A., & Pedersen, W. C. (2002). Men's and women's mating preferences: Distinct evolutionary mechanisms. *Current Directions in Psychological Science, 11,* 88–93.

Miller, L. J. (2001). Psychiatric disorders during pregnancy. In N. L. Stotland & D. E. Stewart (Eds.), *Psychological aspects of women's health care* (2nd ed., pp. 51–66). Washington, DC: American Psychiatric Press.

Miller, S. K. (1992). Asian-Americans bump against glass ceilings. *Science, 258,* 1224–1228.

Miller, W. C. (1999). Fitness and fatness in relation to health: Implications for a paradigm shift. *Journal of Social Issues, 55,* 207–219.

Mills, J. (1984). Self-posed behavior of females and males in photographs. *Sex Roles, 10,* 633–637.

Mills, R. S. L., Pedersen, J., & Grusec, J. E. (1989). Sex differences in reasoning and emotion about altruism. *Sex Roles, 20,* 603–621.

Millstein, S. G., & Halpern-Felsher, B. L. (1998). Adolescent sexuality. In E. A. Blechman & K. D. Brownell (Eds.), *Behavioral medicine and women: A comprehensive handbook* (pp. 59–63). New York: Guilford.

Min, P. G. (1993). Korean immigrants' marital patterns and marital adjustment. In H. P. McAdoo (Ed.), *Family ethnicity: Strength in diversity* (pp. 287–299). Newbury Park, CA: Sage.

Minow, M. (1999). Violence against women: A challenge to the Supreme Court. *New England Journal of Medicine, 341,* 1927–1929.

Minton, H. L. (2000). Psychology and gender at the turn of the century. *American Psychologist, 55,* 613–615.

Mintz, B., & Rothblum, E. D. (1997). Introduction. In B. Mintz & E. D. Rothblum (Eds.), *Lesbians in academia: Degrees of freedom* (pp. 1–11). New York: Routledge.

Mintz, L. B., & Kashubeck, S. (1999). Body image and disordered eating among Asian American and Caucasian college students. *Psychology of Women Quarterly, 23,* 781–796.

Mir-Hosseini, Z. (2001). Iran: Emerging feminist voices. In L. Walter (Ed.), *Women's rights: A global view* (pp. 113–125). Westport, CT: Guilford.

Mischel, W. (1966). A social-learning view of sex differences in behavior. In E. Maccoby (Ed.), *The development of sex differences* (pp. 56–81). Stanford, CA: Stanford University Press.

Mischel, W. (1970). Sex-typing and socialization. In P. Mussen (Ed.), *Carmichael's manual of child psychology* (Vol. 2). New York: Wiley.

Moen, P., Kim, J. E., & Hofmeister, H. (2001). Couples' work/retirement transitions, gender, and marital quality. *Social Psychology Quarterly, 64,* 55–71.

Mogil, J. S., Sternberg, W. F., Kest, B., Marek, P., & Liebeskind, J. C. (1993). Sex differences in the antagonism of swim stress-induced analgesia: Effects of gonadectomy and estrogen replacement. *Pain, 53,* 17–25.

Mohamed, C., & Smith, R. (1999). Race in the therapy relationship. In M. Lawrence & M. Maquire (Eds.), *Psychotherapy with women: Feminist perspectives* (pp. 134–159). New York: Routledge.

Money, J., & Ehrhardt, A. A. (1972). *Man and woman, boy and girl.* Baltimore: Johns Hopkins University Press.

Monsour, M. (1992). Meanings of intimacy in cross- and same-sex friendships. *Journal of Social and Personal Relationships, 9,* 277–295.

Mood disorders: An overview, part II. (1998, January). *Harvard Mental Health Letter,* pp. 1–5.

Mookherjee, H. N. (1997). Marital status, gender, and perception of well-being. *Journal of Social Psychology, 137,* 95–105.

Moore, D. P., & Buttner, E. H. (1997). *Women entrepreneurs: Moving beyond the glass ceiling.* Thousand Oaks, CA: Sage.

Moore, J., & Smith, D. K. (2001). Women and HIV infections. In N. L. Stotland & D. E. Stewart (Eds.), *Psychological aspects of women's health care* (2nd ed., pp. 331–361). Washington, DC: American Psychiatric Press.

Moraga, C. (1993). Women's subordination through the lens of sex/gender, sexuality, class, and race: Multicultural feminism. In A. M. Jaggar & P. S. Rothenberg (Eds.), *Feminist frameworks: Alternative theoretical accounts of the relations between women and men* (3rd ed., pp. 203–212). New York: McGraw-Hill.

Moran, J. P. (2000). *Teaching sex: The shaping of adolescence in the 20th century.* Cambridge, MA: Harvard University Press.

Morawski, J. G. (1994). *Sex matters? The unending search for a valid psychology of sex differences.* Paper presented at the annual meeting of the History of Science Society, New Orleans, LA.

Morawski, J. G., & Agronick, G. (1991). A restive legacy: The history of feminist work in experimental and cognitive psychology. *Psychology of Women Quarterly, 15,* 567–579.

Morawski, J. G., & Bayer, B. M. (1995). Stirring trouble and making theory. In H. Landrine (Ed.), *Bringing cultural diversity to feminist psychology: Theory, research, and practice* (pp. 113–137). Washington, DC: American Psychological Association.

Morgan, B. L. (1998). A three generational study of tomboy behavior. *Sex Roles, 39,* 787–800.

Morgan, L., & Kunkel, S. (2001). *Aging: The social context* (2nd ed.). Thousand Oaks, CA: Pine Forge Press.

Morokoff, P. J. (1998). Sexual functioning. In E. A. Blechman & K. D. Brownell (Eds.), *Behavioral medicine and women: A comprehensive handbook* (pp. 440–446). New York: Guilford.

Morokoff, P. J. (2000). A cultural context for sexual assertiveness in women. In C. B. Travis & J. W. White (Eds.), *Sexuality, society, and feminism* (pp. 299–319). Washington, DC: American Psychological Association.

Morokoff, P. J., Mays, V. M., & Coons, H. L. (1997). HIV infection and AIDS. In S. J. Gallant, G. P. Keita, & R. Royak-Schaler (Eds.), *Health care for women: Psychological, social, and behavioral influences* (pp. 273–293). Washington, DC: American Psychological Association.

Morokoff, P. J., et al. (1997). Sexual Assertiveness Scale for women: Development and validation. *Journal of Personality and Social Psychology, 73,* 790–804.

Morris, J. F. (2000, August). *Lesbian women of color in communities: Social activities and mental health services.* Paper presented at the annual convention of the American Psychological Association, Washington, DC.

Morris, J. F., Waldo, C. R., & Rothblum, E. D. (2001). A model of predictors and outcomes of outness among lesbian and bisexual women. *American Journal of Orthopsychiatry, 71,* 61–71.

Morris, L. A. (1997). *The male heterosexual.* Thousand Oaks, CA: Sage.

Morrison, D. (1987). *Being pregnant: Conversations with women.* Vancouver, Canada: New Star.

Morrow, S. L. (2000). First do no harm: Therapist issues in psychotherapy with lesbian, gay, and bisexual clients. In R. M. Perez, K. A. DeBord, & K. J. Bieschke (Eds.), *Handbook of counseling and psychotherapy with lesbian, gay, and bisexual clients* (pp. 35–55). Washington, DC: American Psychological Association.

Morry, M. M., & Staska, S. L. (2001). Magazine exposure: Internalization, self-objectification, eating attitudes, and body satisfaction in male and female university students. *Canadian Journal of Behavioural Science, 33,* 269–279.

Muehlenhard, C. L., Highby, B. J., Phelps, J. L., & Sympson, S. C. (1997). Rape statistics are not exaggerated. In M. R. Walsh (Ed.), *Women, men, and gender: Ongoing debates* (pp. 243–246). New Haven, CT: Yale University Press.

Mueller, K. A., & Yoder, J. D. (1997). Gendered norms for family size, employment, and occupation: Are there personal costs for violating them? *Sex Roles, 36,* 207–220.

Mueller, K. A., & Yoder, J. D. (1999). Stigmatization of non-normative family size status. *Sex Roles, 41,* 901–919.

Mulac, A. (1998). The gender-linked language effect: Do language differences really make a difference? In D. J. Canary & K. Dindia (Eds.), *Sex Differences and similarities in communication* (pp. 127–153). Mahwah, NJ: Erlbaum.

Mulhauser, D. (2001, August 10). Dating among college students is all but dead, survey finds. *Chronicle of Higher Education,* p. A51.

Muller, C. F. (1990). *Health care and gender.* New York: Russell Sage Foundation.

Murphy, J. D., Driscoll, D. M., & Kelly, J. R. (1999). Differences in the nonverbal behavior of men who vary in the likelihood to sexually harass. *Journal of Social Behavior and Personality, 14,* 113–128.

Murphy, P. A., & Cleeton, E. C. (2000). *In the best interest of the child: Good mothers behaving badly and the law.* Unpublished manuscript, SUNY Geneseo.

Murray, B. (1998, July). Workplace harassment hurts everyone on the job. *APA Monitor,* p. 35.

Murray, S. L., Meinholdt, C., & Bergmann, L. S. (1999). Addressing gender issues in the engineering classroom. *Feminist Teacher, 12,* 169–183.

Murry, V. M. (1996). Inner-city girls of color: Unmarried, sexually active nonmothers. In B. J. R. Leadbeater & N. Way (Eds.), *Urban girls: Resisting stereotypes, creating identities* (pp. 272–290). New York: New York University Press.

Mwangi, M. W. (1996). Gender roles portrayed in Kenyan television commercials. *Sex Roles, 34,* 205–214.

Myaskovsky, L., & Wittig, M. A. (1997). Predictors of feminist social identity among college women. *Sex Roles, 37,* 861–883.

Myers, D. G. (1999). Close relationships and quality of life. In D. Kahneman, E. Diener, & N. Schwarz (Eds.), *Well-being: The foundations of hedonic psychology* (pp. 374–391). New York: Russell Sage Foundation.

Myers, D. G. (2000). *The American paradox.* New Haven, CT: Yale University Press.

Nadien, M. B., & Denmark, F. L. (1999). Aging women: Stability or change in perceptions of personal control. In M. B. Nadien & F. L. Denmark (Eds.), *Females and autonomy: A life-span perspective* (pp. 130–154). Boston: Allyn & Bacon.

Naidoo, J. C. (1990). *Multicultural and gender issues on aging in Canada.* Paper presented at the 22nd International Congress of Applied Psychology, Kyoto, Japan.

Naidoo, J. C. (1999). The experience of contrasting subjective cultures: The case of South Asian women in Canada. In J. Adamopoulos & Y. Kashima (Eds.), *Social and cultural context* (pp. 125–137). Thousand Oaks, CA: Sage.

Naidoo, J. C. (2000). The problem of Canada in the new millennium: Sociopsychological challenges for visible minority women. *Psychologia, 8,* 1–19.

Napier, L. A. (1996). Nine native women: Pursuing the doctorate and aspiring to positions of leadership. In K. D. Arnold, K. D. Noble, & R. F. Subotnik (Eds.), *Remarkable women: Perspectives on female talent development* (pp. 133–148). Creeskill, NJ: Hampton Press.

Naples, N. A. (Ed.). (1998). *Community activism and feminist politics: Organizing across race, class, and gender.* New York: Routledge.

Nash, H. C., & Chrisler, J. C. (1997). Is a little (psychiatric) knowledge a dangerous thing? *Psychology of Women Quarterly, 21,* 315–322.

Nathan, P. E., & Gorman, J. M. (Eds.). (2002). *A guide to treatments that work* (2nd ed.). New York: Oxford University Press.

The nation: Faculty and staff. (2001, August 31). *Chronicle of Higher Education* (Almanac Issue, 2001–2002), pp. 26–29.

The nation: Students. (2001, August 31). *Chronicle of Higher Education* (Almanac Issue, 2001–2002), pp. 20–25.

The nation: Students. (2002, August 30). *Chronicle of Higher Education, Almanac 2002–2003,* p. 23.

National Foundation for Women Business Owners. (1994). *Styles of success: The thinking and management styles of women and men entrepreneurs.* Washington, DC: Author.

National Institute of Mental Health. (2001). *Eating disorders: Facts about eating disorders and the search for solutions.* Bethesda, MD: Author.

National Institute of Mental Health. (2002). *Stories of depression.* Bethesda, MD: Author.

National Labor Committee. (2001). *Bangladesh: Ending the race to the bottom.* New York: Author.

National Mobilization Against Sweatshops. (2000). *Welcome to the U.S.A.: The United Sweatshops of America* [Brochure]. New York: Author.

Neft, N., & Levine, A. D. (1997). *Where women stand: An international report on the status of women in 140 countries.* New York: Random House.

Neill, C. M., & Kahn, A. S. (1999). The role of personal spirituality and religious social activity on the life satisfaction of older widowed women. *Sex Roles, 40,* 319–329.

Nelson, A. (2000). The pink dragon is female: Halloween costumes and gender markers. *Psychology of Women Quarterly, 24,* 137–144.

Nelson, H. D. (1998). Osteoporosis prevention. In A. Blechman & K. D. Brownell (Eds.), *Behavioral medicine and women: A comprehensive handbook* (pp. 221–227). New York: Guilford.

Nelson, T. D. (Ed.). (2002). *Ageism: Stereotyping and prejudice against older persons.* Cambridge, MA: MIT Press.

Ness, R. B., et al. (1999). Cocaine and tobacco use and the risk of spontaneous abortion. *New England Journal of Medicine, 340,* 333–339.

Neto, F., & Pinto, I. (1998). Gender stereotypes in Portuguese television advertisements. *Sex Roles, 39,* 153–164.

Nevill, D. D. (1995). The work importance study in the United States. In D. E. Super & B. Šverko (Eds.), *Life roles, values, and careers: International findings of the work importance study* (pp. 204–221). San Francisco: Jossey-Bass.

Nevill, D. D., & Calvert, P. D. (1996). Career assessment and the salience inventory. *Journal of Career Assessment, 4,* 399–412.

Newtson, R. L., & Keith, P. M. (1997). Single women in later life. In J. M. Coyle (Ed.), *Handbook on women and aging* (pp. 385–399). Westport, CT: Greenwood Press.

NICHD Early Child Care Research Network. (1999). Contexts of development and developmental outcomes over the first seven years of life. In J. Brooks-Gunn & J. Berlin (Eds.), *Young children's education, health, and development: Profile and synthesis project report.* Washington, DC: Department of Education.

NICHD Early Child Care Research Network. (2001). Nonmaternal care and family factors in early development. *Applied Developmental Psychology, 22,* 457–492.

NICHD Early Child Care Research Network. (2002). Child-care structure → process → outcome: Direct and indirect effects of child-care quality on young children's development. *Psychological Science, 13,* 199–206.

Nicolson, P. (1997). *Against their will? Analysing women's accounts of first sexual intercourse.* Unpublished manuscript, Sheffield, England.

Nicotera, A. M. (1997). *The mate relationship: Cross-cultural applications of a rules theory.* Albany, NY: State University of New York Press.

Niemann, Y. F., et al. (1994). Use of free responses and cluster analysis to determine stereotypes of eight groups. *Personality and Social Psychology Bulletin, 20,* 379–390.

Nikolic-Ristanovic, V. (2000, Winter). Victimization by war rape. *Canadian Woman Studies/Les cahiers de la femme, 19,* 28–35.

Nolen-Hoeksema, S. (1990). *Sex differences in depression.* Stanford, CA: Stanford University Press.

Nolen-Hoeksema, S. (2001). Gender differences in depression. *Current Directions in Psychological Science, 10,* 173–176.

Nolen-Hoeksema, S., & Girgus, J. S. (1995). Explanatory style and achievement, depression, and gender differences in childhood and early adolescence. In G. M. Buchanan & M. E. P. Seligman (Eds.), *Explanatory style* (pp. 57–70). Hillsdale, NJ: Erlbaum.

Nolen-Hoeksema, S., & Jackson, B. (2001). Mediators of the gender difference in rumination. *Psychology of Women Quarterly, 25,* 37–47.

Nolen-Hoeksema, S., & Larson, J. (1999). *Coping with loss.* Mahwah, NJ: Erlbaum.

Nolen-Hoeksema, S., Larson, J., & Grayson, C. (1999). Explaining the gender difference in depressive symptoms. *Journal of Personality and Social Psychology, 77,* 1061–1072.

Nonnemaker, L. (2000). Women physicians in academic medicine. *New England Journal of Medicine, 342,* 399–405.

Noor, N. M. (1996). Some demographic, personality, and role variables as correlates of women's well-being. *Sex Roles, 34,* 603–620.

Noor, N. M. (1999). Roles and women's well-being: Some preliminary findings from Malaysia. *Sex Roles, 41,* 123–145.

Norcross, J. C., Hanych, J. M., & Terranova, R. D. (1996). Graduate study in psychology: 1992–1993. *American Psychologist, 51,* 631–643.

Nordvik, H., & Amponsah, B. (1998). Gender differences in spatial activity among university students in an egalitarian educational system. *Sex Roles, 38,* 1009–1023.

Notebook. (1999, June 18). *Chronicle of Higher Education*, p. A43.

Novack, L. L., & Novack, D. R. (1996). Being female in the eighties and nineties: Conflicts between new opportunities and traditional expectations among White, middle class, heterosexual college women. *Sex Roles, 35*, 57–77.

Nussbaum, M. (2000, September 8). Globalization debate ignores the education of women. *Chronicle of Higher Education*, pp. B16–B17.

Obeidallah, D. A., et al. (2000). Socioeconomic status, race, and girls' pubertal maturation: Results from the Project on Human Development in Chicago Neighborhoods. *Journal of Research on Adolescence, 10*, 443–464.

O'Brien, M., et al. (2000). Gender-role cognition in three-year-old boys and girls. *Sex Roles, 42*, 1007–1025.

Ocampo, C., et al. (2003). Diversity research in *Teaching of Psychology:* Summary and recommendations. *Teaching of Psychology, 30*, 5–18.

Ochman, J. M. (1996). The effects of nongender-role stereotyped, same-sex role models in storybooks on the self-esteem of children in grade three. *Sex Roles, 35*, 711–735.

O'Connell, A. N. (2001). *Models of achievement: Reflections of eminent women in psychology* (Vol. 3). Mahwah, NJ: Erlbaum.

O'Connor, P. G., & Schottenfeld, R. S. (1998). Patients with alcohol problems. *New England Journal of Medicine, 338*, 592–602.

Oerton, S. (1998). Reclaiming the "housewife"? Lesbians and household work. In G. A. Dunne (Ed.), *Living "Difference": Lesbian perspectives on work and family life* (pp. 69–83). New York: Haworth.

Oggins, J., Veroff, J., & Leber, D. (1993). Perceptions of marital interaction among Black and White newlyweds. *Journal of Personality and Social Psychology, 65*, 494–511.

O'Hara, M. W., & Stuart, S. (1999). Pregnancy and postpartum. In R. G. Robinson & W. R. Yates (Eds.), *Psychiatric treatment of the medically ill* (pp. 253–277). New York: Marcel Dekker.

O'Hara, M. W., Stuart, S., Gorman, L. L., & Wenzel, A. (2000). Efficacy of interpersonal psychotherapy for postpartum depression. *Archives of General Psychiatry, 57*, 1039–1045.

Oinonen, K., & Mazmanian, D. (2001). *Structure of affect across the human menstrual cycle.* Paper presented at the annual convention of the Canadian Psychological Association.

Okamura, A., Heras, P., & Wong-Kerberg, L. (1995). Asian, Pacific Island, and Filipino Americans and sexual child abuse. In L. A. Fontes (Ed.), *Sexual abuse in nine North American cultures* (pp. 67–96). Thousand Oaks, CA: Sage.

Okazaki, S. (1998). Teaching gender issues in Asian American psychology. *Psychology of Women Quarterly, 22*, 33–52.

O'Leary, K. D., & Maiuro, R. D. (Eds.). (2001). *Psychological abuse in violent domestic relations.* New York: Springer.

O'Leary, V. E., & Flanagan, E. H. (2001). Leadership. In J. Worell (Ed.), *Encyclopedia of women and gender* (pp. 645–656). San Diego: Academic Press.

Oliver, M. B., & Hyde, J. S. (1993). Gender differences in sexuality: A meta-analysis. *Psychological Bulletin, 114*, 29–51.

Olson, E. (1994). Female voices of aggression in Tonga. *Sex Roles, 30*, 237–248.

O'Mahen, H. A., Beach, S. R. H., & Banawan, S. F. (2001). Depression in marriage. In J. H. Harvey & A. Wenzel (Eds.), *Close romantic relationships* (pp. 299–319). Mahwah, NJ: Erlbaum.

O'Neil, J. M., & Nadeau, R. A. (1998). Men's gender role conflict, defense mechanisms, and self-protective defensive strategies: Explaining men's violence against women from a gender role socialization perspective. In M. Harway & J. M. O'Neil (Eds.), *New perspectives on violence against women.* Thousand Oaks, CA: Sage.

O'Neil, J. M., & Nadeau, R. A. (1999). Men's gender-role conflict, defense mechanisms, and self-protective defensive strategies. In M. Harway & J. M. O'Neil (Eds.), *What causes men's violence against women?* (pp. 89–116). Thousand Oaks, CA: Sage.

Onyx, J., & Benton, P. (1999). What does retirement mean for women? In J. Onyx, R. Leonard, & R. Reed (Eds.), *Revisioning aging: Empowering of older women* (pp. 93–108). New York: Peter Lang.

Orbuch, T. L., House, J. S., Mero, R. P., & Webster, P. S. (1996). Marital quality over the life course. *Social Psychology Quarterly, 59*, 162–171.

O'Reilly, P., Penn, E. M., & deMarrais, K. (Eds.). (2001). *Educating young adolescent girls.* Mahwah, NJ: Erlbaum.

Orozco, A. E. (1999). Mexican blood runs through my veins. In D. L. Galindo & M. D. Gonzales (Eds.), *Speaking Chicana: Voice, power, and identity* (pp. 106–120). Tucson, AZ: University of Arizona Press.

Osland, J. A., Fitch, M., & Willis, E. E. (1996). Likelihood to rape in college males. *Sex Roles, 35,* 171–183.

O'Sullivan, L. F. (1995). Less is more: The effects of sexual experience on judgments of men's and women's personality characteristics and relationship desirability. *Sex Roles, 33,* 159–181.

O'Sullivan, L. F., & Gaines, M. E. (1998). Decision-making in college students' heterosexual dating relationship: Ambivalence about engaging in sexual activity. *Journal of Social and Personal Relationships, 15,* 347–363.

O'Sullivan, L. F., Graber, J. A., & Brooks-Gunn, J. (2001). Adolescent gender development. In J. Worell (Ed.), *Encyclopedia of women and gender* (pp. 55–67). San Diego: Academic Press.

Otis, G. (2001, April/May). Casas maternas. *Ms. Magazine,* pp. 32–35.

Ottens, A. J., & Hotelling, K. (Eds.). (2001). *Sexual violence on campus: Policies, programs, and perspectives.* New York: Springer.

Owens, R. E., Jr. (1998). *Queer kids: The challenges and promise for lesbian, gay, and bisexual youth.* Binghamton, NY: Haworth.

Paik, H. (2001). The history of children's use of electronic media. In D. G. Singer & J. L. Singer (Eds.), *Handbook on children and the media* (pp. 7–27). Thousand Oaks, CA: Sage.

Pajares, F., Miller, M. D., & Johnson, M. J. (1999). Gender differences in writing self-beliefs of elementary school students. *Journal of Educational Psychology, 91,* 50–61.

Paludi, M. A. (2000). Sexual harassment of college students. In J. C. Chrisler, C. Golden, & P. D. Rozee (Eds.), *Lectures on the psychology of women* (2nd ed., pp. 306–320). Boston: McGraw-Hill.

Paludi, M. A., & Barickman, R. B. (1998). *Sexual harassment, work, and education: A resource manual for prevention* (2nd ed.). Albany, NY: State University of New York Press.

Paludi, M. A., et al. (1995). Academic sexual harassment: From theory and research to program implementation. In H. Landrine (Ed.), *Bringing cultural diversity to feminist psychology* (pp. 177–191). Washington, DC: American Psychological Association.

Pappas, G., Queen, S., Hadden, W., & Fisher, G. (1993). The increasing disparity in mortality between socioeconomic groups in the United States, 1960 and 1986. *New England Journal of Medicine, 329,* 103–109.

Park, J., & Liao, T. F. (2000). The effect of multiple roles of South Korean married women professors: Role changes and the factors which influence potential role gratification and strain. *Sex Roles, 43,* 571–591.

Parks, J. B., & Roberton, M. A. (1998a). Contemporary arguments against nonsexist language: Blaubergs (1980) revisited. *Sex Roles, 39,* 445–461.

Parks, J. B., & Roberton, M. A. (1998b). Influence of age, gender, and context on attitudes toward sexist/nonsexist language: Is sport a special case? *Sex Roles, 38,* 477–494.

Parks, J. B., & Roberton, M. A. (2000). Development and validation of an instrument to measure attitudes toward sexist/nonsexist language. *Sex Roles, 42,* 415–438.

Parrot, A. (1996). Sexually assertive communication training. In T. L. Jackson (Ed.), *Acquaintance rape: Assessment, treatment, and prevention* (pp. 215–242). Sarasota, FL: Professional Resource Press.

Parrot, A. (1999). *Coping with date and acquaintance rape.* New York: Rosen Publishing Group.

Pascarella, E. T., et al. (1997). Women's perceptions of a "chilly climate" and their cognitive outcomes during the first year of college. *Journal of College Student Development, 38,* 109–124.

Pasch, L. (2001). Confronting fertility problems: Current research and future challenges. In A. Baum, T. A. Revenson, & J. E. Singer (Eds.), *Handbook of health psychology* (pp. 559–570). Mahwah, NJ: Erlbaum.

Pasch, L. A., & Dunkel-Schetter, C. (1997). Fertility problems: Complex issues faced by women and couples. In S. J. Gallant, G. P. Keita, & R. Royak-Schaler (Eds.), *Health care for women: Psychological, social, and behavioral influences* (pp. 187–201). Washington, DC: American Psychological Association.

Pasupathi, M., Carstensen, L. L., & Tsai, J. L. (1995). Ageism in interpersonal settings. In B. Lott & D. Maluso (Eds.), *The social psychology of interpersonal discrimination* (pp. 160–182). New York: Guilford.

Pasupathi, M., & Löckenhoff, C. E. (2002). Ageist behavior. In T. D. Nelson (Eds.), *Ageism: Stereotyping and prejudice against older persons* (pp. 201–246). Cambridge, MA: MIT Press.

Pate, K. (1999, Spring/Summer). Young women and violent offences: Myths and realities. *Canadian Woman Studies/Les cahiers de la femme, 19,* 39–43.

Pattatucci, A. M. (Ed.). (1998). *Women in science: Meeting career challenges.* Thousand Oaks, CA: Sage.

Pattatucci, A. M., & Hamer, D. H. (1995). Development and familiality of sexual orientation in females. *Behavior Genetics, 25,* 407–420.

Patterson, C. J. (1995). Sexual orientation and human development: An overview. *Developmental Psychology, 31,* 3–11.

Patterson, C. J. (1998). Family lives of lesbians and gay men. In A. S. Bellack & M. Hersen (Eds.), *Comprehensive clinical psychology* (Vol. 9, pp. 253–273). Amsterdam: Elsevier.

Patterson, C. J., & Chan, R. W. (1999). Families headed by lesbian and gay parents. In M. E. Lamb (Ed.), *Parenting and development in "nontraditional" families* (pp. 191–221). Mahwah, NJ: Erlbaum.

Patton, W., & Mannison, M. (1995). Sexual coercion in high school dating. *Sex Roles, 33,* 447–456.

Paul, E. L., McManus, B., & Hayes, A. (2000). "Hookups": Characteristics and correlates of college students' spontaneous and anonymous sexual experiences. *Journal of Sex Research, 37,* 76–88.

Pauwels, A. (1998). *Women changing language.* London: Longman.

Payne, K. E. (2001). *Different but equal: Communication between the sexes.* Westport, CT: Praeger.

Paz, J. J. (1993). Support of Hispanic elderly. In H. P. McAdoo (Ed.), *Family ethnicity* (pp. 177–183). Newbury Park, CA: Sage.

Pearce, J. L. (1993). *Volunteers: The organizational behavior of unpaid workers.* London: Routledge.

Pearson, P. (1998). *When she was bad: Violent women and the myth of innocence.* New York: Viking.

Pediatrician testifies on impact of sexuality in media. (2001, October). *American Academy of Pediatrics News,* p. 141.

Peirce, K. (1990). A feminist theoretical perspective on the socialization of teenage girls through *Seventeen* magazine. *Sex Roles, 23,* 491–500.

Peña, M. (1998). Class, gender, and machismo: The "treacherous-woman" folklore of Mexican male workers. In M. S. Kimmel & M. A. Messner (Eds.), *Men's lives* (4th ed., pp. 273–284). Boston: Allyn & Bacon.

Penelope, J. (1990). *Speaking freely: Unlearning the lies of the fathers' tongues.* Elmsford, NY: Pergamon Press.

Penn, M., & Schoen, D. (1998, March 30). The single files. *New York Magazine,* pp. 24–32.

Peplau, L. A. (1983). Roles and gender. In H. H. Kelley et al. (Eds.), *Close relationships* (pp. 220–264). San Francisco: Freeman.

Peplau, L. A. (1994). Men and women in love. In D. L. Sollie & L. A. Leslie (Eds.), *Gender, families, and close relationships: Feminist research journeys* (pp. 19–49). Thousand Oaks, CA: Sage.

Peplau, L. A. (2001). Rethinking women's sexual orientation: An interdisciplinary, relationship-focused approach. *Personal Relationships, 8,* 1–19.

Peplau, L. A., & Beals, K. P. (2001). Lesbians, gay men, and bisexuals in relationships. In J. Worell (Ed.), *Encyclopedia of women and gender* (pp. 657–666). San Diego: Academic Press.

Peplau, L. A., Cochran, S. D., & Mays, V. M. (1997). A national survey of the intimate relationships of African-American lesbians and gay men. In B. Greene (Ed.), *Ethnic and cultural diversity among lesbians and gay men* (pp. 11–38). Thousand Oaks, CA: Sage.

Peplau, L. A., DeBro, S. C., Veniegas, R. C., & Taylor, P. L. (1999). *Gender, culture, and ethnicity: Current research about women and men.* Mountain View, CA: Mayfield.

Peplau, L. A., & Garnets, L. D. (2000a). A new paradigm for understanding women's sexuality and sexual orientation. *Journal of Social Issues, 56,* 329–350.

Peplau, L. A., & Garnets, L. D. (Eds.). (2000b). Women's sexualities: New perspectives on sexual orientation and gender [Special issue]. *Journal of Social Issues, 56*(2).

Peplau, L. A., Padesky, C., & Hamilton, M. (1982). Satisfaction in lesbian relationships. *Journal of Homosexuality, 8,* 23–35.

Peplau, L. A., & Spalding, L. R. (2000). The close relationships of lesbians, gay men, and bisexuals. In C. Hendrick & S. S. Hendrick (Eds.), *Close relationships* (pp. 111–123). Thousand Oaks, CA: Sage.

Peplau, L. A., Spalding, L. R., Conley, T. D., & Veniegas, R. C. (1999). The development of sexual orientation in women. *Annual Review of Sex Research, 10,* 70–99.

Peplau, L. A., Veniegas, R. C., & Campbell, S. M. (1996). Gay and lesbian relationships. In R. C. Savin-Williams & K. Cohen (Eds.), *The lives of lesbians, gays, and bisexuals: Children to adults* (pp. 250–273). Fort Worth, TX: Harcourt Brace.

Peplau, L. A., Veniegas, R. C., Taylor, P. L., & DeBro, S. C. (1999). Sociocultural perspectives on the lives of women and men. In L. A. Peplau et al. (Eds.), *Gender, culture, and ethnicity: Current research about women and men* (pp. 23–37). Mountain View, CA: Mayfield.

Peplau, L. A., et al. (1998). A critique of Bem's "exotic becomes erotic" theory of sexual orientation. *Psychological Review, 105,* 387–394.

Percy, C. (1998). Feminism. In K. Trew & J. Kremer (Eds.), *Gender and Psychology* (pp. 27–40). New York: Oxford University Press.

Perkins, H. W., & DeMeis, D. K. (1996). Gender and family effects on the "second shift" domestic activity of college-educated young adults. *Gender and Society, 10,* 78–93.

Perloff, R. M. (2001). *Persuading people to have safer sex: Applications of social science to the AIDS crisis.* Mahwah, NJ: Erlbaum.

Peterson, G. (1996). Childbirth: The ordinary miracle: Effects of devaluation of childbirth on women's self-esteem and family relationships. *Pre- and Perinatal Psychology Journal, 11,* 101–109.

Pezdek, K. (2001). A cognitive analysis of the role of suggestibility in explaining memories for abuse. In J. J. Freyd & A. P. DePrince (Eds.), *Trauma and cognitive science: A meeting of minds, science, and human experience* (pp. 73–85). New York: Haworth.

Philbin, M., Meier, E., Hoffman, S., & Boverie, P. (1995). A survey of gender and learning styles. *Sex Roles, 32,* 485–494.

Philipp, D. A., & Carr, M. L. (2001). Normal and medically complicated pregnancies. In N. L. Stotland & D. E. Stewart (Eds.), *Psychological aspects of women's health care: The interface between psychiatry and obstetrics and gynecology* (2nd ed., pp. 13–32). Washington, DC: American Psychiatric Publishing.

Phillips, C. R. (2000, Summer). Supportive language in family-centered maternity care. *Advances in Family-Centered Care,* pp. 16–18.

Phillips, K., Glendon, G., & Knight, J. A. (1999). Putting the risk of breast cancer in perspective. *New England Journal of Medicine, 340,* 141–144.

Phillips, L. (1998). *The girls report.* New York: National Council for Research on Women.

Phillips, S. D., & Imhoff, A. R. (1997). Women and career development: A decade of research. *Annual Review of Psychology, 48,* 31–59.

Philpot, C. L., Brooks, G. R., Lusterman, D. D., & Nutt, R. L. (1997). *Bridging separate gender worlds.* Washington, DC: American Psychological Association.

Phinney, J. S., & Alipuria, L. (1990). Ethnic identity in college students from four ethnic groups. *Journal of Adolescence, 13,* 171–183.

Phinney, J. S., & Rosenthal, D. A. (1992). Ethnic identity in adolescence: Process, context, and outcome. In G. R. Adams, T. P. Gullota, & R. Montemayor (Eds.), *Adolescent identity formation* (pp. 145–172). Newbury Park, CA: Sage.

Phizacklea, A. (2001). Women, migration, and the state. In K. Bhavnani (Ed.), *Feminism and "race"* (pp. 319–330). New York: Oxford University Press.

Physicians for Human Rights. (1998). *The Taliban's war on women: A health and human rights crisis in Afghanistan.* Boston: Author.

Pickup, F. (2001). *Ending violence against women: A challenge for development and humanitarian work.* Oxford, England: Oxfam.

Pierce, J. L. (1995). *Gender trials: Emotional lives in contemporary law firms.* Berkeley, CA: University of California Press.

Pierce, R. L., & Kite, M. E. (1999). Creating expectations in adolescent girls. In S. N. Davis, M. Crawford, & J. Sebrechts (Eds.), *Coming into her own: Educational success in girls and women* (pp. 175–192). San Francisco: Jossey-Bass.

Pierce-Baker, C. (1998). *Surviving the silence: Black women's stories of rape.* New York: Norton.

Pilkington, N. W., & D'Augelli, A. R. (1995). Victimization of lesbian, gay, and bisexual youth in community settings. *Journal of Community Psychology, 23,* 34–56.

Pincus, J. (2000). Childbirth advice literature as it relates to two childbearing ideologies. *Birth, 27,* 209–213.

Pinzone-Glover, H. A., Gidycz, C. A., & Jacobs, C. D. (1998). An acquaintance rape prevention program. *Psychology of Women Quarterly, 22,* 605–621.

Pipher, M. (1994). *Reviving Ophelia: Saving the selves of adolescent girls.* New York: Ballantine.

Pipher, M. (1995). *Hunger pains: The modern woman's tragic quest for thinness.* New York: Ballantine.

Piran, N. (2001). Eating disorders and disordered eating. In J. Worell (Ed.), *Encyclopedia of women and gender* (pp. 369–378). San Diego: Academic Press.

Plant, E. A., Hyde, J. S., Keltner, D., & Devine, P. G. (2000). The gender stereotyping of emotions. *Psychology of Women Quarterly, 24,* 81–92.

Pleck, J. H. (1997). Paternal involvement: Levels, sources, and consequences. In M. E. Lamb (Ed.), *The role of the father in child development* (pp. 66–103). New York: Wiley.

Pleck, J. H., Sonenstein, F. L., & Ku, L. C. (1998). Masculinity ideology and its correlates. In B. M. Clinchy & J. K. Norem (Eds.), *The gender and psychology reader.* New York: New York University Press.

Pogrebin, L. C. (1996). *Getting over getting older.* Boston: Little, Brown.

Pogrebin, L. C. (1997, September/October). Endless love. *Ms. Magazine,* pp. 36–37.

Polce-Lynch, M., Myers, B. J., Kliewer, W., & Kilmartin, C. (2001). Adolescent self-esteem and gender: Exploring relations to sexual harassment, body image, media influence, and emotional expression. *Journal of Youth and Adolescence, 30,* 225–244.

Polce-Lynch, M., et al. (1998). Gender and age patterns in emotional expression, body image, and self-esteem: A qualitative analysis. *Sex Roles, 38,* 1025–1048.

Polivy, J., & Herman, C. P. (2002). Causes of eating disorders. *Annual Review of Psychology, 53,* 187–213.

Polivy, J., & McFarlane, T. L. (1998). Dieting, exercise, and body weight. In E. A. Blechman & K. D. Brownell (Eds.), *Behavioral medicine and women: A comprehensive handbook* (pp. 369–373). New York: Guilford.

Pollack, W. (1998). *Real boys.* New York: Random House.

Pollack, W. S., & Levant, R. F. (1998). *New psychotherapy for men.* New York: Wiley.

Pomerantz, E. M., & Ruble, D. N. (1998). The role of maternal control in the development of sex differences in child self-evaluative factors. *Child Development, 69,* 458–478.

Pomerleau, A., Bolduc, D., Malcuit, G., & Cossette, L. (1990). Pink or blue: Environmental gender stereotypes in the first two years of life. *Sex Roles, 22,* 359–367.

Pomerleau, C. S., Zucker, A. N., & Stewart, A. J. (2001). Characterizing concerns about postcessation weight gain: Results from a national survey of women smokers. *Nicotine and Tobacco Research, 3,* 51–60.

Pomerleau, C. S., Zucker, A. N., Namenek, R. J., et al. (2001). Race differences in weight concerns among women smokers: Results from two independent samples. *Addictive Behaviors, 26,* 651–663.

Pomfret, J. (2001, June 3). China's boy boom tied to ultrasound machines. *Dallas Morning News,* p. 31A.

Pope, K. (2001). Sex between therapists and clients. In J. Worell (Ed.), *Encyclopedia of women and gender* (pp. 955–962). San Diego: Academic Press.

Pope, R. L., & Reynolds, A. L. (1991). Including bisexuality: It's more than just a label. In N. J. Evans & V. A. Wall (Eds.), *Beyond tolerance: Gays, lesbians, and bisexuals on campus* (pp. 205–221). Lanham, MD: American College Personnel Association.

Popenoe, D., & Whitehead, B. D. (2002). *The state of our unions.* Piscataway, NJ: National Marriage Project.

Porter, M., & Judd, E. (Eds.). (1999). *Feminists doing development.* London: Zed Books.

Porzelius, L. K. (2000). Physical health issues for women. In M. Biaggio & M. Hersen (Eds.), *Issues in the psychology of women* (pp. 229–249). New York: Plenum.

Posavac, H. D., Posavac, S. S., & Posavac, E. J. (1998). Exposure to media images of female attractiveness and concern with body weight among young women. *Sex Roles, 38,* 187–201.

Potts, L. K. (Ed.). (2000). *Ideologies of breast cancer: Feminist perspectives.* New York: St. Martin's Press.

Powell, G. N. (1999). Reflections on the glass ceiling. In G. N. Powell (Ed.), *Handbook of gender and work* (pp. 325–345). Thousand Oaks, CA: Sage.

Powlishta, K. K. (1995). Intergroup processes in childhood: Social categorization and sex role development. *Developmental Psychology, 31,* 781–788.

Powlishta, K. K. (2000). The effect of target age on the activation of gender stereotypes. *Sex Roles, 42,* 271–282.

Powlishta, K. K., et al. (2001). From infancy through middle childhood: The role of cognitive and social factors in becoming gendered. In R. K. Unger (Ed.), *Handbook of the psychology of women and gender* (pp. 116–132). New York: Wiley.

Pozner, J. L. (2001a, March/April). Cosmetic coverage. *Extra!,* pp. 8–9.

Pozner, J. L. (2001b, December 24). Missing since 9-11: Women's voices. *Liberal Opinion Week,* p. 23.

Pozner, J. L. (2001c, July/August). Power shortage for media women. *Extra!,* pp. 8–9.

Premenstrual mood disturbance. (2001, June). *Harvard Mental Health Letter,* pp. 4–6.

Prezbindowski, K. S., & Prezbindowski, A. K. (2001). Educating young adolescent girls about lesbian, bisexual, and gay issues. In P. O'Reilly, E. M. Penn, & K. deMarrais (Eds.), *Educating young adolescent girls* (pp. 47–80). Mahwah, NJ: Erlbaum.

Price, C. A. (2000). Women and retirement: Relinquishing professional identity. *Journal of Aging Studies, 14,* 81–101.

Price, J. M. (2002, June). *Obesity and stigma in women's health.* Paper presented at the symposium "Cross-

Cultural Issues in Women's Health," Missillac, France.

Price-Bonham, S., & Skeen, P. (1982). Black and White fathers' attitudes toward children's sex roles. *Psychological Reports, 50,* 1187–1190.

Prout, P. I., & Dobson, K. S. (1998). Recovered memories of childhood sexual abuse: Searching for the middle ground in clinical practice. *Canadian Psychology/Psychologie canadienne, 39,* 257–265.

Pryzgoda, J., & Chrisler, J. C. (2000). Definitions of gender and sex: The subtleties of meaning. *Sex Roles, 43,* 553–569.

Ptacek, J. (1999). *Battered women in the courtroom.* Boston: Northeastern University Press.

Pulford, B. D., & Colman, A. M. (1997). Overconfidence: Feedback and item difficulty effects. *Personality and Individual Differences, 23,* 125–133.

Purcell, D. W., & Hicks, D. W. (1996). Institutional discrimination against lesbians, gay men, and bisexuals: The courts, legislature, and the military. In R. P. Cabaj & T. S. Stein (Eds.), *Textbook of homosexuality and mental health* (pp. 763–782). Washington, DC: American Psychiatric Press.

Pyke, S. W. (1994). CPA achievements and weather trends in academe. *SWAP Newsletter, 21,* 12–15.

Pyke, S. W. (1998, June). *The inferior sex: Psychology's construction of gender.* Paper presented at the annual convention of the Canadian Psychological Association, Edmonton, Canada.

Pyke, S. W. (2001). Feminist psychology in Canada: Early days. *Canadian Psychology/Psychologie canadienne, 42,* 268–275.

Quatman, T., Sokolik, E., & Smith, K. (2000). Adolescent perception of peer success: A gendered perspective over time. *Sex Roles, 43,* 61–84.

Quatman, T., & Watson, C. M. (2001). Gender differences in adolescent self-esteem: An exploration of domains. *Journal of Genetic Psychology, 162,* 93–117.

Quick, B. (2000). *Under her wing: The mentors who changed our lives.* Oakland, CA: New Harbinger.

Quina, K. (1996). Sexual harassment and rape: A continuum of exploitation. In M. A. Paludi (Ed.), *Sexual harassment on college campuses: Abusing the ivory power* (pp. 183–197). Albany, NY: State University of New York Press.

Quina, K., Cotter, M., & Romenesko, K. (1998). Breaking the (plexi)glass ceiling in higher education. In L. H. Collins, J. C. Chrisler, & K. Quina (Eds.), *Career strategies for women in academe: Arming Athena* (pp. 215–245). Thousand Oaks, CA: Sage.

Quindlen, A. (2001a, July 2). Playing God on no sleep. *Newsweek,* p. 64.

Quindlen, A. (2001b, December 17). The terrorists here at home. *Newsweek,* p. 78.

Quirouette, C. C., & Pushkar, D. (1999). Views of future aging among middle-aged university educated women. *Canadian Journal on Aging, 18,* 236–258.

Raag, T. (1999). Influences of social expectations of gender, gender stereotypes, and situational constraints on children's toy choices. *Sex Roles, 41,* 809–831.

Raag, T., & Rackliff, C. L. (1998). Preschoolers' awareness of social expectations of gender: Relationships to toy choices. *Sex Roles, 38,* 685–700.

Rabinowitz, F. E., & Cochran, S. V. (2002). *Deepening psychotherapy with men.* Washington, DC: American Psychological Association.

Rabinowitz, V. C. (1996). Coping with sexual harassment. In M. A. Paludi (Ed.), *Sexual harassment on college campuses* (pp. 199–213). Albany, NY: State University of New York Press.

Rabuzzi, K. A. (1994). *Mother with child.* Bloomington, IN: Indiana University Press.

Raffaelli, M., & Ontai, L. (2001). "She's 16 years old and there's boys calling over to the house": An exploratory study of sexual socialization in Latino families. *Culture, Health, and Sexuality, 3,* 295–310.

Raffaelli, M., & Suarez-Al-Adam, A. (1998). Reconsidering the HIV/AIDS prevention needs of Latina women in the United States. In N. L. Roth & L. K. Fuller (Eds.), *Women and AIDS: Negotiating safer practices, care, and representation* (pp. 7–41). New York: Haworth.

Ragan, J. M. (1982). Gender displays in portrait photographs. *Sex Roles, 8,* 33–43.

Raine, N. V. (1998). *After silence: Rape and my journey back.* New York: Three Rivers Press.

Raitt, F. E., & Zeedyk, S. (2000). *The implicit relation of psychology and law: Women and syndrome evidence.* London: Routledge.

Rajagopal, I. (1990). The glass ceiling in the vertical mosaic: Indian immigrants in Canada. *Canadian Ethnic Studies, 22,* 96–101.

Rajecki, D. W., et al. (1993). Gender casting in television toy advertisements: Distributions, message content analysis, and evaluations. *Journal of Consumer Psychology, 2,* 307–327.

Ralston, P. A. (1997). Midlife and older Black women. In J. M. Coyle (Ed.), *Handbook on women and aging* (pp. 273–289). Westport, CT: Greenwood Press.

Rand, C. S. W., & Resnick, J. L. (2000). The "good enough" body size as judged by people of varying age and weight. *Obesity Research, 8,* 309–316.

Rand, C. S. W., & Wright, B. A. (2000). Continuity and change in the evaluation of ideal and acceptable body sizes across a wide age span. *International Journal of Eating Disorders, 28,* 90–100.

Randhawa, B. S., & Hunter, D. M. (2001). Validity of performance assessment in mathematics for early adolescents. *Canadian Journal of Behavioural Science, 33,* 14–24.

Reese, L. A., & Lindenberg, K. E. (1999). *Implementing sexual harassment policy.* Thousand Oaks, CA: Sage.

Regan, P. C. (1996). Sexual outcasts: The perceived impact of body weight and gender on sexuality. *Journal of Applied Social Psychology, 26,* 1803–1815.

Regan, P. C., & Berscheid, E. (1997). Gender differences in characteristics desired in a potential sexual and marriage partner. *Journal of Psychology and Human Sexuality, 9,* 25–37.

Regan, P. C., & Berscheid, E. (1999). *Lust: What we know about human sexual desire.* Thousand Oaks, CA: Sage.

Regan, P. C., & Sprecher, S. (1995). Gender differences in the value of contributions to intimate relationships: Egalitarian relationships are not always perceived to be equitable. *Sex Roles, 33,* 221–238.

Reid, P. T. (2000). Foreward. In L. C. Jackson & B. Greene (Eds.), *Psychotherapy with African American women* (pp. xiii–xv). New York: Guilford.

Reid, P. T., & Bing, V. M. (2000). Sexual roles of girls and women: An ethnocultural lifespan perspective. In C. B. Travis & J. W. White (Eds.), *Sexuality, society, and feminism* (pp. 141–166). Washington, DC: American Psychological Association.

Reid, P. T., Haritos, C., Kelly, E., & Holland, N. E. (1995). Socialization of girls: Issues of ethnicity in gender development. In H. Landrine (Ed.), *Bringing cultural diversity to feminist psychology: Theory, research, and practice* (pp. 93–111). Washington, DC: American Psychological Association.

Reid, P. T., & Kelly, E. (1994). Research on women of color: From ignorance to awareness. *Psychology of Women Quarterly, 18,* 477–486.

Reid, P. T., & Zalk, S. R. (2001). Academic environments: Gender and ethnicity in U.S. higher education. In J. Worell (Ed.), *Encyclopedia of women and gender* (pp. 29–42). San Diego: Academic Press.

Reis, H. T. (1998). Gender differences in intimacy and related behaviors: Context and process. In D. J. Canary & K. Dindia (Eds.), *Sex differences and similarities in communication* (pp. 203–231). Mahwah, NJ: Erlbaum.

Reis, S. M. (1998). *Work left undone: Choices and compromises of talented females.* Mansfield Center, CT: Creative Learning Press.

Reis, S. M., Callahan, C. M., & Goldsmith, D. (1996). Attitudes of adolescent gifted girls and boys toward education, achievement, and the future. In K. Arnold, K. D. Noble, & R. F. Subotnik (Eds.), *Remarkable women: Perspectives on female talent development* (pp. 209–224). Cresskill, NJ: Hampton Press.

Reiser, C. (2001). *Reflections on anger: Women and men in a changing society.* Westport, CT: Praeger.

Remafedi, G., et al. (1998). The relationship between suicide risk and sexual orientation: Results of a population-based study. *American Journal of Public Health, 88,* 57–60.

Rennells, J. (2001). *The focus of the content of teen magazine articles.* Unpublished manuscript, SUNY Geneseo.

Renzetti, C. M. (1998). Violence and abuse in lesbian relationships: Theoretical and empirical issues. In R. Q. Bergen (Ed.), *Issues in intimate violence* (pp. 117–141). Thousand Oaks, CA: Sage.

Reskin, B. F. (1998). *The realities of affirmative action in employment.* Washington, DC: American Sociological Association.

Reskin, B. F., & Padavic, I. (1994). *Women and men at work.* Thousand Oaks, CA: Pine Forge Press.

Revenson, T. A. (2001). Chronic illness adjustment. In J. Worell (Ed.), *Encyclopedia of women and gender* (pp. 245–255). San Diego: Academic Press.

Reynolds, A. L., & Hanjorgiris, W. E. (2000). Coming out: Lesbian, gay, and bisexual identity development. In R. M. Perez, K. A. DeBord, & K. J. Bieschke (Eds.), *Handbook of counseling and psychotherapy with lesbian, gay, and bisexual clients* (pp. 35–55). Washington, DC: American Psychological Association.

Rhoades, K. A. (1999). Border zones: Identification, resistance, and transgressive teaching in introductory women's studies courses. In B. S. Winkler & C. DiPalma (Eds.), *Teaching introduction to women's studies* (pp. 61–71). Westport, CT: Bergin & Garvey.

Rhode, D. L. (1997). *Speaking of sex: The denial of gender inequality.* Cambridge, MA: Harvard University Press.

Rice, J. K. (2001a, Summer). Cross-cultural perspectives: Global divorce and the feminization of poverty. *International Psychology Reporter,* pp. 14–16.

Rice, J. K. (2001b). Family roles and patterns, contemporary trends. In J. Worell (Ed.), *Encyclopedia of women and gender* (pp. 411–423). San Diego: Academic Press.

Rich, A. (1980). Compulsory heterosexuality and lesbian existence. *Signs, 5,* 631–660.

Rich, M., et al. (1998). Aggressors or victims: Gender and race in music video violence. *Pediatrics, 101,* 669–674.

Rich, P., & Mervyn, F. (1999). *The healing journey through menopause.* New York: Wiley.

Richardson, H. R. L., Beazley, R. P., Delaney, M. E., & Langille, D. B. (1997). Factors influencing condom use among students attending high school in Nova Scotia. *Canadian Journal of Human Sexuality, 6,* 185–197.

Richardson, J. T. E. (1997a). Conclusions from the study of gender differences in cognition. In P. J. Caplan, M. Crawford, J. S. Hyde, & J. T. E. Richardson (Eds.), *Gender differences in human cognition* (pp. 131–169). New York: Oxford University Press.

Richardson, J. T. E. (1997b). Introduction to the study of gender differences in cognition. In P. J. Caplan, M. Crawford, J. S. Hyde, & J. T. E. Richardson (Eds.), *Gender differences in human cognition* (pp. 3–29). New York: Oxford University Press.

Richardson, V. E. (1999). Women and retirement. In J. D. Garner (Ed.), *Fundamentals of feminist gerontology* (pp. 49–66). New York: Haworth.

Richins, M. L. (1991). Social comparison and the idealized images of advertising. *Journal of Consumer Research, 18,* 71–83.

Richman, E. L., & Shaffer, D. R. (2000). "If you let me play sports": How might sport participation influence the self-esteem of adolescent females. *Psychology of Women Quarterly, 24,* 189–199.

Rickabaugh, C. A. (1994). Just who is this guy, anyway? Stereotypes of the men's movement. *Sex Roles, 30,* 459–470.

Riger, S., & Galligan, P. (1980). Women in management: An exploration of competing paradigms. *American Psychologist, 35,* 902–910.

Riggs, J. M. (2001). *Who's going to care for the children? College students' expectations for future employment and family roles.* Paper presented at the annual meeting of the Eastern Psychological Association.

Rimer, B. K., McBride, C., & Crump, C. (2001). Women's health promotion. In A. Baum, T. A. Revenson, & J. E. Singer (Eds.), *Handbook of health psychology* (pp. 519–539). Mahwah, NJ: Erlbaum.

Rinfret-Raynor, M., & Cantin, S. (1997). Feminist therapy for battered women. In G. K. Kantor & J. L. Jasinski (Eds.), *Out of the darkness: Contemporary perspectives on family violence* (pp. 219–234). Thousand Oaks, CA: Sage.

Rintala, D. H., et al. (1997). Dating issues for women with physical disabilities. *Sexuality and Disability, 15,* 219–242.

Risman, B. J. (1998). *Gender vertigo: American families in transition.* New Haven, CT: Yale University Press.

Roach, R. (2001, May 10). Where are the Black men on campus? *Black Issues in Higher Education,* 18–20.

Roades, L. A., & Mio, L. A. (2000). In J. S. Mio & G. I. Awakuni (Eds.), *Resistance to multiculturalism: Issues and interventions* (pp. 63–82). Philadelphia: Brunner/Mazel.

Roberto, K. A., Allen, K. R., & Blieszner, R. (1999). Older women, their children, and grandchildren: A feminist perspective on family relationships. In J. D. Garner (Ed.), *Fundamentals of feminist gerontology* (pp. 67–84). New York: Haworth.

Roberts, A. R. (1996a). Introduction: Myths and realities regarding battered women. In A. R. Roberts (Ed.), *Helping battered women* (pp. 3–12). New York: Oxford University Press.

Roberts, A. R. (1996b). Police responses to battered women: Past, present, and future. In A. R. Roberts (Ed.), *Helping battered women* (pp. 85–95). New York: Oxford University Press.

Roberts, J. A., & Chonko, L. B. (1994). Sex differences in the effect of satisfaction with pay on sales force turnover. *Journal of Social Behavior and Personality, 9,* 507–516.

Roberts, T. (1991). Gender and the influence of evaluations on self-assessments in achievement settings. *Psychological Bulletin, 109,* 297–308.

Roberts, T., & Nolen-Hoeksema, S. (1989). Sex differences in reactions to evaluative feedback. *Sex Roles, 21,* 725–747.

Roberts, T., & Nolen-Hoeksema, S. (1994). Gender comparisons in responsiveness to others' evaluations in achievement settings. *Psychology of Women Quarterly, 18,* 221–240.

Robin, L., & Hamner, K. (2000). Bisexuality: Identities and community. In V. A. Wall & N. J. Evans (Eds.), *Toward acceptance: Sexual orientation issues on campus* (pp. 245–259). Lanham, MD: American College Personnel Association.

Robins, R. W., Gosling, S. D., & Craik, K. H. (1999). An empirical analysis of trends in psychology. *American Psychologist, 54,* 117–128.

Robinson, D. (2001). Differences in occupational earnings by sex. In M. F. Loutfi (Ed.), *Women, gender, and work* (pp. 157–188). Geneva, Switzerland: International Labour Organization.

Robinson, G. (2002). Cross-cultural perspectives on menopause. In A. E. Hunter & C. Forden (Eds.), *Readings in the psychology of gender* (pp. 140–149). Boston: Allyn & Bacon.

Robinson, G. E., & Stewart, D. S. (2001). Postpartum disorders. In N. L. Stotland & D. E. Stewart (Eds.), *Psychological aspects of women's health care* (pp. 117–139). Washington, DC: American Psychiatric Press.

Robinson, M. D., & Johnson, J. T. (1997). Is it emotion or is it stress? Gender stereotypes and the perception of subjective experience. *Sex Roles, 36,* 235–258.

Robinson, M. D., Johnson, J. T., & Shields, S. A. (1998). The gender heuristic and the database: Factors affecting the perception of gender-related differences in the experience and display of emotions. *Basic and Applied Psychology, 20,* 206–219.

Robinson, P. (1997). Puberty: Am I normal? *Pediatric Annals, 26,* S133–S136.

Robinson-Walker, C. (1999). *Women and leadership in health care.* San Francisco: Jossey-Bass.

Rodríguez, C. E. (1997). Promoting analytical and critical viewing. In C. E. Rodríguez (Ed.), *Latin looks: Images of Latinas and Latinos in the U.S. media* (pp. 240–253). Boulder, CO: Westview Press.

Rodriguez, H. (1998, May). *Cohabitation: A snapshot.* Retrieved January 2002 from http://www.clasp.org/pubs/familyformation/cohab.html

Rogers, S. J. (1996). Mothers' work hours and marital quality: Variations by family structure and family size. *Journal of Marriage and the Family, 58,* 606–617.

Rogers, T. B., Kuiper, N. A., & Kirker, W. S. (1977). Self-reference and the encoding of personal information. *Journal of Personality and Social Psychology, 35,* 677–688.

Rogers, W. S., & Rogers, R. S. (2001). *The psychology of gender and sexuality.* Buckingham, England: Open University Press.

Romaine, S. (1999). *Communicating gender.* Mahwah, NJ: Erlbaum.

Romo-Carmona, M. (1995). Lesbian Latinas: Organizational efforts to end oppression. *Journal of Gay and Lesbian Social Services, 3,* 85–93.

Rongé, L. J. (1996, November). Keeping young female athletes on a healthy track. *American Academy of Pediatrics News,* pp. 14–15.

Roos, P. A., & Gatta, M. L. (1999). The gender gap in earnings: Trends, explanations, and prospects. In G. N. Powell (Ed.), *Handbook of gender and work* (pp. 95–123). Thousand Oaks, CA: Sage.

Root, M. P. P. (1995). The psychology of Asian American women. In H. Landrine (Ed.), *Bringing cultural diversity to feminist psychology: Theory, research, and practice* (pp. 265–301). Washington, DC: American Psychological Association.

Root, M. P. P. (1998). Women. In L. C. Lee & N. W. S. Zane (Eds.), *Handbook of Asian American psychology* (pp. 211–231). Thousand Oaks, CA: Sage.

Rosado-Majors, E. (1998, Summer). Black men against sexism. *Hues,* p. 45.

Roschelle, A. R. (1998). Gender, family structure, and social structure. In M. M. Ferree, J. Lorber, & B. B. Hess (Eds.), *Revisioning gender* (pp. 311–340). Thousand Oaks, CA: Sage.

Rose, A. J., & Montemayor, R. (1994). The relationship between gender role orientation and perceived self-competency in male and female adolescents. *Sex Roles, 31,* 579–595.

Rose, S. (2000). Heterosexism and the study of women's romantic and friend relationships. *Journal of Social Issues, 56,* 315–328.

Rose, S., Zand, D., & Cini, M. A. (1994). Lesbian courtship scripts. In E. Rothblum & K. A. Behony (Eds.) *Boston marriages: Romantic but asexual relationships among contemporary lesbians* (pp. 70–85). Amherst, MA: University of Massachusetts Press.

Rosen, R. (2000). *The world split open: How the modern women's movement changed America.* New York: Viking.

Rosenbaum, M. E., & Roos, G. M. (2000). Women's experiences of breast cancer. In A. S. Kasper & S. J. Ferguson (Eds.), *Breast cancer: Society shapes an epidemic* (pp. 153–181). New York: St. Martin's.

Rosenthal, D. A., Smith, A. M. A., & de Visser, R. (1999). Personal and social factors influencing age at first sexual intercourse. *Archives of Sexual Behavior, 28,* 319–333.

Rosenthal, R. (1976). *Experimenter effects in behavioral research* (enlarged ed.). New York: Halsted.

Rosenthal, R. (1993). Interpersonal expectations: Some antecedents and some consequences. In P. D. Blank (Ed.), *Interpersonal expectations: Theory, research, and applications* (pp. 3–24). New York: Cambridge University Press.

Rostosky, S. S., & Travis, C. B. (2000). Menopause and sexuality: Ageism and sexism unite. In C. B. Travis & J. W. White (Eds.), *Sexuality, society, and feminism* (pp. 181–209). Washington, DC: American Psychological Association.

Rostosky, S. S., Welsh, D. P., Kawaguchi, M. C., & Galliher, R. V. (1999). Commitment and sexual behaviors in adolescent dating relationships. In J. M. Adams & W. H. Jones (Eds.), *Handbook of interpersonal commitment and relationship stability* (pp. 323–338). New York: Kluwer Academic/Plenum.

Roter, D. L., & Hall, J. A. (1997). Gender differences in patient-physician communication. In S. J. Gallant, G. P. Keita, & R. Royak-Schaler (Eds.), *Health care for women* (pp. 57–71). Washington, DC: American Psychological Association.

Rothbart, B. (1999). Venus and the doctor. In G. Null & B. Seaman (Eds.), *For women only: Your guide to health empowerment* (pp. 1397–1400). New York: Seven Stories Press.

Rothblum, E. D. (2000a). Sexual orientation and sex in women's lives: Conceptual and methodological issues. *Journal of Social Issues, 56*, 193–204.

Rothblum, E. D. (2000b). "Somewhere in Des Moines or San Antonio": Historical perspectives on lesbian, gay, and bisexual mental health. In R. M. Perez, K. A. DeBord, & K. J. Bieschke (Eds.), *Handbook of counseling and psychotherapy with lesbian, gay, and bisexual clients* (pp. 57–79). Washington, DC: American Psychological Association.

Rothblum, E. D. (2002). Gay and lesbian body images. In T. F. Cash & T. Pruzinsky (Eds.), *Body images: A handbook of theory, research, and clinical practice.* New York: Guilford.

Rothblum, E. D., & Factor, R. (2001). Lesbians and their sisters as a control group. *Psychological Science, 12*, 63–69.

Rotheram-Borus, M. J., Dopkins, S., Sabate, N., & Lightfoot, M. (1996). Personal and ethnic identity, values, and self-esteem among Black and Latino adolescent girls. In B. J. R. Leadbeater & N. Way (Eds.), *Urban girls: Resisting stereotypes, creating identities* (pp. 35–52). New York: New York University Press.

Rountree, C. (1999). *On women turning 70: Honoring the voices of wisdom.* San Francisco: Jossey-Bass.

Rousar, E. E., III, & Aron, A. (1990, July). *Valuing, altruism, and the concept of love.* Paper presented at the Fifth International Conference on Personal Relationships, Oxford, England.

Rowland, J. H. (1998). Breast cancer: Psychosocial aspects. In E. A. Blechman & K. D. Brownell (Eds.), *Behavioral medicine and women: A comprehensive handbook* (pp. 577–587). New York: Guilford.

Royak-Schaler, R., Stanton, A. L., & Danoff-Burg, S. (1997). Breast cancer: Psychosocial factors influencing risk perception, screening, diagnosis, and treatment. In S. J. Gallant, G. P. Keita, & R. Royak-Schaler (Eds.), *Health care for women: Psychological, social, and behavioral influences* (pp. 295–314). Washington, DC: American Psychological Association.

Rozee, P. D. (2000a). Freedom from fear of rape: The missing link in women's freedom. In J. C. Chrisler, C. Golden, & P. D. Rozee (Eds.), *Lectures on the psychology of women* (2nd ed.) Boston: McGraw-Hill.

Rozee, P. D. (2000b). Sexual victimization: Harassment and rape. In M. Biaggio & M. Hersen (Eds.), *Issues in the psychology of women* (pp. 93–113). New York: Kluwer Academic/Plenum.

Rubin, D. L., & Greene, K. (1992). Gender-typical style in written language. *Research in the Teaching of English, 26*, 7–40.

Rubin, D. L., & Greene, K. (1994). The suppressed voice hypothesis in women's writing: Effects of revision on gender-typical style. In D. L. Rubin (Ed.), *Composing social identity in written language* (pp. 133–149). Hillsdale, NJ: Erlbaum.

Rubin, L. B. (2000). *Tangled lives: Daughters, mothers, and the crucible of aging.* Boston: Beacon Press.

Ruble, D. R., & Martin, C. L. (1998). Gender development. In W. Damon (Series Ed.) & N. Eisenberg (Vol. Ed.), *Handbook of child psychology: Vol. 4. Social, emotional, and personality development* (pp. 933–1016). New York: Wiley.

Rudman, L. A. (1998). Self-promotion as a risk factor for women: The costs and benefits of counterstereotypical impression management. *Journal of Personality and Social Psychology, 74*, 629–645.

Rudman, L. A., & Glick, P. (1999). Feminized management and backlash toward agentic women: The hidden costs to women of a kinder, gentler image of middle managers. *Journal of Personality and Social Psychology, 77*, 1004–1010.

Rúdólfsdóttir, A. G. (2000). "I am not a patient, and I am not a child": The institutionalization and experience of pregnancy. *Feminism and Psychology, 10*, 337–350.

Ruether, R. R. (1994). Christianity and women in the modern world. In A. Sharma (Ed.), *Today's woman in world religions* (pp. 267–301). Albany, NY: State University of New York Press.

Ruksznis, E. (1998, January). Women's health research goes "where no man has gone before." *APS Observer*, pp. 14–15, 18.

Runions, D. (1996). HIV/AIDS: A personal perspective. In L. D. Long & E. M. Ankrah (Eds.), *Women's experiences with HIV/AIDS* (pp. 56–72). New York: Columbia University Press.

Runté, M. (1998). Women with disabilities: Alone on the playground. *Canadian Women Studies/Les cahiers de la femme, 18,* 101–105.

Ruscio, J., Whitney, D. M., & Amabile, T. M. (1998). Looking inside the fishbowl of creativity: Verbal and behavioral predictors of creative performance. *Creativity Research Journal, 11,* 243–263.

Russell, D. E. H. (1998). *Dangerous relationships: Pornography, misogyny, and rape.* Thousand Oaks, CA: Sage.

Russo, N. F. (1999). Putting the APA *Publication Manual* in context. *Psychology of Women Quarterly, 23,* 399–402.

Russo, N. F. (2000). Understanding emotional responses after abortion. In J. C. Chrisler, C. Golden, & P. D. Rozee (Eds.), *Lectures on the psychology of women* (2nd ed., pp. 112–126). Boston: McGraw-Hill.

Russo, N. F., & Green, B. L. (1993). Women and mental health. In F. L. Denmark & M. A. Paludi (Eds.), *Psychology of women: A handbook of issues and theories* (pp. 379–436). Westport, CT: Greenwood, Press.

Russo, N. F., Green, B. L., & Knight, G. (1993). The relationship of gender, self-esteem, and instrumentality to depressive symptomatology. *Journal of Social and Clinical Psychology, 12,* 218–236.

Russo, N. F., Kelly, R. M., & Deacon, M. (1991). Gender and success-related attributions: Beyond individualistic conceptions of achievement. *Sex Roles, 25,* 331–350.

Rust, P. C. (1995). *Bisexuality and the challenge to lesbian politics: Sex, loyalty, and revolution.* New York: New York University Press.

Rust, P. C. (1996a). Managing multiple identities: Diversity among bisexual women and men. In B. A. Firestein (Ed.), *Bisexuality: The psychology and politics of an invisible minority* (pp. 53–83). Thousand Oaks, CA: Sage.

Rust, P. C. (1996b). Monogamy and polyamory: Relationship issues for bisexuals. In B. A. Firestein (Ed.), *Bisexuality: The psychology and politics of an invisible minority* (pp. 127–148). Thousand Oaks, CA: Sage.

Rust, P. C. (2000). Bisexuality: A contemporary paradox for women. *Journal of Social Issues, 56,* 205–221.

Ruth, S. (2001). *Issues in feminism: An introduction to women's studies* (5th ed.). Mountain View, CA: Mayfield.

Ryan, K. M., Frieze, I. H., & Sinclair, H. C. (1999). Physical violence in dating relationships. In M. A. Paludi (Ed.), *The psychology of sexual victimization* (pp. 33–54). Westport, CT: Greenwood Press.

Rynes, S., & Rosen, B. (1995). A field survey of factors affecting the adoption and perceived success of diversity training. *Personnel Psychology, 48,* 247–270.

Saadawi, N. (1998). Nawal: "I had to find my own answer to the question." In M. C. Ward (Ed.), *A sounding of women: Autobiographies from unexpected places.* Boston: Allyn & Bacon.

Sadker, M., & Sadker, D. (1994). *Failing at fairness: How America's schools cheat girls.* New York: Scribner's.

Saffron, L. (1998). Raising children in an age of diversity: Advantages of having a lesbian mother. In G. A. Dunne (Ed.), *Living "difference": Lesbian perspectives on work and family life* (pp. 35–47). New York: Haworth.

Saguaro, S. (Ed.). (2000). *Psychoanalysis and woman: A reader.* New York: New York University Press.

Saldívar-Hull, S. (2000). *Feminism on the border.* Berkeley, CA: University of California Press.

Sánchez-Ayéndez, M. (1993). Puerto Rican elderly women: Shared meanings and informal supportive networks. In L. Richardson & V. Taylor (Eds.), *Feminist frontiers III* (pp. 270–278). New York: McGraw-Hill.

Sanderson, C. A., Darley, J. M., & Messinger, C. S. (2002). "I'm not as thin as you think I am": The development and consequences of feeling discrepant from the thinness norm. *Personality and Social Psychology Bulletin, 28,* 172–183.

Sanderson, W. C., & McGinn, L. K. (2001). Cognitive-behavioral therapy of depression. In M. M. Weissman (Ed.), *Treatment of depression: Bridging the 21st century* (pp. 249–279). Washington, DC: American Psychiatric Press.

Sandler, B. R., & Shoop, R. J. (1997). What is sexual harassment? In B. R. Sandler & R. J. Shoop (Eds.), *Sexual harassment on campus: A guide for administrators, faculty, and students* (pp. 1–21). Boston: Allyn & Bacon.

Sandnabba, N. K., & Ahlberg, C. (1999). Parents' attitudes and expectations about children's cross-gender behavior. *Sex Roles, 40,* 249–263.

Sapp, S. G., Harrod, W. J., & Zhao, L. (1996). Leadership emergence in task groups with egalitarian gender-role expectations. *Sex Roles, 34,* 65–80.

Sarafino, E. P. (2002). *Health psychology: Biopsychosocial interactions* (4th ed.). New York: Wiley.

Saris, R. N., & Johnston-Robledo, I. (2000). Poor women are still shut out of mainstream psychology. *Psychology of Women Quarterly, 24,* 233–235.

Satterfield, A. T., & Muehlenhard, C. L. (1997). Shaken confidence: The effects of an authority figure's flirtatiousness on women's and men's self-rated creativity. *Psychology of Women Quarterly, 21,* 395–416.

Sattler, C. L. (2000). *Teaching to transcend: Educating women against violence.* Albany, NY: State University of New York Press.

Saucier, D. M., et al. (2002). Are sex differences in navigation caused by sexually dimorphic strategies or by differences in the ability to use the strategies? *Behavioral Neuroscience, 116,* 403–410.

Savin-Williams, R. C. (1998). The disclosure to families of same-sex attractions by lesbian, gay, and bisexual youths. *Journal of Research on Adolescence, 8,* 49–68.

Savin-Williams, R. C. (2001). *Mom, Dad. I'm gay. How families negotiate coming out.* Washington, DC: American Psychological Association.

Savin-Williams, R. C., & Diamond, L. M. (2000). Sexual identity trajectories among sexual-minority youths: Gender comparisons. *Archives of Sexual Behavior, 29,* 607–627.

Savin-Williams, R. C., & Dubé, E. M. (1998). Parental reactions to their child's disclosure of a gay/lesbian identity. *Family Relations, 47,* 7–13.

Savin-Williams, R. C., & Esterberg, K. G. (2000). Lesbian, gay, and bisexual families. In D. H. Demo, K. R. Allen, & M. A. Fine (Eds.), *Handbook of family diversity* (pp. 197–215). New York: Oxford University Press.

Saywell, C. (2000). Sexualized illness: The newsworthy body in media representations of breast cancer. In L. K. Potts (Ed.), *Ideologies of breast cancer* (pp. 37–62). New York: St. Martin's Press.

Saywitz, K. J., Mannarino, A. P., Berliner, L., & Cohen, J. A. (2000). Treatment for sexually abused children and adolescents. *American Psychologist, 55,* 1040–1049.

Scali, R. M., & Brownlow, S. (2001). Impact of instructional manipulation and stereotype activation on sex differences in spatial task performance. *Psi Chi Journal of Undergraduate Research, 6,* 3–13.

Scali, R. M., Brownlow, S., & Hicks, J. L. (2000). Gender differences in spatial task performance as a function of speed or accuracy orientation. *Sex Roles, 43,* 359–376.

Scarborough, E. (1992). Women in the American Psychological Association. In R. B. Evans, V. S. Sexton, & T. C. Cadwallader (Eds.), *100 years: The American Psychological Association, a historical perspective* (pp. 303–325). Washington, DC: American Psychological Association.

Scarborough, E., & Furumoto, L. (1987). *Untold lives: The first generation of American women psychologists.* New York: Columbia University Press.

Scarbrough, J. W. (2001). Welfare mothers' reflections on personal responsibility. *Journal of Social Issues, 57,* 261–276.

Scarr, S. (1997). Rules of evidence: A larger context for the statistical debate. *Psychological Science, 8,* 16–17.

Scarr, S. (1998). American child care today. *American Psychologist, 53,* 95–108.

Schacter, D. L. (1996). *Searching for memory: The brain, the mind, and the past.* New York: Basic Books.

Schacter, D. L., Koutstaal, W., & Norman, K. A. (1999). Can cognitive neuroscience illuminate the nature of traumatic childhood memories? In L. M. Williams & V. L. Banyard (Eds.), *Trauma and memory* (pp. 257–269). Thousand Oaks, CA: Sage.

Schafer, E., Vogel, M. K., Veigas, S., & Hausafus, C. (1998). Volunteer peer counselors increase breastfeeding duration among rural low-income women. *Birth, 25,* 101–106.

Scharrer, E. (1998, December). *Men, muscles, machismo, and the media.* Paper presented at the Department of Communication Research Colloquium, SUNY Geneseo.

Schein, V. E. (2001). A global look at psychological barriers to women's progress in management. *Journal of Social Issues, 57,* 675–688.

Schellenberg, E. G., Hirt, J., & Sears, A. (1999). Attitudes toward homosexuals among students at a Canadian university. *Sex Roles, 40,* 139–152.

Schiebinger, L. L. (1999). *Has feminism changed science?* Cambridge, MA: Harvard University Press.

Schlenker, J. A., Caron, S. L., & Halteman, W. A. (1998). A feminist analysis of *Seventeen* magazine: Content analysis from 1945 to 1995. *Sex Roles, 38,* 135–149.

Schmidt, P. J., et al. (1998). Differential behavioral effects of gonadal steroids in women with and in those without premenstrual syndrome. *New England Journal of Medicine, 338,* 209–216.

Schmitz, S. (1999). Gender differences in acquisition of environmental knowledge related to wayfinding behavior, spatial anxiety, and self-estimated environmental competencies. *Sex Roles, 41,* 71–93.

Schneider, M. S. (2001). Toward a reconceptualization of the coming-out process for adolescent females. In A. R. D'Augelli & C. J. Patterson (Eds.), *Lesbian, gay, and bisexual identities and youth* (pp. 71–96). New York: Oxford University Press.

Schreier, B. A., & Werden, D. L. (2000). Psychoeducational programming: Creating a context of mental health for people who are lesbian, gay, or bisexual. In R. M. Perez, K. A. DeBord, & K. J. Bieschke (Eds.), *Handbook of counseling and psychotherapy with lesbian, gay, and bisexual clients* (pp. 359–382). Washington, DC: American Psychological Association.

Schroeder, D. A., Penner, L. A., Dovidio, J. F., & Piliavin, J. A. (1995). *The psychology of helping and altruism.* New York: McGraw-Hill.

Schuklenk, U., Stein, E., Kerin, J., & Byne, W. (2002). The ethics of genetic research on sexual orientation. In I. Grewal & C. Kaplan (Eds.), *An introduction to women's studies* (pp. 48–52). Boston: McGraw-Hill.

Schwartz, M. D., & DeKeseredy, W. S. (1997). *Sexual assault on the college campus: The role of male peer support.* Thousand Oaks, CA: Sage.

Schwartz, P. (1994). *Peer marriage: How love between equals really works.* New York: Free Press.

Schwartz, P., & Rutter, V. (1998). *The gender of sexuality.* Thousand Oaks, CA: Pine Forge Press.

Scott, B. A. (2000). Women and pornography: What we don't know can hurt us. In J. C. Chrisler, C. Golden, & P. Rozee (Eds.), *Lectures on the psychology of women* (2nd ed., pp. 270–287). Boston: McGraw-Hill.

Scott, J. P. (1997). Family relationships of midlife and older women. In J. M. Coyle (Ed.), *Handbook on women and aging* (pp. 367–384). Westport, CT: Greenwood Press.

Scott-Jones, D. (2001). Reproductive technologies. In J. Worell (Ed.), *Encyclopedia of women and gender* (pp. 919–931). San Diego: Academic Press.

Seccombe, K., & Ishii-Kuntz, M. (1994). Gender and social relationships among the never-married. *Sex Roles, 30,* 585–603.

Segraves, R. T., & Segraves, K. B. (2001). Female sexual disorders. In N. L. Stotland & D. E. Stewart (Eds.), *Psychological aspects of women's health care* (2nd ed., pp. 379–400). Washington, DC: American Psychiatric Press.

Séguin, L., Potvin, L., St.-Denis, M., & Loiselle, J. (1999). Depressive symptoms in the late postpartum among low socioeconomic status women. *Birth, 26,* 157–163.

Selinger, M. (1998, November 18). Labor group charges harsh conditions persist. *Washington Times,* pp. B7–B8.

Sellers, T. A., et al. (1997). The role of hormone replacement therapy in the risk for breast cancer and total mortality in women with a family history of breast cancer. *Annals of Internal Medicine, 127,* 973–980.

Seppa, N. (1997, January). Young adults and AIDS: "It can't happen to me." *APA Monitor,* p. 38.

Sered, S. S. (1998). "Woman" as symbol and women as agents: Gendered religious discourses and practices. In M. M. Ferree, J. Lorber, & B. H. Hess (Eds.), *Revisioning gender* (pp. 193–221). Thousand Oaks, CA: Sage.

Sex and brain differences: Why the female brain is like a Swiss army knife. (1999, January 1–3). *USA Today Weekend,* pp. 8–14.

Seymour, S. C. (1999). *Women, family, and child care in India: A world in transition.* New York: Cambridge University Press.

Sgoutas, A. (2001). Curriculum reform, women's studies, and women of color. In D. L. Hoeveler & J. K. Boles (Eds.), *Women of color: Defining the issues, hearing the voices* (pp. 177–189). Westport, CT: Greenwood Press.

Shafii, T. (1997, March). Resident's viewpoint: I'm not a nurse. *Pediatric News,* p. 5.

Shanahan, J., & Morgan, M. (1999). *Television and its viewers.* New York: Cambridge University Press.

Shandler, S. (1999). *Ophelia speaks.* New York: Harper Collins.

Sharps, M. J., Price, J. L., & Williams, J. K. (1994). Spatial cognition and gender: Instructional and stimulus influences on mental image rotation performance. *Psychology of Women Quarterly, 18,* 413–425.

Sharratt, S., & Kaschak, E. (Eds.). (1999). *Assault on the soul: Women in the former Yugoslavia.* New York: Haworth.

Shaw, L., & Hill, C. (2001, May 15). *The gender gap in pension coverage: What does the future hold?* (IWPR Publication E507). Washington, DC: Institute for Women's Policy Research.

Shaw, S. M., & Lee, J. (2001). *Women's voices, feminist visions.* Mountain View, CA: Mayfield.

Shaywitz, B. A., et al. (1995). Sex differences in the functional organization of the brain for language. *Nature, 373,* 607–609.

Shaywitz, S. E., Shaywitz, B. A., Fletcher, J. M., & Escobar, M. D. (1990). Prevalence of reading disability in boys and girls. *Journal of the American Medical Association, 264,* 998–1002.

Shear, M. (2001, June). Great grandmother [Review of the book *Granny D: Walking across America in my ninetieth year*]. *Women's Review of Books,* p. 16.

Shellenbarger, T., & Lucas, D. (1997). An examination of nursing students' perception of classroom climate. In American Association of University Women (Ed.), *Gender and race on the campus and in the school: Beyond affirmative action* (pp. 151–159). Washington, DC: Author.

Shenk, D., & Fullmer, E. (1996). Significant relationships among older women: Cultural and personal constructions of lesbianism. *Journal of Women and Aging, 8,* 75–89.

Shepela, S. T., & Levesque, L. L. (1998). Poisoned waters: Sexual harassment and college climate. *Sex Roles, 38,* 589–611.

Shernoff, M. (Ed.). (1997). *Gay widowers: Life after the death of a partner.* New York: Haworth.

Sherwin, B. B. (2001). Menopause: Myths and realities. In N. Stotland & D. E. Stewart (Eds.), *Psychological aspects of women's health care* (2nd ed., pp. 241–259). Washington, DC: American Psychiatric Press.

Shields, S. A. (1975). Functionalism, Darwinism, and the psychology of women: A study in social myth. *American Psychologist, 30,* 739–754.

Shields, S. A. (1995). The role of emotion beliefs and values in gender development. In N. Eisenberg (Ed.), *Review of Personality and Social Psychology* (Vol. 15, pp. 212–232). Thousand Oaks, CA: Sage.

Shields, S. A. (2002). *Speaking from the heart: Gender and the social meaning of emotion.* New York: Cambridge University Press.

Shields, S. A., Steinke, P., & Koster, B. A. (1995). The double bind of caregiving: Representation of gendered emotion in American advice literature. *Sex Roles, 33,* 417–438.

Shih, M., Pittinksy, T. L., & Ambady, N. (1999). Stereotype susceptibility: Identity salience and shifts in quantitative performance. *Psychological Science, 10,* 80–83.

Shimp, L., & Chartier, B. (1998, June). *Unacknowledged rape and sexual assault in a sample of university women.* Paper presented at the annual convention of the Canadian Psychological Association, Edmonton, Alberta.

Ship, S. J., & Norton, L. (2001, Summer/Fall). HIV/AIDS and Aboriginal women in Canada. *Canadian Woman Studies/Les cahiers de la femme, 21,* 25–31.

Shoichet, C. E. (2002, July 12). Reports of grade inflation may be inflated, study finds. *Chronicle of Higher Education,* p. A37.

Sidorowicz, L. S., & Lunney, G. S. (1980). Baby X revisited. *Sex Roles, 6,* 67–73.

Siegel, M., Brisman, J., & Weinshel, M. (1997). *Surviving an eating disorder: Strategies for family and friends* (Rev. ed.). New York: HarperCollins.

Siegel, R. J., Choldin, S., & Orost, J. H. (1995). The impact of three patriarchal religions on women. In J. C. Chrisler & A. H. Hemstreet (Eds.), *Variation on a theme: Diversity and the psychology of women* (pp. 107–144). Albany, NY: State University of New York Press.

Sigmon, S. T., Dorhofer, D. M., et al. (2000). Psychophysiological, somatic, and affective changes across the menstrual cycle in women with panic disorder. *Journal of Consulting and Clinical Psychology, 68,* 425–431.

Sigmon, S. T., Rohan, K. J., et al. (2000). Menstrual reactivity: The role of gender-specificity, anxiety sensitivity, and somatic concerns in self-reported menstrual distress. *Sex Roles, 43,* 143–161.

Signorella, M. L., Bigler, R. S., & Liben, L. S. (1997). A meta-analysis of children's memories for own-sex and other-sex information. *Journal of Applied Developmental Psychology, 18,* 429–445.

Signorielli, N., & Bacue, A. (1999). Recognition and respect: A content analysis of prime-time television characters across three decades. *Sex Roles, 40,* 527–544.

Signorielli, N., & Lears, M. (1992). Children, television, and conceptions about chores: Attitudes and behaviors. *Sex Roles, 27,* 157–170.

Sikkema, K. J. (1998). HIV prevention. In E. A. Blechman & K. D. Brownell (Eds.), *Behavioral medicine and women: A comprehensive handbook* (pp. 198–202). New York: Guilford.

Silverstein, B., & Lynch, A. D. (1998). Gender differences in depression: The role played by paternal attitudes of male superiority and maternal modeling of gender-related limitations. *Sex Roles, 38,* 539–555.

Silverstein, L. B. (1996). Fathering is a feminist issue. *Psychology of Women Quarterly, 20,* 3–37.

Silverstein, L. B., & Auerbach, C. F. (1999). Deconstructing the essential father. *American Psychologist, 54*, 397–407.

Silverstein, L. B., Auerbach, C. F., Grieco, L., & Dunkel, F. (1999). Do Promise Keepers dream of feminist sheep? *Sex Roles, 40*, 665–688.

Silverstein, L. B., & Goodrich, T. J. (2001). Feminist family therapy. In J. Worell (Ed.), *Encyclopedia of women and gender* (pp. 447–456). San Diego: Academic Press.

Simi, N. L., & Mahalik, J. R. (1997). Comparison of feminist versus psychoanalytic/dynamic and other therapists on self-disclosure. *Psychology of Women Quarterly, 21*, 465–483.

Simonds, S. L. (2001). *Depression and women: An integrative treatment approach.* New York: Springer.

Simoni-Wastila, L. (1998). Gender and psychotropic drug use. *Medical Care, 36*, 88–94.

Simonson, K., & Subich, L. M. (1999). Rape perceptions as a function of gender-role traditionality and victim-perpetrator association. *Sex Roles, 40*, 617–634.

Sincharoen, S., & Crosby, F. J. (2001). Affirmative action. In J. Worell (Ed.), *Encyclopedia of women and gender* (pp. 69–79). San Diego: Academic Press.

Singer, D. G., & Singer, J. L. (2001). Introduction: Why a handbook on children and the media? In D. G. Singer & J. L. Singer (Eds.), *Handbook on children and the media* (pp. xi–xvii). Thousand Oaks, CA: Sage.

Singh, S., & Darroch, J. E. (2000). Adolescent pregnancy and childbearing: Levels and trends in developed countries. *Family Planning Perspectives, 32*, 14–23.

Singleton, C. H. (1987). Sex roles in cognition. In D. J. Hargreaves & A. M. Colley (Eds.), *The psychology of sex roles* (pp. 60–91). New York: Hemisphere.

Sinnott, J. D., & Shifren, K. (2001). Gender and aging: Gender differences and gender roles. In J. E. Birren & K. W. Schaie (Eds.), *Handbook of the psychology of aging* (pp. 454–476). San Diego: Academic Press.

Skodol, A. E. (2000). Gender-specific etiologies for antisocial and borderline personality disorders? In E. Frank (Ed.), *Gender and its effects on psychopathology* (pp. 37–58). Washington, DC: American Psychiatric Press.

Skrypnek, B. J., & Snyder, M. (1982). On the self-perpetuating nature of stereotypes about women

and men. *Journal of Experimental Social Psychology, 18*, 277–291.

Skucha, J., & Bernard, M. (2000). "Women's work" and the transition to retirement. In M. Bernard, J. Phillips, L. Machin, & V. H. Davies (Eds.), *Women ageing: Changing identities, challenging myths* (pp. 23–39). London: Routledge.

Sleeper, L. A., & Nigro, G. N. (1987). It's not who you are but who you're with: Self-confidence in achievement settings. *Sex Roles, 16*, 57–69.

Slipp, S. (1993). *The Freudian mystique: Freud, women, and feminism.* New York: New York University Press.

Smetana, J. G. (1996, August). *Autonomy and authority in adolescent-parent relationships.* Paper presented at the International Society for the Study of Behavioral Development Conference, Quebec City, Canada.

Smith, A. (2001). The color of violence: Violence against women of color. *Meridians: Feminism, Race, Transnationalism, 1*, 65–72.

Smith, C. J., Noll, J. A., & Bryant, J. B. (1999). The effect of social context on gender self-concept. *Sex Roles, 40*, 499–512.

Smith, G. J. (1985). Facial and full-length ratings of attractiveness related to the social interactions of young children. *Sex Roles, 12*, 287–293.

Smith, S. E., & Walker, W. J. (1988). Sex differences on New York state regents examinations: Support for the differential course-taking hypothesis. *Journal for Research in Mathematics Education, 19*, 81–85.

Smith, T. J., Ellis, B. R., & Brownlow, S. (2001, March). *Does science interest negatively influence perceptions of women?* Paper presented at the annual meeting of the Southeastern Psychological Association, Atlanta, GA.

Smock, P. J. (2000). Cohabitation. *Annual Review of Sociology, 26*, 1–20.

Smolak, L., & Levine, M. P. (2001). Body image in children. In J. K. Thompson & L. Smolak (Eds.), *Body image, eating disorders, and obesity in youth* (pp. 41–66). Washington, DC: American Psychological Association.

Smolak, L., & Striegel-Moore, R. H. (2001). Body-image concerns. In J. Worell (Ed.), *Encyclopedia of women and gender* (pp. 201–210). San Diego: Academic Press.

Snell, T. L. & Morton, D. C. (1994). *Women in prison.* Washington, DC: U.S. Department of Justice.

Snyder, M., & Miene, P. (1994). On the functions of stereotypes and prejudice. In M. P. Zanna & J. M.

Olson (Eds.), *The psychology of prejudice: The Ontario Symposium* (Vol. 7, pp. 33–54). Hillsdale, NJ: Erlbaum.

Sohn, D. (1982). Sex differences in achievement self-attributions: An effect-size analysis. *Sex Roles, 8,* 345–357.

Sokol, M. S., & Gray, N. S. (1998). Anorexia nervosa. In E. A. Blechman & K. D. Brownell (Eds.), *Behavioral medicine and women: A comprehensive handbook* (pp. 350–357). New York: Guilford.

Soldatenko, M. A. G. (1999). Berta's story: Journal from sweatshop to showroom. In M. Romero & A. Stewart (Eds.), *Untold stories: Breaking silence, talking back, voicing complexity* (pp. 256–270). New York: Routledge.

Solheim, B. O. (2000). *On top of the world: Women's political leadership in Scandinavia and beyond.* Westport, CT: Greenwood Press.

Sommer, B. (2001). Menopause. In J. Worell (Ed.), *Encyclopedia of women and gender* (pp. 729–738). San Diego: Academic Press.

Sommer, B., et al. (1999). Attitudes toward menopause and aging across ethnic/racial groups. *Psychosomatic Medicine, 61,* 868–875.

Sommers, C. H. (1994). *Who stole feminism?* New York: Simon & Schuster.

Song, H. (2001). The mother-daughter relationship as a resource for Korean women's career aspirations. *Sex Roles, 44,* 79–97.

Spain, D., & Bianchi, S. M. (1996). *Balancing act: Motherhood, marriage, and employment among American women.* New York: Russell Sage Foundation.

Sparks, E. E. (1996). Overcoming stereotypes of mothers in the African American context. In K. F. Wyche & F. J. Crosby (Eds.), *Women's ethnicities: Journeys through psychology* (pp. 67–86). Boulder, CO: Westview Press.

Sparks, E. E. (1998). Against all odds: Resistance and resilience in African American welfare mothers. In C. G. Coll, J. L. Surrey, & K. Weingarten (Eds.), *Mothering against the odds* (pp. 215–237). New York: Guilford.

Sparks, E. E., & Park, A. H. (2000). The integration of feminism and multiculturalism: Ethical dilemmas at the border. In M. M. Brabeck (Ed.), *Practicing feminist ethics in psychology* (pp. 203–224). Washington, DC: American Psychological Association.

Spence, J. T., & Hahn, E. D. (1997). The Attitudes Toward Women Scale and attitude change in college students. *Psychology of Women Quarterly, 21,* 17–34.

Spender, D. (1989). *The writing or the sex.* New York: Pergamon.

Sperberg, E. D., & Stabb, S. D. (1998). Depression in women as related to anger and mutuality in relationships. *Psychology of Women Quarterly, 22,* 223–238.

Spitz, E. H. (1999). *Inside picture books.* New Haven, CT: Yale University Press.

Spotlight on Canada. (2000, Summer). *Advances in Family-Centered Care, 6,* 26–29.

Sprecher, S., & Sedikides, C. (1993). Gender differences in perceptions of emotionality: The case of close heterosexual relationships. *Sex Roles, 28,* 511–530.

Sprecher, S., Sullivan, Q., & Hatfield, E. (1994). Mate selection preferences: Gender differences examined in a national sample. *Journal of Personality and Social Psychology, 66,* 1074–1080.

Springen, K. (1998, June 1). The bountiful breast. *Newsweek,* p. 71.

Sprock, J., & Yoder, C. Y. (1997). Women and depression: An update on the report of the APA Task Force. *Sex Roles, 36,* 269–303.

SPSMM mission statement. (2002, Spring). *SPSMM Bulletin,* p. 17.

Stacey, J. (2000). The handbook's tail: Toward revels or a requiem for family diversity? In D. H. Demo, K. R. Allen, & M. A. Fine (Eds.), *Handbook of family diversity* (pp. 424–439). New York: Oxford University Press.

Stacey, J., & Biblarz, T. J. (2001). (How) does the sexual orientation of parents matter? *American Sociological Review, 66,* 159–183.

Stack, C. B. (1994). Different voices, different visions: Gender, culture, and moral reasoning. In M. Baca Zinn & B. T. Dill (Eds.), *Women of color in U.S. society* (pp. 291–301). Philadelphia: Temple University Press.

Stahly, G. B. (2000). Battered women: Why don't they just leave? In J. C. Chrisler, C. Golden, & P. D. Rozee (Eds.), *Lectures on the psychology of women* (2nd ed., pp. 288–305). Boston: McGraw-Hill.

Stake, J. E. (1997). Integrating expressiveness and instrumentality in real-life settings: A new perspective on the benefits of androgyny. *Sex Roles, 37,* 541–564.

Stake, J. E. (2000). When situations call for instrumentality *and* expressiveness: Resource appraisal, coping strategy choice, and adjustment. *Sex Roles, 42,* 865–885.

Stake, J. E., & Hoffmann, F. L. (2000). Putting feminist pedagogy to the test. *Psychology of Women Quarterly, 24,* 30–38.

Stake, J. E., & Hoffmann, F. L. (2001). Changes in student social attitudes, activism, and personal confidence in higher education: The role of women's studies. *American Educational Research Journal, 38,* 411–436.

Stampfer, M. J., et al. (2000). Primary prevention of coronary heart disease in women through diet and lifestyle. *New England Journal of Medicine, 343,* 16–22.

Stange, M. Z. (2002, June 21). The political intolerance of academic feminism. *Chronicle of Higher Education,* p. B16.

Stanko, E. A. (1993). Ordinary fear: Women, violence, and personal safety. In P. B. Bart & E. G. Moran (Eds.), Violence against women: *The bloody footprints* (pp. 155–165). Newbury Park, CA: Sage.

Stanton, A. L. (1995). Psychology of women's health: Barriers and pathways to knowledge. In A. L. Stanton & S. J. Gallant (Eds.), *The psychology of women's health: Progress and challenges in research and application* (pp. 3–21). Washington, DC: American Psychological Association.

Stanton, A. L., & Danoff-Burg, S. (1995). Selected issues in women's reproductive health: Psychological perspectives. In A. L. Stanton & S. J. Gallant (Eds.), *The psychology of women's health* (pp. 261–305). Washington, DC: American Psychological Association.

Staples, R. (1995). Socio-cultural factors in Black family transformation: Toward a redefinition of family functions. In C. K. Jacobson (Ed.), *American families: Issues in race and ethnicity* (pp. 19–27). New York: Garland.

Starr, T. (1991). *The "natural inferiority" of women: Outrageous pronouncements by misguided males.* New York: Poseidon Press.

Statham, H., Green, J. M., & Kafetsios, K. (1997). Who worries that something might be wrong with the baby? A prospective study of 1072 pregnant women. *Birth, 24,* 223–233.

Statistics Canada. (1993, November 18). The violence against women survey. *The Daily,* pp. 1–9.

Statistics Canada. (1995). *Women in Canada: A statistical report* (3rd ed.). Ottawa, Canada: Author.

Statistics Canada. (1996a). *Ten most frequent jobs for men, Canada, 1996.* Retrieved December 20, 2001, from http://www.statcan.ca/Daily/English/980317/c980317g.gif

Statistics Canada. (1996b). *Ten most frequent jobs for women, Canada, 1996.* Retrieved December 20, 2001, from http://www.statcan.ca/Daily/English/980317/c980317h.gif

Statistics Canada. (2000). *Women in Canada 2000: A gender-based statistical report.* Ottawa, Canada: Author.

Statistics Canada. (2001a). *Average earnings by sex and work pattern.* Retrieved December 19, 2001, from http://www.statcan.ca/english/Pgdb/People/Labour/labor01b.htm

Statistics Canada. (2001b). *Labour force, employed and unemployed, numbers and rates.* Retrieved December 12, 2001, from http://www.statcan.ca/english/Pgdb/People/Labour/labor07a.htm

Statistics Canada. (2001c). *1996 census: Ethnic origin.* Retrieved July 18, 2001, from http://www.statcan.ca/english/census96/feb17/ethnic.htm

Statistics Canada. (2001d, August). *Women in Canada: Work chapter updates.* Ottawa, Canada: Author.

Status of Women Canada. (2000). *Statistics on women in Canada throughout the 20th century.* Retrieved January 22, 2002, from http://www.swc-cfc.gc.ca/whm/whm2000/whmstats-e.html

Steele, C. M. (1997). A threat in the air: How stereotypes shape intellectual identity and performance. *American Psychologist, 52,* 613–629.

Steele, J., & Barling, J. (1996). Influence of maternal gender-role beliefs and role satisfaction on daughters' vocational interests. *Sex Roles, 34,* 637–648.

Steenbergen, C. (2001, Winter/Spring). Feminism and young women: Alive and well and still kicking. *Canadian Woman Studies/Les cahiers de la femme, 2,* 6–14.

Steil, J. M. (1997). *Marital equality: Its relationship to the well-being of husbands and wives.* Thousand Oaks, CA: Sage.

Steil, J. M. (2000). Contemporary marriage: Still an unequal partnership. In C. Hendrick & S. S. Hendrick (Eds.), *Close relationships: A sourcebook* (pp. 125–136). Thousand Oaks, CA: Sage.

Steil, J. M. (2001). Marriage: Still "his" and "hers"? In J. Worell (Ed.), *Encyclopedia of women and gender* (pp. 677–686). San Diego: Academic Press.

Steil, J. M., McGann, V. L., & Kahn, A. S. (2001). Entitlement. In J. Worell (Ed.), *Encyclopedia of women and gender* (pp. 403–410). San Diego: Academic Press.

Stein, M. D., et al. (1998). Sexual ethics: Disclosure of HIV-positive status to partners. *Archives of Internal Medicine, 158,* 253–257.

Steinberg, L., & Morris, A. S. (2001). Adolescent development. *Annual Review of Psychology, 52,* 83–110.

Steinhausen, H. (1995). The course and outcome of anorexia nervosa. In K. D. Brownell & C. G. Fairburn (Eds.), *Eating disorders and obesity: A comprehensive handbook* (pp. 234–237). New York: Guilford.

Steinpreis, R. H., Anders, K. A., & Ritzke, D. (1999). The impact of gender on the review of the curricula vitae of job applicants and tenure candidates: A national empirical study. *Sex Roles, 41,* 509–528.

Stephens, M. A., & Franks, M. M. (1999). Parent care in the context of women's multiple roles. *Current Directions in Psychological Science, 8,* 149–152.

Stephenson, J. (2000). *Women's roots: The history of women in Western civilization* (5th ed.). Fullerton, CA: Diemer, Smith Publishing.

Stern, D. N., & Bruschweiler-Stern, N. (1998). *The birth of a mother.* New York: Basic Books.

Stern, M., & Karraker, M. K. (1989). Sex stereotyping of infants: A review of gender labeling studies. *Sex Roles, 20,* 501–522.

Sternberg, K. J., & Lamb, M. E. (1999). Violent families. In M. E. Lamb (Ed.), *Parenting and child development in "nontraditional" families* (pp. 305–325). Mahwah, NJ: Erlbaum.

Sternberg, R. J. (1998). *Cupid's arrow: The course of love through time.* New York: Cambridge University Press.

Stewart, A. J. (1994). Toward a feminist strategy for studying women's lives. In C. E. Franz & A. J. Stewart (Eds.), *Women creating lives: Identities, resilience, and resistance* (pp. 11–35). Boulder, CO: Westview Press.

Stewart, A. J. (1998). Doing personality research: How can feminist theories help? In B. M. Clinchy & J. K. Norem (Eds.), *The gender and psychology reader* (pp. 54–77). New York: New York University Press.

Stewart, A. J., Ostrove, J. M., & Helson, R. (2001). Middle aging in women: Patterns of personality change from the 30s to the 50s. *Journal of Adult Development, 8,* 23–37.

Stewart, A. J., & Vandewater, E. A. (1999). "If I had it to do over again . . .": Midlife review, mid-course corrections, and women's well-being in midlife. *Journal of Personality and Social Psychology, 76,* 270–283.

Stewart, D. E., & Robinson, G. E. (2001). Eating disorders and reproduction. In N. L. Stotland &

D. E. Stewart (Eds.), *Psychological aspects of women's health care* (pp. 441–456). Washington, DC: American Psychiatric Press.

Stewart, M. (1998). Gender issues in physics education. *Educational Research, 40,* 283–293.

Stewart, S., & Jambunathan, J. (1996). Hmong women and postpartum depression. *Health Care for Women International, 17,* 319–330.

Stewart, T. L., & Vassar, P. M. (2000). The effect of occupational status cues on memory for male and female targets. *Psychology of Women Quarterly, 24,* 161–169.

St. Jean, Y., & Feagin, J. R. (1997). Racial masques: Black women and subtle gendered racism. In N. V. Benokraitis (Ed.), *Subtle sexism* (pp. 179–205). Thousand Oaks, CA: Sage.

Stohs, J. H. (2000). Multicultural women's experience of household labor, conflicts, and equity. *Sex Roles, 42,* 339–361.

Stoler, L., Quina, K., DePrince, A. P., & Freyd, J. J. (2001). Recovered memories. In J. Worell (Ed.), *Encyclopedia of women and gender* (pp. 905–917). San Diego: Academic Press.

Stoltz-Loike, M. (1992). *Dual career couples: New perspectives in counseling.* Alexandria, VA: American Association for Counseling and Development.

Stoney, C. M. (1998). Coronary heart disease. In E. A. Blechman & K. D. Brownell (Eds.), *Behavioral medicine and women: A comprehensive handbook* (pp. 609–614). New York: Guilford.

Stoppard, J. M., & Gruchy, C. D. G. (1993). Gender, context, and expression of positive emotion. *Personality and Social Psychology Bulletin, 19,* 143–150.

Storm, C., & Gurevich, M. (Eds.). (2001). Looking forward, looking back: Women in psychology [Special issue]. *Canadian Psychology/Psychologie canadienne, 42*(4).

Stotland, N. L. (1998). *Abortion: Facts and feelings.* Washington, DC: American Psychiatric Press.

Stotland, N. L., & Stewart, D. E. (Eds.). (2001). *Psychological aspects of women's health care* (2nd ed.). Washington, DC: American Psychiatric Press.

Stout, K., & Dello Buono, R. A. (1996). Birth control and development in three Latin American countries. In P. J. Dubeck & K. Borman (Eds.), *Women and work: A handbook* (pp. 505–509). New York: Garland.

Straus, M. A., Kantor, G. K., & Moore, D. W. (1997). Changes in cultural norms approving marital violence from 1968 to 1994. In G. K. Kantor & J. A. Jasinski (Eds.), *Out of the darkness: Contemporary perspectives on family violence* (pp. 3–16). Thousand Oaks, CA: Sage.

Street, S., Kimmel, E. B., & Kromrey, J. D. (1995). Revisiting university student gender role perceptions. *Sex Roles, 33,* 183–201.

Street, S., Kromrey, J. D., & Kimmel, E. (1995). University faculty gender roles perceptions. *Sex Roles, 32,* 407–422.

Streissguth, A. P., et al. (1999). The long-term neurocognitive consequences of prenatal alcohol exposure: A 14-year study. *Psychological Science, 10,* 186–190.

Streit, U., & Tanguay, Y. (1994). Professional achievement, personality characteristics, and professional women's self-esteem. In J. Gallivan, S. D. Crozier, & V. M. Lalande (Eds.), *Women, girls, and achievement* (pp. 63–75). North York, Canada: Captus University Publications.

Streitmatter, J. (1994). *Toward gender equity in the classroom: Everyday teachers' beliefs and practices.* Albany, NY: State University of New York Press.

Striegel-Moore, R. H., & Cachelin, F. M. (1999). Body image concerns and disordered eating in adolescent girls: Risk and protective factors. In N. G. Johnson, M. C. Roberts, & J. Worell (Eds.), *Beyond appearance: A new look at adolescent girls* (pp. 85–108). Washington, DC: American Psychological Association.

Stroebe, M., Stroebe, W., & Schut, H. (2001). Gender differences in adjustment to bereavement: An empirical and theoretical review. *Review of General Psychology, 5,* 62–83.

Strouse, J. (1999, August 16). She got game. *New Yorker,* pp. 36–40.

Stumpf, H. (1995). Gender differences in performance on tests of cognitive abilities: Experimental design issues and empirical results. *Learning and Individual Differences, 7,* 275–287.

Stumpf, H., & Stanley, J. C. (1998). Stability and change in gender-related differences on the College Board Advanced Placement and Achievement Tests. *Current Directions in Psychological Science, 7,* 192–196.

Subrahmanyam, K., & Greenfield, P. M. (1994). Effect of video game practice on spatial skills in girls and boys. *Journal of Applied Developmental Psychology, 15,* 13–32.

Subrahmanyam, K., et al. (2001). The impact of computer use on children's and adolescents' development. *Journal of Applied Developmental Psychology, 22,* 7–30.

Sugihara, Y., & Katsurada, E. (1999). Masculinity and femininity in Japanese culture: A pilot study. *Sex Roles, 40,* 635–646.

Sugihara, Y., & Katsurada, E. (2000). Gender-role personality traits in Japanese culture. *Psychology of Women Quarterly, 24,* 309–318.

Sugihara, Y., & Warner, J. A. (1999). Endorsements by Mexican-Americans of the Bem Sex-Role Inventory: Cross-ethnic comparison. *Psychological Reports, 85,* 201–211.

Sumner, K. E., & Brown, T. J. (1996). Men, women, and money: Exploring the role of gender, gender-linkage of college major, and career-information sources in salary expectations. *Sex Roles, 34,* 823–839.

Susin, L. R. O., et al. (1999). Does parental breast-feeding knowledge increase breastfeeding rates? *Birth, 26,* 149–156.

Susman, J. L. (1996). Postpartum depressive disorders. *Journal of Family Practice, 43,* S17–S24.

Sutton, M. J., Brown, J. D., Wilson, K. M., & Klein, J. D. (2002). Shaking the tree of knowledge for forbidden fruit: Where adolescents learn about sexuality and contraception. In J. D. Brown, J. R. Steele, & K. Walsh-Childers (Eds.), *Sexual teens, sexual media* (pp. 25–55). Mahwah, NJ: Erlbaum.

Swann, W. B., Jr., Langlois, J. H., & Gilbert, L. A. (Eds.). (1999). *Sexism and stereotypes in modern society: The gender science of Janet Taylor Spence.* Washington, DC: American Psychological Association.

Sweet, H. (2000). A feminist looks at the men's movement: Search for common ground. In E. R. Barton (Ed.), *Mythopoetic perspectives of men's healing work* (pp. 229–245). Westport, CT: Bergin & Garvey.

Sweetman, C. (1998a). Editorial. In C. Sweetman (Ed.), *Gender, education, and training* (pp. 2–8). Oxford, England: Oxfam.

Sweetman, C. (Ed.). (1998b). *Gender, education, and training.* Oxford, England: Oxfam.

Sweetman, C. (Ed.). (2000). *Gender in the 21st century.* Oxford, England: Oxfam.

Swim, J. K., Borgida, E., Maruyama, G., & Myers, D. G. (1989). Joan McKay versus John McKay: Do gender stereotypes bias evaluations? *Psychological Bulletin, 105,* 409–429.

Swim, J. K., Hyers, L. L., Cohen, L. L., & Ferguson, M. J. (2001). Everyday sexism: Evidence for its incidence, nature, and psychological impact from three daily diary studies. *Journal of Social Issues, 57,* 31–53.

Swim, J. K., & Sanna, L. J. (1996). He's skilled, she's lucky: A meta-analysis of observers' attributions for women's and men's successes and failures. *Personality and Social Psychology Bulletin, 22,* 507–519.

Switzer, J. Y. (1990). The impact of generic word choices: An empirical investigation of age- and sex-related differences. *Sex Roles, 22,* 69–82.

Symonds, P. V. (1996). Journey to the land of light: Birth among Hmong women. In P. L. Rice & L. Manderson (Eds.), *Maternity and reproductive health in Asian societies* (pp. 103–123). Amsterdam: Harwood Academic.

Szinovacz, M. E. (2000). Changes in housework after retirement: A panel analysis. *Journal of Marriage and the Family, 62,* 78–92.

Szymanski, D. M., Baird, M. K., & Kornman, C. L. (2002). The feminist male therapist: Attitudes and practices for the 21st century. *Psychology of Men and Masculinity, 3,* 22–27.

Tamres, L. K., Janicki, D., & Helgeson, V. S. (2002). Sex differences in coping behavior: A meta-analytic review and an examination of relative coping. *Personality and Social Psychology Review, 6,* 2–30.

Tang, T. N., & Dion, K. L. (1999). Gender and acculturation in relation to traditionalism: Perceptions of self and parents among Chinese students. *Sex Roles, 41,* 17–29.

Tapert, S. F., Stewart, D. G., & Brown, S. A. (1999). In A. J. Goreczny & M. Hersen (Eds.), *Handbook of pediatric and adolescent health psychology* (pp. 161–178). Mahwah, NJ: Erlbaum.

Tarkka, M., Paunonen, M., & Laippala, P. (1998). What contributes to breastfeeding success after childbirth in a maternity ward in Finland? *Birth, 25,* 175–181.

Tasker, F. L., & Golombok, S. (1995). Adults raised as children in lesbian families. *American Journal of Orthopsychiatry, 65,* 203–215.

Tasker, F. L., & Golombok, S. (1997). *Growing up in a lesbian family: Effects on child development.* New York: Guilford.

Tassinary, L. G., & Hansen, K. A. (1998). A critical test of the waist-to-hip-ratio hypothesis of female physical attractiveness. *Psychological Science, 9,* 150–155.

Tatum, B. D. (1992, Spring). Talking about race, learning about racism: The application of racial identity development theory in the classroom. *Harvard Educational Review, 62,* 1–24.

Tavris, C. (1992). *The mismeasure of woman.* New York: Simon & Schuster.

Tavris, C. (2002, July/August). The high cost of skepticism. *Skeptical Inquirer,* pp. 41–44.

Tavris, C., & Wade, C. (1984). *The longest war: Sex differences in perspective* (2nd ed.). New York: Harcourt Brace Jovanovich.

Taylor, J. M., Gilligan, C., & Sullivan, A. M. (1995). *Between voice and silence: Women and girls, race and relationships.* Cambridge, MA: Harvard University Press.

Taylor, L. E. (1995). Home brutal home. *Canada and the World, 60,* 24–28.

Taylor, P. L., Tucker, M. B., & Mitchell-Kernan, C. (1999). Ethnic variations in perceptions of men's provider role. *Psychology of Women Quarterly, 23,* 741–761.

Taylor, R. L. (2000). Diversity within African American families. In D. H. Demo, K. R. Allen, & M. A. Fine (Eds.), *Handbook of family diversity* (pp. 232–251). New York: Oxford University Press.

Taylor, S. E., & Langer, E. J. (1977). Pregnancy: A social stigma? *Sex Roles, 3,* 27–35.

Taylor, V. (1996). *Rock-a-by baby: Feminism, self-help, and postpartum depression.* New York: Routledge.

Tenenbaum, H. R., & Leaper, C. (1997). Mothers' and fathers' questions to their child in Mexican-descent families: Moderators of cognitive demand during play. *Hispanic Journal of Behavioral Sciences, 19,* 318–332.

Tepper, C. A., & Cassidy, K. W. (1999). Gender differences in emotional language in children's picture books. *Sex Roles, 40,* 265–280.

Testa, M., & Livingston, J. A. (1999). Qualitative analysis of women's experiences of sexual aggression: Focus on the role of alcohol. *Psychology of Women Quarterly, 23,* 573–589.

Thase, M. E., Frank, E., Kornstein, S. G., & Yonkers, K. A. (2000). Gender differences in response to treatments of depression. In E. F. Frank (Ed.), *Gender and its effects on psychopathology* (pp. 103–129). Washington, DC: American Psychiatric Press.

Thomas, V. G., & Miles, S. E. (1995). Psychology of Black women: Past, present, and future. In H. Landrine (Ed.), *Bringing cultural diversity to feminist psychology* (pp. 303–330). Washington, DC: American Psychological Association.

Thompson, B. (1994). Food, bodies, and growing up female: Childhood lessons about culture, race, and class. In P. Fallon, M. A. Katzman, & S. C.

Wooley (Eds.), *Feminist perspectives on eating disorders* (pp. 355–378). New York: Guilford.

Thompson, H. B. (1903). *The mental traits of sex.* Chicago: University of Chicago Press.

Thompson, J. K., & Heinberg, L. J. (1999). The media's influence on body image disturbance and eating disorders: We've reviled them, now can we rehabilitate them? *Journal of Social Issues, 55*, 339–353.

Thompson, J. K., Heinberg, L. J., Altabe, M., & Tantleff-Dunn, S. (1999). *Exacting beauty: Theory, assessment, and treatment of body image disturbance.* Washington, DC: American Psychological Association.

Thompson, J. K., & Smolak, L. (Eds.). (2001). *Body image, eating disorders, and obesity in youth: Assessment, prevention, and treatment.* Washington, DC: American Psychological Association.

Thompson, S. H., Sargent, R. G., & Kemper, K. A. (1996). Black and White adolescent males' perceptions of ideal body size. *Sex Roles, 34*, 391–406.

Thompson, T. L., & Zerbinos, E. (1995). Gender roles in animated cartoons: Has the picture changed in 20 years? *Sex Roles, 32*, 651–673.

Thompson, T. L., & Zerbinos, E. (1997). Television cartoons: Do children notice it's a boy's world? *Sex Roles, 37*, 415–432.

Thorne, B. (1993). *Gender play: Girls and boys in school.* New Brunswick, NJ: Rutgers University Press.

Thornton, B., & Leo, R. (1992). Gender typing, importance of multiple roles, and mental health consequences for women. *Sex Roles, 27*, 307–317.

Thorpe, K., Barsky, J., & Boudreau, R. (1998, April). *Women's health: Occupational and life experiences— Women in transition.* Paper presented at the International Research Utilization Conference, Toronto, Canada.

Thrupkaew, N. (1999). Breakthrough against female genital mutilation. In G. Null & B. Seaman (Eds.), *For women only: Your guide to health empowerment* (pp. 1223–1230). New York: Seven Stories Press.

Tiefer, L. (1995a). [Review of the book *The sexual brain*] *Psychology of Women Quarterly, 18*, 440–441.

Tiefer, L. (1995b). *Sex is not a natural act and other essays.* Boulder, CO: Westview Press.

Tiefer, L. (1996). Towards a feminist sex therapy. *Women and Therapy, 19*, 53–64.

Tiefer, L. (2000). The social construction and social effects of sex research: The sexological model of sexuality. In C. B. Travis & J. W. White (Eds.),

Sexuality, society, and feminism (pp. 79–107). Washington, DC: American Psychological Association.

Tiefer, L. (2001). A new view of women's sexual problems: Why new? Why now? *Journal of Sex Research, 38*, 89–96.

Tiefer, L., & Kring, B. (1998). Gender and the organization of sexual behavior. In D. L. Answelmi & A. L. Law (Eds.), *Questions of gender: Perspectives and paradoxes* (pp. 320–328). New York: McGraw-Hill.

Tjaden, P., & Thoennes, N. (1998). *Prevalence, incidence, and consequences of violence against women: Findings from the National Violence Against Women Survey.* Washington, DC: National Institute of Justice, Office of Justice Programs, United States Department of Justice.

Tobias, S. (1997). *Faces of feminism: An activist's reflections on the women's movement.* Boulder, CO: Westview Press.

Tobin, D. L. (2000). *Coping strategies for bulimia nervosa.* Washington, DC: American Psychological Association.

Todd, A. D. (1989). *Intimate adversaries: Cultural conflict between doctors and women patients.* Philadelphia: University of Pennsylvania Press.

Todd, J. L., & Worell, J. (2000). Resilience in low-income, employed, African American women. *Psychology of Women Quarterly, 24*, 119–128.

Todoroff, M. (1994). Defining "achievement" in the lives of a generation of midlife single mothers. In J. Gallivan, S. D. Crozier, & V. M. Lalande (Eds.), *Women, girls, and achievement* (pp. 96–105). North York, Canada: Captus University Publications.

Tolman, D. L. (1999). Female adolescent sexuality in relational context: Beyond sexual decision making. In N. G. Johnson, M. C. Roberts, & J. Worell (Eds.), *Beyond appearance: A new look at adolescent girls* (pp. 227–246). Washington, DC: American Psychological Association.

Tolman, D. L., & Diamond, L. (2001). Sexuality and sexual desire. In J. Worell (Ed.), *Encyclopedia of women and gender* (pp. 1005–1021). San Diego: Academic Press.

Tong, R. P. (1998). *Feminist thought* (2nd ed.). Boulder, CO: Westview Press.

Toubia, N. (1995). Female genital mutilation. In J. Peters & A. Wolper (Eds.), *Women's rights, human rights: International feminist perspectives* (pp. 224–237). New York: Routledge.

Townsend, K., & Rice, P. L. (1996). A baby is born in Site 2 camp: Pregnancy, birth, and confinement among Cambodian refugee women. In P. L. Rice

& L. Manderson (Eds.), *Maternity and reproductive health in Asian societies* (pp. 125–143). Amsterdam: Harwood Academic.

Tozer, E. E., & McClanahan, M. K. (1999). Treating the purple menace: Ethical considerations of conversion therapy and affirmative alternatives. *Counseling Psychologist, 27,* 722–742.

Tozzo, S. G., & Golub, S. (1990). Playing nurse and playing cop: Do they change children's perceptions of sex-role stereotypes? *Journal of Research in Childhood Education, 4,* 123–129.

Tran, C. G., & Des Jardins, K. (2000). Domestic violence in Vietnamese refugee and Korean immigrant communities. In J. L. Chin (Ed.), *Relationships among Asian American women* (pp. 71–96). Washington, DC: American Psychological Association.

Tran, T. V. (1991). Family living arrangement and social adjustment among three ethnic groups of elderly Indochinese refugees. *International Journal of Aging and Human Development, 32,* 91–102.

Trautner, H. M., & Eckes, T. (2000). Putting gender development into context: Problems and prospects. In T. Eckes & H. M. Trautner (Eds.), *The developmental social psychology of gender* (pp. 419–435). Mahwah, NJ: Erlbaum.

Travis, C. B., & Compton, J. D. (2001). Feminism and health in the decade of behavior. *Psychology of Women Quarterly, 25,* 312–323.

Travis, C. B., Gressley, D. L., & Adams, P. L. (1995). Health care policy and practice for women's health. In A. L. Stanton & S. J. Gallant (Ed.), *The psychology of women's health: Progress and challenges in research and application* (pp. 531–565). Washington, DC: American Psychological Association.

Travis, C. B., Gressley, D. L., & Crumpler, C. A. (1991). Feminist contributions to health psychology. *Psychology of Women Quarterly, 15,* 557–566.

Travis, C. B., & Meginnis-Payne, K. L. (2001). Beauty politics and patriarchy: The impact on women's lives. In J. Worell (Ed.), *Encyclopedia of women and gender* (pp. 189–200). San Diego: Academic Press.

Treatment of depression: A consumer report. (2001, July). *Harvard Mental Health Letter,* pp. 7–8.

Trotman, F. K. (2002). Old, African American, and female: Political, economic, and historical contexts. In F. K. Trotman & C. M. Brody (Eds.), *Psychotherapy and counseling with older women* (pp. 70–86). New York: Springer.

Trotman, F. K., & Brody, C. M. (2002). Cross-cultural perspectives: Grandmothers. In F. K. Trotman &

C. M. Brody (Eds.), *Psychotherapy and counseling with older women* (pp. 41–57). New York: Springer.

True, R. H. (1990). Psychotherapeutic issues with Asian American women. *Sex Roles, 22,* 477–486.

True, R. H. (1995). Mental health issues of Asian/Pacific Island women. In D. L. Adams (Ed.), *Health issues for women of color: A cultural diversity perspective* (pp. 89–111). Thousand Oaks, CA: Sage.

Tsui, L. (1998). The effects of gender, education, and personal skills self-confidence on income in business management. *Sex Roles, 38,* 363–373.

Twenge, J. M. (1997). Attitudes toward women, 1970–1995. *Psychology of Women Quarterly, 21,* 35–51.

Twenge, J. M., & Zucker, A. N. (1999). What is a feminist? Evaluations and stereotypes in closed- and open-ended responses. *Psychology of Women Quarterly, 23,* 591–605.

Tyrka, A. R., Graber, J. A., & Brooks-Gunn, J. (2000). The development of disordered eating. In A. J. Sameroff, M. Lewis, & S. M. Miller (Eds.), *Handbook of developmental psychopathology* (2nd ed., pp. 607–624). New York: Kluwer Academic/Plenum.

Uba, L. (1994). *Asian Americans: Personality patterns, identity, and mental health.* New York: Guilford.

Ullman, S. E. (2000). Psychometric characteristics of the social reactions questionnaire: A measure of reactions to sexual assault victims. *Psychology of Women Quarterly, 24,* 257–271.

Ullman, S. E., & Breclin, L. R. (2002). Sexual assault history and suicidal behavior in a national sample of women. *Suicide and Life-Threatening Behavior, 32,* 117–130.

Ullman, S. E., & Knight, R. A. (1993). The efficacy of women's resistance strategies in rape situations. *Psychology of Women Quarterly, 17,* 23–38.

Unger, R. K. (1981). Sex as a social reality: Field and laboratory research. *Psychology of Women Quarterly, 5,* 645–653.

Unger, R. K. (1983). Through the looking glass: No wonderland yet! (The reciprocal relationship between methodology and models of reality). *Psychology of Women Quarterly, 8,* 9–32.

Unger, R. K. (1997). The three-sided mirror: Feminists looking at psychologists looking at women. In R. Fuller, P. N. Walsh, & P. McGinley (Eds.), *A century of psychology: Progress, paradigms, and prospects for the new millennium* (pp. 16–35). New York: Routledge.

Unger, R. K. (1998). *Resisting gender: Twenty-five years of feminist psychology.* London: Sage.

Unger, R. K. (Ed.). (2001). *Handbook of the psychology of women and gender.* New York: Wiley.

UNICEF. (2002). *The state of the world's children 2002.* New York: United Nations Publications.

United Nations. (1995). *The world's women, 1995: Trends and statistics.* New York: Author.

United Nations. (1999). *Women and health: Mainstreaming the gender perspective into the health sector.* New York: Author.

United Nations. (2000). *The world's women 2000: Trends and statistics.* New York: Author.

U.S. Bureau of the Census. (1997). *Statistical abstract of the United States* (117th ed.). Washington, DC: Author.

U.S. Census Bureau. (2000, March). *America's families and living arrangements* (Report P20-537, Table A1). Retrieved January 6, 2001, from http://www.census.gov/population/www/socdemo/hh-fam/p20-537_00.html

U.S. Census Bureau. (2001a). *Overview of race and Hispanic origin: Census 2000 Brief.* Retrieved July 18, 2001, from http://www.census.gov/population/www/socdemo/race.html

U.S. Census Bureau. (2001b). *Statistical abstract of the United States: 2001* (121st ed.). Washington, DC: Author.

U.S. Department of Labor. (1994). *1993 Handbook on women workers: Trends and issues.* Washington, DC: U.S. Government Printing Office.

Valcarcel, C. L. (1994). Growing up Black in Puerto Rico. In E. Tobach & B. Rosoff (Eds.), *Challenging racism and sexism* (pp. 284–294). New York: Feminist Press.

Valian, V. (1998). *Why so slow: The advancement of women.* Cambridge, MA: MIT Press.

Van Blyderveen, S., & Wood, J. (2001). *Gender differences in the tendency to generate self-evaluations based on the views of others in the autobiographical memories of events.* Paper presented at the annual convention of the Canadian Psychological Association.

Vance, E. B., & Wagner, N. N. (1977). Written descriptions of orgasm: A study of sex differences. In D. Byrne & L. A. Byrne (Eds.), *Exploring human sexuality* (pp. 201–212). New York: Thomas Y. Crowell.

Van den Hoonaard, D. K. (1999). Navigating in unknown waters: Canadian widows negotiating relationships. In K. Judd et al. (Eds.), *Ageing in a gendered world: Women's issues and identities* (pp. 345–366). Santo Domingo, Dominican Republic: International Research and Training Institute for the Advancement of Women.

Vangelisti, A. L., & Daily, J. A. (1999). Gender differences in standards for romantic relationships: Different cultures or different experiences? In L. A. Peplau, S. C. DeBro, R. C. Veniegas, & P. L. Taylor (Eds.), *Gender, culture, and ethnicity* (pp. 182–199). Mountain View, CA: Mayfield.

Van Olphen–Fehr, J. (1998). *Diary of a midwife: The power of positive childbearing.* Westport, CT: Bergin & Garvey.

Vargas, J. A. G. (1999). Who is the Puerto Rican woman and how is she?: Shall Hollywood respond? In M. Meyers (Ed.), *Mediated woman: Representations in popular culture* (pp. 111–132). Cresskill, NJ: Hampton Press.

Vasquez, M. J. T. (1999, Winter). President's message: Reaffirming affirmative action. *Psychology of Women Newsletter, 26,* 1–4.

Vasquez, M. J. T., & De las Fuentes, C. (1999). American-born Asian, African, Latina, and American Indian adolescent girls: Challenges and strengths. In N. G. Johnson, M. C. Roberts, & J. Worell (Eds.), *Beyond appearance: A new look at adolescent girls* (pp. 151–173). Washington, DC: American Psychological Association.

Vasta, R., Knott, J. A., & Gaze, C. E. (1996). Can spatial training erase the gender differences on the water-level task? *Psychology of Women Quarterly, 20,* 549–567.

Veniegas, R. C., & Peplau, L. A. (1997). Power and the quality of same-sex friendships. *Psychology of Women Quarterly, 21,* 279–297.

Vickers, J. F., & Thomas, B. L. (1993). *No more frogs, no more princes: Women making creative choices at midlife.* Freedom, CA: Crossing Press.

Vigorito, A. J., & Curry, T. J. (1998). Marketing masculinity: Gender identity and popular magazines. *Sex Roles, 39,* 135–152.

Villani, S. L. (1997). *Motherhood at the crossroads: Meeting the challenge of a changing role.* New York: Plenum.

Vincent, P. C., Peplau, L. A., & Hill, C. T. (1998). A longitudinal application of the theory of reasoned action to women's career behavior. *Journal of Applied Social Psychology, 28,* 761–778.

Vitulli, W. F., & Holland, B. E. (1993). College students' attitudes toward relationships with their parents as a function of gender. *Psychological Reports, 72,* 744–746.

Vogeltanz, N. D., & Wilsnack, S. C. (1997). Alcohol problems in women: Risk factors, consequences, and treatment strategies. In S. J. Gallant, G. P. Keita, & R. Royak-Schaler (Eds.), *Health care for women: Psychological, social, and behavioral influences* (pp. 75–96). Washington, DC: American Psychological Association.

Vollman, W. T. (2000, May 15). Letter from Afghanistan: Across the divide. *New Yorker*, pp. 58–73.

Voyer, D., Nolan, C., & Voyer, S. (2000). The relation between experience and spatial performance in men and women. *Sex Roles, 43,* 891–915.

Voyer, D., Voyer, S., & Bryden, M. P. (1995). Magnitude of sex differences in spatial abilities: A meta-analysis and consideration of critical variables. *Psychological Bulletin, 117,* 250–270.

Wade, C., & Cirese, S. (1991). *Human sexuality* (2nd ed.). San Diego: Harcourt Brace Jovanovich.

Wade, C., & Tavris, C. (1999). Gender and culture. In L. A. Peplau et al. (Eds.), *Gender, culture, and ethnicity: Current research about women and men* (pp. 15–22). Mountain View, CA: Mayfield.

Waehler, C. A. (1996). *Bachelors: The psychology of men who haven't married.* Westport, CT: Praeger.

Wainer, H., & Steinberg, L. S. (1992). Sex differences in performance on the mathematics section of the Scholastic Aptitude Test: A bidirectional validity study. *Harvard Educational Review, 62,* 323–336.

Waldram, J. B. (1997). The aboriginal peoples of Canada: Colonialism and mental health. In I. Al-Issa & M. Tousignant (Eds.), *Ethnicity, immigration, and psychopathology* (pp. 169–187). New York: Plenum.

Walker, A. E. (1998). *The menstrual cycle.* New York: Routledge.

Walker, L. E. A. (2000). *The battered woman syndrome* (2nd ed.). New York: Springer.

Walker, L. E. A. (2001). Battering in adult relations. In J. Worell (Ed.), *Encyclopedia of women and gender* (pp. 169–188). San Diego: Academic Press.

Wallace, H. (1999). *Family violence: Legal, medical, and social perspectives* (2nd ed.). Boston: Allyn & Bacon.

Wallen, J. (1998). Substance abuse and health care utilization. In E. A. Blechman & K. D. Brownell (Eds.), *Behavioral medicine and women: A comprehensive handbook* (pp. 309–312). New York: Guilford.

Wallis, L. A. (1998). Medical curricula and training. In E. A. Blechman & K. D. Brownell (Eds.), *Behavioral medicine and women: A comprehensive handbook* (pp. 303–308). New York: Guilford.

Walsh, M. (1999, Summer). Working past age 65. *Perspectives,* pp. 16–20.

Walsh, M., Duffy, J., & Gallagher-Duffy. J. (2003). *A conservative approach to measuring the prevalence of sexual harassment among high school students.* Manuscript submitted for publication.

Walsh, M., Hickey, C., & Duffy, J. (1999). Influence of item content and stereotype situation on gender differences in mathematical problem solving. *Sex Roles, 41,* 219–240.

Walsh, M. R. (1977). *Doctors wanted: No women need apply.* New Haven, CT: Yale University Press.

Walsh, M. R. (1987). Introduction. In M. R. Walsh (Ed.), *The psychology of women: Ongoing debates* (pp. 1–15). New Haven, CT: Yale University Press.

Walsh, M. R. (1990). Women in medicine since Flexner. *New York State Journal of Medicine, 90,* 302–308.

Walter, L. (2001). *Women's rights: A global view.* Westport, CT: Greenwood Press.

Walters, K. L., & Simoni, J. M. (1993). Lesbian and gay male group identity attitudes and self-esteem: Implications for counseling. *Journal of Counseling Psychology, 40,* 94–99.

Walton, M. D., et al. (1988). Physical stigma and the pregnancy role: Receiving help from strangers. *Sex Roles, 18,* 323–331.

Wang, N. (1994). Born Chinese and a woman in America. In J. Adleman & G. Enguídanos (Eds.), *Racism in the lives of women* (pp. 97–110). New York: Haworth.

Ward, C. A. (1995). *Attitudes toward rape: Feminist and social psychological perspectives.* London: Sage.

Ward, C. A. (2000). Models and measurements of psychological androgyny: A cross-cultural extension of theory and research. *Sex Roles, 43,* 529–552.

Ward, L. M. (1999). [Review of the book *The two sexes: Growing up apart, coming together.*] *Sex Roles, 40,* 657–659.

Warin, J. (2000). The attainment of self-consistency through gender in young children. *Sex Roles, 42,* 209–230.

Warner, J., Weber, T. R., & Albanes, R. (1999). "Girls are retarded when they're stoned": Marijuana and the construction of gender roles among adolescent females. *Sex Roles, 40,* 25–43.

War Resisters League. (2003). *Where your income tax money really goes.* Retrieved February 10, 2003, from the War Resisters League Web site: http://www.warresisters.org/piechart.htm

Warshaw, C. (2001). Women and violence. In N. L. Stotland & D. E. Stewart (Eds.), *Psychological aspects of women's health care* (2nd ed., pp. 477–548). Washington, DC: American Psychiatric Press.

Wasserman, E. B. (1994). Personal reflections of an Anglo therapist in Indian country. In J. Adleman & G. Enguídanos (Eds.), *Racism in the lives of women* (pp. 23–32). New York: Haworth.

Waters, M. C. (1996). The intersection of gender, race, and ethnicity in identity development of Caribbean American teens. In B. J. R. Leadbeater & N. Way (Eds.), *Urban girls: Resisting stereotypes, creating identities* (pp. 65–81). New York: New York University Press.

Watrous, A., & Honeychurch, C. (1999). *After the breakup: Women sort through the rubble and rebuild lives of new possibilities.* Oakland, CA: New Harbinger.

Watson, M. S., Trasciatti, M. A., & King, C. P. (1996). Our bodies, our risk: Dilemmas in contraceptive information. In R. L. Parrott & C. M. Condit (Eds.), *Evaluating women's health messages: A resource book* (pp. 95–108). Thousand Oaks, CA: Sage.

Watson, P. J., Biderman, M. D., & Sawrie, S. M. (1994). Empathy, sex role orientation, and narcissism. *Sex Roles, 30,* 701–723.

Way, N. (1998). *Everyday courage: The lives and stories of urban teenagers.* New York: New York University Press.

Wear, D. (1997). *Privilege in the medical academy: A feminist examines gender, race, and power.* New York: Teachers College Press.

Weaver, G. D. (1998, August). *Emotional health of older African American women with breast cancer.* Paper presented at the annual convention of the American Psychological Association, San Francisco, CA.

Websdale, N. (1998). *Rural woman battering and the justice system.* Thousand Oaks, CA: Sage.

Webster, J., et al. (2000). Measuring social support in pregnancy: Can it be simple and meaningful? *Birth, 27,* 97–101.

Wechsler, H., et al. (1994). Health and behavioral consequences of binge drinking in college: A national survey of students at 140 campuses. *Journal of the American Medical Association, 272,* 1672–1677.

Weedon, C. (1999). *Feminism, theory, and the politics of difference.* Malden, MA: Blackwell.

Weinberg, M. S., Lottes, I. L., & Shaver, F. M. (1995). Swedish or American heterosexual college youth: Who is more permissive? *Archives of Sexual Behavior, 24,* 409–437.

Weinberg, M. S., Williams, C. J., & Pryor, D. W. (1994). *Dual attraction: Understanding bisexuality.* New York: Oxford University Press.

Weinraub, M., Hill, C., & Hirsh-Pasek, K. (2001). Child care: Options and outcomes. In J. Worell (Ed.), *Encyclopedia of women and gender* (pp. 233–244). San Diego: Academic Press.

Weissman, M. M. (Ed.). (2001). *Treatment of depression: Bridging the 21st century.* Washington, DC: American Psychiatric Press.

Weitzman, S. (2000). *"Not to people like us": Hidden abuse in upscale marriages.* New York: Basic Books.

Welsh, D. P., Rostosky, S. S., & Kawaguchi, M. C. (2000). A normative perspective of adolescent girls' developing sexuality. In C. B. Tavris & J. W. White (Eds.), *Sexuality, society, and feminism* (pp. 111–166). Washington, DC: American Psychological Association.

Wendell, S. (1997). Toward a feminist theory of disability. In L. J. Davis (Ed.), *The disability studies reader* (pp. 260–278). New York: Routledge.

Wenniger, M. D., & Conroy, M. H. (2001). *Gender equity or bust! On the road to campus leadership with women in higher education.* San Francisco: Jossey-Bass.

Wessely, S. (1998). Commentary: Reducing distress after normal childbirth. *Birth, 25,* 220–221.

West, C., & Zimmerman, D. H. (1998a). Doing gender. In B. M. Clinchy & J. K. Norem (Eds.), *The gender and psychology reader* (pp. 104–124). New York: New York University Press.

West, C., & Zimmerman, D. H. (1998b). Women's place in everyday talk: Reflections on parent-child interaction. In J. Coates (Ed.), *Language and gender: A reader* (pp. 165–175). Malden, MA: Blackwell.

West, C. M. (1998). Lifting the "political gag order": Breaking the silence around partner violence in ethnic minority families. In J. L. Jasinski & L. M. Williams (Eds.), *Partner violence: A comprehensive review of 20 years of research* (pp. 184–209). Thousand Oaks, CA: Sage.

West, C. M. (2000). Developing an "oppositional gaze" toward the images of Black women. In J. C. Chrisler, C. Golden, & P. D. Rozee (Eds.), *Lectures on the psychology of women* (2nd ed., pp. 220–233). Boston: McGraw-Hill.

West, C. M., Williams, L. M., & Siegel, J. A. (2000). Adult sexual revictimization among Black women sexually abused in childhood: A prospective examination of serious consequences of abuse. *Child Maltreatment, 5,* 49–57.

West, M., & Fernández, M. (1997). *Reflexion Cristiana: ¿Como ayudar a una mujer maltratada?* [Christian reflection: How to help an abused woman.] Managua, Nicaragua: Red de Mujeres contra la Violencia.

Westen, D. (1998). The scientific legacy of Sigmund Freud: Toward a psychodynamically informed psychological science. *Psychological Bulletin, 124,* 333–371.

Wester, S. R., Crown, C. L., Quatman, G. L., & Heesacker, M. (1997). The influence of sexually violent rap music on attitudes of men with little prior exposure. *Psychology of Women Quarterly, 21,* 497–508.

Westkott, M. C. (1997). On the new psychology of women: A cautionary view. In Walsh, M. R. (1997). *Women, men, and gender: Ongoing debates* (pp. 362–372). New Haven, CT: Yale University Press.

Whalen, M. (1996). *Counseling to end violence against women: A subversive model.* Thousand Oaks, CA: Sage.

Whatley, M. H., & Henken, E. R. (2000). *Did you hear about the girl who . . . ? Contemporary legends, folklore, and human sexuality.* New York: New York University Press.

Wheelan, S. A., & Verdi, A. F. (1992). Differences in male and female patterns of communication in groups: A methodological artifact? *Sex Roles, 27,* 1–15.

Wheeler, C. (1994, September/October). How much ink do women get? *Executive Female,* p. 51.

Whelehan, P. (2001). Cross-cultural sexual practices. In J. Worell (Ed.), *Encyclopedia of women and gender* (pp. 291–302). San Diego: Academic Press.

Whiffen, V. E. (2001). Depression. In J. Worell (Ed.), *Encyclopedia of women and gender* (pp. 303–314). San Diego: Academic Press.

Whitbourne, S. K. (1996). *The aging individual: Physical and psychological perspectives.* New York: Springer.

Whitbourne, S. K. (1998). Identity and adaptation to the aging process. In C. Ryff & V. Marshall (Eds.), *Self and society in aging processes* (pp. 122–149). New York: Springer.

Whitbourne, S. K. (2001). *Adult development and aging: Biopsychosocial perspectives.* New York: Wiley.

Whitbourne, S. K., & Hulicka, I. M. (1990). Ageism in undergraduate psychology texts. *American Psychologist, 45,* 1127–1136.

Whitbourne, S. K., & Sneed, J. R. (2002). The paradox of well-being, identity processes, and stereotype threat: Ageism and its potential relationship to the self and later life. In T. D. Nelson (Ed.), *Ageism: Stereotyping and prejudice against older persons* (pp. 247–273). Cambridge, MA: MIT Press.

White, J. W. (2001). Aggression and gender. In J. Worell (Ed.), *Encyclopedia of women and gender* (pp. 81–93). San Diego: Academic Press.

White, J. W., Bondurant, B., & Travis, C. B. (2000). Social constructions of sexuality: Unpacking hidden meanings. In C. B. Travis & J. W. White (Eds.), *Sexuality, society, and feminism* (pp. 11–33). Washington, DC: American Psychological Association.

White, J. W., Donat, P. L. N., & Bondurant, B. (2001). A developmental examination of violence against girls and women. In R. K. Unger (Ed.), *Handbook of the psychology of women and gender* (pp. 343–357). New York: Wiley.

White, J. W., & Kowalski, R. M. (1994). Reconstructing the myth of the nonaggressive woman: A feminist analysis. *Psychology of Women Quarterly, 18,* 487–508.

White, J. W., & Kowalski, R. M. (1998). Male violence toward women: An integrated perspective. In R. G. Geen & E. Donnerstein (Eds.), *Human aggression: Theories, research, and implications for social policy* (pp. 203–228). San Diego: Academic Press.

White, J. W., & Sorenson, S. B. (1992). A sociocultural view of sexual assault: From discrepancy to diversity. *Journal of Social Issues, 48,* 187–195.

White, L. (2001). Japan: Democracy in a Confucian-based society. In L. Walter (Ed.), *Women's rights: A global view* (pp. 141–154). Westport, CT: Greenwood.

White, L., & Rogers, S. J. (2000). Economic circumstances and family outcomes: A review of the 1990s. *Journal of Marriage and the Family, 62,* 1035–1051.

Whitley, B. E., Jr., & Ægisdóttir, S. (2000). The gender belief system, authoritarianism, social dominance orientation, and heterosexuals' attitudes toward lesbians and gay men. *Sex Roles, 42,* 947–967.

Whitley, B. E., Jr., & Hern, A. L. (1992). *Sexual experience, perceived invulnerability to pregnancy, and the use of effective contraception.* Paper presented at the annual meeting of the Eastern Psychological Association, Boston, MA.

Whitley, B. E., Jr., McHugh, M. C., & Frieze, I. H. (1986). Assessing the theoretical models for sex differences in causal attributions of success and failure. In J. S. Hyde & M. C. Linn (Eds.), *The psychology of gender: Advances through meta-analysis* (pp. 102–135). Baltimore: Johns Hopkins University Press.

Whooley, M. A., & Simon, G. E. (2000). Managing depression in medical outpatients. *New England Journal of Medicine, 343,* 1942–1950.

Why don't I have a boyfriend? (And how do I get one?). (2001, August). *Twist*, pp. 26–27.

Whyte, J. (1998). Childhood. In K. Trew & J. Kremer (Eds.), *Gender and psychology* (pp. 97–106). New York: Oxford University Press.

Widaman, K. F., et al. (1992). Differences in adolescents' self-concept as a function of academic level, ethnicity, and gender. *American Journal on Mental Retardation, 96,* 387–404.

Widmer, E. D., Treas, J., & Newcomb, R. (1998). Attitudes toward nonmarital sex in 24 countries. *Journal of Sex Research, 35,* 349–358.

Wile, J., & Arechigo, M. (1999). Sociocultural aspects of postpartum depression. In L. J. Miller (Ed.), *Postpartum mood disorders* (pp. 83–98). Washington, DC: American Psychiatric Press.

Willemsen, T. M. (1998). Widening the gender gap: Teenage magazines for girls and boys. *Sex Roles, 38,* 851–861.

Willetts-Bloom, M. C., & Nock, S. L. (1994). The influence of maternal employment on gender role attitudes of men and women. *Sex Roles, 30,* 371–389.

Williams, C. L. (1998). The glass escalator: Hidden advantages for men in the "female" positions. In M. S. Kimmel & M. A. Messner (Eds.), *Men's lives* (4th ed., pp. 285–299). Boston: Allyn & Bacon.

Williams, J. E., Bennett, S. M., & Best, D. (1975). Awareness and expression of sex stereotypes in young children. *Developmental Psychology, 11,* 635–642.

Williams, J. E., & Best, D. L. (1990). *Measuring sex sterotypes: A multinational study* (Rev. ed.). Newbury Park, CA: Sage.

Williams, J. E., Satterwhite, R. C., & Best, D. L. (1999). Pancultural gender stereotypes revisited: The five factor model. *Sex Roles, 40,* 513–525.

Williams, L. M., & Banyard, V. L. (Eds.). (1999). *Trauma and memory.* Thousand Oaks, CA: Sage.

Williams, M. J. K. (1999). *Sexual pathways: Adapting to dual sexual attraction.* Westport, CT: Praeger.

Williams, R., & Witting, M. A. (1997). "I'm not a feminist, but . . .": Factors contributing to the discrepancy between pro-feminist orientation and feminist social identity. *Sex Roles, 37,* 885–904.

Williams, S. S., et al. (1992). College students use implicit personality theory instead of safer sex. *Journal of Applied Social Psychology, 22,* 921–933.

Willingham, W. W., & Cole, N. S. (1997). *Gender and fair assessment.* Mahwah, NJ: Erlbaum.

Willis, C. E., Hallinan, M. N., & Melby, J. (1996). Effects of sex role stereotyping among European American students on domestic violence culpability attributions. *Sex Roles, 34,* 475–491.

Wilsnack, S. C. (1995). Alcohol use and alcohol problems in women. In A. L. Stanton & S. J. Gallant (Eds.), *The psychology of women's health: Progress and challenges in research and application* (pp. 381–443). Washington, DC: American Psychological Association.

Wilson, C. C., II, & Gutiérrez, F. (1995). *Race, multiculturalism, and the media: From mass to class communication.* Thousand Oaks, CA: Sage.

Wilson, C. T., & Fairburn, C. G. (2002). Treatments for eating disorders. In P. E. Nathan & J. M. Gorman (Eds.), *A guide to treatments that work* (2nd ed., pp. 559–592). New York: Oxford University Press.

Wilson, J. F. (1997). Changes in female students' attitudes toward women's lifestyles and career choices during a psychology of women course. *Teaching of Psychology, 24,* 50–52.

Wilson, S. R., & Mankowski, E. S. (2000). Beyond the drum: An exploratory study of group processes in a mythopoetic men's group. In E. R. Barton (Ed.), *Mythopoetic perspectives of men's healing work* (pp. 21–45). Westport, CT: Bergin & Garvey.

Windle, M., Shope, J. T., & Bukstein, O. (1996). In R. J. DiClemente, W. B. Hansen, & L. E. Ponton (Eds.), *Handbook of adolescent health risk behavior* (pp. 115–159). New York: Plenum.

Wing, R. R., & Klem, M. L. (1997). Obesity. In S. J. Gallant, G. P. Keita, & R. Royak-Schaler (Eds.), *Health care for women: Psychological, social, and behavioral influences* (pp. 115–131). Washington, DC: American Psychological Association.

Wing, R. R., & Polley, B. A. (2001). Obesity. In A. Baum, T. A. Revenson, & J. E. Singer (Eds.), *Handbook of health psychology* (pp. 263–279). Mahwah, NJ: Erlbaum.

Wingert, P. (1998, May 11). The battle over falling birthrates. *Newsweek,* p. 40.

Wingert, P., & Snow, K. (1998, June 22). Using the bully pulpit? *Newsweek,* p. 69.

Winstead, B. A., Derlega, V. J., & Rose, S. (1997). *Gender and close relationships.* Thousand Oaks, CA: Sage.

Winstead, B. A., & Griffin, J. L. (2001). Friendship styles. In J. Worell (Ed.), *Encyclopedia of women and gender* (pp. 481–492). San Diego: Academic Press.

Winter, D. D. (1996). *Ecological psychology: Healing the split between planet and self.* New York: Harper-Collins.

Winters, A. M., & Duck, S. (2001). You ****! Swearing as an aversive and a relational activity. In R. M. Kowalski (Ed.), *Behaving badly* (pp. 59–77). Washington, DC: American Psychological Association.

Wise, E. A., et al. (2001). Women's health: A cultural perspective. In S. Kazarian & D. R. Evans (Eds.), *Handbook of cultural health psychology* (pp. 445–467). San Diego: Academic Press.

Wolf, N. (1991). *The beauty myth: How images of beauty are used against women.* New York: Doubleday.

Wolf, N. (2001). *Misconceptions.* New York: Doubleday.

Wolk, S. I., & Weissman, M. M. (1995). Women and depression: An update. *Review of Psychiatry, 14,* 227–259.

Women and HIV/AIDS [Special issue]. (2001, Summer/Fall). *Canadian Woman Studies/Les cahiers de la femme, 21*(2).

Women and poverty: An unequal burden. (2000, April). *Friends Committee on National Legislation Washington Newsletter,* pp. 1–7.

Women in Action. (2001). Violence against women: An issue of human rights. In S. M. Shaw & J. Lee (Eds.), *Women's voices, feminist visions* (pp. 407–408). Mountain View, CA: Mayfield.

Women of Color Resource Center. (2000). *Women of color organizations & projects: A national directory.* Berkeley, CA: Author.

Women's health centers. (1997, October). *Harvard Women's Health Watch,* p. 1.

Wood, M. D., Vinson, D. C., & Sher, K. J. (2001). Alcohol use and misuse. In A. Baum, T. A. Revenson, & J. E. Singer (Eds.), *Handbook of health psychology* (pp. 281–318). Mahwah, NJ: Erlbaum.

Wood, W., Rhodes, N., & Whelan, M. (1989). Sex differences in positive well-being: A consideration of emotional style and marital status. *Psychological Bulletin, 106,* 249–264.

Woodfield, R. (2000). *Women, work and computing.* Cambridge, England: Cambridge University Press.

Woods, N. F. (1999). Midlife women's health: Conflicting perspectives of health care providers and midlife women and consequences for health. In A. E. Clarke & V. L. Olesen (Eds.), *Revisioning women, health, and healing* (pp. 343–354). New York: Routledge.

Woods, N. F., & Jacobson, B. G. (1997). Diseases that manifest differently in women and men. In F. P. Haseltine & B. G. Jacobson (Eds.), *Women's health research: A medical and policy primer* (pp. 159–187). Washington, DC: Health Press.

Woods, N. F., et al. (1999). Depressed mood and self-esteem in young Asian, Black, and White women in America. In C. Forden, A. E. Hunter, & B. Birns (Eds.), *Readings in the psychology of women* (pp. 328–339). Boston: Allyn & Bacon.

Woodzicka, J. A., & LaFrance, M. (2001). Real versus imagined gender harassment. *Journal of Social Issues, 57,* 15–30.

Woollett, A., & Marshall, H. (1997). Discourses of pregnancy and childbirth. In L. Yardley (Ed.), *Material discourses of health and illness* (pp. 176–198). London: Routledge.

Woolley, H. T. (1910). Psychological literature: A review of the recent literature on the psychology of sex. *Psychological Bulletin, 7,* 335–342.

Word, C. H., Zanna, M. P., & Cooper, J. (1974). The nonverbal mediation of self-fulfilling prophecies in interracial interaction. *Journal of Experimental Social Psychology, 10,* 109–120.

Worell, J. (Ed.). (2001). *The encyclopedia of women and gender* (Vols. 1 and 2). San Diego: Academic Press.

Worell, J., & Johnson, D. (2001). Therapy with women: Feminist frameworks. In R. K. Unger (Ed.), *Handbook of women and gender* (pp. 317–329). New York: Wiley.

Worell, J., & Remer, P. P. (1992). *Feminist perspectives in therapy: An empowerment model for women.* New York: Wiley.

Worell, J., & Remer, P. P. (2003). *Feminist perspectives in therapy: Empowering diverse women* (2nd ed.). New York: Wiley.

Workman, J. E., & Freeburg, E. W. (1999). An examination of date rape, victim dress, and perceiver variables within the context of attribution theory. *Sex Roles, 41,* 261–277.

World Health Organization. (2002). *AIDS epidemic update 2002.* Retrieved February 7, 2003, from the World Health Organization Web site: http://www/who.int/hiv/en

Wosinska, W., Dabul, A. J., Whetstone-Dion, M. R., & Cialdini, R. B. (1996). Self-presentational responses to success in the organization: The costs and benefits of modesty. *Basic and Applied Social Psychology, 18,* 229–242.

Wright, K. (1997, February). Anticipatory guidance: Developing a healthy sexuality. *Pediatric Annals,* S142–S145.

Wright, P. H. (1998). Toward an expanded orientation to the study of sex differences in friendship. In D. J. Canary & K. Dindia (Eds.), *Sex differences and similarities in communication* (pp. 41–63). Mahwah, NJ: Erlbaum.

Wright, R. (1998, May 12). Iran a model of population control. *San Jose Mercury News,* p. A7.

Writing Group for the Women's Health Initiative Investigators. (2002). Risks and benefits of estrogen plus progestin in healthy postmenopausal women. *Journal of the American Medical Association, 288,* 321–333.

Wu, X., & DeMaris, A. (1996). Gender and marital status differences in depression: The effects of chronic strains. *Sex Roles, 34,* 299–319.

Wu, Z. (1999). Premarital cohabitation and the timing of first marriage. *Canadian Review of Sociology and Anthropology, 36,* 109–127.

Wuitchik, M., Hesson, K., & Bakal, D. A. (1990). Perinatal predictors of pain and distress during labor. *Birth, 17,* 186–191.

Wyche, K. F. (2001). Sociocultural issues in counseling for women of color. In R. K. Unger (Ed.), *Handbook of the psychology of women and gender* (pp. 330–340). New York: Wiley.

Wyche, K. F., & Rice, J. K. (1997). Feminist therapy: From dialogue to tenets. In J. Worell & N. Johnson (Eds.), *Shaping the future of feminist psychology: Education, research, and practice* (pp. 57–71). Washington, DC: American Psychological Association.

Wymelenberg, S. (2000). *Breast Cancer: Strategies for living.* Cambridge, MA: Harvard Health Publications.

Yarkin, K. L., Town, J. P., & Wallston, B. S. (1982). Blacks and women must try harder: Stimulus persons' race and sex attributions of causality. *Personality and Social Psychology Bulletin, 8,* 21–30.

Ybarra, L. (1995). Marital decision-making and the role of *machismo* in the Chicano family. In A. S. López (Ed.), *Latina issues* (pp. 252–267). New York: Garland.

Yeh, C. J. (1998). Ethnic identity development. In T. M. Singelis (Ed.), *Teaching about culture, ethnicity, and diversity* (pp. 165–173). Thousand Oaks, CA: Sage.

Yoder, J., Schleicher, T. L., & McDonald, T. W. (1998). Empowering token women leaders: The importance of organizationally legitimated credibility. *Psychology of Women Quarterly, 22,* 209–222.

Yoder, J. D. (2000). Women and work. In M. Biaggio & M. Hersen (Eds.), *Issues in the psychology of women* (pp. 71–91). New York: Kluwer Academic/Plenum.

Yoder, J. D. (2001). Military women. In J. Worell (Ed.), *Encyclopedia of women and gender* (pp. 771–782). San Diego: Academic Press.

Yoder, J. D., & Aniakudo, P. (1996). When pranks become harassment: The case of African American women firefighters. *Sex Roles, 35,* 253–270.

Yoder, J. D., & Aniakudo, P. (1997). "Outsider within" the firehouse: Subordination and difference in the social interactions of African American women firefighters. *Gender and Society, 11,* 324–341.

Yoder, J. D., & Berendsen, L. L. (2001). "Outsider within" the firehouse: African American and White women firefighters. *Psychology of Women Quarterly, 25,* 27–36.

Yoder, J. D., & Kahn, A. S. (1993). Working toward an inclusive psychology of women. *American Psychologist, 48,* 846–850.

Yoder, J. D., & McDonald, T. W. (1998). Measuring sexist discrimination in the workplace: Support for the validity of the schedule of sexist events. *Psychology of Women Quarterly, 22,* 487–491.

Young, D. (1982). *Changing childbirth: Family birth in the hospital.* Rochester, NY: Childbirth Graphics.

Young, D. (1993). Family-centered maternity care. In B. K. Rothman (Ed.), *Encyclopedia of childbearing: Critical perspectives* (pp. 140–141). Phoenix, AZ: Oryx Press.

Young, J., & Bursik, K. (2000). Identity development and life plan maturity: A comparison of women athletes and nonathletes. *Sex Roles, 43,* 241–254.

Young, J. R. (2002, September 6). Average SAT scores hold steady, while ACT scores slip. *Chronicle of Higher Education,* p. A50.

Yurek, D., Farrar, W., & Andersen, B. L. (2000). Breast cancer surgery: Comparing surgical groups and determining individual differences in postoperative sexuality and body change stress. *Journal of Counseling and Clinical Psychology, 68,* 697–709.

Zahm, M. (1998). Creating a feminist mentoring network. In L. H. Collins, J. C. Chrisler, & K. Quina (Eds.), *Career strategies for women in academe: Arming Athena.* Thousand Oaks, CA: Sage.

Zalk, S. R. (1996). Men in the academy: A psychological profile of harassers. In M. A. Paludi (Ed.), *Sexual harassment on college campuses* (pp. 81–113). Albany, NY: State University of New York Press.

Zandy, J. (2001). "Women have always sewed": The production of clothing and the work of women. In J. Zandy (Ed.), *What we hold in common: An introduction to working-class studies* (pp. 148–153). New York: Feminist Press.

Zarbatany, L., McDougall, P., & Hymel, S. (2000). Gender-differentiated experiences in the peer culture: Links to intimacy in preadolescence. *Social Development, 9,* 62–79.

Zebrowitz, L. A., & Montepare, J. M. (2000). "Too young, too old": Stigmatizing adolescents and elders. In T. F. Heatherton et al. (Eds.), *The social psychology of stigma* (pp. 334–373). New York: Guilford.

Zeiss, A. M. (1998). Sexuality and aging. In E. A. Blechman & K. D. Brownell (Eds.), *Behavioral medicine and women: A comprehensive handbook* (pp. 528–534). New York: Guilford.

Zemore, S. E., Fiske, S. T., & Kim, H. J. (2000). Gender stereotypes and the dynamics of social interaction. In T. Eckes & H. M. Trautner (Eds.), *The developmental social psychology of gender* (pp. 207–241). Mahwah, NJ: Erlbaum.

Zerbe, K. J. (1999). *Women's mental health in primary care.* Philadelphia: W. B. Saunders.

Zhou, M. (1994, June 10). China: Speaking out against sexual harassment. *Women's Feature Service.* Available by E-mail from wfs@igc.apc.org

Zhou, Q., et al. (1999). Severity of nausea and vomiting during pregnancy: What does it predict? *Birth, 26,* 108–114.

Zia, H. (1996, January/February). Made in the U.S.A. *Ms. Magazine,* pp. 67–73.

Zia, H. (2000). *Asian American dreams.* New York: Farrar, Straus & Giroux.

Zilbergeld, B. (1999). *The new male sexuality* (Rev. ed.). New York: Bantam Books.

Zillman, D. (1998). *Connections between sexuality and aggression* (2nd ed.). Mahwah, NJ: Erlbaum.

Zorza, J. (2001). Drug-facilitated rape. In A. J. Ottens & K. Hotelling (Eds.), *Sexual violence on campus* (pp. 53–75). New York: Springer.

Zucker, K. J., Wilson-Smith, D. N., Kurita, J. A., & Stern, A. (1995). Children's appraisals of sex-typed behavior in their peers. *Sex Roles, 33,* 703–725.

Zuckerman, D. M. (2000). The evolution of welfare reform: Policy changes and current knowledge. *Journal of Social Issues, 56,* 811–820.

Zuckerman, D. M., & Kalil, A. (2000). Introduction: Welfare reform—Preliminary research and unanswered questions. *Journal of Social Issues, 56,* 579–586.

Name Index

This index includes names of people, government agencies, and organizations.

Subject Index

For names of both people and organizations, see the Name Index.

Maquiladoras, 226
Marianismo, 261–262, 338, 405
Marijuana, 382
Marital rape, 426
Marriage. *See also* Family
  age at first marriage, 257
  characteristics of happy
    marriages, 259–260
  death of life partners and,
    475–477
  and decision whether to have
    children, 344–346
  depression and, 388
  egalitarian marriage, 261
  ethnicity and, 257–258, 261–263
  gender comparisons on
    satisfaction with, 258–259
  household tasks and, 233–235
  individual differences in,
    256–257
  living together before, 254
  modern marriage, 260–261
  rape in, 426
  responsibility and power in,
    260–261
  salary and power in, 260
  satisfaction with, 235–236,
    257–260, 347
  stresses in, following
    childbirth, 336
  traditional marriage, 260
  work coordinated with,
    233–236
Masculine generic, 40–42
Masochism, 408
Masturbation, 299–30
Maternity blues, 340
Mathematics ability, 151–153
Mathematics education, 128, 152,
  158, 159
Matriarchy, Black, 262, 337–338,
  406, 477
Mayan communities, 329
Media
  on abortion, 314
  on abuse of women, 447
  activism against gender
    stereotypes in, 401, 500
  on affirmative action, 214
  on androgyny, 66
  on attractiveness, 121, 122

birth control and, 312–313
on cognitive abilities, 143–144
culture of slimness and,
  397–398, 401
on education of girls, 95, 96
effects of stereotyped
  representations in, 46–47
on employed women, 44, 233
on feminism, 494, 495–496
gender bias and stereotyped
  representations in, 42–47,
  97–101, 173
on gender comparisons, 24–25,
  143–144
gender typing and, 97–101
on housework, 44
inaudibility of women in, 44
invisibility of women in, 43
on love relationships, 136, 245
on menopause, 467–470
older women in, 458, 459–460
on pregnancy, childbirth, and
  motherhood, 322
on prisons, 197
on rape, 429, 435
research findings reported by,
  24–26
on sexuality, 287, 297–298
sexually aggressive media, 46
on social class, 45–46
violence in, 441, 452
on women of color, 45
on women's and men's bodies,
  45, 397–398
Medicaid, 356
Medical profession. *See also*
  Physical health
  attitudes of, toward
    menopause, 469, 471
  biases against women in,
    354–356
  care for abused women by,
    451
  cesarean section (C-section)
    and, 330
  frequency of women's visits
    to health care providers,
    358
  gender stereotypes and, 355
  and male-as-normative model,
    355, 372, 377

neglect of women in medicine
  and medical research,
  354–355
older women and, 458
physician-patient
  communication patterns,
  356
pregnant women and, 326
pregnant women as medical
  residents, 327
and prescriptions for sedatives
  and tranquilizers, 382,
  409–410
retirement from, 465
salary discrimination in, 216
women physicians, 35, 39,
  208–209, 216, 229, 239, 354
Medications. *See* Drug therapy
Memory
  gender comparisons on, 148
  gender stereotypes and, 64
  recovered-memory/false-
    memory controversy,
    436–437
Men. *See also* Fathers; Gay males;
  and headings beginning with
  Gender
  abuse of, by women, 443
  action against sexual
    harassment by, 424
  alcohol abuse and, 353,
    380–381
  as allies, 423, 441, 451, 492
  antisocial personality disorder
    and, 387, 446–447
  bodies of, as portrayed by
    media, 45
  characteristics of male abusers,
    446–447
  circumcision of boys, 357
  culture of slimness and, 399
  entitlement and, 92, 219, 418,
    447
  as feminists, 5
  feminists' attitudes toward, 6,
    494
  household tasks and, 233–235
  income of older men, 465, 466
  life expectancy for, 358, 359
  machismo and, 261–262, 405
  men's movement and, 491–493

Credits

This page constitutes an extension of the copyright page. We have made every effort to trace the ownership of all copyrighted material and to secure permission from copyright holders. In the event of any question arising as to the use of any material, we will be pleased to make the necessary corrections in future printings. Thanks are due to the following authors, publishers, and agents for permission to use the material indicated.

Chapter 2. 55: From Glick & Fiske, *Ambivalent Sexism Inventory.* Copyright © 1995 by Peter Glick and Susan T. Fiske. 68: Auster, C. J., & Ohm, S. C. (2000). Masculinity and femininity in contemporary American society: A reevaluation using the Bem Sex Role Inventory. *Sex Roles, 43,* 499–528.

Chapter 3. 93: From Powlishta, K. (1995). Intergroup processes in childhood. *Developmental Psychology, 31,* 781–788. © 1995 by the American Psychological Association. Reprinted with permission. 105: G. D. Levy et al. (2000).

Chapter 5. 152: From Hyde, J. S. et al. (1990). Gender differences in mathematics performance: A meta-analysis. *Psychological Bulletin, 107,* 139–155. © 1990 by the American Psychological Association. Reprinted with permission.

Chapter 6. 182: From Bonebright, T. L., Thompson, J. L., & Leger, D. W. (1996). Gender stereotypes in the expression and perception of vocal effect. *Sex Roles, 34,* 429–445 (Figure 1). Reprinted with permission of Kluwer.

Chapter 8. 248: From Regan, P. C., & Berscheid, E. (1997). Gender differences in characteristics desired in a potential sexual and marriage partner. *Journal of Psychology and Human Sexuality, 9,* 32, (Table 1). © 1997 Haworth Press, Inc. 10 Alice Street, Binghamton, NY 13904. 271: From Kurdek, L. A. (1995). Assessing multiple determinants of relationship commitment in cohabiting gay, cohabiting lesbian, dating heterosexual, and married heterosexual couples. *Family Relations, 44,* 261–266 (Table 1). Copyright 1995 by the National Council on Family Relations, 3989 Central Ave. NE,

Suite 550, Minneapolis, MN 55421. Reprinted with permission.

Chapter 9. 301: From Morokoff, P. J. et al. (1997). Sexual Assertiveness Scale (SAS) for women: Development and validation. *Journal of Personality and Social Psychology, 73,* 804 (appendix). © 1997 by the American Psychological Association. Reprinted with permission. 308: Reproduced with the permission of The Alan Guttmacher Institute from Singh, S., & Darroch, J. E. (2000). Adolescent pregnancy and childbearing: Levels and trends in developed countries. *Family Planning Perspectives, 32,* 14–23 (data selected from Table 2, p. 16).

Chapter 10. 345: From Mueller, K. A., & Yoder, J. D. (1997). Gendered norms for family size, employment, and occupation: Are there personal costs for violating them? *Sex Roles, 36,* 211. Reprinted by permission of Kluwer. 346: From Mueller, K. A., & Yoder, J. D. (1997). Gendered norms for family size, employment, and occupation: Are there personal costs for violating them? *Sex Roles, 36,* 216. Reprinted by permission of Kluwer.

Chapter 11. 363: American Cancer Society (2003).

Chapter 13. 419: From Bursik, K. (2002). Perception of sexual harassment in an academic context. *Sex Roles, 27,* 401–412. Reprinted by permission of Kluwer.

Chapter 14. 472: From Gannon, L., & Ekstrom, B. (1993). Attitudes toward menopause: The influence of sociocultural paradigms. *Psychology of Women Quarterly, 17,* 275–288 (Figure 1, p. 283). Reprinted by permission of Blackwell Publishing Ltd.

DEAR STUDENT:

I hope that you have enjoyed reading *Psychology of Women* (5th edition) as much as I have enjoyed writing it! I would like to know your thoughts and experiences about the book. In what ways did it help you, and how can I make it better for future readers?

School and address: _____

Department: _____

Instructor's name: _____

1. What did you like most about *Psychology of Women,* 5th edition? _____

_____

_____

2. What did you like least about the book? _____

_____

_____

3. Did your instructor assign all of the chapters of the book for you to read? _____

   If not, which ones were not assigned? _____

4. Were the Demonstrations interesting and useful? _____

5. Were the Section Summaries and Review Questions helpful to you? Why or why not?

_____

_____

6. In the space below, or on paper attached, please let me know any additional reactions that you may have. (For example, did you find any of the chapters particularly difficult?) I would be delighted to hear from you!

_____

_____

_____

_____

OPTIONAL:

Your name: _____ Date: _____

May Wadsworth quote you, either in promotion for *Psychology of Women,* 5th edition, or in future publishing ventures?

Yes: _____ No: _____

Sincerely,

Margaret W. Matlin, PhD

BUSINESS REPLY MAIL

FIRST CLASS   PERMIT NO. 34   BELMONT, CA

POSTAGE WILL BE PAID BY ADDRESSEE

NO POSTAGE
NECESSARY
IF MAILED
IN THE
UNITED STATES

ATTN: Editor, Marianne Taflinger

WADSWORTH PUBLISHING
10 DAVIS DRIVE
BELMONT, CA   94002